THE OXFORD HANDBOOK OF

AMERICAN POLITICAL PARTIES AND INTEREST GROUPS

THE

OXFORD

HANDBOOKS

OF

AMERICAN

POLITICS

GENERAL EDITOR: GEORGE C. EDWARDS III

The Oxford Handbooks of American Politics is a set of reference books offering authoritative and engaging critical overviews of the state of scholarship on American politics.

Each volume focuses on a particular aspect of the field. The project is under the General Editorship of George C. Edwards III, and distinguished specialists in their respective fields edit each volume. The *Handbooks* aim not just to report on the discipline, but also to shape it as scholars critically assess the current state of scholarship on a topic and propose directions in which it needs to move. The series is an indispensable reference for anyone working in American politics.

THE OXFORD HANDBOOK OF

AMERICAN POLITICAL PARTIES AND INTEREST GROUPS

Edited by

L. SANDY MAISEL

and

JEFFREY M. BERRY

OXFORD
UNIVERSITY PRESS

OXFORD

UNIVERSITY PRESS

Great Clarendon Street, Oxford OX2 6DP

Oxford University Press is a department of the University of Oxford.
It furthers the University's objective of excellence in research, scholarship,
and education by publishing worldwide in

Oxford New York

Auckland Cape Town Dar es Salaam Hong Kong Karachi
Kuala Lumpur Madrid Melbourne Mexico City Nairobi
New Delhi Shanghai Taipei Toronto

With offices in

Argentina Austria Brazil Chile Czech Republic France Greece
Guatemala Hungary Italy Japan Poland Portugal Singapore
South Korea Switzerland Thailand Turkey Ukraine Vietnam

Oxford is a registered trade mark of Oxford University Press
in the UK and in certain other countries

Published in the United States
by Oxford University Press Inc., New York

© The several contributors 2010

The moral rights of the author have been asserted
Database right Oxford University Press (maker)

First published 2010
First published in paperback 2012

British Library Cataloguing in Publication Data
Data available

Library of Congress Cataloging in Publication Data
Library of Congress Control Number: 2009938565

Typeset by SPI Publisher Services, Pondicherry, India
Printed in Great Britain
on acid-free paper by
Ashford Colour Press Ltd., Gosport, Hants.

ISBN 978–0–19–954262–8 (hbk);
978–0–19–960447–0 (pbk)

1 3 5 7 9 10 8 6 4 2

ACKNOWLEDGMENTS

WE have consulted with many colleagues as we have undertaken the task of editing this volume. Each of us is honored to have served as chair of the Political Organizations and Parties Organized Section (POP) of the American Political Science Association. The extent to which members of that group share their work and their ideas enriches our field and represents the best tradition of social scientists building on the work of those who have come before. We are grateful to the members of POP, many of whom have written for this volume and many more of whose work is referenced in these pages, for being colleagues in the best sense of the word. Of course, we are particularly grateful to our colleagues and friends who have contributed to this volume.

We are also among a small subset of academics who have spent virtually our entire careers at one institution—Colby College in the case of Maisel; Tufts University for Berry. We want to thank our institutions and our departmental colleagues for their support as we have developed as scholars in this field. Maisel would also like to thank Sarah Whitfield, his research assistant, who accepted the responsibility for compiling the List of References that follows the chapters in this book.

George Edwards, the general editor for the series of handbooks of which this volume is a part, flattered us by asking us to undertake this work. We are grateful for the confidence he showed in us and for his assistance and guidance throughout. We also would like to thank Dominic Byatt, our editor at Oxford University Press. We have each worked with a series of editors throughout our career. We have rarely come across an editor who has been as accommodating as has he. We would also like to thank Lizzy Suffling, Louise Sprake, and Laurien Berkeley.

Finally, as is always the case, producing a work like this requires blocks of time that might have been spent with others. Our wives know how much we appreciate their understanding at these times—but we want to say it in any case.

L.S.M.
J.M.B.

CONTENTS

PART I INTRODUCTION

PART II THEORETICAL AND METHODOLOGICAL PERSPECTIVES

PART III PARTY HISTORY

PART IV PARTIES IN THE ELECTORAL PROCESS

PART V PARTY ORGANIZATION

PART VI PARTY IN GOVERNMENT

PART VII INTEREST GROUPS: BIAS AND REPRESENTATION

PART VIII INTEREST GROUPS:
DIMENSIONS OF BEHAVIOR

LIST OF FIGURES

LIST OF TABLES

Abbreviations

AARP	(formerly) American Association of Retired Persons
ACT	America Coming Together
ADA	Americans for Democratic Action
AFL–CIO	American Federation of Labor–Congress of Industrial Organizations
ANES	American National Election Study
BCRA	Bipartisan Campaign Reform Act 2002
BIPAC	Business Industry Political Action Committee
CCES	Cooperative Congressional Election Study
COS	Conservative Opportunity Society
CPG	conditional party government
CPI	Committee on Public Information
DADT	don't ask, don't tell
DCCC	Democratic Congressional Campaign Committee
DNC	Democratic National Committee
DSCC	Democratic Senatorial Campaign Committee
EITM	Empirical Implications of Theoretical Models
ESA	energy, stability, area
FAQ	frequently asked question
FDA	Food and Drug Administration
FEC	Federal Election Commission
FECA	Federal Election Campaign Act 1971
GAO	General Accounting Office
HSA	Health Savings Account
IRS	Internal Revenue Service
LCV	League of Conservation Voters
LGBT	lesbian, gay, bisexual, transgender
MGJ	Mobilization for Global Justice
MLE	maximum likelihood estimation
MMA	Medicare Modernization Act 2003
MSA	Medical Savings Account
NAACP	National Association for the Advancement of Colored People
NAFTA	North American Free Trade Agreement
NFU	National Farmers' Union

NLRB   National Labor Relations Board
NMA   National Medical Association
NOW   National Organization for Women
NRA   National Rifle Association
NRCC   National Republican Congressional Committee
NRSC   National Republican Senatorial Committee
NTU   National Taxpayers' Union
OPEC   Organization of the Petroleum Exporting Countries
PAC   political action committee
PLEO   party leaders and elected officials
POP   Political Organizations and Parties Organized Section
PR   proportional representation
PTA   parent teacher association
RINO   Republican in Name Only
RNC   Republican National Committee
SEIU   Service Employees' International Union
SES   socio-economic status
TPO   traditional party organization
UCA   unanimous consent agreement

About the Contributors

Scott Ainsworth is an Associate Professor of Political Science at the University of Georgia School of Public and International Affairs.

John H. Aldrich is the Pfizer–Pratt University Professor of Political Science at Duke University.

Frank R. Baumgartner is the Richard Richardson Distinguished Professor of Political Science at the University of North Carolina at Chapel Hill.

Jeffrey M. Berry is the John Richard Skuse Professor of Political Science at Tufts University.

David W. Brady is Bowen H. and Janice Arthur McCoy Professor of Political Science and Leadership Values in the Graduate School of Business, Morris M. Doyle Centennial Chair in Public Policy, and Deputy Director and Davies Family Senior Fellow, Hoover Institution, Stanford University.

Mark D. Brewer is an Associate Professor of Political Science at the University of Maine, Orono.

M. David Forrest is a Ph.D. candidate in the Department of Political Science at the University of Minnesota.

Virginia Gray is the Robert Watson Winston Distinguished Professor of Political Science at the University of North Carolina, Chapel Hill.

John C. Green is a Distinguished Professor of Political Science at the University of Akron and Director of the Ray C. Bliss Institute of Applied Politics.

Jeffrey D. Grynaviski is an Assistant Professor of Political Science at the University of Chicago.

Michael T. Heaney is Assistant Professor of Organizational Studies and Political Science at the University of Michigan.

Paul S. Herrnson is a Professor of Government and Politics at the University of Maryland and Director of the Center for American Politics and Citizenship.

Rentaro Iida is a graduate student in political science at Georgetown University.

Raymond J. La Raja is an Associate Professor of Political Science at the University of Massachusetts, Amherst.

Beth L. Leech is an Associate Professor of Political Science at Rutgers University.

David Lowery is a Professor of Public Administration at the University of Leiden, the Netherlands.

Andrew McFarland is a Professor of Political Science at the University of Illinois at Chicago.

David B. Magleby is Distinguished Professor of Political Science and Dean of the College of Family, Home and Social Sciences at Brigham Young University.

L. Sandy Maisel is William R. Kenan Jr. Professor of Government and Director of the Goldfarb Center for Public Affairs and Civic Engagement at Colby College.

William G. Mayer is an Associate Professor of Political Science at Northeastern University.

Sidney M. Milkis is the White Burkett Miller Professor of the Department of Politics and Assistant Director for Academic Programs at the Miller Center of Public Affairs at the University of Virginia.

Hans Noel is a Robert Wood Johnson Scholar in Health Policy Research at the School of Public Health, University of Michigan.

Ronald B. Rapoport is the John Marshall Professor of Political Science at the College of William and Mary.

Jesse H. Rhodes is a Ph.D. candidate in the Department of Politics at the University of Virginia.

David W. Rohde is the Ernestine Friedl Professor of Political Science at Duke University and Director of the Political Institutions and Public Choice Program.

Kay L. Schlozman is the J. Joseph Moakley Professor of Political Science at Boston College.

Byron E. Shafer is the Glenn B. and Cleone Orr Hawkins Chair of Political Science at the University of Wisconsin.

Daniel M. Shea is a Professor of Political Science at Allegheny College and Director of the Center for Political Participation.

Joel H. Silbey is Professor Emeritus of History at Cornell University.

Barbara Sinclair is a Professor Emeritus of Political Science at the University of California, Los Angeles.

Mark A. Smith is an Associate Professor of Political Science at the University of Washington.

Walter J. Stone is a Professor of Political Science at the University of California, Davis.

Dara Z. Strolovitch is an Associate Professor of Political Science at the University of Minnesota.

Clyde Wilcox is a Professor of Government at Georgetown University.

Gerald C. Wright is a Professor of Political Science at Indiana University.

PART I

INTRODUCTION

CHAPTER 1

THE STATE OF RESEARCH ON POLITICAL PARTIES AND INTEREST GROUPS

L. SANDY MAISEL
JEFFREY M. BERRY

HANDBOOKS have long played an important role in many disciplines. In medicine and the sciences in particular, they are invaluable compendiums of the most recent and reliable scholarship. It's fair to say that handbooks have not played the same role in political science. Occasionally a handbook has emerged and enjoyed a well-deserved half-life as an important overview and commentary on one of our subfields. Nevertheless, there is no tradition in our discipline of periodic handbooks that aggregate the most important recent work and stand as signposts in the development of political science.

This is unfortunate. Handbooks not only tell us where we've been but how well we've been accomplishing our scholarly objectives. Most presumptuously—the Brits might say "cheekily"—handbooks can point toward the paths we should follow in our next research projects.

Political science as a discipline is indebted to Oxford University Press for recognizing this lacuna in the collective body of our scholarship and stepping in to fill it. First, under the general editorship of Robert E. Goodin, the ten-volume Oxford Handbooks of Political Science, the first of which was published in 2006, was a massive undertaking, presenting a critical review of the state of the sub-disciplines within political science. Now OUP is publishing a series of handbooks on American politics, with George Edwards serving as general editor for the series.

The editors of this volume were honored to be asked to edit a work on American political parties and interest groups. We were somewhat daunted by the recognition that the contributions and future direction of our subfield within American politics had never been examined with the critical eyes that had examined other subfields. And we were cheeky enough to believe that we and over thirty other contributors could serve as an intellectual bridge between recent research and a research agenda for the immediate future.

In this day and age of online databases and immediate access to the most recent scholarship, is there still a need for a thick tome of chapters examining the fields of both political parties and interest groups? Isn't such a book, to use the vernacular, so very "last-century"? We think not.

Our task as editors was threefold: to organize the volume, to solicit authors, and to challenge them to produce important work that would inform future generations of scholars. We did not seek exhaustive and uncritical literature reviews. Quite the opposite. Instead, we wanted the chapters to assess critically both the major contributions to a literature and the ways in which the literature itself has developed. We wanted to encourage contributions that expressed a clear point of view. This handbook was not designed to provide scholars with a fast fact or quick citation. The authors were encouraged not to think about encyclopedic coverage, but to identify both opportunities for advancement and lines of inquiry where continued labors are not likely to bear additional fruits. The chapters in this book are intended to be read and reflected upon. Their goal is to set the agenda for the next generation, to plant seeds in the hope of stimulating new and important scholarship.

To write these chapters we solicited contributions from the most talented people writing in the fields of American parties and groups. Given their heft and expense, handbooks only gain a readership if they are written by the most distinguished scholars in the field. We consciously chose a mix of scholars. Most are senior scholars at the top of the profession, men and women who have driven scholarship forward. To fully capture where these two fields may be headed we have also included many younger scholars. These individuals have already published important work and seem destined to be central figures in the development of the parties and interest group subfields in the years to come. A quick glance at our Table of Contents attests to our success in attracting the most interesting and influential collaborators for this handbook. What is less obvious is the willingness of the vast majority of those asked to participate in the project, their enthusiasm for the goal, and their incredible cooperation in its reaching fruition. We are deeply appreciative of these individuals' commitment to the project, the time they spent producing these chapters, and for sharing their thoughtful insights with the profession.

In organizing this volume, we quickly realized that the literatures on political parties and on interest groups are separate more often than they are combined—though overlaps are evident throughout. We begin with a series of four chapters on theoretical and methodological perspectives.

John Aldrich and Jeffrey Grynaviski open with an examination of the role of formal theory in the study of political parties. They describe the mechanisms by which two important sets of political institutions—a polity's constitutional structures and the rules that political parties choose to regulate the behavior of their own members—interact to give structure to political outcomes in democratic polities. They note two important distinctions—first between two very different types of institutions—(1) constitutional structures, which are exogenous institutions in this context, and (2) the rules that political elites choose in order to regulate one another's behavior within a party organization to promote shared interests, endogenous institutions. The second distinction is between two different strands of research on politics that might be considered formal theory. The first applies concepts from rational choice theory, the core assumptions of which are that people have well-defined preference functions and seek to make the best choices possible given the constraints they face. The second uses mathematical concepts to provide formal representations of behavior that are not consistent with the assumptions of rational choice theory. With these distinctions in mind, their chapter is organized around the insights that formal theory provides to three main questions. First, how do constitutional rules shape the number of parties that contest elections? Second, how do constitutional institutions and party rules impact the choices that party elites present to the electorate? Third, how do constitutional structures and party rules affect politicians' incentives to follow through on their campaign promises in office?

Andrew McFarland provides a parallel examination of the role of theory in the study of interest groups. He outlines four successive stages of theory building, with each succeeding theory retaining elements of the preceding stage while discarding other elements, seen as mistakes. The first stage was exemplified by David Truman's group theory, emphasizing the need to conduct empirical study of groups, which he considered to be the most important factor in defining public policy. The second stage was Robert Dahl's pluralism, depicting the causal role of interest groups as less central, while portraying the political system as fundamentally decentralized. The third stage was the multiple elitist theory exemplified by Mancur Olson and Theodore Lowi, in which decentralized systems are largely in the control of policy-specific special-interest coalitions among groups, government agencies, and legislative committees. This is largely due to the difficulty in organizing widely diffused constituencies. The fourth stage is neopluralism, which holds that countervailing power groups check such subgovernmental coalitions. The countervailing groups mobilize in reaction to the advocacy of policy networks, lobbying coalitions, patrons, and social movements. McFarland treats concepts such as niche theory, coalition formation, social networks, lobbying influence, and internal democracy in relation to neopluralism and identifies these as promising areas for further research.

Hans Noel and Scott Ainsworth have written chapters on research methodology that similarly examine political parties and interest groups in parallel ways. Noel notes that parties are difficult to study for at least two reasons: first, because they are often informal and often extralegal institutions that do not follow transparent and universal rules; and, second, because they permeate so many domains of politics—all branches of the government at the state and federal level, the electorate, and other organizations concerned with governing. He then focuses on methods used to study parties, particularly quantitative approaches that attend to these difficulties, addressing methodological issues within various domains as well as the question of party cleavage and realignment that bridges the domains. In each case he outlines the various methods that have been used to study the key questions, presents the strengths and weaknesses of each, and deals with the claims of competing models. Noel concludes with a plea for creativity in exploring new methods and with the assertion that party scholars must be familiar with the wide variety of methods used to study questions across the entire expanse of the field.

Ainsworth utilizes many interest group classics as well as a wide range of new works to illustrate key methodological concerns for the interest group subfield. In his view methodological advances are helpful when they illuminate puzzles in new ways. Each of the three main sections of the chapter starts with a condensed discussion of classical approaches to interest group studies and then introduces newer research encompassing important methodological advances. For example, Ainsworth couples his discussion of pluralism and social capital with an introduction to partitioning games, social decisions, and event history analysis. In the second section he examines the strengths and weaknesses of descriptive work, coupling this with discussion of maximum likelihood econometric methods and the methodological issues stemming from unobserved actions and counterfactuals. In the last section Ainsworth analyzes the role of information, noting that many recent lobbying models focus on information transmission. It is often thought that information from interest groups is hopelessly biased. Ainsworth, however, argues that interest groups and lobbyists must compete with numerous sources for information, including elections, public opinion, markets, and bureaucracies, and these alternative sources for information may themselves be biased. He predicts that scholars will move toward developing more comprehensive information-screening models because government officials are simply awash with information.

These chapters are followed by three on party history. Joel Silbey opens this part with a sweeping analysis of the history of American political parties. Silbey uses the lens of critical election theory to examine scholarly treatment of the development of parties as institutions, of the relationship between parties and the electorate, of the means that parties have used to communicate with and build relationships with the electorate, and of the existence and definition of party systems. He concludes that forces have been mounting to challenge the primacy of party as the organizing element of American politics for more than a century, with some concluding that their long history would end in fragmentation and irrelevance, not realignment and renewal. But others have claimed that increased polarization of recent decades signals party revitalization. Silbey lays out the agenda for future scholars—to rethink what this recent history means and possibly to develop new organizational paradigms.

Mark Brewer argues that, at their most fundamental level, political parties have one primary goal: the construction of a coalition that enables them to win elections and exercise governmental power. Groups are the building blocks of these coalitions, and in each election cycle parties and their politicians devote an enormous amount of thought, time, and resources to determining which groups in American society might be enticed to support them and then to making this possible support a reality. Assembling a winning electoral coalition is marked by high levels of risk and uncertainty. Brewer examines the composition and evolution of the electoral coalitions of the Republican and Democratic parties since the 1930s, finding both constancy and change over time. Both parties' electoral bases continue to reflect in some ways the political divides of the New Deal—the less affluent, Americans residing in union households, and urban dwellers have consistently been key elements of the Democratic coalition while the Republicans have long enjoyed support from more affluent Americans and non-southern white Protestants. But each party has also seen significant change to its coalition, especially since the 1980s. The Democratic Party now relies much more on African Americans, women, and those with low levels of religious salience to win elections, while today's GOP is more reliant on southern whites, evangelical Protestants, those with high levels of religious salience, and Roman Catholics.

John Green's "The Party Faithful: Religion and Party Politics in America" looks at religious groups as one of the basic building blocks of party coalitions. After exploring why religion is relevant to party politics in conceptual terms, he compares the religious character of the major party coalitions in the past with those in the contemporary context, explicitly comparing data from 1952 with those from 2008, discussing separately ethno-religious groups and theologically religious groups as they divide between the parties. He concludes that religious voting blocs are an integral part of American politics and that the faith-based elements of the major party coalitions have changed as the country changed, sometimes in degree and sometimes in kind. Finally, Green describes "party faithful" in the early years of the twenty-first century, distinguishing the Democratic coalition, based on various kinds of religious minorities, led by black Protestants, along with less observant white Christians and people unaffiliated with organized religion, from the Republicans, the core of whom is made up of various kinds of Protestants, especially white Evangelicals, and observant white Christians. His speculation suggests that the relationship between religious groups and the major political parties will evolve in interesting ways during the Obama years.

The next four chapters revolve around parties in the electoral process. For most of the nation's first century political parties controlled access to the ballot. Nomination procedures changed radically during the Progressive era, with the advent and spread of direct primaries, and have been evolving ever since. Two chapters look at the role of political parties in nominations. Raymond La Raja examines the roles that parties play in state and local nominations and the research on those roles, finding a relative dearth of scholarship despite the opportunities for important comparative work. He explores three separate sets of questions. He turns first to different institutional rules and laws and how different recruitment practices can determine who runs for office. La Raja notes that two schools of thought have dominated the work in this area, with some scholars following a traditional utility model and others a sociological approach. Despite this research, however, we still have no clear answers as to who fills this gap when party organizations lose their dominant position in recruiting and selecting candidates for office. Next he turns to a series of questions regarding how different selection schemes affect the political parties as institutions—power distribution within the organizations, the extent to which parties are ideologically coherent, their electoral success or failure. Finally, looking at the broader picture, La Raja explores the implication of different nominating procedures for voter participation, for representation, and for governing. Throughout his chapter La Raja points to the variation in key factors that can be studied when one compares the experiences of the fifty states in determining partisan candidates.

In his chapter on the role of parties in presidential nominations, William Mayer traces the evolution of the presidential nominating process and the role of party in securing presidential nominations from the founding to the modern era. He notes, as do others in this volume, that the role of party qua organization has given way to a plebiscitary process that operates under the party mantle and rules set by the national parties. After describing the modern nominating process and identifying five generalizations about the process that one can derive from recent experience— that the process starts inordinately early, that Iowa and New Hampshire have influence out of proportion to their populations, that many candidates drop out of the race either before or just after the first delegates are selected, that the process normally ends by March, and that the national conventions' role in decision making is negligible—Mayer raises questions that remain about the nominating process. Specifically, he directs scholars' attention to exploring how citizens make choices among multiple candidates without the benefit of the cue of party and to focusing on the question of how politics and governance in the United States are different from those in other nations because of the way our chief executive is nominated.

Daniel Shea reviews the seemingly paradoxical positions that, at the same time, party organizations have been revitalized while citizen attraction to party has declined. He cites a number of explanations for this phenomenon that scholars noted late in the twentieth century and then focuses on how the 2000 election marked a significant transformation in partisanship and in citizen activity. Shea argues that recent changes in the electoral process have afforded party organizations with the opportunity to bring citizens back under the party rubric. While in the past parties focused on a top-down strategy to attract activists by following a charismatic leader, the 2008 Obama campaign combined Obama's charisma with grassroots efforts using the Internet and web-based communications—the first truly Net roots campaign, a bottom-up effort. These techniques provide local, state, and national party organizations the chance to energize citizens under their labels for governing purposes as well as for political gain. But whether party organizations take advantage of this opportunity is less than clear. Revitalized party organization that did not connect with the citizens led to low turnout elections and general citizen apathy. Shea argues that technological changes—the opportunity for parties to mobilize citizens for governing as well as voting—can lead to a new role for party, an engaged citizenry, and a healthier democracy.

The role and fate of political parties other than the two major parties in our two-party system have attracted a great deal of scholarly attention. As Ronald Rapoport notes, even categorizing these as "third parties" is deceptive; often more than three parties contest an election, and all minor parties are certainly not alike. Rapoport analyzes the challenges faced by those seeking to launch third parties, focusing on the nature of our electoral system and differing findings on the impact of changing ballot access requirements. Turning to the factors that lead to electoral success or failure, Rapoport notes both factors that "push" voters away from the two major parties and those that "pull" voters toward third party candidates. He emphasizes both proximity of the stand taken by a third party to those of the voter (as compared to those of the major party candidates) and the priority that both the voter and the candidate give to issues. Perhaps the most important question regarding third parties relates to their impact on the existing party system. Rapoport lays out a "dynamic of third parties," moving consequentially from a third party with a large and identifiable issue constituency from which it receives substantial support, to one of the major parties bidding for that constituency, and to the response of the third party's supporters to that effort.

Since the early writing of V. O. Key, political scientists have examined party not only in terms of party in the electorate and the electoral process, but also in terms of party organization. Paul Herrnson has contributed the first of our four chapters in this area, focusing on the development of national party organizations, their relationship with other party committees, and their evolving role in contemporary elections. Herrnson traces the parties' organizational response to their gradual, but nonetheless evident, decline from their peak of power and influence in the late nineteenth century. He highlights how party institutionalization has resulted in a nationalization of politics in two ways: in terms of rules that govern party procedures and in terms of campaign activities. Today's parties are characterized as fiscally solvent, organizationally stable, well staffed, and professionally decisive. They play important roles in all aspects of modern campaigning, working with consultants, recruiting some candidates and discouraging others, providing campaign expertise and services, assisting in fundraising, running independent advertising on their own. Political parties are, above all else, electoral institutions. The national party organizations have responded to changes in the electoral environment in ways that permit them to remain important players on the contemporary political scene.

Byron Shafer focuses attention on national party conventions, the "pure partisan institutions" of American politics. Shafer begins with the conceptual distinction between the convention as an institutional *mechanism* for making decisions and the convention as an institutional *arena* for reflecting social forces, on his way to an argument that the changed institution still functions as a window on major aspects of American politics. A series of social changes following the First World War did draw the nomination outside the convention, leading ultimately to reform of the process of delegate selection as well. What resulted was the convention as "infomercial." Yet the contents of its message continue to reflect important aspects of modern American politics, aspects effectively studied within its confines. Thus, conventions present composite portraits of the two parties—normally quite different portraits—for the American electorate. Their delegates offer a collective portrait of the active party, in its own right and in relationship to the general public. And the inevitable differences between conventions—between the two parties' conventions in one year or between the same party's conventions over time—function as both a concise snapshot of the context of presidential politics in a given year and a focused sample of the larger and ongoing politics around them.

Activists in political parties potentially have more influence over the directions that parties take, the outcomes of elections, and party role in governance than they would have were they just ordinary citizens and voters. Walter Stone discusses the place of party activists in the electoral process, focusing first on why they become involved, how they influence party nominations, and how they influence the general elections. The central question for scholars of party activists has been the extent to which their influence is problematic for democracy because they lack formal constituencies, are not accountable to others for their actions, and are unrepresentative of their party's rank and file not only in their resources and commitment but also in their policy positions. Activists have the potential to undermine the integrative function of the parties that democratic theorists value so highly. Stone argues that we as a discipline need research designs capable of linking activist participation to electoral outcomes before we can conclude that distortion actually occurs, an organic approach to the study of parties and elections, rather than focusing on one or another set of actors, such as voters, candidates, or activists. He then presents new empirical evidence from an integrated study of the 2006 congressional elections to demonstrate the potential for such an approach. He concludes with a call for work on the micro foundations of activists' behavior, including their links to groups external to parties, in order to understand better how activists' roots affect party behavior.

David Magleby examines the development of political consultants in American politics and the increasing interaction of consultants and political parties, first tracing the history and describing the broader role that consultants play in American politics and then discussing in more detail specific functions that consultants have taken over for parties and for individual campaigns. Money has been a key factor in the developing role of consultants due to the cost of specialized functions and the limitations placed on spending by various regulations under the Federal Election Campaign Act of 1971 (amended in 1974) and the Bipartisan Campaign Reform Act of 2002. Magleby then lays out a typology of consultant functions and discusses the growing interdependency between parties and consultants. A controversy in the scholarly literature on the impact of the rise of consultants on political parties has arisen around the nature of this interdependency. Some argue that the rise of consultants has weakened parties; a second group contends that the rise of consultants is a sign of weak parties, but not a cause of party decline; and a third group suggests that strong parties would still rely on consultants because of the development of campaign technology. Finally, Magleby lays out an ambitious agenda for scholars to examine as this relationship develops in upcoming campaigns.

The next four chapters focus on the party in government. David Rohde and Barbara Sinclair look at the development and current state of party organization in the House and Senate respectively. They each examine existing theories that explain party influence in legislatures, applying them to the quite different contexts of the two houses of the US Congress.

Rohde notes how party organizations are visibly stronger and majority party influence over the agenda, member behavior, and legislative outcomes has increased since the time, thirty-five years ago, when David Mayhew argued that congressional parties were of little consequence. He provides a critical overview of the major theoretical perspectives on party leadership, organization, and activity in the House. He does so by reviewing Mayhew's and Fiorina's work that emphasized the electoral connection, his own conditional party government model (amplified by and with Aldrich and others) that expanded the electoral concern to include other member incentives (e.g., policy preferences, influence within the chamber, etc.), Krehbiel's critique that explains congressional behavior based on member preferences without including party as an explanatory variable (because the two parties' actions were offsetting), and Cox and McCubbins's cartel theory, which emphasizes the importance of party in electoral outcomes for members and of the majority party's role in agenda setting. Rohde then raises major issues for future research into the role of party in the House that emerge from his review, including, among others, the centrality of control of the congressional agenda and the mechanisms of agenda control, including the Rules Committee. Rohde concludes his chapter with a call for students of congressional behavior not only to include a discussion of the findings of earlier work as they pursue their studies, but also to ask whether those findings remain accurate, given the changing nature of our political institutions and processes.

Barbara Sinclair notes that treating the Senate separately from the House in discussing party effects is justified because of the unusual rules that govern Senate consideration of legislation. Thus, the extent to which party controls the agenda in the Senate is limited; given this limited agenda control, incentives for senators to follow their party and the reasons that senators contribute to party endeavors when they are a collective good on which individuals could free-ride require explanation. Sinclair reviews the development of party organization in the Senate and conflicting explanations of why the Senate has not developed majority agenda-control mechanisms—with some arguing that inherited rules have been the best explanation while others counter that the costs of changing the rules outweigh the benefits for a majority of the senators. She notes that party plays a lesser role in the Senate than in the House, but because of the agenda-setting influence of the majority leader, a significant one nonetheless. Sinclair also examines the question of negative agenda setting in the Senate, noting research that shows that the majority party is rarely rolled in the Senate. She calls for more nuanced theory building in studying party influence in the Senate. It is important to understand agenda setting in a broader context, not just in terms of bringing bills to the floor (or even preventing them from coming to the floor), but also in terms of writing proposals. And, it is necessary to take the multiple-goals aspect of existing theory seriously, exploring the implications of senators' multiple goals for party influence within the chamber.

David Brady looks at intra-party and inter-party coalitions in the Congress over the nation's history, noting, first, that a degree of heterogeneity within our parties has been a constant of our government and, second, that because of our congressional voting procedures and means of elections, intra-party differences are more difficult to capture in the American context by examining legislative votes than they are in parliamentary systems. He turns to an examination of bipartisan coalitions in the last three decades, a period of acknowledged increased polarization between the parties and increased party line voting in Congress. Brady asserts that legislative outcomes, such as the tax cut during President George H. W. Bush's administration, the failure of health care reform during the Clinton administration, or the passage of the $900 billion stimulus package at the beginning of the Obama administration, cannot be adequately explained without examining intra-party coalitions. While the profession has rightly sought to explain the observed increase in partisanship, political scientists will not achieve a clear picture of the relationship between elections, the distribution of preferences over party, and the policy coalitions that can be formed without continued examination of the nature of the limited bipartisan coalitions that still form, the policy areas in which these do form, limited examples of bipartisanship as seen, for example, in co-sponsoring of legislation, and the nature of preferences and factions within, as opposed to between, the parties.

Sidney Milkis and Jesse Rhodes's chapter investigates the troubled relationship between the presidency and the political parties. As they suggest, this relationship has never been easy; but its dynamics have varied over the course of American political history. Patronage politics that emphasized grassroots mobilization and subordinated executive administration to party control held sway for most of the nineteenth century. Party dominance limited the scope of federal activity, but it also promoted a vigorous democratic politics grounded in state and local affairs. The Progressive era witnessed the stirrings of a new order that would raise the administrative presidency to primacy and challenge locally based party politics. This order was consolidated during the New Deal, which institutionalized a modern presidency that would govern above party in the name of national welfare and national security. Milkis and Rhodes contend that the powerful presidency that permitted the nation to address economic and foreign policy challenges also threatened the practice of American democracy by undermining the party ties linking citizens to government. In recent decades, however, yet another relationship between the president and the parties has emerged. This system holds both promise and perils for American citizenship, Milkis and Rhodes argue. Recent presidents are active party builders, articulating party doctrine, raising funds, and mobilizing citizens. While these behaviors may promote a more vigorous and participatory democracy, presidents' party leadership may devolve into party domination, enervating the capacity of the party to hold the president accountable for his actions.

Gerald Wright notes the difficulty in studying state party organizations because of the conceptual complexity of the subject—there are fifty separate and different state party systems, each with a party organization, a party electorate, and party in government. Not only do these component parts vary from state to state, but the interrelationships among them vary as well. Scholarly efforts are further hampered because of the difficulty in gathering data to analyze these differences. Two reform traditions can be identified: the progressive movement that led to state efforts to regulate the political process and weaken what were seen as corrupt patronage-driven political parties, and the mid-twentieth-century efforts by political scientists to strengthen political parties by advocating a more responsible party model. All helped to shape both the current contours of state parties and the scholarly efforts to study them. Wright contends that political science research has focused too narrowly on strength and competitiveness of political parties and thus has ignored important questions concerning the impact of strong parties and party principles and goals. Examining both existing research and future research directions, he concludes that important questions remain to be tackled, that conceptual complexity must still be resolved. These include looking beyond assumptions inherent in the model of traditional party organizations and the implications of increasingly polarized political parties for representation of relatively moderate state electorates. Fortunately, the availability of new data sources is cause for optimism about continued progress on these questions.

The first of two parts on interest groups offers five chapters on bias and representation. Kay Schlozman's contribution to this collection addresses perhaps the most central and compelling question of the subfield: who is represented by interest groups and is that representation equitable or biased? Her analysis builds on a unique database that she and her colleagues have built over the years. Using *Washington Representatives*, a directory of lobbying organizations in Washington, she is able to outline the contours of the Washington interest group system. Schlozman's longitudinal database is revealing. Despite all the changes that have taken place in American politics, the conclusion drawn by E. E. Schattschneider a half century ago that the pressure system is fundamentally biased in favor of business and professional interests is still accurate. Her data do point toward a much more diverse interest group system but the have-nots and have-a-littles seem no better represented today than they were in 1981, the first of her data points. Schlozman identifies two culprits for this continuing bias: the collective action problem and the lack of resources on the part of those underrepresented in the interest group universe. Given the continuity of her findings over four separate data points over a quarter of a century, she is not optimistic that change is on the way. Public interest groups, for example, were 3.8 percent of all interest groups in 1981. The 2006 data show them to constitute just 4.1 percent of the universe. She concludes that "as the heavenly chorus has gotten bigger, neither its accent nor the mix of voices has been transformed."

Many scholars have begun research endeavors with the goal of documenting business influence, through its lobbying, campaign contributions, and the shared class-wide interests among elites. In his chapter, "The Mobilization and Influence of Business Interests," Mark Smith cautions against this view of business as a powerful monolith. Rather, Smith emphasizes, business is highly diverse, with conflicting interests and facing many significant obstacles to exercising power. Although the discipline has made some progress in documenting the degree to which influence is exercised by business, the research constitutes a surprisingly modest literature. Indeed, Smith calls the study of business a "niche area" in the discipline. Given the centrality of business in the lobbying world, this is certainly a counterintuitive claim. One reason political scientists have not done more extensive work on business is that the actual substance of business lobbying, policy areas such as taxation and finance, are ones that elicit little excitement within the profession. He offers a second reason, too: the sheer difficulty of doing empirical research on business lobbying. With the exception of political action committee

(PAC) statistics, there is little in the way of existing databases that can easily be drawn upon by political scientists studying business. And this is where Smith makes his most emphatic argument. In his mind the study of business will not progress significantly until more political scientists design projects based on extensive empirical research. We need more scholars in the field armed with sharper measuring instruments.

In their chapter "Social and Economic Justice Movements and Organization," Dara Strolovitch and David Forrest analyze the representation of chronically marginalized constituencies, especially women, racial minorities, gays and lesbians, and the poor. There has certainly been a growth of organizations representing these constituencies in recent decades, yet the extent to which these groups have fulfilled their promise to equalize representation "is the source of much debate." To various degrees these movement organizations have become institutionalized and yet retain many characteristics of their earlier roots. Strolovitch and Forrest find that in comparison to interest groups in general, organizations representing marginalized groups are distinctive as they are far less likely to use professional lobbyists, employ a legal staff, or have an affiliated PAC. The authors also stress that advocacy organizations in these broad identity areas do not typically represent "unitary constituencies" but rather ones that are "intersectional" in nature. As multiple interests of race, gender, or social class come together in individual organizations, the most marginalized constituencies within these groups often receive the least active representation.

Despite the difficulties they face, these organizations play a vital role in the policymaking process. They do sometimes prevail and influence the government in ways that benefit the disadvantaged. Looking to the future, Strolovitch and Forrest call on scholars to draw on policy feedback and social constructionist frameworks and to identify the circumstances under which these organizations are most effective in representing their constituencies.

David Lowery and Virginia Gray draw a contrast between the "explosion of large-n studies" and the more modest progress in theory building and hypothesis testing in research on state-level interest groups. What they term the "logic of segmentation" has created boundaries which have raised barriers to progress in the development of normal science and the evolution of broader theories. They criticize the national-level literature for ignoring many important questions about interest representation. Indeed, they believe there is a "one-way pattern of influence" between national interest group studies and state-level studies. For example, the relationship between groups and political parties has received relatively little attention by scholars of Washington politics, while the state politics literature has had a focus on this subject since Belle Zeller's time. Another area where state interest group scholars are ahead of their national counterparts is in the relationship between public opinion and organized interests. Lowery and Gray also note that state-level research is well suited for understanding how institutional design affects interest group communities and advocacy. The variation that states provide allows more sophisticated and ambitious inquiry into this problem. Lowery and Gray do, however, end on a note of optimism, concluding that the state literature is no longer as isolated from the more general research on interest groups.

Following Lowery and Gray's examination of interest groups in the states, Jeffrey Berry moves down the federal system to urban politics. Although the study of groups in cities was the source of pluralist theory, which catalyzed the most enduring debate in the subfield, recent research on urban interest groups has had relatively limited impact on theory. Instead work on interest groups is dominated by research on national politics. Berry argues forcefully that studying local groups through the lens of theories about national groups is perilous. He says city groups are not merely smaller versions of national lobbies but, rather, they are fundamentally different. He outlines four basic structural differences, the understanding of which should serve as a foundation for future research on urban interest group politics. First, there are usually low barriers to entry for urban groups. Second, urban politics is highly sensitized to planning for projects in neighborhoods and this locational basis of policymaking enhances the influence of small neighborhood associations. These groups, in turn, play a much larger role in city politics than their meager resources would otherwise suggest. A third difference is that citizen participation requirements provide neighborhood groups and citywide citizen groups significant leverage in negotiations with developers and city planners. Fourth and finally, he notes that state and local agencies are highly dependent on non-profits. In cities, collaborative policymaking tying together non-profit and agency leaders is very much the norm in the area of social services.

The final part, on dimensions of behavior, analyzes different interest group roles and forms of advocacy. Frank Baumgartner begins his chapter paying homage to E. E. Schattschneider, crediting him with initiating the study of interest groups and agenda building. Schattschneider encouraged us to think about how interest groups try to expand conflict when they are in a disadvantageous position in the development of a policy decision. Baumgartner proceeds systematically to demonstrate how this literature on agenda building has come together to illuminate lobbying strategies. He cautions against the common assumptions about the power of interest groups, noting for example, that recent research has demonstrated that groups are very limited in their ability to reframe issues. Rather, they are more effective at protecting the status quo. Baumgartner also notes that there is an enormous disparity between what lobbyists are working on in Washington and the priorities of the American public. He is most forceful in drawing out the biases of interest group mobilization and linking those advantages to the politics of agenda setting. He notes, "bias comes from the fact that some segments of society mobilize powerfully and speak with amplified voices and others mobilize little or

not at all." Baumgartner outlines some fruitful areas of research on agenda building, including interest groups and venue shopping and the relative effectiveness of
coalitions of interest group advocates and government officials.

Beth Leech's chapter examines the influence of interest groups on public policy
making. Despite the substantial amount of research that has been done in this area,
her review of the literature demonstrates that findings are often contradictory;
some scholars find substantial interest group influence while others find groups to
be relatively weak. PAC studies are an interesting case in point. Reviews of the
research reveal that a significant portion of published work find PAC contributions
unrelated to legislative votes, others find a mixed picture, and still others find that
money does influence votes. From her analysis Leech argues that "We have been
measuring the wrong things in the wrong ways." She supports this contention by
explicating key methodological problems. Such flaws include case selection bias;
focusing on a single stage of the policymaking process; and incorrect assumptions
about how the policymaking process works. Leech identifies three general means
by which interest groups might influence legislation: effectively purchasing votes
with campaign contributions; mobilizing constituencies or signaling constituency
preferences to the legislator; and providing information or otherwise subsidizing
those in office. What she concludes is that available evidence is most supportive of
the third of these possibilities, supplying useful information to elected officials. In
the end, though, interest group influence through this channel is highly contingent.

Clyde Wilcox and Rentaro Iida explore the myriad ways that interest groups are
active in American elections, and the difficulties that scholars face in answering
basic questions about this activity. Although PAC formation and contributions
data are accessible and accurate, these authors note that PACs do not constitute the
only way that interest groups give, and that contributing is not the only way that
groups are active in elections. Studies of group strategies, of the impact of group
activities in elections, and of the impact of interest group electoral activities on
policy making must take into account an increasing amount of activity that is not
fully disclosed. The authors note that the way groups have been active in the past
few election cycles raises important questions about how to conceive of interest
group involvement. Networks of interest group leaders, partisan activists, and
donors have collaborated on strategies and shifted resources, sometimes based on
studies on efficacy of past strategies.

Since this is a handbook on both political parties and interest groups, we
conclude the collection with Michael Heaney's examination of the relationship
between groups and parties. In Heaney's mind the two are "inextricably linked."
He proceeds along four tracks to analyze these ties and to point toward the next
stages of research. The first relationship he identifies is that of *co-evolution*. Over
the course of American history parties and groups have changed partially in
response to each other. Second, parties and groups attempt to *discipline* each
other, by trying to control what kinds of agents act on their behalf. Heaney's

third relationship is that of *brokerage*. Within each other's networks, operatives from groups or parties may play a key role in bringing various factions to the bargaining table. Fourth, parties and groups are linked by *political identities*. Ideology may bring groups and a party together but may also create tensions as each sector tries to define the boundaries of the identity they share. Although scholars are increasingly aware of these links, Heaney is critical of the scholarship that has emerged so far. The case study approach has dominated and Heaney says that it is time for research to push toward systemic knowledge and more sophisticated theory building. He encourages political scientists to think not so much of party coalitions or interest group coalitions, but to focus instead on "political coalitions."

The parties and interest group fields are dynamic and this handbook reflects judgments about research at a particular point in time. New research will quickly come to the fore and will work to reshape such evaluations. Yet the chapters in this book have analyzed long-term developments in various specialties and the challenges our authors have identified are sure to remain as central issues as our discipline moves forward. Each of our authors has offered valuable insights into the kinds of problems that are central to the next stages of research. We hope that these chapters prove to be valuable guides as readers ponder their own research agendas.

New databases and new research techniques are expanding opportunities and enabling researchers to rigorously and systematically test their ideas. For reasons of space and coherence we limited the subject matter in the chapters that follow to parties and groups in the United States. Nevertheless, comparative research that includes the United States is likely to expand greatly in the years to come. In particular, research on the European Union has exploded and it's assuredly the case that there will be increasing cross-fertilization of ideas across the pond as well as more directly collaborative work. This is an exciting time to be working in fields of political parties or interest groups.

PART II

THEORETICAL
AND
METHODOLOGICAL
PERSPECTIVES

CHAPTER 2

....

THEORIES OF
PARTIES

....

JOHN H. ALDRICH

JEFFREY D. GRYNAVISKI

POLITICAL parties present an interesting challenge to formal theorists. First, they are nearly ubiquitous in democracies. Second, they are institutions, and therefore they are appropriate for study in the style of the new institutionalism, that is, the study of the effects of institutional rules on electoral or policy outcomes through the application of rational choice, game-theoretic reasoning. Third, they are unusually endogenous institutions. In the US, for instance, they have historically been self-defined (rather than defined through law or regulation). For example, their national organizations adopt their defining rules each time they meet, and they do so by simple majority rule, making them as subject to what Riker (1980) called "inheritability" as any major political institution can be. Finally, they can be studied in a variety of institutional settings, particularly electoral, legislative, or both, and they can be considered as single political parties or as a set of parties forming a "party system." Only slowly did formal theorists pick up this challenge.

The early contributions of formal theory to political science sought instead to understand, in a very general and abstract way, how political actors arrived at collective outcomes and whether these outcomes had desirable properties. In their quest for generality, these researchers ignored the details of the institutions in which political actors conducted business. Their results included:

Arrow (1951): the famous impossibility result for aggregating individual preferences into coherent collective choices;

McKelvey (1976)–Schofield (1978): the nearly invariable existence of the capability of agenda-setting agents for getting their way;

Gibbard (1973)–Satterthwaite (1975): the essentially generic manipulability of voting rules by strategic actors;

Olson (1965): the ubiquitous free-rider effects that limit collective action and the provision of public goods.

Taken as a whole, this work paints a very bleak picture for the possibility of fair and effective democratic governance.

Beginning in the late 1970s, a series of papers by Shepsle (especially 1979, otherwise often written in collaboration with Weingast, e.g., 1987) revolutionized the way that scholars employ formal theory in their study of politics. Drawing upon the basic insights of the nascent field of the new institutional economics, he demonstrated that formal theory could be put to good use studying how institutions structure interactions among political actors in order to solve the collective dilemmas identified by the previous generation of scholars. Early applications of this literature focused on how institutions—especially the structures of the US Congress, such as its committee system—could provide solutions to social choice problems inside legislatures. In the years since, formal theory has been used to analyze how institutions structure human interactions in a much wider assortment of political domains. See Weingast and Wittman (2006) for a recent review of this literature.

Our purpose in this chapter is to identify the contributions of formal theory to the study of political parties. Or, perhaps more accurately, we intend to describe the mechanisms by which two important sets of political institutions—a polity's constitutional structures and the rules that political parties choose to regulate the behavior of their own members—interact to give structure to political outcomes in democratic polities.

In pursuing this goal, we believe that it is useful to make two important distinctions. The first distinction is between two very different types of institutions: constitutional structures and the rules that political elites choose to regulate one another's behavior within a party organization to promote shared interests. On the one hand, we believe that it is appropriate to consider a polity's constitutional structures to be exogenous institutions: these are institutions that theorists can treat current political actors as having no say in their design.[1] Under this interpretation, one might usefully characterize constitutions as creating the game tree in

---

[1] Riker's general point (1980) was that, in the long run, all rules are endogenous, in the sense that the outcomes of rules (actual or anticipated) feed back into preferences over rules, which then should shape the choice of rules, in addition to whatever other considerations go into preferences over rules. Thus, anticipated outcomes are a part of the bases for preferences over rules. This differs from the immediate sense of endogeneity in which the selection of rules is in close proximity to their use in choosing outcomes, the same actors choose the rules and the outcomes, and they use close approximation of the same methods for choosing rules as for choosing outcomes. In this case, the inheritability of preferences over outcomes into preferences for the rules is, at least theoretically, direct and decisive; one chooses the rules for the purpose of obtaining one's preferred outcomes.

which political actors operate. On the other hand, we treat the rules that parties choose to regulate the behavior of their own members as purely endogenous institutions: we therefore treat the rules that party elites choose to govern one another's behavior as an optimal response to the strategic situation created by a polity's constitution and the anticipated reactions of all relevant actors (voters, party activists, candidates, elected officials, etc.) of the polity.

The second distinction is between two different strands of research on politics that might be considered formal theory. On the one hand, there is the strand of research that applies concepts from rational choice theory, the core assumptions of which are that people have well-defined preference functions and seek to make the best choices possible given the constraints they face, to the study of politics. Work done in this tradition is often very mathematical, but it need not be (Downs's classic application of rational choice theory (1957), for example, had very little math). On the other hand, there is a strand of research that uses mathematical concepts to provide formal representations of behavior that are not consistent with the assumptions of rational choice theory. A good example of this is Adams, Merrill, and Grofman's recent efforts (2005) to model candidate strategies when voters are assumed to obey non-"rational" psychological processes. While we believe that the latter approach offers valuable insights, we have chosen to limit our attention in this chapter to the former category of scholarship, with an eye toward illustrating how rational choice theory provides a unified framework for understanding how partisan institutions emerge and structure political actors' interactions for a wide assortment of constitutional forms.[2]

With these distinctions in mind, our chapter is organized around the insights that formal theory provides to three main questions. First, how do constitutional rules shape the number of parties that contest elections? Second, how do constitutional structures and party rules structure the choices that party elites present to the electorate? Third, how do constitutional structures and party rules affect politicians' incentives to follow through on their campaign promises in office?

FORMAL THEORIES OF ELECTORAL RULES
AND THE NUMBER OF PARTIES

Most formal theories of politics treat the number of parties that contest elections to be given a priori. That is, they begin from a set of assumptions about the number of parties and conduct their analysis from there. However, formal theory provides some

---

[2] One reason is that the non-rational formalizations are of more recent vintage and are fewer in number at this time than the "traditional" rational choice accounts.

insights into how a polity's electoral rules influence the number of viable political parties in elections. Since the number of parties has a profound effect on party and voter strategies in equilibrium, we think a discussion of how constitutional rules shape the number of parties is a useful place to begin our survey of the literature.

A famous empirical regularity is Duverger's Law (Duverger 1954). Indeed, Riker, the founder of formal modeling in political science, wrote an essay about it as the sort of regularity from which a science of politics might be built (1982). Duverger's statement is that when its constitution requires that elections be conducted by plurality or majority rule (or, in current parlance, it is a first-past-the-post system), a polity tends toward having exactly two major parties. Duverger offered two reasons for this. The first is the "mechanical effect" of electoral laws, by which he meant that the translation of votes into seats under virtually all electoral laws ordinarily advantages the plurality-winning party, but that this effect is magnified tremendously by single-member districts and related features of first-past-the-post systems. Thus, in Britain, for example, the plurality party (Conservative or Labour) rarely wins a majority of the public's votes: indeed, it often is far short of it. Since the 1920s, however, the mechanical effect has been sufficiently strong that the plurality party captures a majority of seats in Parliament simply by winning a plurality of votes in a majority of single-member electoral districts. The second is what Duverger called the "psychological effect," in which those who support third parties (such as the UK's Liberal Party and its successors) will realize their vote for that third party will be "wasted" on a certain loser. At least some will therefore defect from their most preferred choice to support whichever of the two major parties is their second-most preferred option, to seek to avoid their least liked alternative from winning. This claim resonates in part because there is substantial, if imperfect, empirical evidence for it and in part because what Duverger called his "hypothesis" pairs with his "Law" to cover party systems. The "Hypothesis" is that, under proportional voting, multiparty systems are likely (where "multi" means "at least three").

This "Law" was, to Duverger, an empirical regularity for which he offered plausible explanations, but not a theory. Rae (1967) and many others explored the mechanical effect, but while the results are very interesting, the translation rules do not involve human decision making. The psychological effect is therefore where theorists turned. They need not have been rational choice theorists.[3] But they were. Indeed, two closely related but still differing streams of rational-choice-theoretic research sought to provide a formal derivation of Duverger's Law. One examined

---

[3] Indeed, one could argue that not only is a vote for the third most popular party wasted, it is also effectively just as certain that one's vote for *any* party or candidate, including the two most popular, is just as wasted. Avoiding a wasted vote could alternatively be explained by psychological concepts far removed from rational choice theory. It is just that wasted voting hasn't been explained thus.

the preferences over the choices, that is, the voters' utility for parties winning, combined with beliefs about the likelihood of each party winning (as surrogate for the likelihood of one's vote affecting the outcome). This focus, therefore, was on the voter. The second looked more carefully at the parties themselves, using their positioning in a spatial model, the question to which we turn first.

Party Positioning in a Spatial Model

Palfrey (1984, 1989) derived the first example of what has come to be known as a "Duvergerian equilibrium" from application of spatial modeling, primarily in contrast to Downsian convergence results (1957). Thus, Palfrey used the spatial model, in which parties take a point position for any given election. Voters select the party they most prefer (is closest to them in space). The question is whether there is an equilibrium pair of positions for two parties such that, should they adopt those two positions, there is no position for a third party to enter the election and win. In addition, the positions of the two parties must be "rational" in the sense that they would adopt them in competition against each other. In such equilibrium, the two existing parties tie in expectation, and there is no winning position for any third party to select and so none enters. In showing this result, he also assumed a sort of spatial symmetry of entry. That is, a third party is equally likely to enter and compete as a "left" party as it is to enter and compete as a "right" party. Palfrey found that there is such an equilibrium in a unidimensional policy space with divergence, e.g., if ideal points are uniform over [0,1] the equilibrium is at [¼,¾]. This was true regardless of whether voters were themselves strategic or "sincere" (that is, always voted for the closest party) in their voting behavior. In that sense, he proved Duverger's Law without the psychological effect Duverger invoked. Note that, while each party would like to converge to the median voter if they were confident that there would be no third party, the equilibrium is Nash (i.e., no player can move without harming his position), because if one party did move toward the center, a third party could enter and win by adopting a position just to the outside of the moving party's new position.

Palfrey's result remains pretty much state of the science. In a recent working paper, Aldrich and Lee (n.d.) find that there are often Palfrey-like equilibriums in multidimensional space, although with potentially interesting conditions in which at least three parties can coexist. For example, if three parties are located such that at least two are tied for second (or all three are tied) in support, this is also a Nash equilibrium, because there is a "coordination problem" multiparty equilibrium, consistent with that found in the second stream of research reviewed below.

There is a sort of impossibility result affecting this first stream of research. In its most general form, if voters have spatial preferences, any single party's support is entirely vulnerable. That is, any party can expect to have essentially zero votes.

For example, suppose that two parties enter together, one just to the left, the other just to the right of the original party. In that case, the original party's votes will converge to zero in expectation.[4] The general problem of entry of parties was studied by Shepsle (1991) and Greenberg and Shepsle (1987). They look at the problem of entry in spatial models, examining races for legislative seats. As they show, the primary effect of general and open rules for entry is that "entry may disrupt spatial equilibria" (1987, 525, abstract).

While this leads to something of a dead end in the literature that seeks to derive Duvergerian equilibrium from examination only of the rational choices made by parties, it has led to a suggestion of how we might define a "party system." A party system can be defined as the set of parties whose behavior is contingent, in equilibrium, on the set of other parties in the equilibrium, and vice versa. Thus, for spatial games, the party system is the set of parties whose spatial location depends upon the set of other parties in the equilibrium and whose behavior is in turn taken into account by the rest of the parties. Thus, in Palfrey's case, there is a two-party equilibrium, in which the choice of both depends upon the actions of each other. It also depends upon an ill-defined set of "any other party that might enter" and, thus, a two-party system really is a multiparty system with "latent" (not entering) third parties.

Voters and Duvergerian Equilibrium

The second stream of research on "derivations" of Duverger's Law has remained more lively. This stream examines voters and their evaluation of the parties, both in terms of preferences over parties and in terms of expectations, often expressed in terms of how close the party is to winning, but actually examining how likely it is that one's vote will affect the outcome. These may, of course, be tied to a spatial framework, but need not. The key point of difference is that the modeling takes the electorate's preferences and choices as the key moving parts, letting the parties and their actions fade more into the background.[5] In this sense, it is closer to Duverger's Law as originally stated. To the best of our knowledge, Feddersen (1992) is the first word on the derivation of the Law, per se, from this perspective. What he shows is that, if voters are strategic, in equilibrium only two parties will receive any votes. Thus, it appears to be the strategic calculation of voters that drives the result— pretty much as Duverger anticipated.

The ideas are, perhaps, best known through Cox (especially 1997). He offers a general result that is the by now well-known "$m + 1$" rule. He focuses on the effect of the district

---

[4] The earliest proof that we know of is due to Brams (1978). He derived it in thinking about multi-candidate nomination politics, where this form of entry is quite plausible.

[5] Feddersen, Sened, and Wright (1990) is an exception, in which both sets are strategic actors in a unidimensional spatial model, and convergence is implied.

magnitude, that is, on how many seats are elected from the individual district. If there are *m* of them, then there is room for exactly *m* + *1* parties. That is, rational, strategic voters will only vote for *m* + *1* parties, in equilibrium. The important new wrinkle in all of these sorts of results is that voters' information must meet what are sometimes called "rationality" conditions. Basically, that means that they must assimilate information according to Bayesian principles and, in addition, the information must be in balance across the electorate, in accord with the requirements of the Bayesian perfect equilibrium solution. In common terms, voters must agree on who is ahead and by how much as election day nears. Under these conditions, Duvergerian equilibriums are common.[6] Cox (1997) emphasizes that the Law applies only at the individual district level, however. It is therefore a separate question whether the same two parties will be found in any given set of districts, whether this will aggregate up to a two-party system at the national level, or whether it is possible to sustain a multiparty system in a world with two-party systems in each district or at least most districts. Chhibbar and Kollman (2004) argue something very like this account for explaining apparently multiparty systems in India and perhaps Canada.

Proportional Systems

Duverger's "tendency" was that under proportional systems, there was a tendency for multiparty systems to emerge. That is a weaker claim on his part for at least three reasons. First, "multiparty" does not tell us a precise number, just that there is a tendency for at least three parties to form. Second, there are many kinds of proportional systems and they have varying degrees of strength to any "mechanical" effect.[7] Most scholars seem to anticipate that the degree of psychological effect is reduced considerably (perhaps or perhaps not to zero). Abramson et al. (forthcoming) find that, empirically, "strategic voting" of this sort is nearly as common even under "very" proportional systems, although their evidence at least seems consistent with the claim that the aggregate effect is more dispersed over parties and thus less forceful in reducing the number of parties in the national system. Cox (1997), for example, notes that proportional systems are also governed by the *m* + *1* rule, implying an upper bound to the number of parties in the system. He also argues that strategic voting in such systems can occur for somewhat differing reasons, implying some of

---

[6] If there are three parties in a district with *m* = 1, and all three are tied or one party is ahead but the other two are tied, then there is also an equilibrium with all three parties receiving votes. This happens owing to the inability of voters to be certain of "coordinating" on which second place candidate to support. Such an interpretation of pre-2000 Mexico can be found in Díaz-Cayeros and Magaloni (1996).

[7] All proportional systems have some degree of mechanical effect, and, indeed, as district magnitude shrinks, the effect converges exactly to the two-party effect when *m* = 1, even if the system is otherwise "proportional."

the dispersion Abramson et al. (forthcoming) note. Kselman (forthcoming) develops a game-theoretic model in a proportional voting system in which the likelihood of entry is inversely related to the number of currently existing parties, and shows that, when two existing parties are appropriately polarized in a unidimensional space (following Palfrey's model), third party entry might not happen even in a proportional system. The reason is that by dividing the ideologically similar parties' votes, the disparate large party increases its chances of winning the executive. In short, the work on proportional systems is less fully developed than under plurality systems. Similar kinds of results, however, seem most often to be found, suggesting that the important differences between the two types of voting systems (which are generally the strongest institutional variable in empirical accounts of party systems) remain to be developed.

FORMAL THEORIES OF PARTIES IN ELECTIONS

The formal analysis of parties and elections is usually traced to Anthony Downs's classic *An Economic Theory of Democracy* (1957), which, famously, asks what platform a rational (by which Downs means solely election-motivated) party presents the public when it contests office.[8] Downs's answers to this question, and the subsequent refinements to these answers by formal theorists to model the political process in different institutional environments, are the focus of this section.

The starting point for Downs's analysis of party platform choice is Hotelling's (1929) famous median voter theorem. His analysis proceeds from the following set of assumptions about motivations, information, and the institutional environment: (1) there are two parties, (2) which are motivated solely by the desire to win today, (3) who contest a single-round election within a single constituency, (4) decided by plurality rule, (5) by announcing platforms that can be assigned spatial locations along a left–right ideological continuum representing the percentage of the economy the party would leave in private hands in the event of its election; (6) that citizens do not look beyond the next election, (7) do not have the option of abstention, and (8) prefer the party that is closest to them along this ideological continuum; and finally, (9) there is no uncertainty about party platforms or voters' ideal points. If these conditions are satisfied, then, in equilibrium, both parties will announce the policy position most preferred by the voter with the median ideology. The logic of the median voter theorem is that a party which chooses a platform at the ideal point of the median voter is assured at least a majority of the votes if its opponent chooses any other platform: knowing that it guarantees victory if it adopts that platform and its

[8] Although, the application of the familiar spatial model of voting dates at least to Lowell (1913).

opponent does not, and it would not benefit from adopting a platform other than the median voter's ideal point if its opponent chooses the median voter's ideal point as its platform, when the above conditions are satisfied an office-motivated party always chooses the median voter's ideal point.

In light of the family of impossibility results noted in the Introduction, it is widely accepted among formal theorists that Hotelling's theorem is knifed-edged in the sense that a violation of any one of its many assumptions may lead to non-median party platform choices (cf. Grofman 2004). Downs himself addresses one such possibility when he considers what might occur if citizens are given the opportunity to abstain from voting and they are future-oriented. In such cases, candidates might choose divergent platforms in a two-party system. His rationale is that if extremist voters are future-oriented, they might withhold their support from a party that converges to the ideal point of the median voter (knowing that their utility differential from voting for the two parties is zero if both parties have centrist platforms): if enough voters act this way, then an office-motivated party hoping to win elections might adopt a non-centrist platform in order to induce ideological extremists to turn out to vote. He argues that this process is especially likely to occur if there are large numbers of voters at the ideological extremes. Hinich and Ordeshook (1969) have expressed a variant of Downs's intuition in a more rigorous way (see also Hinich and Munger 1997).

Much of the subsequent work exploring the behavior of candidates and parties has retained Downs's assumptions of two-party competition and a unidimensional policy space to explore when parties might adopt platforms other than that most preferred by the median voter. Some particularly fertile areas of inquiry have been to understand how equilibrium party and voter strategies change when there is a non-spatial component to voter behavior (e.g., Enelow and Hinich 1982), policy-motivated parties (e.g., Wittman 1983), or uncertainty about voter ideal points or candidate locations (Calvert 1985). Much of this work, however, has been motivated by the effort to explain how the Downsian spatial model can be reconciled with the empirical observation that candidates and parties rarely (never?) adopt identical policy platforms when contesting elections. Rather than providing a lengthy survey of this literature (see Grofman 2004 for an excellent review), our focus in this section is on understanding how party organizations give structure to electoral competition in the context of the spatial model of elections in settings (more than two parties and/or more than one dimension of competition) where the early impossibility results suggest that structure should not exist.

Nomination Procedures

The possibility that party organizations might provide structure to elections was first anticipated by a pair of models examining how party nomination procedures might affect platform choices.[9] In particular, this work showed that if candidates must first win a primary election, where the actors responsible for choosing the candidate are not themselves office-motivated, then it is likely that candidates will choose non-median platforms. Aranson and Ordeshook (1972) consider the case where voters cast ballots sincerely in both the primary and general election and candidates choose non-median platforms that maximize their probability of winning both races. Coleman (1971, 1972) examines the setting where primary election voters take into account a candidate's probability of winning an election as a function of their platform and who cast their votes in the primary strategically in the sense that they want to nominate the candidate whose platform is closest to their ideal point who is also able to win an election.

Activists and Ideologues

Both of these accounts treat the preferences of party activists as exogenous parameters. Aldrich (1983a, 1983b) considers the more primitive question of why voters choose to become party activists. In Aldrich (1983a) he demonstrates that if activists have policy preferences in a unidimensional policy space and follow ordinary spatial preference rules for deciding whether to become active and in which party to be active, but choose the party on the basis of the distribution of activists already engaged in the two parties, then even in a unidimensional space, the distribution of activists will be polarized in equilibrium. Aldrich (1983b) extends this model to the case where voters have policy preferences in more than one dimension. The fundamental result in this paper is that there exist equilibriums and these will be polarized, as in the unidimensional case. In general, the parties will polarize along the most salient dimension, "converging" on less salient dimensions. One key result, therefore, is that there are equilibrium distributions for the two parties even when there is no equilibrium in voting.

Aldrich and McGinnis (1989) use this framework to understand how party activists' decisions to contribute to their party's nominee affect her platform choice. They show that when candidates' electoral fortunes are aided by support from their party (and the parties have activist bases with distinct sets of preferences), then there exist equilibriums where candidates adopt divergent policy platforms in multidimensional policy spaces. Aldrich and McGinnis argue that party organizations create a structure-induced equilibrium in electoral

---

[9] Depending on the setting, nomination procedures may be usefully thought of as being exogenous or endogenous institutions. To the best of our knowledge, however, researchers have not addressed why a party organization that is free to select its own nomination procedure would choose a set of rules that induce its candidates to choose non-centrist policy positions, especially when its opponent (who is not necessarily selected by a primary election constituency) may be free to adopt a platform that is optimal in the general election without regard to its primary election constituency.

games that solves social choice problems in elections. This conclusion is similar to the role that Congress's committee structure plays in solving social choice problems in legislatures in the manner suggested by Shepsle.

Roemer (2001) develops an alternative model of two-party competition in a multidimensional policy space that also yields equilibrium behavior. In his account, there are internal party divisions between hard-core ideologues, purely office-motivated politicians, and a group which cares about both policy and office. He assumes that these actors must mutually agree to changes to an existing party platform, taking into account whether the new platform makes all members of the organization better-off. He finds that in many (but not all) circumstances, the parties settle on an equilibrium pair of platforms where either the ideologues or the purely office-motivated politicians reject any modification to the party platform.

A final model is by Schofield and Sened (2006), in which they consider the case of multiple parties in a multidimensional policy space. They assume that voter choices may be stochastic (in the manner suggested by Hinich 1977), that each party is endowed with a valence advantage describing how much voters favor the organization for non-policy reasons, and that each party is motivated to maximize its vote share. Under relatively restrictive circumstances, they find that there is a Local Nash Equilibrium where all parties converge to the mean (as opposed to the median) voter; otherwise, there is often a Local Nash Equilibrium in which parties locate along a common axis with the parties with the weakest valence advantage adopting positions furthest from the political center. The intuition for this result is that the parties with the weakest valence advantage have a lower probability of winning votes at the center than parties with higher valences, so the weaker parties adopt more extreme platforms (where there are fewer voters whose votes they have a higher probability of winning because of spatial proximity). In elaborations of the model, Sened and Schofield build on Aldrich and McGinnis's (1989) model of party activism to make valence advantages endogenous to parties' platform choices. A natural implication of this extension is that parties, hoping to secure a valence advantage, may need to adopt non-mean platforms in order to motivate party activists to contribute to the organization's electoral success.

FORMAL THEORIES OF THE CREDIBILITY OF PARTY PROMISES WHEN IN GOVERNMENT

Recent chapters by Laver (2006) and Diermeier (2006) in the Oxford Handbooks of Political Science series have admirably demonstrated the power of formal models of political parties in government. One important contribution of formal theory that they identify is that of the implications of constitutional structures such as the separation of powers (e.g. Krehbiel 1998) or the confidence vote procedure (Huber 1996; Diermeier and Feddersen 1998) for the level of party discipline (and discipline within the ruling coalition in multiparty settings) exhibited in government. A second important contribution concerns the ways in which parties provide institutional solutions to social choice problems in legislatures (e.g., Laver and Schofield 1990; T. Schwartz 1977; see also Rohde, Chapter 17 in this volume, for an assessment of applications of theories of parties in the US Congress). Therefore, we consider a question that links the electoral promises made by parties and candidates considered above to the actions of parties when in office, as in the works cited above. This critical question is how political parties *credibly* promise to fulfill their campaign promises in office given that office-motivated politicians have incentives to mislead the electorate about the policies they intend to pursue once in office. Answers to this question have important implications both for the possibility of representative democracy with regard to the question of how votes for officeholders translate into public policy and for the scholarly understanding of why voters depend on partisan cues at the ballot box.

Downs (1957) may have been the first to consider the possibility that parties might not follow through on their electoral promises. He argues that parties' electoral motivations over the long term provide them with incentives to be reliable (to keep campaign promises if elected) and responsible (to campaign on the basis of past policy accomplishments). Parties have incentives to be reliable because they want voters to believe that they keep their campaign promises. Having a reputation for being reliable is especially important for out-parties who cannot campaign on the basis of their recent performance in office and, given that a reputation for reliability can only be earned by a party while in office, the current ruling party has incentives to follow through on its campaign promises to ensure that it can contest future elections when it is out of office on the basis of a credible party platform. Similarly, a party has incentives to be responsible because voters observing frequent changes in its issue positions will conclude that it is unlikely to follow through on its campaign promises that require implementation over the long run. Grynaviski (2009) describes Downs's mechanism by which parties maintain their brand names as being akin to how firms of the early twentieth century solved the adverse selection problem in consumer markets through one-product, one-brand-name, branding strategies.

Downs's discussion of how parties maintain brand names was not explicitly linked to his formal analysis of voter behavior. Bernhardt and Ingberman (1985) rectify this. They describe a two-party system where the incumbent has established a reputation for pursuing particular types of policies (a reputation that the challenger does not possess), which means, all else equal, that incumbents will be viewed by voters as the less risky choice. By implication, the incumbent's reputation gives rise to the incumbency advantage when voters are risk-averse and the ideal point of the median voter does not change from one election to the next. On the other hand, if the ideal point of the median voter changes between elections, then the incumbent has incentives to change her platform to appeal better to the political center. In this case, the incumbent party's decision to distance itself from its past actions makes it the riskier bet—the greater the move, the greater the increase in voter uncertainty. An office-motivated incumbent party must therefore balance policy distance from the median voter with the greater uncertainty that voters feel when responding to changes in the incumbent's behavior. The authors demonstrate that the need to maintain a reputation for being responsible (in Downs's sense) induces parties to be reasonably consistent in their platforms over time, and, with the ideal point of the median voter changing over time, gives rise to divergent policy platforms.

A common element of the above-mentioned work on party platform credibility is the notion that a party is a single, infinitely lived team worried about maintaining its reputation over the long term. Relaxing this assumption greatly complicates modeling how parties credibly signal their intent to implement their platform in office because it is no longer possible to treat parties analytically as if they were analogous to firms trying to maximize their long-run profits by maintaining their brand name.

To the best of our knowledge, Alesina and Spear (1988) were the first to examine the case where there is more than one party member. Their model begins from the observation that a politician whose career has a known finite endpoint has strong incentives to adopt the policies she most prefers in her last term in office and cannot credibly commit to a centrist platform (see also Alesina 1988). They argue that political parties provide an institutional solution to this problem. Specifically, an incumbent politicians' successor in her party may provide her with some form of payment (e.g., advocating for her policies; raising funds for a presidential library) to prevent her from behaving opportunistically in office. Thus, intergenerational transfers allow the party's candidates to credibly commit to a centrist platform.

Harrington (1992) argues that parties can credibly commit their lame duck members to campaign promises even without this kind of transfer. He argues that policy-motivated incumbents care about both the policies implemented today and those implemented in the future. To the extent that a party's future candidates compete on the basis of the incumbent's reputation, the incumbent has incentives to adopt more centrist policies than she sincerely prefers in order to boost the organization's chances in future elections. Such an equilibrium, however, is quite sensitive to the rate at which the incumbent discounts future policy payoffs—the greater the discounting of the future, the more extreme the laws adopted by a policy-motivated lawmaker.

Snyder and Ting (2002) examine the more interesting case where there exists more than one party member seeking office at the same time (a legislative party, perhaps). In their work, candidates for office join parties because they provide a brand name that conveys a credible signal about the types of policies they would support. The way parties perform this function is by providing institutions that penalize candidates whose sincere preferences disagree with the party platform—the penalty that candidates incur is increasing in the distance between their preferences and the party platform. Voters, observing these institutions, infer that the only types of candidates who will join the party in equilibrium are those individuals whose sincere preference is to adhere to the party platform. In subsequent work, Snyder and Ting (2002) extend the model to allow incumbents within the party to develop personal reputations through their voting behavior that is distinct from that of their co-partisans.

Levy (2004) applies similar intuitions to model how parties might commit their members to a platform in a multidimensional policy space. Similar to Alesina and Spear (1988), she assumes that no individual candidate can credibly commit to a platform that disagrees with her sincere preferences—this is problematic for office-motivated candidates who are fully willing to compromise ideology for office. They join political parties because, she assumes, they have the ability to coerce group members into toeing the party line once in office. Political parties can therefore credibly commit to pursuing any policy in the Pareto set of its members (much like the case of the individual politician, parties cannot credibly commit to any policy outside the Pareto set because all organization members, once in office, would prefer to pass laws in the Pareto set). This is obviously advantageous to ambitious politicians who, acting alone, cannot credibly commit to such a platform.

Taking a different tack on how legislative parties commit their members to a set of policy positions, Grynaviski (2009) places the emphasis on a party's reputation. He argues that a party forms a reputation about the range of issue positions that its nominees will support, that it values this reputation because it decreases the costs of winning office, and the lesser the variation in party members' issue positions the greater the benefit to the party's office-seekers. As a result, voters infer that it is costly for a party to allow its members to cross party lines too often. Since voters understand that parties want to avoid this penalty, it is rational for them to infer that party organizations create a control apparatus to effectively whip group members and to treat a party affiliation as a credible signal about the kinds of policies officeholders might pursue (even if they do not observe these institutions themselves). Nicely, this model simultaneously accounts for how multi-candidate parties with a seemingly weak party control apparatus might provide brand names to office-seekers and for the stability of party programs over time.

FORMAL THEORIES OF PARTIES IN GOVERNMENT

Thus far, this chapter has sought to identify the contributions of formal theory to the study of parties as electoral institutions, that is, to the study of institutions that structure the choices presented to voters on election day. Specifically, we have tried to reveal the insights that formal theory provides about the nature of a polity's electoral rules and the number of parties; how the internal characteristics of party organizations (such as its nominations procedures, or the nature of its activists' base) affects party platform choices; and how party reputations and a party's control apparatus affect whether voters find party platforms to be credible signals about the performance of its nominees in office. We have largely neglected models of parties in government, except inasmuch as the activities of parties in government are embedded (often implicitly) in the work that we have reviewed in a blunt—once in office the party implements platform X—kind of way.

Given recent excellent contributions to the Oxford Handbooks in Political Science series by Laver (2006) and Diermeier (2006) that address formal models of parties in government, and, for the US case, by Rohde (Chapter 17 in this volume), we have chosen to focus on elections and on credibility. It is worthwhile to dedicate some attention to the linkage between formal models of parties in elections and those of parties in government. In particular, we want to highlight the ways in which formal models of parties in elections are essentially models of important inputs—notably, the number of parties in the chamber and office-holders' policy commitments—which, in addition to constitutional provisions regarding the organization of the government, formal models of parties in government often treat as primitive concepts.

The formal analysis of legislative parties is complicated by the vast array of constitutional structures that, in combination, determine the role of parties in government. Three institutions stand out as especially important. The first is the electoral rules governing elections, which, as we noted above, have a substantial effect on the number of parties in government and whether some form of coalition government is required because a single party does not control a majority of seats in government. The second such institution is the rules governing the legislature's ability to dissolve the government through a vote of confidence (or no confidence). As the literature cited above notes, such a vote provides a powerful stimulus for high levels of party discipline in voting on legislation. It is thought to be a significant institutional feature in explaining the differences for so long observed between the relatively low levels of party voting found in the US Congress, for example, and those found in most parliamentary democracies. Of course, saying so is different from showing the comparative statistics and estimating relevant equations flowing from them. The third such institution is whether there is a significant degree of separation of powers, particularly between the legislative and executive branches, and a significant degree of federalism in contrast to unitary concentrations (see Tsebelis 1997, 2002). If we divide this set into plurality versus proportional electoral systems, vote of confidence or not, and many veto points versus few, then there are eight cases. Results are available for some, but not all, of these cases. And, of course, in time these should serve as the variables from which continuous deductions are drawn.

CONCLUSIONS

Rational-choice-based models of political parties (a subset of formal models of political parties) have developed coherent streams of research about two very different sorts of questions. One sort is best exemplified by the search for a rigorous theoretical basis for Duvergerian conclusions. Here the question was well posed in advance (indeed, perhaps for over a century), but the theoretical basis for the empirical observations was recognized by all scholars as underdeveloped. The second sort of question, well exemplified in our discussion of the credibility of party promises, is one that had eluded serious investigation until the new institutional theorists began serious study of it. The general point, then, in both cases is that rational choice theorists have tackled complex problems in the study of political parties, questions where no particularly strong theory existed, but areas where there were either extensive systematic empirical studies or sufficiently developed empirical understandings to serve as guiding intuitions for the development of rigorous theories. More importantly, the results derived from the accounts have yielded new and valuable insights for the empirical understandings of political parties. Thus, the elucidation of the forces underlying Duverger's Law demonstrated how the problem was not to generate forces toward forming a two-party system under plurality rule but how political party leaders faced the rather different problem of aggregating the within-district tendencies toward two-partyism into a national two-party system. Similarly, the problem with credibility of party promises becomes less how to understand polarization of American party politics at the end of the twentieth and beginning of the twenty-first century: once polarized, it is now easy enough to understand its reinforcing nature. The question is, how did such a diverse Democratic majority as existed from the early to mid-twentieth century sustain itself as long as it did?

CHAPTER 3

INTEREST GROUP THEORY

ANDREW MCFARLAND

IN this chapter, following the book's emphasis on American politics, I focus on interest group theory as it applies to American politics and deemphasize topics of greater relevance to other political systems or to international relations. This emphasis is represented in the four-step framework describing interest-group theory building stated below. After the four-step framework, I consider various developing themes in interest group theory, especially as it applies to American politics.

THE FOUR-STEP THEORETICAL FRAMEWORK

The *Federalist Papers*, particularly contributions by James Madison, set forth a theory of the constitutional order which has influenced Americans ever since. In particular the *Federalist Papers* set forth a type of theory of interest groups later known as "countervailing power," or that could be referenced with the term "balance of interests." Madison was concerned with the problem that in a republic, personal liberty allowed citizens to band together to pursue rash passions or special interests which might be opposed to the general good. Repressing the liberty to pursue selfish interests is authoritarian, but the constitutional order can be constructed to balance the adverse effects of selfishness if one expands the political order from the particular local unit to a more general government, encompassing the local units. Within the more general unit, different interests will offset the ill effects of a locally dominant interest opposed to the general good. This was not, however, a modern consideration of special-interest politics, because Madison was concerned with the problem of "majority tyranny," that is, the ill effects of a temporary, rash local majority opposed to the long-run, general good in both the local and the hypothetical general constituency. After adopting the concept of judicial review, Madison's developing constitutional order left it to the US Supreme Court and the federal judicial system to restrict the effects of majority tyranny. Not substantially treated by Madison, the problem of minority tyranny, the question of minority interests triumphing over the general good, was not so clearly dealt with by the courts. Nevertheless, Madison's model of countervailing power constitutes an interest group theory applying to both majority and minority tyranny (J. Berry and Wilcox 2007).

Madison's view about ordinary politics involving the pursuit of interests is reflected in the first step in the evolving framework of interest group theory. This first step has been termed *group theory* (not interest group theory) by American political science. Political science recognizes Arthur F. Bentley as the original proponent of group theory with the publication of *The Process of Government* in 1908, although, strictly speaking, Bentley was not widely read until revived by the chief proponent of group theory, David Truman, in 1951. American graduate education in the social sciences was heavily influenced by the German graduate school model and German social theory in the period 1885–1905. German social theory regarded "the state" as an entity above the behavior of individuals; the state was seen as sovereign, embodying the law as an idealized cultural statement, and certainly the state and law were autonomous from influence from everyday political factors. Bentley reacted strongly against such Germanic ideals, and stated an interest group theory that went to the other extreme. He viewed all politics and government as based on group actions seeking interests, with interest defined as economic interest. The governmental process, then, was a process of interaction and power among economic interests, while the state and the law were ultimately reducible to representations of interest. This was, however, different from Marx, as such interests were group economic interests, not class interests. In any event, Bentley's fundamental political reality was the process of group interaction in the pursuit of evolving, often conflicting, economic interests (Bentley 1908, 1967; Truman 1951).

Group theory reached its apogee in 1951–61 after the publication of David Truman's *The Governmental Process*. Like Bentley, Truman stated that the process of interaction among political groups is the fundamental basis for understanding American politics. Truman backed off somewhat from Bentley's extreme emphasis on economic interests, as Truman preferred to state that political groups are organizations of social and political attitudes, opinion predispositions that might not be economic in nature. Truman did not make definite statements as to whether the structure of political institutions and the law is solely epiphenomenal to the group struggle, although *The Governmental Process* leaves the impression that the balance of power among groups is usually much more important than legal or institutional structure factors. Thus, Truman was often taken to mean that the law and political institutions simply acted as referees, adjudicating the rules of the process of the group struggle for power, with the balance of power among groups as the fundamental political factor. Truman based his study on numbers of empirical studies, particularly in the period 1945–50, describing political reality as a process of interaction among political groups, as in describing "how a bill becomes a law." Accordingly, during the 1950s, Truman's group theory was taken to be the cutting edge of realistic political science, and for a while "group theory" was "interest group theory" and the idea that political groups are the fundamental variable of politics and government was widely accepted.

However, in the 1960s group theory was displaced on the mantelpiece of theory by "pluralism," or more appropriately "Robert A. Dahl's pluralism" (Dahl 1961). Group theory was the first stage of American interest group theory; pluralism was the second stage. Dahl developed pluralist theory in distinction to C. Wright Mills's power elite theory (1956), widely circulated throughout academia. Essentially Mills argued that a national power elite dominated America; this elite consisted of a generally allied group of perhaps a thousand top national government officials, executives of the biggest corporations, and leading military officers. Mills described this power elite as having the money, the power in the federal government, and the control over force to have the most power in America. Dahl argued that one needed to do case studies to show that an elite actually controlled decisions. A widely read study by Floyd Hunter (1953) argued that a power elite ruled the city of Atlanta; in *Who Governs?* Dahl showed there was no power elite in New Haven. In this oft-reprinted book, Dahl put forth a theory of power, focusing on the role of competitive elections in controlling social and political elites. He argued that citizens had variable motivations to use resources such as money and time to pursue political power, and that sometimes these resources might be contributed to the organizing of interest groups. Dahl's pluralism was not foremost a theory of interest groups; instead, it was an overall theory of power. But because Dahl's pluralism was the dominant theory in the American politics research during the 1960s, it was also the dominant interest group theory during that time. Dahl's perspective was that group theory overstated the role of political groups, and his emphasis on political parties and elections implied that these factors were more important than interest groups. Nonetheless, *Who Governs?* indicates that interest groups have significant influence in politics, as was the case of teachers in New Haven school policy. Dahl also showed that in the pluralist process, citizens could readily mobilize into interest groups which had the potential to wield power over policy. Essentially Dahl found the American political process to have decentralized political power, and a significant amount of this power was wielded by interest groups, representing the interests of citizens motivated to contribute political resources to the groups (Dahl 1961, 192–9).

Dahl's pluralism stresses the role of competitive elections, and he did not state that public policy is solely determined by the balance of power among interest groups, a misreading common in the political science literature, especially during 1975–85 (noted by Krasner 1984). This was a semantic error as Bentley and Truman were sometimes called "pluralists," meaning they affirmed the influence of groups as opposed to doctrines and observations of state sovereignty and dominance. It was Bentley and Truman who came close to saying that public policy was solely determined by the interaction of groups. Dahl was called a "pluralist" as opposed to Mills' power elite theory, but Dahl's pluralism was a different theory than Truman's pluralism. In *Who Governs?* political parties, politicians, government agencies, and interest groups are all seen as influencing public policy (Dahl 1961, 153–5, 192–9, 120–30).

A more trenchant criticism of Dahl's pluralist theory and its attendant interest group theory is that it does not provide for an unequal capacity to organize interest groups. This is the third step in the theoretical framework of interest group theory which I term "multiple-elitism," the position that multiple special interests tend to rule American politics. Dahl's pluralist theory leaves the impression that individuals are free to contribute their political resources to interest groups, which will then give contributing individuals some form of satisfactory representation in the policymaking process. Dahl's pluralist theory indicates that a plurality of interests are satisfactorily represented (another reason for the use of "pluralism" in reference to this theory). However, Dahl's theory of interest groups was undermined by a fundamental critique by Mancur Olson, Jr., known as "the logic of collective action" (M. Olson 1965). Olson noted that public policy frequently produces "public goods," benefits such that if one person in an area receives the benefit, then, by its very nature, all persons in that area receive the benefit. The archetypical case is clean air.

If an interest group lobby succeeds in influencing policy to obtain a public good, then it will go to everyone in the area, regardless of whether they contributed to the lobby (e.g., getting an amendment to air pollution regulations). Then if we model individuals as economically rational, it does not pay the individual to contribute to the lobby, because the individual will get the benefit anyway. As a consequence, only lobbies with a few beneficiaries (such as a few corporations) will organize, because this is the case in which the individuals or contributing groups get a positive payoff for contributing. On the other hand, groups with perhaps a hundred or more potential beneficiaries will not organize, as individuals will not get a positive payoff if they contribute, since either they will get the public good anyway, or else the benefit is smaller than the contribution (a consumer supporting a lobby to eliminate sugar import quotas to reduce the price of sugar). It follows that groups representing a few businesses or professional associations will organize, but diffused groups of millions of consumers, taxpayers, residents of the environment, and so forth will not organize. Thus, in the world of interest group politics, according to the logic of collective action, the few defeat the many. And thus, the plurality of satisfactory representation in Dahl's pluralism cannot be expected to exist. Instead, Olson's interest group theory posits rule by the few, or rule by "special interests," each in its own particular area of public policy. This is not Mills's elitism, nor Dahl's pluralism, but rule by multiple elites, each in its own policy area (M. Olson 1965).

During the 1970s, the dominant interest group theory of American politics was Theodore Lowi, Jr.'s, "interest group liberalism," a form of multiple-elite theory congruent with Olson's collective action theory of groups (Lowi 1969, 1979). Lowi used the term "liberalism" in its European sense, meaning a political philosophy stressing the privacy of individuals, individual rights, and free markets and thus opposed to doctrines of state sovereignty and expansion of governmental power. Lowi argued that since the 1930s, American jurisprudence and legislation had become dominated by the interest group liberal theory of a weak state and vague, flexible legislation, delegating policymaking to administrators, who, not constrained by specific legislative language in the process of policy implementation, form coalitions with like-minded interest groups and interested legislators. According to Lowi, organized special interests are thus able to control specific areas of policymaking of concern to themselves, and deflect policy implementation to reflect their own particular goals, rather than those of a much larger public.

Lowi has been extraordinarily influential (Roettger 1978) in stating a concept of distributive politics, a type of interest group theory. Lowi stated a well-known threefold typology of public policy: regulatory (business versus labor), redistributive (upper class versus lower class), and "distributive politics," in which specific, tangible benefits are distributed by government, such as construction projects, subsidies, and grants. Lowi argued that distributive politics is characterized by special-interest rule in which coalitions of interests, government agencies, and friendly legislators work together to distribute benefits to particular constituencies, such as specific local areas or economic producer groups. Interest group behavior in distributive politics is different from group behavior in the regulatory policy area, in which there is a greater tendency to have policy battles among broad coalitions of groups, rather than logrolling among special interests as in distributive politics (Lowi 1964).

Another influential contributor to multiple-elite theory was E. E. Schattschneider, the author of a study of the Smoot–Hawley tariff of 1930, the textbook example of a policymaking disaster in which legislators submitted to the influence of hundreds of particular economic interest groups, each seeking its own tariff protection (Schattschneider 1935). The aggregate import policy, derived from a huge logroll among interest groups, led to retaliation by foreign countries against US exports, making the Great Depression even worse. Schattschneider subsequently argued (1960) that interest groups are unrepresentative, reflecting the interests of an upper class, and that strong political parties are needed to represent the general public to countervail the power of unrepresentative interest groups.

A compendium of the theories of Olson, Lowi, and Schattschneider can be called "multiple-elite theory," as their general theory of interest group politics is that separate coalitions, based on interest groups, separately dominate numerous different areas of public policy. The theories of interest group liberalism, distributive politics, the logic of collective action, and class dominance in groups contributed to multiple-elite theory, the third theoretical step after group theory and Dahl's pluralism. Other writers had contributed to multiple-elite theory (e.g. Cater 1964; Edelman 1964; McConnell 1966; Selznick 1953; Stigler 1975), which was the leading interest group theory in the 1970s.

However, in the 1980s and 1990s, a *fourth step* in interest group theory appeared: *neopluralism*. Case studies of public policymaking often did not reveal the pattern of some special-interest coalition dominating an area of policy, but instead showed a plurality of interests influencing policy, with none of such interests being dominant (J. Berry 1985; Bosso 1987; C. Jones 1975; J. Wilson 1980). Observations of such a plurality of interests differed from the observations of group theory and Dahl's pluralism, however, in that the neopluralist scholars did not come close to saying that the observed plurality fairly represented all of the interests. The new case studies did indicate a special difficulty in organizing widely diffuse interests, even if public interest groups and citizens' groups did have some countervailing power against business groups and professional associations. The neopluralists admitted the possibility that elitist group coalitions might dominate numbers of public policy areas, even while a plurality of groups appeared in most such areas. The neopluralists all observed that the state was not just a dependent variable in a power struggle among groups, and all neopluralists observed that the state and its component institutions often acted autonomously, initiating components of public policy on their own, although such initiatives might be challenged by groups (J. Wilson 1980).

Neopluralist research findings may be defined as accepting Dahl's pluralism in finding power and interest groups in American politics to be held by multiple groups and individuals. But neopluralism is further defined as giving priority emphasis (unlike Dahl) to the existence of hundreds of policy issue areas, and to the finding that while many issue areas are characterized by a plurality of groups, some issue areas are elitist, ruled by a single coalition or perhaps having just a handful of influential groups. Concomitant to definition, neopluralists stress the coincident autonomy of many governmental agencies, and also stress that the plurality of separate issue areas is not equivalent to a system of fair representation.

In addition to case studies of policymaking processes, a number of scholars studied the various environmental groups, Common Cause, and other citizens' groups that were organized or surged in membership particularly during 1968–75. Political scientists concluded that such newly mobilized "public interest groups" did indeed exercise significant influence over public policy and wielded a degree of countervailing power to special-interest coalitions (J. Berry 1999; Bosso 2005; McFarland 1984; Rothenberg 1992).

Neopluralists had to deal with a major question: why did public interest groups, citizens' groups, and other large membership groups exist in spite of the logic of collective action? They derived at least three theoretical answers. The first of these was Hugh Heclo's observations about "issue networks" (Heclo 1978). He observed the existence of communication networks among public policy elites acting in the same area of policymaking; such elites include interest group leaders, concerned legislators, administrators of public agencies, business executives, scholars researching that area of policy, journalists, social movement activists, and so forth. Such individuals are concerned on a full-time basis about a type of public policy. Issue area activists have the resources to form interest coalitions which can exercise countervailing power against the special-interest coalitions described by Olson and Lowi. Paul Sabatier and Hank Jenkins-Smith extended the concept of issue network activists with the observation that much public policy is influenced by the struggle of relatively permanent (say ten years) "advocacy coalitions" of activists, such as environmentalists versus developers in many areas of the West (Sabatier and Jenkins-Smith 1993).

Neopluralists observe that social movements have spun off interest groups seeking to represent widely diffused interests, such as representing the environment, women, and so forth (see below).

Jack Walker, Jr.'s, major neopluralist contribution was the observation that "patrons" often exist to provide money and other resources to organize interest groups. Walker's concept of patron applied not only to wealthy individuals, but also to government agencies, foundations, and previous groups spinning off new groups. In fact, Walker argued, in the United States a surprising number of major interest groups spring from original organizational efforts by the federal government including the US Chamber of Commerce, the Business Roundtable, the Farm Bureau, the National Organization of Women, and the National Rifle Association. The Ford Foundation played a prominent role in organizing environmental lobbies around 1970 (Walker 1991). The National Retired Teachers' Association and the Colonial Penn Life Insurance Company founded the American Association of Retired Persons (AARP); Common Cause developed from the previous Urban Coalition and the entrepreneurial efforts of John W. Gardner; the Sierra Club spun off Friends of the Earth, etc. (Bosso 2005; McFarland 1984; Pratt 1976). Patrons may provide money to the political entrepreneur who actually organizes a group; however, political entrepreneurs might be forced to provide most of their own group organizing resources, in order someday to reap the reward of heading an influential group (Salisbury 1969; J. Berry 1978).

This, then, is the neopluralist theory of interest groups, the fourth step in the succession of theories. The logic of collective action, special-interest control over particular policy areas, and distributive politics are important theoretical factors, but countervailing power results from issue networks, advocacy coalitions, social movements, political patrons, and group entrepreneurs. Usually one observes a plurality of interest groups in American politics, but this should not be confused as observing fair representation in the political process. Political parties, the electoral process, autonomous actions of state agencies and public institutions are areas of public action each about equal in influence to that of interest groups, in neopluralist theory. The four steps of interest group theory leading to neopluralism are considered to be mainstream political science, and David Truman, Robert Dahl, Theodore Lowi, and E. E. Schattschneider all were elected presidents of the American Political Science Association. (Mancur Olson was an economist.)

Let us consider a few theoretical contributions from other disciplines.

SOCIOLOGY AND ECONOMICS

One basis of neopluralist theory is the observation that social movements lead to the formation of interest groups. Before 1985 (approximately), there was a disciplinary hiatus between political science and the political sociology of social movements (but see Jo Freeman 1975). However, Jack Walker (1983, 1991) began to put forth an argument influenced by the resource mobilization theory of social movements—the need to focus on the resources for political mobilization derived from patrons, such as governments, foundations, and the wealthy. After a landmark work by Doug McAdam (1982, 1999), political sociologists developed a synthesis of social movement theory focusing on four variables: (1) resource mobilization, (2) the existence of political opportunities, (3) issue framing, identity, and cultural variables, (4) the general context of grievances (Tarrow 1994). This "political opportunities" theory of social movements bolsters the neopluralist theory of a plurality of groups. "Political opportunities" refers to the observation that movements are partially induced by conditions in the political system, such as the favorability of the US Supreme Court and the presidency to the civil rights movement after 1946.

A second contribution of sociology to neopluralism is network theory. The network analysis eschews the framework of resources and goals, most common among interest group scholars, and substitutes the graphics of communication patterns among principal actors. Data are gathered about who communicates with whom, and such data are displayed graphically, usually in terms of lines among dots, whose density and arrangement display a social structure. For instance, among Washington lobbies we normally observe lobbies communicating with like lobbies, similarly acting in a specialized area of public policy. On the other hand, almost no lobbies communicate in a general way through a general area of policy, such as agriculture or health. The data rich network study *The Hollow Core* displayed this pattern, with general area networks shown as a wheel, with similar groups networked together at the periphery, but with almost no groups located at the center of the network, communicating in a general way, as spokes around a hub. At first such data might seem to support multiple-elite theory, as it shows multiple clusters of interaction among similar groups, but such a cluster may be checked in political influence by some other cluster on the other side of the general-area network (Heinz et al. 1993).

A further contribution of network theory is usefulness in indicating the structure of lobbying coalitions, because we can say intuitively about half of the action in Washington lobbying is conducted by coalitions of interest groups, not by groups acting alone. A network analysis of coalitions is indicative of their overall strength in mobilizing groups into the coalition, as well as indicating their potential for selecting different paths of action as related to the various strength of internal clusters within the whole (Heaney 2004a; Shapiro 2004).

The main contribution of economics to neopluralist theory is Olson's logic of collective action. Olson's perspectives on political groups were derived from the theory of oligopoly, in which a few firms collude to restrict production to raise the price of their product, thereby increasing profits. (OPEC is the famous example.) A few firms may succeed in such collaboration, but as the number of firms increases, there is an increasing incentive to become a "free-rider," that is, a firm which increases its production, rather than decreases it, but still benefits from the price increase. Olson observed that a similar pattern applies to political groups.

A second contribution of economics is simply the language of basic economic concepts. In general, political science research uses such language in discussing interest groups: resources, patron, entrepreneur, rational decision making in pursuit of goals, and so forth. Basic economic terminology is used in preference to physics vector terminology, in which action is modeled in terms of interacting force vectors, a mode preferred by Bentley (although his vectors represented economic interests), and by David Truman, who preferred the social-psychological analog of interacting individual attitudes. Dahl's pluralism, on the other hand, was based on individuals expending political resources in the course of strategies to achieve political goals. His language came in general use among interest group scholars in the political science field. Interest groups came to be described in terms of mobilized political resources, and group survival depicted in terms of the efficient mobilization and use of resources (Dahl 1961). Another type of economic language is decision-making incentives. James Q. Wilson (1980) based his observations about group behavior in terms of the incentives of group members, whether they were material or ideological. More elaborate than the use of basic concepts in language, some interest group scholars state economic equations of group behavior (see Ainsworth, Chapter 5 in this volume).

The Chicago School of Economics put forth a special-interest theory of groups analogous to multiple-elite theory in political science. In particular George Stigler, and as a secondary effort, Milton Friedman, described the tendencies of those regulated by government agencies to capture the agencies themselves, and then to enact special interest policies. To economists, such policies included the promotion of monopolistic behavior, in particular governmental price setting, subsidies to existing producers, tariffs and import quotas, and setting forth barriers to entry and to competition by new producers. The Chicago School described this as done through the organization of interest groups, which then influence legislative bodies and administrative agencies. The conclusion of the Chicago School is, of course, to get government out of markets, thereby decreasing the influence of interest groups over prices and production (Stigler 1975; M. Friedman 1962).

Theoretical Developments

In the rest of this chapter I discuss ways in which interest group theory might be developed, especially in considering American politics. In considering scholarly development, I tend to be more theoretical than other chapters, emphasizing trends in research programs.

If we have arrived at the point of neopluralist theory, what has been accomplished? Political writers, journalists, and other citizens will continue to state observations of a single power elite (i.e., the only interests that really count are large corporations), pluralism, and the general power of special interests, but neopluralism places these in useful perspective. Political scientists might explore how other models of power in this family of ideas apply to the United States. In particular, the corporatist model of power and interest groups (Schmitter 1974; Katzenstein 1985), usually applied to certain European societies but not to the United States, might be useful in certain limited areas of American politics. In the corporatist model (contrasted to the atomistic model of pluralism), policies are negotiated among centralized segments of groups and government, e.g., a centralized business group, a centralized labor group, and centralized government. Corporatism might be an alternative to neopluralism in some cities, or particular areas of state government policymaking (McFarland 1984). Similarly Arend Lijphart's model of consociationism, applied to certain foreign societies, might be a better means to describe interest politics in some local governments. In consociationism, interest groups are organized in centralized segments, but unlike corporatism, one or more such segments are based on ethnic or religious affiliation (Lijphart 1969). In US local government, it might be that interest politics is negotiated among centralized African American, Latino, and predominately white upper-middle-class segments. This might be true of local schools policy. Another one of this family of ideas is "statism." This occurs when relatively autonomous government agencies dominate interest groups, as opposed to groups tending to dominate the state in multiple elitism. Statism, however, has been well covered theoretically, as it was a priority research topic in the 1980s, especially if one refers to the wealth of writing on institutionalism (P. Evans, Rueschemeyer, and Skocpol 1985). Probably little new about interest groups can be said from this perspective.

Neopluralism, aside from being a theory of interest groups and political power, is also a theory of the political process, meaning the complex interaction of various political factors, acting in systems and subsystems over time (McFarland 2004). In other words, neopluralism pertains to the theory of complex political systems, and the two theories might interact, in mutual development. A particularly promising theory of complex political and policymaking systems is termed "the politics of attention" (B. Jones and Baumgartner 2005), which overlaps with other theoretical notions of policy change, the political agenda, and issue framing. The theory of political attention depicts public policy in its particular areas as ordinarily not changing much, while sometimes the technical and political context of a policy changes rapidly. In an onrush of political attention, a particular public policy suddenly changes in adaptation to the changed context, an event known as "policy punctuation" (F. Baumgartner and Jones 1993). It would seem that interest groups both act to maintain an equilibrium in a policy area (as in multiple-elite theory), but at times are one of several factors acting to bring about a policy punctuation. How can this be stated theoretically? Interest groups have an issue-framing function, setting forth an interpretation of events in some situation and the meaning of such events to individuals, together with action proposals to deal with problems posed by the issue frame (F. Baumgartner et al. 2009; Snow et al. 1986; Goffman 1974). For instance, a public health group might frame the issue of public smoking as having secondary effects on non-smokers and propose a ban on such public smoking. The interaction of policy punctuation, political attention, groups, and issue framing in complex systems is an important theoretical topic. Surprisingly, empirical research has found that issue framing by interest groups in the Washington lobbying process seldom occurs, even though we might have the expectation that effective issue framing is at the core of the lobbying process (F. Baumgartner et al. 2009).

THEORY OF INTEREST GROUPS AND ELECTIONS

Theoretical attention is needed to bring together neopluralism and other contemporary interest group concepts together with research about political parties and elections in the United States. Interest group theory and election theory in political science have had different histories. Interest group theory started with the work of

Bentley and Truman, proceeded with contributions from Dahl and Schattschneider, and in the main went in the direction of Olson and Lowi. Bentley and Truman had little to say about elections; Dahl and Schattschneider give more emphasis to elections and interest groups; while Olson and Lowi said little about elections. Neopluralist interest group theorists, such as Heclo and Walker, have little to say about elections. In the generation of the 1940s and 1950s, the leading scholar of American politics, V. O. Key, Jr., wrote mostly about parties and elections, but included a major section about interest groups into his advanced introduction to political science research, *Politics, Parties, and Pressure Groups* (Key 1964).

The preceding paragraph can imply that the discipline should emulate Schattschneider in considering both parties and elections, and interest groups as having somewhat equal treatment in a discussion of American democracy. This needs to go beyond the listing of factors and partial theories. Students of campaign finance have produced a great deal of research indicating the effects of interest groups acting in campaign finance, and even the causation going in the other direction. Stating a definitive pattern about groups and campaign finance is difficult due to the complexity of the variables (see Chapter 28). We have information about donations, which groups give, what types of groups give, relations to political incumbents, relations to congressional committees, different mechanisms of giving (political action committees, independently organized fundraising committees, etc.), relations to role call voting in different areas, relations to distributive politics. Elected politicians may induce contributions from groups through the threat of paying no attention to non-contributors. Campaign contributions from groups appear to reinforce special-interest politics in some areas of national policymaking, enhancing multiple-elitism, although the effect is limited by factors producing neopluralism (e.g., contributions from both business and labor to the same politician).

Political science theory might be advised to follow further in the footsteps of E. E. Schattschneider, who closely combined political parties, elections, and interest groups in his work (Schattschneider 1960). However, some scholars might regard Schattschneider as too negative in his treatment of interest groups in America. He was not impressed by the democratic potential of interest groups, which he saw as having "an upper class bias," as prone to special-interest logrolling, and as blocking the will of the majority in the US Congress. Schattschneider was famous for his advocacy of a reordering of American political institutions along the lines of a "responsible party system," in which nationally centralized political parties would give the voters clear-cut choices between alternative platforms, which could be enacted by the president and Congress in the manner of disciplined parties as seen from an idealized perspective on the British political system (American Political Science Association 1950). Such proposals have been debated among political scientists, but are generally seen as not realistic within the context of an American political culture stressing individualism and local control (Ranney 1962). The Schattschneider tradition continues, however, in influential writings about political participation by Kay Lehman Schlozman and Sidney Verba and their associates (Verba, Schlozman, and Brady 1995). Political participation scholars gathered data to show more active voting and participation in interest groups by the better-off citizens in income and education stratification. This leads to a perspective on the need to mobilize working-class citizens, and those of low or average income, to greater activity in electoral campaiging and voting to counter the upper-class bias of interest groups. For a generation many looked to American labor unions, and the New Deal Democratic Party to so mobilize average-income citizens, but in the last generation unions have declined in membership and influence, and are less significant within the Democratic Party.

On the other hand, Schattschneider stressed the power of corporate business within the realm of interest groups in America as part of the picture of political inequality and upper-income rule. Political scientists have produced a good number of useful studies of public interest groups, citizens' groups, and transnational advocacy networks—organizations having a reform outlook and often criticizing business (J. Berry 1999; Walker 1991; Keck and Sikkink 1998). In addition to the overall goal of explaining interest group politics, to deal with a Schattschneider-type argument political science needs to conduct more research into business lobbying in Washington (Schlozman and Tierney 1986; Schlozman et al. 2008; Vogel 1989).

Interest group theory need not be a Pollyanna-ish defender of the group status quo to argue that we might take a look at pessimistic conclusions about the fairness of group representation in light of neopluralist findings. The critical heaven of a responsible two-party system, with a powerful labor-oriented party, competing with a capitalist party oriented to elimination of wasteful distributive politics, is subject to the politics of attention. Power must be delegated to administrators, legislative staff, and to courts who may not always be dedicated to serving the original intent of responsible-party legislation, even if such intent were always clear. In policy implementation, of course, interest groups reassert their influence, and owing to the politics of attention, voters and leaders of centralized parties cannot pay attention to everything at once. This is one theoretical reason to support public interest lobbies to continue to represent the interests of the general public during the implementation process.

However, Theda Skocpol argues that such public interest groups are also not representative, in that such Washington lobbies are managed by professional, upper-middle-class elites (Skocpol 2004). The neopluralist position might be that this is empirically true, but that such elites are still making the policy system more representative of widely diffused interests. Further, the neopluralist can argue that the great disparity of interest organization in some policy areas may reflect the control of higher-income managers, but a disparity of interest representation is at least fairer than control by a special-interest coalition of a single group and its administrative and legislative allies. In any case, interest group theory might draw on data and theory from neopluralism to deal with questions regarding the representative role of interest groups in the context of parties, elections, public administration, and the enforcement of law by the courts.

A similar theoretical development, relying on a greater degree of description and empirical analysis, might deal with the question of trends of interest group power within the overall American political system. It is reasonable for the undergraduate or for the journalist to ask, are interest groups gaining or losing power in American politics? Perhaps this is too difficult to answer, but a few scholars might try. There are two conflicting observations of trends. Neopluralist researchers have apparently shown that many of the policy areas controlled by special-interest coalitions in the 1950s now contain a greater diversity of influential interest groups and thus exhibit neopluralism (Walker 1991; Heclo 1978). It can be argued that one reason neopluralism now seems to be a more useful theory than multiple-elitism is simply that the reality of group politics has changed in the last fifty years. On the other hand, some might argue that the increasing role of campaign finance is playing into the hands of interest groups as politicians become more reliant on funding from groups. Interest group theory might take steps to deal with such issues of historical change within the framework of representative processes.

POLITICAL PARTICIPATION

Participation in interest groups is seen to be one of four standard modes of participation in American politics—the others being voting, electoral campaigning, and direct contacting of government officials (Verba, Schlozman, and Brady 1995). A concept which has attracted enormous attention in recent years, civic engagement might be viewed as another mode of participation, both social and political. Civic engagement refers to face-to-face participation in social groups by which individuals learn social trust, an important foundation for cooperation needed in a democracy. Discussion of interest group theory and civic engagement theory is largely parallel to the discussion of the role of groups and political parties (Putnam 2000). At least one disciplinary leader, Theda Skocpol, describes a decline in engagement in social groups crossing social classes (such as lodges or the PTA), while the decline in labor unions enhances the relative influence of public interest groups managed by professional elites (Skocpol 2004). On the other hand, the leading engagement theorist Robert Putnam calls for a revival of Theodore Roosevelt era Progressivism to revive civic engagement, even though historians usually describe Progressivism as activism by middle-class professionals (Putnam 2000; Wiebe 1967). Interest group theory in America must take some note of the classic *Democracy in America* by Alexis de Tocqueville, whose outlook directly preceded current civic engagement theory, even if written in the early 1830s (Tocqueville 1969). Tocqueville anteceded work by political sociologists such as William Kornhauser, who argued the necessity of a rich organization of groups in civil society to protect democratic institutions against authoritarian social movements (Kornhauser 1959). This Tocquevillean observation became dated in light of the African American civil rights movement, but Tocqueville is now particularly relevant as the antecedent of the civic engagement discussion.

Interest group theory now implies an important role for participation in social movements, as one of the mobilizers of groups necessary to represent diffuse interests. There may be little to say that is new about this idea (McAdam 1999; Walker 1991; Bosso 2005; Costain and McFarland 1998).

American writers about interest groups need to consider the theory of political consumerism, which has been of interest to at least a score of European researchers (Micheletti, Føllesdal, and Stolle 2003). Political consumerism occurs when segments of the public protest policies of business corporations, but such publics do not act through standard political institutions, but attempt to act directly against the corporate business, especially through boycotts, switching shopping to politically correct businesses, through protest communication on the Internet, and so forth. Political consumerism can be considered to be one type of "creative political participation," when scattered individuals act to pursue general-interest goals through creating new forms of political participation, believing that established political institutions do not provide effective means for such action. Other forms of creative political participation include the formation of transnational advocacy networks in which citizens of one country attempt to pressure the government of a country not their own, and types of protest against government corruption when existing modes of participation are seen as the issue of the protest (Keck and Sikkink 1998; Micheletti and McFarland 2009).

COALITIONS, LOBBYING, AND POWER

Recently interest group researchers have generally realized that groups form coalitions to influence Congress, as well as at other decision-making sites. Some coalitions are actually institutions, and could be understood within some type of institutional theory—for instance, the Leadership Conference on Civil Rights was founded in 1950, has 190 member interest groups, and has a staff and offices. Another mode of studying coalitions is network theory, which might be combined with institutional theory. The general prediction is that dense portions of networks are correlated with the existence of lobbying coalitions. In turn, network theory can be used to predict cooperation and divisiveness within coalitions, and overall coalitional stability (Shapiro 2004).

A direct way to understand coalitions is in terms of models of rational decision making, which might include straightforward observations that groups with like goals form coalitions. Such straightforward observations of goals is useful in understanding the formation of ad hoc lobbying coalitions, when groups get together within a relatively limited time to lobby for one particular bill or legislative approach to an issue (J. Berry and Wilcox 2007; Bosso 1987). Accordingly, short-term versus long-term lobbying coalitions can be compared on the basis of whether agreement is over core values (long-term) or just agreement as to the need to pass some particular bill (ad hoc) (Hula 1999). From a rational choice standpoint, a group may refuse to join a coalition in order to maintain its autonomy and organizational distinctiveness, seen to be useful in recruiting and retaining members and resources (Hojnacki 1997).

Coalitional activity outside of Washington probably can be largely explained using similar approaches and models to Washington lobbying. Local advocacy coalitions are based on shared values, networks, and rational decision making about similarity of goals and the need to share political resources. Writers on advocacy coalitions place more emphasis on coalition members who are government officials and others who are not interest group leaders than tends to be found in congressional lobbying studies. Studies of "getting to yes" among opposing local advocacy coalitions are particularly interesting. Here the main questions are why opposing coalitions, such as environmentalists and developers, might agree to negotiate their differences, and how such agreements can be enforced in light of incentives of some parties not to cooperate. If negotiation among opposing advocacy coalitions becomes frequent in some area, then elements of European-style corporatism enter American policymaking (Sabatier 1999; McFarland 1993).

Not surprisingly, interest group scholars have been particularly interested in the variations in power of those seeking to influence the national Congress. Quite precise measurement of power is difficult to do, and often does not seem to be a wise allocation of scarce research resources. Precise measurement entails projecting an expected vote by congresspersons, likely based on constituency characteristics, political party affiliation, and past behavior. The scholar might then ascertain which congresspersons are lobbied by a group, and determine which of these departed from their expected vote (Rothenberg 1992). Normally this is just too much to do. However, case studies and contextual analysis usually gives a pretty good idea of relative power, especially if one is just concerned with three to five points on a scale. We can give convincing evidence that the National Rifle Association or the AARP have "a lot" of power in influencing Congress.

A theory of lobbying power must be joined to a theory of Congress and a theory of voting behavior. Powerful lobbies generally combine the lobbying skill of Washington insiders with a network of communications to members in a large number of districts and states, who in turn communicate with their congresspersons their support for a lobby on some measure (Kollman 1998). Intensity of preference of constituents as reflected in voting behavior (gun owners) leads to lobbying power. Lobbyists normally first approach members of Congress who agree with them to enhance the priority the member gives to the lobbyist's issue (the politics of attention). Usually in coalition with friendly congresspersons, the lobbyist then approaches the undecided, while normally not approaching congresspersons known to be "against," except sometimes when that member has numerous contributors to the group in his or her district (F. Baumgartner and Leech 1996; Hojnacki and Kimball 1998). Lobbyists try to develop positive relationships with members having key roles on legislative committees or in the party leadership; they also pay more attention to senators having a pivotal vote (that is, numbers 58, 59, 60 possibly in favor) (Krehbiel 1998).

Such views of lobbying, with neopluralism and the politics of attention as a background, rely on straightforward rational choice theory. Lobbyists pursue goals using strategies to use effectively their potential power to persuade legislators. A major publication having this outlook is being published by researchers coordinated by Frank Baumgartner at Penn State University (F. Baumgartner et al. 2009). The Penn State group has drawn about a hundred issues at random and intensely studied the congressional policy process on each issue. This has never been done before. Findings include: that groups defending the status quo win more often; a great variation in the number of groups active on an issue (some issues have hundreds of groups active while other issues have only a few groups active); issue reframing seems hard to do and is rare. Others are not likely to conduct such a large study until 2020 or later.

The anthropological study of the role of the lobbyist, conducted either figuratively or literally by following the lobbyist on his or her duties (Dexter 1969; Kersh 2002), is neglected in political science, because such studies are thought to be difficult to publish in journals and are thus avoided by the non-tenured. Anthony Nownes indicates that the greater number of lobbyists do not work to influence the US Congress but work on such seemingly humdrum matters as influencing the contracting practices of state-level and local governments, while many other lobbyists are dedicated to influencing land use and permitting policies of local government (Nownes 2006; Thomas and Hrebenar 2003). Interest group theorists need to pay more attention to this.

NICHE THEORY AND RESOURCE MOBILIZATION

Niche theory was developed by political scientists Virginia Gray and David Lowery in their effort to apply ecological theory to communities of interest groups (1996a). Agricultural policy scholar William Browne independently came up with the term "niche theory" in explaining why agricultural interest groups reflected the separate interests of scores of different agricultural commodities, from mohair to walnuts (Browne 1990). In ecology the species develop separately while interacting with other species, with each species tending to locate an ecological niche, in which a species can maintain itself effectively in its environment in its competition for sustenance with other species.

The ecological niche is a parallel concept to the economic niche of the firm, each firm competing with other firms for scarce resources, leading to firm specialization with firms locating a special production and sales activity in which it is most efficient and thereby manages to maintain itself. In niche theory, the interest group is viewed in the context of other similar interest groups and its competition with them for resources of money and membership for group maintenance. Gray and Lowery applied this idea to communities of groups attached to state-level government; Browne so described agricultural lobbies; Christopher Bosso analyzes the competition for support among the variety of environmental lobbies (Gray and Lowery 1996a; Browne 1990; Bosso 2005). The basic observation of niche theory is a trend to group specialization in adaptation to its environment. Niche theory is related to coalition theory, in that the evolving specialized groups still maintain some similarities of interest in the group community (agriculture etc.), and niche groups are most likely to form lobbying coalitions in support of a community interest. Niche theory should be developed further with insights from ecology or from the theory of the firm.

Niche theory pertains to group resource mobilization and group maintenance. As noted, neopluralists also point to the resource concepts of the patron and the political entrepreneur which can be combined with niche observations. On the other hand, neopluralists refer to sociological concepts such as network theory, issue networks, and aspects of social movement theory to account for the mobilization of resources in groups, especially when we do not expect such mobilization in light of Olson's logic of collective action.

Internal Democracy

The theory of internal democracy in groups dates back a century to Italian sociologist Robert Michels, whose famous "iron law of oligarchy" stated that internal group democracy is nearly impossible. Michels argued that an initial elite within a group would pyramid its political resources within the group in a positive feedback process, while the non-elites' capacity to challenge the initial elite would get progressively weaker (Michels 1959). Dahl made a similar point about power in New Haven, but pluralist Dahl saw that the elite would be controlled in the process of competitive elections (Dahl 1961, 102). Sociologists had observed that competitive elections are rare within unions and other civil society groups. A study of a printers' union having competitive elections showed that these were based on autonomous groups within the union, as printers spent an unusual amount of time networking with themselves, as opposed to immersion in outside society (Lipset, Trow, and Coleman 1956). This conclusion was extended to unions of miners and longshoremen (Lipset 1963). One might call the printers' union study an early version of civic engagement theory, as in face-to-face interactions the printers built up social capital in the form of interpersonal trust that facilitated a more democratic process in electing union leadership.

A theory of internal democracy thus has two poles. One is that such democracy is reliant upon face-to-face interaction with others within the group: the sociological civic engagement view. A second is that group leaders anticipate that followers will quit the organization, and take their resources out of the organization, if group leaders violate the preferences of the followers. Followers thus through anticipated reactions exercise a type of control through "the exit option," in the terminology of economist Albert Hirschman (1970). The difference in perspective is indicated in civic engagement writer Theda Skocpol's criticism of public interest groups as often not having local chapters for face-to-face interaction and as controlled by Washington-based elite professionals (Skocpol 2004).

The elite versus follower terminology omits an important segment in the middle—activists within an interest group. Within many mass membership groups, only 5 percent or less do anything more than contribute a check. But within that 5 percent, at any one time a few hundred or a few thousand members will be active within group affairs, meeting in a face-to-face manner with other group members, and contributing time and money resources to group activities, so that the central leadership becomes concerned about the activists' responses to group policies (Rothenberg 1992). There is more internal democracy from the standpoint of group activists than from that of the average contributor or member.

CONCLUSION

American political scientists have developed interest group theory in four steps: group theory, Dahl's pluralism, multiple-elite theory, and neopluralism. The fourth step, neopluralism, basically indicates a variation in patterns of interest group action among scores of issue areas of politics, as well as among the numerous state-level and local jurisdictions. The basic theoretical statement is one of complex political action. This is a useful finding, but political scientists want to develop interest group theory to make more specific statements about how such complexity operates and its meaning to citizens and political actors.

Perhaps a first priority to advance interest group theory is to view groups within the processes of policymaking; such a priority might be to cross-fertilize policy theory with interest group theory. In this case groups would be viewed as acting within a process or flow of public policy events. Especially thought-provoking is the new theory of the politics of attention (B. Jones and Baumgartner 2005). Within the processes of the politics of attention, interest groups can be seen as framing issues, having a causal role in policy punctuations, and a role in changing policy venues in changing patterns of political attention among branches of government and among levels of government. How do groups bring issues to the attention of politicians acting in electoral processes? Research into the politics of attention and the role of groups might be a first priority, but of course there are several other promising areas to develop interest group theory.

Political scientists should of course keep remembering that attention must be paid to the role of interest groups in the theory and practice of democracy in America.

CHAPTER 4

....

METHODOLOGICAL ISSUES IN THE STUDY OF POLITICAL PARTIES*

....

HANS NOEL

THE empirical study of political science is difficult. We have concepts that can defy easy measurement, subjects whose strategic behavior can confound explanation, and actions that take place in privacy, hidden from the public and the researcher alike. While these issues vex all social scientists, they are especially challenging for the study of political parties.

Political parties are difficult to study for at least two reasons. First, parties are informal and sometime extralegal organizations. The US Constitution makes no mention of them, and their regulation is minimal in many countries. Instead of following formal, transparent, and agreed-upon rules, they make decisions based on "customary processes"[1] that are often subject to interpretation and debate.

* I would like to thank Gregory Koger, Seth Masket, Chloé Miller, and especially Jonathan Ladd for helpful comments.

[1] The term is British Prime Minister Harold Macmillan's, who said that his successor should "emerge" from "the customary processes of consultation" that Macmillan claimed prevailed (Bogdanor 1995, 96).

Where the rules and players are not clear, it is hard to collect data or even observe some of the most important activity.

Moreover, in the United States, the rules that do exist were often written by anti-party Progressive reformers who aimed to hinder parties rather than help them. Campaign finance laws and rulings *prohibit* some groups that are working for the same end as a party from coordinating with that party. If they do coordinate, then they must do so informally or secretly. In such an environment, parties have reason to become even more informal and unobserved. The political party has even been called a "conspiracy" of the organized against the unorganized (Schattschneider 1942, 43–4). Even when the "conspiracy" is conducted in plain sight, its members can be reluctant to admit they are cooperating.

A second feature of parties that makes them hard to study is that they permeate so many different domains of politics. V. O. Key (1952) usefully divided these into the party in government, the party in the electorate, and the party as organization. These three elements can be studied separately, depending on the research question. But their interaction is also important in understanding parties. Even work that focuses on one element often needs insight into others. So while it can be helpful to organize the subfield with these categories, parties scholars can sometimes feel like blind men discovering an elephant, understanding one part of parties without fully grasping any other part. Comprehensive understanding requires an integration of methods well adapted to each domain. The parties scholar may need to understand both public opinion and legislative rules; both legal strategy and organizational behavior; both media markets and voter mobilization. There is probably no aspect of politics where parties or partisanship is not relevant.

Of course, neither of these problems is unique to the study of parties. Thus, a great deal of good parties work employs the same methods as other work in political science. The early work on the role of parties in the legislature engaged directly with existing work on the organization of Congress, and so used many of the same methods, from quantitative analysis of committee memberships to detailed case histories of legislation. The study of party organizations is deeply connected to the study of nominations and elections. Much of the seminal work in public opinion focuses on the construct of party identification.

Because so many different methods can and should be used to study parties, I will focus in this chapter on methods that creatively tackle the problems mentioned above, and especially on those that are on the frontier of research and that pose important challenges in the future. I will also focus on quantitative methods, with some exceptions. Almost all work on parties makes use of qualitative methods in some way. This use is probably inevitable, if parties are as hard to pin down as I argue. We can not get reliable measures of the bargains struck inside a smoke-filled room, but we can interview those who were there and compare their accounts. Excellent qualitative work has addressed the history of the parties, the politics surrounding key transformations, and the source of current party rules. The advantages of quantitative work, its rigor, its breadth, its replicability, can be harder to bring to bear on parties questions. I focus on those issues here.

The chapter proceeds as follows. In the first three sections, I work through the most important methodological issues concerning the study of parties in V. O. Key's three main domains—in the government, as an organization, and in elections. In the fourth section, I examine the question of party cleavages and realignment, highlighting how this question bridges the three domains.

Party in Government: Inference from Voting Patterns

Parties are at the center of many of the debates in the Congress literature. Some scholars find parties to be central in the organization and operations of Congress, while others say that party affiliation is nothing more than a rough proxy for preferences (Krehbiel 1993), and perhaps, under the "pivotal politics" model, legislation passes when it satisfies those legislators whose votes would be pivotal in reaching a majority or required supermajority (Krehbiel 1998). For those who think parties matter, there are differing theories about why they matter. They might operate like a "cartel," controlling the agenda by controlling procedures (Cox and McCubbins 1993, 2005). Or the members of a party might, when their preferences are similar enough, delegate more power to their leaders to ensure that those preferences are satisfied (Rohde 1991; Aldrich and Rohde 2000a). In this "conditional party government" model, parties are strong when the condition of homogeneous preferences is satisfied.

All of these theories have been thoroughly tested empirically. In fact, the study of Congress is among the better success stories of the Empirical Implications of Theoretical Models movement in political science. The EITM approach links theoretical models of politics with rigorous empirical analysis based on those models. Theories of Congress, building on a general spatial model of voting (D. Black 1958), make predictions that could be tested if we had empirical data on that policy space. Thus, a common strategy is to estimate features of the policy space from the voting records of legislators, with techniques like the widely used NOMINATE scores (Poole and Rosenthal 1997) and other scaling estimates of legislators (e.g., Clinton, Jackman, and Rivers 2004; Heckman and Snyder 1997). These methods produce empirical estimates of the legislators' ideal points in a policy space, as well as some information about the alternatives being voted on. The congressional theories that build on the spatial model make different predictions about those quantities. The theories also make predictions about other measures of congressional behavior, but I focus here first on NOMINATE and other scaling methods.

Early work typically used interest group ratings, which are based on a smaller set of votes, often in only one issue area. Early theories made predictions about the ideological makeup of committees. If we know the preferences and party of each member, for example, we can tell whether committee members are outliers, as predicted by distributive theory (e.g., Weingast 1979; Weingast and Marshall 1988), representative of the chamber, as predicted by informational theory (e.g., Krehbiel 1991, 1993), or loyal to the majority party, as predicted by party cartel theory (e.g., Cox and McCubbins 1993).

Interest group ratings were based on a set of votes identified by the group as revealing. The set of votes could be small, and each vote is typically treated as equally important. Since the interest group that chose the votes is itself a political actor, the choice of votes might be strategic, or simply imperfect. Scaling techniques like NOMINATE instead make use of every contested vote. The ith legislator's vote on the jth bill, y_{ij}, is a function of the latent scale, or ideal point, of the legislator x_i, and of vote-specific parameters θ_j. It is akin to estimating a logit or probit model predicting each vote, where both the xs and the θs are unknown. The procedure can recover estimates because, for each θ, there are many xs, and for each x, there are many θs. This procedure frees the researcher from imposing any interpretation on the votes and lets the data speak instead.

This improved measurement has been applied to the next generation of theoretical questions, which have revolved around the pivotal politics, party cartel, and conditional party government models. Each of these models, when expressed in the context of a unidimensional model of Congress, makes competing claims about the locations of the bills and the cutting lines, and who wins and who loses. However, NOMINATE methods can identify the cutting line between the alternatives being voted on, but not the locations of the alternatives themselves. Thus, researchers have had to get clever with their tests.

For instance, the cartel model predicts that the majority party will never make proposals that move policy away from a point that the majority of the majority prefers to the position favored by the median voter. Similarly, the pivotal politics model predicts that policy cannot be changed if it already lies in the middle of the policy space. These regions of policy stability—"gridlock intervals"—can be identified empirically from the ideal points of the legislators. But since the NOMINATE model does not produce estimates of the status quos, we cannot directly observe whether status quos in this interval are challenged. Instead, scholars have looked at the cutting lines of votes, assuming that proposals are the equilibrium proposal given a certain status quo (Krehbiel, Meirowitz, and Woon 2005; Chiou and Rothenberg 2003). This strategy requires careful thought not only about measurement, but also about the subtler features of the models themselves, and the predictions they generate.

Relatedly, Lawrence, Maltzman, and Smith (2006) point out that dropping "party" and "ideology" into a model with votes on legislation as the outcome will not necessarily help to distinguish the effects of the two concepts. Party leaders might want to *encourage* some members to vote against their party if the members' vote is not pivotal and voting against the party will help re-elect a member of the caucus. Of course, if our measure of ideology is a NOMINATE score, then that right-hand-side variable was computed from the vote, which is now the dependent variable. Lawrence, Maltzman, and Smith instead look at which members are on the winning sides of votes, on the grounds that different theories predict that members with different ideal points should "get their way." They find evidence that parties do control the agenda.

Since the "condition" in conditional party government is a feature of preferences, ideal point estimates can also help get leverage on this as well. Conditional party government theorists have developed a set of related measures to capture variability of the condition in a one- (Aldrich, Berger, and Rohde 2002) and two-dimensional (Aldrich, Rohde, and Tofias 2008) spatial policy space. Moving to a two-dimensional space is important, they argue, because the theory does not rely on a single policy dimension. Making the "conditions" more concrete requires measures of (1) interparty heterogeneity, or how far apart are central tendencies of the two parties, (2) intraparty homogeneity, or how similar are members of the same party, (3) party separation, or how little overlap is there between the two parties, and (4) party label fitness, or how well a member's ideology corresponds to their party. These four concepts can all be measured with NOMINATE scores, in one or two dimensions, but, as Aldrich, Rohde, and Tofias (2008) argue, more dimensions capture the variation more accurately.

All of these approaches, however, take ideal points at face value as measures of ideology. This assumption would follow if parties did not manipulate the agenda or influence members. Otherwise NOMINATE scores will not be clean estimates of ideology. Snyder and Groseclose (2000) consider the possibility that party might have an effect on the estimates themselves. They estimate ideal points using only lopsided votes, on the assumption that party leaders will not pressure members when the movement of a few votes will not be decisive. Then they use those estimates to predict, along with party, the votes on the closer votes. They find that party has an added influence. McCarty, Poole, and Rosenthal (2001) argue that this method is inadequate,[2] and they propose several alternatives, including examining party switchers, whom they find do change their ideal points. They do not find evidence of systematic pressure across the caucus, however.

---

[2] Specifically, they argue that omitting close votes will misestimate the preferences of moderates, because no cutting lines would be found to distinguish them with perfect spatial voting. Snyder and Groseclose (2001) contend that, with stochastic voting, this is not empirically the case.

The key lesson from this exchange is that it is very difficult to get leverage on the difference between parties and preferences (or any other influences) from a measure that is based on votes. The Snyder and Groseclose and McCarty et al. strategies are clever, because they attempt to find places where the influence of party might vary: in the first case, because party leaders will vary the pressure they impose, and in the second, because members who switch parties trade the influence of one party for the influence of the other. Neither strategy takes scaling estimates as unambiguous measures of preference.

Too often, scholars do just that. The problem can perhaps best be seen with an example from American history. In the middle part of the twentieth century, when southern Democrats often split from the Democratic Party to vote with conservative Republicans, legislators are said to be in a two-dimensional space, where one dimension is economic ideology, and the second is a race or regional dimension of conflict.

Suppose instead, however, that voting decisions are always a function of ideological positions and partisanship. Sometimes, preferences and party coincide, in which case they cannot be distinguished. But when they do diverge, legislators make a trade-off. Suppose this trade-off were systematic, so that legislators were more likely to diverge from their party on civil rights and foreign policy issues, and more likely to agree with their party on economic issues. This interpretation is rarely front and center in the literature, but it is in fact the one offered by Poole and Rosenthal (e.g., 1991, 233; 1997, 45–6).

Under this interpretation, the ideological space only appears to be defined by two issue dimensions. A different underlying mechanism has generated the data. Today, when party and ideology both push in the same direction, the problem is perhaps more difficult. Our mistaken estimation is a kind of omitted variables bias, in which the effect of the (two-dimensional) ideal point on the vote is overestimated, since the effect of party has been constrained to be 0. Recall that scaling simultaneously estimates the ideal point, x_i, and the effect of that ideal point θ_j, on the vote y_{ij}. So, the specification cannot be corrected by adding party to the model, because we are inferring the ideal points from the dependent variable (the vote). We could put party into the model, and we would get a different estimate of the ideal points. But we would not get leverage on which variable mattered, because without knowing independently what x is, we get no leverage from the places where ideal points and party diverge.

Further, in the case where party and ideology are highly related, as today, it is even more difficult to disentangle them. The bottom line is that NOMINATE scores, or any other scaling measures, are not measures of ideology. They are summaries of voting behavior that *might be* highly related to ideology. But they might also be determined by other factors. Indeed, those factors might not even be unrelated. A member's ideology probably has a great deal to do with which party she will choose. And parties might influence a member's preferences, especially on those issues on which she is less committed or less informed (Sinclair 2002a).

This conclusion does not mean that ideal point estimates cannot be used as a measure of preferences. There is variation in voting records not captured by the member's party, and that variation is plausibly seen as some kind of preference, whether induced by the member's district or by their conscience. They do tend to fit well with estimates of ideology from outside the legislative context. Indeed, such cross-validation (e.g., Snyder and Groseclose 2001) is useful. But the application matters. For the understanding of parties, these issues of the complex sources of voting records are important, and ought to be kept in mind.

PARTY AS ORGANIZATION: SOCIAL NETWORKS ANALYSIS

If the study of the party in government is among the most theoretically and empirically sophisticated work in political science, the study of party organization may be the opposite. So much of the behavior of legislators is on the record and in front of the camera. Party activists, on the other hand, work in an ill-defined domain, often deliberately out of the public eye.

For that reason, the great works in party organization and party campaigning are often qualitative. Theodore H. White (1961, 1965, 1969, 1973, 1982) pioneered an approach to understanding presidential nominations that has set the standard for much of the best work on the subject since (Crouse 1973; Witcover 1977; Cramer 1992). Much of this work has involved nominations and elections, which are exciting. But much of it also lets the political party fade into the shadow of the candidate. If the party really is subservient to the candidate (Wattenberg 1991; Aldrich 1995), this reflects a realistic allocation of attention in the study of elections. But it does mean the party is less understood. And that, in turn, may mean we do not really understand the party's role in elections.

One approach that has seen increasing attention recently is Social Networks Analysis. Social Networks Analysis (e.g., Wasserman and Faust 1994) examines the patterns in the connections among a set of actors or other nodes. The idea is that something important can be observed by understanding not only the individual actor, but also its place in a network of other actors, as well as the architecture of that network.

Technically, Social Networks Analysis deals with actors or other entities in the network, called "nodes," and the links between them, called "edges."[3] Some nodes

---

[3] The techniques for this sort of analysis have developed in other disciplines, notably mathematics, specifically graph theory, and sociology. Terminology varies across disciplines and applications.

are connected to many other nodes, and some are connected to few. Some clusters of nodes are heavily connected, others are sparse. Edges can be directed or not and vary in intensity and type. The network can have one or more kinds of nodes. The framework is flexible enough to be able to examine everything from marriage or sexual relationships to trade or war.

Parties are a promising application. It is widely understood that the formal offices and hierarchies of the political parties do not reflect importance or any sort of chain of command. V. O. Key notes that "the party organization constitutes no disciplined army," and that the national party only loosely unites the real centers of power, the largely independent local and state parties (Key 1952, 329). These local parties are no more disciplined, he argues:

> The discussion of the confederative nature of national party organization has proceeded as if tightly organized party machines would be found in the states and cities. In fact, behind the façade of the formal party organization the widest variety characterizes the actual organization of the political activists in the states and cities. . . . Moreover, the extent to which the formal party organization—the formal mechanism prescribed by rule or statute—is the real organization differs from place to place. In some states it coincides with the working party organization; in other localities, manned by hacks, it is moribund, and groups of political workers completely outside the formal organization stir up candidates and advance their cause. (334–5)

Key was describing parties in the 1940s and 1950s. Today, formal party organizations are even less likely to serve as the locus of local politics. David Mayhew (1986) surveyed formal party organizations across the American states *circa* 1960 and found traditional machines dead or dying. This could be (and has been) interpreted as the death of political parties, but it need not be. Party activity may simply be more informal and thus harder to observe.

If we believe the actual party is more complicated than the official leadership, the network model is a natural place for leverage. If political parties are endogenous institutions that form in response to various problems, in and out of the legislature, and during and between elections, then a good way to get a handle on those institutions is to look at the individual actors who decide to make connections and coordinate with one another. The formal and informal institutions they create, follow, and renegotiate make up the party; those institutions cannot be understood without understanding their relationships. This approach has been applied by a number of scholars recently.

Conceptually, the social networks model is straightforward. The parties consist of their candidates for office, from the top of the ticket to the bottom, and of the formal party leadership, chairs of key house campaign committees, local party officials, and so forth. But they also consist of important consultants, notables, and influential figures. Bill Clinton and James Carville continue to have a major influence on the Democratic Party, even though they are no longer the center of its efforts. So in the terms of Social Networks Analysis, every political actor is a node, and the connections between them trace out the shape of the party. Bill Clinton has strong ties to Hillary Clinton, and many ties to many important figures from the period he was president. He has weaker ties to the next generation of political activists, especially those who opposed Hillary Clinton's nomination bid. This network of ties sheds light on a host of conflicts at the 2008 Democratic Convention and in the state primaries leading up to it. That is, assuming the conventional wisdom about who is allied with whom is correct.

Empirically, applying the model is not that straightforward. What counts as a link? Working for or with someone surely does. But does serving on the same board of directors? Appearing at the same rally? Is it things that are unobserved? Unobservable? Who counts as in the network? Candidates and officeholders surely do. But do campaign consultants? Pollsters? Interest groups? How do we get at the importance of players whose power is informal?

These issues can limit Social Networks Analysis, but they may also be best addressed by the framework. The importance of informal players would emerge if we could see their connections. The application of Social Networks Analysis in political science is in its infancy, but there are a number of scholars applying the method to political parties. Many stop short of formal Social Networks Analysis, while others identify a subset of actors whose ties can be formally analyzed.

Schwartz (1990), for instance, argues that the Republican Party in Illinois is best understood as an informal network, and Monroe (2001) and Masket (2009) explore informal party organizations in California, but none use formal social networks tools. Likewise, Cohen et al. (2008), Dominguez (2005), and Dominguez and Bernstein (2003) address the influence of informal party endorsements in nominations, and Skinner (2005) examines the campaign roles of 527 committees, but again, this work all stops short of using the network as more than a metaphor.

Bernstein (1999) and Doherty (2006a) use formal Social Networks Analysis to examine the links among campaign consultants. Consultants almost never cross the aisle, but they do move from office to office. They are more loyal to the party than to their candidate. Candidate- or campaign-centered scholarship tends to miss the degree to which forces that last beyond the campaign influence consultants.

Koger, Masket, and Noel (2009, forthcoming) use the trade in fundraising mailing lists to trace party networks. They donated small sums to a variety of formal party organizations, candidates, interest groups, and political publications, each with a unique donor name. Those diverse organizations form two well-connected networks, with little overlap. Moreover, ties within the network are made without much regard to internal factions.

Heaney and Rojas (2007) examine the network of activists in antiwar rallies. While these activists are the furthest from the formal party of any group described here, they argue that they are best understood as the "party in the street," where social movements and party organization interact.

All of this work is highly suggestive of a party organization that includes formal and informal members. However, a number of important issues with the application of networks analysis to political parties remain unaddressed.

First, the network cannot detect the motivation of the actors. They could be working in concert informally. Or they could be individually motivated in common ways, so that actors who are similar appear to be cooperating. Much depends on how much each node in the network knows about the goals of parts of the network far from it. If each node acts myopically, that is a different organization than if each node is trying to build a coalition. It is possible that common preferences—for types of candidates or types of donors, for instance—drive much of the results.

Second, we cannot always tell how much information or influence travels through the connections we observe. If two actors have a "tie," does that mean that they influence each other equally? Ties can be directed, but the way in which the tie was measured (they solicited the same potential donor) may not reflect directly everything that is important about that tie (who initiated their relationship, and could one party have declined?).

Finally, we cannot be sure of the relationship between network features and individual characteristics. Do certain places in the network make actors important, or do important actors demand certain places in the network? Does an actor who is positioned to coordinate with others actually do so?

These sorts of problems, of course, arise in any observational data. The patterns can be observed, and theories make sense of those patterns. Some theories will predict one outcome; others, another; and the data can adjudicate. The difficulty so far has been to sharpen those theories. Social Networks Analysis has been around for some time in sociology, but its application in political science, especially for understanding political parties, is much newer. The social networks theory of parties is nowhere near the level of rigor or predictive precision that the spatial voting theories of Congress have achieved.

PARTY IN THE ELECTORATE: WHY AND HOW?

The study of parties in the electorate has perhaps the longest pedigree of any area of parties research. Early work on voter behavior (Angus Campbell et al. 1960) identified the voter's party identification as a key variable, and work has explored this construct extensively. The literature since then has ranged widely, but two closely related questions involve the origins of party identification and its effects. Most would agree that party identification influences the vote, but scholars debate whether party has a mediating effect on the reception of new information, which in turn affects the formation of party identification.

On the first question, the literature debates whether party identification is a stable identification, or whether voters adjust their attachment in response to changes in party platforms, etc. The evidence is mixed. Some scholars (e.g., Angus Campbell et al. 1960; D. Green and Palmquist 1994; D. Green, Palmquist, and Schickler 2002; Petrocik 2006) argue that partisan attachment is like a group identity. People see their identity defined through their membership in various groups—Catholics, Jews, feminists, Red Sox fans, Trekkies . . . and Democrats or Republicans. This identity is not set in concrete, but it will be very stable. Other scholars (e.g., Fiorina 1981; Achen 1992; Abramowitz and Saunders 1998) argue that voters make a more rational assessment of the two parties, and so may change parties as they learn from their experience with successive administrations, or as they observe changes in party platforms.

Distinguishing these approaches is difficult. It is hard to measure abstract identity, and it is hard to know what voters have observed. And at the heart of the debate is an endogeneity problem. Identity might shape party identification, and it might also shape, directly or indirectly (through a partisan screen), policy preferences or evaluations of the candidates. Or, demographic and regional differences might shape issue positions, which in turn shape party preferences. This sort of endogeneity is then similar to the problem of disentangling the effects of preferences from the effects of party in the legislature. We are again without many of the best tools. We cannot conduct experiments in which we manipulate the variables we most think are important—a voter's policy preferences or social identity—because those constructs are not easily changed in the lab.

One approach is to use panel data, in which the same subjects are interviewed repeatedly. In that case, we can observe on which measures they change and on which they remain the same. But most datasets span only a handful of years. Work leveraging short panels tends to show a great deal of party stability, and less stability in other variables (D. Green, Palmquist, and Schickler 2002; W. Miller 2000). But major changes in party identification, even those driven by other events, might take a long time to develop, as the changes voters respond to slowly accumulate.

Another approach has been to use structural equation models and instrumental variables (John E. Jackson 1975; Markus and Converse 1979; Page and Jones 1979; Fiorina 1981). In this work, scholars attempt to disentangle the part of a variable, say party identification, that causes the vote from the part that is merely caused by something else that causes the vote. The researcher develops a system of equations that captures all of the relationships, and then estimates each relationship, simultaneously accounting for the others. However, this approach can be very sensitive to what is considered exogenous. As Page and Jones put it (1979, 1071): "in the absence of accepted theory many specifications are open to controversy." But in this case, it is exactly this sort of absence we are attempting to get leverage on. For this reason, scholars have largely abandoned structural equations, although the problems they were meant to address persist.

Another approach, akin to the EITM work on Congress, is to develop a model tied closely to a theoretical approach. For example, Achen (1992) builds on Fiorina's (1977; see also Calvert 1980) conception of party identification as a running tally and models the voter's party preference as a Bayesian updating. Voters wish to derive a prospective evaluation about which party is better for them. They are not sure which party is, but they have an estimate, with some uncertainty. Voters might begin with the beliefs they learn from their parents, and then update as they observe the performance of the current parties. Over time, a more stable preference will evolve. Achen's model is an improvement over previous linear regression models, which did not attempt to model the real functional from linking their variables to the outcome. The model incorporates the meaning usually captured by demographic variables, which are a proxy for the voter's experience with the parties, through their previous party identification.

Achen's model is an improvement, but it can also be improved upon. For instance, the model assumes a stable party system, which is inaccurate. Secular realignment might be modeled with an autoregressive term to the noise around the voter's estimate of the party that is best for them (A. Gerber and Green 1998). The best explanation of the underlying process may not yet be available, but the key is to develop models that fit the theories, rather than simply testing routine, linear regressions.

The fact that the parties do change so much leads some (e.g., D. Green, Palmquist, and Schickler 2002) to conclude that party identification must be a more fundamental identity than a rational prospective evaluation. Since the parties do change, and we observe stability, the learning model must be incorrect. Alternatively, it may be that there is biased learning, which leads to the second debate mentioned above: the way in which partisanship mediates other behaviors.

The public opinion literature has long held (c.f., Zaller 1992) that partisan predispositions filter information. Zaller's model was primarily concerned with effects at different levels of information: people without much exposure are unlikely to learn anything, while people with a lot of exposure will hear new messages but are more likely to resist new material that conflicts with earlier messages. This dynamic is partisan, because, especially for the highly informed, people are more likely to accept messages from friendly sources and reject those from disagreeable sources. Zaller's model, like Achen's, moves away from a simple linear regression, and instead builds on a basic theoretical microfoundation of information flows.

Just how much this sort of partisan screen leads to different perceptions is debated. As new information is received, partisanship matters, but there are uniform effects as well. For example, as information about scandal affecting a

Democrat is disseminated, Democrats will remain more supportive of that Demo-crat than Republicans will, but both groups will trend, almost in parallel, toward less support. Some (A. Gerber and Green 1999) would interpret this parallel trending as a lack of a partisan screen, as both groups are affected by new information. Others might say this defines a partisan screen, as the Democrats remain more supportive than the Republicans, even though they are receiving the same information. The Bayesian model would predict convergence (Bartels 2002). Bartels also finds parti-san divergence on a great number of factual questions, such as whether the economy has or has not improved, which is consistent with perceptual bias.

In the end, this debate about a perceptual screen, like the debate about prospec-tive evaluations versus group identity, rests to a great degree on definitions, interpretation, and attempts to address endogeneity. And so, it rests a great deal on theoretical leverage. We shouldn't forget that almost all of these analyses are ultimately averaging across large samples. It's not impossible that, for some, party identification is a group identity, while others do not "identify" with a party so much as have evaluations of them. Some respondents might have a perfect perceptual screen, while others are perfectly responsive to new events. If that heterogeneity does not map to any measure we have, the aggregate indicators will be hard to interpret.

Public opinion is the area of political science that showed the most promise and the most initial progress, a half-century ago. Today, progress continues in a number of areas, where manipulation is possible. The study of political communication and campaigns, for instance, can leverage laboratory experiments as well as large natural variation in campaign treatments. Party identification, however, cannot be manipulated. Scholars can prime or not prime partisanship, but they cannot directly manipulate it.

PARTY CLEAVAGES: VOTES, VOTERS, AND TEXT

It is surprisingly complicated to get a very good handle, empirically, on what the parties stand for. If parties matter in politics, surely part of what matters is that policy would be different if a different party controlled policy. And in the early twenty-first century, we are fairly certain that the parties differ on a great many things. If we think of the parties as coalitions of different interests (e.g., T. Schwartz 1989; Aldrich 1995; M. Cohen et al. 2008; Karol 2009), then it is important to know who is in those coalitions.

The issue is not that there are no good methods, but that there is a surfeit of methods, and a surfeit of places to look, each with potential weaknesses. So scholars have become increasingly sophisticated about using them.

One straightforward method for identifying the differences between the parties is to look at congressional voting records. The same scaling methods that generate ideal points also generate bill parameters, which can define which votes—which issues—divide the parties. Those issues with cutting lines between the parties are party issues (Poole and Rosenthal 1997; Noel 2007). The nice thing about this party measure is that it can reveal behavior that may be at odds with electoral coalitions or political rhetoric.

However, using voting cleavages can ignore important strategic variation. For one thing, parties might vote against something that they prefer, in the hopes that something better may be possible. The 2003 prescription drug benefit vote is a prime example (Lee 2005). The Democratic Party is more in favor of increasing government benefits in health care than is the Republican Party, but the Republicans voted for the bill, and the Democrats against it, for several reasons. The Democrats saw the prospect of what they viewed as a better bill dim if this was passed, and the Republicans got to take credit for a bill that may have moved policy away from their collective preferences, but only slightly. In this case, the cutting line would accurately note that the parties are split on this issue (and in many analyses, that would be sufficient), but the direction of the cutting line might be in the wrong direction.

Parties can also obscure differences by controlling the agenda. Under Cox and McCubbins's (2005) party cartel model, the majority party prevents votes that would divide its coalition. If there are many such potential votes on an issue, but only the ones that have been negotiated or otherwise adjusted to be appealing to the whole party are observed, we would get a misleading picture of the party's position on that issue. Issues that split moderates from conservatives will not appear, or will only appear when the differences have been worked out. Wedge issues that split two wings of the party—say, social conservatives and economic conservatives—will also not be observed.

For most applications, these nuances may not be important. The aggregate voting records of the parties will accurately show which broad issue areas divide the parties. And the fact that the agenda hides some disagreement is itself relevant, and it is important that scaling capture it. However, applications that want to explore the specifics of an issue may need some outside leverage on the party differences.

Party platforms or manifestos are a natural place to go for such leverage. After all, the platform is the party's own statement of its position. They are publicly available and are designed to speak directly to the question of what the party stands for. However, platforms can be even more strategic than votes, amounting to little more than cheap talk. They are not binding on any elected official, and candidates routinely distance themselves from them. They are, in Ostrogorski's (1982, 138) word, a "farce." Or, as politicos put it, platforms are built "to run on, not to stand on." In that light, researchers should be cautious when reading platforms.

But read with caution, platforms can be as useful to study as any other political behavior. Gerald Pomper (1967a) conducted content analysis of twelve major-party platforms from 1944 to 1964, looking for evidence that the platforms were written to serve the needs of voters and of party leaders. He argues that the platforms are light on rhetoric and heavy on specifics, allowing voters to make the kind of judgments about the parties that a Downsian (1957) rational voter model would require.

Platforms can be studied qualitatively, as in Pomper's example, and quantitatively. Qualitative analysis can be easily integrated into other analyses (qualitative or quantitative) of the crafting, context, or reception of the platform. Carmines and Stimson (1989), for instance, augment their quantitative discussion of the timing of the issue evolution on race with reference to the changes in the party platforms during the presidential elections that frame the key changes in public opinion.

Quantitative analysis of platforms allows for systematic comparison across different periods, places, and parties. One simple quantitative approach is just to count words or sentences. For instance, John Gerring (1998) studied the shifting ideologies of the parties by collecting party platforms, as well as acceptance speeches and other publications produced by the major political parties. He then counted the number of sentences in those sources that were devoted to specific subjects or arguments. He finds that the parties do differ, systematically, on the fundamental principles of the day. The platform measures trace how those differences have changed through American history.

Quantitative measures allow for comparison across space as well as time. Feinstein and Schickler (2008) examine state party platforms on civil rights issues. They code each platform on a variety of civil rights measures and then compare Democratic and Republican platforms from the same state. They find that the Democratic Party began taking pro-civil rights positions, relative to the Republicans, across many non-southern states long before the realignment at the national level. This observation casts doubt on accounts of that realignment (e.g., Carmines and Stimson 1989) that focused on national elites.

This sort of analysis of party platforms has been conducted on a larger scale in a comparative setting. Laver and Hunt (1992) used surveys of experts, where the researcher essentially outsources the content analysis to policy experts, who know not only what is contained in the party manifesto, but also speeches, voting patterns, media coverage, and anything else in the context. They then use those surveys to identify the policy space for further analysis.

Building on this approach, the Comparative Manifestos Project (Budge et al. 2001; Budge, Robertson, and Hearl 1987) has used human coding to create summary measures of manifestos from fifty-four countries. Coders count the number of quasi-sentences that fall into one of fifty-six different issues. The result is something similar to what Feinstein and Schickler do, but for a comprehensive set of issues. The Comparative Manifestos dataset is thus well suited to that kind of analysis: which parties care more about one issue versus another, or which issues are primary or secondary to party differences?

The dataset has also been used to create a left–right ideological summary measure. This is less straightforward. Laver and Budge (1992), for instance, categorize some of the fifty-six issues as "left" and others as "right," and then compare the frequency of each category in a party's manifesto. If we are comfortable assigning issues to the left–right dimension, this provides a reasonable approximation. However, one nice feature of most scaling methods is that the ideological character of the issues emerges from the estimation. If the right starts talking about a new issue, or ceases talking about a once central issue, that does not necessarily mean they are no longer on the right.

This concern suggests a need for a different method. Systematic analysis with experts or other human coders is potentially powerful. However, it has two drawbacks. First, it is hard to apply to larger datasets. Reading a very large number of platforms can be time-consuming. Further, conducting identical expert surveys across many countries can be logistically complicated. Both methods are also open to human biases and cognitive limitations. Confirmation bias toward the researcher's theory or perhaps erroneous conventional wisdom can contaminate the data. For this reason, scholars have recently sought to develop a number of methods to process large quantities of language in a potentially unbiased way. Two useful programs have applied this approach to comparative manifestos: Wordscores (Laver, Benoit, and Garry 2003) and Wordfish (Slapin and Proksch 2008; Proksch and Slapin forthcoming). Both approaches can be implemented in standard statistical packages.

Wordscores begins with a few sample texts that anchor ideological positions in a policy space. The program, available for implementation in Stata, compares the frequency of words in a manifesto with their frequency in the anchoring text. The procedure then places those manifestos on a continuum between the anchoring texts.

Wordfish echoes the NOMINATE procedure, in that it estimates a latent space from the specifics contained in the manifestos. Instead of estimating the effect of the latent space on a vote, Wordfish estimates its effect on the choice of words used in the manifesto. That latent space might be interpreted in the same way as the ideological space that NOMINATE seeks to recover. Wordfish is available for implementation in R.

The principal difference between the approaches is how the researcher defines the ideological dimension.[4] In Wordscores, this is done through the anchoring texts. That choice can be both advantageous and limiting. On the one hand,

---

[4] There are other, more technical differences, of course. But the substantive consequences derive from this difference.

Wordscores assume that the researcher knows what differentiates the left from the right, or, at the very least, who is on the right and the left, and what of their works represent their ideological position. If the goal is to understand that space, we should not constrain our estimation of it with sample texts that might not be perfect. This is especially true if the space might change over time.

On the other hand, if simply applied to the entire text, Wordfish will estimate a space without regard for the substantive meaning of its dimensions. Just as NOMINATE is an amalgam of everything that goes into a vote, so too is Wordfish an amalgam of everything that goes into a manifesto. The left–right dimension can be confounded with other motivations, and it can lie in some diagonal through the higher-dimensional space. Proksch and Slapin refine this technique by choosing a subset of the manifesto that refers to a chosen research area. That makes the dimension more interpretable, but it is based on the issue area rather than on a general left–right ideology.[5] Wordscores may also be confounded with other differences between the anchor texts, but the result can be interpreted in light of texts with known qualities.

There is no reason to limit the quantitative analysis of text to party manifestos. Monroe, Colaresi, and Quinn (forthcoming) have developed a model identifying the lexical differences between Democrats and Republicans using the Congressional record.

As noted, these quantitative methods for text have some similarities to the scaling methods discussed in the previous section. These similarities mean that they can have the same class of shortcomings—that factors other than what the researcher hopes to measure can play a role in determining text or votes. However, those "other" factors may not be the same across different applications. Thus, comparing party platforms and voting records can help to identify both the common ideological environment and the differences from one domain to another.

For all their potential limitations, these approaches do get some traction on what separates the parties. They look at the parts of the party that are probably most important for understanding the party coalition: the party in government, or possibly (in the case of platforms) the party organization. Some scholars have also looked at voting coalitions. This approach makes some sense. When we refer to the New Deal coalition, for instance, we refer to the southern whites and northern liberals who *voted for* Roosevelt.

The voting coalition is meaningful, but it is not the same as the governing coalition, or the coalition of interests that shape the party. A useful illustration demonstrates the problem. In recent US elections, African Americans have overwhelmingly identified with and voted for the Democratic Party. (In the 2004

---

[5] A similar approach can be taken for NOMINATE and other ideal point estimation techniques, limiting the votes to those on, for example, civil liberties issues (Bailey 2005).

National Election Study, 81 percent of African Americans identified with or leaned toward the Democrats.) Meanwhile, while union members are still vastly more Democratic than Republican, they are more divided (only 58 percent of respondents from union households identified with or leaned toward the Democrats in the 2004 NES). Does this mean that pro-labor positions are less associated with the Democratic Party than pro-black positions are? Probably not. It is hard to imagine a Democratic Party without labor as a key component.

This discussion raises three concerns. First, looking at the identities of voters ignores any potential internal conflict within the voters. Working-class voters who vote for Republicans (and there are few) do not do so because they see the Republican Party as the party of the working class. They do so because something else—perhaps a socially conservative religion—is more important to them. The second problem is that different demographic characteristics do a better or worse job of identifying a voter's interest. Race is immutable and highly visible. An African American almost certainly has a high stake in African American policies. Union membership is fluid. There are union members who are not really working-class, and working-class voters who are not in unions. Indeed, income not only "still" predicts party votes, it does so better than it used to (e.g., Bartels 2006; Gelman et al. 2008). But identifying that pattern requires sophisticated thoughts on defining "the working class." So that construct is harder to measure than race, and as a result, it appears less related.

Finally, and most importantly, scholarly attention should be directed at the *relationship* between the voting coalition and the ultimate policy coalition. The latter is defined more by the elites who are active in the party than by who votes for it. Nevertheless, it is not uncommon for commentators to slip from describing voting patterns to describing what the "coalition" of elite activists must be like.

Indeed, this problem is prevalent in the realignment literature, which focuses on the voting coalitions. Political scientists have a great faith in the importance of the voter, and it tends to shape our choice of subject. Thus, while the extensive representation literature makes clear that the link between voters and officials is sketchy, we still focus a great deal on who votes for which party when we think about lasting transitions in politics. The New Deal coalition dates from 1932, even though voting patterns in Congress (Poole and Rosenthal 1997, 106) and party platforms (Gerring 1998, 187–231) began reflecting the economic divide that characterizes the New Deal coalition much sooner.

It may be that there are so many definitions of a "realignment," and thus little empirical traction on them (Mayhew 2002), precisely because we focus so much on the differences among the voters. The "realignment" of the parties (or their "evolution") from about 1950 to the present was tricky to detect among voters, although with the long view it now seems evident. What should be less tricky is to note how the policy activists on race changed sides, and the activists on other social issues became more involved in party politics. These changes were, in ways, facilitated by the electorate. But the electorate did not drive them. Indeed, if party identification is sticky, as we saw above, it would be surprising if it did. Politicians forget voters at their peril, but remembering voters is not the same as being a slave to them. It may be blasphemy to say in a democracy, but politics can be (and maybe even sometimes should be) driven by considerations that go beyond the ballot box.

The literature on polarization highlights this point. It is hard to argue that legislators today are not more "polarized" than they were a half-century ago. Political rhetoric also seems polarized. The literature is less clear about voters. Party identification seems to matter more today, but the great mass of voters do not seem to be as polarized as elites. These possibly contradictory patterns make more sense when we look at the interplay between voters and candidates. Voters might not be very polarized, but if they must choose between polarized elites, they may appear to be (Fiorina 2006). And then, if elites influence voters, their polarization might eventually be transferred (John Coleman 1996), and voters will be more polarized (Abramowitz and Saunders 2005). Understanding polarization requires studying multiple levels of the party.

DISCUSSION

These four areas of parties research—the party in government, party organization, party identification, and party cleavages—nicely illustrate several important problems in the study of parties.

First, as with most social science research, creativity is required in observing empirical implications in parties. Because party behavior is often hidden, we need to think carefully about what the observable implications will be. The implication of this conclusion is that theory needs to play a very important role in methodological decisions. In the study of party in Congress, a widely accepted spatial model of voting has been leveraged to produce a variety of sometimes quite precise testable implications. In the study of party organization, a social networks model has the potential to produce such implications, but more theoretical work is needed. In the study of party identification, models that explicitly draw on theoretical microfoundations give better leverage than linear, additive models. In the study of party cleavages, theory helps to distinguish party divisions between legislators from divisions between platforms and between voters. Which division is needed depends on the question being asked.

Second, the study of parties covers a great deal of ground, and so parties scholars must be familiar with a variety of methods. Those who focus on only one domain—in the government or in elections, for example—must still be aware of the literature from other domains. Those who ask questions that bridge domains must master diverse methods.

Putting these two points together, we need theory to help us identify how methods suited to one question will interact with those suited to another question. If parties are, as I have argued, both particularly murky and crossing many domains, studying them requires a great deal of creativity.

CHAPTER 5

....

METHODOLOGICAL PERSPECTIVES ON INTEREST GROUPS*

....

SCOTT AINSWORTH

A HISTORY of lobbying and interest groups provides a nearly complete history of American political development, touching upon each branch of government. Further removed from the halls of government, interest groups have long been active in social movements as well as electoral politics and the affairs of political parties. In a similar fashion, one could argue that the study of interest groups has been a centerpiece of the discipline of political science throughout the 1900s and early 2000s. The study of interest groups remains exciting for scholars today for at least two reasons. First, there are a wealth of topics and opportunities for careful analysis. Interest group scholars may be behavioralists, focusing on virtually any part of elections, or they may be institutionalists, focusing on virtually any aspect of Congress, the courts, or the bureaucracy. Interest group scholars may study grassroots mobilization efforts or the implementation of public policies. The domain of interest group scholarship encompasses nearly the entire political science discipline. Virtually any course in American politics, whether it is focused on campaigns and elections, judicial procedures, the Congress or the presidency,

* Thanks are due to Jeff Berry, Tony Bertelli, Jamie Carson, Bob Grafstein, and Susan Nees for their comments and discussions, which strengthened this work. The usual caveats apply.

public policy, or political parties, devotes some time to discussing the roles that interest groups play.

Aside from its tremendous scope, there is a second major reason to be excited about the interest group subfield: scholars freely employ a wide range of methodo-logical approaches, which dovetails nicely with the diversity of topics for explora-tion. In this chapter, I refer to a wide range of works to help illustrate key methodological concerns that are of particular relevance to interest group scholar-ship. My hope is to focus on a small number of important advances that have the potential to affect the course of interest group scholarship in the future. Of course, predicting future promise is a risky endeavor. Some academic trends are short-lived, appearing and disappearing as quickly as weakly talented pop stars. To be certain, the prominence of interest group scholarship waned after the heydays established by the scholarship of Truman (1951), Olson (1965), Dahl (1956, 1961), Polsby (1963) and others. Some scholars might look to the inner weaknesses within a subfield to explain its lost prominence. However, the strengths and weaknesses of a subfield are also affected by the gains, opportunities, and overall excitement in other fields. Talented scholars move into and out of various subfields as opportunities and circumstances change. For instance, the Cuban missile crisis and the early successes of the Soviet space program likely prompted a shift in interests away from American politics and toward comparative politics and international relations. Within American politics, the prominence of the American National Election Studies program no doubt bolstered the careers of countless scholars who eagerly awaited every new release of data. In the midst of a behavioral revolution, one should not be surprised when scholars move toward subfields with readily available data. The interest group subfield may have fallen from its pinnacle due to its inabilities to understand power, to handle normative or empirical concerns in a convincing fashion, or to develop a clear sense of appropriate research agendas, but some scholars moved from the subfield due to the exciting developments elsewhere.[1]

What methodological approaches warrant attention from interest group scho-lars working today? How do new methodological approaches connect to the substantive concerns of interest group scholars? Each of the main sections of this chapter starts with a highly condensed discussion of some classical approaches to interest group studies and then introduces some newer work with important methodological advances. The next section discusses pluralism and sociological models. Issues addressed relate to networks, social capital, partitioning games, social decisions, and event history analysis. The second main section discusses descriptive work. The barriers to entry for scholars developing descriptive work are fairly low, making descriptive work attractive to pursue. That said, the benefits from descriptive work are sometimes limited by conceptual or methodological

---

[1] For a recent critique of the interest group subfield, see Baumgartner and Leech (1998).

shortcomings. In this section, I discuss how adopting some of the same reasoning that underpins maximum likelihood econometric methods can strengthen descriptive work. I also suggest that scholars need to be more sensitive to the strategic underpinnings of group behaviors. Methodological issues related to unobserved actions and counterfactuals are also addressed in this section. The last main section of the chapter discusses the role of information for interest groups and interest group scholarship. Hansen (1991) argues that the very emergence of interest groups stemmed from their comparative advantages over parties in providing information to legislators. Many recent lobbying models focus on information transmission. In the future, scholars will need to develop more comprehensive information-screening models because government officials are awash in information, and interest groups and lobbyists must compete with numerous sources for information.

Studies of interest groups are seldom far from the forefront of American political science. With the careful employment of new methodologies, interest group scholarship can enhance its relevance to the other subfields of political science and offer new insight into society, politics, and public policy.

PLURALISM AND SOCIOLOGICAL MODELS

Early Works

Liberal scholars of the nineteenth century often focused their work on the individual. A prominent concern of the liberal tradition of the late 1800s was the structuring of government to preserve individual rights and individual sovereignty. Whereas the classical liberal tradition was centered around individuals and placed considerable faith in the abilities of individuals to make reasoned choices, "One of the central thrusts of . . . pluralism [and early group theories] had been to redefine democracy along group lines precisely to avoid the rationalist assumptions" of individual behavior (Garson 1978, 125). Early group theories evolved from the conservative tradition of the nineteenth century, which was more organic and more sensitive to the community as a whole (or at least large segments of the whole). Individuals existed first and foremost within classes or groups however defined. Arthur Bentley, remembered as the initial intellectual driving force behind group theories, argued the case particularly strongly. "The individual stated for himself, and invested with an extra social unity of his own, is a fiction" (1908, 215). Any truly individual concern or activity is "of trifling importance in interpreting society" (215). Garson (1978, 125) and others connected the disregard of the individual with a distrust of the individual. Pluralists deemed individuals "restless and immoderate" (Garson 1978, 125), but groups could be a moderating influence. These early group scholars adopted a sociological approach that emphasized individuals' quest for meaning and purpose through group attachments.

For David Truman, the most prominent pluralist of the 1950s, groups naturally emerged through a network of interactions between individuals. Individual choice was secondary to an individual's social context. Truman sought to establish fundamental social and political underpinnings that would explain the omnipresence of political interest groups. He suggested that the group precedes the interest. Groups are a product of our social tendencies. To disavow groups is to disavow what makes us social beings. "Man is characteristically human only in association with other men" (Truman 1951, 15). For Truman, all of the defining features of human existence are group-related. Regular social interactions at home provide the basis of the family unit or group. Ultimately, even for the family unit, the biological ties are less important than the daily social interactions. Regular association with individuals provides the basis for the natural establishment of groups in society.

Networks and Partitions

Truman recognized that individuals often establish myriad group affiliations, some more direct and some more tangential. Numerous scholars have struggled with the possibilities and implications of overlapping and crosscutting cleavages tied to our memberships (e.g., D. Rae and Taylor 1970). Today, these issues are most directly reflected in work on networks or social capital. Networks and social capital have been linked to the aggregation and dissemination of information, the promotion of cooperative efforts, and the trust and efficiency inherent in some transactions. Numerous sociologists have focused on the role that individuals' memberships in various groups play in the construction of social networks. Bain (1997), Frank and Yasumoto (1998), and Granovetter (1973, 1974) argue that social networks are comprised of a series of "strong ties," with people we know directly, and "weak ties," with those we know primarily through others. As Granovetter notes, "weak ties ... are ... indispensable to individuals' opportunities and to their integration into communities" (1973, 1378). "[T]hose to whom we are weakly tied are more likely to move in circles different from our own, and will thus have access to information different from that which we [ordinarily] receive" (Granovetter 1973, 1371). Weak ties connect individuals to new sources of information and allow for the diffusion of ideas to a larger number of people than would occur if information were diffused among immediate associates (Lin 2001).

More recently, networks have been linked with information gathering and sharing, collective action, and group stability. Using network analysis, Carpenter, Esterling, and Lazer (2004) reevaluated a longstanding question in the interest group subfield. With whom do lobbyists interact? Many works addressing this issue focused on the preferences of lobbyists and legislators (e.g., Bauer, Pool, and Dexter 1963; Austen-Smith and Wright 1994; Groseclose and Snyder 1996). Carpenter et al. find that network effects remain important even after considering preferences. In addition, Carpenter et al. find that the communications between two lobbyists are most likely to be brokered by a third, commonly known party. Network analysis was also used by Heinz et al. in *The Hollow Core*(1993) to assess the array of interactions among Washington brokers. Their data, drawn from hundreds of interviews of Washington brokers, are truly monumental. However, as the title of their book hints, in the policy areas they investigated, there were no wholly dominant brokers and there were no brokers through whom all other actors tended to interact. The cores of the policy networks were hollow—more akin to a doughnut than a spoke and wheel.

Networks are often studied as static structures, but some of the newest work highlights the growth or development of networks, allowing for dynamic changes. The expansion of a network is often tied to the viability of collective efforts. As networks become more and more inclusive, the self-enforcement mechanisms that facilitate cooperation among network members become strained (e.g., Annen 2003; Kandori 1992) and networks may collapse upon themselves. Consider that large organizations, whether they are professional organizations, interest groups, or political parties, sometimes have a hard time maintaining their numbers. Often when a large organization (say the American Medical Association) shrinks, other smaller professional organizations (say the American Society of Nephrology or the American College of Cardiology) expand. In other words, networks spin off from one another. Chwe (2000) develops a formal model in which cliques may exist within networks. Chwe's focus is on the coordination of collective efforts within a network. Information flows readily within the separate cliques, and as information flows from one clique to another, individuals develop a clearer sense of the viability of a collective effort.

Partitioning games provide another means to analyze the opportunities for new group or clique emergence. Milchtaich and Winter (2002) develop a game in which individuals seek to join a group of like-minded individuals. In the spirit of Truman, shared attitudes are the sole basis of joining. Milchtaich and Winter show that if individuals are characterized by a single, one-dimensional attribute, then a stable partition always exists. That is, all individuals join a group and are content to remain in that group. However, if individuals are more than one-dimensional, then the presence of a stable group partition depends on whether there is some upper bound on the number of groups that can be formed. Whenever an upper bound on the number of groups exists, no stable partition exists. Group memberships keep shifting. This formal theoretic result leads one to consider various empirical implications. Can there be a limit on the number of groups in a society? In a number of works evaluating state-level lobbying, Gray and Lowery (1996a) argue that there is a limit to the number of groups likely to develop in a state. Some states have a greater "carrying capacity" for groups than others. If Gray and Lowery are correct, then the Milchtaich and Winter result is particularly intriguing. As virtually every interest group text reminds us, Truman argued that groups emerged from disturbances in society; but the work of Milchtaich and Winter suggests that under some circumstances disequilibrium is the norm. The observation of a disturbance may be coincidental to the underlying, ever-present disequilibrium. If one looks hard enough, there are always disturbances and there are always changes within the group environment.[2]

Private Acts and Public Consequences

Joining groups is a private act with public consequences. Increasingly, scholars look at the array of memberships and groups within whole communities as a means to measure what is sometimes termed "social capital." Putnam (2000, 197) suggests that social capital builds from the "features of social life—networks, norms, trust— that facilitate cooperation and coordination." Although the notion of social capital is sometimes beleaguered with ambiguity (Sobel 2002), social capital does merit careful attention if it affects the behavior within or effectiveness of social, political, or economic transactions. If trust is an element of social capital, then interactions within a circle of trust are less costly because transaction costs are reduced. One need not evaluate every aspect of each new interaction. Engaging in costly searches for information related to reputations or expertise is unnecessary because a network of trust is already in place. Proponents of social capital argue that various formal and informal relationships can mitigate potential conflicts and create opportunities for broad-ranging communications.

Though the work was wildly popular, not everyone was satisfied with the social science procedures adopted in Putnam's *Bowling Alone*. Sobel argues that cause and effect were conflated and social capital was at times simply equated with good outcomes (Sobel 2000, 140). There are important instances when the notions of social capital fail to increase our understanding. Let us focus, as Putnam does, on memberships. Suppose our memberships are largely reinforcing. As individual A joins more and more groups, her attitudes and ideologies are reinforced, and as individual B joins a different set of more and more groups, her attitudes and ideologies are reinforced. A and B seldom join the same group, so their differences cumulate with every new membership. Given that circumstance, multiple memberships might simply harden views and create inflexibility. Gridlock, inaction, and

---

[2] Miller (1983) develops another view of disequilibrium in an interest group society. The continual bargaining in an interest group society and the ever-changing coalitions might provide an element of systemic stability that a stable division with set winners and losers would not provide (Miller 1983). For other work on the stability of group memberships, see Johnson (1990, 1996).

bitterness may prevail. An "us versus them" attitude is easiest to imagine when there are strong social ties among the "us" individuals and strong social ties among the "them" individuals. *Less* social capital in those "us" and "them" cliques might promote a greater social harmony. Now, suppose our memberships are largely crosscutting, so that our differences do not cumulate with each new group membership. That is, individuals A and B join some of the same groups. For either A or B, the array of group memberships might include some strange bedfellows. Conforming to one group's expectations may limit an individual's ability or willingness to participate actively with other groups. Cognitive dissonance may reign. These sorts of multiple memberships may cause individuals to feel so cross-pressured that they avoid active participation (e.g., Mutz 2002).

Social capital remains too ambiguous to help us to address the effects of crosscutting and reinforcing cleavages in group memberships. That said, many works on social capital did reemphasize the fact that group memberships have social implications. The Nobel Laureate George Akerlof (1997) was one of the first social scientists to explore the social implications of individuals' decisions. For Akerlof, private decisions have no social consequences. As Akerlof notes, we can buy an apple or an orange for our lunch and there are few if any social consequences. In contrast, social decisions are those decisions with clear social consequences. "While my network of friends and relatives are not affected in the least by my choice between apples and oranges, they will be affected by my educational aspirations, my attitudes and practices toward racial discrimination" or any of a myriad other social decisions (Akerlof 1997, 1006). Therefore, an individual's choice (say about education) may be affected by the social consequences of that choice. Attention to the social consequences of a choice may help or hurt an individual. In one set of examples, Akerlof considers high school students. Students may underinvest in their education because they are rewarded with an expanded circle of friends. The individual, private returns to education are not independently maximized when strong social rewards for underachievement exist. Akerlof's goal was to assess individuals' behaviors when they are rewarded for their status in society and when they are rewarded for their ability to conform to the rest of society. These models define the bounds of important social interactions because status seekers attempt to be as different as possible from everyone else and conformers try to mimic everyone else. Akerlof's models provide representations of social distance and show that people overinvest in status and may either over- or underinvest in conformity.

Surely, joining a group has social consequences. If a member's sense of belonging is accompanied with a public display or recognition, then joining has a social consequence. Indeed, some group members proudly display their affiliations. Their expressive benefits from joining appear quite tangible. Our group memberships have both private and public consequences, but scholars have not fully explored this area. When are our group memberships private decisions and when are they social decisions? Surely, there are important distinctions between (privately) identifying with an interest and (publicly) mobilizing with a group (e.g., Gartner and Segura 1997).[3] At times, we model joining as a simple, private exchange (Olson 1965; Salisbury 1969). At times, we develop models in which joining publicly signals group viability to others and facilitates coordination with others (Ainsworth and Sened 1993; Lohmann 1994), but these signals are of no social consequence for those "outside of the group."

Critics of Pluralism

The normative tinge in Putnam's work has been seen before in interest group scholarship. In the 1960s, some group scholars were so enamored of pluralism that they considered pluralism as an antidote for all sorts of societal ills. These scholars moved from *describing* politics from a pluralist perspective to *prescribing* pluralist solutions for societal ills.[4] For prescriptive pluralists, enhanced participation, especially from traditionally underrepresented groups, improved the governing process. Such pluralists were quick to recall Madison's admonitions in the tenth *Federalist* paper about controlling the "tyranny of the majority." Pluralism, it was argued, ensured the dispersion of power among organized groups. The inclusion of more and more interests was deemed beneficial because it provided a brake on majority tyranny as well as other forms of concentrated power. To many pluralists, greater inclusion was considered a part of the natural process of political development. Greater inclusiveness broadened the negotiation process, which in and of itself was beneficial because the voicing of interests and concerns enhanced the deliberative process (e.g., Mansbridge 1992).

For another set of scholars, the *promise* of pluralism was of little concern. Key issues and fundamental questions were never directly addressed. The deliberations and bargains inherent to pluralism were really quite limited (see, for example, Bachrach and Baratz 1962, 1963; Gaventa 1982; Schattschneider 1960; Walker 1966). In *Who Governs* (1961), Robert Dahl examined various local, community organizations. Some critics wondered whether Dahl's conclusions about a local parent teacher association (PTA) offered meaningful insights into other issues or other, larger, more powerful organizations? Could a study of the local PTA offer insights into the governmental process? Most critics of pluralism were not opposed to studying groups, per se, but

---

[3] A related issue arises in other areas. In the PAC literature, scholars often use Heckman procedures to distinguish between a choice to contribute and the level of a contribution. The standard thinking is that the binary decision to contribute (yes or no) is different than the decision that affects the level of a contribution. The connections to identification and mobilization are straightforward. The binary decision to identify or not must precede the decision affecting one's extent of mobilization. Selection bias may occur if the mobilization process is evaluated without first considering the identification process.

[4] The distinctions between descriptive and prescriptive pluralism are made by Berry (1997).

they did dispute the purported benefits of prescriptive pluralism. These critics argued that all interests were seldom included in the deliberative process, and often deliberations addressed only minor issues. Was American politics too elitist, too socialist oriented, or too enamored with the free market? These fundamental concerns about the nature of American politics and society did not arise within the pluralist paradigm. For many students of interest groups, these critiques were all related to "non-decisionmaking" (Bachrach and Baratz 1963).

Bachrach and Baratz (1963) suggested that the manipulation of community norms and values and the structuring of governing procedures effectively limited the scope of decision making. For many social scientists, the notion of non-decision making was initially quite powerful, but this work has fallen out of favor within the political science community. In the political science literature, few references (whether central or token) are made today to Bachrach and Baratz's work. The lack of favor stemmed from conceptual weaknesses and measurement and methodological problems. Bachrach and Baratz failed to specify how one might distinguish minor issues from fundamental issues. To suggest that PTAs and educational policies are minor is to belittle the issues of equal opportunity and equal access, integration, choice, immigration and assimilation, and a host of other defining issues. Bachrach and Baratz's work was also stymied by the discipline's inability to model the absence of actions or decisions.

Today, there are a wide array of models that evaluate the timing of decisions and non-decisions. The empirical analyses designed to handle such situations are often called event history models.[5] Though I cannot in this space detail the econometrics underpinning event history analysis, I can lay out the general framework.[6] Consider a congressional committee. Numerous legislative proposals are referred to the committee, and most of those will die from inattention. Which proposals are addressed and which are left to die? When are proposals addressed—early or late in a session or just before a recess? To conduct an event history analysis, one first must consider the relevant time frame for decisions. One could divide the two-year congress into year-long congressional sessions, months, weeks, or days. Suppose we divide a congress into twenty-four month-long periods. Within each of those periods, there is a decision or non-decision for each legislative proposal. Whether the committee moves forward with a proposal may depend on the period, lobbying pressure, public opinion, media attention, economic conditions, or any of a number of other independent factors. Carpenter (2002) used event history procedures to evaluate drug approval actions taken by the Food and Drug Administration (FDA). The covariates included such things as media attention and the number of disease-related groups concerned about a drug's approval. Bachrach and Baratz might not consider the

---

[5] Other terms include "duration analysis" and "survival analysis."
[6] Box-Steffensmeier and Jones (2004) is a very good reference for more information on event history models.

timing of drug approvals by a federal agency to be a major issue, but the speed and timing of FDA decisions have far-reaching implications for health policy, affecting patients and medical procedures as well as the profitability of pharmaceutical firms. Event history procedures do allow one to analyze empirically questions related to how and when one "decides to decide" (Bachrach and Baratz 1962; 1963, 644).

DESCRIPTIVE WORK

Descriptive work never seems to go out of style. Social scientists often begin work in new areas of study with descriptive statistics. For an interest group scholar, a steady flow of new, descriptive work may appear particularly important if there is no equilibrium in the set of extant interests or groups. If the environment is ever-changing, the demand for new work describing those changes remains strong. Descriptive work is often considered the most straightforward and objective of methods. Catalogs of interests and interest groups may seem straightforward, but the actual cataloguing process forces one to establish criteria for acceptance or rejection of relevant data. Which facts are appropriate for cataloguing and which are of no significance? The very best descriptive work is very explicit about such criteria, but as often as not, criteria remain implicit. Relying heavily on Quine's *Methods of Logic*, the historian David Fischer (1970, 5) notes that "if a fact is a true statement about past events, then there is no practicable limit to the number of facts which are relevant to even the smallest . . . problem. 'Truths are as plentiful as falsehoods,' [but] 'scientific activity is not the indiscriminate amassing of truths; science is selective and seeks the truths that count most.'" Compiling "just the facts" is problematic because there are an infinite number of facts, and one seldom fully specifies why some facts are compiled while others are not.

Descriptive work is plagued by another potential problem for interest group scholars. One can only describe what is observed, but interest group scholars often refer to unobserved interests (Bentley), potential groups (Truman), or decisions not made (Bachrach and Baratz). Bentley (1908, 199) categorically stated that when there is no observable action, there is no interest. Bentley would only catalog actions. Earl Latham, a contemporary of Truman's, chose only to catalog organized interests (1952a). In contrast, Truman felt that there was a role for potential groups, latent, unorganized, and inactive interests. If we accept a role for potential groups, how do we distinguish unrepresented and unimportant "feelings" or interests from the interests of important potential groups? Simply cataloguing interests and interest groups is not an easy task.

Recognizing Patterns in Descriptive Data

Descriptive interest group analyses provide snapshots of an event or situation. Snapshots of the interest group environment provide a static recording of the interest group environment, but they fail to discern any of the fluidity in the group environment. Consider one of the most important works on interest group organization and maintenance in the 1980s. In his oft-cited 1983 *American Political Science Review* article, Jack Walker included a graph that has been reproduced in numerous books and articles. Walker's graph displays the cumulative count of groups listed by founding date. These founding dates extend over a one-hundred-year period. The graph rises moderately from the mid-1800s to about 1920, and then makes a sharp upward trajectory. By the 1960s, there appears to be a tremendous explosion in the number of groups active in politics. There may have indeed been an explosion in the number of groups in the 1960s and 1970s, but the graph provides no clear information in that regard. It appears that relatively few groups catalogued in the 1980s were founded in the early 1900s and many, many groups were founded in the 1960s and 1970s. The graph is a snapshot that simply fails to reflect the processes that produced the data illustrated in the figure. As Walker himself acknowledges (395), the appearance of the graph may be driven by higher "death rates" among older groups founded in the 1800s and early 1900s or by higher "birth rates" in the 1960s and 1970s.

Is the common interpretation of Walker's graph still "mostly right"? There is no way to know how the probable explosion in groups in the 1960s compares to the explosions after the Civil War, during the Progressive era, or just after the Second World War. How far "off the mark" can the graph be? Suppose we looked at the growth in the United States population over the same time period and chose to attribute that growth to increases in the birth rate. For some periods of time, population growth is reasonably attributed to increased birth rates, but for other eras the population growth might have more to do with immigration patterns or improved health care. To further complicate the issue, the number of live births from year to year can increase even as the birth rate decreases.

Of course, we are not all methodologists, and no one can become a methodologist overnight. However, we can ask, "Why do we see the patterns we do?" To strengthen descriptive analyses one should consider a thought process that mirrors the underpinnings of maximum likelihood estimation (MLE) procedures. MLE procedures are fast becoming the dominant econometric tools in political science.[7] In classical ordinary least squares regressions, we simply accept the data as truth and attempt to fit a straight line to them. With MLE procedures, we consider what sort of function would lead to the array of data that has been observed. What type of function would be most likely to leave the observed data trail? The political

---

[7] For an introduction to MLE reasoning and methods, see King (1989).

science discipline engages in considerable data collection, while largely overlooking methodological advances (G. King 1989, 3). Such an oversight is particularly unfortunate because sophisticated methods allow one to correct for various problems that might occur in the data (G. King 1989, 3). If our data were perfect, our methods could be weaker.

Of course, different explanations might plausibly explain the same patterns in the observed data. Distinct theories might be observationally equivalent. For instance, Lowery, Gray, and Monogan (2008) note that either their ESA model (energy, stability, area) or Olson's collective action model (1965) could explain observed aggregate-level interest group data. "[R]esults [and implications] of one model can equally support the other" (1173). Even though the micro-level foundations in the models are very different, the theories predict similar patterns in aggregate-level data. Though some questions remain unresolved, Olson (1965) and Lowery, Gray, and Monogan (2008) move well beyond merely reporting what interests are observed.

Any number of conditions might affect the array of interests observed in a community. Many scholars extend their analyses to other areas, sometimes well removed from the interests or group members themselves. Most traditional scholarship focuses on what could be termed the "supply of interests," but there is also a "demand for groups" that extends beyond any sort of membership base. Fluidity in the interest group environment is partly affected by the patrons and large foundations who underwrite groups and who usually stand well apart from the group members themselves (e.g., Lowry 1999; Nownes and Cigler 2007; Strolovitch 2006). Bertelli and Wenger (forthcoming) link the emergence of think tanks to demands for information as well as a rising stock market that bolsters foundations' and patrons' abilities to fund group efforts. Bertelli and Wenger hypothesize that as ideologies in the US became more polarized, the demand for specialized, partisan information also increased. One might also consider the competition for attention that groups face. Some groups secure attention by occupying an ever-narrowing niche within the ideological spectrum. Finally, one might consider the effects of new microtargeting technologies on the emergence of new groups.

Lists of Group Behaviors

Studies of lobbyists and lobbying, dating back to at least Lester Milbrath's path-breaking work on lobbyists (1963), often list a set of activities in which lobbyists engage. Such lists provide insights into the day-to-day activities of lobbyists, but they do not tell us anything about lobbying strategies per se. Consider a lobbying campaign. Even seemingly inconsequential activities, such as constituent fly-ins, may be important if they are a costly signal of issue salience (Ainsworth 1993). A lobbyist's activities might make sense only in light of other people's actions or conditions. A lobbyist's contacting behavior may be a function of legislators' preferences or of other lobbyists' activities (Austen-Smith and Wright 1994). Under different circumstances, lobbyists may engage in activities with an eye toward their opponents or their allies (Ainsworth 1997; Hall and Wayman 1990; Hall and Deardorff 2006). With an eye toward building and maintaining coalitions, Groseclose and Snyder (1996) suggest that supermajorities limit the ability of any particular member of a coalition to threaten defection in an attempt to secure additional resources. In a supermajority, no single legislator is crucial, so no legislator can extract excessive rewards for his or her support. Supermajorities may be cheaper to secure and maintain than bare majorities. Typically, scholars link lobbying activities to policy goals, but Groseclose and Snyder's work suggests that lobbying activities and contacting behaviors may be linked to policy goals or to coalition maintenance and cost concerns. A simple list of activities fails to explain whether some activities reinforce others. Kollman (1998) and Hojnacki and Kimball (1999) find that grassroots lobbying and direct lobbying are often used in combination. Scholars increasingly examine the combined effects of lobbying and contributions (e.g., Ansolabehere, Snyder, and Tripathi 2002; Bennedsen and Feldmann 2006; Esterling 2007). The simple point is that lobbying does not occur in a vacuum, so lists of lobbying activities are barely illuminating. Instead of lists, one must construct theories that address what prompts certain types of lobbying activities and consider how those activities interact with one another.

Unobserved Interests and Actions

One cannot describe what cannot be observed. However, in the tradition of Sherlock Holmes, sometimes interest group scholars are most concerned about the dog that did not bark in the night. Game-theoretic models allow scholars to consider the implications of actions taken as well as those not taken. Game-theoretic applications to the study of interest groups have been among the most controversial of methodological approaches employed. Nearly every interest group scholar develops a throwaway line for a discussion of Olson's work on the collective action problem. Olson's work tightly focused on a central question for interest group scholars. Which interests organize and which remain latent? Olson also introduced a new question for interest group scholars. Are like-minded individuals invulnerable to squabbles and internecine competitions? The quest for group affiliation is countered with the quest for individual economic survival. It is not that groups fail to emerge; it is that many more groups could emerge. Groups are not seen as the "automatic fruit" of interests (Salisbury 1969). It is not that affiliation is irrational; it is that affiliation is fragile. Given Truman's claim that political interest groups make claims upon others, it is only natural to think that groups and group members might be strategic in their pursuits of policy gains.

Game-theoretic advances have been especially helpful when considering the unobserved action or interest, the very unobserved action that Bentley derided. Games require that one define a set of players and a set of options or actions available to the players. Depending on the actions chosen by the players, a particular outcome obtains and payoffs are distributed. Game-theoretic models are often amenable to comparative statics, whereby one can see how changes in exogenous variables affect endogenous variables. An exogenous variable is simply a variable over which no player has any control. Suppose a lobbyist wants to consider how much pressure to apply to a legislator (e.g., Denzau and Munger 1986). Various costs and benefits are ascertained, and some equilibrium level of pressure is applied. Now suppose that media coverage suddenly becomes much more favorable for the lobbyist's argument. Favorable media coverage ought to make the lobbyist's endeavors in persuasion easier (and therefore less expensive). Given its reduced cost, one might expect greater lobbying pressure.[8] Comparative statics allow us to develop testable hypotheses about how a change in an exogenous variable (favorable media coverage) affects a change in an endogenous variable (lobbying pressure). The comparative statics in the Denzau and Munger work suggests that potential groups are still represented even as extant groups work to buy influence.

Games of incomplete information allow scholars to address players' beliefs. All along the equilibrium path of chosen actions in a game tree, players refine their information and update their beliefs about one another. Actions and inactions affect those beliefs, and ultimately the game's equilibrium is consistent with those beliefs. Testing strategic interactions directly has proven to be much more vexing than testing hypotheses derived from comparative statics. We face a problem related to the independence of observations, which is a crucial assumption in most econometric methods. In a game-theoretic scenario, players' choices are seldom truly independent from other players' choices, so our observations of actions taken are no longer independent. Game-theoretic methods generally lack stochastic elements, and wholly deterministic processes are less amenable to statistical evaluations. Thomas Palfrey and the late Richard McKelvey (McKelvey and Palfrey 1995, 1998) began work to address this problem, and Curtis Signorino (2003) has developed statistical techniques to address this problem.[9] Signorino's methodological corrections have been applied most often in the international relations subfield, but they are also being applied in analyses of congressional elections (Carson 2005) and wherever strategic interactions may occur. Signorino's work is not the only econometric route possible under these circumstances. Switching

[8] For the moment, I ignore the income and substitution effects. If political pressure is an inferior good rather than a normal good, the relative strengths or the income and substitution effects are crucial.

[9] Rebecca Morton's *Methods and Models* (1999) provides a very good introduction to the McKelvey and Palfrey quantal response equilibrium concept.

regressions allow one to derive information that is related to the choices not made. The economists Pablo Spiller and Rafael Gely (1992) use a switching regression in their article on indirect group influence in the National Labor Relations Board. If one proceeds without the derived information from the counterfactual (that is, the choice not made), the observed variables are vulnerable to selection bias. The dog that did not bark in the night can be as important as observed signals.

Institutions and the Scope of Analysis

Using purely descriptive methods provides no bounds to the scope of one's analysis. However, when group scholars focus on particular institutions, they establish clearer boundaries to their analysis. Even if their work is what one might still call descriptive, the institutional context provides crucial structure. The cataloguing of interests and the listing of behaviors are somewhat easier because of the defining rules and procedures of the institution. For instance, to study groups and the courts, scholars can focus on groups as litigants or groups as authors of amicus curiae briefs (Caldeira and Wright 1988, 1990). The different roles help to define the scope of the analysis. The scope of analysis may also be limited by the fact that the number of individuals tied to an institution is limited. There are only 435 House members. To assess who lobbies whom, one can consider every possible legislator–lobbyist dyad (Hojnacki and Kimball 1998). Each observation is a legislator–lobbyist dyad, but these observations violate the standard statistical independence assumption because the same actors appear in many different dyads. The econometric corrections are fairly simple—in some statistical software programs they are just a click away.[10] The larger point is that methodological advances can enhance our abilities to address basic substantive issues such as "Who lobbies whom?"

Institutions also provide opportunities to refine our descriptions of strategic behavior. That is, different stages of a decision-making process in an institution create different strategic concerns for a group. Lobbying to secure a spot on the congressional agenda may be very different than lobbying for votes (Austen-Smith 1993). A raft of new scholarship, including both published and forthcoming work, examines how interests and pressures in one institution affect other behaviors in other institutions. Shipan (1997) examines how interest groups are affected by opportunities for judicial review. Balla and Wright (2001) explore whether the array of interests in Congress is reflected in an agency's advisory councils. Gordon and Hafer (2005, 2007) and Hall and Miler (2008) consider how pressure on legislators can affect agency oversight and agency behavior. If interest group activities in the first branch of government are designed to elicit behavior in

---

[10] A standard reference for cluster options is Wooldridge (2002).

another branch, then we must be especially careful when we interpret lists of activities or describe behaviors related to interest groups in Congress.

INFORMATION AND INTEREST GROUPS

States require good information to govern effectively. There are several channels for information transmission to government officials, including bureaucracies, markets, elections and public opinion polls, and interest groups. Information has permeated every aspect of interest groups discussed so far in this chapter. It is often thought that information from interest groups is hopelessly biased. In this last main section of this chapter, I address two issues. First, providing information is just one activity out of many in which groups engage, and that provision of information may interact with other interest group activities. How might information interact with other group activities? There is some evidence to suggest that good information derived from lobbying is crowded out by a group's financial contributions (Bennedsen and Feldmann 2006), especially when the information is expensive to collect or validate. However, Esterling (2007) finds that contributions may enhance the willingness of legislators to advance their own expertise. As noted earlier, informative legislative lobbying may be tied to grassroots campaigning. Information might be the coin of the realm, but the real questions are "How does information interact with other group activities?" and "How are legislators affected by the overall interest group presence?"

The second point is that groups have incentives to withhold or contort information, but distortion affects information from all other sources as well. Bias in group information should be measured in relation to the bias inherent in other sources. Recall that Hansen (1991) argued that interest groups provided information at a comparative advantage over the political parties. Party information can be helpful, but it is not always state- or district-specific. Parties generally focus more broadly, and sometimes legislators prefer more narrowly oriented information. Groups have a comparative advantage over other sources as well, which I believe will receive greater attention in the future. Group information must compete with other (biased) sources for information, including bureaucracies, markets, and elections and public opinion.

Let us briefly consider the biases in information. Information from a bureaucrat may be skewed because there are strong incentives to exaggerate bureaucratic successes and bolster clientelism. The bureaucrat at the Department of Agriculture need not consider the views of the interests more closely aligned with the Department of Commerce or the Environmental Protection Agency. Groups as well as bureaucrats strive to promote their own clients. Almost every market has some sort of imperfection, and government intervention in a market often creates a moral hazard thereby stimulating behaviors the government sought to limit. For instance, a bank bail-out might encourage riskier banking practices. An investment in higher-education grants and loans might spur automobile consumption (Cornwell and Mustard 2006) as well as college attendance. If there is an imperfection, prices are poor signals. If there is an intervention, prices and behaviors are skewed.

Public opinion polls presume issue salience. That is, respondents can only answer the questions they are asked—whether those questions are salient to them or not. When political interest groups mobilize, there are fewer questions of salience. The choice to mobilize indicates salience and signals electoral mobilization potential (J. Wright 1996). Public opinion polls also rely heavily on average responses and provide less information about the distribution of responses. The average response may be determined from either a highly bifurcated bimodal distribution or a normal distribution. Upon reflection, the interpretation of polls is never straightforward. Interest group information may indeed be biased, but one should not presume that polling data is devoid of problems in interpretation. Elections provide regular feedback to governing officials, but they may not provide information about the desired shifts in policies. If voting is retrospective (Fiorina 1981), then the electoral outcome expresses clearer information about past policies as opposed to future direction. In contrast, lobbying efforts are always prospective. There are many sources of information for government officials, but each of the four sources evaluated here has shortcomings. Sometimes the state actually has too much information to evaluate. Whenever there is a cacophony of demands, states must rely on costly signals, audits, screening devices, and reputations to separate the good information from the bad information.

CONCLUSION

Whether scholars focus on politics inside of the beltway or on the political lives of those far removed from Washington, the shadows cast by interest groups are readily apparent. The immense domain of interest group studies virtually ensures that scholars will continue to be fascinated by interest groups. The tremendous scope of the domain for interest group research has at times also been the root of weaknesses in interest group research. Successful research projects most often have a narrow scope, with a well-defined set of actors and actions. An immense domain invites poorly defined research projects. "The awkwardness of... political phenomena ... [stems from the lack of a] beginning or end .... It cannot really be said that we have seen a subject until we have seen its outer limits" (Schattschneider

1960, 22). Smaller, more manageable events allow for clearer logical connections and greater precision in language and analysis. In his trenchant critique of pluralism, E. E. Schattschneider stated that his goal was simply "to define general propositions more precisely" (1960, 22).

If limiting the scope of one's analysis is important for scientific advancement, then descriptive work must be thoroughly reworked because, as Fischer noted, there are no bounds to descriptive work. To establish boundaries to descriptive analysis, I have argued that one adopt MLE-like reasoning and seriously consider data generation processes. One can also use institutions to demarcate the boundaries of research. "Constitutional rules are mainly significant because they help to determine what particular groups are to be given advantages or handicaps in the political struggle" (Dahl 1956, 137). Constitutional rules can also narrow a scholar's focus, thereby strengthening her work. A consideration of the strategic underpinnings of group behaviors dovetails nicely with MLE reasoning. The adoption of new methods sometimes appears faddish, but often in political science methods emerge to address problems that might otherwise remain intractable. As new tools emerge, we will be able to address crucial substantive questions more directly.

PART III

PARTY HISTORY

CHAPTER 6

AMERICAN POLITICAL PARTIES

HISTORY, VOTERS, CRITICAL ELECTIONS, AND PARTY SYSTEMS

JOEL H. SILBEY

POLITICAL parties have been an enduring element on the American landscape since the 1790s. In all but a very few presidential contests early in the nation's history two major parties have organized and fought elections on behalf of the policy initiatives that each advocated and the candidates that each supported. These were, first, the Federalists and the Republicans; then there were the two branches of a swollen and divided Republicans, labeled the National Republicans and Democratic Republicans; these morphed, in turn, into the Whigs and Democrats, and, finally, after the mid-1850s, the Republicans and Democrats, plus a range of minor parties. Their efforts provided a guide for voters and legislators to follow as the parties sought to win control of the government and then bring their policy goals to fruition through congressional and state legislative action.

There is a rich library of scholarly monographs dealing with aspects of party activities at different moments (e.g., Holt 1999; Gienapp 1987; among many) as well as more general surveys (e.g., Beard 1929; Binkley 1943; Polakoff 1981; A. Schlesinger 1973) recounting the full history of these parties. They have recognized the shifting contexts of American politics over time, as well as the continuities and regularities in the evolution of parties on the nation's landscape. Much about them has remained constant. Whatever their name or time frame, the parties have been much alike, acting in similar ways throughout the two centuries since they first appeared: in their focus on elections and governing, and in articulating a perspective about their society and where they stand on the issues of the day (see, for example, Key 1942; Rossiter 1960; Sindler 1966).

Despite their general similarity over more than 200 years, political parties have not been stable entities. Alongside their constant elements, changes have occurred at different moments in how they organized themselves to nominate candidates and campaign on their behalf owing to changes in society's values, its technology, needs, and the rules under which the parties operated, as well as the necessity of organizing and campaigning across an expanding land expanse as the nation grew into a continental empire. Similarly, the substance of the arguments that they offered to the voters shifted, often dramatically, as did their sources of electoral support. American political history has been punctuated throughout by these changes, and, as a result, historians and political scientists have collaborated to go beyond the descriptive in search of the underlying patterns of party history, mark their shifts over time, and develop a way of framing their story (Aldrich 1995).

The most persuasive result of their consideration has been for scholars to argue that the best way to proceed is by tracing the history of American political parties through the critical election–realignment–party system approach (Rosenof 2003). Originally put forward by the political scientist V. O. Key (1955, 1959), this was extended by his student Walter Dean Burnham in a series of seminal articles and books (1965, 1970, 1982). In this perspective, voters are the center of the party system. All else flows from their presence and behavior. As a result of their actions, there has been a life cycle and rhythm to party history, first, in their support base, where in most elections voting coalitions consisting of different blocs of voters come together and remain steadfast in support of their party in election after election for a generation (Sundquist 1968; Burnham 1970; Clubb, Flanigan, and Zingale 1980). This preeminent voter stability is disrupted by a critical election, sometimes several in a row, which results in an electoral realignment when a proportion of the voters rearrange themselves in response to some extraordinary event or crisis that severely shakes their world. The result is the emergence of a new alignment of supporters for each party, usually a new majority party, and a change in the nation's policy agenda, which last for a significant time period thereafter. In between, there are occasional deviating elections where the normal support pattern is temporarily shaken, and reinstating elections in which the normal pattern in a particular era is reestablished (Angus Campbell et al. 1960, 1966; Pomper 1967b).

Beside the particular voter mix present, each new party system added a number of new ingredients to the nation's politics as well; for example, in the size, complexity, and capabilities of their organizations, in the nature of their leadership, in the numbers pulled into their orbit, in the intensity of the commitment to them by those involved, and in the style, as well as the content, of their campaign arguments. Most of all, the extent of the parties' reach into the population and political authority has shifted over time as their power on the national scene has increased, waned, and finally, as some have argued, all but fragmented (Pomper 1977; Silbey 1991).

The rhythms and patterns present at different moments have led scholars to identify five different party systems throughout our history as defining what Burnham called "the changing shape of the American political universe" (Burnham 1965). Each party system is about a third of a century long. The first lasted from the 1790s to the aftermath of the war of 1812, the second existed from the 1820s to the 1850s, the third was present from the 1850s to the 1890s, the fourth from then into the early 1930s, and the fifth lasted from the 1930s to the late 1960s. In each of these periods, as noted, popular voting behavior remained quite stable from election to election and across different offices, although there were always some defections, third party activity, and failure of some supporters to come to the polls (Chambers and Burnham 1967, 1975; Kleppner et al. 1981; Argersinger 1992).

These durable voter alignments were badly shaken by the occurrence of critical elections (not all of them presidential contests) which bounded each system: in 1796–1800, 1828–36, 1854–60, 1894–6, 1932–6, and, finally, perhaps in 1968–72, that redefined the nation's political course as new durable voter alignments and issue agendas emerged and came to dominate the political scene (Kleppner et al. 1981; Burnham 1965; McCormick 1982; Sundquist 1968).

WHY PARTIES?

The critical election–realignment organizing scheme has been both widely accepted (and, more recently, increasingly challenged) (Rosenof 2003; Mayhew 2002; H. Price 1976). To sort out and clarify the issues involved leads us back to the beginning of American national politics. Political parties were an unexpected creation since a powerful ideological antipartyism dominated early American political thought because, it was alleged, they corrupted the political independence of citizens by demanding submission to a party's dictates, and because they were generators of conflict when societies needed consensus and non-confrontational ways of deciding the issues that faced them. Parties elsewhere, particularly in

England, had always been dangerously divisive; the persistent conflicts that they bred as a normal aspect of their activities threatened the well-being, the liberty, and even the survival, of a nation or, at least, presage its decline into formidable difficulties (Hofstadter 1969; Wallace 1968).

But political parties emerged in America despite the strong resistance to them. Persistent contentiousness bred parties. They rose out of the reality of a divided political landscape in the nation's first years under the new federal Constitution and the need to tame the dissonance and the threat it posed to the nation. The founding generation sharply differed over what policies were desirable once the Constitution was in place. Finding ways to order and direct disagreements into channels that would lead to winning control of the government became necessary (Charles 1956; Formisano in Kleppner et al. 1981; Chambers and Burnham 1975; Elkins and McKitrick 1993; Sharp 1993).

That necessity continued thereafter, because of the ongoing contentiousness of American politics. There was always something to fight about. Bringing people together to confront others not once, but again and again, in the many elections that occurred at both the federal and state levels, necessitated establishing some kind of organizational framework, and the articulating of a frame of reference that explained what people were fighting for, and why they should march under the banners of one group of leaders or the other. However ideologically painful that recognition of necessity was, what emerged was all but inevitable given the frequency of elections in every year, year in and year out (Van Buren 1867; Hofstadter 1969; Nichols 1967; Heale 1982).

POLITICAL PARTIES IN A NEW NATION

Specifically, the first parties emerged in the 1790s in response to Secretary of the Treasury Alexander Hamilton's push to build up an expansive national government and the consequent resistance by those defending the primacy of state authority. Hamilton sought legislation calling for a powerful national bank and a high tariff to deal with the economy, a foreign relations based on America's close ties with England (and consequent hostility to France), and to control conflict between the states from threatening national unity. Advocates of the primacy of the states against the center, led by Thomas Jefferson and James Madison, opposed Hamilton and saw his plans as a threat to the states' well-being and control over their own interests. The opposition was, at first, scattered and fragmented, without much national focus to their efforts. The states' rights leaders needed to build up an array of support across the nation that would come together as a disciplined cohort large enough to attain an electoral college majority and take control of Congress. The reality of frequent elections in the new nation underscored that need even further. Much was at stake—all of the time (Charles 1956; Chambers 1963; Goodman 1975; Banning 1978).

Madison and Jefferson did not begin with a full blueprint of what they intended to create, and in many ways they still resisted the idea of organized, disciplined parties. But necessity trumped traditional beliefs (Nichols 1967; Heale 1982). They set to work, establishing contact among the different state groups coalescing under the name Republicans, and founded "Democratic–Republican" clubs and newspapers in key areas to propagandize and electioneer on behalf of their cause. Unlike the presidential elections of 1788 and 1792, when no one ran against George Washington, Jefferson challenged John Adams in 1796 in a campaign to decide who would be the next president. Candidates for other offices, state and federal, who shared similar policy outlooks joined in behind his candidacy (Cunningham 1957; Chambers 1963; Elkins and McKitrick 1993; Sharp 1993).

Hamilton's supporters were slower off the mark, refusing at first to think in terms of the despised notion of a political party. But, as the Jeffersonians moved ahead, their opponents ultimately responded with their own counteracting efforts to protect the policies that they believed were necessary to enact. As a result, political confrontations such as the first contested efforts to win office from the mid-1790s onward were highly charged efforts (Nichols 1967). The bitter election of 1800 in particular set the tone with widespread expressions by both sides of fear for the country (if the other side won), intense anger against what their opponents threatened, and the need to prevail if the country was to survive (Ferling 2004).

As the parties spread their wings, the voters were drawn into the ranks of one or other of the combatants. The reasons for their choices originated in several places, their economic interests and outlook, their particular group identity, or because they followed the lead of their community leaders caught up in the party wars. Although there were sectional tensions in these first divisions, both parties received support throughout the nation, albeit in different proportions. The Jeffersonians were particularly strong in the southern states, the Hamilton group in New England. The nation's largest economic interest group, farmers, including slave owners, were to be found in both parties. Their market orientation often determined their choice. Those who produced for distant markets and were part of the trade nexus (primarily tobacco planters and the growing number of cotton producers) differed in their political orientation from those who produced primarily for themselves or only for limited nearby markets. Other economic groups on the ground, bankers and merchants at one end of the spectrum, laborers of various kinds at the other, made similar choices as their interests dictated (Chambers 1963; Formisano 2001).

Other voters selected their party home based on ethnic and religious identity. Friction between such identity groups was commonplace and divisive in their society and potential voters reacted to that reality. Still others had security concerns, especially about the Indian tribes along the frontier who, abetted by the English in Canada, were resisting American expansion into the trans-Appalachian region. They wanted the government to confront their enemies and remedy the threatening situation. As a result of the voter distribution between the two parties, some states were basically one-sided politically on election day. Others, such as the key large state of New York, fielded robust two party competition throughout the 1790s and in 1800 (Formisano 2001; Shade 1981).

Parties were more than organizers and mobilizers in the electoral arena. Once in office, members of the states and federal governments, the executive branches, state legislators and congressmen, elected under partisan labels, were expected to follow their party's lead as they dealt with the issues and policy choices before them. Some resisted such discipline but more and more came to accept it. Party unity was usually quite high when legislative votes were taken. The reach and control of the parties was never as complete as their leaders desired. Not every legislator was caught up in this system. But their impact on policymaking was clear and direct (Chambers 1963; Broussard 1978; Elkins and McKitrick 1993; Sharp 1993).

INTERREGNUM AFTER 1815

The first parties had limited penetration into the political world (Formisano 1981). Federalists and Republicans did not arrive on the scene fully formed and never became so. They were not organizationally robust, nor did they need to be, since the American electorate remained small primarily owing to suffrage restrictions that limited the numbers eligible to vote (Nichols 1967). Although there was clearly a popular element in the politics of party warfare, this was far from a democratic situation. Popular pressure existed but was not usually decisive. The nation's elites ran things and dominated elections. Most critically, commitment to the system existed but was not widespread. Turnout among potential voters remained low during the period despite the efforts of party leaders to get everyone they could to the polls. At best, whatever commitment there was, was intermittent and viewed with a casual attitude by many. A good number of Americans remained unaligned with either party. Most continued to believe that the two parties were temporary expedients needed to confront a particular situation. Even party leaders remained hesitant about what had emerged. Although they, too, had begun to organize and electioneer, the Federalists, as they came to be labeled, clearly remained less eager to engage in such activity, despite the constant conflicts with the Republicans, than were their opponents. And, the Jeffersonians in power proved to be as hostile as the

Federalists had been to the norms of party conflict, particularly the unseemly and divisive attempts by the opposition to challenge them at the polls. As a result, some modern analysts are not comfortable calling this political world the first party system because of the incomplete, ad hoc, and shallow nature of the parties, and the strong persistence of antiparty attitudes throughout (Formisano 1974, 1981; Hofstadter 1969).

After 1800, party tumult continued for a time, stimulated by the impact of the Napoleonic wars on American trade and security interests. The Jeffersonian Republicans grew stronger while the Federalists, although continuing to fight on, faded, first because of the deaths of their great leaders, George Washington and Hamilton, and then because of the reaction against the pro-British behavior of many of them during the War of 1812. As a result, a basically one-party arrangement replaced the contentiousness of the nation's first twenty-five years under the Constitution. The Republicans ruled the roost, even enjoying an all but unanimous victory in the electoral college in the presidential election of 1820 (Banner 1970; Fischer 1965).

State-level politics continued to be more divided and confrontational than was the national scene, but even at the latter there were moments of angry battle, in reaction to the economic collapse of 1819 for one, and over the admission of Missouri as a state a year later (Rothbard 1962; Forbes 2007). But there was little national organization or discernible, sustained party groupings in this. Factions fought factions, changing sides from one issue to the next; volatility of support dominated the scene. American politics had become fragmented, neither coherent nor organized. Four Republican candidates, representing different factions of the Jeffersonian coalition, won electoral votes in the presidential election of 1824, a contest only settled through a so-called "corrupt bargain" between two of the candidates and the action of the House of Representatives that followed because no one was able to organize a disciplined majority for a candidate in the voting in the electoral college (Hopkins 1973).

ROUND TWO: JACKSONIANS VERSUS WHIGS

But this "era of good feelings" and political fragmentation was short-lived. A new party system arose in the late 1820s and 1830s in circumstances similar to those earlier, that is, not through a realignment (there was no alignment to realign from), but because of the coming together of national coalitions to confront one another. Once again, a strong nationalist power surge pushed by political leaders in Washington, this time emanating from one part of the swollen post-1815 Jeffersonian coalition, the so-called National Republicans. President John Quincy Adams and Secretary of State Henry Clay urged the enactment of an even more ambitious nationalizing program than had their predecessors in the 1790s. And, once again, state-power-centered politicians desiring to uphold the Jeffersonian conception of limited power at the center realized that they had to revive effective collective organizations in their own defense. Once more, their argument went, national parties were needed to mobilize and organize the electorate, this time across a much broader geographic expanse. Led by New York Senator Martin Van Buren, a national coalition of the so-called Democratic–Republicans came together and successfully elected Andrew Jackson as president in 1828 (Remini 1959; Holt 1999).

What distinguished this system from its predecessor was, first, the fuller organization of the parties, with committees to organize and run elections being formed at every level from the national down to counties, towns, and urban wards, with local, state, and congressional district conventions called to nominate candidates. All of them came together at a national convention that met every four years where delegates worked out differences, agreed on their campaign program, nominated candidates, drafted platforms, and organized the party's campaign activities (rallies, speeches, etc.) necessary to energize the voters and get them out to the polls in the upcoming presidential contest (McCormick 1967; Silbey 1991).

The second distinguishing characteristic of these emerging parties was their deeper penetration into the political world, with more interests in conflict and making demands on the government, interests who had to be organized for electoral warfare. Third was the new reality of an expanding mass electorate as states did away with most suffrage restrictions for adult white males. Fourth was the extensive and sustained support of voters for each of the two major coalitions. Finally, there was a significant transformation in the political culture, that is, a widespread, and eventually all but total, acceptance of parties as legitimate institutions in the American republic with the growing agreement with Martin Van Buren's argument that political conflict was a normal aspect of American life and would inevitably continue into the future so that parties had to become a permanent part of the nation's political terrain. These distinguishing elements of this party system did not appear all at once but evolved over time as the pace and reach of politics dramatically quickened (Hofstadter 1969; Nichols 1967; Formisano 1983; Silbey 1991, 2001).

New political leaders, many of them newspapermen such as Thurlow Weed, Horace Greeley, Francis P. Blair, and Thomas Ritchie, alongside others who were lawyers or local political activists, came to the fore to run the enlarged political organization under construction. The editor's role was crucial in presenting the parties' arguments as well as getting out the instructions and suggestions for local leaders to follow. The lawyers and local leaders, in turn, looked to the organizing and managing of electoral efforts within their spheres and contributing to the building of a national party network of committees and conventions at the different levels of political activity. These organizations were never as complete as political leaders hoped they would be. But they accomplished their purpose (Nichols 1967; Silbey 1991).

Strong party loyalty among officeholders was a major aspect of the system. Parties staffed what government institutions there were at both the state and national levels. The Jacksonians believed that the only way to ensure what they wanted done would be by the appointment of political allies into government positions to carry out their heavily resisted policies. "To the victors belong the spoils of office" was the cry, and party-dominated government became as important as the other elements emerging. Their opponents disagreed, although they too were not hesitant about utilizing patronage when they came into office (Nichols 1967; Silbey 1967, 1991).

The Jacksonian Democrats articulated a more populist appeal than the Jeffersonians ever had. There had been an increase in the society of democratic ideas and claims especially in the political world, and both the Democrats and their Whig opponents responded to such in the way that they operated. A political culture of popular participation (albeit only for white males) replaced the more elite focused notions previously dominant. Suffrage restrictions continued to be eased with a concomitant growth in the numbers to be won over. As the electorate grew, styles of campaigning had to change. A much more democratic perspective was advanced, first by the Democrats, who presented Andrew Jackson to the electorate as "the tribune of the people," personifying all that they stood for. He was the embodiment of democratic values and a leader who would root himself in the people and their needs. He would increase popular participation and control of the government (Shade 1981; Heale 1982; Keyssar 2000; Gerring 1998; Baker 1998).

Despite their initial hesitations, the Whigs joined their opponents soon enough and used the new style of campaign rhetoric and the massing of an organized army of voters to win the presidency in the "hurrah" campaign of 1840 (Gunderson 1957; Holt 1999). In the campaign discourse of both parties from then on there was a coarsening and simplifying of argument and language and the substitution of symbols for explanations to deal with a less educated electorate. Important differences between the parties were magnified into chasms by the rhetorical flourishes used to attract and hold the increasing number of potential voters. To be sure, neither party was a model of democratic practice, especially in their leadership circles. Elites continued to dominate matters. But they interacted more widely with their followers in shaping party decisions, given the increase in the number of voters and party members who were now part of the political equation in these mass party organizations. The voice of the people was not all that counted in politics but it was important to listen to it by those trying to lead their party to victory (Benson 1961; Heale 1982; Holt 1999; Silbey 1991).

The basic structure and influence of political parties had emerged by the 1840s. A key indicator of the successful party penetration into popular consciousness and their success in organizing the electorate for the battles they were to fight was the soaring voter turnout in national elections. The effort to mobilize partisan supporters led to 80 percent and more of those eligible to vote coming to the polls. While such high levels had occasionally occurred in local and state elections before the 1830s, participation at the national level had always been much lower. Now the high levels became a regular feature of national elections as well, and would remain so for many years (Census 1975; McCormick 1967; Silbey 1991).

The Jacksonians dominated the era, the Democrats winning six of the eight presidential elections between 1828 and 1856 and controlling Congress most of the time. As in the first party battles of the 1790s, the Whigs and Democrats attracted different supporters to their camps. Both were national in appeal, winning blocs of voters throughout most of the country, with fewer one-party states and areas than in the predecessor system. The basic parameters of the support that each party drew were generally similar to that of the Republicans and Federalists before them, its roots in economic and ethnic and religious identity issues, with the Whigs articulating more commercially minded and developmental policies that attracted those interests that found their policy advocacy useful and necessary (Benson 1961; Shade 1981; Holt 1999; Watson 2006).

The Democrats had their share of commercially minded interests among their adherents (such as the many state bankers opposed to the Whig push for a national bank), but they articulated a less commercial notion of American society than did their opponents. They continued to press for limited national government authority on the domestic scene, in economic matters and in areas of people's beliefs and behavior as well, which they charged the Whigs (like the Federalists before them) wanted to regulate and reshape in their own image and enforce what beliefs and behavior that they considered correct and permissible. Despite differences and disagreements within each coalition, the central policy thrust of each party was always present (Howe 1979; Ashworth 1983; Gerring 1998).

Most of all, as they settled in during the late 1830s, the parties came into their own as the dominating organizing and directing force in the electoral, legislative, and other parts of the governing arena. There were shortcomings in their activities. But they carried the day despite their imperfections. Whatever made voters and officeholders distinct, class identities, religion, ethnicity, ideology, these were subsumed within their party identities. There were few independent voters in these years: "To one or another of these parties every man belongs" was how one partisan editor summed up (*Nashville Union*, Nov. 9, 1838; Gienapp 1982). Moreover, the tools of politics were all partisan, such as the party ballots prepared by the party organizations and given to voters for them to use at the polls (McCormick 1986; Silbey 1991).

At the same time, there were also anomalies, elements that did not fit within what one historian has called "the partisan imperative" that dominated these years (Silbey 1985). Ambivalence toward the parties continued to exist. So did the continuation of resistance to them as a dominant feature of the American system, particularly from a number of minor parties, the Antimason, Liberty, American Republican, Free Soil, and Know Nothing, who organized against the mainstream coalitions to challenge the dominant themes of the political world. Each of them had notions of their own about what was necessary and proper in their society and worked hard to achieve their goals against the resistance of the major parties. Some of them were local; others ran candidates for national offices, including the presidency. Most survived only for an election or two, then disappeared or were absorbed by the major parties (A. Schlesinger 1973; Voss-Hubbard 2002).

A number of scholars have suggested that such antiparty hostility and the persistent resistance to them challenges the notion of the depth of the involvement and commitment of Americans to the parties (Altschuler and Blumin 2000; Voss-Hubbard 2002; Formisano 1969, 1999). But despite the presence of countervailing forces, this was not a fragile system. These years were the foundation of the party-dominant period in American political history. The two parties that had emerged into dominance set the agenda for policy conflict and marked out the channels for the voters to follow. Their role and importance was widely recognized, accepted, and, in most quarters, celebrated. There was nothing temporary or haphazard about what was emerging (McCormick 1986; Holt 1999; Silbey 1991).

A Sectionalized Party System

There was another shift in the political world in the 1850s, this time due to a powerful electoral realignment. There had always been sectional tensions in American society resulting in occasional political outbursts. Parties with their intersectional composition had served as barriers to any persistent division along sectional lines. In the early and mid-1850s that stability cracked wide open. An explosive reaction among northerners against southern overreach when they tried to introduce slavery into previously free western territories intersected with a nativist political challenge to the frightening surge of immigrants, particularly Catholics from Ireland and Germany, who had been entering the United States in great numbers. Hostility to the existing parties erupted because of their apparent indifference to, or their encouragement of, the immigrant wave as they sought new sources of electoral support among these newcomers (Gienapp 1987; Voss-Hubbard 2002; Anbinder 1992).

The Know Nothing and Republican parties appeared in response to these seismic provocations and made significant gains in the off-year elections of 1854, winning support from disaffected members of both major parties already on the scene and from the ranks of antislavery and nativist third parties. As the new coalitions grew, they severely weakened the Whigs in particular, whose remnant eventually faded from the scene (Gienapp 1987; Holt 1978). The Republicans ultimately won out as the major second party as the sectional dynamic grew more powerful. Both northern and southern sectional policy demands became an important aspect of the partisan warfare despite the resistance of the Democrats to such a focus (Gienapp 1987; Holt 1978; Nichols 1948).

All of this indicated the significant shift in the substance of the battles over the issues championed by the two main parties although the Republicans sounded like the Whigs in their arguments over the traditional issues of the previous era while the Democrats retained their longstanding hostility to the powerful central state thrust of their opponents. The Republicans worked successfully to absorb many northern Know Nothings into their ranks as well, and triumphed in the presidential election of 1860 over the Democrats badly hurt by an internal sectional schism over the territorial issue (Nichols 1948; Holt 1978; Potter 1976).

The realignment of the 1850s, whatever its power, did not sweep everything away. Rather, so far as political parties were concerned, much remained from the previous system amid the marked changes in the way that many voters behaved. Specifically, the new party system was, in its structure, reach, and widespread acceptance by contemporaries, much like its predecessor. Parties continued to dominate the political terrain, their organizational structures to manage, exhort, and direct, were still seen as necessary instruments in order to accomplish anything in the political world. They campaigned with the same force and approaches as they had in the previous years (Kleppner 1979; Silbey 1991).

The Civil War added a great deal to the dynamics of party warfare. There was a strong attempt by those directing the war in both North and South to argue for a "no party now" policy because of the need for national unity in wartime (A. Smith 2006). At first there was a positive response to that call and a suspension of partisan politics. But this did not last (Silbey 1977; Neely 2002). In the North, the Republicans added to the Whigs' vision of the importance of national power by arguing that the necessities of wartime demanded that the government exercise power beyond anything seen before. They did not hesitate to organize and regulate, and create and build new institutions as needed. They made great strides in imposing federal control over finances and the economy. The military draft forced men to serve in the army. Governments censored, and occasionally imprisoned, critics of their policies. Finally, the Lincoln administration went far beyond any previous claims to the reach of the national government by adopting a policy of emancipation of slaves in the states in rebellion (Richardson 1997; Foner 1988).

Despite the pressure demanding non-partisan acquiescence, therefore, party warfare continued in the North as the Democrats, with their deep hostility to too much national power, vigorously resisted the expansion of government activities as unnecessary, arguing that the Lincoln administration was going far beyond what needed to be done even in the face of the emergency. The Republicans fought back, branding the Democrats as defeatists, even traitors, so that wartime campaigns and legislative activity were as hard-fought and as bitter as ever despite the changed conditions. The partisan imperative retained its force. In the South, in contrast, organized party warfare did not take hold although there was a great deal of protest against the policies of the Confederate government. But it was scattered, without effective national leadership, and never became united into a full-fledged partisan confrontation (Silbey 1977; McKitrick 1975; Holt 2001).

The issues raised by the wartime (and earlier) party warfare, real and extravagant, continued to play important roles in the post Civil War years as well. Both parties' ideologies were hardened by the intensity of their wartime experience. In the early years of Reconstruction, central government authority continued to expand in dealing with the situation in the South as a result of its defeat and large-scale destruction, and the shock of emancipation (Foner 1988). The Democrats continued to oppose as sharply as they could, and the Republicans, in response, continued to extol their leadership in the war to save the Union, labeling the Democrats, as they had throughout the war, as unpatriotic and calling upon northern voters to vote the way they shot (Summers 2000; Marcus 1971; Jensen 1971).

The Republicans reaped significant benefits at the polls from their assault on their opponents' wartime behavior. Voter commitment to them was intensified by the memories of the war and the issues created by the conflict and gave the Republicans an advantage in postwar elections. They won all but two of the ten presidential elections between 1860 and 1896, and at least held their own in Congress. Not accidentally, all but one Republican presidential candidate between 1868 and 1896 had been a Union army officer, and their campaigning centered on "waving the bloody shirt" (allegedly of a dead Union soldier) to flay the Democrats as unworthy of holding office (Kleppner 1979; Summers 2000). The Democrats responded by adding to their usual resistance to the Republicans' expansive commitment to federal power virulent racial assaults on the policies of the "Black Republicans" in a nation that remained deeply racist (L. Grossman 1976).

After the war, the Democrats reunited with their southern brethren and were joined by some former Whigs in that section hostile to Republican policies. The latter countered by bringing the emancipated African Americans into their ranks. For a time this worked to the Republicans' advantage as they took political control of many of the seceding states' restored governments. Nevertheless, electoral stalemate settled on the national scene. The parties settled down into the most sustained competitive situation they had ever experienced. The Republican advantage in presidential elections from the mid-1870s to the early 1890s was by quite small margins—which put a premium on maximizing the turnout of one's supporters (Kleppner 1979).

These years were the so-called golden age of parties as their effective organizations were more in charge of the political process than they had ever been. As a result, highly committed voting blocs marched together like the disciplined political armies they were, roared and cheered as their leaders urged them on, and turned out at the polls in the highest percentage yet seen of those eligible to cast ballots (Kleppner 1979). Beyond the surface indicators of party success, however, there were the first stirrings of impending challenge to the dominant role that they played in American politics. The late nineteenth century was characterized by economic and social changes of enormous impact. The industrial revolution, with its great expansion of railroads into a national transportation network and the building of a large-scale manufacturing base in steel mills and similar enterprises, which led, in turn, to the growth of large urban centers populated by great numbers of native-born and immigrant laborers, now defined the central reality of the nation's economy and society. None of this occurred entirely peacefully. Transformative changes were accompanied by social and political upheavals, industrial unrest, and the growth of dismal, overcrowded slums which shocked and frightened their neighbors, particularly as the political system proved to be incapable of coping with these rising dangers (Summers 1997).

Party leaders paid attention to what was happening on the economic and social landscape—to a degree, and in their own style. They acted to bring the new immigrants and other industrial workers into the parties' orbits. The Democratic and Republican organizations further expanded to deal with the swelling urban population and became more systematized and in command than ever. From the 1860s on, urban political organizations, the political machines such as Tammany Hall in New York, developed a new prominence. Party bosses gained more power as their networks expanded. New sources of money for running campaigns were sought—and found. Party leaders demanded contributions from those seeking government favors—as so many did in the exploding economy. Party appointees to government positions paid over part of their salaries to their party as well. In America's new industrial order corruption seemed more prevalent than it had ever been, with the bribery of political officials widespread and the granting of government largesse based on matters other than merit growing in scope and amount (Callow 1966; Buenker 1973; Marcus 1971; Keller 1977).

Such evidence of malfeasance and partiality created a backlash against the perceived corruption and its political progenitors, despite the parties' penetration, place, and power in the political realm. As a result, ideological and cultural hostility to parties which had never completely died out revived and grew more pressing. A growing rhetorical assault on both the Democrats and Republicans began to be heard—enough to become a major part of the era's political equation. Good government advocates, the Mugwumps, argued, in the 1870s and 1880s, that the parties and their leaders were corrupt in their activities, in how they conducted elections, and the way they organized all levels of government. They worked only for their own benefit. Too much that went on in politics occurred under the pretense, but not the reality, of democratic involvement. Party bosses benefited, but few others did as they followed their own selfish agendas, and preserved their power by their control of decisions made in secret, in "smoke-filled rooms," not out in the open where they could be vetted. They were answerable to no one (McFarland 1975; Summers 1993).

The party bosses were able to get away with such behavior thanks to the intense loyalty of their supporters, who did not question what party leaders told them and blindly followed their dictates (Kleppner 1979). The bosses degraded the voting process, allowing many to vote who were not eligible. Their chicanery affected electoral outcomes and preserved their power. In sum, the bosses' behavior was a challenge to republican ideals of what constituted good government and the reach of the democratic ethos that defined the nation (Sproat 1968; Keller 1977).

Furthermore, as the American economic and social landscape grew larger and more complex, some asked whether political parties were relevant in this new age. Could they solve the problems of an urban society? Could they provide the personnel with the skills necessary to deal with an industrial urban nation? Some important skeptics did not think so. The reformers saw the key to better government and more efficiency in delivering services and promoting further economic growth in the weakening of the unresponsive parties' control over the American political process. Thus, the argument ran, politics in a rapidly changing and modernizing society meant overcoming the road blocks present by reforming party practices and replacing the spoils system and other forms of partisan intervention in governing with technical expertise. Experts would now decide what needed to be done and do it rather than leaving decisions to the manipulable mass parties relying on illegal or ignorant voters and the execution of policies to ill-prepared partisan appointees (Hoogenboom 1961; McGerr 1986; Keller 1977).

The case against party was made by both reformers and the leaders of the new industrialism emerging on the scene. The old parties basically held their ground but, in a very close electoral climate, defections to reform parties, or interfering with the partisan-run voting process, had the potential to have a disproportionate impact on electoral results. A level of uncertainty had crept in among the sureties of the well-entrenched partisan system (Jensen 2001; Kleppner 1981).

These non-partisan notions of government grew stronger among opinion leaders and the public and began to be enacted into law by legislatures and other governing bodies as good government reformers and their economically elite allies gained leverage over the system. They began well-financed and well-publicized campaigns to loosen the party bosses' control by changing the rules for nominating candidates and managing the campaigns and elections. States began to consider laws mandating the official registration of those who were eligible to vote to guard against the party bosses' alleged allowing non-eligibles, including non-citizens, to vote. In order to prevent other ballot chicanery, reformers also sought to substitute state-supplied non-partisan ballots in place of the party-provided tickets then in use. In the government area, the first steps toward a non-partisan civil service were taken in order to limit the major parties' control of the appointments process (Argersinger 1992, 2001; Keller 1977; Keyssar 2000).

As the spokesmen for the reform impulse made their case for cleaning up the system, other challenges added to the uneasiness and unrest. There was another outbreak of third party activity in the 1870s, and thereafter, amid worker unrest and strikes, and growing fear about the diluting of American values because of the nation becoming more awash in immigrants than ever, Prohibitionist, anti-immigrant nativist, Greenback, and various industrial labor-based coalitions articulating their dissent from the major parties on economic and cultural behavior grounds appeared with their own vigorously promoted programs. All of them agreed that much was going wrong in the nation and the old parties with their hidebound ways and harping on long-dead issues could no longer be tolerated (Kleppner 1979).

THE SYSTEM OF 1896

Another electoral realignment occurred in the 1890s, this time rooted in the voters' reaction to a severe economic downturn and the failure of the government of the day to address the emergency in adequate fashion. Farm prices tumbled, resulting in rising anger and protests in agricultural areas. There was labor unrest, as well, fueled by unemployment and their employers' anti-labor practices, which led to strikes in urban centers and threats of more to come (Jensen 2001). The Democratic president Grover Cleveland, who entered office just before the economic collapse, remained true to his party's traditional outlook and refused to use federal government machinery or its financial resources to alleviate the impact of the economic disaster on people in different parts of the country (R. Welch 1988; Argersinger 2001; Morgan 1963).

The result of economic breakdown and political inadequacy was a noisy, potent threat to the partisan stability of the era. As in the realignment of the 1850s, a significant third party, the Populists, arose to challenge the policies and dominance of the traditional parties, demanding economic redress by the government in the face of a depression of some magnitude. They offered significant opposition to the major parties in the election of 1892. By 1896, many of them, along with some of their provocative ideas, had united with radical Democrats in several southern and western states to seize control of the party there and then triumph at its national convention. But the Republicans fended them off and, running on the promise of "a full dinner pail," swept the critical elections of 1894 and 1896 (McSeveney 1972; Goodwyn 1976; Jensen 1971; Kleppner 1979).

Organizationally, and in practice, the system that arose in the 1890s looked and behaved much like its predecessor. Political parties were as ubiquitous as ever, and their basic parameters, both organizationally and in terms of the policies each party supported, were familiar. Party activity encapsulated much of the patterns of the previous age and contained the same management and campaign structure. There had been, however, changes in the mix of voter support, and, as a result, a further increase in the sectionalizing of political warfare. The Democrats gained important additions to their ranks because of the extension and settling in of an anti-Republican Solid South. Republicans improved their lot in the fast-growing urban areas in the Northeast and Middle West (Marcus 1971; Kousser 1974; Keller 1977).

Most critically, the realignment converted the very close, often stalemated electoral system of previous decades into a Republican-dominant era. The rural and southern tilt that the Democrats adopted from 1896 onward repelled some of their previous urban support, both elites and working-class. The assault by the Populists and the radicalized Democrats in 1896 frightened the emerging economic elites headquartered in the big cities and many members of the new urban professional and managerial middle class. Some defectors drifted back after a time, but others did not, and their absence continued to hurt the Democrats badly. Republicans won six of the eight presidential elections from 1896 to 1928, usually by substantial margins. They only lost when they split badly in 1912 and 1916, with a significant defection from their ranks to the reformist Progressive Party. But they regained their footing in the next three elections. As the dust settled, clearly the Republicans were the party of the traditional cultural values of much of small-town America, big business, and parts of urban America, the Democrats of the outsider elements in American society, economic and cultural (Kleppner 1987; Harbaugh 1961).

In the midst of this electoral reaction, the size of the voter pool significantly changed. Some of the changes reflected the nineteenth century's march toward removing existing restrictions on the right to vote. Women were enfranchised, first in several states, beginning in the late nineteenth century, then nationally by the Nineteenth Amendment to the Constitution in 1920. But, in contrast, there were successful moves to remove other voters from the list of those eligible to participate. African Americans in the South were largely disfranchised by a range of restrictive laws including literacy tests and state poll taxes, as were many poor whites by the same means. Voter eligibility requirements were tightened by Republican legislators in northern states in ways that affected recent immigrants throu~ the imposition of English language literacy tests among other rules that pl~ barriers in front of those who sought to vote (Keyssar 2000; Kousser 1974).

Coterminous with the emergence of the system of 1896, structural ch~ partisan activities and organizations also became part of the politica~ One result of different parts of the country becoming increasingly d~ one party was that party organizations in those areas weakened in~ the need to prepare for and fight frequent competitive elections a~ do before. This began a long-term process of the general v~ organizations through their neglect and disuse. New ways new sources of money from economic interest groups, outside the party bosses' orbit and span of control, also had an impact on the bosses' control of the political situation (Jensen 2001; Gidlow 2004).

At the same time, the realignment of the 1890s renewed the challenge to the role that the parties played in American life. There was a reinvigorated assault on the way the parties operated and because of what they had turned into—the language of antipartyism was once more heard as the Progressive movement, rising up after 1900, sought to tame their excesses once and for all. Like the Mugwumps earlier, the Progressives believed that they had the key to creating the good society and clean, efficient, democratic, politics and government. To them, like their predecessors, the parties, their leadership, and their practices were a major barrier to creating the new and better America, economically and socially, that they envisioned. The Republicans' and Democrats' ossified outlook, and their obsolete, corrupt, parochial ways of acting, had to go. Breathing a most moralistic fire, "corruption became a sin" in Progressive arguments (Jensen 2001, 161), they were determined "to banish all forms of traditionalism—boss control, corrupt practices, big business intervention in politics, 'ignorant' voting and excessive power in the hands of hack politicians" (Jensen 1971; see also Sanders 1999; McCormick 1981).

Increasingly the Progressives were able to pass legislation instituting procedures that would limit the power of the parties and the control of the system by the bosses. The notion of administrative institutions staffed by non-partisan experts as superior to patronage and party government in running things began to bear fruit with the creation of various commissions to provide unprejudiced information to legislators to make decisions themselves and to supervise how various government agencies were managed. By the First World War several of these existed to deal with, and regulate, such important economic matters as tariff policy and corporate monopoly issues. During the war the government created other such administrative organizations, staffed by experts to deal with the problems of production and manpower, and ensure the people's commitment to the war. These wartime additions were considered temporary but did establish their non-partisan markers on the political scene (Link and McCormick 1983; Ballard Campbell 1995).

Some reforms to the nominating process were instituted. But most decisions about candidates continued to be made by bosses at their controlled party conventions. At the polls, despite the continuing intensity of voter commitment, the restrictions and barriers to participation that had become part of the political world had their effect. Turnout began to decline significantly in presidential, congressional, and state elections from its very high numbers of the previous party system. The impact of non-partisan ballots was also felt as split-ticket voting increased (Kleppner 1982; Burnham 1986).

Again, however, their impact was not as great as might it have been, given the gility of political bosses in figuring out how to limit it. Throughout these years uch remained as before as real changes came slowly. Voters in the main remained loyal and partisan when they went into the voting booth. The reinforcing party instruments were weaker than earlier but still operative. Third parties continued to try to break the majors' hold. Marxist Socialist and Socialist Labor organizations pushed radical economic agendas; the Prohibitionists continued their crusade, as well. But these parties drew a comparatively small portion of the vote, as such organizations usually had. Still, elections had different qualities to them in this party system from what they had had in the preceding era. There was now, in short, a mixture of attitudes and procedures affecting political parties that would last throughout the first half of the twentieth century (Kleppner 1987). American politics had crossed a significant divide. It appeared to a number of analysts that "the party period" that distinguished the years from the 1830s to the 1890s had ended (McCormick 1986; Keller 2007; Silbey 1991).

THE NEW DEAL PARTY SYSTEM

Another electoral realignment changed the political equation once again. A devastating depression beginning in 1929 was the initiating moment, followed by the refusal of the incumbent Republican administration to accept the need to help those most deeply hurt by rising unemployment and dislocation. Out of it came significant shifts in the parties' approach to governing. Pushed by the very popular President Franklin D. Roosevelt's program, there was a sharp change in the Democratic attitude toward federal power in these years. Combining progressive ideas of economic regulation with state-level advances in social welfare delivery to those in need, the party, for the first time, pushed for a much larger role for the federal government in American society (Hawley 1966; Romasco 1983; Leuchtenburg 1963).

The New Deal program established, or extended, federal institutions to meet their goals and staffed them with those political figures and technicians sympathetic to the programs they pushed forward. Most significantly among these actions, Democrats provided expanded aid and security to the poor and unemployed, establishing social policies not earlier seen at the federal level. The New Deal Democrats also used federal power to try to get the economy moving again through government loans, guarantees, subsidies, and similar interventions (Leuchtenburg 1963; Hawley 1966; Romasco 1983).

The Republicans recoiled in horror and fought against the New Deal's regulative expansion of the federal government and development of the Social Security state, accompanied as they were by increased taxes and government actions indicating the Democrats' strong commitment to labor. Largely under big business control through the 1920s, they became more the party that asserted the propriety of state power over the federal in dealing with the kinds of issues—regulation and welfare—that were now at the center of national politics (J. Patterson 1972; Leuchtenburg 1963).

There was a significant rupture of existing voter commitments as the New Deal took hold. The impulses that led voters to choose one or the other party—economic interest, cultural values, attitudes toward government authority—continued to operate. For the first time, however, there was a widespread class dimension to party support—certainly more than had existed at earlier moments of party history. Republicans drew strength from the middle class in their base in the small-town Protestant heartland, and from industrial elites fearful of Democratic radicalism and challenge to big business. The Democrats retained from the previous system their hold on the Solid South, and much of the urban working class and Irish Catholics mobilized by the big city machines. They also began to attract African American voters who had been loyal Republicans since the days of Abraham Lincoln but who now were benefiting from the New Deal's security programs. All of these reacted positively to the Democrats' blaming the Republicans for the economic collapse so that running against the failed president Herbert Hoover became the stock-in-trade of Democratic campaigning for more than twenty-five years (Anderson 1979; Leuchtenburg 1963).

There were always some anomalies in these patterns, to be sure, and both parties had internal conflicts because of their mixed support (southern Democrats were uncomfortable with their party's commitment to an expansive federal authority, for example) (Leuchtenburg 2005; Lichtman 1976). But, whatever differences existed among party groups, the Democrats' approach clearly caught the mood, and needs, of the country in the 1930s. Franklin Roosevelt's appeal was, at first, partisan and continued to be so to a great extent thereafter. It was also personal. Republicans hated him, but many Americans adored him and what he had done for them whatever his party identification. Like earlier presidents in trying times, Jackson, Ulysses S. Grant, and William McKinley, Roosevelt became a powerful positive political symbol who, for a time, rose above normal political adulation to something much greater and more intense. The programs that he championed, while more limited than many of his supporters hoped for owing to the resistance of powerful conservative influences within his party, were seen as the most critically important that had ever been enacted on the domestic scene (so powerful was the appeal of the New Deal's programs that some Republicans began to support such legislation as well) (Leuchtenburg 1983; Donald Johnson 1960).

The hothouse years of the 1930s reinvigorated the party system. The New Deal drew committed millions to both parties' ranks because of the economic policies of the Roosevelt government. The surge to the Democrats from 1932 onward was dramatic. They routed the Republicans in the next presidential election and commanded Congress by large margins. That was only the beginning. For the first time since the Civil War era, they enjoyed a majority of the two-party popular vote in the country. They won five straight presidential elections between 1932 and 1948, a feat that had never occurred before, and controlled Congress for an even longer time span. Even where there was a reaction against them, they kept their command, with the Republicans only breaking through in 1946 (briefly) and in 1952 and 1956. After each Republican gain they fell back again and the Democrats regained control. The American voters (or at least the largest bloc of them) had become Democrats (Angus Campbell et al. 1960). The Republicans, who had ruled for so long, were bewildered, frustrated, hostile to FDR's dominance, and, in their bitterness, internally contentious. But they could do little to escape their situation (J. Patterson 1972; R. Smith 1982).

Roosevelt benefited his party in another way beside his appeal. As the institutions of government expanded and grew in power and scope, he did not hesitate to use the organizations run by urban political bosses and their counterparts in rural America to push and manage his programs and get out the vote on their behalf in the face of the bitter opposition of the Republicans. The technological and bureaucratic values that had dominated reformers' hope for better government remained—in fact, they were reinvigorated. But the Democrats believed that only they were willing to nurture the kind of government that had grown up during the economic emergency. They were not ashamed to staff the agencies with their partisans as being in the best interests of the country (Dorsett 1977; Leuchtenburg 1963).

The Democrats' administrative state grew further during the Second World War and was reinforced and further expanded during the Cold War that followed. During the war the nation's economy boomed, opportunities opened up that had not been present earlier, and employment surged. The Social Security state expanded even further with the passage of the GI Bill providing educational and other benefits for military veterans and the further extension of government assistance in promoting the economy and protecting the less fortunate. These were the golden years of federal government authority, and the Democrats reaped full benefits from their championing of it as the party of Roosevelt, the party of the common man. It was a powerful attraction to many Americans (J. Patterson 2001).

Things Fall Apart

In the 1950s, Democratic control temporarily weakened as postwar readjustments, angst and fear based on the onset of the Cold War, the threat of internal subversion, and the exposure of political corruption cost the Roosevelt coalition the presidency to a wildly popular Republican candidate, Dwight Eisenhower. Not for the first time, a military hero propelled a party forward. Normally Democratic voters flocked to him in great numbers. But they were won back to their party homes and the Democrats quickly regained control of Congress, and then the presidency in what analysts call John F. Kennedy's close "reinstating election" in 1960, followed by a rout of their opponents in 1964. The New Deal party system was still alive as the Democrats reached the height of their support and achievements with the further extension of their domestic policy goals in the mid-1960s. President Lyndon Johnson's war on poverty, and the federal government' vigorous support of the civil rights revolution, all kept the party dominant for a generation after the Second World War (Angus Campbell et al. 1960, 1966).

Then things fell apart. As the New Deal faded from memory and its influence on a new generation of voters sagged, the Democrats did as well, intensified by the power of a number of long-range and immediate realities. First, the New Deal's administrative state, with its focus on welfare, employment, unemployment, and Social Security, replaced the political machines as the basic provider of services for voters in need (S. Fraser and Gerstle 1989). Second, the civil rights revolution alienated southern whites, who feared the growing power of the federal government to alter social norms (E. Black and Black 2002). Third, there was, in the midst of the Vietnam War and the further development of the civil rights revolution, a sharp backlash against conventional politics and their institutions. Neither party was seen by both angry dissenters and some formerly loyal supporters as better than the other in its willingness to face up to the nation's foreign and domestic problems. To many, political decisions had to be made more in protest marches, picketing, and disruption than by working through the two parties and voting regularly. A solid core resisted such negative behavior, but for a time it seemed to dominate the political world. And it had a significant impact in the years that followed (Petrocik 1981; Jensen 2001; Burnham 1982).

The chaos of the riotous 1968 Democratic national convention seemed to symbolize the collapse of organizing and mediating institutions in American politics. Democrats reacted to the disorder by passing internal reforms to open up their party and its nominating process further than it had ever been. But in doing so they made things even more difficult for themselves to forge unity and encourage realistic campaign efforts. To many voters liberalism and its ways had brought on social turmoil, frustration, and the threat of chaos on the home front. Their anger was manifested at the polls. Beginning in 1968, the Republicans won four out of the next five presidential elections (Ladd with Hadley 1975; S. Fraser and Gerstle 1989; Jensen 2001).

The period since the late 1960s presents a challenging problem for the long-dominant way of thinking about the patterns of party history (Bruce Campbell and Trilling 1979). The sharp reaction against the Democrats did not result in a critical realignment and a new, supposedly the sixth, party system. The Democrats remained in control of Congress much of the time even as the Republicans dominated presidential elections. Amid continued falloff in turnout at the polls, split-ticket voting rose as voters no longer automatically supported party tickets, and choosing an attractive candidate became more important as many voters moved from one party nominee to the other party's choice as they voted for different offices. The number of voters who declared themselves independent of either major party increased. The electorate, or at least part of it, was not realigning but dealigning instead (Nie, Verba, and Petrocik 1970; Ladd 1980, 1991).

The explosion of challenges to the system and the loudly expressed disdain for the parties and their conventional ways severely shook the normal patterns of New Deal era politics. The force of the assault lasted into the next decade and beyond. Changes in campaign finance laws and the rise of political action committees independent of parties, candidate-centered nominating and campaigning organizations, and of single issue groups, similarly unanchored to either party, had their effect. There was a continuation of the decline in party loyalty. And as people thought of themselves as not being loyalists to one or the other of the major parties, and engaged in more candidate-centered, as against partisan, voting behavior, active hostility to the parties continued to grow as well. Candidates often masked their party identity when they campaigned with their literature, emphasizing their individual virtues instead. There was an increase in the number of safe seats in Congress and the waning of the importance of presidential coattails so that significant across-the-board electoral overturns or an across-the-board electoral realignment was not as possible. All of this had an impact beyond the voting booth. The parties' mediating function between the demands of society and the government significantly lessened. Whatever else was happening, all of it demonstrated a lack of commitment to the main political parties (Keller 2007; Wattenberg 1984; Ladd 1978; Pomper 1977; Ware 1985).

Despite such outbursts and their downward spiral as positive institutions in the minds of the American people, the two parties continued to operate in the post-1968 years and remained important to many Americans. Intense partisan cadres remained on the scene and were influential in primaries, campaigns, Congress, and other government offices. But it became increasingly clear that much about them was very different from what had been the norm in earlier years. Their role had clearly significantly narrowed. They were no longer alone on the political playing fields. Party leaders lost control of the nomination of candidates, party-centered campaigns continued to fade before the success of the proliferation of many more sources of campaign arguments outside the parties; and there was more federal regulation of their activities and in the realm of campaign finance. There was clear fragmenting of parties and the ways they appealed to voters. The rise of the importance of non-partisan, often anti-partisan, media, television for example, in the shaping and communicating of political messages, and in defining the virtues and deficiencies of a candidate and his or her policies, became the norm, an especially important one given its generally skeptical attitude toward political parties and their product. Later, the growth of the Internet opened up an easily accessible world of blogs, commentary, and insider information, available to all, unrefined by party leaders (Keller 2007; Milkis 1993; Pomper 1977).

The force of all of this further hastened the continued loss of party primacy in American politics, a degenerative pattern that had been going on, with an occasional uptick along the way, since the 1890s. They seemed to be fading into irrelevance. Their long history seemed to be ending in confusion, fragmentation, and irreversible decline—not realignment, renewal, and continued relevance. As the journalist David Broder summed up the situation in the title of his book about these matters, "the party's over" (Wattenberg 1984, 1991; McCormick 1982; Lichtman 1982; Broder 1972). To be sure, there were contrary arguments offered (Clubb, Flanigan, and Zingale 1980). Not every scholar believed that matters had changed all that much from earlier times. Burnham titled an article on the subject "Realignment Lives" (Burnham 1996; but compare Ladd 1980). There was increased partisan polarization in the 1990s as the Republicans regained control of the House of Representatives and vigorously set themselves against a Democratic president. But the perceived revival of party was a limited one. Whatever the intensity of the partisan commitment and behavior of party leaders and some of their followers, such did not penetrate deeply into the American psyche as had been the norm in earlier times (Wattenberg 1991; Lewis-Beck et al. 2008). Parties remained necessary. But they had clearly lost many of the weapons and attitudes that gave them the kind of role that they had played throughout the history of the United States under the Constitution—and sent scholars back to the drawing board to think through what this checkered ending to a compelling story suggests about our understanding and the possible need to develop a new organizational paradigm (Shafer 1991; Maisel 1994).

CHAPTER 7

THE EVOLUTION AND ALTERATION OF AMERICAN PARTY COALITIONS

MARK D. BREWER

THE existing rules of the game dictate that party competition in the United States is a two-player affair. Since the end of the Civil War, the Democratic and Republican parties have been those two players, engaged in a fierce competition for electoral success and control of government power. The nature of this competition, however, has changed over time. One of the biggest examples of change involves the parties' electoral coalitions. America's two-party system, combined with the highly hetero-geneous nature of American society, almost by necessity means that the two parties that comprise that system at any one time will be big-tent and multi-winged in nature, with each exhibiting a good deal of internal diversity. This has been true of both the Republicans and the Democrats over the course of their respective histories.

As John Petrocik (1981) correctly points out, American electoral politics is a group-based politics, at least from the perspective of the parties. As they approach each election cycle, the leaders of the Democratic and Republican parties survey the American populace with an eye toward determining which social and demographic groups they might be able to draw into their respective ranks successfully. It is worth remembering that while parties and their candidates are after the votes of *individuals*, they most often pursue these individual votes with messages and appeals directed toward specific *groups.* Voters recognize the group nature of the parties; as Donald Green and his colleagues (2002) demonstrate, voters think about and understand parties as being both collections and champions of particular groups present in American society. It is this collection of groups that accounts for their internal diversity of American parties.

While intraparty diversity has been constant, the groups that make up the parties' variegated coalitions have not. The electoral coalitions of both the Republican and Democratic parties have changed a good deal over time. Part of this coalitional evolution is due to the social change that has been a constant feature of American society. Immigration, changes in residential patterns, alterations in socioeconomic status, policy changes that contract or (in most cases) expand the electorate, shifts in family structure—the list could go on and on—are all examples of instances in which social change creates at least the possibility of party coalition change. Change in a party's mix of group support can also come about as a consequence of specific events. Events of unusually high importance or magnitude—such as the Great Depression or the civil rights movement of the 1960s—are especially likely to create an opportunity for the alteration of partisan coalitions. The rise of new issues in the American public dialogue also opens the door for shifts in the parties' coalitions, especially if the new issues become highly salient. Another source of coalition change lies within the parties themselves; any time a party decides to support and pursue a particular policy goal, it creates at least the possibility of a change in the existing patterns of group support as groups do not evaluate and react to individual policies in a similar fashion. In many instances these opportunities for change work in combination, thereby increasing the likelihood that change in the parties' electoral coalitions will actually occur.

Looked at in this fashion, stability in partisan coalitions is often not in the cards; indeed, the deck appears to be heavily stacked in favor of change. The nature of change at any particular time, however, is highly uncertain, especially to the parties themselves. Party leaders spend inordinate amounts of time speculating on what change will look like, trying to determine its source(s), timing, magnitude, and duration, among other characteristics. But the reality is that the high levels of uncertainty present make nailing down the specifics of change—at least before it happens—extremely difficult, even for those party leaders whose very success or failure depends on their ability to do just that. Indeed, it seems as though the best calculations of even the most perceptive party leaders are just as likely to be wildly off the mark as they are spot on. American party history is littered with the wreckage of what seemed to be perfectly reasonable (at the time) plans for electoral success that instead resulted in failure on election day. The 1896 presidential election provides a perfect example of this reality. In that contest the Democrats and their presidential nominee, William Jennings Bryan, designed a plan aimed at combining the agrarian interests of the South and West and the urban working class of the Northeast and Midwest into a broad-reaching coalition of the less affluent in American society. These groups had been ignored by the Republican

Party, so such a strategy on the part of the Democrats seemed, and indeed was, entirely reasonable. But this plan failed, some would say in spectacular fashion.

It is the uncertain nature of change in American electoral politics that, at least in part, makes the subject so interesting. The Democratic and Republican parties are constantly taking the measure of American society, trying to determine how—given the broad, programmatic goals of the party—they can best appeal to voters and gain control of government through victory on election day. A key component of this process involves deliberation among party leaders as to what is the most feasible way to construct a winning electoral coalition. Correct answers are not easy to come by. Widespread agreement among the various leaders and factions present within a particular party is rare, and competition and disagreement among supporters of various plans of attack often become quite intense. Such a situation is more likely to be seen in the party that is out of power at a particular point in time, but can manifest itself within the party that currently holds power as well. The bottom line is that even under the best of circumstances a party can never be certain that its plan for constructing a winning electoral coalition will be successful. In American politics, opportunities for both the Democrats and Republicans to cobble together successful coalitions are always present (even when things might seem darkest for a party), but these opportunities always come with a certain amount of risk involved. Clearly more risk is present in some situations than in others, but risk is always there. Parties can never know for sure how voters will react to a particular policy stand or candidate; they can never be certain how an appeal to one group in society will play with other groups that the party may also want to attract; they can never know for sure how social change has altered the electorate, how a new issue will affect voters, or what events might occur that have the potential to alter the electoral playing field. In addition to all of these unknowns, there is also the fact that the opposing party is involved in the exact same process, and its decisions also have the potential to change the equation. Uncertainty abounds, and it is this uncertainty that makes the American party system so fluid and dynamic (M. Brewer and Stonecash 2009).

This chapter examines the electoral coalitions of both the Republican and Democratic parties. A heavy emphasis will be placed on mapping partisan change from the 1930s to the present, explaining how and why change took place, and examining the meaning of change. Finally, the chapter will close with a discussion of what this dynamic tells us about electoral change, and a bit of speculation about what the partisan change of the future might look like.

THE LINGERING IMPACT OF THE NEW DEAL

To a certain degree the origins of contemporary American party coalitions lie in the politics of the 1930s, when Franklin Roosevelt gained control of the Democratic

Party and over time assembled what came to be known as the New Deal coalition. Indeed, more than sixty years after his death, both parties continue to be shaped by FDR's actions and his opponents' responses to these actions. The continued influence of the New Deal on today's politics reminds us of an important lesson regarding party alignments and coalitions: existing partisan arrangements rarely, if ever, disappear completely. Even when party relationships and coalitions change, the old patterns often remain discernible in the new arrangements, intermingling to a certain extent with the newly established order (Schattschneider 1960; Sundquist 1983).

The Democratic Party of the 1920s was, simply put, a mess. The party had been in the minority nationally since the mid-1890s, and other than Theodore Roosevelt's fracturing of the GOP in 1912 allowing Woodrow Wilson to win the White House (which he won again in 1916), the Democrats had been consistently shut out of power at the national level. No other major party in American history suffered consecutive defeats like the drubbings the Democrats received in the three presidential elections from 1920 to 1928, and only in the South was the party able to win elections consistently.

These were the circumstances inherited by Franklin Roosevelt when he secured the Democratic presidential nomination in 1932. But FDR and the Democrats had reason for optimism. Al Smith, the party's 1928 presidential candidate, had done well among immigrant-stock and urban Americans, two increasingly important segments of the electorate and also two groups that Democrats could reasonably hope to bring into their coalition. The Great Depression was also in full swing by 1932, making it difficult for the Republican Party and its incumbent president, Herbert Hoover, to hang onto power.

Roosevelt won the presidency in 1932, and the Democrats also added to their advantage in the House of Representatives and took control of the Senate. Initially, however, it was unclear what exactly the Democratic victories actually meant. Given the depth of economic suffering in 1932, it was incredibly unlikely that the party in power—in this case, the Republicans—would be left in place by voters, and FDR's 1932 campaign was extremely light on the details of what he planned to do if he won the election. Hope was what Roosevelt promised voters, and in 1932 that was enough for him and his party to return to power after a long period in the electoral wilderness.

Once in office, however, FDR began laying the groundwork for the New Deal coalition and approximately three decades of electoral success for the Democratic Party. The first piece of puzzle assembled by Roosevelt was the one that the Democrats had been able to count on since the end of Reconstruction—the South. Some white southerners had abandoned the party in 1928 owing to Smith's Catholicism, but they returned to the fold for the safely Protestant Roosevelt. FDR made sure these southern whites remained in party, being careful not to make waves on racial issues and accommodating southern Democrats when necessary on elements of the New Deal (Leuchtenburg 2005).

In addition to securing the traditionally Democratic South, FDR and the Democrats moved quickly to appeal to lower- and working-class Americans. By mid-1935, it was clear that Roosevelt intended to craft a coalition anchored by America's have-nots, and he succeeded to a remarkable degree. Indeed, the party system created by the New Deal was perhaps the height of class-based politics in the United States, with the Democrats as the party of the less affluent and the Republicans attracting those who were better-off financially (Ladd 1970; Ladd with Hadley 1975).

Roosevelt also built on the success first realized by Smith in 1928 and assembled massive Democratic advantages in the big cities of the Northeast and Midwest, attracting high levels of support from those with immigrant backgrounds, organized labor, Catholics, and Jews, all groups with a heavy presence in America's urban areas. FDR was even able to attract black voters in these areas, despite the Democrats' strong anti-African American southern wing. After Roosevelt retained the presidency and Democrats increased their majorities in both houses of Congress in 1936, the contours of the New Deal coalition were clear: white southerners, the less affluent, organized labor, Catholics, Jews, urban dwellers, and blacks living outside of the South (Leuchtenburg 1963; Lubell 1956; A. Schlesinger 1960; Sundquist 1983).

FDR and the Democrats did not assemble this coalition out of whole cloth. Each of these groups gravitated to the Democratic Party for a reason, and the manner in which they were brought into the Democratic fold is indicative of how parties try to craft their coalitions. Heading into the 1932 and then 1936 election cycles, Roosevelt and the Democratic Party surveyed the electorate in hopes of determining which groups they might be able to bring into their coalition, and also thought about how best to attract the members of these groups.

Southern whites' support of the Democrats stretched back to the Civil War, and as long as they were left to handle internal race relations as they saw fit their allegiance to the party was secure. For the have-not portion of the New Deal coalition Roosevelt and the Democrats delivered specific public policy programs that benefited the groups in the coalition and locked in their support. The various alphabet soup programs of the First New Deal, combined with prominent Second New Deal policies like the establishment of Social Security, the guaranteeing of organized labor's right to organize and bargain collectively, and the huge tax increase on the most affluent provided tangible benefits to the less fortunate groups within the Democratic coalition and also sent a clear message to these groups that the Democrats were the party looking out for their interests. Republican indifference to have-nots in American society during the 1920s combined with the Great Depression to provide the opportunity for the Democrats to craft a new majority coalition in 1932, but this opportunity was realized and the coalition cemented only when the Democrats used their control of government to enact policies that benefited these groups (Milkis 1993; Plotke 1996; Ware 2006). In becoming the majority party in the 1930s, the Democrats saw their opportunities and took advantage.

PARTY COALITIONS IN THE IMMEDIATE POST-FDR ERA

With FDR winning four presidential elections in a row from 1932 to 1944 and the Democrats maintaining control of Congress by healthy margins in both chambers, it is clear that the Republican coalition of the New Deal era was smaller than the one possessed by the Democrats. But the GOP's situation in the 1940s was not as dire as it appeared at first glance. Not all groups became New Deal Democrats. Even at the height of Roosevelt's and the Democrats' popularity and success, Republicans enjoyed strong support from more affluent Americans, those working in professional or managerial occupations, rural dwellers (outside of the South), and non-southern white Protestants. By the mid-1940s Republicans were highly competitive with the Democrats everywhere other than the South, and in 1946 they were able to retake control of Congress. While they remained the minority party, it was clear that GOP fortunes were improving.

Republicans were presented with an opportunity to further grow their coalition in the late 1940s. By that time it was evident that the Democratic Party outside of the South had become a relatively liberal party, increasingly primed for government action on a variety of fronts (Sundquist 1983). One of the primary areas of interest for these liberals was the issue of race, particularly increasing equality for African Americans. Roosevelt's successor, Harry Truman, was more willing to act on civil rights issues than Roosevelt had been, establishing a presidential commission on the subject in 1946 and desegregating the US military by executive order in 1948. When the Democratic Party inserted a strong (for the time) civil rights plank in its 1948 platform (which Truman opposed because he feared losing the South), the door was opened for the Republicans to make inroads in the South. It would take the party over fifty years to capitalize on this opportunity fully, but the eventual Republicanization of the South began in 1948 (E. Black and Black 2002; Carmines and Stimson 1989; Leuchtenburg 2005). Some white southerners voted for Dixiecrat presidential candidate Strom Thurmond in 1948, and more voted for Republican Dwight Eisenhower in 1952 and 1956.

The Democrats opened the door for the Republicans in the South, and the GOP cautiously peeked in. But the party did not barge through the door and embrace the South as part of its coalition, and it would not do so in full until 1964. Indeed, although the Republicans won the two presidential elections of the 1950s with Eisenhower as their candidate, they did so with very little change to the party's coalition, and thus very little change to the party's status in the overall political alignment of the time. A good deal of Republican success in the presidential contests of the 1950s can be attributed to the personal popularity of Eisenhower, rather than to any programmatic goals or policy agendas offered by the GOP (Angus Campbell et al. 1960). The Republican Party of the late 1940s and 1950s—at least the wing that supported presidential candidates like Thomas Dewey and Eisenhower—was a moderate party, one that was purposely not proposing radical new policy directions nor attempting to remake its electoral coalition in any meaningful way. The Republican Party of the 1950s is often described as an "us too" party, one that presented itself to voters as largely accepting of the Democrats' New Deal policy changes but as being able to direct these changes more efficiently. Such descriptions are for the most part accurate, and despite the GOP control of the presidency in the 1950s, it was clear that the Democrats were still the majority party and that the New Deal coalition remained largely intact (Milkis 1993; Plotke 1996).

This began to change in the 1960s. Emboldened by their increasing presence within the party, liberals pushed the Democratic Party further and further left on a variety of issues as the decade progressed (Mackenzie and Weisbrot 2008). At the same time a number of changes were taking place that were radically altering the traditional makeup of American society. The African American civil rights movement often justifiably gets the most attention here, but social change was unfolding on many other fronts as well. Religion was removed from public schools by the federal courts, while at the same time sex education was being introduced into the classroom. Traditional family arrangements were changing as an increasing number of women were leaving the home and entering the paid workforce as the so-called second wave of the feminist movement gathered steam. Births to unmarried women skyrocketed, especially among teenagers. The number of divorces began to rise as well. By the end of the 1960s the sexual revolution was in full force, the counterculture was firmly ensconced among young people on college campuses across the nation, and the first stirrings of a homosexual rights movement had manifested themselves. Together these issues would come to be referred to collectively as social or cultural issues, and over time their emergence would have a large impact on American politics (J. Hunter 1991; Leege et al. 2002; Scammon and Wattenberg 1970). But this development would take time, and to discuss it here would be getting ahead of ourselves. For now it is enough to note that much change took place in a short period of time, resulting in an incredibly unsettled environment (M. Brewer and Stonecash 2007).

The unsettled nature of 1960s America eventually moved into the political realm as well. As the Democratic Party became increasingly liberal, a growing number of voices within the Republican Party argued that the way for the GOP to regain the majority status it had last possessed in the 1920s was for the party to remake itself as a clearly conservative alternative to the Democrats. These conservative voices claimed that a growing number of Americans were unhappy with the Democrats' increasingly liberal direction, opposed to a large and activist federal government, and uncomfortable with many of the social changes that were occurring. If the Republicans presented themselves as a clearly conservative party, it was argued, they would be able to attract the support of those who were disenchanted. These

Republicans got their wish in 1964 when they gained control of the party and nominated conservative Barry Goldwater for president. Goldwater was not Thomas Dewey or Dwight Eisenhower; he was a conservative across the board, as was made clear in his 1960 statement of principles *The Conscience of a Conservative.* Goldwater's opposition to the 1964 Civil Rights Act marked him (and by extension the Republican Party) as conservative on race issues, and it is clear that this shift by the GOP was crucial in ratcheting up the process of bringing white southerners into the party (Carmines and Stimson 1989; Carter 1996; Leuchtenburg 2005; Pomper 1972; N. Rae 1989). But Goldwater was also conservative on other issues such as taxes and government spending, the proper size and scope of the federal government, and defense and foreign policy. He was also the first Republican presidential candidate to present himself as a conservative on cultural issues (Leege et al. 2002).

Goldwater of course suffered one of the worst defeats in American presidential election history. But in so doing he set the stage for partisan change to come. By the end of the 1960s the new issues that emerged in that decade had disrupted the existing partisan alignment (Nie et al. 1976; Petrocik 1981). The way in which these 1960s disruptions ultimately played out proved crucial to future American politics, and continue to have relevance today (Aldrich 1995, 1999).

THE HEIGHT OF AMBIGUITY AND THE RESTORATION OF CLARITY

There is no doubt that issues surrounding the question of race disturbed the partisan alignment that had grown out of the New Deal (Carmines and Stimson 1989; Huckfeldt and Kohfeld 1989; Jackman and Jackman 1983). It is also undeniable that the newly emerging cultural issues of the 1960s served to further destabilize the political environment, a situation that was exacerbated when the Supreme Court legalized abortion in 1973 with its decision in *Roe v. Wade* (Layman 2001; Leege et al. 2002). But in a classic example of the uncertainty discussed at the outset of this chapter, neither party was quite sure how to react to changed social and political realities. The clear differentiation between the parties offered in the 1964 presidential contest between the Republican Goldwater and Democrat Lyndon Johnson was largely gone by the time the 1968 contest rolled around. In that election Alabama governor and independent presidential candidate George Wallace regularly claimed that there was not a "dime's worth of difference" between Republican candidate Richard Nixon and Democratic candidate Hubert Humphrey. Clearly Wallace's statement was not entirely accurate; there were some meaningful differences between

Nixon and Humphrey (and by extension their political parties) in 1968, and the differences between the parties' presidential candidates were extended in the 1972 contest between Nixon and Democratic nominee George McGovern. However, Nixon did not campaign as a thorough conservative, as Goldwater had done, nor did he consistently govern as one. The Democrats reacted to the defeat of the liberal McGovern in 1972 by nominating southern born-again Christian Jimmy Carter in 1976. While Carter is clearly seen as a liberal today, he was not perceived as one nor did he run as one in 1976. Indeed, it was difficult to see large-scale meaningful differences between Carter and his Republican opponent in 1976, Gerald Ford. In some ways Wallace's difficulty in distinguishing between the Democrats and Republicans in 1968 could be seen as extending throughout the 1970s as well. Despite rhetoric to the contrary, the Republican Party continued to essentially go along with the taxing and spending patterns established by the Democrats during the New Deal era. The Democratic Party did the same. Neither party seemed to know where it stood on increasingly controversial cultural issues, except to agree that neither wanted to get caught on the wrong side of this set of issues. There was greater difference on racial issues, but even here the racial conservatism of the Republican Party fronted by Nixon and Ford was not as clear as it had been in the Goldwater GOP. There may have been a dime's worth of difference between the parties, but one would have been hard-pressed to extend that figure to a dollar's worth of distinction.

Voters noticed this lack of difference between the parties in the 1970s. During that decade split-ticket voting went up and party identification went down, especially in the category of self-proclaimed "strong" partisans. Many scholars examining the electoral politics of that time argued that the electorate had become "dealigned," and that voters were increasingly detached from and uninterested in political parties (Beck 1977, 1979). Elections, it was claimed, were now "candidate-centered," meaning that voters ignored partisan labels and determined their vote choice based on the personal characteristics and issue positions of the individual candidates for office (Wattenberg 1987, 1998). Parties, it was often argued at the time, had lost their meaning to voters, and were well on their way to becoming irrelevant.

As James Campbell (2006) recently noted, the benefit of hindsight allows us to see that claims of dealignment and the fading away of partisanship were overblown and off course. Partisanship is resurgent in American politics, with its effect on shaping election outcomes currently at a level not seen for decades (Bartels 2000; Hetherington 2001; Stonecash 2006). It is the case, however, that Americans relied less on partisan cues to structure their vote choice in the 1970s, and it is likely that a good deal of this decline had to do with the perceived lack of meaningful difference between the parties.

This all changed in the 1980s. Just as they had in 1964, the Republicans nominated a clear conservative for president in 1980, former actor and California governor Ronald Reagan. Reagan had long been a favorite of the conservative wing of the Republican Party, first rising to national attention (at least for his politics) with an impassioned televised speech in support of Goldwater in the waning days of the 1964 campaign. Doing as Goldwater had done in 1964, Reagan campaigned as a staunch conservative, and the Republican Party had provided Reagan with a platform to match. Incumbent Jimmy Carter was once again nominated by the Democrats—although not without a spirited challenge from Massachusetts Senator Edward Kennedy—and while Carter was certainly not a liberal in the mold of George McGovern, he still provided a stark contrast with Reagan. In 1980, voters had a clear choice when they went to the polls on election day.

For all of their similarities, there was of course one crucial difference between Goldwater in 1964 and Reagan in 1980: Reagan won. With Reagan's victory in 1980 and landslide reelection in 1984, conservatives' control of the Republican Party was solidified. In addition, Reagan governed in such a way that made the conservative nature of the GOP difficult to miss, even for the most inattentive voters. On fiscal policy, he successfully enacted what was at the time the largest tax cut in American history, and desperately (although not terribly successfully) tried to cut government spending in areas other than defense. He railed against a big federal government, famously saying in his 1981 inaugural address, "government is not the solution to our problem; government is the problem." On racial issues Reagan was adamantly opposed to affirmative action and was perceived by African Americans as at best indifferent and at worst hostile to their interests. On cultural issues, Reagan's opposition to the Equal Rights Amendment, his support of a constitutional amendment banning abortion, and his desire to return prayer to public schools all served to identify him, and his party, as conservative. By the time he left office in January 1989 it was clear that the Republicans were the conservative party, and that the Democrats were the liberal option (Milkis 1993; N. Rae 1992). This clarity was reflected in the two parties' coalitions at the end of the Reagan era, and indeed remains evident in the coalitions of today. In the same way that Franklin Roosevelt shaped the partisan divisions of his era and beyond, Ronald Reagan's influence on America's party politics is still present two decades after he left office.

CURRENT PARTISAN COALITIONS

From the mid-1980s forward, there was no more ambiguity about where the Republicans stood on the ideological spectrum: the party was plainly and coherently conservative. Democrats too did their part in making party divisions clearer to voters. Already widely seen as a liberal party in the early 1980s, the Democrats strengthened this image by nominating two very liberal candidates for president in 1984 and 1988: Walter Mondale and Michael Dukakis respectively. Bill Clinton tried and to a certain extent succeeded in moderating the Democrats' image in the 1990s, but if anything the ideological distinction between the parties grew in that decade as the Newt Gingrich-led Republican Revolution of 1994 both further cemented conservatives' control of the GOP and allowed the Republicans to take over control of Congress for the first time since the 83rd Congress of 1953–5. The clashes between Clinton and Gingrich provided Americans with a clear picture of partisan difference. Images and partisan distinction sharpened still more in the first years of the twenty-first century as conservative President George W. Bush and his fellow Republican conservatives in Congress governed in a highly partisan and ideological manner, drawing the ire of a Democratic Party that remained firmly liberal, perhaps even more so than it had been in the Clinton years. Voters did not miss these developments. They recognized that the ideological divide between the parties had grown significantly from the 1980s forward, and these same voters increasingly sorted themselves on the basis of these ideological divisions. The impact of individuals' ideology on their party identification and vote choice has increased substantially in recent years (Abramowitz and Saunders 1998; Saunders and Abramowitz 2004).

The ideological difference between the parties was not limited to only one or even a few issue areas; rather, it extended pretty much across the board, in many ways covering the broad spectrum of issues present in the American polity. By the 1990s the clear economic differences and conflict between the parties that had existed at least since the New Deal had been joined by equally clear differences and conflict between Republicans and Democrats over issues surrounding race and cultural–social concerns. Voters recognized these differences and over time racial and cultural concerns joined economic ones as significant factors in determining Americans' vote choice and partisanship (M. Brewer 2005; Layman and Carsey 2002a, 2002b). This development is demonstrated in Table 7.1, which presents unstandardized logistic regression coefficients for a conservative position on one economic concern (the role of the government in providing individuals with jobs and a good standard of living), one racial concern (government aid to blacks), and one cultural concern (abortion) on Republican presidential vote and also for a liberal position on these same issues on Democratic presidential vote since 1972 (the first year all three questions were asked in the American National Election Study, ANES).[1] All variables (both dependent and independent) are coded as

[1] All independent variables are coded as present-absent dichotomies. Guaranteed jobs and standard of living is derived from vcf0809, with a conservative position indicated by a choice of 5, 6, or 7 on a 7-point scale where 1 is delineated "government see to job and good standard of living" and 7 is "government let each person get ahead on his own" and a liberal position indicated by a choice of 1, 2, or 3 on the same scale. Aid to blacks is derived from vcf0830, with a conservative position indicated by a choice of 5, 6, or 7 on a 7-point scale where 1 is delineated "government should help

Table 7.1 Logistic regression coefficients for a conservative issue position on Republican presidential vote and a liberal issue position on Democratic presidential vote, 1972–2004

Year	Republican presidential vote			Democratic presidential vote		
	Guaranteed jobs and standard of living	Aid to blacks	Abortion	Guaranteed jobs and standard of living	Aid to blacks	Abortion
1972	1.04 (0.12)	0.69 (0.12)	0.26 (0.11)	1.28 (0.13)	0.78 (0.12)	0.26 (0.11)
1976	0.72 (0.12)	0.47 (0.12)	0.06 (0.11)	1.18 (0.15)	0.34 (0.13)	−0.04 (0.11)
1980	0.96 (0.14)	0.90 (0.14)	0.21 (0.14)	0.94 (0.16)	0.84 (0.18)	−0.32 (0.14)
1984	1.27 (0.12)	0.73 (0.13)	0.49 (0.12)	1.03 (0.14)	0.83 (0.13)	0.35 (0.12)
1988	1.08 (0.13)	0.61 (0.13)	0.49 (0.12)	0.99 (0.16)	1.02 (0.16)	0.39 (0.12)
1992	0.83 (0.11)	0.60 (0.11)	0.84 (0.11)	0.99 (0.13)	0.76 (0.14)	0.56 (0.11)
1996	1.39 (0.15)	0.78 (0.15)	1.01 (0.14)	1.17 (0.18)	1.08 (0.21)	0.80 (0.13)
2000	0.34 (0.16)	0.23 (0.17)	0.91 (0.12)	1.03 (0.24)	0.39 (0.25)	0.86 (0.12)
2004	1.31 (0.16)	0.97 (0.16)	0.88 (0.16)	1.34 (0.19)	1.37 (0.23)	0.75 (0.16)

Note: Presidential vote is coded 1 for Republican (or Democratic) vote and 0 if otherwise. See n. 1 for coding of independent variables. Figures presented are unstandardized logistic regression coefficients with standard errors in parentheses. Coefficients significant at the .05 level or better are in italic.

Source: American National Election Studies (2005).

presence–absence dichotomies and no control variables are utilized, which means that all coefficients are comparable. As Table 7.1 shows, conservative and liberal positions on these issues are significant predictors of Republican and Democratic presidential vote respectively in all but five of fifty-four instances possible here. These results also indicate that the impact of views on aid to blacks and abortion has grown over time and now approaches (and in a few instances exceeds) that of individuals' opinion on the role of government in providing jobs and ensuring a good standard of living.

minority groups/blacks" and 7 is "minority groups/blacks should help themselves" and a liberal position indicated by a choice of 1, 2, or 3 on the same scale. For 1972 and 1976 abortion position is derived from vcf0837 with a conservative position delineated by a choice of "by law, abortion should never be permitted" or "abortion should be permitted only if the life and health of the woman is in danger" and a liberal position delineated by a choice of "abortion should be permitted if, due to personal reasons, the woman would have difficulty in caring for the child" or "abortion should never be forbidden, since one should not require a woman to have a child she doesn't want." For 1980-2004, abortion position is derived from vcf0838 with a conservative position delineated by a choice of "by law, abortion should never be permitted" or "the law should permit abortion only in case of rape, incest, or when the woman's life is in danger" and a liberal position delineated by a choice of "the law should permit abortion for reasons other than rape, incest, or danger to the woman's life, but only after the need for the abortion has been clearly established" or "by law, a woman should always be able to obtain an abortion as a matter of personal choice." For a similar analysis involving party identification, see Brewer (2005).

This extension of partisan conflict can also be seen in the evolution of the parties' coalitions. Table 7.2 illustrates this evolution for the Democratic Party's coalition by focusing on twelve social and demographic groups that have been critical to the party's success for at least some portion of the years 1952–2004. Table 7.2 presents the percentage of each group that voted for the Democratic presidential candidate in each year (the first figure in each cell) and the percentage of all Democratic presidential voters who possessed the group characteristic in question (the figure in parentheses).[2] The first figure represents the Democratic preference or bias of the group in question, while the second figure demonstrates the group's place in the overall Democratic coalition. The groups in the first seven columns are those that formed the core of the Democrats' New Deal coalition, while those in the last five are groups that have become more important components of the party over time.

Unfortunately the ANES did not begin in full until 1952 (there was a very small pilot study in 1948); therefore, we cannot begin our empirical examination at the height of the New Deal coalition. But even with the immense personal popularity of Republican Dwight Eisenhower cutting into the traditional support groups, the outline of the New Deal coalition crafted by FDR is still visible in Table 7.2. Those in the bottom third of the income distribution, southern whites, individuals residing in union households, Roman Catholics, and urban dwellers were all relatively large components of the party's coalition even as they drifted toward Eisenhower, while Jews and African Americans (mostly outside of the South because the overwhelming majority of blacks in that region could not vote until after the civil rights movement and legislation of the 1960s) were smaller but highly supportive groups within the party. Indeed, in 1960—the election that may reasonably be seen as the last where the entire New Deal coalition was intact—these groups all remained key components of the Democrats' base (southern whites less so and Roman Catholics more so in that particular election owing to Kennedy's Catholicism).

We see the Democratic Party's coalition slowly begin to change in the 1960s. Part of this change involved the gradual decay of the New Deal coalition (Stanley, Bianco, and Niemi 1986; Stanley and Niemi 1991, 2001). The most glaring element of this decay was the rapid decline in Democratic support among southern whites as both their support of the party's presidential candidates and their percentages of

---

[2] A case can be made that party identification would have been the more appropriate dependent variable here, as the primary focus of this analysis is on the coalitions of the Democratic and Republican parties as wholes. This is the approach taken by Stanley and Niemi (1991, 2001) and Stanley, Bianco, and Niemi (1986) in their examination of partisan coalitions. Presidential vote is used here instead primarily for two reasons. First, what ultimately matters in determining election outcomes and control of government power is vote choice, not party identification. Second, changes in presidential voting patterns among groups often manifest themselves well before changes in group partisanship. The recent shifts in the South are an example of this.

Table 7.2 Group components of the Democratic presidential coalition, 1952–2004

Year	Bottom income third	Southern Whites[a]	Union households	Roman Catholics	Jews	Urban dwellers	African Americans	Women	Low religious salience	Northeast Residents[b]	Latinos	Not married or widowed
1952	44 (29)	50 (16)	55 (36)	52 (29)	72 (7)	49 (39)	80 (8)	41 (47)	44 (41)	41 (27)		44 (10)
1956	43 (32)	51 (22)	52 (37)	46 (27)	77 (8)	45 (28)	64 (6)	37 (48)	42 (38)	32 (23)		44 (10)
1960	47 (25)	52 (20)	63 (33)	82 (38)	91 (7)	63 (29)	74 (7)	47 (49)	55 (38)	49 (30)		46 (8)
1964	73 (34)	58 (14)	83 (32)	79 (29)	89 (4)	73 (31)	100 (13)	69 (56)	69 (36)	74 (27)		70 (11)
1968	42 (31)	26 (11)	48 (29)	56 (31)	84 (6)	53 (33)	97 (20)	43 (58)	38 (38)	46 (28)		47 (17)
1972	41 (28)	20 (10)	42 (31)	39 (28)	69 (4)	50 (35)	86 (21)	38 (60)	40 (51)	40 (27)		52 (27)
1976	60 (31)	46 (16)	64 (31)	57 (29)	70 (3)	55 (30)	94 (15)	51 (56)	51 (43)	54 (24)		56 (22)
1980	52 (34)	35 (20)	50 (33)	41 (23)	48 (4)	56 (39)	92 (26)	42 (59)	38 (45)	38 (19)		44 (27)
1984	56 (31)	31 (13)	56 (31)	46 (30)	69 (4)	59 (32)	87 (21)	45 (61)	43 (46)	39 (18)	53 (6)	48 (32)
1988	57 (26)	32 (12)	58 (26)	52 (29)	73 (3)	62 (32)	90 (20)	50 (59)	47 (44)	45 (18)	70 (9)	54 (34)
1992	60 (32)	38 (14)	54 (29)	50 (26)	76 (4)	63 (33)	91 (22)	52 (58)	53 (50)	54 (22)	64 (6)	59 (37)
1996	68 (30)	41 (17)	67 (25)	55 (27)	92 (4)	61 (31)	96 (18)	59 (60)	60 (47)	61 (19)	75 (8)	61 (33)
2000	59 (34)	35 (17)	60 (18)	50 (27)	89 (5)	69 (20)	91 (18)	56 (61)	56 (46)	55 (19)	56 (5)	59 (39)
2004	57 (33)	33 (14)	64 (24)	50 (25)	76 (5)		87 (26)	52 (57)	54 (51)	51 (18)	57 (7)	55 (44)

Note: First figure represents the percentage of a particular group voting Democratic for president, while the figure in parentheses represents the percentage of all Democratic presidential voters who possessed the group characteristic in question. Low religious salience is those who attend religious services seldom, never, or did not have a religious preference (1972–2004). Certainly it would be desirable to have an indicator of religious salience that encompasses more than just church attendance, as Wald and Smidt (1993) and Guth and Green (1993) point out. However, church attendance is the only measure of religious salience available in the ANES for all of the years under examination in this study. Jews are marked by small Ns, and thus readers are urged to use caution when examining the results for this group.

[a] South is defined as the eleven states of the Confederacy.
[b] Northeast is defined as Conn., Me., Mass., NH, NJ, NY, Pa., RI, and Vt.
Source: American National Election Studies (2005).

total Democratic voters dropped precipitously (E. Black and Black 2002; Lublin 2004; Shafer and Johnston 2006). The same was true, although to a much lesser extent, for voters in union households and Roman Catholics. Among the other traditional New Deal coalition groups, support among those in the bottom income third, Jews, and urban dwellers remained relatively stable during this period, while African Americans became a much larger component of the party's base, a development that reflected both the increased clarity of differences between the parties on racial issues and the growth in the ability of blacks in the South to actually vote. It was also during these years that women first began their move into the Democratic coalition, a trend that would become increasingly evident in future years (Box-Steffensmeier, De Boef, and Lin 2004; Sanbonmatsu 2002a; Wolbrecht 2000).

Table 7.2 starkly demonstrates the strong impact of the Reagan era on partisan coalitions—in this case for the Democratic Party. Reagan's—and by extension the Republican Party's—strong preference to rely on free markets to determine economic outcomes and equally strong opposition to most social welfare programs reenergized Democratic support among those in the lower third of the family income distribution. The same is true among union household voters and urban dwellers, and to a lesser extent for Catholics as well. Blacks and Jews remained important parts of the Democratic coalition, and support for the party among women continued to slowly increase as well. All of these groups had good policy-related reasons for siding with the Democrats and against the increasingly conservative GOP, again highlighting the important place of public policy in partisan change.

The groups that were important to the Democratic coalition in the 1980s remain central elements of the party's base today. Less affluent Americans, voters from union households, Jews, those who reside in urban areas, African Americans, and women are all highly supportive of Democratic presidential candidates, and each of these groups (with the exception of Jews) also represents a sizeable percentage of all Democratic presidential voters. Democratic support is not as high among Roman Catholics as it once was, but this group does still account for a relatively large percentage of Democratic voters.

We also see that the partisan and ideological clarity discussed earlier in this chapter has brought some new groups into the Democratic fold. Those Americans with low levels of religious salience—both attracted by the Democrats' liberalism on social issues and repelled by the GOP conservatism on this same front—have increased their Democratic support (Layman 2001), as have residents of the Northeast, a region of the US where social liberalism is more likely to be warmly received (Speel 1998). Latinos—a rapidly growing segment of the American electorate—have shown themselves to be relatively Democratic, attracted by the party's stand on economic issues and its image as more sympathetic to the concerns and issues of immigrants (de la Garza 2004).

Following the model of Table 7.2, Table 7.3 presents the Republican presidential vote (first figure) and total percentage of all GOP presidential voters (figure in

Table 7.3 Group components of the Republican presidential coalition, 1952–2004

Year	Top income third	Non-southern white Protestants	Rural dwellers	Professional and managerial	Southern whites	White men	High religious salience	White evangelical Protestants	Roman Catholics	Suburban dwellers	Married or widowed
1952	61 (47)	71 (60)	62 (38)	68 (20)	50 (11)	59 (45)	59 (40)		48 (19)	62 (33)	
1956	62 (36)	71 (60)	59 (47)	66 (21)	47 (14)	57 (45)	59 (45)		54 (21)	64 (30)	60 (91)
1960	52 (46)	71 (71)	54 (55)	58 (21)	45 (17)	48 (43)	50 (47)	60 (22)	18 (8)	54 (29)	50 (90)
1964	41 (50)	43 (61)	32 (39)	46 (29)	42 (20)	36 (48)	33 (45)	35 (19)	21 (16)	38 (37)	32 (90)
1968	50 (38)	65 (63)	51 (46)	54 (26)	43 (16)	51 (43)	50 (44)	50 (22)	37 (18)	50 (33)	47 (86)
1972	68 (40)	74 (51)	69 (45)	65 (24)	80 (22)	71 (45)	71 (33)	80 (23)	59 (24)	68 (36)	67 (86)
1976	57 (47)	61 (53)	51 (39)	58 (31)	53 (18)	53 (42)	51 (32)	54 (22)	41 (21)	50 (37)	50 (83)
1980	56 (35)	61 (43)	57 (38)	53 (31)	60 (27)	60 (46)	58 (32)	59 (21)	50 (22)	58 (44)	54 (80)
1984	69 (42)	72 (45)	61 (35)	61 (30)	69 (20)	67 (43)	60 (30)	74 (23)	54 (25)	65 (49)	61 (75)
1988	61 (43)	66 (46)	56 (33)	54 (34)	68 (22)	62 (43)	54 (32)	72 (25)	47 (23)	58 (50)	56 (75)
1992	39 (45)	44 (42)	37 (33)	34 (32)	46 (23)	38 (44)	46 (40)	43 (37)	30 (22)	37 (48)	39 (80)
1996	48 (42)	49 (38)	38 (31)	43 (45)	51 (29)	49 (50)	51 (40)	43 (33)	37 (26)	43 (47)	41 (77)
2000	51 (35)	53 (29)	51 (18)	45 (42)	61 (34)	54 (42)	58 (38)	64 (27)	49 (30)	48 (24)	51 (74)
2004	57 (36)	64 (35)		43 (31)	67 (27)	60 (41)	59 (29)	77 (34)	48 (24)		55 (67)

Note: First figure represents the percentage of a particular group voting Republican for president, while the figure in parentheses represents the percentage of all Republican presidential voters who possessed the group characteristic in question. High religious salience is those who attend religious services every week.

Source: American National Election Studies (2005).

parentheses) for eleven groups that have been important elements of the Republican party's coalition for at least some period of time since 1952. The groups in the first four columns—voters in the upper third of the income distribution, non-southern white Protestants, rural dwellers, and those with professional or managerial occupations—were the GOP's counter of the Democrats' New Deal coalition, as evidenced by both the support and size percentages for these groups from 1952 to 1960. As was the case for the Democrats, the Republicans have also seen changes to this coalition over time. Two of these core groups—more affluent individuals and non-southern white Protestants—have remained quite supportive of the GOP over time. More affluent voters did reduce their support of Republican presidential candidates in the 1990s, but they returned to the Republican fold in 2004. The haves in American society remain critical components of the Republican coalition (Stonecash 2000). Non-southern white Protestants followed almost the same pattern, but it is important to note that the percentage of all Republican presidential voters accounted for by this group has declined dramatically over time. Those who work in managerial or professional occupations were for years highly supportive of the Republican presidential candidate. This changed in 1992, and to this point has stayed changed although the group does still account for a relatively large percentage of all Republican voters. Rural voters follow essentially the same pattern as the managers and professionals, although their percentage of all GOP voters has shrunk over time, likely owing at least in part to the decrease in the percentage of Americans living in rural areas.

While these elements of continuity are certainly important, the perhaps more interesting components of the GOP coalition lie in the groups that have been added over time. Remember, the Republicans were the minority party in the New Deal party system, and thus they were under the most pressure to alter and expand their coalition. The fact that the GOP has won seven of eleven presidential elections since 1968 shows that the party was able to accomplish these tasks. One of the most important groups that Republicans have added to their coalition is southern whites. In some ways the GOP's addition of white southerners began with Eisenhower in the 1950s, but as Black and Black (2002) make clear, it was Reagan who finally locked these voters into the party's coalition. Indeed, only white southerner Bill Clinton was able to prevent the Republican candidate from receiving at least 60 percent of the vote among this group since 1980.

The size of white southerners in the overall Republican coalition has grown as well.[3] In a group with a fair amount of overlap with southern whites, white

---

[3] From 1960 to 1988 white evangelical Protestant religious tradition is determined using vcf0128a in combination with the variable for race of the respondent in the ANES Cumulative Data File (American National Election Studies 2005). This classification scheme is not without problems. The most significant has to do with the classification of Baptists. Prior to 1972 the ANES survey instrument did not differentiate among Baptists, meaning that during this period some Baptists are misclassified in the division of Protestants into mainline and evangelical traditions. There is simply no

evangelical Protestants have also become increasingly important elements of the Republican coalition. When this development is combined with the increased GOP support by voters for whom religion is highly salient, we can see how the increased cultural conservatism of the Republicans enabled them to increase the size of their electoral coalition (Layman 2001; Leege et al. 2002). Cultural issues also likely account for at least some of the growth in Republican support among Catholics, although the increasing affluence of this group is relevant as well.

We also see that white men have been quite supportive of Republican candidates since 1972 (with the exception of 1992), although their overall contribution to the Republican coalition does not match that of women to the Democratic coalition (Edsall 2006; Kaufmann and Petrocik 1999). Suburban voters—always relatively supportive of Republican candidates—increased their total contribution to the party's base from the 1960s through the 1990s (Lassiter 2006; McGirr 2001).

satisfactory way to deal with this problem. From 1990 to 1996, the revised classification scheme represented by vcf0128b is utilized. Beginning in 1998, ANES officials stopped dividing Protestants into "mainline" and "evangelical" categories as they began a review and reevaluation of the construction of the religious tradition variable. This review apparently has yet to be completed, and thus the last four versions of the ANES Cumulative Data File offer no variable differentiating Protestants by religious tradition after 1996. In an attempt to provide at least some differentiation among Protestants for 2000 and 2004, white Protestants were identified as evangelical by denomination only. None of the other characteristics that the ANES used to create its categories from 1990 to 1996, such as charismatic or fundamentalist identification, born-again status, or frequency of church attendance, have been included here. The reasons for this decision are as follows. Charismatic or fundamentalist identification was not asked in 2000 or 2004, born-again status was not asked in 2004, and classifying a respondent as "evangelical" or "mainline" based on frequency of attendance at worship services requires assumptions that are not warranted. For a useful discussion of classifying the religious tradition of Protestants based solely on denominational identification, see Steensland et al. (2000). For 2000 and 2004, denominations were classified as "evangelical" or "mainline" following the guidelines used by the ANES from 1990 to 1996, with two exceptions. Those identifying themselves as members of the American Baptist Churches USA or Jehovah's Witnesses were removed from the evangelical category. Classifying by denomination only obviously results in undifferentiated Protestants and Christians being excluded from these analyses. This resulted in eighty-nine respondents being removed in 2000 and eighty-five in 2004. This is particularly problematic given the recent growth in the number of non-denominational Protestants in the US. As Steensland et al. (2000) and Woodberry and Smith (1998) point out, this group is one of the fastest-growing religious groups in America, and individuals in this group tend to exhibit beliefs that are different from those Protestants who identify themselves as having "no denomination" (as opposed to "non-denominational"). The religious beliefs of non-denominational Protestants resemble those held by evangelicals much more than those possessed by mainliners. However, without information on these beliefs in a dataset it is unwise to classify non-denominational Protestants into either Protestant tradition. Steensland et al. (2000) do classify some non-denominational Protestants into the evangelical tradition solely on the basis of church attendance, with those who attend services once a month or more being classified as evangelicals and those who attend less than once a month being omitted from further analysis. I am reluctant to follow this example because, as noted above, this requires making assumptions that are not clearly warranted or justified. In future versions of the ANES survey researchers can hope that sufficient belief and identification questions will be asked so that this important and growing component of the American religious landscape can be more fully analyzed. Full classification schemes are available from the author upon request.

Suburbanites' vote percentages, however, declined in the 1990s and have yet to rebound to previous levels.

Finally, Table 7.3 presents the Republican presidential vote figures for individuals who are either married or widowed. While the pattern is not as clear as it was for the non-married or non-widowed and the Democrats, we do see that since 1972 voters who are either married or widowed tend to favor the Republicans over the Democrats. Only Jimmy Carter (1976 only) and Bill Clinton (1992 and 1996) were able to alter this pattern. Again, married or widowed voters are not a group in the same sense as the others examined here, but their increased GOP proclivities do demonstrate the increased Republican rhetorical emphasis on the family.

While informative, the results presented in Tables 7.2 and 7.3 are bivariate in nature, and thus there is the possibility they could be misleading. This is particularly true owing to the high degree of overlap between some of the group characteristics included here, such as African American and urban residence, or southern whites and white evangelical Protestants. In order to obtain a truer understanding of the place of these groups in the parties' respective coalitions multivariate analyses are necessary. Tables 7.4 and 7.5 present the results of these analyses for the Democratic presidential vote and the Republican presidential vote respectively. In each case presidential vote is coded as a dichotomy of a vote for the party in question or some other presidential vote, and all of the independent variables are coded as present or absent dichotomies. This allows the unstandardized logistic regression coefficients presented in the tables to be compared with each other and over time *within* a party but not *between* parties. Data are pooled and results presented by decade in order to get a clearer picture of change over time.

Looking first at the Democratic coalition, the multivariate results for the most part confirm those presented earlier from the bivariate analyses. African Americans and Jews are strongly supportive of Democratic presidential candidates throughout the entire period under examination here, and the same is true to a lesser extent among those residing in union households. Those in the bottom third of the family income distribution have consistently been important to the Democrats, and this support has grown over time. The same pattern is present, but in reverse, for Roman Catholics. Urban dwellers, women, and those with low levels of religious salience have increased their support of the party since the 1960s, while southern whites have moved from being a significant component of the Democrats' coalition to be significantly opposed to the party's presidential candidates. Latinos were strong supporters of the party in the 1980s and 1990s but less so in the 2000s (perhaps because of Bush's appeals to these voters), while the coefficients for Northeast residents and those neither married nor widowed do not show much of a pattern.

The results for Republican presidential vote in Table 7.5 also for the most part support the earlier results. The importance of southern whites to the party has

Table 7.4 Logistic regression coefficients for group components of the Democratic presidential coalition, by decade, 1950s–2000s

Decade	Bottom income third	Southern whites	Union households	Roman Catholics	Jews	Urban dwellers	African Americans	Women	Low religious salience	Northeast residents	Latinos	Not married or widowed
1950s	0.26 (0.10)	0.86 (0.12)	0.79 (0.10)	0.82 (0.11)	2.16 (0.26)	0.05 (0.10)	1.61 (0.24)	−0.19 (0.09)	0.17 (0.09)	−0.51 (0.11)		0.13 (0.20)
1960s	0.26 (0.09)	0.19 (0.11)	0.70 (0.10)	1.49 (0.11)	2.62 (0.32)	0.08 (0.10)	3.10 (0.29)	0.03 (0.08)	0.28 (0.09)	−0.30 (0.10)		−0.11 (0.13)
1970s	0.38 (0.10)	−0.03 (0.11)	0.61 (0.09)	0.50 (0.10)	1.49 (0.28)	0.19 (0.10)	2.67 (0.22)	0.23 (0.08)	0.31 (0.08)	0.04 (0.10)		0.35 (0.11)
1980s	0.53 (0.09)	−0.01 (0.10)	0.80 (0.09)	0.46 (0.09)	1.26 (0.23)	0.41 (0.09)	2.61 (0.19)	0.31 (0.08)	0.22 (0.08)	−0.27 (0.10)	0.72 (0.18)	0.05 (0.09)
1990s	0.53 (0.10)	0.07 (0.11)	0.61 (0.11)	0.41 (0.10)	1.76 (0.34)	0.31 (0.10)	2.91 (0.24)	0.46 (0.09)	0.67 (0.09)	0.21 (0.12)	0.98 (0.20)	0.23 (0.10)
2000s	0.42 (0.12)	−0.38 (0.13)	0.64 (0.14)	0.32 (0.11)	2.02 (0.36)	0.67 (0.19)	2.41 (0.23)	0.50 (0.10)	0.56 (0.10)	−0.12 (0.14)	0.33 (0.22)	0.16 (0.11)

Note: All variables are coded in the same fashion as for Tables 7.2 and 7.3. Figures presented are unstandardized logistic regression coefficients with standard errors in parentheses. Coefficients significant at the .05 level or better are in italic.

Source: American National Election Studies 2005.

Table 7.5 Logistic regression coefficients for group components of the Republican presidential coalition, by decade, 1950s–2000s

Decade	Top income third	Non-southern white Protestants	Rural dwellers	Professional and managerial	Southern whites	White men	High religious salience	White evangelical Protestants	Roman Catholics	Suburban dwellers	Married or widowed
1950s	0.11 (0.09)	1.71 (0.16)	0.09 (0.11)	0.57 (0.12)	0.66 (0.18)	−0.26 (0.09)	0.20 (0.09)		0.80 (0.17)	0.24 (0.12)	0.08 (0.12)
1960s	0.23 (0.09)	2.20 (0.15)	0.06 (0.11)	0.47 (0.11)	1.55 (0.17)	0.08 (0.08)	0.30 (0.08)	−0.14 (0.11)	0.50 (0.16)	0.27 (0.11)	−0.20 (0.13)
1970s	0.36 (0.09)	1.54 (0.12)	0.22 (0.11)	0.14 (0.10)	1.41 (0.15)	0.21 (0.08)	0.26 (0.09)	0.07 (0.12)	0.68 (0.13)	0.30 (0.10)	0.30 (0.10)
1980s	0.49 (0.08)	1.36 (0.10)	0.50 (0.10)	0.05 (0.08)	1.19 (0.13)	0.39 (0.08)	0.22 (0.08)	0.22 (0.11)	0.65 (0.11)	0.64 (0.09)	0.08 (0.08)
1990s	0.32 (0.09)	1.11 (0.12)	0.13 (0.12)	0.09 (0.09)	1.14 (0.13)	0.32 (0.09)	0.65 (0.09)	0.30 (0.10)	0.51 (0.13)	0.27 (0.11)	0.35 (0.10)
2000s	0.40 (0.13)	1.18 (0.18)	−0.19 (0.19)	−0.08 (0.12)	1.34 (0.18)	0.24 (0.12)	0.37 (0.13)	0.78 (0.17)	1.01 (0.16)	−0.11 (0.16)	0.25 (0.13)

Note: All variables are coded in the same fashion as for Tables 7.2 and 7.3. Figures presented are unstandardized logistic regression coefficients with standard errors in parentheses. Coefficients significant at the .05 level or better are in italic.

Source: American National Election Studies (2005).

grown significantly over time, as has that of those with high levels of religious salience, white evangelicals, and Catholics. The support of those in the top income third has been relatively steady, and although non-southern white Protestants have declined in their tendency to support the GOP on election day, they remain a sizeable element of the party's coalition. Those in professional and managerial occupations were significant sources of party support in the 1950s and 1960s, but not since. Suburban dwellers were consistently supportive of Republican presidential candidates until the candidacies of George W. Bush. If there are any surprises in Table 7.5 they can be found in the results presented for rural residents and white men. The coefficients for white men are significant, but relatively small for the 1970s–1990s, and fail to achieve significance in the 2000s. Rural dwellers fail to show much of a pattern at all. But for the most part, the multivariate results support the pictures of the Democratic and Republican coalitions presented in this chapter.

CONCLUSION

The Republican and Democratic parties of the early twenty-first century are very different from each other, offering Americans relatively clear policy choices across the board. These differences exist, to a certain extent, because the two parties have very different electoral coalitions. A Democratic Party whose electoral success is rooted in the support of the less affluent, union households, urbanites, women, blacks, Latinos, and those with low levels of religious salience will—if it wants to maintain the support of these groups—possess very different issue positions and champion very different public policy options than a Republican Party whose success on election day comes in large part from more affluent voters, southern whites, men, white Protestants (especially evangelicals), individuals for whom religion is highly salient, and rural and suburban dwellers. A properly functioning representative democracy requires the representation of diverse interests, and at least in the American context it is political parties that fulfill this representative function. Indeed, as Schattschneider (1942, 1) famously noted, American democracy would be "unthinkable" without parties.

Because of the dynamic nature of American society, political parties cannot be static and still adequately perform their representative responsibilities. They must adapt and evolve as society changes; otherwise relevant interests and groups will be left out and important issues will not be addressed in the public dialogue. Fortunately, parties are highly concerned with these processes of adaptation and evolution; their ability to win elections and exercise governmental power rests on their success in properly interpreting and responding to change. As noted at the outset of this chapter, this is not an easy process, and parties and their leaders are never certain what they should do. Opportunities for partisan success are always there, but so too are risks.

The results of the 2008 election cycle are a perfect example of this dynamic. Democratic candidate Barack Obama won the presidency by a comfortable margin, and the Democrats added to their majorities in both the House and the Senate. But there is a certain amount of ambiguity in terms of how this success should be interpreted by the party. Some Democrats believe that the 2008 results represent a mandate for a renewed era of liberalism and activist government. Others in the party caution that much of the party's 2008 success resulted from the high disapproval ratings of Republican President George W. Bush combined with the dramatic economic downturn that occurred in 2008. In short the Democrats are at least somewhat uncertain where the party should go next.

The Republicans are in a similar situation. Were the party's losses in 2008 a repudiation of basic GOP principles, or simply the electorate registering its deep displeasure with the Bush administration? Which of these explanations is more accurate is of obvious importance for the future of the GOP, but the answer is unclear and thus the party is racked by uncertainty. Parties constantly evaluate election returns, examine their opportunities, and evaluate the risks as best they can, and eventually they act. Sometimes their moves pay off and sometimes they don't, but when taken together these partisan successes and failures combine to produce representation and political change in the United States.

A good deal of this political change lies in alteration of the parties' electoral coalitions (Petrocik 1981). In most instances this change unfolds slowly over time, more closely resembling Key's theory of secular realignment (1959) rather than his perhaps more famous concept of critical realignment (1955).[4] New groups rise in American society, new issues enter the public debate, the parties present new policy options—all of these phenomena come together to produce a dynamic for change. As new groups and issues arise, parties and their politicians slowly and cautiously respond to them. The masses then assess these partisan responses, and eventually they respond as well. The end result is a feedback loop where both the elites and masses each create and respond to political change (Aldrich 2003; M. Brewer and Stonecash 2009). The process is often messy and for many people it moves far too slowly, but in the end the American political system almost always responds to calls for change, at least in part owing to the search of political parties for a winning electoral coalition.

---

[4] For an excellent examination of realignment theory, see Rosenof (2003).

CHAPTER 8

....

THE PARTY
FAITHFUL

RELIGION AND PARTY
POLITICS IN AMERICA

....

JOHN C. GREEN

RELIGION was a major preoccupation of the 2008 presidential campaign. Would Democrat Barack Obama's outreach to white Christians be successful? Or would Obama's association with black Protestantism—and the false rumor he was a Muslim—keep such voters at bay? And from another angle, would Obama's religious outreach alienate non-religious voters?

Similar questions were raised about Republican John McCain. Would he be able to effectively mobilize white evangelical Protestants, despite the deep skepticism of many of their leaders? Would the tensions between Evangelicals and Mormons evident in the presidential primaries cost McCain votes in the West? And would McCain's pursuit of white religious conservatives drive away minority and moderate religious voters?

This interest in religion and the presidential vote may surprise some readers. After all, wasn't the 2008 election all about the economy and thus not about other factors, such as religion? In fact, both things were true: the troubled economy certainly influenced the vote, as has often been the case in presidential elections, but at the same time, religious groups were a key element of the major party presidential coalitions—as has been the case throughout American history. In this regard, it is important to distinguish between social groups in the electorate and the issues that motivate such groups to vote in a particular way.

Religious groups are an important feature of the American electorate, and group membership influences how voters respond to campaign issues. During the 2008 campaign, nearly all religious groups reported the economy was their top concern, but some of these groups strongly backed Obama at the polls and others voted strongly for McCain. One reason for this pattern was the underlying partisanship of the religious groups, with the Democrats likely to see their party's nominee as cogent on the economy, while the Republicans were likely to have the opposite appraisal. A geological metaphor is apt here: religion is part of the political bedrock over which the flood of campaign issues ebb and flow.

In fact, one source of continuity in President Obama's historic victory was the partisanship of his religious supporters: the faith-based elements of Obama's vote looked remarkably like the Democratic Party coalitions of the late twentieth century. Likewise, the religious segment of the McCain vote closely resembled the Republican Party coalitions of the recent past. There were, of course, details peculiar to 2008, as in every election. But the basic structure of faith-based politics was rooted in the history of the major political parties, with some aspects dating back to the nineteenth century and others being of more recent vintage. To continue the geologic metaphor, the political bedrock of which religion is a part was laid down in previous eras.

This chapter describes the religious elements of the major party coalitions in the American public. After briefly discussing why religion is relevant to party politics at a conceptual level, it reviews the religious character of the major party coalitions in the past and present. The most attention will be paid to more recent party coalitions, comparing the Democratic and Republican faith-based supporters in 1952 and 2008. The conclusions are straightforward. First, religious groups have been one of the basic building "blocs" of major party coalitions, an integral part of the bedrock of American politics. Second, the faith-based elements of the major party coalitions have changed as the country changed, sometimes in degree and sometimes a change of kind. The former and more typical change is like the slow erosion of bedrock by electoral floods, but the latter is more like the appearance of a new fault line in the bedrock.

Finally, this chapter describes the "party faithful" in the early years of the twenty-first century. The Democratic coalition was based on various kinds of religious minorities, led by black Protestants, along with less observant white Christians and people unaffiliated with organized religion. Meanwhile, the core of the Republican coalition was made up of a variety of white Christians, especially white Evangelicals and the religiously observant.

Why Religion Matters in Party Politics

A good place to begin is with a brief review of the role of religion in party politics at a conceptual level. Simply put, religion matters politically for the same reasons that many other demographic characteristics matter, including gender, age, region, or social class. All such traits are associated with values and interests that can be politically relevant. Some such values and interests derive from ideas about the nature of the world held by social groups, while others arise from the regular activities of different kinds of people, and still others develop from the interaction among diverse populations.

However, religion has often had special linkage with such values and interests. For one thing, religion is strongly associated with special ideas in the form of religious beliefs, including basic views of the divine and its relationship to humanity. Such beliefs can be an important source of values and interests. In addition, religious beliefs typically motivate special activities in the form of religious practices, including public worship and private devotion. Such activities can help individuals assign political priority to their values and interests. Taken together, religious beliefs and practices can also foster a special sense of belonging among co-religionists in the form of affiliation with congregations, denominations, and religious traditions. Such affiliations can help connect individuals' values and interests to politics. For all these reasons, religious groups regularly display distinctive values and interests that can be relevant to politics. Such distinctiveness typically has political effects that are independent of other demographic factors, but it is also true that other demographic characteristics—such as gender, age, region, and social class—can influence the politics of religious people as well (see Olson and Green 2008a).

American Religion: Diverse and Dynamic

The political distinctiveness of religious groups has been important to politics in part because of the great diversity and dynamism of American religion (Marsden 1990). Indeed, the original colonial settlement included diverse religious communities, principally various kinds of Protestants. Subsequent immigration dramatically increased this diversity to eventually include Catholics and other Christian groups as well as Jews and other non-Christians. From the beginning this religious diversity was closely associated with ethnicity and race, so that many of the most important religious communities were distinctive "ethno-religious" groups (Swierenga 1990; Barone 1990). Scottish Presbyterians, Irish Catholics, and German Jews are all good examples of such groups arising from European immigration. The impact of immigration continues to this day, bringing new kinds of ethno-religious groups into the country from other parts of the world, such as Korean Methodists, Mexican Catholics, and Arab Muslims. Black Protestants are a special case of this phenomenon, being the product of slavery, segregation, and internal migration.

The repeated waves of immigration also produced religious dynamism as the various religious communities interacted with one another (Finke and Stark 2006). For example, many ethno-religious groups eventually assimilated into the broader society, losing some of their ethnic and religious distinctiveness in the process, but at the same time modifying society's overall character. In this context, some groups sought to regularize religious life by building large and sophisticated institutions, some national and even international in scope. But other groups resisted such institutionalization, and one form of such resistance was religious movements promoting innovative approaches to faith.

In addition, the urge to proselytize on behalf of a particular faith has been strong in an open society with many potential converts, and as a result there have been repeated "awakenings" and "revivals" (McLoughlin 1978). At the same time, religious faiths regularly encountered non-religious perspectives, producing both accommodation and conflict. This confrontation encouraged secularization, aided by economic and technical modernization (Norris and Inglehart 2004). Although secularization has not had as large an influence in America as in Europe, it has contributed to a degree of entropy in religious life, producing some people unaffiliated with organized religion (and sometimes hostile to it).

The consequence of this dynamism was the creation of new kinds of ethno-religious groups, including the founding of new denominations and entirely new religions. But sometimes it has also helped create other kinds of religious groups, such as the recent development of "ethno-theological" groups, based on levels of religious observance. Both ethno-religious and ethno-theological groups can be associated with politically relevant values and interests.

Religious Groups, Government, and Politics

American government has been hospitable to this religious diversity and dynamism (Jelen and Wilcox 1995). The First Amendment to the US Constitution prohibits an official state religion ("an establishment of religion") and also guarantees freedom of religion ("the free exercise thereof"). Although the exact meaning of these statements has changed a good bit over the course of American history, the net impact has been to foster a "marketplace" in religion, with many religious "sellers" and "buyers" (see Jelen 2002 for a fuller discussion of this topic). The absence of an official state religion meant that there was no religious monopoly in such a religious marketplace. But more importantly, it meant that all religious groups had to compete with one another for a voluntary following in the public, producing an extensive set of sophisticated religious organizations. At the same time, the guarantee of free exercise of religion created a strong presumption against regulating religion for its own sake, and in particular, the faith-based activities designed to compete for followers. Just as importantly, individuals rarely faced legal barriers to joining the religion of their choice—or changing religions if they chose. As a consequence, many Americans became deeply engaged in a wide variety of faiths.

Thus, the combination of religious diversity, dynamism, and constitutional structure has produced numerous religious groups holding distinctive values and interests that can be relevant to politics. Sometimes religious groups have taken the initiative in politicizing their values and interests by supporting politicians, and sometimes politicians have politicized religion by seeking the support of religious groups on the basis of their values and interests. The major political parties have been a crucial forum for this kind of faith-based politics, performing the same kind of brokerage for religious groups as for other social groups, largely in order to win elections and influence the personnel of government (see Reichley 1985a, Layman 2001, and Leege et al. 2002 for descriptions of this process).

Although the constitutional structure encouraged a diverse marketplace in religion, it had an opposite effect on political parties, fostering a two-party rather than a multiparty system. Thus, most of the religious diversity of the country—and for that matter, all other kinds of diversity—has been funneled into politics through the two major parties. Under these conditions, the major parties built broad, complex, and loosely organized coalitions of social groups, representing diverse (and sometimes contradictory) values and interests. From the beginning of the two-party system, such coalitions developed a dynamism of their own, in which the diverse religious groups played an important role (Noll and Harlow 2007).

As a consequence, religious groups were woven into all levels of partisanship (Koopman 2001). The diversity of religious groups has been especially prominent in the partisanship of the mass public or party in the electorate, with the major parties developing strong religious constituencies. This diversity has often not been quite as evident among major party leaders and activists, in party organization, nor among public officials elected under each party's label, or party in government. The difference between the partisan publics and elites derives from other factors besides religion that determine access to party organizations and governmental offices. For example, the "iron law of oligarchy" has advantaged higher-status religious groups, while federalism favored religious groups that were concentrated geographically. Still, the contours of the parties' religious constituents have been regularly visible among such party activists and office-holders (for contemporary party activists, see J. Green and Jackson 2007; for members of Congress, see Guth and Kellstedt 2001).

RELIGIOUS GROUPS AND MAJOR PARTY COALITIONS

What have the faith-based elements of American party coalitions actually looked like in the past and in the present? Such coalitions have been primarily based on religious affiliation, with each of the major parties drawing strong support from a different set of ethno-religious groups (McCormick 1974). In part, the partisanship of religious affiliation reflected the observance of religious beliefs and practices, but these aspects of religion typically reinforced the linkage between religious affiliation and party affiliation. As a consequence, the most observant members of the ethno-religious groups tended to most fully exemplify the groups' partisan disposition. In this regard, the level of religious observance often had an indirect impact on party coalitions through the level of members' political activity, including voter turnout. However, religious affiliation was the primary connection to the major political parties.

The partisanship of ethno-religious groups also arose in part from the internal dynamics of coalition building itself: groups often backed one of the major parties because a rival group supported the other party. Such negative references resulted from the combination of intense group identification with the great diversity of such groups, where every group was a potential rival. In a politics where ethnic and religious identity was a potent resource, then ethnic and religious disparagement— and prejudice—were potent weapons. Such a complex politics confronted party leaders with the challenge of building coalitions from disparate and fractious ethno-religious groups.

Not surprisingly, such coalitions were characterized by considerable short-term instability. But there were sources of long-term instability as well: changes in religion (especially shifts in the size and variety of ethno-religious groups) and changes in politics (particularly the rise of new issues). Thus, the exact nature of the ethno-religious coalitions varied over time. For the most part this variation represented differences in degree, not kind: although the particular ethno-religious groups in the coalitions changed, religious affiliation remained the basis for the coalition.

Ethno-Religious Groups and Party Coalitions

A brief sketch of past ethno-religious party coalitions is in order, noting key points of change and continuity. Such coalitions appeared shortly after independence during the first party system, when the Republican Party (the forerunner of the modern Democrats) opposed the Federalist Party. Here each party drew support from key groups of white Protestants that had settled the original colonies

(Formisano 1981). The Republicans had more diverse faith-based coalitions, including Presbyterians (largely Scottish), Baptists (many who were Scottish Irish), and Methodists (including German and Welsh adherents), groups that had grown as the result of revivals on the frontier and in the South beginning before the American Revolution. They were also backed by religious minorities of the era, such as Catholics, Jews, and Nonconformists. Meanwhile, the Federalists had strong backing from English Congregationalists and Episcopalians, remnants of the religious "establishments" in New England and the middle Atlantic colonies. Thus, the initial politics of nation building involved divisions among more or less socially prominent Protestants, a pattern that has persisted in one form or another throughout American history.

This pattern became more complex in the 1830s and the second party system, when the Democratic Party took its present name and the Whig Party replaced the Federalists (Benson 1961). The Democrats drew strong support from new immigrants, including Irish Catholics, Lutherans, and other kinds of Protestant churches from continental Europe, adding these groups to their support from other religious minorities. They also benefited from some Methodists and Baptists, especially in the South, where support for slavery was strong. Meanwhile, the Whigs were backed strongly by Anglo-Protestant groups influenced by a set of revivals that occurred after the revolution, including many Congregationalists, Presbyterians, and Baptists. This coalition favored economic modernization and the abolition of slavery, but also a tendency toward nativism and anti-Catholicism. Indeed, the reforming thrust of the revivalists was a source of political conflict, a tendency still evident in contemporary politics.

This complex ethno-religious politics shifted yet again with the advent of the Civil War and the third party system, where the Democratic Party faced the modern Republican Party, which had replaced the Whigs (Kleppner 1979). The rebellious and then defeated South became solidly Democratic, and its white Protestants developed a distinctive religious outlook (still evident today among evangelical Protestants). The legacy of slavery and the imposition of segregation solidified the unique religious perspective of African American politics (still evident today in the black Protestant churches). In the North, Democrats received backing from Catholics and Protestant groups, such as Episcopalians and Lutherans. Swelled by continued immigration, these groups had in common a "ritualist" approach to religion. Meanwhile, a core constituency of the Republican Party was abolitionists rooted in northern Anglo-Protestant churches, and after the war, many other northern Protestants became Republicans, including Methodists and other previously Democratic groups. Bolstered by continued revivals, these churches shared a "pietist" approach to religion. Economic individualism and moral reform were points of contention between the ritualists and pietists.

The major party coalitions shifted again after the 1896 election and into the fourth party system, where tensions between the burgeoning industrial cities and declining rural communities altered the religious elements of the Democratic and Republican coalitions (Kleppner 1987). The Democrats maintained their bastions of support among Catholics, immigrants, and religious minorities in the North, and with white Protestants in the South. They also drew some support from northern "fundamentalist" Protestants, who sought to defend the "old-time religion" against cosmopolitan culture (a movement that would eventually contribute to evangelical Protestantism). Much of the energy in Protestant revivalism turned in this direction. One set of carriers of the cosmopolitan culture was that of the largest and most institutionalized "mainline" Protestant denominations in the North, some of which preached a "social gospel" of economic and cultural reform. This diverse "Protestant mainline," including both ritualists and pietists, was the backbone of the Republican coalition in this era. Republicans also made some inroads among urban non-Protestants and non-religious people uncomfortable with the values of southern and fundamentalist Protestants. These complex coalitions warred over economic issues (tariffs, trade unions) and cultural matters (prohibition, teaching of evolution); the outlines of these disputes can still be seen in faith-based politics.

New shifts took place in the fifth party system beginning in the 1930s, when Democrats and Republicans confronted the economic calamity of the Great Depression (Kellstedt et al. 2007). In the North, the Democrats reinvigorated their support from Catholics, Jews, and other religious minorities, including new immigrants from southern and eastern Europe. The Democrats benefited to some extent from black Protestants who had migrated to the northern cities, and also from the emergence of an alternative to mainline Protestants, evangelical Protestants, a diverse set of traditional churches. The Democrats maintained their support from white southern Protestants, many of which began to identify as Evangelicals as well. A new wave of revivalism helped mold this emerging identity. Although the Republican Party enjoyed some support from Evangelicals and other white Christians in the North, the party's major source of faith-based support was the diverse white Protestant mainline. Economic issues, such as unemployment and social welfare programs, were central to these coalitions, but so were cultural issues, such as prohibition and segregation. These New Deal party coalitions were the backdrop for the faith-based coalitions of contemporary parties.

Ethno-Theological Groups and Party Coalitions

The religious elements of the Democratic and Republican coalitions shifted again after the 1960s, in the less well-defined sixth party system (Aldrich 1995, ch. 8). To some extent, this shift involved a typical change in degree among ethno-religious groups. But the shift also involved a change in kind: religious observance began to play a role in party politics independently of religious affiliation, creating distinctive ethno-theological groups within some of the existing ethno-religious groups (Kohut et al. 2000; Layman and Green 2005). For example, the most observant white Catholics became one politically distinctive group and less observant white Catholics another one. Some observers include the religious unaffiliated population as part of this pattern on the grounds that non-religious people are the least religious observant group in the public (J. Green 2007, ch. 3).

It is possible that changes of this sort had occurred in past eras but have not been recognized because of the absence of detailed information on individual voters available from public opinion surveys. In fact, the best evidence of ethno-theological groups comes from survey data. A well-known example is the "God gap" in the presidential vote based on the frequency of worship attendance (Olson and Green 2008b). However, many measures of religious beliefs and practices show a similar association between level of religious observance and politics (J. Green et al. 2007).

Not surprisingly, the new ethno-theological groups became building "blocs" of party coalitions, with the Democrats obtaining the backing of less observant white Christians and the unaffiliated—and losing support from observant white Christians—and the Republicans showing the opposite pattern. If ethno-religious groups had helped "structure" the major party coalitions in the past, then ethno-theological groups helped "restructure" the party coalitions in recent times. Sociologists of religion noticed this restructuring in the 1980s and 1990s (Wuthnow 1988), but there is evidence that this shift began in the early 1970s (J. Green 2007, 65).

These new faith-based coalitions were widely associated with the "culture wars," disputes over issues such as abortion and same-sex marriage, as opposed to the "ethnicity wars" of the previous eras (J. Hunter 1991; Petrocik 2006). The key difference was not so much the type of issue that was salient—after all, cultural disputes are hardly new in American politics and economic issues remained important to these new coalitions—but rather how religion was connected to political parties. Religious observance no longer simply reinforced the link between religious affiliation and party affiliation, but instead created separate partisan dispositions within religious communities. In this context, religious affiliation has an indirect impact on partisanship, a reversal of the pattern with ethno-religious groups. In this situation, people with moderate levels of religious observance were the least likely to be strong partisans. Indeed, in a politics where religious beliefs and practices are a resource, ideological attacks—and intolerance—are potent weapons. Such strife can contribute to the polarization of party politics, bringing its own kind of short- and long-term instability to party coalitions (Dionne 2006).

CONTEMPORARY FAITH-BASED PARTY COALITIONS

Contemporary faith-based party coalitions can be usefully illustrated with survey data from 1952 and 2008.[1] Of course, a comparison of survey results over such a long time period must be viewed with caution: much has changed in religion and politics over the nearly six decades between the two presidential election years. However, such a comparison covers a long enough period to observe both the structure and the restructuring of faith-based party coalitions, and the time frame is recent enough to be relevant to party coalitions in the twenty-first century. In addition, the 1952 and 2008 elections had similar political contexts. These elections were unusual in that neither party nominated an incumbent president or vice-president, so there was a completely open race for the White House. Each election also produced a change in party control of the presidency and united party control of the executive and legislative branches, with the winners obtaining a modest majority of the popular vote and a landslide victory in the electoral college.

Of course, there were important differences between these election years as well. In 1952, Dwight Eisenhower led the Republicans to their first presidential victory in twenty years, while in 2008 Barack Obama put the Democrats back into the White House after eight years of Republican rule. The modern civil rights movement was just getting under way in 1952, while 2008 represented a culmination of the movement with the election of the first African American president. But the most relevant difference was the nature of the faith-based party coalitions: the ethno-religious politics of the New Deal era was still in operation in 1952 and the ethno-theological politics of the post-New Deal era was clearly visible in 2008.

Faith-Based Party Coalitions in 1952

Table 8.1 lists fourteen major religious groups in 1952 (down the side of the table) in order of the net Democratic partisanship of each group (the first column). A positive figure means that the group on balance identified as Democrats, while a negative number means that the group on balance identified as Republicans.

---

[1] The 1952 data come from Roper Commercial Poll 1952–059, conducted in May 1952 (N=3,006). The 2008 data come from the pre-election survey of the National Survey of Religion and Politics, conducted at the University of Akron in June 2008. In both surveys, the religious groups were calculated on the basis of denominational affiliation, race, and ethnicity (see J. Green 2007, app. A, for the content of the categories). In the 1952 data, religious observance was defined by church membership and a high level of knowledge and involvement in the congregation. A comparison of this measure with other, contemporary surveys showed that this measure resembles weekly or greater worship attendance. In 2008, weekly or greater worship attendance was used to define religious observance.

Table 8.1 Religious groups and partisanship in the public, 1952 (%) (N = 3,006)

Religious groups	Net Democratic partisanship	Democratic	Independent	Republican	Entire electorate
Jews, other faiths	50.5	67.9	14.7	17.4	3.6
Old ethnic Catholics	39.0	63.4	12.2	24.4	11.2
Observant white Catholics	32.9	62.7	7.6	29.8	7.5
Less observant white Catholics	31.3	56.6	18.1	25.3	2.8
Observant white evangelical Protestants	28.0	60.3	7.4	32.3	13.0
Unaffiliated	28.0	49.3	29.4	21.3	7.0
Black Protestants	26.9	55.4	16.1	28.5	8.1
Less observant white evangelical Protestants	25.0	57.1	10.9	32.1	5.2
ALL	13.3	51.2	10.9	37.9	100.0
Liberal faiths	0.0	44.4	11.1	44.4	1.5
Other Christians	−5.0	40.0	15.0	45.0	2.0
Less observant white mainline Protestants	−8.5	41.0	9.5	49.5	13.0
Observant white mainline Protestants	−16.2	39.4	5.0	55.6	20.7
Old ethnic Protestants	−16.7	38.0	7.3	54.7	4.6

Source: 1952 Roper Survey (see n. 1).

These figures are based on the next three columns in the table, which listed the percentage of each group that identified as Democratic, Independent, and Republican (including partisan leaners). Net Democratic partisanship for each group was calculated by subtracting the Republican percentage from the Democratic percentage. As can be seen in the "All" row, the country was on balance Democratic in 1952, with a net partisanship of 13.3 percentage points. The final column lists the size of the religious groups as a percentage of the adult population.

The first four religious groups at the top of the table were strongly Democratic. The composite category of Jews and other faiths had the highest score (the small number of other non-Christians closely resembled Jews in this regard), and the second largest was old ethnic Catholics, primarily from eastern and southern

Europe.[2] By this measure, ethnic Catholics were on balance more Democratic than the white Catholic categories which follow in the table. But note that there was very little difference between the observant and less observant white Catholics, with the former slightly more Democratic.

These four groups represented the religious core of the New Deal Democratic coalition in the North, including the new ethno-religious groups mobilized in the 1920s and 1930s. These groups are an example of the longstanding support for Democrats by religious minorities of various kinds. Taken together, these groups accounted for nearly one-sixth of the adult population in 1952. Largely assimilated, the other white Catholic categories accounted for about one-tenth of the population. All told, these non-Protestant groups made up one-quarter of the population in 1952.

The next four categories also on balance identified as Democrats, but to a lesser extent. White evangelical Protestants made up the first and last of these groups. As with white Catholics, there was little difference between the observant and less observant Evangelicals, and the former were slightly more Democratic. The two remaining groups, the religiously unaffiliated and black Protestants, had a similar net Democratic score, but with a larger number of independents compared to the Evangelicals.

The figures for white Evangelicals contain a strong regional pattern: southern Evangelicals strongly identified as Democrats, while Evangelicals outside of the South were more evenly divided. In 1952, white Evangelicals accounted for more than one-sixth of the electorate—a bit more than the combination of Jews and other faiths and ethnic Catholics. The unaffiliated and black Protestants also combined for about one-sixth of the adult population—about the same size as Jews and other faiths and ethnic Catholics. Both of these groups had an urban focus, the first reflecting the cosmopolitan culture of large metropolitan areas, and the latter reflecting the migration of African Americans into the northern cities. In many respects, white Evangelicals and black Protestants date from the Civil War era, but were both part of the New Deal Democratic coalition.

The remaining categories in the table were markedly more Republican than the population as a whole. The composite category of liberal faiths (Unitarians, Christian Scientists) was divided evenly between the major parties (with a net partisan score of zero). The composite category of other Christians (Mormons, Eastern Orthodox) was modestly Republican. White mainline Protestants were more Republican, with the observant being among the most Republican groups in the table. But here, too, note the small differences between these two categories of mainline Protestants. The final category of old ethnic Protestants (defined the

---

[2] In 1952, old ethnic Catholics included non-whites and individuals who reported that their grandparents were born in eastern or southern Europe. Old ethnic Protestants were defined the same way, except that African Americans were included in the black Protestant categories.

same way as old ethnic Catholics) was the most Republican category by a small margin. This group is a reminder that Protestants were influenced by immigration as well.

The liberal faiths and other Christians are examples of religious innovations arising in the context of American Protestantism, which may account for their GOP leaning in 1952. Despite a long tradition to the contrary, not all religious minorities were Democrats. Taken together, these small groups were about as numerous as Jews and other faiths. In contrast, white mainline Protestants were among the largest categories in the table, with the observant accounting for one-fifth of the adult population, and the two categories combined for one-third. Most of these ethnic Protestants were within the orbit of the mainline Protestant churches, so adding them to the mainline groups produces a sum nearly equaled to the combination of white Catholics and Evangelicals. Ethnic Protestants were, however, less than half the size of ethnic Catholics. These patterns are examples of the link between socially prominent Protestant communities and the Republican Party—a pattern that extends in one form or another back to the origins of the party system.

All told, these patterns illustrate the ethno-religious character of the New Deal party coalitions. The Democrats drew strong support from Catholics and other non-Protestants, the less prominent white Evangelical and black Protestant churches, and the unaffiliated. Meanwhile, the Republicans' strongest supporters came from the most prominent Protestant churches and related groups. The Protestant–Catholic division was pronounced—well illustrated by the large differences between ethnic Catholics and Protestants—and other ethnic and racial differences mattered as well. However, differences between ethno-theological groups, such as the observant and less observant in the three largest white Christian traditions, were not very large, and where such differences did occur, the observant were the stronger partisans.

The political impact of these patterns can be seen in the proportion of Democratic and Republican partisans in the public contributed by these religious groups. The first four Democratic groups in Table 8.1 accounted for three of every ten self-identified Democrats in 1952; white Evangelicals provided a little more than one-fifth; and the combination of the unaffiliated and black Protestants a little less than one-sixth. Thus, religious groups that on balance identified with the party provided two-thirds of its identifiers. Of course, this means that one-third of self-identified Democrats came from religious groups that did not favor the party. In regards to the GOP, more than one-half of self-identified Republicans came from the bottom four groups in Table 8.1 (and nearly three-fifths if the liberal faiths are included). The combination of white Evangelicals, black Protestants, and the unaffiliated provided another one-quarter of Republican identifiers, while Jews and other faiths and Catholics made up the final one-sixth.

Faith-Based Party Coalitions in 2008

Table 8.2 provides similar information for 2008, calculated in the same fashion (for an overview of religion and the 2008 election, see Espinosa 2009). The religious categories have been made as similar as possible to 1952, but vast changes in American society mean that comparisons between the two years need to be made with caution. One difference is that the composite category of other faiths had become large enough to have a separate entry, reflecting the increase in size of groups such as Muslims, Buddhists, and Hindus. Another difference is the definition of the ethnic categories: in Table 8.2, the new ethnic Catholics and new ethnic Protestants reflected changes in immigration, especially the presence of Hispanics

Table 8.2 Religious groups and partisanship in the public, 2008

Religious groups	Net Democratic partisanship	Democratic	Independent	Republican	% Electorate
Black Protestants	71.0	79.1	12.8	8.1	9.0
Other faiths	67.2	75.4	16.4	8.2	1.5
Jews	50.0	65.0	20.0	15.0	1.5
Ethnic Catholics	41.2	59.3	22.6	18.1	9.0
Liberal faiths	38.9	59.3	20.4	20.4	1.4
Unaffiliated	26.5	47.7	31.1	21.2	14.9
Less observant white Catholics	17.5	49.7	18.0	32.2	8.4
ALL	9.2	44.9	19.4	35.7	100.0
Less observant white mainline Protestants	7.9	45.1	17.8	37.2	9.2
Ethnic Protestants	−4.7	37.4	20.4	42.1	5.9
Observant white Catholics	−8.2	38.4	15.0	46.6	7.4
Less observant white evangelical Protestants	−7.8	35.4	21.4	43.2	9.9
Observant white mainline Protestants	−10.0	39.5	11.0	49.5	5.3
Other Christians	−39.8	17.4	25.4	57.2	3.5
Observant white evangelical Protestants	−43.3	21.9	12.9	65.2	13.4

Source: 2008 National Survey of Religion and Politics (N=4000).

and Asians.[3] As in 1952, Americans were on balance Democratic in 2008 (9.2 percentage points in the "All" row). Overall, there were more independents in 2008 than 1952, and also evidence of greater partisan polarization within many of the religious categories.

Once again the top four groups in Table 8.2 were strongly Democratic. Black Protestants were by far the most Democratic group, followed by the composite category of other faiths. Jews and ethnic Catholics (largely Hispanics) came next, at somewhat lower levels of net Democratic partisanship. So the top four Democratic religious groups in 2008 were more diverse than in 1952, with Protestants added to Catholics, Jews, and other faiths.

One important change from 1952 was the increased net Democratic partisanship of black Protestants. This pattern was not new to 2008, having developed over time largely as the consequence of the civil rights movements. Black Protestants were a larger group in 2008 than in 1952. The new ethnic Catholics were a smaller group than the old ethnic Catholics, and largely a product of new kinds of immigration. Such immigration had its largest relative effect on the growth of the other faiths group. At the same time, however, the relative size of the Jewish population declined, so that the combination of Jews and other faiths was about the same relative size in both election years. In 2008, all these groups combined for one-fifth of the electorate—about the same proportion as the top four Democratic groups in 1952. So the historic affinity of many minority faiths for the Democrats persisted in 2008, even though the particular groups had changed.

The next three categories in Table 8.2 were also on balance Democratic, but at a lower level. In relative terms, the composite category of liberal faiths had moved from being evenly divided in 1952 to having a Democratic bias in 2008 (but had not changed in relative size). The unaffiliated remained Democratic and also retained their relative position compared to other groups in terms of net partisanship. Less observant white Catholics came next in Table 8.2, having dropped in the relative level of net Democratic partisanship compared to 1952. And note the sharp difference between the less observant and observant Catholics, with the latter in the Republican camp.

Another major change was the relative size of the unaffiliated category, which was more than twice the percentage of the electorate in 1952 (on the change in the size of the major religious groups in the post-war period, see J. Green and Dionne 2008). The less observant Catholic category was substantially larger in 2008 as well, reflecting in part the growth of the white Catholic community over the period. In part, these changes reflect the impact of secularization on American religion in the form of an increase in less observant and non-religious populations.

---

[3] In 2008, new ethnic Catholics were defined as Hispanics and other non-whites. New ethnic Protestants were defined the same way, except that African Americans were included in the black Protestant categories.

Two groups on the Republican side of net partisanship had moved in a Democratic direction from 1952: less observant white mainline Protestants and new ethnic Protestants (largely Hispanic). This pattern resembles the path of the less observant Catholics, but with the opposite partisan implications. Here, too, note the sharp difference between the less observant and observant mainline Protestants. The former group was smaller in relative terms, owing in large part to the decline in the relative size of mainline Protestants as a whole. The new ethnic Protestants were more evenly divided in partisan terms in 2008 rather than solidly Republican as in 1952. The key difference may be the ethnicity of the group, with Hispanic Protestants being more open to the Democrats than European ethnicities in the past. These new ethnic Protestants of 2008 were modestly larger in relative terms than the old ethnic Protestants in 1952.

The remaining five groups showed net Republican partisanship. Two of these groups, observant white Catholics and less observant white evangelical Protestants, had moved from the Democratic to the Republican camp between 1952 and 2008. This substantial shift puts their modest level of net Republican partisanship in proper perspective. Observant Catholics were about the same proportion of the adult population as in 1952 and less observant Evangelicals were substantially larger; in both cases, the change was part of the relative growth of white Catholics and Evangelicals since 1952.

In 2008, observant mainline Protestants were still among the strong Republican groups, but at a lower relative level than in 1952, largely owing to an increase in the proportion of independents in their ranks. More importantly, their relative size had fallen dramatically—from one-fifth to about one-twentieth of the adult population, reflecting the overall decline of white mainline Protestants. The final two groups reported the highest net Republican partisanship, the composite category of other Christians and observant white Evangelicals. The other Christians were substantially more Republican in relative terms than in 1952—and also larger in relative terms. Here the key trend appears to be a Republican shift and steady growth among Mormons.

Observant white Evangelicals were about the same relative size in 2008, but shifted their partisanship from being solidly Democratic to being the strongest Republican group. But even here, note the substantial difference between the observant and less observant Evangelicals. In sum, the most Republican religious groups were also more diverse in 2008 than in 1952, with observant white Evangelicals and Catholics joining other Christians and observant mainline Protestants. In some respects, Evangelicals enjoyed higher levels of social status by 2008, continuing the link between socially prominent Protestants and the GOP.

These patterns illustrate the ethno-theological politics of the post-New Deal era, with a new feature being the sharp differences based on religious observance. These differences substantially restructured the partisanship of white Catholics and evangelical and mainline Protestants compared to 1952. It may also help account for other changes, such as the increased net Democratic partisanship of the liberal faiths; the increased relative size of the unaffiliated; and the net Republican partisanship of the other Christians.

However, the move of all white Evangelicals to the GOP reveals that more typical ethno-religious shifts had occurred as well. Other such ethno-religious changes may include the increased Democratic partisanship of black Protestants; the Democratic bias of the new ethnic Catholics and Protestants; and the swelling ranks of the other faiths. And the partisan differences between the three largest white Christian traditions did not entirely disappear. For example, note that the white Catholic groups were more Democratic than their evangelical and mainline counterparts at both levels of observance.

The political impact of these patterns can be seen in the proportion of Democratic and Republican partisan publics that came from these religious groups. The first four Democratic groups accounted for one-third of all self-identified Democrats in 2008, with black Protestants the single largest source of partisans. The next five groups (including less observant mainline and new ethnic Protestants) made up some two-fifths of all Democrats, with the unaffiliated being the single largest contributor (and second largest source overall). These figures sum to a little less than three-quarters of all self-identified Democrats. Thus, a little more than one-quarter of the party's partisans came from groups that on balance identified with the Republicans.

With regard to the GOP, the five strongest groups accounted for three-fifths of all self-identified Republicans, with observant white Evangelicals the single largest source of partisans. Meanwhile, the middle five categories in Table 8.2 made up another third of the Republican public, for a total of more than 90 percent. The strongest Democratic groups provided only about one-fourteenth of self-identified Republicans. Thus, ethnicity and race were still crucial parts of faith-based coalitions in 2008. But it is worth noting the impact of the ethno-theological groups: in 2008 less observant white Christian groups and the unaffiliated contributed more than two-fifths of all self-identified Democrats, while the observant white Christian groups and other Christians provided more than two-fifths of self-identified Republicans.

THE PARTY FAITHFUL

The questions asked about religion and politics in the 2008 presidential campaign presumed the current faith-based party coalitions. The query about Obama's outreach to white Christians concerned the possibility of drawing votes away from the Republican coalition. One reason these voters might have been hard to reach was Obama's special appeal to black Protestants and other religious minorities, groups already at the heart of the Democratic coalition. And such appeals could have damaged Obama's support from unaffiliated voters, another Democratic constituency. Likewise, the question about McCain reflected his need to mobilize a key part of the GOP base (observant white evangelical Protestants) without alienating another part (Mormons and other Christians), while at the same time securing voters that leaned Democratic (such as less observant white mainline and new ethnic Protestants).

In fact, Obama did make some gains among white Christians who had supported Republicans in the past, but even larger gains among the Democratic-leaning groups.[4] However, Obama's biggest success came in mobilizing the Democratic base of religious minorities, and the unaffiliated. The case of black Protestants is instructive: Obama received about the same percentage of the black Protestant vote as his predecessors in 2004 and 2000, but their turnout at the polls was much higher. In this sense, the Obama victory represents a modest turn toward ethno-religious politics. However, McCain largely held onto the Republican religious constituencies, keeping the election closer than might have been anticipated given the poor economy, but otherwise losing ground among other kinds of religious voters necessary for a victory. So the religious elements of the major party coalitions were part of the political bedrock over which the 2008 campaign ebbed and flowed. In 2008, these flows benefited the Democrats, unlike in the 2004 election, when they favored the GOP.

In the broadest sense, such faith-based politics were not new in 2008. After all, similar patterns obtained in 1952 when the Eisenhower campaign sought to add Catholic and evangelical votes to the Republican base of mainline Protestants— and the Democratic campaign tried to do the opposite (Reichley 1985a: 224–35). As we have seen, religious groups played similar roles back to the beginning of the two-party system: religion has been an important source of politically relevant values and interests, and consequently, religious groups have been among the basic building "blocs" of the major party coalitions. The particular impact of religious groups has changed as American religion and American politics changed. Sometimes these shifts were changes in degree (resembling the erosion of the political bedrock by campaigns), but sometimes there have been changes in kind (more like the opening of a new fault line in the political bedrock).

The 2008 election revealed evidence of one such change in kind, which began to develop near the end of the New Deal party system. This change was from coalitions based on ethno-religious groups (and religious affiliation) to coalitions where ethno-theological groups (and religious observance) were important. The

---

[4] For an early assessment of the faith-based vote in 2008, see Pew Forum on Religion and Public Life 2008.

major party coalitions in 1952 were good examples of ethno-religious politics, and in that sense, resembled the faith-based coalitions of past eras. In contrast, the major party coalitions in 2008 represented a difference from past eras due to a prominent role for ethno-theological groups. This change helps explain some of the political foment of the last quarter of the twentieth century and the initial years of the twenty-first century, including the much debated "culture wars."

The comparison of 1952 and 2008 reveals that faith-based coalitions can change, and quite dramatically, over relatively short periods of time. So it is worth asking: what will the structure of faith-based politics look like in the future? Three scenarios suggest themselves (see J. Green 2007, ch. 8, for a fuller discussion of these scenarios).

First, the present ethno-theological politics could continue, with deepening divisions based on religious observance. Such a trend could eventually extend to all religious communities, including the religious minorities, so that observant black Protestants, Jews, and Hispanics would back one party, while their less observant co-religionists would support the other. It could be that the election of the first African American president would reduce the power of race and ethnicity, allowing the "culture wars" to spread across the religious landscape. If taken to its logical conclusion, this scenario would render religious affiliation and ethno-religious groups irrelevant to party coalitions.

A second scenario is the opposite of the first: a return to ethno-religious politics, with divisions based on religious affiliation becoming more important. Such a trend could involve the appearance of new ethno-religious groups fostered by immigration, institutionalization, and religious revivals. As in the past, an increased pluralism in American society could make racial, ethnic, and religious identities more salient politically. In such a context, white Christians might find common ground with each other, reducing divisions based on religious observance. Perhaps the "culture wars" would revert to "ethnicity wars" as in the past, fueled by economic issues. If taken to its logical conclusion, this scenario would render religious observance and ethno-theological groups irrelevant to party coalitions.

A third scenario is the most speculative. It is possible that a new aspect of religion will become politicized in much the same way that religious observance became politically relevant in recent times. For example, suppose that spirituality became associated with distinct values and interests, perhaps linked to heightened concerns about the environment. Then "spiritual" voters from many religious affiliations and levels of observance would be attracted to one party, while less "spiritual" voters of all sorts would support the other party. Hence faith-based coalitions would be characterized by "ethno-spiritual" groups of one kind or another. This speculation may seem odd, but in 1952 the future politicizing of religious observance might have seemed just as odd. In any event, it is likely that religion will continue to be a key element of party coalitions as long as some aspect of faith is associated with politically relevant values and interests.

PART IV

PARTIES IN THE ELECTORAL PROCESS

CHAPTER 9

PARTY NOMINATING PROCEDURES AND RECRUITMENT— STATE AND LOCAL LEVEL

RAYMOND J. LA RAJA

THE candidate selection process lies at the heart of democratic politics. It concerns nothing less than choosing potential leaders of the government who will shape and implement policies. Most democracies have developed a complex, multistage process involving peer review of candidates for the party nomination and mass support in general elections to select government leadership. In the United States, the party nomination happens to be more inclusive than most democracies because of the widespread use of direct primaries. American states, however, vary considerably with respect to inclusiveness, potentially affecting who runs for office and succeeds. The selection process may also shape how such leaders will govern in terms of ideology and responsiveness to constituencies.

No selection process, even in the relatively open system found in the US, gives citizens unbounded choice in determining who runs for office. Instead, political leaders use various institutions and practices to winnow potential leadership. At the general election, candidates have already been filtered based on characteristics related to ideology, campaign skills, or other political resources, including access to campaign funds. Thus, the electorate is presented with a limited range of choices for picking leaders to govern and pursue policies. Quite obviously, the winnowing process raises important questions about democratic theory and practice.

The selection process also engages normative questions related to democracy. On one side, there is the perspective that democracy simply requires voters to choose among teams of potential officeholders (Downs 1957). The composition of those teams reflects decisions made by political elites who desire to control government through winning elections. The voters indirectly shape the party team because pragmatic elites are inclined to put forward candidates and policies acceptable to a majority of voters. On the other side of the debate, there are those who support a view that democracy requires grassroots participation at various stages of political decision making (see, for example, Barber 1984). Viewed this way, participation in the nomination allows citizens to hold elites accountable (Geer and Shere 1992) and, more symbolically, to provide civic meaning and regime legitimacy.

The locus for these contending perspectives of democracy is the political party. Through this essential mediating institution, choices get made about who will run for posts in the government. Since candidates use the party label when running for office, the political parties are positioned uniquely as gatekeepers in a procedure that distinguishes them from all other political organizations (Sartori 1976; Schattschneider 1942; Ranney 1965). To be sure, interest groups and informal social networks influence candidate selection in the US, but the party label remains indispensable when seeking office. For this reason, parties are guaranteed a place at the table, and analysis of the selection process provides insights into their linkage function in American politics.

Observing how parties award their label also reveals essential aspects about the party system. Battles over the party nomination suggest the nature of factional disputes within and outside the organization. The degree to which factional battles over nominations take place within parties indicates opportunities or obstacles for third party movements. Additionally, the ideologies of party candidates who succeed in the nomination suggest the range of ideological conflict in the party system. Ultimately, of course, the quality of candidates emerging from either party influences the intensity of partisan competition.

In the subsequent sections I discuss how the literature addresses three sets of questions about the selection process. First, I look at how the selection process affects *who runs for office*. The central concern here is how different nominating institutions or recruitment practices affect which citizens emerge as candidates. The second set of questions examines *political parties*, asking how the selection process affects the distribution of power in the organization, its ideological coherence, and electoral success. Third, I ask about the effect of selection processes on *political campaigns, representation, and governing.* Here, I explore its impact on voter behavior and how nomination practices influence elite behavior in public office.

*

Overall, the study of non-presidential nominations and recruitment remains surprisingly underexplored given how important it is. With the exception of research on candidate emergence and incumbency advantages in congressional elections, I am puzzled that more work has not been done for state and local elections. The field is dominated by theory and analysis of presidential nomina- tions (see Mayer, Chapter 10 in this volume), where we have learned in exquisite detail how nomination rules matter for who gains advantages securing the party label. For presidential elections, a steady stream of research explains how reforms, technological innovation, and shifts in partisan coalitions affects who runs for office, how candidates campaign, and how winners govern (Reiter 1985; Shafer 1983; Polsby 1983; Ceaser 1979; W. Mayer and Busch 2004). Much has also been written about political parties, and the intrafactional struggles to change nomination rules to favor to some elites (Ranney 1975; Eldersveld 1982; Jewell 1984; Shafer 1988; Leon Epstein 1986).

The lack of a solid and consistent body of work on state and local nominating process is particularly surprising given that data are available to test propositions about how individuals enter politics and who succeeds. The fifty states provide a rich source of institutional and cultural variation regarding recruitment methods, electoral laws, composition of the nominating electorate, and political traditions. In 2008, 127 candidates sought the party nomination for the US Senate and 2,038 for the US House; and more than 8,000 sought it for state legislatures across the nation. A well-designed comparative study of the distinctive practices across the American states has the potential to discover causal links between selection prac- tices and characteristics of those who choose to run, how they campaign, and how they govern. To be sure, variations in state primary election laws and political party rules make classification of data difficult (Galderisi, Ezra, and Lyons 2001), but this has hardly been an obstacle to studying the process at the presidential level. And true, state-level election data have been much more difficult to come by than federal-level data, but this is changing swiftly as states put election records online and scholars build large time series datasets for public use (Ansolabehere et al. 2007a).

This is not to say that good research on the local and state nominations has been entirely lacking (as I describe below). We possess a fairly solid grasp of the process at the congressional level, particularly district-level factors that affect who runs for the nomination. Recent work on candidate emergence in congressional elections shows the profound influence of incumbency in deterring quality challengers from seeking the nomination. However, even at the congressional level, we know little about how different institutional structures affect candidacies. And we know even less about how the process shapes internal dynamics of political parties, voting behavior, and governing. This gap in knowledge is especially true for non-federal offices where the vast majority of citizens get their start in elective politics.

The knowledge gap is not isolated to studies of the US system. There are relatively few comparative studies, even though more attention has been given to the subject elsewhere than in the American states. Observing the state of the field, one of the leading comparativists put it well, saying that "although we have well-developed theories of voting behavior and elections, which have been examined and replicated in many different national contexts, as a result of this neglect it sometimes appears as if candidates are born by miraculous conception, politically fully clothed, the day the campaign is announced" (Norris 1997: 8). There is little doubt that scholars need to go back further in the process to investigate how candidates arrive on the electoral stage. At the same time, more work must be done to understand the impact of selection practices on political parties, elections, and governing. Keeping this in mind, I turn to the four questions about recruitment and nominations.

How Does the Selection Process Affect Who Runs?

Research on candidacies in the US typically concentrates on the ambitious office-seeker—the so-called "self-starter"—who chooses to run for office on his or her own. The conceptual emphasis among scholars on the candidate-centered campaign reinforces this perspective. Thus, the selection process tends to be viewed in terms of the costs and benefits facing the individual candidate, rather than as a dynamic process engaging various political elites and organizations (but see Dominguez 2005). The dominant perspective, with its narrow focus on individual ambition, fails to capture how such ambition is kindled or extinguished prior to announcing one's candidacy. We are then left wondering why certain kinds of individuals choose to run at all (Maisel and Stone 1997; Fox and Lawless 2005). For this reason, some additional effort needs to be made examining political recruitment *before* candidates appear on the stage.

A less glaring gap in knowledge concerns the effect of institutional variation on candidate selection. Given that ambitious individuals seek office, we need to know more about how different nominating processes and recruitment patterns figure into candidate calculations to run. Moncrief, Squire, and Jewell (2001) set out a practical framework to evaluate the process, urging consideration of systemic, district, and individual variables in assessing the impact on who runs. To date, scholars have done an excellent job understanding district variables (incumbency, partisanship). The profession, however, has done less adequate work in understanding individual-level factors (skills, resources, background, gender, and personal networks), and especially systemic variables (nominating systems, recruitment patterns, and party organizations). In short, much work needs to be done before we understand how, where, and why candidates arrive on election day.

Utility Models

Over the past three decades, the dominant approach to understanding candidate emergence has been economic analysis that applies rational actor or "utility" models. This approach has generated fruitful work beginning with two seminal studies setting forth "ambition theory." Schlesinger (1966) and Black (1972) posited that potential candidates evaluate the availability of political opportunities, which are structurally determined by short-term factors, e.g., the range of offices, political competition, and long-term factors, e.g., prior careers available to the candidate.[1]

Utility models were developed further by Jacobson and Kernell (1981) under the rubric of strategic-actor theory, which demonstrated that quality candidates emerge when they think they can win. In other words, before choosing to run, candidates assess local conditions, such as the incumbent's previous margin of victory, shifts in district partisanship, and contingent events such as scandals (Bond, Covington, and Fleisher 1985; Jacobson 1989; Krasno and Green 1988; Hetherington, Larson, and Globetti 2003). National conditions may also influence the decision, usually measured as an indicator of economic health or some other salient policy issue that favors a party (Jacobson and Kernell 1981; Jacobson 1989). Overall, the decision to seek office is a function of the benefits of the office, the probability of winning, and the cost of running (Abramson, Aldrich, and Rohde 1987; G. Black 1972; Rohde 1979; Jacobson and Kernell 1981; Maestas et al. 2006). It follows from these models that the higher the quality of the incumbent, the lower the chances that a quality challenger will take the risk of jumping into the race (Mondak 1995; Zaller 1998).

Only recently has research examined how *primary* elections figure into the strategic calculus of quality congressional candidates (W. Stone and Maisel 2003). Beyond incumbency factors, this work begins to model candidate emergence as a multistage process that involves both the nomination and general election. Although similar factors help a candidate in both elections (like being a quality candidate), it appears that district partisanship and incumbency have different

---

[1] Although this work acknowledged the importance of long-term factors, there has been little effort to study such factors systematically.

effects at each stage. Specifically, quality challengers in the out-party are less likely to emerge in the nomination when the partisan makeup of the district favors the potential candidate (precisely because they are likely to face more competition at this stage), but more likely to emerge in the general as district partisanship becomes more favorable. The logic is that quality candidates consider the joint conditional probability of winning both stages.

Scholars have also observed how potential challengers in statewide races use information in both election stages to make decisions about running. Looking at senate and gubernatorial elections from 1976 through 1998, one study finds that incumbent-party challengers run against incumbents who did poorly in the previous primary election, whereas out-party challengers run against incumbents who did poorly in the previous general election (Lazarus 2008). In the primary stage, *weak* out-party challengers enter when they believe they will not face strong out-party challengers.

With few exceptions, the structure of primaries on candidate decisions has not been a major subject of study. One nominating structure that has received a lot of attention is the use of runoffs in primaries when no candidate receives a majority of the vote. It has attracted scrutiny because seven of the original eleven confederate states use the runoff, with Florida eliminating it only as recently as 2002 (Glaser 2006). V. O. Key observed that the runoff in the South likely ensures a candidate cannot win the nomination without garnering majority support. Thus, factional candidates would have a difficult time winning, although the runoff system might entice more of them to run (Rice 1985; W. Berry and Canon 1993; B. Canon 1978; S. Wright and Riker 1989). After all, even losers can earn influence in the subsequent round by bargaining and supporting a candidate in the runoff.

Recent work supports Key's argument (Glaser 2005, 2006) by demonstrating in congressional elections that the runoff primary in most southern states serves the purpose of blocking the nomination of fringe candidates who might win the most votes in the first round of primary voting. Such candidates subsequently lose to a more centrist candidate who picks up support from voters who backed failed candidates in the first round. However, a study of runoff primaries for statewide offices suggests that runoffs have a small effect on candidate entry (Engstrom and Engstrom 2008). Indeed, the vast majority of nominations under plurality rule (roughly, three-fourths of nominations) are made by a majority support of voters. In runoff primary states, about one-third of contested primaries require runoffs, and of these, in about one-third of the races the first-round winner loses in the runoff (Engstrom and Engstrom 2008).

According to several scholars, ambition theory adequately explains candidate behavior regardless of the nominating system. As evidence they point to minimal differences in the motivations and quality of candidates before and after primaries were implemented in American states (Carson and Roberts 2005). The inference is based on the observation that incumbents fared no worse against "quality" challengers, here defined as those who held previous elective office. This measure, introduced by Jacobson (1989), has been used extensively in studies of elections. Nonetheless, the quality of candidates may still matter more today under combination of nomination rules and new campaign dynamics (Cox and Katz 1996). Surely the contemporary media environment places different demands on candidates than previously. Moreover, higher pay and status—and longer hours—for state legislatures likely attract different kinds of candidates (Hogan 2003b; Squire 2000). It remains far from clear that the introduction of primaries had no effect on the qualities necessary to succeed in elections.

The fact that contemporary candidates require so much money to succeed in potentially competitive primaries should suggest that the nomination process has a different effect on candidate emergence than previously. An analysis of campaign finance laws for state legislative elections during the 1990s shows that low contribution limits increase challenger emergence in general elections because they likely restrain fundraising advantages of incumbents (Hamm and Hogan 2008). Curiously, however, such limits seem to decrease candidate emergence in primaries. The impact of public financing is even less clear. A three-state study suggests that public financing hinders entry into primaries but likely boosts candidate entry in the general election (Hamm and Hogan 2008). Other recent work suggests that the effect of public subsidies on candidate entry is modest (La Raja 2004; K. Mayer, Werner, and Williams 2006).

Sociological Approaches

An alternative to utility models are sociological approaches that emphasize the way political culture and institutional biases shape recruitment and candidacy. This work focuses primarily on the candidacies of women who continue to be underrepresented in American legislatures. The conventional wisdom is that institutional barriers to women's success have been largely broken down, and it is a matter of time before women occupy roughly 50 percent of elective offices. Research points to the fact that women win at the same rates as men once they decide to run for office (Burrell 1994; Darcy, Welch, and Clark 1987; Seltzer, Newman, and Leighton 1997). Consequently, once the supply of women pursuing political careers expands at the grassroots, more of them will fill the ranks at higher offices until they reach their proportion in the population. This "pipeline theory" assumes that women and minorities serving in lower levels of political office accumulate the same political resources and experience as men to advance to higher office.

The pipeline theory of candidate emergence has been challenged on several fronts. First, survey research suggests that women tend to express significantly lower levels of political ambition than similarly situated men (Fox and Lawless 2004, 2005; Lawless and Fox 2005). Moreover, the gender gap is reflected in patterns of recruitment, namely that women are less likely than men to be asked to run, or to view themselves as qualified to run. In short, the findings point to the continuing influence of traditional sex-role socialization in suppressing the selection of women for public office.

More fundamentally, this argument disputes the underlying assumption of rational choice models that assume ambition is exogenous, merely an attribute that one possesses independently of the political and social environment. Personal circumstances matter, aside from political interest, experience, or resources. For example, female state legislators are less likely to advance to Congress than their male colleagues owing to gender-related differences in occupational backgrounds, family situations, and stages in the life cycle (Mariani 2008). And although women generally win primaries they enter at roughly the same rates, they tend to face greater competition. This suggests that women must be better candidates than their male counterparts in order to fare equally well (Lawless and Pearson 2008).

The influence of political culture is evident in recruitment patterns of the Democratic and Republican parties. Sanbonmatsu (2006a) demonstrates that the differing social bases and opportunity structures in the major parties account for variations in the political careers of women. Whereas women make up a greater proportion of the pool of eligible candidates in the Democratic Party, they face tougher competition getting the nomination and are not recruited as actively as Republican women by gatekeepers in the party.[2] Women are also less likely to hold office in higher-status legislatures (Rule 1981), though more likely to be in the legislature when residing in a state with high proportions of professional women (Hill 1981; Norrander and Wilcox 1998; A. Nelson 1991; Rule 1990; C. Williams 1990).

Beyond District-Level Factors

These studies suggest that political scientists need to do a better job of understanding the systemic variables that affect candidacy, as well as develop more fine-grained analyses of individual-level factors that shape ambition and willingness to run. The profession has done an excellent job of explaining the impact of district-level variables, especially incumbency, on candidate emergence. The holy grail, it seems,

---

[2] But see Elder (2008) for an analysis of the decline of Republican women in Congress, which she attributes to the growing partisan imbalance for women in state offices (the congressional pipeline), the regional realignment of the parties, and gains made by non-white women (virtually all Democrats) in obtaining congressional seats.

is to fully understand how incumbents possess the kind of electoral advantages that ward off challengers. While this path of research has been successful, future gains in knowledge are likely to be marginal. Instead, scholars should look further back in the process to understand why some kinds of potential candidates never consider running at all. Or exploit time-series data to understand how the political environment has affected the quality of candidates running for office. Such analyses are more difficult because they involve semi-heroic efforts to collect data and to develop concepts that aid in making stronger claims about causality, even as we move back further in the "funnel."

The opportunity exists to exploit fifty-state variation that would allow a shift in focus from individual to system-level analysis. This strategy would provide insights into how (or if) different nominating systems produce different kinds of candidates. In the European context, research on party recruitment has shown how electoral and party rules allocate political resources, enabling some political elites to emerge over others (R. Katz and Mair 1995; Carty 2004; Kirchheimer 1966; Panebianco 1988). Indeed, comparativists have made the claim that institutional variation matters more in explaining women candidacies than cultural explanations (Norris 2004). In the US, this kind of work has been confined to the study of presidential nominations with few exceptions (Sanbonmatsu 2006a).[3] The findings have implications for studies of minority recruitment, about which there is minimal work (but see Branton 2008) beyond the literature pertaining to the Voting Rights Act and the effects of redistricting on minority candidacies (La Raja forthcoming).

In short, we have a tenuous grasp of the institutional and cultural aspects of the selection process at the state and local level. It remains somewhat of a mystery who fills the gap left behind by local party organizations in recruiting candidates. To be sure, we know that state legislative leaders and the congressional campaign committees are active recruiters, particularly in competitive states (Herrnson 2004; Sanbonmatsu 2006b; Shea 1995). But presumably, local notables help party legislative party committees identify quality candidates (Carey, Niemi, and Powell 1998). To the extent that clusters of elites serve as gatekeepers in the process, the tools of social network analysis could be useful. We know that being asked matters (Maisel, Stone, and Maestas 2001) but we have not identified patterns of recruitment and candidate emergence that might be linked to nominating structures or local political cultures. And there is much more to learn

---

[3] Interestingly, Norris's findings come to the opposite conclusion with respect to the role of gatekeepers. Norris finds that when party leaders, rather than rank-and-file members, choose candidate lists or assign gender quotas, more women enter politics. Sanbonmatsu, however, finds that cultural biases among party elites keep women out of politics. Comparative work in the US context might help explain the different findings.

about the role of political parties and allied interest groups in the selection process, a subject to which I turn next.

What Is the Effect of Nominating Processes on Political Parties?

Until the end of the nineteenth century, party leaders and their cliques chose who would run for office with decision making shrouded from public view. The introduction of direct primaries cleared some air in these smoke-filled rooms by forcing parties to open the selection process to voters. Practices changed swiftly between 1896 and 1915 when all but a few states moved from caucus systems to direct primaries to nominate candidates for federal, state, and local offices (Ansolabehere et al. 2007a). In most states, primaries were imposed by the state governments, though occasionally with support of party officials (Ware 2002). In other states, mostly in the South, party officials moved to adopt the primary without state actions.

Much good work on the relationship between the selection process and internal party dynamics was done decades ago (Ranney 1965; Eldersveld 1964; Epstein 1967), but there has been little follow-up. One possible reason is that the dominant approach, ambition theory, gives little weight to party organizational behavior in the nomination process, except in rare cases (Kazee and Thornberry 1990; Sanbonmatsu 2002b; Maisel, Stone, and Maestas 2001). Collectively, the profession remains in the grip of the candidate-centered paradigm. To move forward, it is worth drawing on theoretical constructs from comparative studies of European parties to help understand the distribution of power within party organizations in the United States (Panebianco 1988; Ware 1996; R. Katz and Mair 1994).

A great deal has changed for party organizations in the past two decades that warrants renewed scrutiny on the relationship between the party organization and selection process. The national committees are wealthier, more unified, and more engaged in elections than perhaps in their collective histories (Herrnson 1988; Aldrich 1995; Kolodny 1998). Many state parties have undergone similar changes (Aldrich 2000; Frendreis and Gitelson 1999; Cotter 1989; La Raja 2008) and party committees and allied interest groups at all levels appear more engaged in candidate selection and nomination (Francia et al. 2003b; Frendreis, Gibson, and Vertz 1990). With state legislatures becoming more professional, leaders have greater institutional capacity to recruit and support party candidates (Jewell and Whicker 1994; Gierzynski 1992; Cindy Simon 1995; Moncrief, Squire, and Jewell 2001). Not least, the legal environment has changed considerably, with the courts giving greater deference to party associational rights, even allowing them to reject state-mandated primary rules that party officials find objectionable (Lowenstein 1993; Jewell and Whicker 1994). These transformations make it worthwhile to pursue research in the following areas.

Factional Power

In presidential nominations, party officials and activists pay considerable attention to nomination rules. Much has been written about the causes and consequences of the McGovern–Fraser reforms of the early 1970s (see, for example, Polsby 1983). This kind of analysis has rarely been applied systematically to the study of nominating institutions and party dynamics below the office of the presidency. In theory, at least, control over nomination rules and resources should give leverage to some factions over others (Panebianco 1988). Since the nomination process reflects a core function of party organizations, those who control this process should have significant power to shape the party.

The conventional wisdom is that the onset of primaries weakened the party organization and ushered in an era of candidate-centered campaigns. With direct primaries, candidates typically decide when to run and organize their own campaign (Herrnson 2004). To file for candidacy in most states, candidates need to collect signatures from local voters and pay a small filing fee. In only ten states are nominations partially controlled at a convention. For example, in several states candidates must receive a percentage of support from convention delegates in the district or statewide (usually around 15 percent).[4] Once the campaign begins, candidates might rely for support on friends and neighbors, interest groups, and favorable media coverage to boost their prospects. Thus, it would seem that the current system of direct primaries is capable of allowing candidates with factional support to flourish (Key 1954). However, I know of only a handful of studies that examine how direct primaries affect the degree of factional politics in local and state politics (Ware 2002; Glaser 2006). Glaser (2006) suggests that runoff primaries can be crucial in tamping the emergence of radical factions. Centrist factions in the Republican Party might counter intense minority factions such as the Christian Right, which mobilized in the 1980s and 1990s to nominate candidates and control state party organizations (Rozell and Wilcox 1995).

A favorable legal environment for political parties may encourage factions to contend more aggressively for control over the party. In *Tashjian v. Republican Party of Connecticut*, 479 U.S. 208 (1986), the Court ruled that the state could not prevent political parties from allowing independent voters to vote in their primary

---

[4] But even this rule has been watered down in states like Connecticut where the candidate in either party can collect 2 percent of signatures of district voters to get on the primary ballot.

for the state legislature, even though closed primaries were state law. In another decision with far-reaching implications, *Eu v. San Francisco County Democratic Central Committee*, 489 U.S. 214 (1989), the court overturned California laws that prevented the party from endorsing candidates in the primary, and proscribing its governing structure. Subsequently, the court struck down a law passed by voters for blanket primaries in *California Democratic Party v. Jones*, 530 U.S. 567 (2000). Collectively, these court decisions create an opportunity for partisans to change nomination procedures to advance particularistic or ideological goals. As far as I know, there have been no studies that observe intraparty deliberations over the nomination process or whether changes strengthen the hand of one faction or another. The subject appears ripe for historical analysis through methods in American political development, akin to Mickey's work on the White Primaries in the South (2008).

Party Loyalty and Ideology

Political scientists have long assumed that the decentralized nature of American party nominations creates political parties lacking ideological and policy coherence. Not being reliant on the party leadership for electoral support, American legislators can vote against the party when expedient to do so (Dalton and Wattenberg 2000). Single-member districts and candidate-centered elections motivate them to nurture a personal constituency that makes them less vulnerable to electoral challenges and demands of the legislative leadership (Fenno 1978; Cain, Ferejohn, and Fiorina 1987), although some studies suggest that the structure of nominations has no effect on party loyalty (Ansolabehere, Hirano, and Snyder 2007b; Haeberle 1985).

Dismay over the policy incoherence of parties spurred an unprecedented effort by political scientists, led by E. E. Schattschneider, to recommend reforms to make political parties more responsible. They suggested that leaders in the national party have more influence in the selection process—and hence more control over members—through a mechanism of peer review for nominations and control over campaign funds (see American Political Science Association 1950). Not surprisingly, the advice of political scientists was ignored. The nomination process in the US remains highly decentralized and the institutionalization of direct primaries precludes significant party intervention. In spite of this, however, American parties have become the kind of responsible organizations that Schattschneider and his colleagues sought. Party voting in Congress is as high as ever and the electorate perceives greater differences between the two parties since the American National Election Studies began tracking voters (Layman, Carsey, and Horowitz 2006).

Some have argued that ideological polarization of the parties is attributable, in part, to the primary system (Burden 2001; Fiorina, Abrams, and Pope 2005). The claim is that closed primaries, in particular, attract the most ideological voters in either party, especially in districts favoring one of the major parties. Consequently, candidates get elected by a small, ideological core that tends to vote in primaries rather than the median voter in districts with two-party competition. The process makes the party ideologically purer because it hollows out the moderate positions in the legislature by reducing the number of crossover politicians who might be conservative Democrats or liberal Republicans.[5] Fearing that voters in primaries might nominate candidates who are too extreme to win the general election, several state parties have adopted open primary rules to make the nominating electorate more representative of the general electorate.

But is it true that direct primaries have these effects on party ideology? Ranney (1968) noted that the preferences of primary voters and non-voters are similar, regardless of demographic differences. Subsequent studies support this view (Norrander 1989b; Geer 1989). However, the weight of research points in the opposite direction, namely, that the structure of primaries affects voter demographics and preferences. Exit poll data for presidential primaries, from 1988 through 2000, indicate that open and modified-open primaries attract voters that are ideologically more centrist and representative of the electorate than in closed primaries (Kaufmann, Gimpel, and Hoffman 2003). Others have found that closed primaries are associated with greater extremism (Geer 1988, 1989; E. Gerber and Morton 1998; Grofman and Brunell 2001), although curiously, semi-open and semi-closed appear more moderating than either pure closed and open primaries (Kanthak and Morton 2001). Moreover, interest groups seeking to promote an ideological agenda now have the resources and technology to sponsor primary challenges against incumbents who dissatisfy them. Even if the candidates they support lose, these "party purity" groups send a message to warn other party members from straying (Murakami 2008).[6]

More recently, work by Abramowitz (2008) challenges the prevailing consensus about primaries and party polarization. Using exit poll data for the 2006 elections, he demonstrates that ideologies of primary and general election voters in either party are not significantly different. The source of ideological polarization, he argues, is the concrete fact that partisans are deeply divided on a range of policy issues (D. King 1997; Jacobson 2000; Layman, Carsey, and Horowitz 2006). Thus, the polarization debate continues, with no consensus yet on the sources of sharp partisan division.

---

[5] Paradoxically, the theoretical expectation, at least in studies of European parties, is that inclusiveness leads to factionalism, while giving greater influence to party leaders, increasing ideological unity and hence "responsible" parties. In the US, however, the primary may, in fact, create the opposite effect because American party leaders, who occupy positions in government, tend to be pragmatic as a strategy to win elections, while primary voters tend to be ideological and less concerned about nominating candidates who may lose in the general election.

[6] Lieberman lost the primary, but because Connecticut lacks a sore-loser provision he was able to win the general election as an independent candidate.

Partisan Competition and the Party System

Not surprisingly, V. O. Key was among the first to give serious thought to how direct primaries shaped party competition and the party system. In *Southern Politics in State and Nation* (1949) Key discussed how the primary was used to create meaningful electoral choice in one-party states in the South. But in his article in the *American Political Science Review* (Key 1954), he fleshed out in greater detail how primary elections affected the minority party and party systems in the North as well. Key observed that direct primaries caused institutional decay of the minority party in districts where they were disadvantaged by eliminating the necessity to maintain local party organizations in all counties for the purpose of state nominating conventions. When electoral competition occurs only within the majority party, the second party loses its monopoly on opposition and the party starts to unravel. It is drained of talent as the politically ambitious migrate to the majority party, and fails to hold itself accountable through consistent critique of the majority party. Consequently, the minority party is in such shambles that it can hardly govern responsibly even if it is swept into office by scandal in the majority party.

Given that so many legislative districts have become lopsided in the past two decades, it is worth revisiting Key's arguments about how primaries may exacerbate institutional decay of the minority party. As of this writing, there are no Republican members of Congress from New England. How has this process of decay unfolded, and what are the prospects for Republican renewal? And what of Democrats in the South where Republicans have established seemingly insurmountable strongholds outside of urban districts? To a large extent, these trends toward lopsided districts may reflect ideological realignments in the electorate (Carmines and Stanley 1992; Levine, Carmines, and Huckfeldt 1997; Abramowitz and Saunders 1998; Fleisher and Bond 2001), or the possibility that partisans are more polarized on core policy issues (Layman and Carsey 2002b). In future work, close inspection of intrapartisan dynamics during the nomination in lopsided districts might reveal the possibilities for genuine two-party competition. For example, Black (2004) has observed that Democrats are unlikely to fare well because the Democratic Party in the electorate, which influences the nomination, is so different from the median voter in the general election.[7]

As V. O. Key argued, the strength of the opposition party determines intraparty competitiveness in both party primaries (Rice 1985). An alternative view contends that the structure of the nominations determines competition, with runoff

---

[7] According to Black, the contemporary southern Democratic Party is majority female, approximately 52 percent white, 38 percent African American, and 10 percent Hispanic. This demographic, he argues, will put increasing pressure on party leadership to recruit and support candidates who share liberal ideologies—as well as the gender, race, and ethnicity—of most Democratic voters. Since Democratic voters are considerably different than the median southern voter, the party will be disadvantaged in general elections.

primaries enticing more candidates to run, at least in the South (S. Wright and Riker 1989; B. Canon 1978). A subsequent study demonstrated an interactive effect, namely that both structure and partisan strength matter (W. Berry and Canon 1993). Runoff primaries help increase competitiveness when the party opposition is weak, but this dynamic attenuates significantly as the opposition gains strength, i.e., there is less of a difference in competitiveness between runoffs and single primaries.

If two-party competition wanes in parts of the nation, then direct primaries might, presumably, provide a mechanism to hold political elites accountable through competitive intraparty elections. But the literature suggests that primaries are rarely competitive. One study shows that only half of open seats in congressional primaries were competitive and just a handful for races with incumbents who rarely lost (Goodliffe and Magleby 2001). It was not always this way. Primaries were competitive in the first thirty or forty years after they were introduced (Ansolabehere et al. 2007a). But then competition declined precipitously. Why? To be sure, incumbents had advantages in primaries even in the first decades of the twentieth century when they were introduced. But the so-called "sophomore surge" advantage grew significantly, albeit gradually, over time (Ansolabehere et al. 2007a). Explanations for why incumbent advantages grew during this period remain speculative. Was it the weakening of party organizations, or increased role of media? Regardless, more work could be done here to understand the implications for candidate emergence and political competition in the general election.

Given that primaries are so infrequently contested, does this mean they are irrelevant to political competition for office and fail to serve the purpose of holding political elites accountable? Not necessarily. The very existence of primaries figures into the considerations of potential candidates and the behavior of incumbents (W. Stone and Maisel 2003; Maestas et al. 2006). Incumbents, of course, do not want to face a primary challenge so they will do everything possible to create the appearance of invulnerability (Grofman and Brunell 2001). Even if they win, incumbents fear the challenge will weaken them in the general election and, at the very least, cost them time and money in waging the internal party battle.

The behavior of incumbents raises the obvious question of whether competitive primaries affect the prospects of the party nominee in the general election. Do hard-fought primaries help or hurt the party nominee? There has been quite a bit of work in this "divisive primary" literature. One causal argument is that voters loyal to the primary loser may find it difficult to switch over to the candidate they voted against (Kenney and Rice 1987; Southwell 1986) or that activists supporting the primary loser's campaign may not work for the primary winner (Comer 1976; W. Stone, Atkeson, and Rapoport 1992; but see Atkeson 1998). There is also the argument that hard-fought primaries tend to flesh out negative issues that could hurt the party nominee in the general election. At first blush, the findings in this literature seem muddled. Several studies find that divisive primaries hurt candidates in the general election (Abramowitz 1988; R. Bernstein 1977; Segura and Nicholson 1995). Others say there is no relationship (A. Hacker 1965; Kenney 1988) or that it is inconclusive (Born 1981; Hogan 2003a; Kenney and Rice 1984). Recent scholarship now finds that divisive primaries may actually *help* House challengers (Alvarez, Canon, and Sellers 1995; Herrnson 2000).

Lazarus (2005) seems to put his finger on why findings are discrepant. He points out convincingly that most studies do not distinguish the implications of divisive primaries for incumbents and challengers. If scholars modeled challengers and incumbents *independently* they would find that divisiveness hurts incumbents but helps challengers. The difference can be attributed to candidate strategic behaviors. Non-incumbents tend to emerge when they think they can win. Hence, more candidates enter the race with a vulnerable incumbent, creating the divisive primary. The better performance of challengers in the general election is thus correlated with divisiveness simply because the race attracts more quality challengers. Conversely, the incumbents who survive tend to do more poorly in the general election precisely because they are vulnerable and attract tougher challengers. It is not the divisive primary per se that causes poorer results in the general election but the quality of the challengers. Other recent work extends the concept of strategic behavior to the actions of political elites who support (or withdraw support from) primary candidates depending on the competitiveness of the general election (Dominguez 2005).

Third Parties

Although primaries may weaken party organizations, it has been argued that direct primaries reduce the possibility of third party challenges to the major parties. Candidates dissatisfied with a party's policy may choose to capture a major-party nomination in primaries, rather than pursue office under a third party label with a smaller probability of winning the general election (Bibby and Maisel 2003; Leon Epstein 1986; Rosenstone et al. 1996). Certainly, there has been a decline of third party electoral support over the past century (Hirano and Snyder 2007). It is unclear, however, the degree to which electoral reforms such as the introduction of direct primaries or the Australian ballot affected third party decline.

Crespin (2004) finds evidence that the introduction of direct primaries reduced the total number of candidates competing in congressional elections (ostensibly because fewer individuals ran as third party candidates). The logic is that direct primaries make major-party politicians more responsive to constituents, rendering third parties less meaningful. However, recent research attributes the decline of third parties during the twentieth century to New Deal era policies that co-opted electoral support of left-wing parties (Hirano and

Snyder 2007). The introduction of sore-loser laws and antifusion laws probably also matter in shrinking third party activity (on the latter, see Masket 2007).

Voter Participation, Representation, and Governing

Voter Participation

Theory suggests that open primaries, which are more inclusive, increase turnout relative to closed primaries. This is supported by empirical work on gubernatorial primaries (Jewell 1984). Competitive primaries also appear to boost general election turnout (Kanthak and Morton 2001), which runs against findings that divided primaries make supporters of losing candidates stay home on election day. The type of primary may also affect the degree to which states' residents consider themselves independents (Norrander 1989a). There is limited research on the relationship between primary elections and voter loyalty, although Harvey and Mukherjee (2006) find that ticket splitting increased following the introduction of the direct primary in the 1910s and 1920s.

Otherwise, studies of voter behavior in non-presidential primaries are minimal. Knowledge comes mostly from studies of non-partisan elections (Schaffner, Streb, and Wright 2001; Squire and Smith 1988), and presidential nominations (Bartels 1988). This work indicates that the absence of the party label motivates voters to use other information shortcuts, especially incumbency. Since primary voters in non-presidential campaigns typically receive relatively little political information, it is likely that non-party heuristics (incumbency, race, gender, age) are even more important than in presidential nominations. The low information environment may also increase the significance of media coverage or endorsements by interest groups, parties, and other political elites (Bardwell 2002; Jewell and Morehouse 2001; Ansolabehere et al. 2006; Iyengar 2002; Shields, Goidel, and Tadlock 1995). As far as I know, there has been no work on how endorsements and media coverage matter for different kinds of primaries in state and local elections.

Representation and Governing

Finally, I turn to the literature that addresses the question of how recruitment and nominations affect governing. Does the greater inclusiveness of American direct primaries produce better democratic outcomes in areas of policy, political leadership, responsiveness, or popular legitimacy? As stated previously, the response depends considerably on various conceptions of democracy. If the concern is substantive, then perhaps the inclusiveness of American primaries is not necessarily an important feature in the democratic process. If, on the other hand, the concern is about participation or procedural transparency, then primaries assume greater importance.

From a substantive perspective, the use of primaries should be more important when rank-and-file legislators have significant power in policymaking (Cross 2008). Lacking certitude that a politician will conform to the party platform once elected, voters possess an additional check on candidates in the nomination. The importance of this check increases as the degree of interparty competition wanes. Given that US general elections are infrequently competitive and that politicians can ignore party leadership (relative to other democratic systems), there is a strong argument for inclusiveness in selecting party candidates.

Another argument for inclusiveness is the two-party system. When voters in a general election have significant choices among political parties, then inclusive nominations are probably less important and voters may be more willing to let parties control the nomination process. A good test of this hypothesis is to observe the relationship between states with restrictive primary laws and the ease with which third parties or independent candidates can enter general elections. For example, New York and Connecticut have relatively restrictive primary laws (both are closed, both require party registration many months before the primary), yet each is relatively open to third party entrants for the general election. New York allows fusion laws, and Connecticut does not have a sore-loser provision, enabling candidates who lose the primary to run in the general election as independents. To understand the impact of party nomination rules, I recommend a study that observes the relationship between degree of inclusiveness in major-party nominations and the potential for third party candidacies.

Ware (2002) argues that too much inclusiveness may weaken the capacity of parties to function as intermediaries between citizens and government. The inclusiveness actually causes lower levels of competition and representation. In theory, at least, the most internally democratic parties may produce candidates that are least representative. Conversely, organizations that lack internal democracy may contribute to democratic practices at the system level, i.e., in general elections and governing coalitions (Rahat, Hazan, and Katz 2008).

Aside from these important normative questions, there are studies that consider in concrete terms how multistage elections affect the relationship between constituency preferences and policy positions of winning candidates (Aldrich and McGinnis 1989; Aranson and Ordeshook 1972; James Coleman 1971; Wittman 1983). The research on ideology cited previously covers much of this ground so I will not repeat it here, except to emphasize the point there is no consensus yet about how much nominating structures affect policy positions. Zaller (1998) argues that the multistage system produces talented politicians. Like prize-fighters, the many successful electoral battles they endure and win confirm their prowess in representing constituents. While this may be true, it is reasonable to wonder whether this system generates effective campaigners rather than individuals who can legislate. King (1997), for example, argues that primary elections (and the frequency of all elections) make American candidates overly concerned with winning the next campaign. Since they fear electoral challenge from either the opposing party or a challenger in their own party, they are unlikely to spend as much time governing or making difficult decisions that could make them vulnerable in the district. His arguments have not been challenged directly and much remains to be said—theoretically, conceptually, and empirically—about the link between nominations and democratic outcomes.

CONCLUDING REMARKS

I reiterate my surprise about the dearth of research in a field where empirical work has so many implications for democratic politics. The grooming of political leadership, especially in the early stages, raises fundamental questions about the relationship between elites and masses. Who is better-off by various forms of participation through direct primaries? And what does it mean to have influence when competition appears limited to a few contests? From a normative perspective, we need to explore whether inclusiveness produces "better outcomes," however defined. At the very least, the research should be more attentive to how nominating and recruiting practices potentially undermine some political values while supporting others.

The nomination process also raises meat and potato questions about power. It is central to understanding Lasswell's (1936) formulation of politics: who gets what, when, and how. Through the nomination process, intraparty factions contend for their vision of the party, trying to benefit the candidate who reflects their material interests or ideological aspirations. For this reason elites attend closely to nominating rules that might favor preferred candidates. The profession should do more to understand the relationship between reform of local and state nominating systems and political outcomes favored by factions in each of the parties.

The timing is good for such research. Non-federal electoral data are now widely available and the theoretical ground has been ploughed with studies of the presidential nomination process. Moreover, recent changes experienced by the political parties—especially in terms of their financial strength and legal standing—warrant closer scrutiny of the selection process. The subject appears ripe for all kinds of methodological approaches, but especially historical analysis, akin to recent work on the White Primaries in the South that illustrates the remarkable dynamics involving institutional change, elite behavior, and democratic outcomes (Mickey 2008).

It is also worth revisiting Key's arguments about how primaries in some regions exacerbate institutional decay of the minority party. As of this writing, there are no longer any Republican members of Congress from New England. To what extent have institutions of recruitment and nomination affected Republicans in the region? And what of the prospects for Democrats in the South where Republicans have established seemingly insurmountable strongholds outside of urban districts? Solid work here can illuminate much about the present and future American party system (or systems, if you think in terms of fifty states).

Even at the congressional level, we know little about how different nominating structures affect candidacies. Where do they obtain resources, skills, and networks to launch political careers (Dominguez 2005)? How are different kinds of candidates affected by different nominating institutions? To be sure, incumbents have enormous advantages (everywhere), as the research has amply demonstrated, but additional work should increase knowledge about the effect of institutions and political culture in drawing out or suppressing quality challengers. In short, the study of selection practices will tell us much about the winnowing of American political leadership through its political parties, interest groups, and elections.

CHAPTER 10

....

HOW PARTIES NOMINATE PRESIDENTS

....

WILLIAM G. MAYER

OF all the many functions political parties perform for democratic political systems, perhaps none is more crucial than nominating candidates for elective office. And of all the candidates American political parties nominate, none is more important than the president of the United States. This, in a nutshell, is why the American presidential nomination process is so significant.

For most of the twentieth century, however, presidential nominations received relatively little attention from political scientists, at least when compared to presidential general elections. As recently as about 1974, one could master the academic literature on presidential nominations by reading about a half-dozen books and five or ten significant articles. Even V. O. Key (1958), in his celebrated text on parties and pressure groups, devoted just one chapter to national conventions.

This situation began to change in large part because the nomination process itself changed, and political scientists naturally tried to understand why the changes occurred and what consequences they had. In the last three decades, considerable progress has undoubtedly been made. When Barbara Norrander wrote a "field essay" on "Presidential Nomination Politics in the Post-Reform Era" in 1996, she concluded her article with a 224-item bibliography.

As this chapter tries to demonstrate, we now know a lot about the basic structure of the contemporary presidential nomination process: the rules, the key decision points, the candidate strategies, and the roles played by the media and other outside actors. Yet, inevitably, there remain important gaps in our knowledge. In the final sections of this chapter, I highlight two of them: our understanding of how voters reach decisions in presidential primaries; and the larger consequences of the presidential nomination process for the functioning of the American political system.

A BRIEF HISTORY OF PRESIDENTIAL NOMINATION PROCEDURES

Most political scientists and historians who have studied the presidential nomination process agree that in the approximately 220 years since the writing of the US Constitution, that process has gone through five distinct stages or systems.

The Framers' System, 1787–1792

When the members of the Constitutional Convention gathered in Philadelphia in May 1787, they had, by the standards of the eighteenth century, a remarkable amount of experience in electing and working in legislatures. Every state except Georgia had been electing some kind of representative assembly for at least ninety years. By contrast, up until 1776, almost all of the executives early Americans were familiar with had acquired their titles either by inheritance (the British monarchy) or by appointment (most colonial governors). Against that background, it should come as no great surprise that the presidential selection process proved to be one of the most difficult and contentious issues the convention considered.

The story of how the Constitutional Convention finally settled upon the Constitution's intricate executive selection procedure has already been told (see McCormick 1982; Slonim 1986; and W. Mayer 2008b). As detailed in Article II, Section 1, each state was to choose a number of presidential "electors" equal to its number of representatives plus its number of senators. (How these electors were to be chosen was left to the discretion of the state legislatures.) These electors would then meet in their own states, and each elector would cast ballots for *two* presidential candidates. If any candidate received a vote from a majority of the total number of electors, that person would become president of the United States. If no person received a majority, the choice would then be made by the House of Representatives, which had to choose among the top five finishers in the electoral college voting.

This system was designed to achieve a number of objectives. In part, the members of the convention were desperately concerned that the new nation's choice of a chief executive not be susceptible to intrigue and corruption, from both domestic and foreign sources. This explains why, for example, the electors met in their own states rather than in a central location, why no elector could hold an "Office of Trust and Profit under the United States," and why all electors were required to cast their votes on the same day. A second goal, with more substantial long-term implications, was the framers' determination to make the executive independent of the legislature. This seemed to rule out selection by the legislature, and since a national popular vote was widely considered impracticable, that left an elector-based system as a natural compromise.

The question of immediate relevance is: how were presidential *nominations* to be accomplished under this system? That is to say, did the framers of the Constitution provide or anticipate any specific mechanism for narrowing the set of serious presidential contenders down to a manageable number of alternatives? Given the state of democratic theory and practice as of 1787, it is likely that many framers did not, in fact, see this as a distinct or important question. Among those who did think about the matter, however, there seem to have been two major schools of thought.

On the one hand, a number of members of the Constitutional Convention clearly thought that the electoral college itself would serve as a nominating device. In most years, they believed, the electoral votes would be so scattered among a variety of state and local favorites that no candidate would achieve the majority required by Article II. The final decision would therefore regularly devolve upon the House of Representatives, which, as noted earlier, would be compelled to choose from among the top five finishers in the electoral college. In the extant records of the convention, at least six delegates, including both James Madison and Alexander Hamilton, expressed the view that most presidential elections would wind up in the House. Indeed, both James Madison and Roger Sherman specifically described the system they were creating as one in which the large states, which were expected to dominate the electoral college, would "nominate" the candidates (Farrand 1937, 500, 513).

But there are also some suggestions in the convention records of a second possibility, which might be called *nomination by natural consensus*. Given that the electors were supposed to be a group of political elites, deliberately selected for their "information and discernment" (as Hamilton claimed in *The Federalist*, No. 68), they would know all the leading presidential candidates well and an unforced consensus would gradually emerge around one or two of the candidates. As James Wilson put it, "Continental Characters will multiply as we more & more coalesce, so as to enable the electors in every part of the Union to know & judge of them" (Farrand 1937, 501). It was this second possibility that actually governed the presidential elections of 1788–9 and 1792, the only elections in which the electoral college worked anything like the framers had anticipated. George Washington was an overwhelming favorite to be elected president no matter what the selection procedure; and, in fact, Washington received a vote from every elector in both of the first two elections.

The Rise of Deliberate Coordination, 1796–1828

By the early 1790s, however, political parties had started to emerge in the new nation, and by 1796, these parties were clearly starting to exert their influence in the presidential election process. Precisely because the framers had made it so difficult to coordinate or control the process *after* the members of the electoral college had been selected, the parties' solution was to try to influence who was chosen for the electoral college. What was needed was a mechanism for getting the adherents of each party to agree in advance on their preferred presidential and vice-presidential candidates,[1] and then work within each state to ensure that electors pledged to vote for those candidates were elected by popular vote or by the state legislatures. (Up until the 1830s, both methods were widely used for choosing members of the electoral college.)

The predominant, though not exclusive, mechanism that the early American parties used to unite and coordinate their presidential efforts was the congressional caucus. As its name implies, the congressional caucus was a gathering of a party's adherents in the US Senate and House of Representatives. Why was this particular nominating mechanism used? Perhaps the best answer is simply that there was no practicable alternative. In a large country with a geographically dispersed population and an underdeveloped communications and transportation infrastructure, Congress was the only vehicle for assembling a set of party leaders that could plausibly be described as both national and representative.

A cloud of illegitimacy hung over the congressional caucus throughout the three decades or so of its existence—partly because political parties in general were seen as disreputable, partly because the congressional caucus was seen as an extraconstitutional attempt to unite the legislative and executive powers that the Constitution had so deliberately and intricately separated. Indeed, it is difficult to say just when the first congressional nominating caucuses were held: some historians say 1796, others say 1800 (for a review of the dispute, see Morgan 1969). As historian

---

[1] Though the Constitution, as we have seen, instructed the electors to vote for two, undifferentiated presidential candidates, from the very beginning political parties clearly intended one of their two nominees to be their presidential candidate and the other their vice-presidential candidate. In 1804, the Twelfth Amendment removed any ambiguity by mandating that the electors cast separate votes for president and vice-president.

James Chase (1973) has pointed out, the congressional caucus also never developed a stable set of rules and procedures. Even on such basic matters as who had the authority to organize and convene the caucus, there was surprisingly little continuity from one election to the next.

The congressional caucus lingered on, at least within the Democratic–Republican Party, until 1824. Its other weaknesses notwithstanding, what finally administered the caucus's death blow was the fact that the opposition party, the Federalists, had essentially disappeared, thereby removing all incentive for party unity. So when the congressional caucus threatened to nominate Treasury Secretary William Crawford, three other prospective candidates and their supporters simply boycotted the proceedings and ran for president anyway. (Crawford finished last in the popular vote and a weak third in the electoral college.)

The Pure Convention System, 1832–1908

As two new parties, the Democrats and the Whigs, began to emerge in the late 1820s and early 1830s, they experimented with a variety of mechanisms for unifying their ranks and legitimizing their presidential candidates. In 1832, both held national party conventions for this purpose, and by the 1840s, both were taking steps to institutionalize and regularize this procedure.

Whatever other upheavals American politics went through between 1840 and 1908, including the dissolution of the Whig Party and its replacement by the Republicans, the rules of the presidential nomination process proved remarkably stable. Every four years, delegates representing the state affiliates of each national party gathered in a centrally accessible city to nominate a presidential ticket, adopt a national platform, and perform a small number of other housekeeping tasks. (Almost all of the early conventions were held in Baltimore; beginning in 1860, Chicago became the favored location.) Convention votes were apportioned among the states in proportion to their number of electoral votes; the delegates were usually chosen at state conventions. There was one critical difference between the parties. Whereas the Whigs and then the Republicans nominated their presidential ticket by a simple majority, Democratic rules insisted that a candidate receive two-thirds of the convention votes before being declared the winner.

How did these conventions go about making their decisions? In one of the few systematic studies of the pure convention system, Gerald Pomper (1966, ch. 8) divided conventions into four basic types. Eighteen of the thirty-nine major party conventions held between 1832 and 1908 (48 percent) simply ratified what appeared to be a preexisting consensus: a candidate was nominated on the first ballot and received at least two-thirds of the convention votes. Three other conventions (8 percent) exercised what Pomper called "limited discretion": here, too, the nomination took just one ballot, but the winner received less than two-thirds of the vote. Eleven conventions (28 percent) required multiple ballots, but finally settled upon what Pomper called a "major candidate": one who had received at least 20 percent of the votes on the first ballot. Finally, almost one-fifth of all conventions (seven of thirty-nine) produced a "dark horse" nominee: the eventual winner had less than 20 percent on the first ballot. In a significant number of cases, in short, the pure conventions were the site of real decision making.

The Mixed System, 1912–1968

Beginning in 1912, an important new ingredient was added to the convention system: presidential primaries.[2] In a significant number of states, national convention delegates were selected or bound not by closed, party-run conventions, but by popular vote. Who was eligible to vote in these primaries varied from state to state. Some states opened their primaries only to voters who had previously registered with a particular party; others, such as Wisconsin, allowed in any voter who had taken a temporary interest in a given party's presidential contest. Whatever the precise details, presidential primaries dramatically expanded the number of ordinary voters who could take a meaningful part in a major-party presidential nomination.

Up through 1968, however, the role of presidential primaries—and thus of direct popular participation—remained a limited one. Only about a third of all states held a primary, and many of these operated under rules that were deliberately designed to advantage party regulars and insulate the delegate selection process from insurgent candidates and popular movements.

The classic way to win a presidential nomination under the mixed system is often said to be John Kennedy's march to the Democratic nomination in 1960. Kennedy entered a total of just seven presidential primaries, winning them all, but thereby acquiring just a small fraction of the number of delegates needed to win the nomination. Kennedy then used his success in the primaries to convince skeptical party leaders that he would be the party's strongest candidate in the general election, his youth and Catholicism notwithstanding.[3]

As its name implies, the mixed system created two major "power centers" within each party's presidential nomination process. Presidential primaries allowed for some measure of popular input; but party leaders and elected officials also controlled large blocs of delegates. And if those leaders disliked or distrusted a

---

[2] For further details about the rise of presidential primaries and their role in the mixed system, see Overacker (1926) and David, Goldman, and Bain (1960).

[3] The classic account of the role of primaries in the mixed nomination system is Davis (1967).

candidate, they had the discretion to reject him, no matter how well he did in the primaries. In 1952, Tennessee Senator Estes Kefauver won twelve of the thirteen primaries he entered, but had so little support among party leaders that he never won more than 30 percent of the total convention vote.

THE PLEBISCITARY SYSTEM, 1972–PRESENT

In retrospect, it is hard not to feel that the mixed system served the Democratic Party—and the country—rather well. Between 1928 and 1964, mixed-system conventions nominated, in succession, Franklin Roosevelt, Harry Truman, Adlai Stevenson, John Kennedy, and Lyndon Johnson. This is also one of the few periods in American history when academics, congenitally disposed to find fault, actually wrote spirited defenses of the presidential nomination process (see, for example, Polsby and Wildavsky 1968).

That record notwithstanding, the mixed system was unable to survive the fierce political passions that accompanied the late 1960s and the Vietnam War. In 1968, two major antiwar candidates, Eugene McCarthy and Robert Kennedy, won most of the presidential primaries, but the party leaders didn't like McCarthy, and Kennedy was assassinated on the final night of the primaries, so the nomination went instead to Hubert Humphrey, Johnson's vice-president and a supporter of the war, who hadn't contested a single primary. As is often the case in politics, a process that had previously been judged quite acceptable began to seem illegitimate once it produced the "wrong" outcome. As the Democratic convention approached, part of the antiwar forces' anger focused on the process that, in their view, had denied them a nomination they won in the primaries.

On the second night of the Democratic national convention, partly as a concession to the supporters of the losing candidates, the convention approved a minority report from the rules committee that, as eventually interpreted, authorized a special commission to rewrite the delegate selection rules that were to be used for the 1972 convention. Though commissions are often dismissed as a way to "study" a problem in order to avoid acting on it, the Commission on Party Structure and Delegate Selection—more commonly known as the McGovern–Fraser Commission, after the two men who served as its chairman—met or exceeded the expectations of its most fervent supporters. In just four years, the commission succeeded in putting together a comprehensive set of recommendations that entirely recast the ground rules for delegate selection, got these recommendations accepted by the Democratic National Committee, and then compelled fifty state parties to abide by their provisions. The upshot has been justly described as "the greatest systematic change in presidential nomination procedures in all of American history" (Shafer 1983, 28).

Two major ideas underlie most of the changes instituted by the McGovern–Fraser Commission. First, the new rules represented a dramatic increase in the power of the national Democratic Party vis-à-vis the state parties. Both the pure convention system and the mixed system had been characterized by an extreme decentralization of authority in establishing delegate selection procedures. State parties essentially had the power to select their delegates in any way they wanted. Only if two sets of delegates showed up at the national convention, each claiming to represent a given state, would the national party intervene in such matters. Even the most blatant forms of racial discrimination practiced by southern Democratic parties were not outlawed until 1968. In stark contrast, the centerpiece of the McGovern–Fraser initiatives was a sweeping assertion of the national party's authority to control its state and local affiliates. Specifically, the commission promulgated eighteen "guidelines" that were designed to regulate state delegate selection procedures in remarkable detail. All state parties that hoped to have their delegates seated at the 1972 convention were required to:

- have "explicit, written rules"
- "forbid proxy voting"
- "forbid the use of the unit rule"
- ensure that party meetings were held on "uniform dates, at uniform times, and in public places of easy access"
- "ensure adequate public notice" of all meetings
- "prohibit the ex-officio designation of delegates"
- "conduct the entire process of delegate selection . . . within the calendar year of the Convention."[4]

Still other guidelines took aim at filing fees, petition requirements, quorum provisions, intrastate apportionment, and slate-making procedures.

Second, in the battle between the established, "regular" party organizations and the new issue- and candidate-activists, the McGovern–Fraser Commission came down squarely on the side of the activists. Where the old rules had often been set up with the deliberate intention of assisting the party regulars, the new rules sought to strip away all such advantages. "Full, meaningful, and timely" participation was the commission's goal and mandate, that swept everything else before it. That is why, as we have seen, the McGovern–Fraser guidelines banned ex officio delegates and proxy voting, demanded explicit written rules and advance publicity for all meetings, and even tried to regulate slate-making procedures.

---

[4] All guidelines are quoted from Commission on Party Structure and Delegate Selection (1970).

Taken together, this was no mere tinkering with the rules. Of the eighteen guidelines, *every* state was in violation of *at least* six. Looked at from another perspective, before the commission's formation, there were five basic institutional mechanisms used by state parties for selecting national convention delegates. The commission's final report effectively banned two of the five and severely restricted the use of a third (Shafer 1983, 197–9, 223).

The most conspicuous consequence of the new rules was a significant increase in the number of presidential primaries. In 1968, the Democrats had held just seventeen primaries, a number that had stayed fairly stable since at least 1952. But this number increased to twenty-three in 1972, to twenty-nine in 1976, and then to thirty-three in 1988 (Hagen and Mayer 2000, 11). States that decided not to hold a primary could select their delegates through a caucus-convention process that was superficially similar to the state conventions that most states had used before 1972. But the McGovern–Fraser rules also transformed caucuses, opening them up to any Democrat who wanted to participate and removing any special advantages that had once accrued to the regular party organizations. Though they have far lower participation rates, in most other respects contemporary caucuses are, as one presidential candidate described them, "the functional equivalent of a primary." Indeed, where the pre-reform conventions advantaged candidates with close ties to the established party leadership, present-day caucuses actually provide an edge to insurgent candidates like Jesse Jackson, Pat Robertson, and Barack Obama (W. Mayer 1996).

To this point, my account of changes in the contemporary nomination process has dealt entirely with the Democratic Party. In fact, we lack a good account of what was happening in the Republican Party during these same years and why. Most commentators simply assert (without much evidence) that when Democratic state legislatures rewrote their states' presidential primary laws, they applied these laws to both parties and thus inadvertently "reformed" the Republican Party as well. But the Republicans also established a special commission at their 1968 convention, which recommended a number of significant changes that were eventually adopted by the 1972 GOP convention (Bibby 1980; D. Price 1984, 156–9). Whatever was driving the changes on the Republican side, the bottom line is that while there are some differences between the Democratic and Republican nomination systems, they tend to be rather subtle ones, such as the Republicans' greater use of so-called winner-take-all delegate allocation rules. The most conspicuous features of the plebiscitary system, such as the increased use of presidential primaries, are clearly characteristic of both parties.

In addition to these party-based reforms, one other set of rule changes clearly helped lay the groundwork for the plebiscitary nomination system. Just two years after the 1972 election, Congress passed a law that completely restructured the ways that candidates could raise and spend money while running for president. For the first time, there were limits on the amount of money that a person could contribute to a presidential campaign; candidates were also required to disclose the sources of all the money they raised and how they spent it. To compensate for the money that candidates could no longer raise from large contributions, the 1974 law also established a new source of campaign money—federal matching funds—but candidates who accepted such funds were required to abide by spending limits.[5]

REFORMING THE REFORMS

The work of the McGovern–Fraser Commission proved to be highly controversial, especially after the first presidential candidate nominated under the new rules, South Dakota Senator (and former commission chairman) George McGovern, went down to one of the most lopsided defeats in American presidential history. In each of the next four election cycles, the Democrats established a new "reform" commission that was charged with reexamining and revising the work of one or more of its predecessors.

As the plebiscitary nomination system enters its fifth decade, it seems clear that anyone who had hoped that these later commissions would turn back the clock and "reform the reforms" was sadly disappointed. Almost all of the changes instituted by the McGovern–Fraser Commission have endured. In some cases, indeed, subsequent commissions actually pushed the changes even further in the direction initially sought by reform advocates. For example, the McGovern–Fraser guidelines had merely *urged* state parties to "adopt procedures which will provide for fair representation of minority views on presidential candidates" (Commission on Party Structure and Delegate Selection 1970, 36). By 1992, however, all states were *required* to allocate delegates in direct proportion to the primary or caucus vote.

The only real exception to the claim made in the last paragraph—the only enduring counter-reform—was the creation of superdelegates. With state parties no longer permitted to appoint ex officio delegates or do anything else that seemed to give an advantage to party leaders and elected officials, one effect of the new rules was a sharp decline in the presence of major Democratic officeholders at the party's national conventions. For example, between 1956 and 1968, on average 70 percent of the Democratic members of the US Senate were voting delegates at the national convention. But this number fell to 35 percent in 1972, and then to 18 percent in 1976 (based on data reported in Reiter 1985, 66).

Convinced that this development was negatively affecting both the workings of the presidential nomination process and the Democratic Party's performance in

---

[5] For further details about the campaign finance laws and their effect on the plebiscitary nomination process, see Corrado (1996); Corrado and Gouvea (2004); Magleby and Mayer (2008).

government, in 1982 the Commission on Presidential Nomination (the Hunt Commission) created a new category of delegates, dubbed superdelegates. (Their formal title in the Democratic Party's national rules is "unpledged party leaders and elected officials.") Though the details have changed a bit from election to election, since 1992 all members of the Democratic National Committee, all Democratic governors, and all Democratic members of the US House and Senate have automatically become delegates to the Democratic national convention. In all, superdelegates comprised 19 percent of the delegates to the 2008 convention (for the exact provisions and numbers in all Democratic conventions since 1984, see W. Mayer 2009).

So the ban on ex officio delegates has been repealed. But has this new type of delegate, whose existence was much fought over in the early 1980s, actually had a significant effect on subsequent nomination races? The 2008 nomination contest provided exactly the sort of circumstances where the superdelegates *might* have mattered. On the morning after Super Tuesday (February 5), it was clear that neither Hillary Clinton nor Barack Obama had scored an early knockout, and that the fate of the Democratic nomination might accordingly rest with the large bloc of super-delegates, most of whom were still uncommitted. With Clinton holding a two-to-one advantage among those superdelegates who had declared a preference, many within her campaign openly suggested that the superdelegates might bring her victory even if she didn't fare quite so well in the remaining primaries and caucuses.

It soon became clear, however, that the superdelegates were reluctant to play such a role. As House Speaker Nancy Pelosi put it, "If the votes of superdelegates overturn what's happened in the elections, it would be harmful to the Democratic Party." In the weeks immediately after Super Tuesday, Obama posted a string of ten consecutive primary and caucus victories, and as he established a clear lead in the popular vote and the media delegate counts, the superdelegates slowly but surely swung into line behind him. By early May, most media delegate counters were reporting that a small plurality of the superdelegates now favored Obama; on June 3, he clinched the nomination.[6]

The most striking lesson of the superdelegate saga concerns the difficulty of turning the clock back on party reforms. Over the last four decades—indeed, for most of the twentieth century—Americans have learned to treat political parties as essentially public entities, whose internal deliberations and most important decisions are open to any voter who wants to express an opinion, no matter how little support they have previously given the party. From this perspective, the McGovern–Fraser Commission and its Republican counterpart merely extended a set of norms and rules to presidential nominations that had long been applied to almost every other major office in American politics. Thus, even when a group like the

---

[6] All details in this and the preceding paragraph are taken from Mayer (2009).

superdelegates had the theoretical capacity to influence the outcome of a closely contested nomination race, they were reluctant to exercise that power.

THE CONTEMPORARY NOMINATION PROCESS IN ACTION: FIVE GENERALIZATIONS

How does the contemporary presidential nomination process actually work? How does it finally confer the nomination on a single candidate? In the interests of facilitating further research, I have tried to sum up the state of current knowledge of this subject in terms of five major generalizations.

The process starts early. Before 1972, presidential nomination campaigns were generally confined to the election year. Even the most eager candidates generally did not announce their candidacies until the beginning of the election year or the final months of the preceding year (for the announcement dates of all presidential candidates between 1952 and 1968, see Hagen and Mayer 2000, 22–4). John Kennedy, for example, announced his intention to seek the White House on January 2, 1960. The earliest entrant into the 1960 Democratic field was Hubert Humphrey; he launched his campaign on January 30, 1959. To be sure, many candidates (including Kennedy) had been quietly laying the groundwork for their candidacy for months or years prior to the formal announcement. But as Michael Hagen and I (2000) have shown, this sort of "pre-campaign" activity did not appear to interfere with a potential candidate's governing responsibilities. In 1959, John Kennedy showed up for 77 percent of all Senate roll call votes, not much different from his participation rates in 1957 and 1958. Only in 1960, the election year itself, did his participation rate plunge to 35 percent.

By contrast, contemporary presidential nomination campaigns generally begin a few weeks after the preceding midterm election. By the early spring of the year before the election, twenty months before the general election, one or both parties will generally have a large field of candidates already in the field, working pretty much full-time on their campaigns. Almost the only exception is an incumbent president, who generally does not face any serious opposition in his quest for renomination and can therefore delay his announcement until the election year itself.

So long and potentially significant is this period of intense campaigning that precedes the formal delegate selection season that it now has a name: the invisible primary (Hadley 1976), though some commentators have argued that this is now a misnomer, since a great deal of this campaigning is quite public and closely monitored by the national media. At least three major activities occupy the candidates' time and attention during this period.

First, the new campaign finance regime—in particular, the contribution limits—has turned fundraising into a highly labor-intensive activity. In order to raise the substantial amounts of money required by a contemporary nomination campaign, candidates can no longer call up a few wealthy supporters. Instead, they must solicit contributions from thousands and even millions of individual donors, and even with the assistance of the Internet, this generally requires a huge commitment of the candidate's time. Shortly after the conclusion of the 1996 presidential nomination campaign, former Tennessee Governor Lamar Alexander estimated that fully 70 percent of his time during 1995 was devoted to fundraising (as quoted in W. Mayer and Busch 2004, 157).

Second, and more substantively, the invisible primary is the time when candidates try out the themes and issue appeals that will, they hope, distinguish them from the other candidates and win them votes. The significance of this early campaigning is easiest to appreciate when one candidate clearly reads the mood of the potential electorate better than his or her peers. In 2003, for example, Howard Dean was initially the only major Democratic candidate to come out squarely against the war in Iraq. The result was that during the second quarter of 2003, Dean raised substantially more money than any other candidate and also saw a significant increase in his poll numbers. Belatedly, and with varying degrees of success, all of the other major candidates struggled to shift gears and portray themselves as opponents of the war.

An enormous amount of attention is focused on two early delegate selection events: the Iowa caucuses and the New Hampshire primary. One other invisible primary activity deserves special notice: the candidates spend an enormous amount of time and, increasingly, money in Iowa and New Hampshire, the states that have traditionally held, respectively, the first presidential caucus and the first primary.[7] In the 1988 election cycle, for example, the seven major Democratic candidates spent 547 days campaigning in Iowa, 288 days in New Hampshire, and 441 days in all fourteen of the southern and border-South states that voted on Super Tuesday (i.e., about thirty-two days per state). The figures on the Republican side are similar: the GOP's six major presidential contenders devoted 300 days to Iowa, 367 days to New Hampshire, and just 396 days to the entire South (twenty-eight days per state).[8]

The reason that Iowa and New Hampshire matter is not, of course, the number of delegates at stake there, but all the publicity these states receive and the effect that a win or a "better than expected" showing in one or both of these states can have on the rest of the delegate selection season. This phenomenon, too, has a name: it is called "momentum."

---

[7] For further discussion of the role of Iowa and New Hampshire in the presidential nomination process, see Orren and Polsby (1987); Buell (2000); Mayer and Busch (2004); Busch (2008).

[8] Figures are taken from Norrander (1992, 94).

Momentum, it seems clear, is not a simple phenomenon.[9] It is best defined as the effect that primary and/or caucus outcomes have on subsequent primaries and caucuses. It thus reflects one of the most distinctive features of the primary and caucus season: its sequential nature. Unlike general elections or the primaries that are held for all other elective offices in the United States, primaries are not held on a single day, but over a four- to five-month period. Voters in later primaries may therefore adjust their decisions based on information they learn from earlier primaries.

Specifically, momentum probably derives from all of the following causal mechanisms, in proportions that vary from election to election:

- By winning or running better than expected in one of the much anticipated and highly publicized early delegate selection events, a candidate will probably receive a great deal of additional media coverage and will thus become better known to prospective voters. Since voters rarely vote for someone whom they don't know, this effect alone is likely to increase their share of the vote in subsequent primaries.

- Not only do candidates get a lot of additional publicity from doing well in Iowa and New Hampshire, but this publicity tends, at least in the short term, to be highly positive. "The victorious candidate is portrayed as popular, exciting, confident, in control: in short, a leader. His poll ratings are increasing; his organization is growing; his message is catching on; his crowds are large and enthusiastic. His opponents, by contrast, are dead, dying, or in disarray" (W. Mayer 1987, 14).

- In a large multicandidate field, voters tend to restrict their choice of candidates to those who are seen as *viable*: those who have a reasonable chance of winning the nomination. Although neither Iowa nor New Hampshire is representative of the national electorate, the media and other commentators tend to interpret these early events—overinterpret them, actually—as a sign of how voters in general will assess the candidates and thus of how the rest of the primaries and caucuses will turn out. Successful candidates are accordingly seen as more viable.

- Voters also use the results from early primaries and caucuses to assess the candidates' *electability*: their likelihood of being able to win a general election against the opposition party's candidate. Since a nomination victory is of little value unless it is followed up by a victory in the general election, some voters may decide to vote strategically, casting their ballot for one of their less preferred candidates because he or she has a better chance of winning in November.

- Voters aren't the only ones who use the Iowa and New Hampshire results to assess the candidates' viability and electability. Campaign contributors go

---

[9] The following account draws especially on Patterson (1980); Brady and Johnston (1987); Bartels (1988).

through much the same process. Candidates who do well in Iowa and New Hampshire often receive huge infusions of new campaign money. Losers often find themselves short of funds and thus unable to wage the kind of aggressive campaign needed to recover from an early setback.

The importance of momentum should not be overstated. In most contested nomination races, the winning candidate is the person leading in the national polls on the eve of the Iowa caucuses (W. Mayer 2004). But doing well in Iowa and New Hampshire at least means that a candidate will be taken seriously in subsequent primaries. A candidate who does poorly in both locales, by contrast, will frequently find himself taken down a notch in the estimation of both reporters and voters. Since 1976, only one candidate (Bill Clinton in 1992) has managed to win a presidential nomination without winning either Iowa or New Hampshire.

Within a few days or weeks after the beginning of the delegate selection season, a substantial number of candidates will begin to drop out of the race. In the mixed system, candidates who got into a contested nomination race generally stayed in, at least to the end of the primary season, usually all the way to the convention. In the plebiscitary system, by contrast, most candidates start early but also exit early. In 1984, to take a typical year, the Democrats had eight major candidates competing throughout the invisible primary. Within ten days of the Iowa caucuses, three of them had already announced that they were withdrawing from the race. In the next two weeks, two other candidates exited the field. Thus, for most of the primary and caucus season, Democratic voters had an effective choice among just three of the eight original candidates.

In most years, a candidate will wrap up the nomination by the end of March. Given all the attention lavished on Iowa and New Hampshire, and the early withdrawals of so many candidates, lots of states drew the obvious conclusion that, when scheduling a primary or caucus, early was better. Beginning in the 1980s, more and more states moved their key delegate selection events as close as possible to the start of the delegate selection period allowed by Democratic party rules. (The Republican Party did not adopt a rule that restricted the scheduling of primaries and caucuses until 2000.) The result was a primary and caucus calendar that has become increasingly *front-loaded* (W. Mayer and Busch 2004). In 1996, for example, there were four primaries in the week immediately after New Hampshire, followed by nine more in week 3, seven in week 4, four major midwestern primaries in week 5, and three more primaries, including California, in week 6. Thus, while the primary season technically lasted sixteen weeks, 77 percent of the delegates were already chosen by the end of the sixth week.

And as the calendar became more front-loaded, it became possible for a front-running candidate to clinch his party's nomination quite early in the calendar year, months before the end of the primary season and the opening of his party's national convention. The Democratic nomination race of 2008 is a conspicuous exception to this generalization: Barack Obama and Hillary Clinton continued slugging it out until the beginning of June. But this is the only exception in the last four nomination cycles. In every other contested nomination race during this period, including the 2008 Republican contest, the successful candidate had clinched the nomination by the end of March.

The national conventions no longer make any important decisions. While some nomination contests may linger on into May or June, it is incredibly unlikely that they will still be unresolved by the time a party's national convention begins. National party conventions are still held every four years, and in a formal, legal sense they are still the bodies that officially designate each party's presidential and vice-presidential candidates. But every shred of discretion, every bit of real decision-making power, has gradually been bled out of the conventions.

National conventions, it is important to say, were in decline well before the McGovern–Fraser Commission held its first meeting. The last convention that required more than one ballot to nominate a presidential candidate was the Democratic national convention of 1952. In every convention since then, in both parties, one candidate entered the convention with a large lead among declared delegates and then went on to victory on the first ballot. Nevertheless, in the final years of the mixed system, conventions still had some significance. Of the preconvention front-runners between 1956 and 1968, most non-incumbents had not yet secured a majority of the delegates (see the data in W. Mayer and Busch 2004, 47). The convention therefore became the place where the bargain was sealed: where the front-runner and his campaign organization made and received enough commitments to put him over the top. And the front-runner's opponents thus had at least some hope that they could derail the bandwagon if the front-runner misplayed his cards or lost out on some crucial rules or platform fight.

Conventions could play this sort of role during the mixed system because large numbers of delegates—between 20 and 50 percent in most years—were still uncommitted on the weekend before the convention. One effect of the new rules, however, was a dramatic reduction in the number of uncommitted delegates selected to both parties' conventions. In the 1980 contest between Jimmy Carter and Edward Kennedy, for example, at the end of the primary season only 3 percent of the delegates were uncommitted. In that year's Republican nomination race, just 8 percent of the delegates were selected on an uncommitted basis (all data are from W. Mayer and Busch 2004, 39). With fewer uncommitted delegates available, with most candidates dropping out of the race only weeks after the first delegates were selected, it was almost inevitable that one candidate would achieve a majority well before the convention was gaveled to order.

As conventions became less significant as a decision-making forum, political strategists increasingly came to view conventions in terms of the contribution they could make to a party's general election campaign. At least at the beginning of the plebiscitary nomination period, the three major television networks were still broadcasting "gavel-to-gavel" coverage of the national conventions. Beginning with the Republican convention of 1972, presidential campaign managers tried to turn the conventions into a four-day-long commercial for the victorious candidate.

But this, in turn, meant that every vestige of dissent, every sign that the party was anything less than 100 percent united behind the nominee and his program, had to be resolved behind the scenes, before the convention opened, outside the spotlight of prime-time television. The last convention to hold a contested roll call vote on either the platform or the rules was the 1988 Democratic convention. National conventions, once one of the most enthralling moments in all of American politics, became boring. Ironically but quite predictably, the more conventions were scripted and sanitized for television, the less the major networks wanted to televise them. In recent years, network television coverage of the major party conventions has dwindled to about one hour per night—and a considerable part of this time is usually spent complaining about how little is actually taking place.

WHO WINS AND WHY

Contemporary presidential nominations, then, are won and lost in the primaries and caucuses. In every election cycle since 1976, in both parties, the nomination has *always* gone to the candidate who won the most votes. Though superdelegates have accounted for about one-sixth of the delegates at recent Democratic conventions, they have never shown the capacity to resist a popular favorite.

But this conclusion only pushes the explanatory task one step further back. Why does one candidate win a plurality of the vote? What major factors explain voting behavior in a presidential primary? In addition to its importance in presidential politics, these questions have great theoretical significance. Virtually everything we know about voting behavior in American politics comes from *general elections* contested by *two candidates*, each of whom is explicitly identified as a member of *one of the two major parties*. How might behavior change if one or more of these variables were altered? One way to answer this question, of course, is to analyze data from other countries, but this strategy requires the analyst to grapple with a series of complicated questions about the confounding effects of political culture and national history. By studying presidential primaries, we can, without venturing outside the United States, examine elections that usually involve *more than two candidates*, all of whom are *members of the same party*. Moreover, presidential primaries are only the *first stage* in a multistage electoral process; a successful candidate in the primaries, in order to deliver on most of his promises, must also be capable of winning the general election.

Its practical and theoretical significance notwithstanding, political scientists have made surprisingly little progress in understanding voting behavior in presidential primaries. We know that momentum has something to do with it, but momentum is plainly not a complete theory of primary voting. It cannot explain, for example, why a New Hampshire victory has catapulted some candidates into the national lead (e.g., Gary Hart in 1984), while other candidates never won again (Pat Buchanan in 1996). Nor can it explain why candidates with momentum catch on with some types of voters more than others.

There are a few building blocks available for a larger theory of primary voting. John Geer (1989) has provided strong reason to think that the personal qualities of the candidates matter a lot more in the primaries than they do in presidential general elections. There is also evidence that performance evaluations are a dominant factor in nomination contests involving incumbent presidents and vice-presidents (W. Mayer 2008a). But we still lack a basic understanding as to why, for example, Barack Obama bested Hillary Clinton.

THE PROCESS AND THE POLITY

In what ways, if any, is American politics different for having the kind of presidential nomination process we have? This is, in many ways, a forbidding question to answer in any kind of systematic manner. If the nomination races of the last forty years have taught us nothing else, they have shown the remarkable adaptability of candidates and political parties. No matter what the rules, ambitious candidates and other actors find ways to make them work to their advantage or, at least, to neutralize the disadvantages. When long shots and "outsider" candidates like George McGovern and Jimmy Carter showed the advantages of doing lots of personal campaigning in Iowa and New Hampshire, front-runners such as Walter Mondale and Al Gore responded by doing the same thing. As Marty Cohen and his colleagues (2008) have shown, party leaders have also found ways of exerting influence in the post-reform nomination process.

Yet the question is an important one, and the following are some preliminary answers.

1. The framers, as we have seen, wanted a presidential selection process that would ensure the executive's independence from the legislature. Had the congressional caucus survived, it might have led to a regular pattern of weak executives,

who understood that subservience to the legislature was the price of acquiring and keeping power. But the rise of national conventions, whether in the pure, mixed, or plebiscitary form, has kept the presidential nomination process free from congressional domination. This is not to say that national conventions have been the driving force behind the growth of presidential power; but we can say that when other forces conjoined to strengthen the hand of the presidency, nothing in the presidential nomination process restrained that development.

2. Particularly when compared to the path to power trod by prime ministers in Great Britain, the American presidential nomination process has always been a lot messier. There is no one, well-marked route to a presidential nomination. Of the thirty-seven major party presidential nominations that have been conferred since 1900 (renomination of incumbent presidents excluded), fourteen were won by governors, eight by senators, six by vice-presidents. The remainder went to a general, a businessman, an ambassador, two judges, two cabinet members, and a member of the House.[10] Among other things, this helps explain why any party that is not renominating an incumbent president usually has a large field of declared candidates.

3. While there are many possible routes to a presidential nomination, one strategy with a notably low success rate is to first become part of the congressional leadership. In the United States, legislative leaders rarely win presidential nominations. Since the institutionalization of party nominating conventions in the 1840s, only three former Speakers of the House have ever received a presidential nomination (all were in the nineteenth century). Only one Senate majority or minority leader has been nominated for the presidency. Most twentieth-century speakers of the House appear to have recognized this reality and never seriously considered a run for the White House.

4. As British observers of American politics have frequently noted, the US presidential selection process takes a long time. (Indeed, Harold Laski made this point in 1940, well before the onset of the plebiscitary system.) In recent years, there is increasing evidence that the US political system pays a price for all the time devoted to campaigning rather than governing. When David Mayhew (1991) put together a list of important laws enacted between 1946 and 1990, one of his more striking findings was that a lot more gets done in the first two years of a president's term than in the second two years. As both parties start to turn their attention to the impending presidential election, they get substantially less serious legislating accomplished. Kathryn Dunn Tenpas (1997) has similarly shown how disruptive a presidential election is for the internal workings of the White House.

---

[10] Candidates are classified according to their most recent position held prior to nomination.

....

CHAPTER 11

THE ROAD LESS TAKEN

NEW DIRECTIONS IN AMERICAN PARTY POLITICS

....

DANIEL M. SHEA

HISTORY seems to be unfolding all around us. Beyond the historic candidacies of Barack Obama, Hillary Clinton, and Sarah Palin, the 2008 election set records for candidate spending, the length and intensity of the modern nomination process, and, perhaps most significantly, the use of "new media" in the delivery of campaign news (YouTube, for example) and the mobilization of activists (the so-called "netroots"). There have been dramatically transformative elections in the past, such as in 1828, 1896, and 1960, but when combining *how* the 2008 election was conducted with *who* participated as viable players, there is no question that our recent democratic feast will be studied by many future generations.

Adjustments in party politics also seem to be moving at light speed. There are three significant developments. First, the movement away from party identification—which began in earnest in the 1970s—has turned rather dramatically in another direction. Much to the surprise of scholars, voters seem quite willing to attach themselves to a partisan badge and to vote accordingly. Several indicators suggest both 2004 and 2008 were two of the most partisan elections on record.

In 2004, for instance, some 93 percent of Republicans and 89 percent of Democrats voted for candidates of their respective parties—unprecedented figures since the use of polling (Reichley 2007, 16).

Second, measures of party unity in Congress and in state legislatures have also increased in recent years. Since the 1990s, party unity scores have generally been higher in both the House and Senate than during any other period since the Second World War. While it is not clear that increased partisanship in the electorate triggered higher levels of party unity, especially given that intense in-government levels predate the resurgence in the electorate, these two indicators underscore the weight of contemporary party dynamics.

Third, party organizations have reemerged from the depths of candidate-centered–interest group politics of the 1970s. Most had assumed that party committees were fading and that we were entering a "partyless age." The resurgence of party organizations speaks volumes about their capacity to adjust and remain key players in American electoral politics. The national party organizations, in particular, have more resources and a higher level of technological prowess, and are able to give candidates more help than at any point in history. Even recent campaign finance changes, designed to curtail party-based soft money, do not seem to have drastically altered the mounting influence of the national committees. As noted by a team of scholars some time ago, "the phoenix has risen from the ashes" (Kayden and Mahe 1985, 3).

Combined, it seems that party politics has recaptured its prominent place in American politics, particularly at the national level. Herrnson notes, "Once characterized as poor, unstable, and powerless, national party organizations ... entered the twenty-first century as financially secure, institutionally stable, and highly influential in election campaigns ..." (2002, 47). One might even go so far as to compare our current partisan system with other robust party periods in American history. With some hesitation, A. James Reichley, a leading scholar of party history, noted, "contemporary political parties appear to come close, at least structurally, to the model proposed by the famous 1950 APSR report" (2007, 16).

But is it really the case that the contemporary party system mirrors other periods in American history? Because parties seem increasingly active and influential, does that also imply the strengthening of a "responsible" party system?

The aim of this chapter is *not* to provide additional arguments in support of the resurgence perspective; other chapters in this volume present bushels of important data and convincing arguments that underscore this view. Rather, it will be contended that recent elections have triggered a dramatic change in the electoral system, affording party organizations a unique opportunity to draw citizens into the party rubric in meaningful ways for decades to come. National, state, and local party committees have a rare opportunity to shift their approach from a more rational, service-oriented pole to a voter-centered, responsible model. Put a bit differently, the historic battle between the Hamiltonian and Jeffersonian approaches to party politics is being waged. How party leaders respond to these new conditions will define the nature of the American party system for decades to come.

ORGANIZATIONAL RESURGENCE

Party organizational resurgence can be aptly dubbed one of the great comeback stories of American politics. Most had assumed that America was headed into a partyless age; interest groups were poised to dominate the policy process, and political action committees (PACs) and campaign consultants ruled the roost during elections. David Broder's (1972) claim that "the party's over" was widely accepted. But the parties, struggling to remain players, took a dramatic turn to what has been dubbed a service-oriented position.

The roots of this shift can be traced to the Republican National Committee (RNC) during the 1960s.[1] Headed by Ray C. Bliss and his "nuts and bolts" approach to party politics, the RNC began a concerted effort to raise money and to develop greater campaign prowess. During the 1970s, Bill Brock took GOP fundraising a step further with the refinement of direct mail, and on the Democratic side Charles Manatt turned his organization to a similar path. The parties could once again be real players, they believed, by raising truckloads of money and by helping candidates. Ironically, this revitalization was occurring at the same time many journalists and scholars bemoaned the passing of party politics in America.

By the early 1980s, a growing chorus of scholars challenged the voter-centered notion of party decay. The adjustments of Bliss, Brock, and Manatt had taken hold and the parties were "responding." It was becoming clear that American parties were "resilient creatures" (Bibby 1990, 27). Both parties were developing campaign-centered branch organizations, revamping their internal operations, and devising innovative ways to raise huge sums of cash. Additionally, the number of full-time party employees, the size of their operating budgets, their average financial contribution to individual candidates, and the range of services provided had vastly increased (Cotter et al. 1984; Frendreis et al. 1994; Aldrich 1999; to note just a few).

At the national level, the data could not have been clearer. There were numerous indicators, including the growing list of services parties were providing candidates (see, for example, Herrnson 1988, 1994). Perhaps the best indicator of party vitality was party finance. Resurgent parties should have more money and by the late 1980s

---

[1] Others might stretch things back a bit further, perhaps to the election of 1916. Jensen (1969) suggests this election marked a shift from "militarists'" party activities, focused on grassroots organizations, to "mercantilists'" campaigning, where a premium is placed on the manipulation of symbols and the strategies of advertising.

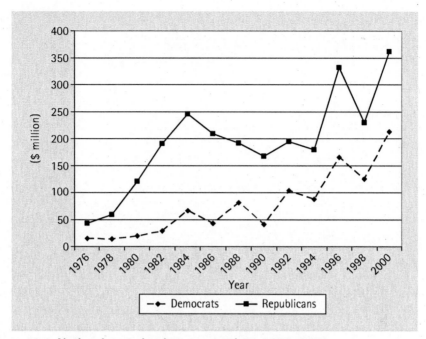

Figure 11.1 National party hard money receipts, 1976–2000

Note: Figures include National Party Committees and both the House and Senate Campaign Committees.

Source: Federal Election Commission press releases.

they surely did. The pace of growth was staggering, even when inflation is considered, as noted in Figure 11.1. Others pointed to the number of paid staff positions, voter contact activities, polling services, candidate recruitment, and nearly every other measure of organizational vitality. The picture is clear. As noted by one observer a few years ago, "the growth chart for this political 'industry' exhibits an ebullience more familiar in Silicon Valley" (Putnam 2000, 37).

At the state level, Aldrich's recent study (2000) was revealing. While focusing most of his analysis on the emergence of state party organizations in the South, he did have the opportunity to survey state party leaders across the nation. He compared his new data with survey material compiled by Gibson and his colleagues in 1983. Table 11.1 provides the results of this analysis. One should bear in mind, also, that the study by Gibson and his colleagues shocked observers by indicating how truly active state parties were. Thus, Aldrich's findings give further weight to the organizational resurgence supposition.

Even though the revivalist perspective challenged traditional wisdom, it was also clear that service-oriented party organizations were different. A flurry of works set their sights on redefining what parties were up to and how they might best be conceptualized. Leading the way was Arterton (1982) and his "Party as PACs" model, Frantzich's (1989) "service-vendor party," and perhaps

Table 11.1 Financial and campaign activities of state party organizations, Aldrich (1999), with comparisons to Gibson et al. (1983)

Variable	Gibson et al. (1983)	Aldrich survey (1999)	Difference
Contributed to governor (%)	47	89	+42
Contributed to other constitutional offices (%)	44	81	+37
Contributed to congressional (%)	48	85	+37
Contributed to state senator (%)	25	85	+60
Contributed to state legislator (%)	47	92	+45
Held fundraising event (%)	19	98	+77
Conducted campaign seminars (%)	89	95	+6
Operated voter ID programs (%)	70	94	+24
Conducted public opinion surveys (%)	32	78	+46
Typical election year budget ($000)	340	2,800	+2,460
Typical election year full-time staff (no.)	7.7	9.2	+1.5

Source: Aldrich (2000, 659).

most notably Herrnson's systematic reviews of the institutionalization of the parties' congressional committees during the 1980s (1988, 1990, 1994). Paralleling each other in many key aspects, these perspectives suggested that parties comprise a small group of elite campaign professionals that hold as their foremost goal raising ever larger sums and becoming more technically advanced at campaigning. They have adapted to "PAC politics" by serving as intermediaries between special-interest groups and candidates. Although winning elections remained the most important outcome of party activity; "successful" parties are also those capable at aiding candidates with new-style elections.[2] After a period of decline, the parties had "attained a degree of institutional preeminence that they have never known before and have carved out a secure niche for themselves by virtue of their fund-raising and campaign capabilities" (D. Price 1984, 297).

This transformation brought with it a collective sigh of relief because it was assumed the new focus would resonate throughout the political system. Herrnson's book *Party Campaigning in the 1980s* (1988) did much to shift scholarly focus from individual behavior (the voter and the candidate) to the organization. He was also quite optimistic about the new party model. Among other things, Herrnson speculated that the institutionalized party system would:

[2] Scores of scholars and journalists commented on the power and sophistication of the RNC during the 1980s, even though their electoral success was limited.

- foster the development of a stronger, more nationally oriented sense of party identification among voters;
- lead to party-centered television commercials, radio advertisements, and press releases;
- strengthen the party's policy-based image;
- create a large group of new-style partisans—ones who were more committed to support a party than are traditional party identifiers;
- and make elections more competitive (Herrnson 1988, 126–7).

Other scholars suggested much the same. Kayden and Mahe (1985) were sanguine in their take of the new party system: "More people will have access to more information than ever before and that, we believe, will lead to an increase in partisan intensity" (199). L. Sandy Maisel, in the parting paragraph of his first collection of essays, *The Parties Respond*, notes that the new parties "stand ready to play a key role in a new electoral alignment; indeed, that part of the renewal is well underway" (1990, 322–3). Anthony Gierzynski, in his path-breaking look at the emergence of state-level legislative campaign committees—a key piece of the resurgence puzzle— is optimistic as well, but also a bit more cautious: "The parties may be moving, however slightly, toward the model of responsible parties . . . allowing voters to more directly select policy alternatives through the selection of party candidates" (1992, 122). It simply made good sense to speculate that as organizations bounced back, so too would voter partisanship. The link between party spheres seemed tight throughout history so why should this new phase be any different?

ENTER THE PARTY SPOILERS

One of the first scholars to call attention to the limits of what he dubbed the "new orthodoxy of party resurgence" was John Coleman (1994). In a piece entitled "The Resurgence of Party Organizations? A Dissent for the New Orthodoxy," Coleman challenged the revivalists' logic. He argued that recent party research had been shortsighted and misdirected. One striking anomaly in the contemporary party system is that scholars view party organizations as vibrant while the public has become increasingly skeptical about the relevance of political parties to governing. More citizens say that interest groups better represent them than do parties, particularly the young. Another nagging issue concerned voter turnout. A party system dubbed resurgent or revitalized would *not* witness sustained declining participation, which has been the case throughout the 1980s and 1990s. Coleman compared parties to a failing business. After all, if things are going so well, why so few customers? Although parties have new marketing schemes, these hardly matter if there are no new customers.

A good deal of my research has centered on a similar theme. In *Transforming Democracy* (1995) I argued the proliferation of state-level legislative campaigns will displace local party organizations. These organizations are well suited for helping candidates, but inept at forging links with voters. They are yet another example of the centralization and professionalization of party politics. In 1999, I published an article suggesting that the traditional realignment process was likely gone; we had entered a "baseless" party system. Here party organizations would remain viable, but rather than attract new voters into the system—thereby expanding the base of the party—national, state, and local organizations would focus their energies on candidate services. In this system, winning the next election is more important than cultivating long-term voter loyalties.

A few years later, in a piece dubbed "Schattschneider's Dismay; Strong Parties and Alienated Voters" (2003), I explored individual-level data that seemed to buttress the claim that average citizens have been left out of the organizational revival process. If party organizations are more active than in the past, we might speculate that citizens would also be more involved. Yet measures of split-ticket voting, electoral participation, trust, and efficacy all seemed to underscore the limit to the resurgence perspective. Many forces had pushed citizens away from the process, but the "reinvigorated" parties had seemed to do little to reverse this trend. "Party scorecards tally only wins and losses after election day," I argued, "rather than any long-term cultivation of voters" (229).

EXPLAINING THE PARADOX

Party scholars were confronted with what seemed to be a paradox: party *organizations* were experiencing a period of dramatic resurgence, while *citizens* seemed to shun party and electoral politics. To be fair, most party organization scholars said their claims of a revitalized party system were not intended to challenge the entire decline perspective, but rather to present information to suggest the behavioral-centered approach was myopic. Some argued it was time to reconceptualize what was meant by "party," which implied a movement toward a more organizational model. In other words, if voters were dropped from the party rubric the picture became less vexing. Parties are akin to firms and the voters are the consumers, suggested John Frendreis (1996).

Many sought to integrate the divergent trends. Schlesinger (1985, 1991) argued that changes in party in the electorate over the last several decades help explain the growth of party organizations. "It is the very weakness of partisan identification among the voters which is a stimulus for the growth of partisan organizations" (J. Schlesinger 1985, 1167). Given that split-ticket voting, a good measure of electoral volatility, hit its peak immediately prior to the organizational buildup of the 1980s, this argument seemed logical. Putnam, in *Bowling Alone*, made a similar argument: "Since their 'consumers' are tuning out from politics, parties have to work harder and spend much more, competing furiously to woo voters, workers, and donations, and to do that they need a (paid) organizational infra-structure" (2000, 40). Aldrich (2000) argued that the growth of electoral competi-tion in the South (declining Democratic loyalties) during the last two decades has led to the creation of aggressive, vibrant party structures.

Another closely related supposition was dubbed the "counteracting model" (Cotter and Bibby 1980; Frendreis, Gibson, and Vertz 1990). Here it was conjectured that organizational resurgence has been so successful that the parties have pulled voters away from their partisan predisposition (Cotter et al. 1984, 103). The causality was inverted from the Schlesinger model. Not to despair, the model suggested that while declining party loyalties were not a positive sign, it was more than counteracted by renewed party organizations. As noted by Frendreis, Gibson and Vertz, "Further analysis should be mindful of the role that party organizations can play in counter-acting declines in areas like mass attitudinal attachments" (1990, 233).

A final perspective was a bit more contentious. Perhaps "revitalized" party organizations turned voters away from party politics. That is, the new parties were simply pushing voters away. As one might imagine, drawing an *empirical* connection between party activities and voter withdrawal was difficult, but there were a number of interesting bits of evidence, including:

Campaign finance shenanigans. Given the public's uneasiness about excessive money in the political process, and also given that money was jet fuel for revitalized party organizations, perhaps many equated "party politics" with corrupt politics. Parties in the 1980s and 1990s bent the limits of finance regulations, to be sure, and trunkloads of survey evidence suggested the public's cynicism (Lehmann 1997).

Going negative, often. While we know that negative campaigning does not demobilize the electorate, it might have a lasting negative impact on less partisan voters (Ansolabehere and Iyengar 1995). Party organizations have shown an increased receptiveness to negative, attack-style electioneering in the 1980s and 1990s (Ginsberg and Shefter 1990; Shea 1999). During the waning days of the 1998 election, for example, both parties spent record-breaking amounts on "issue advocacy" advertisements, nearly all of which were negative. This led one observer to call them "issue attacks" (Abramson 1998).

Scandal politics. Theodore Lowi has argued that "party leaders have responded to gridlock not with renewed efforts to mobilize the electorate but with a strategy of scandal" (1996, 176). Indeed, the list of examples in the 1990s of where parties responded to opposition with personal attacks, rather than policy alternatives, is hefty (see also Ginsberg and Shefter 1990). Might "politics by other means" turn voters off?

Electoral demobilization. Given that party operatives in the 1990s were some of the best-trained new-style campaign consultants, we can imagine that they would pursue new-style tactics and strategies. One such approach is to reduce the size of the electorate to highlight the import of targeting schemes. A smaller electorate is more manageable, and this would not be the first time in American history that party leaders sanctioned, if not endorsed, strategies to shrink the size of the electorate (Piven and Cloward 2000).

Discounting young citizens. In the fall of 2003, John Green and I conducted a telephone survey of 805 local party officials (mostly county chairs) from communities of all sizes and types from across the nation (Shea and Green 2007). One of the most significant findings of the study dealt with young citizens. We asked an open-ended question: "What demographic group of voters is particularly important to the long-term success of your local party?" "Young voters" were mentioned by just 8 percent of party leaders. Senior citizens were mentioned nearly three times as often, even though the question addresses the long-term success of the party. Next, respondents were asked to think of another group. Here young voters were mentioned by only 12 percent. Finally, respondents were asked a third time to mention an important demographic group, at which time 18 percent pointed to younger voters. In all, local party leaders were given three opportunities to suggest younger voters are important to the long-term success of their party, but just a tad over one-third did so. This suggested, we argued, a much sharper focus on electoral success than on long-term party building.

Promotion of "non-partisan" candidates. One of the best ways to win a race with a dealigned electorate is to pitch the candidate as "independent." I can understand that consultants would be anxious to move in this direction, but would service-oriented party operatives reject it?

The breakdown of party tickets. In the waning weeks of the 1996 presidential race, for instance, the National Republican Campaign Committee ran a series of television advertisements that suggested to voters they might feel better about supporting Bill Clinton if they also voted for a Republican for the House. Bob Dole was furious about the commercials, but notions of tickets seemed out of fashion—even for party operatives. Two years later, Charles Rangel, chairman of the board of the Democratic Congressional Campaign Committee, berated Roy Romer, then the general chair of the Democratic National Committee (DNC), for hoarding money for Al Gore's 2000 race. George W. Bush, the GOP establishment candidate from the beginning, refused to campaign with other members of his ticket in 2000. In 2008, we also saw a number of Republican operatives push their candidates to draw some distance from John McCain.

Sacrificing local party structures. Finally, the locus of party rejuvenation has primarily been at the national and state levels (J. White and Shea 2000). As the party system moved from the local structures (the mom and pop shops of politics, so to speak) voters found less of a connection to the entire electoral system. Putnam suggests this shift may have wide repercussions. "There may be nearly as many fans in the political stadium nowadays, but they are not watching an amateur or even a semipro match. Whether the slick professional game they have become accustomed to watching is worth the increasingly high admission is another matter" (2000, 40).

A conservative estimate is that during the 1980s and 1990s the national party committees spent well over $3 billion. What a dramatic turn since the "partyless" age of the 1970s. From the perspective of candidates, the payoff was immense. National party organizations and state-level units had become the largest single contributor to candidate coffers, and their services extend far beyond financing. They had become the repositories of squadrons of new-style consultants and an array of high-technology tools of the trade. The parties had, indeed, responded.

But once again, are candidates the *only* consumers in the party system? Historically, party organizations cultivated voter loyalty and used this base as a resource on election day. Likely this was the logic that compelled some revivalist scholars to make optimistic predictions. Surely voters will be part of any organizational growth. Nonetheless, at precisely the same time that organizations "rose from the ashes," voters moved away from the party system.

Optimistically, we might conclude that service-oriented organizations grew precisely *because* voters abandoned partisanship. It was a way to counteract the growing uncertainty of elections. But that was in the beginning. One would have expected that by the end of the century, after some thirty years of "nucleus building" (J. Schlesinger 1985), party organizational activity would have spread into greater party loyalty and the electorate would have been drawn into the system. Other than strengthen GOP loyalties in the South, as the 1990s drew to a close, scholars seemed hard-pressed to see any significant improvement in attitudes toward either party, the two-party system, or electoral politics in general.

RECENT ELECTIONS

And then things changed. The decline in partisanship and overall interest and faith in the electoral process took a dramatic turn in the 2000 election, and it continued in subsequent elections. Our reservoir of voter survey data only extends back to the 1950s, so it is risky making sweeping historical generalizations, but it is probably

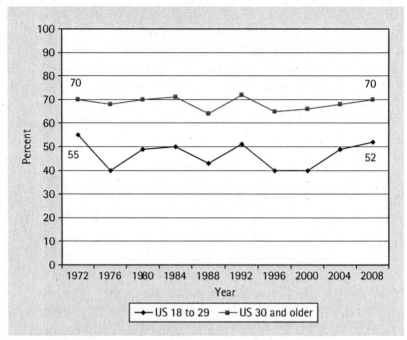

Figure 11.2 National voter turnout in presidential elections, 1972–2008 (%)

Source: Kirby and Ginsbert (2009).

safe to say that the 2000 election triggered one of the most significant transformations in American electoral history.

Let us start with turnout. As Figure 11.2 notes, turnout for all Americans continued to sag throughout much of the 1980s and 1990s (with the modest exception of 1992), but after the 2000 election there was a dramatic rebound. This was especially true for young Americans, as their turnout jumped 11 percent between 2000 and 2004.

Now let us consider a sampling of data from the American National Election Study, as noted in Figure 11.3. As to why there has been such a dramatic turnaround, theories abound. Thomas Patterson, who heads the Vanishing Voter Project at Harvard University, has underscored the importance of issues and voter concerns. "Americans historically have voted in higher numbers when the nation confronts big issues. That was as true in the late 1800s and 1930s as it has been more recently. The meltdown in the financial markets [in the fall of 2008] likely confirmed Americans' belief that 2008 was a watershed election" (Patterson 2008). Another perspective holds that the competitiveness and subsequent importance of the 2000 election drew new participants into the process. David Hill writes, "National elections in the United States since 2000 have been very competitive and thus it is possible that the cohorts entering the electorate during this period will create a footprint...and turnout will increase in future elections" (2006, 5).

One possibility may be changing attitudes toward government and the electoral process. According to ANES data, the percentage of Americans suggesting that the outcome of elections do *not* make public officials listen to the voters shrank from a high of 20 percent in 1984 to 7 percent in 2004. In fact, the 2004 figure matches the lowest level in the survey's history.

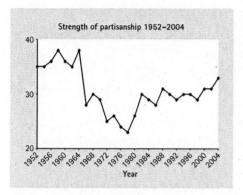

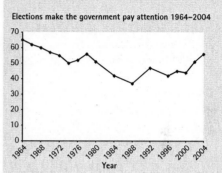

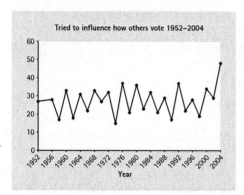

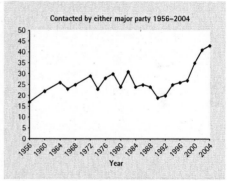

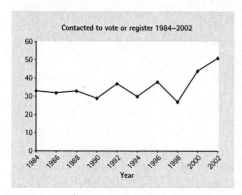

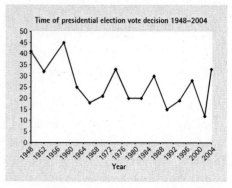

(Continued)

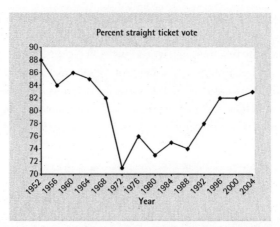

Figure 11.3 Percentage of Americans who split their vote choice, 1952–2004
Source: ANES (2005).

Still another possibility relates to the number of persuadable voters. Throughout much of the last three decades about one-fifth of the electorate "knew all along" who they would vote for. That figure jumped to 33 percent in 2004 (again, using ANES data). Similarly, about 7 percent of voters made up their minds on election day during the revival period. In 2004, this figure had shrunk to just 2 percent. This affects voter mobilization in two ways. First, as more and more voters establish voting preference early in the process, the number of voters who struggle with the "costs" of casting an informed vote declines. Second, and more importantly, as election activists confront a predisposed electorate, resources are shifted from persuasion to mobilization. Put a bit differently, if most voters make up their minds well before the election, then it makes sense to focus on getting the faithful to turn out.

Which brings us to another explanation of increased voter interest in recent elections: perhaps the activities of the revitalized party organizations have finally yielded dividends. Conceivably, the counteracting model, where organizational renewal is spurred by declines in partisanship and voter interest, has swung in the other direction. Aggressive party organizations have done what Schattschneider had hoped: connected in meaningful ways with the electorate. Maybe Herrnson's supposition, detailed above, that revitalized parties would create a large group of new-style partisans, voters even more committed to support a party than traditional party identifiers, has been realized.

There is evidence to suggest this might be the case. One of the figures above suggests nearly twice as many voters contacted by either of the major parties in the 2004 election than were contacted at any point since the ANES began measuring this issue (since 1956). Roughly the same finding emerges when respondents are asked about whether anyone contacted them to register to vote. And while empirical data have not yet been made available for the 2008 election, anecdotal evidence suggests that Barack Obama's historic "ground game" entailed many local party operatives and some local party committees. A reasonable guess is that Obama had four times as many "ground troops" as did John Kerry or Al Gore. This was especially true in swing states. For example, John Kerry had ten field offices in New Mexico, while Obama had thirty-nine.

Indeed, there is little doubt that Obama's neighborhood team and "net-roots" approach has revolutionized electoral politics. As noted by one observer, "The architects and builders of the Obama field campaign have undogmatically mixed timeless traditions and discipline of good organizing with new technologies of decentralization and self-organization" (Exley 2008). Marshall Ganz, a labor organizer who has led training sessions for Obama staff members and volunteers, noted much the same: "They've invested in a civic infrastructure on a scale that has never happened before. It's been an investment in the development of thousands of young people equipped with the skills and leadership ability to mobilize people and in the development of leadership at the local level. It's profound" (UPI.com 2008).

A few months after John Kerry lost the presidential race, fellow Democrat Bill Bradley wrote an insightful op ed in the *New York Times* (March 30, 2005). He argued that while the Republican Party had focused efforts on structural enhancements, the Democrats had neglected organization with the hopes that a strong leader would resurrect the party. The Democrats have been, he argued, "hypnotized by Jack Kennedy, and the promise of a charismatic leader." The Republicans, on the other hand, "consciously, carefully and single mindedly built an organization based on money, ideas, and action." Did the Obama campaign change this dynamic? Galvin (2008) has recently argued that while Obama represents that sort of charismatic leader, his team *also* focused extensively on building grassroots organizations in every state. "Indeed, his commitment to rebuilding the Democratic Party [was] not incidental to his candidacy. It [was] seen as a major selling point, something that attract[ed] Democrats to his campaign."

It is a bit early to say with certainty, but most observers suggest the top-down, microtargeted, television-based model that has dominated American politics since the early 1960s has been transformed—and perhaps even displaced. "They have taken the bottom-up campaign and absolutely perfected it," noted Joe Trippi, a key player in Howard Dean's Internet-based campaign for the presidency in 2004. "It's light-years ahead of where we were four years ago." Trippi further noted, "They'll have 100,000 people in a state who have signed up on their Web site and put in their zip code. Now, paid organizers can get in touch with people at the precinct level and help them build the organization bottom up. That's never happened before. It never was *possible* before" (Dickinson, March 20, 2008).

While this may all be true, the extent to which these new organizations connected with existing party committees is unclear. Obama's ground troops were, for the most part, new activists, likely less inclined to merge their efforts with the "establishment." Second, many (perhaps most) local party leaders endorsed Hillary Clinton during the nomination contest, and there was lingering animosity between the two camps.

To further assess the status of local party structures we might touch upon campaign finance issues. Many expected the Bipartisan Campaign Reform Act of 2002 to greatly diminish the role of party committees in federal elections. The principal goal of the legislation was to end unlimited soft money contributions to the national party committees. How would parties survive without this massive reservoir of funds? In reality, the parties have done just fine, raising enough hard money to compensate for the loss of soft money resources (La Raja 2006; Farrar-Myers and Dwyre 2008). Once again, it seems that the national parties have demonstrated their ability to adapt.

Yet, two issues are worth mention. First, one of mutations of the law has been the mushrooming weight of independent 527 organizations. How these new players will shape the electoral process in the years ahead is anyone's guess. Thus far, they have demonstrated an ability to raise a great deal of money and sophistication on how to spend those resources, and a propensity to engage voters at the grassroots. Might these units usurp local parties in the years ahead?

Second, and of greater importance, BCRA has had a significant impact on state and local parties. Backers of the reform seemed to appreciate the importance of local structures in a viable democracy. Prior to 2002, the national parties channeled much of their soft money down the organizational pyramid, particularly to state and local parties in swing states and in those with competitive congressional and Senate races. To help deflect the impact of declining soft money, the law created higher hard money contribution limits to parties: from $5,000 to $10,000. It also allows state and local parties to raise up to $10,000 from corporations and unions for grassroots activities under what was called the Levin Amendment. But there is little evidence that state and local parties have taken advantage of these provisions. As reported by Farrar-Myers and Dwyre, "Only 17 percent of the state party receipts reported to the Federal Election Commission qualified as soft money in 2004, down from 62 percent in 2000" (2008, 149). It seems that big donors have been reluctant to give to state and local parties, which may explain the dramatic rise of 527 organizations. Some have speculated that local parties would likely link their efforts to like-minded 527 groups, such as some local Democratic organizations did with Americans Coming Together in 2004, but that would seem a tenuous scheme for long-term viability. "State and local parties will likely rely more heavily than in the past on partisan entrepreneurs and interest groups outside the formal party structure," notes Raymond La Raja (2006, 115).

One of the key indicators of how the efforts of the Obama campaign might spill over into party dynamics has centered on the lists garnered by the Obama team in 2007 and 2008. The fact that the Obama campaign compiled an email inventory of over 13 million aggressive, active supporters was not lost on the DNC. Would they hold these contacts close to their vest, drawing them out when they believed important, or would they turn them over to the DNC, and to state and local party committees? Put a bit differently, would the Obama net-root campaign be coupled with party-building efforts—or would it remain a separate entity, to be used by the president when needed?

We know that shortly after the election Obama lead strategist David Plouffe sent an email to 10 million activists soliciting funds to help the DNC retire its 2008 debt. His note stated

The DNC went into considerable debt to secure victory for Barack and Joe. It took unprecedented resources to staff up all 50 states, train field organizers, and build the technology to reach as many swing voters as possible. It worked. But it also left the DNC in debt. So before we do anything else, we need to help pay for this winning strategy.

The success of the note remains unclear.

We also know that Obama's pick for DNC chair, Governor Tim Kaine of Virginia, has publically stated that he expects the lists to be "rolled into the party" for permanent use. Moreover, he intends to use the list to motivate supporters to engage in numerous policy battles. "We're very focused on the notion that engagement should not just be around contributing or being part of election cycles. It should be around governance and social change" (Lawrence 2009). It would seem, then, that not only will Obama's efforts aid party coffers, but they may also bolster the party's policy activities. The extent to which these efforts will aid state and local party efforts remains unclear.

And what about GOP efforts? According to ANES data, in thirteen of sixteen presidential and midterm elections between 1970 and 2004, Republican identifiers were more likely to report being contacted by a political party than were Democratic identifiers. In every one of these elections GOP followers were contacted more often than were independents. This would suggest that Republican outreach efforts were quite robust. Comparable survey data from the 2008 election will not be available for some time, but by most accounts community-based Republican efforts were rare. Not surprisingly, turnout in heavily Republican areas was actually down in 2008. As they regroup to win back some of the local, state, and federal office seats they have lost in recent elections, will Republican organizations shift resources from grassroots mobilization to direct candidate services?

In sum, the precise weight of party mobilization efforts—juxtaposed dynamic candidates, crosscutting issues, a lengthy campaign, massive media buys, and projected close elections—in recent elections is unclear. Did intensifying party identification, due to crosscutting issues, as Patterson suggests, do more to mobilize voters than did party operatives? Did local party organizations have lead roles in recent elections or were they simply members of the Obama chorus?

CONCLUSION

But what does this all mean? Scholars have, for some time, noted a conflict between elite and popular democracy (see Walker 1966; Bachrach 1967; Dahl 1989; Lappé 1989). Elite democracy, or what John White and I dub Hamiltonian nationalism

(2004), holds that so long as there are guarantees of fairness and political opportunity, the system is healthy. After elections, public officials should be left to conduct the business of government. It is best for average citizens to stay out of the way because governance is complex business. As for party politics, this model underscores the role of professional, centralized, national organizations. Ideological and policy purity is sacrificed for the sake of electoral efficiency. In this sense, the best parties are rational-efficient.

Popular democracy, or what we dub Jeffersonian localism, is based on the Rousseauian ideal where a premium is put on civic involvement in the conduct of government. This approach implies an ongoing, meaningful involvement in the political process. When this occurs, citizens develop an affinity for the system because they feel as though they have a stake in the outcome. "[C]itizenship, after all, is an acquired taste or discipline. For the most part, people are drawn to politics by private motives, and only later develop public ones" (McWilliams 2000, 3). Jeffersonian localism, then, is a model where citizens connect with party organizations in their community. These units are amateur-based, localized, and to a good extent, ideologically driven. Clearly, much of what we witnessed among the Obama campaign in 2008 reflected this approach.

Jeffersonian party politics affords citizens numerous meaningful ways to become involved in the political process. Average citizens can work on behalf of their favorite candidate in a Hamiltonian system, but professional operatives are preferred; there is enhanced efficiency and accountability. Candidates need services, and professionals, hired by the national party organizations, will simply do a better job. When political action is amateur-based and localized, the connection between the participant's efforts and "the system" are less abstract, also. Maybe, as suggested by Aristotle, the experience of politics must offer something beyond one's immediate interest: the dignity of being recognized and being heard, the warmth of political friendship, and ultimately, the possibility of noble deeds and the good life (as cited in McWilliams 2000, 3).

While the "revived" parties of the last few decades before the 2008 election afforded candidates cutting-edge services, little of what they did fostered a sense of citizenship. Can anyone really say, with a straight face that is, that a party message via email or television commercial is little different than a local activist knocking on a neighbor's door?

So the parties at the dawn of the twenty-first century are confronted with an opportunity. Recent elections have created a meaningful commitment to party labels, and the renewed interest in grassroots activism has been astonishing. Young citizens, in particular, stand ready to join the political fray, to come off the sidelines onto the political field. Further embracing the Hamiltonian model would likely help the organizations continue to provide candidates services, but a shift to a Jeffersonian model would foster long-term party sympathies and a willingness to remain engaged in the political process.

That is to say, the pathway that parties chart in the years ahead may affect their role in the system—as well as the democratic character of that system. The most consequential outcome of contemporary activities will likely be what it does to the spirit of the electorate. While party organizations will surely continue to provide candidates with new-style services, will their activities foster an affinity for politics among Americans? Several years ago scholar and pundit E. J. Dionne noted in *Why Americans Hate Politics* (1991) that a nation that hates the process of politics will not long thrive as a democracy. Far too many Americans have rejected politics in recent decades.

The revival of party organizations over the past few decades has been impressive. The electorate stands ready to embrace a more participatory, more ideological role. But will the service-oriented parties seize the opportunity? One cannot help but be reminded of the biblical admonition "To whom much is given, much is expected."

CHAPTER 12

WINNING ISN'T EVERYTHING

THIRD PARTIES AND THE AMERICAN TWO-PARTY SYSTEM*

RONALD B. RAPOPORT

THIRD parties in the United States are confusing phenomena. They range from the Republicans who supplanted the Whigs to Kinky Friedman's campaign for governor of Texas. Even the name "third party" is deceptive. They range from parties with clearly defined party organs and structures to ad hoc independent campaigns unaffiliated with other candidates on the ballot. And there are never just third parties in an election, but usually fourth, fifth, and sixth parties as well. Nonetheless, the term has been used to refer to parties other than the two major party organizations since at least 1852.[1] In this chapter I look at the factors that allow the emergence and continuity of third parties; the factors that allow them to succeed; and finally, at the long-term effects that third parties can have on the two-party system.

* I would like to extend thanks to Kira Allmann, Sandy Maisel, Chris Nemacheck, Abby Rapoport, Walt Stone, and Simon Stow for their comments and patience on this project.

[1] *American Whig Review*, 1852, quoting from "The Pittsburg Convention," 1852.

Third parties are those groups in a two-party system that run candidates for office but are themselves not one of the two major parties. Such parties have always been present in election campaigns but are almost always irrelevant to the outcome. There has, for example, been no presidential election in the last 130 years without multiple third parties running; but in the last ninety-six years, only three third parties have gained any electoral votes, and none has ever won electoral votes in sufficient quantity to deprive one of the mainstream parties of a majority victory in the electoral college. In this they still resemble George Ticknor Curtis's (1884, 132) dismissive characterization: "political mushrooms springing up suddenly and suddenly disappearing." Their disappearance, however, does not always imply lack of influence, nor indeed do they always disappear, and the rapidity of their disappearance is often inversely related to their electoral success.

Some parties, like the Prohibition Party, have run presidential candidates in every election since 1872 without ever receiving as much as 3 percent of the vote. On the other hand, the most successful third party since the Civil War, Theodore Roosevelt's Bull-Moose Party, which actually gained more votes than the Republicans in 1912, was barely in evidence four years after it had almost won the presidency. Third parties have very different processes of development (although typologies are rarely clear-cut). At one end of a spectrum, parties may emerge out of pre-existing interest groups (as in the case of the Right to Life Party), with the platform simply extending interest group politics into the electoral arena by highlighting the group's issues. In these cases the interest group sets the agenda, which the party and its candidates then adopt. Such parties stand in stark contrast to the candidate-centered parties of Ross Perot, Teddy Roosevelt, John Anderson, and George Wallace, which comprise the other end of the spectrum. In these cases the candidate creates the party in furtherance of his own agenda—both issue-based and personal. In such cases the party emerges out of the candidacy rather than the reverse. In dealing with third parties, then, the questions of what counts as a third party, and whether third parties can be dealt with as a single category, are crucial.

While recognizing differences among third parties, Rosenstone, Behr, and Lazarus (1996, 11) contend that what is most important is "the commonalities the movements share. Most prominently, they are all expressions of dissatisfaction with the major parties." V. O. Key (1964, 254) had suggested a narrower approach and argued, furthermore, that a "party can best be comprehended in the light of its place in the total political structure." Based on the differential effect of each on the party system, Key distinguishes between "those [third parties] formed to propagate a particular doctrine," most of which have attracted small votes, but many of which have stayed around for multiple elections; and a transient third party movement marked by a "rapid rise and [an] equally rapid decline."[2] Key argues that the first set of parties is

---

[2] Key also divides the short-lived third parties into parties of economic protest and secessionist parties.

"effectively outside the [party] system," while the second "are intimately connected with it" (Key 1964, 255).

Harmel and Robertson (1985) draw a similar distinction in dividing parties into "contender parties" and "promoter parties." Contender parties are often parties initiated by individual candidates as a vehicle for their presidential candidacies (American Independent, Bull-Moose, Perot's 1992 candidacy, and Anderson's 1980 candidacy). They are heavily focused on a positive electoral outcome. If successful, these parties can impact the party system. Focused on the possibility of winning and not just issue promotion, Perot demanded of those who wanted him to run, "register me in fifty states. If it's forty-nine, forget it. If you want to do fifty states, you care that much, fine, then I don't belong to anybody but you" (Germond and Witcover 1993, 217). Similarly, Michael Bloomberg indicated an unwillingness to run in 2008 unless he was likely to win the election. "Promoter" parties, on the other hand, have few illusions about winning. As Benjamin Bubar, presidential candidate of the Prohibition Party in both 1976 and 1980, put it: "The press would ask me if I really planned to go to the White House. I looked back at them and replied, 'Do I look that stupid?' . . . We have a political message that we think America needs. We're not going to the White House and we may not win, but we're having an impact" (Smallwood 1983, 43).

Contender parties differ among themselves as well. Some are formed around a single candidate running for office (usually president or governor). In this case, we often refer to "independent candidacies." Others run candidates across a wide range of offices in an attempt to control the full set of levers of government. Most large third party efforts through the early part of the century (Whigs, Populists, Bull-Moose) did run candidates for Congress and at the state level as well as at the presidential level. But beginning in 1924 with the LaFollette Progressives, and continuing through the present, those third parties attracting 5 percent of the vote or more for president ran few if any candidates for lower office. Our discussion will not differentiate between "independent candidacies" and party candidacies.

CHALLENGES TO OVERCOME

Anyone who studies third parties has to confront the fact that there has not been a fully successful third party (one which became a major party) in more than 150 years. This failure means that the barriers to third party success must be strong indeed, and identifying those barriers and their impacts is important to understanding the life cycle of particular third parties and the conditions under which new third parties emerge, as well as to understanding the levels of success that different third parties have achieved. Explaining the number of third parties able to compete in elections and explaining their electoral success are the two foci of most of the third party literature.

Although one might think that the two are very strongly related, such is not the case. An increase in the number of third parties does not guarantee a strong third party aggregate vote, and neither does a small number of third parties in a given election produce a weak third party vote. In 2008 twenty-one parties received a total of 1.6 percent of the total vote. By comparison, in 1912 with only four third parties qualified in two or more states, two of these got over 5 percent of the vote and the four together totaled 35 percent of the vote. Clearly it is important to view new party emergence and persistence (i.e., the number of third parties in an election) separately from issues of third party vote (Hug 2000).

As Rosenstone, Behr, and Lazarus (1996), Mazmanian (1974), Bibby and Maisel (2003), and others make clear, third parties always face a formidable set of challenges for both party creation and electoral success. Getting on the ballot and attracting a large vote require overcoming significant impediments. Some impediments are challenges to party formation and continuity (e.g., ballot access); others are challenges to party electoral support (e.g., level of partisanship, party organization, ability of major parties to co-opt, campaign finance laws, media exposure); and some are challenges for both (e.g., electoral system). I will examine, first, issues of party formation and then move on to consider bases of and barriers to third party electoral success.

THIRD PARTY FORMATION

In defining parties as organizations that run candidates for office, the distinction between an advocacy or interest group and a party is ballot access. But even when a group has the potential to get on ballots in every state and has a strong candidate, there is still no guarantee that the candidate will be willing to run. In many cases, the prospect that even with an unusually strong third party run there is little chance that he or she will be able to exert influence on government or policy is enough to blunt the candidate's desire. And the winner-take-all system of US presidential elections virtually guarantees that influence goes entirely to the winner.

As a result, the electoral system is a major barrier to third parties, particularly for "contender" parties. We will deal with the electoral system below as a brake on third party electoral success, but, at an even earlier stage, it is a real restraint on third party formation. Because no successful third party in history (with the exception of the Republicans, who did become one of the two major parties in their first presidential election in 1856) has seen its percentage of the vote increase in a subsequent election, the first election may be the best opportunity for success.[3] Supporters of a potential "contender" third party or candidate thus face the almost impossible task of trying to win in their first election. The task of putting together an organization and a campaign that can be successful its first time out, and that can convince voters that the third party's chance merits voter support and is not just a "wasted vote," is, however, enormous. Many who have considered running as third party candidates (e.g., Michael Bloomberg) have balked at the challenge, even when there was a serious constituency for their candidacy.

The challenges posed to third parties by the electoral system are evident in the experience of Ross Perot, who, despite garnering almost 20 percent of the vote, failed to win a single state or vote in the electoral college. One of the few propositions in political science that has even been referred to as a law—although not by its author—states, "The simple-majority single-ballot system encourages a two-party system" (Duverger 1963, 205). Had Perot's party run a slate of candidates for a national legislature under a system of proportional representation, however, it would have received 20 percent of the seats, provided a base on which to build in subsequent elections, and possibly emerged as the party able to determine the composition of government. Similarly, a 2008 Bloomberg party would not have had to win a plurality to emerge as a party with enormous influence on policy, giving Bloomberg an incentive to run. In fact under PR, smaller parties often exercise influence disproportionate to their size (the Free Democratic Party in Germany has frequently been in government even though it has never attracted even 15 percent of the national vote). With the first-past-the-post system advantaging major parties, any change to enhance the possibility of third party success is extremely unlikely.

As important as the electoral system is in party formation, the factor that has received the most attention regarding the ability of parties to develop and compete are ballot access requirements (Winger 1994). Ballot access became a significant formal hurdle after the introduction of the Australian ballot, which was in place in almost every state by 1892. Prior to the Australian ballot, parties printed their own ballots, usually on distinctively colored paper so that anyone who cared to observe was aware of the party being supported. Any party could print a ballot if they wished, or voters could simply write in whomsoever they wished. However, with states printing ballots under the Australian ballot reform, they had to determine rules of access to the ballot so that the ballot could be printed in time for the election.

---

[3] I am defining a successful third party as one gaining 5 percent of the vote or more in line with Burnham's (1970, 28) definition.

But the "golden age" of ballot access prior to the Australian ballot was not necessarily so golden for third parties, as Rosenstone, Behr, and Lazarus (1996, 25) show. Most significantly, prior to the Australian ballot printed and distributed by the state, third parties had to have the resources to print their own ballots and to distribute them across the state. The organizational and financial resources required for such an effort have always been difficult to come by for third parties. In addition, because parties printed their own ballots, it was relatively difficult to split tickets (which further disadvantaged third parties). And since votes were public, support for "non-traditional" parties was limited to the degree that voters might be reticent about admitting to their vote. In fact, after the Civil War until 1912, no third party made it on the ballot in every state.

Even though there were requirements to get on the ballot with the end of party ballots, "Under the early forms of the Australian ballot, third parties and independent candidates could, with relative ease, qualify for a position" (Mazmanian 1974: 90). The immediate effect, at least at the presidential level, was not evident as the Populist Party (with 8.5 percent of the vote) was on the ballot in all but two states in 1892 and the Prohibition Party (with only 2.2 percent of the vote) in all but three. As late as 1916, the Socialists were on the ballot in all states.

By 1924, however, rules had changed. Ten states increased their signature requirements for ballot access, making it more difficult to get on the ballot (Rosenstone, Behr, and Lazarus 1996, 22). California provided no way for a new party to get on the ballot via petition (a position upheld by the California Supreme Court).[4] Other changes were not in number of names needed, but rather in their format. In Florida, Robert LaFollette had to submit petitions from at least twenty-five voters in each of fifty-four Florida counties, and in Louisiana, the petitions could not contain the names of Democratic registrants (which encompassed the vast majority of the electorate), which made ballot access all but impossible. Although, in 1924, LaFollette needed to collect only 75,500 petitions to get on the ballot in forty-seven states (Winger 1988), the difficulties of doing so were such that the *New York Post* commented that "Senator LaFollette will have more difficulty getting his name on the ballots in the various states than he will in getting votes" (*New York Post*, July 11, 1924). And he could only get on the ballot by running under a potpourri of labels— Progressive, Independent, Independent-Progressive, and Socialist. Between 1924 and the George Wallace campaign of 1968, the requirements in number of petitions, format, and date of filing increased in difficulty.

Although we can chart trends in the number of third parties running, the states in which they qualified for the ballot, and the requirements for ballot access, it is far more difficult to impute causality. Indeed, in spite of what appears to be an obvious relationship between difficulty of getting on the ballot and parties that qualify, several

---

[4] LaFollette was able to run as a Socialist—a far less favorable designation, since that party had already been on the California ballot for many years.

scholars fail to find any such effect at the sub-presidential level. Hirano and Snyder (2007) find no overall effect on vote for third party gubernatorial and US House candidates with the introduction of the Australian ballot. In their analysis of 1996 congressional races, Collett and Wattenberg (1999) find no effect of ballot access difficulty on either number of candidates nor votes received. And Tamas and Hindman (2007) actually find a positive relationship between petitions required and vote for third party candidates. However, as Burden (2007) points out, many of these cases use absolute number of signatures rather than the percentage of the electorate. This is clearly a misspecification since it is easier to reach the same number of signatures in a large state than in a small state. Using percentage of voters required rather than number of voters, Burden (2007) does find that state ballot access requirements are significantly related to the number of congressional third party candidates in 2006, but not to the percentage of the vote received by third party candidates.

At the presidential level, Rosenstone, Behr, and Lazarus (1996) argue that ballot access problems had largely disappeared by 1980, although Winger rightly points out that several states have increased their ballot requirements in the past fifteen years. But what was the effect? If ballot restrictions do limit congressional candidacies (which are smaller, less organized, and more ad hoc), then by implication, the effects at the presidential level should be most evident among small third parties, rather than those that generate a large outpouring of support like George Wallace, Ross Perot, and John Anderson.

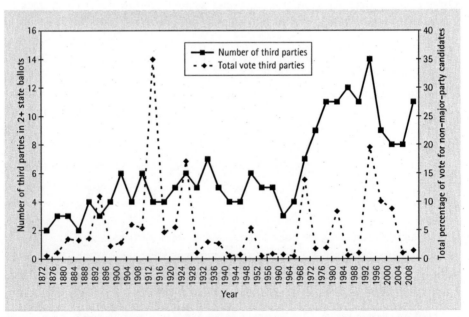

Figure 12.1 Third parties and total third party vote in presidential elections, 1872–2008

Figure 12.1 displays the number of parties qualifying for the presidential ballot in at least two states for each year since 1872, as well as the total percentage of the vote received by all third parties in every presidential election. Several things are clear from the figure. First, there is very little relationship between vote and number of parties, as I suggested earlier. In fact the two are correlated at only 0.12 (p > .5). Second, the number of parties increased slightly (albeit statistically significantly) from 1872 until 1964 at an average rate of one new party every fifty years (a period of time in which ballot access laws became more rigorous). However, the real change occurs after 1964. Those elections between 1872 and 1964 had an average of 4.3 third parties contesting presidential elections in at least two states. Between 1968 and 2008, the average number of parties more than doubled to 10.1 (p < .001).

The reasons for this are twofold. First, some of the most egregious requirements for ballot access were thrown out by the courts. George Wallace found himself denied access to the Ohio ballot, even after he had collected 440,000 petitions (15 percent of the turnout in the previous election), because he did not turn them in by February 7 (prior to either party's primary), as required by Ohio state law. The Supreme Court intervened and ordered Wallace placed on the ballot. Only eight years later, Eugene McCarthy, whose campaign had faltered badly, put much of his energy into ballot access cases, winning thirteen cases before the election and three after. As a result, by the time John Anderson readied his campaign for 1980, requirements for ballot access were significantly less difficult than they had been twelve years earlier. Whereas Wallace had needed around 1,700,000 valid signatures to get on the ballot in all fifty states, Anderson needed slightly fewer than 650,000 (Winger 1988), and Perot needed just over 695,000 petitions to get on the ballot (Winger 2006).[5] If we consider signatures required as a percentage of the actual presidential vote rather than just raw numbers of signatures needed, it is easier to make comparisons across time. In 1924, LaFollette needed signatures from only about 0.25 percent of all voters to qualify, but by 1968, the requirement for Wallace had risen by almost a factor of ten (to 2.4 percent of all voters) to qualify for the ballot. After 1968, petition requirements did diminish thanks to legal challenges from Wallace, Eugene McCarthy in 1968, and John Anderson in 1980, although not to the levels of 1924. Both Anderson in 1980 and Perot in 1992 needed petition signatures from 0.8 percent (less than one-third the percentage required for Wallace).

The problems associated with presidential ballot access, while real, appear currently less problematic than at any extended time in American history.[6] If we take as our starting point the post-Civil War period, it is impressive to note that between

---

[5] These numbers are based on the method that has most frequently been used in each state by candidates to get on the ballot (Winger 2006).

[6] Although petition requirements increased from around 635,000 in 2004 to 690,000 in 2008, the 2008 number is still below that of 1992 with a population that has increased by 20 percent over the same period.

1872 and 1892 (for most states, the pre-Australian ballot period), there were no elections in which any third party received votes in every state. Whereas third party presidential candidates were able to secure ballot access in all states only twice between 1896 and 1964 (the Socialists in 1912 and 1916), between 1968 and 2008 eight parties did so. More remarkably, it was not just parties receiving large shares on the vote in the general election that were able to get on all the ballots. Three did so even though they received less than 0.5 percent of the total presidential vote, and did so without huge expenditures of money (which they lacked in any case).[7]

But has too much has been made of the number of petitions required, without considering how changes in technology might make ballot petition drives cheaper and easier to coordinate? Unfortunately, little research has been done in this area, but it is an important issue for third party scholars, and deserves attention. Developments in communications and transportation might help explain how third parties have achieved increased success in ballot access even as the number of required signatures stayed fairly constant overall (although varying within states) over the past twenty-five years. The difficulty of organizing a Perot-like effort in precomputer days, let alone in pretelephone days, is almost impossible to comprehend. Even in 1968, the Wallace campaign benefited from the increased use of the airplane and direct dialing, among other improvements. More recently, how much has the use of Meetup, Facebook, blogs, and other Internet made ballot access for new third parties increasingly possible?

BALLOT PETITIONS AS AN OPPORTUNITY FOR ACTIVIST MOBILIZATION

While ballot access requirements do present a challenge for small third parties, they may also provide an opportunity for "contender" parties with significant popular appeal to actually expand their visibility and their eventual vote through the mobilization of campaign activists around the ballot petition effort. The difficulty of collecting petitions is often due (especially among twentieth-century third parties) to the lack of organization and of activists. Replacing the stable organizations of nineteenth-century third parties with occasional activists motivated by a new party or candidate is a difficult challenge. Very little work on third parties has focused on third party activists (see Martin and Spang 2001; Canfield 1984; Rapoport and Stone 2005; J. McCann, Rapoport, and Stone 1999), but activists

[7] The Libertarian Party got its nominee on the ballot in all states and the District of Columbia in 1992 for between $600,000 and $700,000, or about a dollar a name (Redpath 1995).

provide the organizational skills and labor that third parties so desperately need. Major parties have continuing activists, but third parties have to create them anew. And ballot access campaigns, although arduous, difficult, and usually expensive, provide the opportunity for the recruitment of activists, particularly as advances in computer technology have made contact with and organization of activists cheaper, less labor-intensive, and far more comprehensive.

The Perot campaign of 1992 is a case in point. It spontaneously formed around hundreds of thousands of volunteers "from Maine to California...opening petition offices and manning petition tables in shopping malls at their own expense to advance the cause" (Germond and Witcover 1993, 306). By creating the campaign around the petition efforts, Perot not only recruited volunteers, but also showed his high level of support, which helped to recruit more volunteers (whose names were entered into computer databases) and to convince voters of his viability. He also ensured significant media coverage in the mass rallies (virtually the only public events he attended prior to his dropping out of the race) that delivered vastly more petitions to state officials than were required by state law (Barta 1993, 479–80).

As a result of these committed volunteers, Perot was able to get on the ballot at least in the early states (through early July) without a vast professional organization. Although many have claimed that the success of the Perot campaign hinged heavily on his financial resources (Rosenstone, Behr, and Lazarus 1996, ch. 9), by the time he had taken the lead in the three-way presidential race, Perot had spent just over $2 million, less than either Buchanan or Tsongas in their failed nomination campaigns, and less than a quarter of what Bush or Clinton had spent (Federal Election Commission 1992). Altogether Perot collected 5,400,000 petitions, more than 5 percent of the 1988 presidential vote total (Barta 1993).

But Perot was not unique in his mobilization of volunteers for ballot access. George Wallace also experienced significant outpouring of spontaneous support, particularly in the South, but also in other states. All told he obtained more than 2.7 million petition signatures (Carter 2000, 307), about 4 percent of the 1964 presidential election turnout in what "was perhaps the most remarkable triumph of participatory democracy at the grass roots in the campaign of 1968, not excluding the McCarthy campaign" (Chester, Hodgson, and Page 1969, 284).

Although Eugene McCarthy in 1976 and John Anderson in 1980 blamed the ballot access fights for their failures, it was also a reflection of their failure to generate spontaneous and enthusiastic support for their campaigns, as well as a failure of strategy. Anderson spent $2.5 million on his ballot access effort, far more than Wallace had spent, even though he needed significantly fewer signatures. His desire to obtain numbers of petitions far beyond that required to generate media coverage turned out to be a serious miscalculation (Germond and Witcover 1981, 236–7), given his limited financial resources.

EXPLAINING THIRD PARTY ELECTORAL SUCCESS

Once third parties are on the ballot, their problems in terms of a significant vote are just beginning.[8] All major studies of third parties agree that third parties almost never control their own fate (Mazmanian 1974; Rosenstone, Behr, and Lazarus 1996; Gillespie 1993). Given that 90 percent of Americans either identify with or lean toward one of the two major parties, a third party's success depends on a significant rejection of both parties. Third parties are always underfunded relative to the major parties (with the possible exception of Ross Perot in 1992); they do not get the same level of media coverage; in only rare instances can they attract a nationally prominent figure to run; and in the forty-eight years that debates have been around, they have been excluded in all but one election.[9] Because of these constraints, third parties face an uphill struggle. Most commonly, when things are going badly, the incumbent party is tarred, and the other major party picks up support and is victorious. For significant third party support, more is required. As Rosenstone, Behr, and Lazarus (1996, 162) put it, 'Overwhelmingly, it is the failure of the major parties to do what the electorate expects of them . . . that most increases the likelihood of voters to back a minor party. Citizens by and large cast third party ballots because they are dissatisfied with the major parties, not because they are attracted to the alternatives.'

Failure of both major parties is rare, since, once aware of the situation of the incumbent party and of the threat from a third party, the non-incumbent party has an incentive to make a strong bid for a potential third party's constituency, so long as it can do so without seriously endangering its ongoing coalition of support. But even major party failure is only necessary but not sufficient for third party emergence. It provides the opportunity for third party success but does not guarantee it. Quality of third party candidates and the ability of those candidates to rally the discontent around their party or candidacy are also important to success. It is for this reason that in times of major party failure some third parties do extremely well, others fail to improve their showings from previous elections, and sometimes no third party emerges to seize the opportunity.

For the most part, then, we need to identify both strong push factors that provide the opportunity for third party success, and pull factors that convert the

---

[8] Most of the discussion of the determinants of third party electoral success focus on the presidential level, because the examples here are better known. It is the case, however, that with a few exceptions (e.g., the electoral college) the same factors that would be important at the presidential level would also be important for lower-level elections so long as the election is a first-past-the-post single-office election (e.g., single-member district legislative representative, governor, attorney general).

[9] Anderson was able to debate Reagan in 1980, but the crucial Reagan–Carter debates excluded him.

potential for protest into actual votes for the third party—a "push–pull" model of third party support (Rapoport and Stone 2005).

Scholars have done a generally good job of identifying push factors: economic stress, unpopular major party candidates, unpopular issue positions taken by major party candidates, marginalization of significant issues by both major parties, and high levels of general alienation (likely related to some of the previously mentioned factors), as well as some of the pull factors (strong third party candidates, successful issue appeals, media access, party membership) (Gold 1995; Rosenstone, Behr, and Lazarus 1996; Bibby and Maisel 2003; Rapoport and Stone 2005).

Systemic Factors Favoring Third Party Success

Historically, it is clear that these push factors all seem to be related to third party success at various times, although in different combinations. In most cases these push factors emerged out of economic, political, and social change, which created challenges for the major parties and created the opportunities for third party success. These challenges included the emergence of new issues not easily assimilated by the current party system, dislocation of sufficiently large groups to form the basis of a third party challenge, and demands for policies more extreme than either major party had heretofore endorsed (Sundquist 1983).

It is significant to note that these opportunities depended not on any of these dislocations being experienced by the system as a whole, but rather their being experienced by a group sufficiently large to be electorally significant. For example, Rosenstone, Behr, and Lazarus (1996, 135–7) emphasize the effect of specifically agricultural depressions (not necessarily associated with the same level of economic distress in the rest of the population) as the impetus for successful farmer-based third parties like the Greenback and Populist parties.

The failure of major parties to respond to a segmental economic disaster is understandable, since to do so may entail greater potential losses than potential gains. On the other hand, general depression (as in 1932) is certain to engage the attention of the non-incumbent party, whose response diminishes the chances of a third party breakthrough. The lack of a successful third party in 1932 is testament to this proposition.

Although there had been antislavery parties dating back to the Liberty Party in 1840, the issue of slavery had been effectively put off through a series of compromises beginning with the Missouri Compromise of 1820. The emergence of slavery as a major issue in the wake of the Kansas–Nebraska Act doomed the Whigs, which with a strong Southern wing could not engage the slavery issue without fracturing their coalition. By taking a strong antislavery position, the Republican Party was able to displace the Whigs within two years.

The role of race as a campaign issue returned in the 1960s, not because the issue was being ignored, but because it had been a major part of Lyndon Johnson's Great Society legislation. George Wallace and his supporters pushed back against the spate of bipartisan civil rights legislation and judicial rulings of the 1960s, and as the role of the federal government in civil rights, specifically in cross-district busing, became more widespread, George Wallace bluntly took extreme positions that neither major party endorsed. While never threatening the dominance of the Democrats or Republicans, Wallace attracted the largest third party vote in almost half a century and grabbed the attention of both major parties.

Factors Favoring Third Party Success: Individual Level

To understand the ways that these third party opportunities translate into third party success we need to focus on individual voter decision making, and ask under what conditions will voters consider and vote for third parties. Given the rarity of third parties votes, it must be assumed that both significant push factors and significant pull factors must be present. Rapoport and Stone (2005, ch. 2) lay out the basic logic of the "push–pull" model of third party support that will be followed here.

If we take an issue which is of paramount importance to a voter, we should expect that she will vote for the major party candidate who is closer to her on that issue. If she is a centrist, she will calculate how extreme each of the two party candidates is and then select the one who is less extreme. If there are a variety of issues which she cares about, she might average how distant she is from the candidate from Party D over the issues, do the same for the candidate from Party R, and vote for the candidate on average closest to her.

But what if both candidates are quite distant from her on the issue? If she hears about a third party candidate who has staked out a position relatively close to her own (as in Figure 12.2), she might consider voting for that candidate. Figure 12.2 represents this situation. We should expect that the further away she is from the closer major party candidate (here the distance from her position to the position of Party R's candidate), the greater the push away from the major parties. On the other hand, the smaller the distance to the closer major party, the less likelihood that a third party will even enter the choice set for the voter. In this case the "push" away from the preferred major party (R) is sufficiently large that the voter considers a third party candidate, but only if there is significant "pull" from the third party candidate by virtue of the issue proximity to the voter. Empirical research from both 1968 (Rosenstone, Behr, and Lazarus 1996, 163; Converse et al. 1969; Gold 1995) and 1992 (Rapoport and Stone 2005) supports our expectation that "push" factors (distance from the closer major party) and pull factors (close-ness to the third party candidate) both affect the propensity of third party voting.

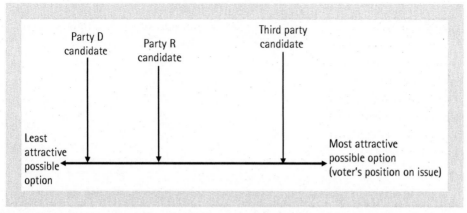

Figure 12.2 Push–pull model of third party support with separated major parties

But not only does the distance from closer major party to voter's position make a difference, so too does how much closer the more proximate major party (R) is to the voter compared with the less proximate major party (D). Because of the first-past-the-post electoral system, a third party victory is unlikely. This means that either party D or party R is going to win. To decide to reject both is a difficult decision. Therefore, even if party D and party R are both relatively distant from the voter but she is significantly closer to party R (as in Figure 12.2), she might decide to vote for Party R, despite her knowledge that she is far closer to the third party. If, in another scenario, she is not only distant from the closer major party but is also almost equally distant from the other (as in Figure 12.3), then her level of indifference between the major parties is quite high and the incentive to support an issue-proximate third party increases. In 1992, Perot activity declined as individuals felt closer proximity to one of the major parties than to the other (Rapoport and Stone 2005, 110).

When voters or activists even slightly prefer one of the major parties to the other (even if they prefer a third party to both), there may still be great concern that voting for that third party will elect the major party that they like less. Since the third party is unlikely to win, they are, therefore, wasting their vote in terms of the actual outcome. This wasted-vote or strategic-voting concern has significant empirical support behind it (e.g., Cain 1978). Abramson, Aldrich, Paolino, and Rohde (1995) show that in 1968, 1980, and 1992, third party candidates were far less likely to receive votes from those who preferred them to the other two candidates than was the case with major party candidates. Fewer than three in five (57 percent) 1980 voters who preferred Anderson to Reagan and Carter actually voted for Anderson, while 97 percent who preferred Carter voted for him and 97 percent of those who preferred Reagan over Carter and Anderson voted for him. The same trend holds for 1968, 1992, and 1996 (Abramson et al. forthcoming).

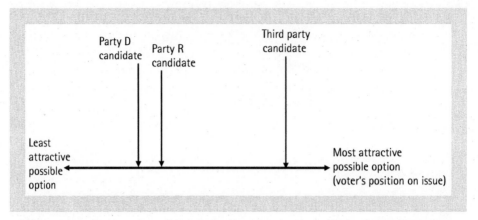

Figure 12.3 Push–pull model of third party support with undifferentiated major parties

However, as discussed above, this problem is diminished where the major parties are equidistant (or almost equidistant) on issue(s) important to the voter. Under such circumstances voting for a third party has only small costs. Another case would be where one's vote or activity is irrelevant to the election outcome. This is the case if the state in which one lives is clearly going to vote for the Democratic candidate or the Republican candidate. Since the election outcome is unaffected by an individual's behavior, she is free to support and work for whichever candidate she prefers. In contrast a close election nationally means that states that are closely contested (and could conceivably affect the national election outcome) should show more strategic voting and more drop-off in the third party candidate's support as election day approaches.

Burden (2005) finds that when an election is close in terms of electoral college likely results (e.g., 2000), voters in states that are close and prefer the third party candidate do in fact reject that candidate and vote strategically for one of the major parties. In 2000, the closeness of the election in a state was significantly related to the drop-off in Nader support between the final survey done and the actual vote Nader received. There was no such drop-off when the election outcome was predictable long before the election (1992, 1996).

The relationship between proximity and closeness of the election raises an interesting point. When parties are relatively centrist (or in agreement at some other point on the issue or ideological spectrum), there is little potential for strong differentiation relative to any given voter. But when parties are ideologically distant from one another, there is great potential for such differentiation. All other things being equal, the more differentiation between the major parties, the greater the pressure on voters to select one of them even in the presence of a preferred third party. The closer the election, the greater the propensity to choose a major party; the more top-heavy the winning margin, the greater the incentive to support third parties. A system that offers one-party dominance but little party differentiation would be most open to third party activity, while a system with highly differentiated parties and close elections should be least hospitable. Right now our system seems to be close to the latter example. American parties are (at least in Congress) more polarized than at almost any point in American history; and, elections have been relatively close in two of the last three cases.

What can a third party do? The issue model in Figures 12.2 and 12.3 is based on candidate and voter placement on issues (similar to the Wallace position on civil rights discussed above), but another dimension of issues that is important in third party support is issue priority. Two voters sharing the same position on an issue may differ in the priority they put on that issue. For some people who want to balance the budget, this is *the* issue, whereas for others who want to do so it may still be less important than lowering taxes. Just as it is with voters and activists, so too is it with candidates. A voter or activist may agree with a candidate on the preferred policy preference but doubt that that candidate will make it a top priority. For example, although most conservative activists did not doubt Ronald Reagan's pro-life sentiments, his lack of action on abortion and other social issues infuriated them (Troy 2005, 154).

Where issues have been relegated to the back burner by the major parties, historically the ability of third parties like the Republicans, Populists, and George Wallace's American Independent Party not only to take issue positions in line with a large constituency, but also to make these their top priority issues, has been effective in the aggregate. We would expect to find the same at the individual level. Voters should be more inclined to be supportive of third party candidates who share their issue position on a voter's high-priority issue if the issue is also a high priority for that candidate (while a low priority for the major party candidates). This becomes a "push" factor away from the major parties and a "pull" factor toward the third party. Even though the parties were highly differentiated on issues like abortion, national health, and affirmative action, these were less important to Perot's supporters than economic nationalism, reform, and the budget. Elevating their importance when the major parties largely ignored them provided a significant impetus for activist support on his behalf (Rapoport and Stone 2005, 110).

In addition to its issue appeals, of course, the Perot campaign offered the voters Ross Perot—the mythic figure, the self-made billionaire, can-do guy. This added greatly to the appeal because, in addition to the role of push and pull of issue factors in third party success, candidate factors are also important. Rosenstone, Behr, and Lazarus (1996) divide third party nominees into "nationally prestigious candidates," "prestigious candidates," and "non-prestigious candidates." They find that two-thirds of nationally prestigious candidates receive more than 9 percent of the vote, compared with only 6 percent of prestigious candidates and none of non-prestigious candidates. The less well regarded both major party candidates are by voters, the greater the likelihood of a vote for the third party. Of course, much of the dislike may be based on issue alienation from the major party candidates, but personal evaluations also affect presidential vote (A. Miller, Wattenberg, and Malunchuk 1986). The 1980 Anderson campaign epitomizes one in which the rejection of the major party candidates and the attraction to Anderson played a significant role, in the absence of distinctive issues which Anderson promulgated. Not surprisingly, Gold (1995) finds that while the degree of rejection of major party candidates is important in predicting third party vote in 1968, 1980, and 1992, the strongest effect is in 1980 (when issue proximity to major parties has no effect at all).

Other factors also play a role in third party voting, and one of the most frequently referenced is alienation. Although it may be an intervening variable reflecting issue and economic dissatisfaction, it has played a role in many third party campaigns. This is not surprising since if both parties are to be rejected in a two-party system, then the political system as a whole is likely to be tainted. In 1892, the Populist platform (*Congressional Quarterly* 1997, 59) decreed that the nation was on "the verge of moral, political, and material ruin. Corruption dominates the ballot-box, the Legislatures, the Congress, and touches even the ermine of the bench." Wallace and Perot both utilized similar populist themes, claiming that the average voter needed to have more access to the levers of power in order to control powerful, often corrupting, interests. In both years alienation had a significant effect on third party support (Gold 1995; Atkeson et al. 1996), emphasizing that both parties were responsible for the problems faced by voters and the country.[10]

THE DYNAMIC OF THIRD PARTIES

If third parties have not won the presidency nor displaced one of the major parties in almost a century and a half, then do third parties really matter? And if so, and under what conditions and in what ways do they affect the political system? And what happens to this influential third party?

Richard Hofstadter (1955, 97) remarked that "third parties are like bees; once they have stung they die," emphasizing the short life span of electorally successful third parties. And as Hofstadter suggests, every party getting more than 6 percent of the vote since the Civil War—the Populist, Bull-Moose, Progressive Party,

---

[10] Koch (1998) finds that alienation actually increased among Perot supporters after he entered the race. Nonetheless, both alienation before he entered and alienation measured later were strongly related to support for him (Peterson and Wrighton (1998).

American Independent, and Anderson campaign—were spent forces by the next presidential election.[11]

But although bees die once they sting, they also leave their stinger in their victim, who finds it hard to ignore. Analogously, third party success grabs the attention of the major parties and forces them to respond (if doing so does not seriously endanger their coalition and electoral prospects). And it is this response which both changes the party system and kills the successful third party. "Usually after a strong showing by a minor party, at least one of the major parties shifts its position, adopting the third party's rhetoric if not the core of its programs. Consequently, by the following election the third-party constituency...has a major party more sympathetic to its demands" (Mazmanian 1974, 143).

It is this process of major party attention, response, and third party supporter response to the major parties' attention that has been labeled "the dynamic of third parties" (Rapoport and Stone 2005). The "dynamic of third parties" requires three conditions to be met:

1. A third party movement must have a large and identifiable issue constituency from which it receives a substantial vote.

2. One or more major parties must make a bid for this support by tailoring their own positions to better reflect those of the third party's supporters.

3. The third party's supporters must respond to the bid by moving their support toward the major party or parties making the bid.

Although the dynamic has been described in similar ways by other third party scholars (Rosenstone, Behr, and Lazarus 1996; Mazmanian 1974), until very recently data at the mass and elite level have not been available to fully test the model. Data gathered from the Perot campaigns of 1992 and 1996 (Rapoport and Stone 2005) allow for such a test of all three requirements underlying the "dynamic of third parties."

Requirement 1: Large and identifiable issue constituency. Unless a third party achieves a significant vote total, the incentive for a major party to make a bid for their supporters is small. Nader's small vote in 2000, pivotal as it was, did not cause the Democratic Party to shift radically between 2000 and 2004. By way of contrast, both the Wallace and Perot supporters attracted much greater interest and much greater response from the Republicans in 1968–72 and 1992–6.

Third parties serve as "political venture capitalists" by identifying issues or issue positions that major parties have ignored. Although many ascribed Perot's success entirely to his money (Rosenstone, Behr, and Lazarus 1996) or to alienation and the

---

[11] Perot's 1992 campaign is a notable exception, but the promise of guaranteed federal funding for a 1996 campaign was a clear incentive to run once again.

economy (Dionne 1992), Perot supporters had distinctive positions around three sets of issues: economic nationalism (e.g., NAFTA, foreign involvement, immigration), reform (e.g., campaign finance reform and a balanced budget amendment), and the budget (cutting programs and increasing taxes). And on those issues, unlike the traditional left–right issues, Perot supporters were more extreme than either Democrats or Republicans (Rapoport and Stone 2005, 86).[12]

But if the third party's appeal is based on a set of distinctive issues, not only must the third party supporters differ from the major parties on these issues, but these issues have to be the basis of third party activity. And this is the case as well. The more extreme on the Perot issues (i.e., closer to Perot), the more activity and support for Perot. And, the greater the distance from the major parties on these issues, the more support for Perot. What made these issues particularly available for activist and voter mobilization around a third party candidacy is that the major parties differed far less on them than on traditional liberal–conservative issues (Rapoport and Stone 2005, 90). So, on these new Perot issues the downside risk of having the less favored major party win was less than on other issues.

These Perot issues not only increased Perot's support based on the agreement of the candidate and his supporters, but Perot's supporters also assigned these "Perot issues" much higher priorities than did the major party candidates. Agreement between Perot and his supporters on the priority of these issues had a strong additional effect on their level of Perot support.[13] Taken jointly, the combined effects of issue proximity and issue priority had an effect on Perot support almost equal to that of candidate evaluations (Rapoport and Stone 2005, 121). The significance of an identifiable set of issues provided a road map for the major parties if they wished to pursue and co-opt Perot's voters. The Republicans without the presidency and in the minority in both houses of Congress had the greater incentive, but could they do what was needed to add Perot supporters to their party without splitting their coalition?

Requirement 2: The Republican bid. The large vote for Perot immediately caught the attention of the Republican leaders, particularly Newt Gingrich. When Frank Luntz, former Perot pollster, spoke at a post-inauguration Republican retreat in early 1993 on the need and the strategy for Republicans to win over Perot voters, Gingrich was convinced. His "Contract with America" in 1994 was a document clearly aimed at Perot and his supporters, with its strong emphasis on reform and its disregard of issues like abortion and free trade, which were strongly opposed by

---

[12] The focus here will be on the 1992 Perot campaign as the "bee which stung" and set in motion the "dynamic of third parties," because the data on the 1992 campaign and its aftermath is most complete. However, there is clear evidence of a similar process in the case of a variety of other third parties as well (Rosenstone, Behr, and Lazarus 1996; Mazmanian 1974).

[13] As well as the perception that the issue was not a high priority for the major parties.

the Perot constituency, although key to important Republican constituencies. Remarkably, the Contract with America looked far more like the checklist at the end of Perot's *United We Stand* than it looked like the Republican platform of only two years earlier (Rapoport and Stone 2005, 152).

The bid was not only at the level of the party leadership. It was made explicit by Republican congressional campaigns across the country, who targeted likely Perot voters with telephone calls, canvassing, and mailings specifically emphasizing Republican commitment to reform and a balanced budget and other Perot issues (Rapoport and Stone 2005, 155).

Requirement 3: The response. The attempt was successful. Perot supporters shifted disproportionately to the Republicans in 1994. Whereas in 1992, about half of Perot's supporters voted Republican for Congress, in 1994 two-thirds did. But not only that, those who had been most active for Perot shifted their activity and support disproportionately toward the Republicans.

The Republican strategy of contacting Perot supporters with targeted communications worked. At every level of 1992 Perot activity, the higher the level of communications from the Republicans in 1994, the greater the level of Republican activity in 1994. And for those who received the most communications from the Republicans, their level of Perot activity from 1992 translated most directly into 1994 Republican activity (Rapoport and Stone 2005, 197). So by 1994, "the dynamic of third parties" had run its full cycle. Perot had shown the resonance of a set of issues that the major parties had had difficulty in articulating. The Republicans seized on the opportunity and fashioned a co-optation strategy which they promulgated through the Contract with America, and Perot's supporters responded as third party supporters in 1896 and 1972 had in forsaking the third party to support a major party.

Clearly, the Perot campaign, like other successful third parties, had not simply been the bee that stung and died, but the bee that left its stinger in the political system. Looking to 2008, Stan Greenberg and James Carville (2005b, 3) identified Perot voters as the swing group, this time encouraging the Democrats to "revisit the Perot voters and their concerns, even if Perot himself has faded from view."

CONCLUSION

We write off the possibility of major third party success at our peril. In the final edition of his masterful text on parties, V. O. Key (1964, 281) opines, "Students of the topic seem to agree that the day of the third party, at least in presidential elections is done." Ironically he wrote this in the election year preceding the 1968 Wallace campaign that seemed to usher in a spate of major third party candidates (in four of the next eight elections, a third party would get more than 6 percent of the vote—as many as had done so in the preceding hundred years). And the number of parties on the ballot in two or more states more than doubled from the pre-1964 era to the post-1964 era.

The extreme candidate-centered nature of the third parties that have emerged since 1964 probably explains some of his failure of prognostication. It also ignores the ways that when major parties ignore issues or fail to engage those on a particular side of important issues, they create opportunities for entrepreneurial candidates. And the entrepreneurial skills of politicians and activists and their ability to create new ways of organizing themselves and voters utilizing technological advances have allowed third parties to form quickly and to overcome the legal impediments to ballot access. This ability extends even to "promoter" third parties, which have achieved ballot access more frequently than in the past.

Third party success looks rather meager if we focus on the ability of a third party to become a permanent part of the party system either by displacing a major party or by establishing itself as a significant and consistent vote getter at the highest (i.e., presidential) level (similar to the Free Democratic Party in Germany or the Liberal Democrats in Britain). However, if we think of third parties as a crucial part of the two-party system, with the ability to appeal to a constituency on issues that the major parties ignore and raise those issues in a public forum, and, when their support is large, to influence one or both of the major parties to respond to those issues and that constituency, then their periodic success is obvious and their important and influential role in the American party system is clear.

PART V

PARTY ORGANIZATION

CHAPTER 13

....

THE EVOLUTION
OF NATIONAL
PARTY
ORGANIZATIONS

PAUL S. HERRNSON

ONCE characterized as poor, unstable, and powerless, national party organizations in the United States entered the twenty-first century financially secure, institutionally stable, and highly influential in election campaigns and in their relations with state and local party committees, political consultants, and interest groups. The national party organizations—the Democratic and Republican national, congressional, and senatorial campaign committees—have adapted to the candidate-centered, money-driven, "high-tech" style of modern campaign politics. This chapter examines the development of the national party organizations, their evolving relations with other party committees, and their role in contemporary elections.

PARTY DEVELOPMENT, DECLINE,
AND REEMERGENCE

....

American political parties are principally electoral institutions. They were created to help meet the needs of candidates for public office (Aldrich 1995), and they continue to focus more on elections and less on initiating policy change than do parties in other Western democracies (Leon Epstein 1986). National party development has been influenced by forces impinging on the parties from the broader political environment and pressures emanating from within the parties themselves. The Democratic National Committee (DNC) was formed during the Democratic national convention of 1848 for the purposes of organizing and directing the presidential campaign and tending to the details associated with setting up future conventions (Cotter and Hennessy 1964). The Republican National Committee (RNC) was created in 1856 for the purposes of bringing the Republican Party into existence and conducting election-related activities similar to those performed by its Democratic counterpart.

The congressional and senatorial campaign committees were created in response to heightened electoral insecurities resulting from factional conflicts within the two parties following the Civil War. The National Republican Congressional Committee (NRCC) was formed in 1866 by Radical Republican members of the House who believed they could not rely on President Andrew Johnson or the RNC for assistance with their elections. Following the Republican example, pro-Johnson Democrats formed their own election committee—the Democratic Congressional Campaign Committee (DCCC). Senate leaders created the senatorial campaign committees in 1916 after the Seventeenth Amendment transformed the upper chamber into a popularly elected body. The Democratic Senatorial Campaign Committee (DSCC) and the National Republican Senatorial Committee (NRSC) were founded to assist incumbent senators with their reelection campaigns. Like their counterparts in the House, the Senate campaign committees were established during a period of political upheaval—the Progressive Movement—to assuage members' electoral insecurities.

The six national party organizations have not possessed abundant power during most of their existence. Throughout most of the parties' history, and during the height of their strength (*circa* the late nineteenth and early twentieth centuries), power was concentrated at the local level, usually in county-wide political machines that possessed a virtual monopoly over the tools needed to run a successful campaign. Power mainly flowed up from county organizations to state party committees and conventions, and then to the national convention. The national, congressional, and senatorial campaign committees had little, if any, power over state and local party leaders.

Nevertheless, party campaigning was a cooperative endeavor. Individual branches of the party organization were primarily concerned with electing candidates within their immediate jurisdictions, but leaders of different party organizations worked together because they recognized that ballot structures and voter partisanship linked the electoral prospects of their candidates (Ostrogorski 1964; Schattschneider 1942). They also understood that electing candidates to federal, state, and local governments would enable them to maximize the patronage and other benefits they could extract for themselves and their supporters. The national party organizations, and especially the national committees, provided the financial, administrative, and communications resources needed to coordinate and set the tone of a nationwide campaign (Bruce 1927; Kent 1923). Local party committees used their proximity to voters to collect electoral information, to conduct voter registration and get-out-the-vote drives, and to organize other grassroots activities (Merriam 1923). State party committees used their relatively modest resources to channel electoral information up to the national party organizations and arranged for candidates and other prominent party leaders to speak at local rallies and events (Sait 1927).

The transition from a party-dominated system of campaign politics to a candidate-centered system was brought about by legal, demographic, and technological changes in American society and reforms instituted by the parties themselves. The direct primary and civil service regulations instituted during the Progressive era deprived party bosses of their ability to handpick nominees and reward party workers with government jobs and contracts (see, for example, Key 1958; Roseboom 1970). They weakened the bosses' hold over candidates and political activists and encouraged candidates to build their own campaign organizations.

Demographic and cultural changes reinforced this pattern. Increased education and social mobility, declining immigration, and a growing national identity contributed to the erosion of the close-knit, traditional ethnic neighborhoods that formed the core of the old-fashioned political machine's constituency. Voters began to turn toward nationally focused mass media and away from local party committees for their political information (Ranney 1975; Kayden and Mahe 1985). Growing preferences for movies, radio, and televised entertainment reduced the popularity of rallies, barbecues, and other types of interpersonal communication at which the machines excelled. These changes deprived the parties of their political bases and rendered many of their campaign techniques obsolete.

The adaptation of technological innovations developed in the public relations field to the electoral arena further eroded candidates' dependence on party organizations. Advancements in survey research, data processing, and mass media advertising provided candidates with new tools for gathering information from and communicating messages to voters. The emergence of political consultants enabled candidates to hire non-party professionals to run their campaigns (Agranoff 1972; Sabato 1981). These developments helped transform election campaigns from party-focused, party-conducted affairs to events that revolved around individual candidates and their campaign organizations.

Two recent developments that initially appeared to weaken party organizations and reinforce the candidate-centeredness of American elections were party reforms introduced by the Democrats' McGovern–Fraser Commission and the Federal Election Campaign Act of 1971 and its amendments (FECA). The McGovern–Fraser reforms, and reforms instituted by later Democratic reform commissions, were designed to make the presidential nominating process more open and more representative. Their side-effects included reducing the roles of long-time party "regulars" at national party conventions and in other party activities and increasing the influence of issue and candidate activists (frequently labeled "purists" or "amateurs") in party politics. The rise of the "purists" also led to tensions over fundamental issues such as whether winning elections or advancing particular policies should have priority (J. Wilson 1962; Polsby and Wildavsky 1984). It also led to schisms with the parties that made coalition building more difficult. The reforms were debilitating to both parties, but they were more harmful to the Democratic Party, which introduced them (Ranney 1975; Polsby and Wildavsky 1984).

The FECA also had some negative effects on the parties. Its contribution and expenditure limits, disclosure provisions, and other regulatory requirements forced party committees to keep separate bank accounts for state and federal election activity. Its immediate effect was to discourage state and local party organizations from fully participating in federal elections (D. Price 1984; Kayden and Mahe 1985). It also set the stage for the tremendous proliferation of political action committees (PACs) that began in the late 1970s (Alexander 1984). Numbering 608 in 1974, PACs soon became the major organized financiers of congressional elections, reaching 5,000 in 2006.

Changes in the parties' environment and internal governance fostered the emergence of a candidate-centered election system. Under this system, most candidates assembled their own campaign organization to compete for their party's nomination and then to contest the general election. In the case of presidential elections, a candidate who succeeded in securing the party's nomination also won control of the national committee. In congressional elections, most campaign activities were carried out by the candidate's own organization both before and after the primary. The parties' seeming inability to adapt to the new "high-tech," money-driven style of campaign politics resulted in their being pushed to the periphery of the elections process. These trends were accompanied by a general decline in the parties' ability to structure political choice (Carmines, Renten, and Stimson 1984; Beck 1984), to furnish symbolic referents and decision-making cues for voters (Nie, Verba, and Petrocik 1979; Wattenberg 1984), and to foster party unity among elected officials (Deckard 1976; Clubb, Flanigan, and Zingale 1980).

Although party decline was a gradual process that took its greatest toll on party organizations at the local level, party renewal occurred over a relatively short period and was focused primarily in Washington, DC. As was the case in earlier periods, national party organizational renewal was shaped by the needs of candidates. Many campaigns did not have the skills or funds needed to meet the demands of the new-style campaigning. Others turned to political consultants, PACs, or interest groups for help. The increased needs of candidates for greater access to technical expertise, political information, and money created an opportunity for national party organizations to become the repositories of these resources (J. Schlesinger 1985). National party leaders responded to these demands after electoral crises that heightened office-holders' electoral anxieties furnished them with the opportunities and incentives to augment the parties' organizational apparatuses (e.g., Herrnson and Menefee-Libey 1990).

The Watergate scandal and the trouncing Republican candidates experienced in the 1974 and 1976 elections provided a crisis of competition that was the catalyst for change at the Republican national party organizations. The GOP lost forty-nine seats in the House in 1974, had an incumbent president defeated two years later, and controlled only twelve governorships and four state legislatures by 1977. Moreover, voter identification with the Republican Party dropped precipitously, especially among voters under 35. This drew party leaders' attention to the weaknesses of the Republican national, congressional, and senatorial campaign committees. GOP leaders initiated a variety of programs to promote the institutional development of their committees, increase the committees' electoral presence, and provide candidates with campaign money and services. They transformed the missions of the national parties and placed them on a path that would strengthen them organizationally.

The institutionalization of the Democratic national party organizations occurred in two phases. The tumultuous 1968 Democratic national convention created a factional crisis between liberal reform-minded "purists" and party "regulars." The crisis and the party's defeat in November created an opportunity for the McGovern–Fraser Commission, and other reform commissions, to introduce rule changes that made the delegate selection process more participatory, led to the proliferation and front-loading of presidential primaries, and increased the size and demographic representativeness of the DNC and the national convention. Later Democratic reform commissions created slots for Democratic elected officials, former elected officials, and party activists to participate in Democratic conventions as so-called "superdelegates" without having to be selected in primaries or caucuses. The roles of superdelegates were hotly debated in 2008 when it appeared that they might cast the deciding votes in the nomination race between Illinois Senator Barack Obama and New York Senator and former First Lady Hillary Rodham Clinton.

The Democrats' reform movement resulted in the DNC gaining responsibility for overseeing state party compliance with national party rules. This shift in power within the party boosted DNC influence in both party and presidential politics. At times this responsibility has appeared to tie the Democratic Party in knots. For example, in its effort to reduce front-loading in the 2008 presidential nomination process, the DNC forbade any state other than Iowa, New Hampshire, Nevada, and South Carolina from holding its primary or caucuses before February 5, 2008.

When Florida and Michigan violated this rule, leading some nomination candidates to remove their names from the ballots in these states, the DNC had to arbitrate whether it would be fair to seat those states' delegations and determine what constituted adequate punishment for the flouting of party rules. After publicly wrangling over the situation for several months, the DNC decided to seat the delegates, but only after Obama had wrapped up the nomination. Faced with a similar situation the RNC acted more decisively, stripping half of the delegates originally allocated to Wyoming, Michigan, Florida, South Carolina, and New Hampshire because they had scheduled their primaries ahead of February 5, 2008.

The second phase of Democratic national party institutionalization followed the party's massive defeat in the 1980 election. The defeat of incumbent President Jimmy Carter, the loss of thirty-four House seats (half of the party's margin), and loss of control of the Senate constituted a crisis of competition that created an opportunity for change at the Democratic national party organizations. Unlike party reform, Democratic Party renewal was preceded by widespread agreement among Democrats that the DNC, DCCC, and DSCC should increase the party's electoral competitiveness by imitating the GOP's party-building and campaign service programs.

INSTITUTIONALIZED NATIONAL PARTIES

The institutionalization of the national party organizations refers to their becoming fiscally solvent, organizationally stable, larger and more diversified in their staffing, and adopting professional-bureaucratic decision-making procedures. These changes were necessary for the national parties to develop their election-related and party-building functions.

National party fundraising improved greatly from the 1970s through 2006. During this period, the national parties set several fundraising records, using a variety of approaches to raise money from a diverse group of contributors. The Republican committees raised more federally regulated "hard" money, which could be spent to expressly promote the elections of federal candidates, than their Democratic rivals throughout this period. However, during the early 1980s the Democrats began to narrow the gap in fundraising. They managed to shrink the Republicans' national party organization's hard money fundraising advantage from 6.7 to 1 in the 1982 election cycle to 1.3 to 1 in the 2006 election cycle. Preliminary figures for 2008 suggest that the DCCC and DSCC are destined to raise more money than their Republican counterparts, even as the RNC and the Republican

Party overall appear to be poised to retain their traditional advantages over the DNC and the Democrats (Federal Election Commission 2008).[1]

The GOP's long-held financial advantage was due to a number of factors. The Republican committees began developing their direct mail solicitation programs earlier and adopted a more business-like approach to fundraising. The demographics of their supporters also made it easier for the Republican committees to raise money. The GOP's supporters possess greater wealth and education, and are more likely to be a business executive or owner. These individuals are accustomed to spending money to improve their material interests (Francia et al. 2003a).

The competitiveness over control of the House and Senate following the Republican takeover of Congress in 1995 helped fuel both parties' campaign fundraising efforts. The close-fought presidential elections of 1992, 2000, and 2004 had similar effects. The national party organizations raised huge sums of money in these election cycles. For example, during the 2004 elections the national Democrats raised a total of $576.2 million and the Republicans raised $657 million.

The national parties raise most of their contributions of under $200 using targeted solicitations. These include direct mail, email, and telemarketing techniques that reach out to individuals who contribute because they care deeply about salient issues or broad causes. Internet websites proved to be a very potent vehicle for fundraising during the 2004 presidential election (Pew Internet and Political Life Project 2005; Hindman 2008, 35–7). Fundraising dinners, receptions, and personal solicitations are important vehicles for collecting contributions of all sizes, and are essential to raising large donations. Events are particularly effective for raising contributions of all sizes from individuals who enjoy the social aspects of politics (C. Brown, Powell, and Wilcox 1995; Francia et al. 2003a).

Prior to the enactment of the Bipartisan Campaign Reform Act of 2002 (BCRA) political parties were able to collect and spend sums of money from sources and in amounts that were prohibited by the FECA's regulations. This so-called "soft money" was collected primarily using personal solicitations that routinely involved the participation of presidents, congressional leaders, and national party chairmen. Traditionally used to purchase or rent the buildings that house party operations, buy equipment, strengthen state and local party organizations, help finance national conventions and voter registration and get-out-the-vote drives, and broadcast generic television and radio advertisements designed to benefit the entire party ticket, the parties began to spend substantial sums of soft money to broadcast so-called "issue advocacy" advertisements on television and radio during the 1996 elections, after the Supreme Court ruled that such ads were permissible (Potter 1997). These ads resemble candidate ads in that they focus on individual candidates, but they are distinct in their financing in that they cannot *expressly* advocate

---

[1] Figures for the 2008 election are for funds collected through Oct. 15, twenty days prior to the general election.

the election or defeat of a federal candidate, and in that they tend to be more negative or comparative than are candidate ads (Herrnson and Dwyre 1999; Goldstein 2004).

Issue advocacy ads increased the pressures on the national parties to raise more soft money. As a result, the parties' soft money receipts escalated dramatically. During the 2000 election cycle, the Democratic national party committees raised $245.2 million in soft money, and the Republicans collected $249.9 million. These figures accounted for 53 and 41 percent of the national Democrats' and the national Republicans' respective receipts in 2000. Following the BCRA's ban on soft money, the political parties reinvigorated their efforts to raise federally regulated "hard" money. They enjoyed considerable success, setting records in the 2004 elections.

Success in fundraising has enabled the national parties to invest in the development of their organizational infrastructures. Prior to their institutionalization, the national party organizations had no permanent headquarters. Their transience created security problems, made it difficult for the parties to conduct routine business, and did little to bolster their standing in Washington (Cotter and Hennessy 1964). All six national party organizations are now housed in party-owned headquarters buildings located only a few blocks from the Capitol. The headquarters buildings provide convenient locations to carry out research, host fundraising events, and hold meetings with candidates, PACs, journalists, and campaign consultants. They also provide a secure environment for the committees' computers, records, radio and television studios, and staffs (see, for example, Herrnson 1988).

Each national party organization has a two-tier structure consisting of members and professional staff. The members of the Republican and Democratic national committees are selected by state parties and the members of the Hill committees are selected by their colleagues in Congress. The national parties' staffs have grown tremendously in recent years. Republican committee staff development accelerated following the party's Watergate scandal, while the Democratic Party experienced most of its staff growth after the 1980 election. National committee staffs typically number in the hundreds, including aides who are paid in part by the national committees and in part by state party organizations. During the 2006 election season, the DCCC, DSCC, NRCC, and NRSC employed 106, fifty-six, seventy-four, and fifty-seven full-time staff, respectively. Committee staffs are divided along functional lines; different divisions are responsible for administration, fundraising, research, communications, and campaign activities. The staffs have a great deal of autonomy in running the committees' day-to-day operations and are extremely influential in formulating their campaign strategies (Herrnson 2008).

Not surprisingly, the institutionalization of the national parties has had an impact on their relationships with interest groups, political consultants, and state and local party organizations. Political observers first believed that the rise of the political consultants and the proliferation of PACs would hasten the decline of parties (Sabato 1981; Crotty 1984; Adamany 1984), but it is now recognized that many political consultants and PACs cooperate with the political parties to advance their common goals (Herrnson 1988; Sabato 1988; Kolodny and Dulio 2003). Fundraising constitutes one area of party–PAC cooperation; the dissemination of information and the backing of particular candidates constitute others (Herrnson 2008). National party organizations handicap races for PACs, arrange "meet and greet" sessions for PACs and candidates, and provide PAC managers with information they can use when making contribution decisions.

Relations between the national party organizations and political consultants also have become more cooperative. The national parties facilitate contacts and agreements between their candidates and political consultants. They also hire outside consultants for polling, advertising, and voter file management, and to provide candidates with campaign services. These arrangements enable the parties to draw upon the expertise of the industry's premier consulting firms and provide the consultants with steady employment, which is especially important between election cycles.

The institutionalization of the national party organizations has provided them with the resources to develop a variety of state and local party-building programs. The vast majority of these were introduced following major electoral defeats. Following their landslide losses in 1976, the RNC began to assist state and local party leaders with modernizing their organizations' fundraising, conducting research, and developing realistic election objectives and strategies (Bibby 1980; Conway 1983). Other programs sponsored by the RNC, NRCC, and NRSC involved candidate recruitment and training and the delivery of campaign services ranging from fundraising to issue and opposition research, voter targeting data, and grassroots organizing (Herrnson 1988). The DNC, DSCC, and DCCC began to emulate the GOP's state and local party-building efforts following their massive losses in 1984. DNC Chairman Howard Dean's "50-State Strategy" represents an attempt to rebuild the Democratic Party from the ground up and increase its ability to contest elections in competitive regions and Republican strongholds.

National committee party-building programs have helped to strengthen, modernize, and professionalize many state and local party organizations. They also have altered the balance of power within the parties' organizational apparatuses. The national parties' ability to distribute or withhold money, party-building assistance, and other help gives them influence over the operations of state and local party committees. They, along with the national committee rule-making and enforcement functions, have complemented the traditional flow of power upward from state and local party organizations to the national committees with a flow of power downward from the national parties to state and local parties. The institutionalization of the national party organizations has led to a greater federalization of the American party system (Wekkin 1985).

Further evidence of the cooperative relationships among the national party organizations, political consultants, interest groups, state and local party committees, as well as candidates' campaign organizations, concerns the careers of political professionals. Employment at one of the national parties can serve as a high point or stepping stone in the career of a political professional. By strengthening the relationships among those who work in a party's network, the "revolving door" of national party employment has enhanced the party's role in its network.

National Party Campaigning

The institutionalization of the national parties has provided them with the wherewithal to play a larger role in elections, and national party campaign activity has increased tremendously since the 1970s. Still, the electoral activities of the national parties, and party organizations in general, remain constricted by electoral law, established custom, and the resources in the parties' possession.

Candidate Recruitment

Candidate recruitment is one of the areas where party influence is limited. Most candidates for elective office in the United States are self-recruited and conduct their own nominating campaigns. The DNC and the RNC have a hand in establishing the basic guidelines under which presidential nominations are contested, but neither expresses a preference for candidates for its party's presidential nomination. National party organizations, however, may get involved in nominating contests for House, Senate, and state-level offices. They actively recruit some candidates to enter primary contests and just as actively discourage others. Most candidate recruitment efforts are concentrated in competitive districts, where a party seeks to nominate the best-qualified candidate for the district. However, party officials also encourage candidates to run in less competitive districts to strengthen its party organizations and candidate pool. During the 1970s, 1980s, and 1990s, the Republicans used this approach to improve their ability to compete in the South. During the early twenty-first century, House Democrats used it in key congressional districts under the guise of its "Red-to-Blue Program."

When participating in candidate recruitment, national party staff in Washington, DC, and regional coordinators in the field meet with state and local party leaders to identify potential candidates. Armed with polls, the promise of party campaign money and services, and the persuasive talents of members of Congress, and even presidents, party leaders and staff seek to influence the decisions of potential candidates. Both parties have had success in encouraging what are typically referred to as quality candidates—those with prior political experience, high name recognition, reputations as problems solvers among local voters, and the ability to raise funds (D. Canon 1990; W. Stone and Maisel 2003; Herrnson 2008).

National party candidate recruitment and primary activities are not intended to do away with the dominant pattern of self-selected candidates assembling their own campaign organizations to compete for their party's nomination. Nor are these activities designed to restore the turn-of-the-century pattern of local party leaders selecting the parties' nominees. Rather, most national party activity is geared toward encouraging or discouraging the candidacies of a small group of politicians who are considering running in competitive districts. Less focused recruitment efforts attempt to arouse the interests of a broader group of party activists (e.g., Herrnson 1988, 2008).

National Conventions

The national conventions are technically a part of the nomination process. After the 1968 reforms were instituted, however, the conventions lost control of their nominating function and became more of a public relations event than a decision-making one. Conventions still have platform writing and rule-making responsibilities, but these are overshadowed by speeches and other events designed to attract the support of voters.

Contemporary national conventions are notable for their choreography (see Shafer, Chapter 14 in this volume). Featuring impressive backdrops, staging, and video presentations tailor-made for television, they are intended to convey messages of unity, energy, and the inevitability of victory in the general election. Disputes among convention delegates over party rules or platforms are relegated to meeting rooms where they attract relatively little media attention. Protesters are directed to special "protest sites" away from the convention halls so as to minimize their press coverage.

The substitution of public relations for decision making at national conventions has not come without costs. Many television networks have responded to what they perceive to be a lack of newsworthiness by providing only limited television coverage. In contrast to the gavel-to-gavel coverage that many twentieth-century conventions safely assumed they would get and actually received, the organizers of the 2008 Democratic national convention had to be careful to schedule their convention around the Olympics and the organizers of the 2008 Republican convention were concerned that their nominee's acceptance speech would have to compete with a Thursday night football game between the Super Bowl Champion New York Giants and the Washington Redskins.

Other convention activities include policy seminars, fundraising, and planning for the general election campaign and future party events. Meetings are arranged for major donors and prospective donors to meet with party leaders and other luminaries to socialize, discuss policy, and find ways to put their resources to best use in the upcoming general election. Non-presidential candidates are given access to television and radio taping and satellite up-link facilities. "Meet and greet" sessions are used to introduce competitive challengers and open-seat candidates to PACs, individual big contributors, party leaders, and the media. The atrophy of the national conventions' nominating function has been partially offset by an increase in its general election-related activities.

The General Election

Candidate recruitment and nominations reinforce the candidate-centered nature of US elections. Rules requiring candidates for the nomination to compete in primaries and caucuses guarantee that successful candidates enter the general election with their own sources of technical expertise, in-depth research, and connections with other political elites. These reforms combine with the federal campaign finance law to limit national party activity and influence in elections. For example, presidential general election candidates who accept public funding are restricted from accepting contributions from any other sources, including the political parties. With the exception of the Democrats' 2008 presidential nominee Barack Obama, every major party presidential candidate has accepted public general election funding since 1976, when it first became available.

Nevertheless, the national parties do assume important roles in contemporary presidential elections. They furnish presidential campaigns with staff, legal and strategic advice, and public relations assistance. National committee opposition research and archives serve as important sources of political information. National committee coordinated expenditures can boost the total resources partially under the candidates' control by over 20 percent. The funds national parties transfer to state parties for voter mobilization drives and party-building activities improve the prospects of presidential candidates. The same is true of the unlimited independent expenditures the national parties are allowed to make to *explicitly* advocate the election of their candidate or an opponent's defeat as long as the expenditures are made with the candidates' advance knowledge or consent. Hybrid campaign ads, first introduced by the GOP in 2004, are a tactic that enables the party and a candidate to jointly pay for an advertisement that features both the candidate and a generic party message (Corrado 2006).

Combined, these forms of party spending can be impressive. In 2004, the DNC made $16.1 million in coordinated expenditures on behalf of Democratic presidential nominee John Kerry, $120.4 million in independent expenditures in support of his candidacy, and $24 million in jointly funded hybrid ads. The DNC also transferred $26.5 million to state and local parties. The RNC made $16.1, $18.3, $45.8, and $45.8 million in expenditures on these same activities. The disparities in independent expenditures are due to the Republicans introducing jointly funded hybrid ads and the Democrats only taking advantage of this new spending opportunity later.

National party organizations also play a big role in congressional elections. They contribute money and campaign services directly to congressional candidates and provide transactional assistance that helps candidates obtain other resources from other politicians, political consultants, and PACs. They also communicate advertisements directly to voters to win voter support for their candidates. Most national party assistance is distributed by the congressional and senatorial campaign committees to candidates competing in close elections, especially to non-incumbents. This reflects the committees' goal of maximizing the number of congressional seats under their control (Jacobson 1985–6; Herrnson 1989, 2008).

As is the case with presidential elections, federal law constrains party activity in congressional races. National party organizations are allowed to contribute a total of $15,000 to House candidates. The parties' national and senatorial campaign committees are allowed to give a combined total of $35,000 to Senate candidates. State party organizations can give $5,000 each to House and Senate candidates. National party organizations and state party committees also are allowed to make coordinated expenditures on behalf of their candidates, giving both the party and the candidate a measure of control over how the money is spent. Originally set at $10,000 per committee, the limits for national party coordinated expenditures on behalf of House candidates were adjusted for inflation and reached $39,600 in the 2006 election cycle.[2] The limits for national party coordinated expenditures in Senate elections vary by the size of a state's population and are also indexed to inflation. They ranged from $79,200 per committee in the smallest states to almost $2.1 million per committee in California during the 2006 elections.[3]

Democratic Party organizations spent $9.4 million in contributions and coordinated expenditures, more in contested House elections, and $10.5 million in contested Senate elections in 2006. The Republicans spent considerably less on House races and slightly less on Senate contests. The Democrats' spending advantage in House races represents a reversal over previous elections; slight party spending advantages have swung back and forth the last few elections. Most party money is distributed as coordinated expenditures owing to the higher limits imposed by the law. Most of these funds originate at one of the congressional or

[2] Coordinated expenditure limits for states with only one House member were set at $79,200 per committee in 2006.

[3] State party organizations are allowed to spend the same amounts in coordinated expenditures in House and Senate elections as are national party organizations.

senatorial campaign committees and are distributed in accordance with the spend-ing strategies they formulate. When a state party committee is short on money, the congressional and senatorial campaign committees may make agency agreements allowing them to assume some of the state party committees' coordinated expen-ditures. These transactions enable the parties to concentrate their resources in close House and Senate races.

"Party-connected" contributions comprise another set of financial transactions involving parties (Herrnson 2008). These are made by current or former members of Congress and the leadership PACs they sponsor rather than formal party committees. Leadership PAC contributions, like other PAC contributions, are limited to $5,000 in each stage of the campaign (primary, general election, and runoff). Contributions from one member of Congress's (or retiree's) campaign account to another candidate's campaign account are limited to $2,000. During the 2006 elections, Democrats contributed $14.1 million in party-connected contribu-tions to House candidates and almost $6 million to Senate candidates; Republicans spent $25.6 and $8.3 million in these elections. Total party-connected spending in House contests reached almost $39.7 million, almost 160 percent more than the party committees distributed in contributions and coordinated expenditures. Senate candidates raised almost $13.9 million in party-connected contributions, about 31 percent less than they raised in party contributions and coordinated expenditures. The comparatively generous ceilings for party-coordinated expendi-tures in Senate races and the small number of senators and senator-sponsored leadership PACs largely account for the differences between House and Senate elections.

The national parties usually target competitive campaigns for their largest contributions and coordinated expenditures, and the 2006 elections were no exception. Both parties distributed roughly one-fourth of their funds to House candidates contesting competitive open seats.[4] The Democrats committed 55 per-cent of their funds to competitive challengers and the Republicans distributed an identical amount to the incumbents the challengers sought to unseat. Democratic incumbents in jeopardy of losing their seats received 9 percent of their party's funds, as opposed to the 12 percent of GOP funds allocated to the Republican challengers running against them. The distributions of funds were informed by party strategists' interpretations of the political environment. Given President Bush's low approval ratings, the unpopularity of the war in Iraq, and concerns about corruption in the federal government, Democrats correctly sensed an op-portunity to pick up Republican-held seats and Republicans accurately predicted that their incumbents would be in danger. Both parties committed only 8 percent

---

[4] Elections decided by 20 percent of the vote are categorized as competitive, given that they may have been close at some point in the election cycle; all others are categorized as uncompetitive. For more information on these categories, see Herrnson (2008).

of their funds to lopsided House races, largely the result of the challenges associated with handicapping elections (Herrnson 2008).

The distributions of party funds in the 2006 Senate elections bear similarities to the House contests. Both parties invested significant resources in open-seat contests, the Democrats allocated more than half of their funds to competitive challengers, and the Republicans allocated more than half of their funds to incumbents in jeopardy. One difference is that the Democratic targeting was weaker in Senate elections, as the party distributed 16 percent of its money to candidates in one-sided Senate contests (Herrnson 2008).

The distribution of party-connected funds to House and Senate candidates shadowed the distribution of party money. The major differences in spending patterns are that party-connected committees distributed more of their funds to incumbents and open-seat candidates, including some in uncompetitive races, and less to challengers. The differences in the parties' and the party-connected committees' spending patterns are informed by differences in their goals. The parties' seat maximization goals inform their targeting close contests, regardless of candidates' officeholding status. The sponsors of party-connected committees are interested in seat maximization, but they also want to collect post-election payoffs, such as support in their bids for leadership posts, committee assignments, and preferred policies (Wilcox 1989a; Heberlig 2003; Currinder 2003; P. Brewer and Deering 2005; Heberlig, Hetherington, and Larson 2006). The latter objective encourages them to support candidates who are likely to serve in the next Congress, mainly current incumbents (who collectively enjoy a better than 90 percent election rate) and candidates for open-seat contests (who as a group have a 50 percent chance of winning).

Party and party-connected funds accounted for roughly 4 percent of the resources collected by House candidates in competitive elections and 7 percent of the funds collected by competitive Senate contestants (Herrnson 2008). Even though individuals and PACs still furnish candidates with most of their campaign funds, political parties are the largest single source of campaign money for most candidates. Party money comes from one, or at most a few, organizations that are primarily concerned with one goal: the election of their candidates. Individual and PAC contributions, on the other hand, come from a multitude of sources that are motivated by a variety of concerns. The inclusion of party-connected money, which is given by a relatively small number of organizations, boosts the level of party support to 12 percent for House candidates and 10 percent for Senate candidates. Of course, party and party-connected money comprise a much larger portion of some candidates' resources than others. The 2006 election for Wyoming's at-large House seat provides an example in which both major party candidates received significant amounts of party support. The winner, Republican incumbent Barbara Cubin, collected $174,000 in party contributions and coordinated expenditures and $221,000 in party-connected contributions from other

House Republicans and their leadership PACs. Combined these funds accounted for 28 percent of her total resources. Her opponent, Democratic challenger Gary Trauner, received $165,000 in Democratic Party contributions and coordinated expenditures and $36,500 in party-connected contributions, accounting for 18 percent of his total resources.[5]

In addition to providing financial support, parties furnish competitive congressional candidates with campaign services, ranging from candidate training to fundraising to independent expenditures. The national parties hold training seminars for candidates and campaign managers, broker relationships between candidates and political consultants, help congressional campaigns file reports with the Federal Election Commission, and perform other administrative and legal tasks. National party staffs in Washington and field coordinators also help candidates formulate strategy and tactics.

The parties' congressional and senatorial campaign committees help candidates raise money from individuals and PACs in Washington, DC, in their districts and states, and around the nation. They provide candidates with direct assistance, including raising money on their behalf at events, through the mail, and on the Internet, and advising them and their consultants on how to solicit PACs and individuals who make large contributions. The national parties also influence the decision making of potential donors. The committees' PAC directors help design the PAC kits many candidates use to introduce themselves to the PAC community, disseminate campaign progress reports, and spend countless hours on the telephone with PAC managers. Other party aides seek to mobilize contributions from individual donors. The goals of this activity are to get money flowing to the party's most competitive candidates and away from their candidates' opponents. National party communications, contributions, and coordinated expenditures serve as decision-making cues that help donors decide which candidates to back. The same is true of the contributions that congressional leaders make from their campaign accounts and leadership PACs and the fundraising efforts these leaders make on behalf of candidates. National party transactional assistance is especially important to non-incumbents running for the House because they typically do not possess fundraising lists from previous campaigns, are less skilled at fundraising than incumbents, have none of the political clout that comes with incumbency, and they begin the election cycle virtually unknown to members of the donor community (Herrnson 1988, 2008).

---

[5] Successful Democratic challenger Heath Shuler, who defeated Republican incumbent Charles Taylor in North Carolina's 11th district, raised the most from his party and members of Congress ($1.6 million in party contributions and coordinated expenditures and $217,200 in party-connected contributions). Taylor's triggering the BCRA's millionaire's provision (now unconstitutional) made it possible for the Democratic Party to make virtually unlimited amounts in coordinated expenditure (Herrnson 2008).

The national party organizations help congressional candidates gauge public opinion by distributing reports on voter attitudes on the issues. Many candidates in competitive contests receive voter files to help them locate and mobilize supporters and potential supporters. The congressional and senatorial campaign committees also commission surveys for a small group of competitive candidates to help them ascertain their name recognition, electoral support, and the impact of their campaign communications on voters (Herrnson 2008).

National party assistance in campaign communications takes many forms. All six national party organizations disseminate issue information on traditional party positions and the policy stances of incumbent presidents or presidential candidates. The congressional and senatorial campaign committees give competitive candidates issue packets consisting of hundreds of pages detailing issues that are likely to attract media coverage and win the support of specific voting blocs. The packets also include suggestions for exploiting an opponent's weaknesses.

Some House and Senate candidates receive party assistance with developing their media strategies, including having their ads pretested. The national parties occasionally make coordinated expenditures to air the finished products. Prior to the BCRA's prohibitions against party soft money, national party organizations spent tens of millions of dollars on issue advocacy ads. During the 2002 elections, the last in which raising and spending party soft money was permissible, the NRCC spent $21 million on issue advocacy to the DCCC's $6 million. The NRSC and DSCC spent $7.3 million and $8 million, respectively.

Following the ban on party soft money, the national parties greatly stepped up their independent expenditures. Most of these ads are either negative or comparative in tone for the simple reason that negative advertising works (Freedman and Goldstein 1999; Goldstein and Freedman 2002). During the 2006 elections, the Democrats spent $8.1 million expressly calling for their House candidates' election and $51.5 million advocating a Republican's defeat. The Republicans spent $5.2 million and $72.3 million for reciprocal purposes. Having few elections in which to become involved, the parties made fewer independent expenditures in contests for the Senate. The Democrats spent $7.3 million advocating the election of their candidates and $34.6 million calling for the defeat of these candidates' opponents. Republicans made $11.5 million in positive independent expenditures and $21.9 in negative ones. As was the case with party contributions and coordinated expenditures, virtually all spending took place in competitive House and Senate contests (Herrnson 2008).

Given the substantial efforts the national parties put forth in congressional elections, it seems reasonable to ask whether they make a difference. When asked, candidates competing in close elections, who receive the lion's share of national party assistance, answered yes. Not surprisingly, party assistance has a greater impact on the campaigns waged by challengers and open-seat candidates, who generally have less campaign experience and fewer advantages in fundraising, than on the campaigns of incumbents (Herrnson 1988; 2008, 124–6).

Although not as active in state and local elections as they are in presidential or congressional contests, national parties provide support to some candidates for lower-level offices. The DNC, the RNC, and affiliated organizations, such as the Democratic Legislative Campaign Committee and GOPAC (a leadership PAC that encourages Republicans to run for public office), work with state party leaders to recruit candidates, formulate strategy, and distribute campaign money and services. The national committees hold workshops to help state and local candidates learn the ins and outs of modern campaigning. The committees also recommend professional consultants, and disseminate strategic and technical information through party magazines and briefing papers. It is important to note that national party strategy for distributing campaign money and services to state and local candidates is influenced by considerations related to House, Senate, and presidential races. In 1999, for example, Democratic Party organizations and members of Congress contributed well in excess of $500,000 to Democratic state legislative candidates in Virginia, and national Republicans contributed roughly $1.3 million to their opponents. The GOP's donations were instrumental in helping the Republicans win control of the statehouse and come to dominate the congressional redistricting process (Mercurio and Van Dongen 1999).

In addition to the candidate-focused campaign programs discussed above, the national parties conduct generic, or party-focused, election activities designed to benefit all candidates on the party ticket. Many of these are concerned with voter registration, helping voters apply for absentee ballots, get-out-the-vote drives, and other grassroots efforts. Many are financed by the national, congressional, and senatorial campaign committees and conducted in cooperation with the parties' federal, state, and local party committees and candidates. National party organizations often provide the money and targeting information needed to perform these activities effectively, while state and local organizations provide the footsoldiers that help carry them out.

CONCLUSION

American political parties are principally electoral institutions, and they develop in response to changes in their environment and the changing needs of their candidates. Major national party organizational change usually occurs in response to electoral instability and political unrest. Gradual changes are made in response to technological advances and changes in the regulatory environment in which the parties operate. The institutionalization of the national parties has made them stronger, more stable, and more influential in their relations with state and local party committees, political consultants, and interest groups. More important, this development has enabled the national parties to play important roles in contemporary elections. They supplement the campaign communications and voter mobilization efforts of presidential candidates. They contribute to congressional candidates, make coordinated expenditures and other campaign communications on their behalf, and provide services in areas of campaigning requiring technical expertise, in-depth research, or connections with political consultants, PACs, or others possessing some of the resources needed to conduct a viable campaign. The national party committees play smaller and less visible roles in state and local elections. Although most national party activity is concentrated in competitive elections, party-sponsored television and radio ads and voter mobilization efforts help candidates of varying degrees of competitiveness. The reemergence of national party organizations has resulted in their becoming important players in twenty-first-century party politics and elections.

CHAPTER 14

THE PURE PARTISAN INSTITUTION

NATIONAL PARTY CONVENTIONS AS RESEARCH SITES*

BYRON E. SHAFER

NATIONAL party conventions are the major, purely partisan, formal institutions of American politics. For a concentrated view of what partisanship implies at a given point in time, then, they might appear to be the inescapable reference point. Yet conventions are widely overlooked—marginalized, even disrespected—as research sites for understanding partisan politics in the United States. Little work focuses *on* them. As a result, little work focuses *through* them. Some attention to this peculiar disjunction is thus the obvious route into an understanding of national party conventions as institutional elements of American politics and as researchable windows on it.

* James A. Barnes of *National Journal*, Charles O. Jones of the University of Wisconsin, and Robert P. Saldin of the University of Montana each read and commented carefully on this chapter. I have shared two conventions with Chuck Jones, two with Rob Saldin, and a remarkable fourteen with Jim

In their role as routes into contemporary partisanship, national party conventions share all the charm of political parties more generally, in a particularly concentrated and easily observed form. That is, they mediate the major societal influences on politics in their time, while making these forces readily visible in a concrete format. National conventions are not just the ultimate—close to the only—pure partisan institutions of American politics, offering an unconflated portrait of the party as social group and as programmatic package. They also sample and exemplify what would be taken elsewhere to be major aspects of the larger structure of contemporary politics. On the other hand, as institutions widely thought to be in precipitous decline, conventions tend in practice to forfeit all these advantages.

As a result, coming to grips with the disjunction between research potential and scholarly neglect requires a small series of analytic steps. It begins by placing the convention within a conceptual framework for analyzing the evolution of the institution itself. It moves on to the practical implications of this evolution, from institutional mechanism to institutional arena. It turns to the politics of the contemporary institution, organized around its role as "infomercial." It looks at the changing partisan content of that infomercial, in effect the substance of its message. It considers the nature of elite-mass linkages at the convention, as well as their contribution to this message. And it closes by taking stock of the distinctions that remain *among* conventions, the place of the generic convention in a larger national politics, and some possible harbingers of further change.

ARENAS VERSUS MECHANISMS

In his overview of legislatures in the volume on institutions from the *Handbook of Political Science* (Greenstein and Polsby 1975), Nelson Polsby builds his argument around the distinction between legislative arenas and transformative legislatures. The former are distinguished by being "formalized settings for the interplay of significant forces in the life of a political system", as opposed to the latter, which "possess the independent capacity, frequently exercised, to mold and transform proposals from whatever source" (Polsby 1975, 277). Expanding this distinction to

Barnes. For the last four conventions, the Democratic and Republican Conventions of 2004 and 2008, I have also had the great good fortune of sharing workspace and insights with Craig Gilbert, national political correspondent for the *Milwaukee Journal—Sentinel*. Amber Wichowsky then dug out some of the material for the tables presented here. And the members of the Political Behavior Group at the University of Wisconsin worked collectively on the result, under the guidance of Kenneth R. Mayer and Sara Dahill-Brown.

cover institutions for collective decision making that are not national legislatures requires only a modest terminological shift, to "arenas" versus "mechanisms" as the terms will be used here. The underlying difference then remains hugely useful in understanding the evolution of the national party convention.

In an arena, the comparative power of the social forces that are assembled inside is the critical factor, so that the nature of their representation is the key consideration. In a mechanism, by contrast, the transformative power of internal structures is the critical factor, so that the nature of a recurrent political process is the key consideration instead. With an arena, you want to know what goes in. With a mechanism, you want to know how it works. An arena privileges the social background of the delegates, while a mechanism privileges the organizational connections that they bring with them. An arena mediates between the general public and the organized party by articulating points of view, while a mechanism mediates by shaping policy products. As a result, the operation of an arena is best understood through a focus on its top leadership, while a mechanism requires more of a focus on its procedural arrangements.

Over 175 years, the national party convention has been transformed from a mechanism into an arena, and it is this trajectory that provides the background essential to understanding its contemporary operation. At bottom, creation of the convention was the response to a fundamental flaw in constitutional design: the framers of the US Constitution simply did not envision separate processes of presidential nomination and presidential election. Yet the very success of the bulk of their handiwork, in creating a stable government worth trying to control, was central to the creation of the key intermediaries of American politics, namely political parties. Moreover, the success of their new presidency gave these parties a reason—and need—for a national focus. That is, the parties needed some means both to produce and to confirm presidential nominees, and from the 1840s onward, the device for doing so has always been the national party convention (McCormick 1982).

For much of this period, the convention also served as a classic example of an institutional *mechanism*, where formal rules produced differentiated processes with powerful impacts on convention products, most especially the identity of its nominee. The rules for selecting convention delegates were devolved to the individual state parties and resulted in a wide array of distinctive arrangements, thereby increasing the importance of mastery of the process. Though it was largely party organizations, not general publics, which were being represented and which thus needed to develop this mastery. Internal convention rules also mattered, however. Most strikingly and for a hundred years, the Democratic Party insisted on a two-thirds majority for nomination, a rule essential to unifying a party whose three great factions—northeastern immigrants, southern regionalists, and western populists—had little to hold them together beyond an aversion to governmental intervention. Yet the rule that provided the essential glue simultaneously magnified the importance of internal convention maneuvering.

Still, the creation of the nomination—the crowning of a nominee within the convention and not, as currently, within the process of delegate selection—was what allowed the analyst to see that the convention was a classic mechanism, while at the same time giving added importance to the elements of internal structure that had other purposes, like judging its own credentials, adopting its own rules, and, most especially, producing a partisan platform. This was sufficient for its first hundred years (David, Goldman, and Bain 1960). Yet by the end of the Second World War, social forces outside the convention had begun to overwhelm its power to make, rather than just ratify, this crucial decision. The result was a transition over the last half-century to being a classic example of an institutional *arena* instead.

A cluster of major social changes came together at the end of the Second World War and effectively precipitated this larger shift. There was the long-term weakening of political parties as field organizations, due partly to other social changes but also to the long-run impact of conscious political reform. There was the coming of truly national media of information, where radio played the crucial role and television subsequently confirmed it. There was the growth of government during the New Deal and the Second World War, giving more and more organized interests a stake in presidential nominations. And there was the growing educational attainment of the American public, which, among other things, encouraged individual Americans to want to make these nominating choices for themselves, rather than cede them to party officials (Shafer 1988).

Seen from one side, the convention was an ideal means of tracking these changes, of seeing such vague and general social forces in a very concrete context. Seen from the other side, all of these social changes gradually but ineluctably drew the calculations of the major players outside the convention hall and into the process of delegate selection. The two conventions of 1952 were to be the last of the old order. Never again, at least as this is written, would the national party convention require so much as a second ballot to confirm its nominee (Table 14.1). Sweeping reforms of the process of delegate selection after the conventions of 1968, originating in the Democratic Party but quickly infusing the Republican Party as well, then formalized this result. In the process, an institution previously tasked with creating a presidential nomination became principally a device for introducing the nominee and reintroducing his party to the general public instead.

Table 14.1 The disappearance of the nomination and the rise of the infomercial

Years	All nominating contests		Contests without incumbent	
	Multi-ballot	First-ballot	Multi-ballot	First-ballot
1956–2008	0	28	0	19
1840–1952	27	30	25	14

THE MODERN EVOLUTION OF THE NATIONAL PARTY CONVENTION

From the creation of the national party convention until the early 1900s, the process of delegate selection was essentially a "pure convention system." States used caucuses of local party officials to select delegates to some higher-level convention, which selected delegates to a statewide convention, which selected the national convention delegates. From the early 1900s until 1968, this arrangement morphed into a "mixed system." The primary election invaded the process of delegate selection in some states, giving the politics of presidential nomination a much more mixed dynamic than it had previously held. Yet state party conventions continued to dominate the process statistically, and successful challenges to a party favorite by way of primary elections remained the practical exception rather than the rule. It was this mixed system that was still very much in operation when the nomination left the convention and lodged in the process of delegate selection after 1952 (Ceaser 1979).

In a sense, it was one specific convention, the disastrous Democratic Convention of 1968, that was responsible for recasting this process into a "dominant primary system." Almost in passing, that convention authorized a subsequent reform exercise. As a result, the overall matrix of institutions for delegate selection changed comprehensively: these reforms effectively locked the nomination outside the convention, except in cases of illness, accident, or dramatic revelation—none of which have yet to come to pass. The old party-based institutions of delegate selection were essentially destroyed, to be replaced by new participatory versions.[1] What resulted was a sequence of state presidential primaries, along with the occasional participatory caucus, in which candidates began largely as unknowns, in which early contests acquired disproportionate influence, and in which sequential

---

[1] The curious exception to this institutional evolution—curious because it approaches delegate selection in such a different way—is the vast bloc of appointed delegates that contemporary Democrats add to their mix, though in practice, these too have helped to remove potential conflicts from the convention. Roughly 30 percent of modern Democratic conventions are comprised of these PLEOs (party leaders and elected officials), who can be formally uncommitted (the, superdelegates) or pledged to one or another candidate.

In the immediate aftermath of reform, major public officials declined sharply as a presence at Democratic conventions, thanks partly to the fortunes of insurgent candidates but largely to the slating rules that were a further part of these reforms. Lacking those rules, the Republican Party did not experience this problem. But a growing sense within the Democratic Party that it was perverse to have a national convention without its major figures eventually produced the current balance. Accordingly, if these individuals were to be treated as the product of a separate selection device rather than as an add-on, then Table 14.2 would show Democratic delegates at the 2008 convention, for example, to have been 60 percent elected in candidate primaries, 10 percent elected in participatory caucuses, and 30 percent unelected superdelegates and PLEOs.

Table 14.2 The changing matrix of delegate selection

Year	Committee selections	Traditional caucuses	Delegate primaries	Participatory caucuses	Candidate primaries
Democrats					
2008	0	0	0	14	86
1976	0	0	9	24	66
1972	2	2	14	36	46
1968	13	24	19	21	23
1952	8	27	26	19	19
1936	8	31	31	15	14
Republicans					
2008	0	0	0	14	86
1976	1	4	11	24	60
1972	3	16	20	24	37
1968	5	24	23	28	20
1952	4	26	25	25	19
1936	4	31	32	20	14

momentum acquired a huge impact on subsequent outcomes. The nominating bandwagon already rolled informally in advance of the convention by the time of these sweeping reforms. In their aftermath, it rolled formally and ineluctably (Bartels 1988; Mutz 1997).

For a time after these reforms locked the nomination outside, there was still substantial conflict inside the convention over its residual activities—over credentials, rules, and a platform. This reflected rearguard efforts by losing candidates and their supporters either to use these conflicts to crack an apparent nominating majority or, failing that, to extract some policy compensation for their loss. At the Republican Convention of 1976 and the Democratic Convention of 1980, the main challenger to the renomination of a sitting president still attempted to change balloting rules in an explicit attempt to block that renomination. These were probably the last conventions where serious analysts entertained the possibility that a nominating majority might yet come apart. The Democratic Conventions of 1984 and 1988 still saw serious platform skirmishes, potentially awarding convention products to the losers from the nominating contest, and disputed policy content remained important at the Republican Convention of 1992, though more from the podium than through any official convention product.

Yet the other side of the fact that these efforts proved reliably futile was the way in which they taught convention managers how to defuse even the remaining potential flash points. By the time the nomination itself had exited the convention, these managers already understood that what they had inherited was an arena, not a mechanism. As a result, what they had really inherited was the opportunity for a giant "infomercial," for using convention coverage to introduce their nominee to the general public, and to tell that public why it should consider voting Democratic or Republican. Or rather, this was what they inherited assuming that they could suppress all those other, residual, tangential conflicts. If they could, success in the manipulation of their incipient infomercial would then be largely dependent on the interaction of their strategic goals with press behavior, so that the critical negotiations over convention content were now between convention managers and media managers, not between supporters of one aspiring nominee and supporters of another (Panagopoulos 2007).

We need to attend to the contours of these negotiations below. But before any of that, success at managing the convention as an infomercial, that is, success at managing this institutional arena, required expunging the residual conflicts left over from the days of the convention as a mechanism. Convention managers became impressively adept at doing so. In opposite fashions, the two parties effectively eliminated conflicts over delegate credentialing, conflicts that had been absolutely central—there had been pivotal credentials contests—at those last true nominating conventions in 1952. The Democrats accomplished this elimination with an extremely detailed code of rules for delegate selection, nationally imposed. The Republicans accomplished it instead by reaffirming the authority of their state parties, in effect a national rule defending local autonomy, and thereby keeping disputes out of the national body.

In the process, both parties effectively squeezed most of the conflict out of party rules more generally, albeit again by very different routes. The Democrats produced a series of reform commissions, successors to the McGovern-Fraser Commission which had locked the nomination outside the convention, elaborating the specifics of their rules in greater and greater detail. What the Republicans did instead was just to confirm that their convention remained the sole body authorized to *amend* the rules, and then only prospectively, so that no further rules challenges could affect any sitting convention. When these same developments reached the party platform, the substantive "emptying" of the convention, a formal but not (as below) an informal emptying, was effectively complete.

To begin with, the victorious candidates paid far more attention to eliminating any slippage in control of their respective platform committees than they would or could have done in an era when delegates were selected with more autonomy from these candidates. Yet when there were issues where the candidate and his own delegates nevertheless differed, most commonly because the candidate wanted to move toward the ideological center for the general election while the delegates wanted to use their residual authority to reaffirm an established and clear-cut partisan position, the candidate simply surrendered. Within some broad limits, candidates allowed delegates to write their preferences into the platform, and then took care to see that platform specifics never appeared in the podium coverage that constituted the external embodiment of the convention infomercial.

At that point, the transformation of the national party convention from institutional mechanism to institutional arena was largely complete. At that point, as a result, it became the public messages sent by the convention, rather than the policy conflicts within it, that were its central product. Just as it became the simple identity of the delegates, rather than their tactical behavior, that came to the fore with regard to the partisan politics of the convention itself. Yet before any of that, what really resulted in this shift from mechanism to arena was a parallel shift in the real and practical negotiations central to convention impact. Once, these negotiations had involved candidate and party organizations, trying to shape a presidential nomination. Now, they involved convention and media managers, trying to shape the amount and content of podium coverage that would go into the infomercial.

THE CONVENTION AS INFOMERCIAL, WITH A POLITICS OF ITS OWN

The last conventions to offer a serious extension of the old order, the Republican and Democratic Conventions of 1952, were also the first to acquire serious television coverage. By the time television had become the leading source of news for American society, in 1960, the nomination had left the convention, though there were just enough subsequent flutters—the Democrats in 1972, the Republicans in 1976—to hide this effect from some participants some of the time. Yet it was the battle over press coverage on television, much more than in the older print media or indeed the newer cyber media to come, that was already central to the key negotiations of modern convention politics. Two major developments shaped the result of these negotiations. One was simple and direct: as the convention moved from being a mechanism to an arena, diminishing the importance of its internal processes and emptying its environs of substantive conflict, conventions became less newsworthy in the eyes of media managers, and simultaneously less interesting to a viewing public.

The other grand influence on the amount and content of this infomercial was an institutional shift largely internal to the mass media itself. When television in particular first began to cover national party conventions, this very coverage served as a badge of achievement, as proof that television news had come of age as a public service. That sense was augmented by the rise of the evening news programs on television, for which convention coverage was a special—and prestigious—extension. It might be a "loss leader" in terms of marketing, but it was the great opportunity to draw fresh viewers to these news programs on a regular basis. The high-water mark both for total televised coverage and for public attention to—and hence ratings for—this coverage then arrived with the national party conventions of 1968, the year that the Democratic Convention exploded and the year that spawned the reforms that would lock the nomination outside subsequent conventions (Shafer 1983).

After that, the same institutional logic began to work in the opposite direction. The emptying out of policy products from the convention proceeded apace. In the absence of dramatic conflict over those products, the audience began to decline. As it did, the television networks came to understand—though here, they were merely a more extreme version of a general press response—that the economics of convention coverage argued for as little, not as much, as professional respectability permitted. Convention coverage was now not just expensive in its own right. It also represented a huge opportunity cost by comparison to the entertainment programming that it replaced in the short run and disrupted in the longer term. In a chicken-and-egg spiral after 1968, viewership fell, coverage declined, viewership fell, and coverage declined. There were idiosyncratic blips along the way: the Republican Convention of 1964 and the Democratic Convention of 1972 were especial ratings disasters; the two conventions of 2008 produced a noticeable uptick in viewership. Yet the trend line was clear enough, and it was exaggerated by network responses, as measured by the amount of convention coverage offered.

What had existed in 1956 and 1960 was essentially gavel-to-gavel coverage, even though conventions were in session for a far longer time than they are in the modern era. An average of 3,400 minutes per network in 1956 seems incomprehensible from the modern perspective. What had stabilized instead by the 1990s was a consensual pattern for the major networks, featuring two hours of coverage on each of the four convention evenings. Convention managers would have liked at least to schedule the full two hours within this radically constricted presentation, but the cuts were effectively much larger than this. For *all* convention news, including everything that had happened since the session of the previous evening and all current reportorial activity, had to fit within this two-hour window. What this meant was that there was the possibility, in effect, of full televised coverage of a maximum of two speeches each evening. If parts of any other speech achieved nationally televised coverage, that ordinarily implied the possibility of full coverage of only *one* speech.

Conventions had always possessed a certain bifurcated nature: the convention on site had never been the same as the convention presented by the news media. This was true in the days of actual nominating decisions, where much of the real negotiations was not public. Though in that era, it was clearly the convention on site that mattered. Yet this bifurcation was, if anything, truer in the era of conventions as infomercials, when the vast bulk of convention proceedings, perfectly open and fully public, never acquired televised coverage by the major national networks. The convention on site was thus hugely different from the convention on TV. In turn, convention managers, recognizing the situation as it unfolded, began to

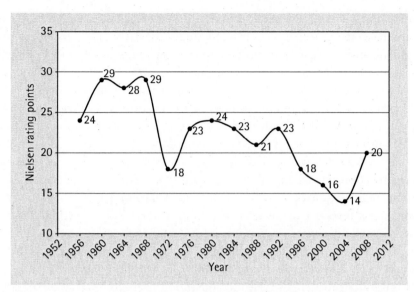

Figure 14.1 Viewing audiences for Democratic conventions in the television era

think about the convention as two separate institutions. One of these was power-fully focused on the viewing audience, and hence on the fall campaign. The other was inescapably focused on delegates, alternates, guests, and the preternaturally attentive. This latter convention also focused on the fall campaign, in a different and more operational fashion. Yet this was also the convention that was much more a register of where the political parties were, as social networks and as policy programs, at a given point in time.

There was still that part of the convention program which might conceivably be covered live by the major television networks, and convention managers picked and scheduled their speakers to capitalize on this as best they could. The point was to have a small set of specific messages, and ideally a progression among them, from Monday through Thursday. In this ideal program, a good convention had one overarching theme, plus four progressive subthemes. Often these latter began with a "passing of the baton" or "unifying the party" on Monday, with Tuesday and Wednesday involving domestic and international affairs, and Thursday combining them all in the themes of the fall campaign, by way of the acceptance speech from the official nominee. When this half of the bifurcated convention was successful, convention managers gauged the response of media managers accurately, while potential themes for the fall campaign became real strategic approaches as that campaign materialized.

The other part of the convention program, the much larger part, was then aimed at the delegates, alternates, and guests in the hall, along with some specialized publics outside, where podium content would never conceivably reach any sub-stantial mass audience. Some of this program was inescapably celebratory and pro forma, as with welcoming the participants, recognizing the hosts, and thanking the staff. Some of it was practically essential but increasingly automatic, as with confirming convention officers and adopting credentials, rules, and a platform. All of it gave the delegates themselves something to do, in an era when neither nominations nor credentials, rules, and platform were much amenable to their impact. Admittedly, this was the modern convention at its most tedious.

Yet some of this programming involved practical impacts of a very different sort. In particular, some of it involved elite education, in a fashion often overlooked by those who dismiss the convention more generally. For part of what these non-televised sessions were really doing was instructing partisan activists about the arguments—the "talking points"—that active partisans would ideally use in response to the opposition party in their locales during the fall campaign. What was droningly repetitive in one sense was thus intentionally educational in another. This was simultaneously the part of the program that constituted a register of where the delegates, and hence party activists, and hence the party as an activist network, resided ideationally—programmatically—at this point in time.

As the mix of media covering the convention changed, there were additional nuances to this picture. PBS, CNN, and Fox News were added to the network television mix, bringing an additional hour or so of convention coverage with them. The arrival of C-SPAN actually restored gavel-to-gavel coverage for those with the necessary fortitude. And the arrival of the cyber press, especially in the form of a handful of bloggers in 2004 and a greatly expanded number in 2008, likewise broadened the range of commentary available to diehard observers. None of this altered the mass audience for conventions in a major way, though it did presumably add some off-scene activists who could be educated by the issue emphases and "proper" positions that the convention was showcasing to those in the hall.

THE SUBSTANCE OF THE MESSAGE

The message or, really, messages that result are much under-studied in their own right. Every convention, no matter how well or badly managed, no matter how modestly or even thinly covered, does succeed in putting some messages—substantive arguments plus operational impressions—in front of a general public that, while viewership and ratings have declined, still registers in the multi-millions. Moreover, while the number varies widely, between 15 and 30 percent of all Americans always tell the National Election Study that they decided how they would vote in November during these infomercials. Needless to say, the vast expanse of the convention that attracts no television coverage from the national networks produces even more of this substantive message by bulk. This is also the convention product that has much greater potential for use by students of partisan politics in the United States: if it is generally unviewed, it is not uncataloged, so that it remains available to those who were never present in the convention hall.

In effect, the convention, especially in this assembled but off-camera incarnation, provides a register of the state of both partisan programs, in three separate but related senses. The grand programmatic differences that distinguish the parties are on display here, convention after convention. It would be hard for a convention observer to miss these fundamental differences. Yet the two parties reliably differ in a larger but more amorphous way, in the way they conceive of the nation itself and thus of the appropriate means to represent it. This is a difference perhaps more easily approached through the national party convention than by any other route. At the other extreme, lastly, there are always fresh adjustments of the main established positions, adjustments to contemporary conditions that can be quite substantial in scope, along with fresh initiatives, tried out for the first time, that may or may not join those ongoing (and defining) partisan differences.

In the first category, of grand programmatic differences that reliably distinguish the two parties, Democrats in convention have long been concerned about, and are always showcasing, issues of social welfare. Just as Republicans in convention have long been concerned about, and are often likewise showcasing, issues of foreign affairs. It is not that the other party does not counter these emphases. Republicans reliably respond to Democratic welfare proposals, often by emphasizing their tax implications. Just as Democrats reliably respond to Republican security concerns, often by emphasizing diplomacy and multilateralism as alternative virtues. These are the concerns that are often described as demonstrating "issue ownership" in the general public (Petrocik 1996; W. Miller and Shanks 1996). The point here is that they are registered very cleanly at the elite level by way of the podium at national party conventions.

These concerns do acquire a further evolution of their own; they are not simply static. The welfare focus of the Democratic Party in convention had already arrived with the national conventions of the 1930s. Differences on national security between the two parties were certainly expanded during the national conventions of the late 1960s and 1970s. Nevertheless, these established positions are constantly tweaked at national party gatherings. The Republican Convention of 1964, the Democratic Convention of 1972, the Republican Convention of 1980, and the Democratic Convention of 1992 each testified to a major attempt to adjust the welfare position of a national party. The Democratic Convention of 1948 was noteworthy for its attempt to adjust the party position on civil rights, in a struggle that proved prescient: the convention was well out ahead of the party as represented in other venues. The Democratic Convention of 1972 and the Republican Convention of 1980 testified to a major attempt—ultimately successful in both cases—to alter party positions on cultural values and social policy.

Those are crucial aspects of the central, ongoing, policy agendas of the major parties, presented in a particularly clean and abstracted fashion at their national party conventions. Yet there are some additional, larger but vaguer differences,

differences that are also perhaps best seen in convention. In these, American political parties—which is to say, their confirmed and active partisans—appear to think of themselves in fundamentally different ways. Democrats think of themselves as opening opportunities to new and further segments of American society, thereby extending its benefits to all. Republicans, by contrast, think of themselves as fostering and protecting a collective national interest, extending its benefits down through the ages.

It would be possible to summarize this as nothing more than the difference between a party that is a coalition of minorities versus one that has a clear central tendency, thereby making the difference an epiphenomenon of the social identities of those who are present in the arena. It will indeed be necessary to inquire into those identities below. But seen and heard from the podium, there is more to it than that. On the one hand, both parties have a vision of themselves as truly "national." This is not the crucial distinction. On the other hand, presentation of this national vision is different in both substance and style. It is as if one party would facilitate wider access to an American Dream, while the other party would sustain that Dream for future generations. There has been some effort to get at these differences by way of political history (Gerring 1998), but they assume their most active contemporary life at national party conventions.

From the other side, these conventions always feature adjustments specific—even idiosyncratic—to a given year, adjustments perhaps registered only in this particular forum. Just as there are always fresh concerns, potentially ongoing, which are best isolated initially in convention. Both require some attention. Even efforts to keep the policy essence of the two parties clear and relevant can produce noteworthy adjustments. Both sides knew, for example, that the general election of 2004 was likely to turn on issues of national security. The Republicans in convention trumpeted their perceived superiority in this realm, over and over. Democrats countered, but they also attempted to link these concerns with their own perceived superiorities: multiple speakers argued that the nation needed universal health care because the returning troops deserved no less!

Alternatively, these efforts can highlight issues that are perceived by party leaders to be up for grabs. Education policy became such an issue for the 2000 conventions; energy independence became such an issue for their 2008 counterparts. This hardly meant that the parties were contending for similar *policies* in these particular realms. For Democrats, educational reform meant resource equalization and better pay for teachers. For Republicans, it meant national standards and school choice. For Democrats, energy independence meant windmills and solar power. For Republicans, it meant offshore (oil) drilling, clean coal, and nuclear power. Afterward, both nominees would attempt to fudge these differences, but in convention they were striking.

Finally, conventions are an obvious theater for noticing the truly new policy initiatives that one or another segments of a political party hope to see evolve into a central element of the party program. Especially in that vast array of convention speeches that will never be covered by the television networks, there are always some new themes, even new proposals, that are "floated" into the hall. In the same fashion, the presentations by organized interests which also come to the convention, presentations made at press conferences and working sessions outside the hall, are even more likely to produce these aspiring future policy shifts.

For example, the Republican Convention of 1984, otherwise memorable chiefly as an extended celebration of the renomination of Ronald Reagan, was the first introduction, to Republican activists and to the national media, of the Conservative Opportunity Society (COS), an intraparty group—Newt Gingrich, Vin Weber, Robert Walker, and others—that would be central to national policy debate for almost a generation. If few such groups acquire the centrality of the COS, many use the convention in their attempts to do so. More familiar is the way that conventions have long been critical to launching the careers of individual political figures. Think of Reagan himself at the Republican Convention of 1964, or of Barack Obama at the Democratic Convention of 2004. Yet the analytic point here is that conventions are critical theaters in doing the same for public policies. Given a general scholarly interest in where policies come from, and how they become attached to political parties, conventions remain curiously under-studied in this regard.

THE CONSTITUENTS OF THE ARENA

The audience for most of this remained, in formal terms, what it had long been: the delegates, alternates, and invited guests that populate the hall itself. Yet as the convention evolved from institutional mechanism to institutional arena, the social backgrounds and partisan characteristics of these individuals changed enormously. All but some members of the Republican National Committee among Republicans and all but the superdelegates among Democrats were now candidate supporters, which helps explain why the nomination was now locked outside the convention and why maneuvers to change that situation by way of credentials, rules, and platform had such miserable prospects. The old supporters of "favorite son" plus truly uncommitted delegates were a thing of the past. This alone was a major change embodied by modern delegates.

Few of these candidate supporters had much personal responsibility for the changing structure of partisan politics in the United States, the structure that had created them in their modern form, with one major exception that is addressed at the end of this section. Yet collectively, they reflected—in essence, helped to constitute—the partisan structure of the modern world. Indeed, as the convention morphed from being a classic mechanism to an even more classic arena, the simple social identity of these delegates became more important, becoming in some sense its main concrete product. Demographically, Democratic and Republican delegates were powerfully different in some ways. To use 2008 as an example: Democratic delegates were 23 percent black, Republican delegates 2 percent, while Republican delegates were 33 percent evangelical, Democrats 14 percent—and the latter would be very close to 33 percent to 3 percent if black delegates were removed from the picture (New York Times/CBS News 2008a, 2008b).

Those figures were comparatively straightforward reflections of the external party coalitions. On the other hand, there were important demographics on which these Democratic and Republican delegates were more like each other than like their own party identifiers. Thus, a third of all Americans had a high-school degree or less, but almost no delegates from either party—less than 5 percent—fell into that category, while at the other end of the educational spectrum, more than half of the delegates in both parties had a postgraduate degree, compared to 12 percent for the nation as a whole. Yet if there was something about these delegates that would either constrain or enable the attempt to use the national party convention as an infomercial, it was more their explicit political views, the policy preferences of these two comparatively extreme embodiments of the active parties. To take only one snapshot, again from 2008:

- On the Iraq War, Republican delegates viewed the US as having done the right thing by a margin of 80 percent–13 percent, while Democratic delegates felt that the US should have stayed out by a margin of 2 percent–95 percent. On the trade-off between health care and taxes, Republican delegates emphasized the latter, 7 percent–77 percent, while Democratic delegates emphasized the former, 94 percent–3 percent. In both cases, it was the Democratic delegates who were closer to mean public opinion.

- On making the Bush tax cuts permanent or letting them expire, Republican delegates favored the former, 91 percent–4 percent, while Democratic delegates favored the latter, 7 percent–80 percent. And on the now-standard fourfold item on abortion policy, Republican delegates preferred the two more conservative options by 67 percent–18 percent, while Democratic delegates preferred the two more liberal options by 12 percent–76 percent. In both these cases, it was the Republican delegates who were closer to mean public opinion.

The simplest way to create a summary measure for all this across time is just to compare the ideological self-identification of these delegates both with the self-identification of their fellow partisans and with that of the general public. When such questions were first broached by way of public opinion surveys in the immediate postwar years, the established wisdom about the structure of preferences in American society was very clear. Democratic identifiers were modestly left of the median voter, while Republican identifiers were modestly right. Democratic

Table 14.3 Ideological representation at national party conventions

Year	Republican delegates	Republican identifiers	All voters	Democratic identifiers	Democratic delegates
2008	+62	+48	0	−20	−50
2004	+48	+39	0	−29	−52
1980	+49	+15	0	−11	−54
1976	+49	+14	0	−8	−42
1972	+24	+12	0	−9	−55
1956	+45	+6	0	−6	−9

Note: Positive scores are conservative and negative scores are liberal; the national median becomes the 0 point; cell entries are then the balance of conservative over liberal or vice versa, as a distance from that national median. For the specifics of creating these measures across time, see Shafer (1988, 100–7).

elites, as represented by convention delegates, were then modestly left of their rank-and-file identifiers, while Republican elites were sharply off to the right of theirs (McClosky, Hoffman, and O'Hara 1960). Recall, however, that as long as the convention was more mechanism than arena, these ideological positions were not necessarily determinative of practical outcomes: these were the years, after all, when Republican conventions reliably endorsed moderate nominees. There were then three recognizable periods thereafter:

- In the immediate aftermath of sweeping structural reform, there was a moment when analysts believed that this situation had been reversed—that Democratic and Republican identifiers were still modestly left and right of the national average, but that Democratic delegates had now jumped far off to the left, while Republican delegates had actually moved back toward the center. This was indeed the situation in 1972, but in short order, the picture that emerged and then reliably recurred, a picture of post-reform delegates within the convention as an institutional arena, became very different.

- The world of mass identifiers still looked much as it always had, with Democrats modestly liberal and Republicans modestly conservative. But now, the two sets of convention delegates were both sharply off to the ideological extremes, indeed farther from their own rank and file than the two sets of mass identifiers were from each other. This was already the situation in 1976 and 1980, and it remained an adequate description for a further generation.

- By 2000, what appeared to be different was a growing distance between *mass bases*, that is, between rank-and-file Democratic and Republican identifiers, with perhaps an added increment for rank-and-file Republicans. As a result, both groups of party identifiers were now closer to their own partisan elites than to the opposite body of party supporters (Abramowitz and Saunders 1998). That was the shape of the modern world as this is written.

The resulting picture—those demographic differences but especially this ideological patterning—did have two further impacts on partisan politics. In one, despite the irrelevance of procedural mechanics within the modern convention, the delegates as a collectivity did set practical limits on what the top leadership could do with its convention. If these limits were usually invisible, because the leadership understood and adapted to them, this adaptation should not obscure their existence. In the other impact, party activists with these demographic but especially ideological characteristics were part and parcel of the process by which new policy positions became integrated into the meaning of partisan attachment in the United States, and in which old positions were shucked away. This is an impact whose consequences are harvested in the American politics outside the convention but whose mechanics are more easily observed inside.

With the first of these, in a convention increasingly emptied of concrete policy decisions, what this overall ideological patterning meant was that the convention leadership had absolutely zero incentive to put resurrected convention decisions, much less strategy for the fall campaign, back into the hands of convention delegates. That could only tie the hands of this leadership, a calculation that reinforced the recurrent decision, for example, to yield the party platform to the delegates if they were restless and then just to bury it from public view. Beyond that, this distribution of delegate preferences meant that there was often a tension behind the scenes over strategy going forward, that is, a recurrent situation where nominees either had to abandon strategic initiatives that could never get past these delegates, or where these nominees would have to adopt those initiatives later and thus apparently shift strategies after the convention, with all the risks of tactical delay plus apparent indecisiveness that this entailed.

Seen the other way around, of course, this distribution of ideological preferences functioned as a powerful anchor for the policy positions of the major parties. From one side, the fact that the delegates (and alternates, etc.) now had to be elected in tandem with presidential candidates was a development that guaranteed some substantial turnover among convention participants in most contests. This made it look as if political parties in national convention could pivot quickly in order to capitalize on new strategic opportunities. From the other side, however, if these delegates had recurrent and predictable preferences for party programs, they nevertheless served as an anchor for those programs—as well as a guarantee of substantial differences *between* the programs of the two major parties. This only emphasizes the role of the partisan activists who turn up at national party conventions in the creation and adaptation of such programs (Miller and Jennings 1986).

The process by which various issues come to be central to partisan self-identification, along with the simultaneous process by which specific positions on these issues become associated with particular parties, are an increasingly consequential dynamic of American politics (Carmines and Wagner 2006). If one wanted to know when these issues and their positions actually came to the top of the legislative agenda—when they were being converted into actual public policy—then the US Congress would be the relevant institutional forum. But if one wanted to know instead when these issues and positions first appeared and then began to characterize the active parties, the national party convention is almost the only institutional forum through which to approach these questions.

Yet as a research site, the convention, by virtue of its loss of concrete policy decisions, has receded as an analytic tool for these ideational concerns as well. Convention observers know anecdotally when the Democratic Party in convention moved away from the Cold War consensus, or when the Republican Party in convention abandoned the cultural progressivism that was once characteristic. But the dynamics of this larger process remain surprisingly under-studied, even as it becomes increasingly implausible to believe that the politics of presidential selection has little to do with these dynamics, which is what the marginalization of the convention as a scholarly focus would otherwise imply.

FROM INSTITUTION TO ARENA: LOOKING IN AND LOOKING OUT

Despite an overarching evolution from institutional mechanism to institutional arena; despite a background politics that reliably privileges convention managers and the mass media; and despite an apparent stability to the partisan positioning of the bulk of convention participants, national party conventions do manage to retain noteworthy differences one from another, even within the same political party. Part of this difference, as above, lies in the constant adjustment of partisan program that is focused in, and sometimes stimulated by, the convention. Some adjustments are idiosyncratic to a particular year or even a particular contest, but others are essentially the updating—the modernization—of what it means to be a self-identified Democrat or a Republican. Yet part of the difference is contextual in another sense: different political contexts provide more or less scope for strategic choice by convention managers, and thus more or less scope for public impact from national party conventions.

The simple comparison of two sequential *pairs* of conventions can make this point concretely. The national party conventions of 2004 were sharply constricted in the presentational choices available to their strategists. The Republicans were renominating a sitting president, George W. Bush, a comparatively polarizing figure. The vast bulk of the electorate would either vote for him or not, regardless of the identity of the Democratic nominee. Under those conditions, all that was left for the Republican Convention was an effort to maximize the mobilization of supporters. The Democrats had more presentational leeway, having a far less well-known candidate, yet Democratic strategists already knew that the election was likely to turn on considerations of national security. Their primary job was thus to make their candidate acceptable on those grounds; their secondary task was to personalize him; anything else was a distraction.

By contrast, the pair of national party conventions in 2008 could hardly have been farther, contextually, from those of 2004. The nominating contests of 2008 were the first since 1952 not to feature either a sitting president or vice-president seeking a major-party nomination, thereby indirectly reducing the name recognition of the nominees. John McCain had run for president before, while Barack Obama had the "advantage" of having waged a six-month struggle for the nomination, yet both needed to be introduced to a much larger public via their conventions. Moreover, both nominees remained programmatically obscure. Obama was a committed partisan who had run for the nomination as a man who would transcend partisan politics, while McCain was an acknowledged maverick, the substance of whose "maverickness" was not obvious going forward.

In such a context, convention strategists had maximum leverage for introducing their candidate and for shaping his intended themes for the fall campaign. Their very leverage, on the other hand, simultaneously emphasizes not just the difference between conventions from year to year, but the conditional relationship between the convention, the fall campaign, and the ultimate outcome in every year. Conventions emerge from one context and lead into another. That much is formally true. Moreover, there is no reason for the candidate and his party not to make every effort to maximize the impact of their convention. Anything not gained from this convention is lost forever. Yet the "bounce" from any given convention, that is, the gain in public support achieved by its nominee, is neither regular in its size nor guaranteed by the surface quality of the convention itself. Much else goes into this impact.

In the end, these differences are still twists and turns on an overall pattern of convention evolution. But does this pattern itself have anything to teach the analyst about the evolution of American politics more generally? Which is to say: can it be treated as a microcosm of something larger than itself? One way to argue that it can is to say that there was an old American politics which featured a set of institutional mechanisms through which discrete localities could send individual representatives to the geographic center to bargain for their policy wishes. Just as there is a new American politics which features a set of institutional arenas in which political elites concentrate on sending policy messages that will allow them to claim to be representing national majorities. The analyst does not need to believe that national party conventions had the power to lead the transition between these worlds in order to suggest that the convention is a particularly clear and bounded theater in which to study that larger transition.

This potential was most immediately and consequentially apparent in the case of those two grand movements, the nationalization of politics and the imposition of procedural reform, which were reshaping not just the national party convention but national political life in the later twentieth century. Both grand movements were very concretely present in the national party convention. Moreover, at the center of politicking within this new political order was the attempt to use the institutions of government to communicate with a differentiated or general public, to build coalitions by mobilizing sectors of that public, and at some point to convert those coalitions into governmental policy. Once more, this was more consequential with the presidency or Congress, but it was easier to see—to conceptualize as a whole—in the case of the national party convention.

At the same time and regardless, the convention continues to evolve in its own right. Seen from inside, the long and winding road from institutional mechanism to institutional arena is not yet at its end. It is always difficult to know whether a twist or turn in convention operations is a harbinger or just an anomaly, but every convention offers some examples, and the two from 2008, the most recent as this is written, were no exception:

- The Democratic Convention of 2008 removed the largest remaining concrete event of the convention from the convention hall, the acceptance speech by its nominee, and placed it in an outdoor amphitheater. In the process, it devalued the orthodox participants—the delegates, alternates, and invited guests—in a remarkable fashion, even as window dressing. It is hard to think of a more symbolic realization of the notion of convention as arena, especially if this change were coupled with a further foreshortening of convention events before the acceptance speech. On the other hand, this same maneuver had been tried once before, with John Kennedy at the Democratic Convention of 1960, so that it had obviously not become established.

- Yet the experiment gained potential consequence in 2008 because a foreshortening of the convention was exactly what the Republican Convention went on to offer. In deference to extreme weather and associated suffering, the Republicans truncated their opening day, such that there was no coverage by network television. The established networks had themselves done this in 2004, dumping Monday for the Republicans and Tuesday for the Democrats. They had actually planned a modest expansion for 2008 by restoring the extra hour on that fourth night, only to have it given back by the Republicans. Since the established television networks had been arguing for years that conventions could be handled as an even shorter—a two-day—extravaganza, they might reasonably argue that they have now repeatedly tested a short format.

The convention is thus in transition as an institution in its own right. It is in transition as a register of the nature of partisanship in its time. And it is in transition, almost in spite of itself, within the larger institutional framework of which it is only one long-established but evolutionary piece. Along the way, it has evolved from classic mechanism to archetypal arena, while remaining the leading pure partisan institution of American politics. It survives because it has proved remarkably malleable and adaptable along the way. As a result, it retains the potential to comment upon—not always to influence, but reliably to observe—the major factors shaping American politics at the time of each particular incarnation. In intellectual terms, then, it is more than a little ironic that this institutional trajectory has coincided with the general disappearance of those professional observers, professional political scientists, who might be thought to be most interested in all these other developments.

CHAPTER 15

....

ACTIVISTS, INFLUENCE, AND REPRESENTATION IN AMERICAN ELECTIONS

....

WALTER J. STONE

THE American political system is susceptible to fragmentation over integration; factionalism over enduring coalitions. Some would say the Madisonian system exploits and encourages factionalism to the detriment of sustained, accountable, and programmatic national policy. Critics of the American system have lamented these tendencies (Dahl 1994; Lowi 1979; Schattschneider 1975), while academic reformers have suggested strengthening the political parties as an antidote (Ranney 1962; Schattschneider 1942). In the view of many political scientists and other observers, the emergence of mass political parties solved critical collective action and policy integration problems left unattended in the American constitutional framework. The parties provide a locus of collective responsibility in an otherwise fragmented and contentious system that encourages politicians to attend to local and factional concerns rather than responding to long-term problems or national conditions (Fiorina 1980).

The political parties may have been a fortuitous invention of politicians in the early years of the republic as they struggled with career, political, and policy pressures, but they have evolved to take a central place in our understanding of how modern democracies work. As Schattschneider famously put it in his defense of party government in the US, "political parties created democracy . . . and democracy is unthinkable save in terms of the political parties" (1942, 1).

If political parties serve broader purposes such as accountability, representation, and integration, it is primarily as a by-product of the more immediate career and political interests of those who create and maintain them. Parties are often seen as bridging or linking institutions between the interests of voters and politicians. Voters need efficient shortcuts in reaching a decision, and the political branding offered by parties serves that end; politicians face collective action problems both in mobilizing the electorate and in governing, and parties are essential to resolving both challenges.

Volunteer party activists are central to the contemporary party organization, the third component of Key's tripartite conception of the parties (Key 1964). Unlike candidates and officeholders, activists do not formally serve constituencies, nor do they typically seek public office, although they may hold competitive positions within the party organization such as national convention delegates. In that, they are like voters because they participate primarily to advance their own interests rather than acting formally on behalf of others. Because they are unusually involved in the political process, they may wield substantial influence. Whereas voters' influence is formally circumscribed by the fact that each citizen has only one vote to cast, activists may exercise disproportionate influence by virtue of their skill, energy, and resources. Because they lack formal constituency or accountability and their influence may distort the egalitarian foundation of popular elections, activists have often been seen as problematic. In this chapter I consider the place of party activists in the electoral process, with attention to questions about whether and how they distort processes of electoral representation in the United States.

Party activists are involved in the electoral process on behalf of candidates or parties in some way beyond voting. They are usually identified by virtue of a party position such as precinct captain or convention delegate, or because of their activity in campaigns, such as displaying a yard sign, contributing money to a candidate, or canvassing.[1] As noted, party activists potentially have influence over party and electoral outcomes that is greater than the influence they would have if they participated only as voters. In the absence of accountability relationships with constituencies activists have been seen by critics as a fragmenting force within the political parties. Party activists bring their own issue priorities and positions, which may arise from allegiances to interest groups, social movements, or nomination

---

[1] As I use the term, anyone actively involved in the electoral process beyond voting is a "party activist" whether for a specific candidate or for the party.

candidates. The parties have evolved away from patronage-based incentives to organizations dependent on or permeated by myriad interests that are not necessarily coterminous with the party organizations' electoral and governance interests. In national politics, for example, the emergence of "amateur" and "purist" activists in presidential nomination campaigns has been interpreted to mean that the parties no longer control the resources necessary to maintain their interests in the nominating process (Polsby 1983; Soule and Clarke 1970; Wildavsky 1965; J. Wilson 1960). Activists whose primary interest is in issues and policy outcomes, the reasoning goes, support candidates who agree with them on the issues, rather than candidates who are well positioned to win the general election. This, in turn, opened the parties to external influences, principally from competing candidates for the party nomination that could threaten party unity, undermine long-term coalitions, and fragment the party in government (Polsby 1983; Ranney 1975). In short, contemporary activists have the potential to undermine the integrative function of the parties by weakening the parties' capacity to mount a coherent campaign and present a united front in governance.

If party activists were representative of the broader electorate, their potential influence in the process might be less worrisome. But their influence, combined with the fact that they have uniformly been shown to be unrepresentative of the voting public, raises concerns. As Verba, Schlozman, and Brady (1995) put it, "Those in public life are more likely to be aware of, and to pay attention to, the needs and preferences of those who are active. Thus, it must matter for the democratic principle of equality that studies of citizen participation in America find political activists to be unrepresentative of the public at large." Thus, the question is whether activists produce, in Adams and Ezrow's phrase, "representational inequality" by virtue of their influence and interests, both of which distinguish them from ordinary voters (Adams and Ezrow 2009).

WHY DO ACTIVISTS DO WHAT THEY DO?

Ultimately, our ability to comprehend the place of activists in the electoral process depends on a micro-level foundation comparable to our understanding of the voter. Why are they active? Why do they support the candidates, issues, and causes that they do? In their exhaustive audit of participation in America, Verba, Schlozman, and Brady (1995) employ a unique design to catalog different types of activism and provide extensive evidence in support of a coherent explanation of political activism. In a book published shortly before the Verba et al. work, Rosenstone and Hansen (1993) offered a comprehensive analysis of the ANES time series to address fundamental issues of political participation and activism. Both books provide insight about why people participate as activists, and how activists might distort outcomes of the electoral process from the interests of an electorate composed only of ordinary voters.

Both works confront the collective action problem associated with most forms of electoral participation, especially in an era when activists are motivated to promote public policies and candidacies, rather than material benefits in the form of party patronage. The problem occurs because public policies and winning candidates are, from the perspective of the voter or activist, public goods that benefit (positively or negatively) all members of the public, whether or not they helped produce the outcome by participating. Because participation is costly in time and other resources, and because the individual participant's contribution is too small to determine the outcome, rational-actor models suggest that citizens ought to enjoy the policy and other benefits of election outcomes without bearing the costs of participating.

Many scholars have taken issue with this logic, not least because it cannot explain why so many citizens and activists bother to participate in electoral politics, and Verba et al. and Rosenstone and Hansen are no exceptions. The Verba et al. study is a more complete explanation of activism, in part because of its uniquely powerful two-stage design. The authors drew a large cross-section of the American electorate, and used filter questions to identify the subset of respondents who engaged in various forms of participation beyond voting. Activists make up a small proportion of any cross-section sample of the American electorate, but the unusually large sample yielded a much larger than normal subset of activists. Their design gave Verba et al. comparable data on activists and non-activists which, combined with the large number of activists, provided statistical leverage to explain activist participation by comparing activists with non-activists on a number of dimensions.

The "Civic Volunteerism Model" Verba et al. employ to explain activism rests on three variables: resources, engagement, and recruitment. Individuals with more resources such as personal wealth, time, and skills are more likely to participate, as are those who are more engaged in politics by virtue of their interest or commitment on the issues. Likewise, individuals who are invited to participate by others are more likely to become involved. Verba et al. emphasize resources because of their political relevance, although engagement and recruitment are also important because they help solve the collective action problem associated with electoral participation. Citizens who are deeply engaged in politics enjoy benefits intrinsic with participation itself, such that the "costs" of participation may be difficult to differentiate from the benefits. Thus, time and money spent (or forgone) by activists also carry benefits linked to being associated with a larger social purpose, which can be deeply rewarding in its own right. Likewise, the interpersonal and social rewards often associated with activism may provide selective compensation to participants, unavailable to those who do not become politically involved. Thus, the satisfactions and rewards come to participants and not to non-participants, even if they recognize that their individual contribution as an activist cannot produce the desired policy or electoral outcome.

A critical contribution Verba et al. make is to demonstrate the potential of their analysis to address questions of representation. By linking the political needs and issue positions of activists to their explanation of why people are drawn to unusual levels of political involvement, they provide a detailed analysis of the potential distortion that results from differences between the policy preferences of activists and those of ordinary voters. For example, higher-income individuals are much more likely to contribute to political causes than lower-income individuals, and income is associated with conservative policy views. Their data demonstrate that the conservative distortion on economic issues linked to activism by financial contribution is more substantial than the bias introduced by any other variable in the Civic Volunteerism Model (Verba, Schlozman, and Brady 1995, 475).[2]

The Verba et al. analysis of potential "representational distortion" based in activism is a subtle and innovative approach. Like all path-breaking research, it raises as many questions as it answers. One is illustrated by way of comparison with the central theme of the Rosenstone and Hansen (1993) book. Rosenstone and Hansen criticize much of the research on political participation for overemphasizing the importance of individual explanatory characteristics (such as socioeconomic resources) at the expense of mobilizing forces, principally as stimulation from the political environment. Mobilization, in Rosenstone and Hansen's view, involves direct and indirect efforts to induce participation by others. Many of these efforts are linked to strategic efforts by politicians and others in political campaigns to alter the calculus of participation by their potential supporters (Aldrich 1993; Leighley 1995).

The Rosenstone and Hansen analysis complements the Verba et al. book by expanding awareness of recruitment and other forms of mobilization. For Rosenstone and Hansen, like Verba et al., direct interpersonal recruitment is an important part of the explanation of why people become active beyond voting. For example, party contact shows a consistent and strong effect on such forms of activism as persuading others, working on a campaign, and contributing money (Rosenstone and Hansen 1993, 130). But over and above these direct mobilization effects, and independent of variables measuring individuals' resources and engagement in politics, Rosenstone and Hansen also find campaign mobilization effects

---

[2] Their data show that the distorting effects of income among contributors are equally conservative in both parties but, whereas most other explanatory variables also push contributors to be more conservative than the Republican rank and file, some variables among Democratic contributors (education and interest) push them more to the left, offsetting the effects of income. The net result in their data within the Democratic Party is zero distortion on economic attitudes linked to financial contributions (Verba, Schlozman, and Brady 1995, 479).

(131–2). These effects not only work directly; they also have indirect effects by stimulating higher levels of party contact (164–5).

Rosenstone and Hansen's approach complements that of Verba et al. by incorporating the political context in their explanation of active participation. Their emphasis draws attention to the links between contact and other forms of mobilization and the resource-based explanation stressed by Verba et al. The different components of the Civic Volunteerism Model are interdependent and interact with the political context in ways that have not yet been fully explored. We know, for example, that higher socio-economic status (SES) individuals are more likely to be contacted by the parties in election campaigns than low SES individuals (Rosenstone and Hansen 1993, 164–5). Mobilization, in addition to reinforcing the SES bias in participation, also can mitigate it by interacting with SES to stimulate participation among those otherwise less inclined to become involved. Likewise, activism itself stimulates future contact and mobilization, and appears to foster greater engagement in the form of stronger commitment on the issues (Claassen 2008; J. McCann 1995).

ACTIVISTS IN THE NOMINATION PROCESS

In addition to explaining why people become activists, a focus on representation in the electoral process points to the question of candidate support in nomination campaigns because it is especially in those contests that activists have disproportionate influence. As noted, pressures on major party candidates to attend to activist preferences are often assumed to push candidates toward the extreme of their party, away from the median voter in the general election. However, contrary to the view that primary activists and voters support the candidate closest to their own extreme issue preferences, my coauthors and I have shown that activists discount their policy preferences by their perceptions of nomination candidates' general election chances (W. Stone and Abramowitz 1983; W. Stone, Atkeson, and Rapoport 1992; W. Stone, Rapoport, and Atkeson 1995).[3] Because activists are aware that the average general election voter is relatively centrist and that their own views diverge rather sharply from those of the typical voter (W. Stone and Rapoport 1994), they balance their policy interests by the competing candidates' electability in deciding whom to support. This often, but not always, pushes activists to

[3] This is as true of activists who identify themselves as "purists" in response to questions about their willingness to compromise their principles to win elections as it is of "pragmatists" who acknowledge a general willingness to compromise in order to win (W. Stone and Abramowitz 1983, 951).

support nomination candidates less extreme than their own preferences.[4] Activists care deeply about their policy preferences, so it would not make sense for them to defer completely to the median general election voter on the issues. At the same time, however, if they vote their sincere preferences during the nomination contest, they may doom their party to defeat, thereby resulting in victory by the opposition with correspondingly severe losses in policy. The result is a process in which candidates are not completely free to offer centrist appeals in the nomination phase, but neither are they necessarily tethered to their party's extreme.

The willingness of nomination activists to discount their policy preferences in deciding which candidate to support suggests that activists may be sensitive to competing electoral interests in other settings as well. Thus, financial contributors to candidates and other activists who have more extreme views than their party's rank and file or the electorate as a whole probably appreciate the competing electoral pressures on those candidates. In short, activists are sophisticated players in politics; they understand that compromise is necessary, and that they cannot simply dictate terms to elected officials (Stacy Gordon 2005). This is not to deny the interests that motivate activists, nor to contradict the claim that representational distortion occurs. Rather, it suggests that the amount of distortion is an empirical question and not a straightforward consequence of the *potential* for distortion.

ACTIVISTS IN THE GENERAL ELECTION: AGENTS OF PARTY CHANGE?

In general elections, activists' strong partisanship is usually seen as pushing them inexorably to support their party's candidate. There are exceptions, as when supporters of losing candidates in the nomination are thought to be alienated during the general election, and in analysis based on movement in and out of the activist stratum over time (Carmines and Stimson 1989; Carmines and Woods 2002; Nexon 1971). These questions are linked because of the importance of nomination candidacies in mobilizing activists into the party, and because activists and other party elites are central actors in explanations of party change (Carmines

[4] Ronald Reagan was a prominent exception in that he was recognized in 1980 by Republican and Democratic activists as both more extreme than his major competitor for the GOP nomination, George H. W. Bush, and more electable. Thus, in the 1980 Republican nomination race, many relatively moderate Republican activists who were closer to Bush in their ideological preferences backed Reagan.

and Stimson 1989; Claassen 2007; Herrera 1995; Rapoport and Stone 1994; W. Stone, Atkeson, and Rapoport 1992).

Carmines and Stimson's theory of issue evolution rests explicitly on the importance of change at the elite level and assigns a primary role to activists in communicating change in party positions to the electorate (Carmines and Stimson 1989, ch. 4). Ordinary voters may react to change but are not sufficiently engaged or attentive to be prime movers of political change. Likewise, officeholders "strain toward consistency rather than change . . . by the constraint of party affiliation, and by the political danger of appearing unsteady of approach" (Carmines and Stimson 1989, 90). In contrast,

Citizen activists, fired by zeal and standing to lose no more than an investment of time committed to the cause, are well situated to respond quickly to new ideas, to be the carriers of new themes . . . the fact that they move in and out of activity frees them to be the dynamic element in issue evolution. Because activity itself is occasional, we expect change between occasions.

In their analysis of the period between 1956 and 1984, Carmines and Stimson find substantial shifts in racial attitudes among campaign activists that seem to reflect the ascendancy of conservative Republican nominees, Barry Goldwater in 1964 and Ronald Reagan in 1980. Their analysis fits well with research on the mobilization effects of nomination-stage activism, and provides a reasonably coherent picture of how party and campaign activists promote party change. While it is true, as Carmines and Stimson point out, that officeholders are reluctant to change their positions on issues, those who contend for their party's nomination have incentives to compete by appealing to and mobilizing different issue constituencies. Barry Goldwater and Ronald Reagan represented a brand of conservatism different from mainstream GOP presidential candidates, and they are generally credited with shifting the Republican Party to the right, partly, as Carmines and Stimson suggest, as a result of the activist base they mobilized. There are many other candidates who have more or less successfully appealed to constituencies that had been disaffected or undermobilized in their party, including George McGovern in 1972, Jesse Jackson in 1984, Pat Robertson in 1988, and Barack Obama in 2008. What effect did these and other candidacies have on their party, whether or not they were able to win the nomination or election?

The purist–amateur conception of party activism strongly suggests that when activists motivated by issue incentives and unaccustomed to compromise support a candidate who loses, especially in the candidate-centered style of politics prevalent in contemporary American politics, they withdraw from party involvement in the general election phase (Lowi 1985; Wattenberg 1991). Early empirical studies tracking activists from the nomination to the general election stage appeared to confirm a drop-off effect among supporters of nomination losers (Donald Johnson and Gibson 1974; Southwell 1986; W. Stone 1984). The alienation of nomination losers from the party is part of political lore, as when commentators breathlessly speculated that Hillary Clinton's disappointed 2008 nomination supporters not only would fail to back Obama's general election candidacy, but would turn to John McCain in the fall campaign.

In contrast, much as we found that party activists did not behave like single-minded "purists" in deciding whom to support for their party's nomination, my collaborators and I have found that activists who become involved in a nomination campaign are actually quite pragmatic about their subsequent support for the general election nominee and other candidates in the parties. In fact, nomination activity actually stimulates general election activism among those who backed a losing nomination contender, even when the nomination stage was a long and bitter contest (W. Stone, Rapoport, and Abramowitz 1992).[5] We have found a comparable mobilization effect of third party activists in ensuing major party campaigns (see Rapoport, Chapter 12 in this volume). The reason for this effect is that active participation in a campaign apparently sensitizes the individual to general election appeals and choices, as well as making the activist a more visible target for subsequent mobilization. The effect generalizes beyond mobilization into a succeeding presidential general election campaign to House races and to campaigns four years or more after the initial mobilizing campaign (J. McCann 1995; Pastor, Stone, and Rapoport 1999; Rapoport and Stone 1994).

Pastor, Stone, and Rapoport (1999) demonstrate the potential these mobilization effects have as a mechanism of party change, consistent with the argument first advanced by Carmines and Stimson (1989). Pat Robertson's unsuccessful bid for the 1988 Republican nomination mobilized neophytes different from core Republican activists in their issue commitments. These newly mobilized activists continued to participate in the 1988 general election campaign as a result of their involvement in the nomination campaign, despite their candidate's defeat by George H. W. Bush. Moreover, the mobilization effects among Robertson activists from the 1988 campaign continued in GOP presidential and sub-presidential campaigns in 1992. Their results suggest the importance of mobilization efforts in one campaign for long-term party change. Robertson's relatively brief nomination campaign helped foster a sea change in the Republican Party toward the Christian Right, mobilizing evangelical Christians who had not previously been involved into long-term activism in the party, and producing notable change in the policy makeup of the activist base in the bargain. Rapoport and Stone (2005) found even longer-term effects from the Perot movement on the Republican Party after

[5] The erroneous conclusion in the early studies that supporting a loser depresses general election support results from the fact that loser backers do, in fact, support the winning candidate less than activists who supported the winner in the nomination fight. Nonetheless, the more involved activists were for the nomination loser (or winner) in the nomination campaign, the more active they are in the general election (Stone, Atkeson, and Rapoport 1992; McCann et al. 1996).

1992 to illustrate the potential for major party change rooted in mobilization by a third party or independent candidate.

The central place of activists in our understanding of party change brings us full circle to the central question of this chapter because it suggests activists exert disproportionate influence over electoral outcomes. Verba, Schlozman, and Brady ask whether activists, because of their extraordinary influence and atypical policy preferences, distort the process of representation away from an egalitarian process based on the preferences and behavior of ordinary voters. They provide detailed evidence about how activist participants have the *potential* to distort processes of representation, but we need research designs capable of linking activist participation to electoral outcomes before we can conclude that distortion actually occurs. That requires an organic approach to the study of parties and elections, rather than focusing on one or the other set of actors, such as voters, candidates, or activists. At a minimum, such designs must include variation in voter behavior and preferences, variation in activist behavior and preferences, and variation in electoral outcomes. Carmines and Stimson's (1989) study of issue evolution in the parties has some of these ingredients by linking mass response to officeholder and activist change. Erikson, Wright, and McIver (1993) accord an important place to party activists in their model of policy response in the states to electoral preferences; Adams and Ezrow (2009) provide an excellent example in a comparative study of the distorting effects of opinion leaders on European parties. To illustrate the potential for such studies, I draw on a study of the 2006 midterm elections in the House of Representatives that includes elements related to these requirements.

CAMPAIGN ACTIVISTS IN THE 2006 US HOUSE ELECTIONS

The spatial model of elections offers a simple framework for assessing claims about the influence of party activists. One reason for this is the regular finding in the literature on party activists that they are more extreme in their issue preferences than the electorate as a whole and more divergent than the party rank and file (John S. Jackson, Brown, and Bositis 1982; J. Kirkpatrick 1976; McClosky, Hoffman, and O'Hara 1960; W. Miller and Jennings 1986; Aldrich 1995).[6] Activist extremism has been used by spatial modelers to explain why candidates from the two major parties do not converge on the preferences of the median voter as the original

---

[6] Activists are usually, but not always, found to be more extreme in their preferences than ordinary voters within their party (cf. W. Miller and Jennings 1986; McClosky, Hoffman, and O'Hara 1960; Nexon 1971).

Downsian model predicted (Aranson and Ordeshook 1972; Baron 1994; Moon 2004; Aldrich 1983a). Activists control resources necessary for candidates to wage successful campaigns, which may make candidates especially attentive to their interests, just as Verba et al. suggest. Because activist candidate support reflects their personal interests, candidates (and ultimately the parties themselves) may have incentives to depart from the preferences of ordinary voters.

In collaboration with University of California, Davis colleagues, I undertook a study of the 2006 US House elections that has some of the design elements necessary to assess the influence of activists in the electoral system. The study was conducted in a random cross-section national sample of ninety-nine US House districts, with a supplementary sample of fifty-five districts that were open or judged to be competitive by close observers of congressional elections.[7] Samples of registered voters were surveyed in these districts in a pre- and post-election design, as part of the omnibus Cooperative Congressional Election Study (CCES) midterm election study conducted by Polimetrix under the direction of Stephen Ansolabehere.[8]

Two features of the study make the data especially appropriate for addressing the implications of activist preferences and participation for electoral representation. First, simultaneous to the voter survey, we conducted an independent survey of district "experts" who could provide information about the two parties' candidates running in each House district. We surveyed by mail and the Internet 2,004 national convention delegates and state legislators in both political parties living in the sample districts because these individuals were assumed to be well informed about the candidates, the politics of their districts, and the campaign.[9] We asked district experts to place the House candidates from both political parties on a 7-point liberal–conservative scale identical to the item included on the registered voter survey. We aggregate expert perceptions of candidate placements to the district level by computing a mean placement of each candidate. This gives us an estimate of each candidate's position on the liberal–conservative scale independent of constituents' self-placements in the identical ideological space.[10]

---

[7] We identified the competitive district sample by consulting projections by *Congressional Quarterly, Cook Report, Sabato Crystal Ball*, and the *National Journal*. If a district was rated as a "toss-up" by any of the sources in June 2006, we included it in the competitive supplemental sample. There was substantial agreement among the four sources, with the correlations among them greater than 0.70.

[8] For details on the study, see <http://web.mit.edu/polisci/portl/cces/index.html>. Candidate and self-placement items on the liberal-conservative scale are from the pre-election wave; items used to identify activists in House campaigns were asked on the post-election wave.

[9] District experts were surveyed during the month of October, before election day so that their perceptions and judgments were not affected by the election outcome. The response rate was 21 percent with an average of 6.2 responses per district.

[10] Candidate placements are subject to modest partisan bias, with experts rating candidates in the opposite party slightly more extreme than candidates in their own party. We statistically correct experts' ratings for this effect prior to aggregating expert ratings to the district mean, which provides the estimate of each candidate's placement. We have conducted extensive analysis on the reliability and validity of the candidate placement data, with reassuring results. Reliability analysis indicates high

The second unusual aspect of our study relates to the identification of the sample of citizen activists from among the registered voters surveyed. We asked a standard battery of questions to identify respondents who had been active in the campaign in some way beyond voting in the election.[11] The unusual aspect of the questions was to inquire about whether the activities were undertaken specifically for one of the major party candidates for the House in the respondent's district.[12] The advantage of asking about activism in House candidates' campaigns is that we can link activists directly to the campaign in our attempt to trace the process of representation in these elections.

Figure 15.1 presents an ideological mapping of House candidates, voters, and activists in 2006. The mapping is roughly consistent with what we would expect from other studies of voters, activists, and candidates, although this is the first such mapping that places candidates, voters, and activists in the ideological space using exactly the same metric for these three critical actors in the electoral and party

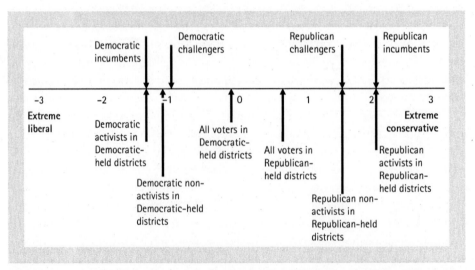

Figure 15.1 Ideological placements of US House candidates, activists, and voters, 2006

Source: 2006 Congressional Election Study, University of California, Davis.

levels of consistency in expert ratings; the correlation between district expert placements and incumbent NOMINATE scores is 0.93, which supports the validity of the informant placements.

[11] Items asked whether the respondent tried to persuade someone to vote for the candidate, worked on the candidate's campaign, attended meetings or election rallies for the candidate, posted a yard sign or bumper sticker, wore a button for the candidate, or contributed money to the candidate. Activists are those who did at least one of these things.

[12] In contrast, the standard ANES activist battery asks whether respondents were active in the campaign for one party or the other, without specifying which campaign (presidential, Senate, House, gubernatorial, local) motivated the activism.

system. As a result, these data are the first to allow a simple descriptive picture of how activists, ordinary voters, and candidates relate to one another on the liberal–conservative scale.[13]

As we would expect from previous studies, both activists and House incumbents were sharply distinguished on the left–right scale. The contemporary Congress has been characterized by partisan polarization, with Democrats on the left and Republicans clearly differentiated on the right (Ansolabehere, Snyder, and Stewart 2001b; Burden 2004; Poole and Rosenthal 1997). Democratic activists in districts represented by Democrats were at almost exactly the same point on the left–right scale on average as their representatives in the House, while Republican activists in Republican-held districts were likewise very close to their House members' positions as determined by district experts.[14] Note as well that Democratic activists were more liberal than registered voters in the same districts and that Republican activists were more conservative than voters in Republican districts. This, too, fits with a mapping we would expect from previous studies showing that activists are typically more polarized by party than ordinary voters (Aldrich 1995; W. Miller and Jennings 1986), although it is also clear from Figure 15.1 that even among ordinary voters partisan differences in 2006 were stark. Finally, it is not surprising to see that Democratic incumbents represent districts that were, as a whole, more liberal than districts represented by Republicans. Much of the difference between districts is due to the fact that Democratic districts tend to have strong pluralities of Democratic identifiers, while districts with Republican majorities elect Republicans to Congress.

The US system of representation is based on geographical districts, and evidence of a district effect is present in the ideological mapping of candidates and districts. District experts saw Democratic challengers as significantly less extreme than Democratic incumbents and Republican challengers as less conservative than Republicans in the House. This too appears to be a general pattern (Burden 2004), although it does not indicate "shirking" on the part of incumbents. Incumbents in each party are more extreme than their co-partisans running for Congress not because incumbents have come down with Potomac fever and depart from their district preferences. Rather, while Democratic incumbents won their seats in relatively liberal districts, Democratic challengers were attempting to unseat Republican incumbents in relatively conservative districts. The same is true in reverse for Republican challengers, and helps explain why they are more moderate than Republican incumbents. In other words, Republican challengers' moderation must be assessed against the

---

[13] As a percentage of the entire sample, 21 percent were active in some way for a Democratic candidate and 15 percent were active for a Republican House candidate; 27 percent of the sample are classified as Democratic non-activists while 28 percent were Republican non-activists.

[14] The resolution in the figure does not allow for the minor differences between activists and their Representatives, which is only 0.03 in the case of Democrats and 0.05 in the case of Republicans. These differences are neither statistically nor substantively significant.

relatively liberal districts in which they ran, compared with Republican incumbents running in significantly more conservative districts.

ACTIVISTS AND ELECTORAL OUTCOMES

Within this framework, how can we understand the place of party activists? Can we conclude that the proximity between activists and representatives resulted from the disproportionate influence of activists compared with ordinary voters? Our results are certainly *consistent* with this story, although they are a long way from definitive evidence in its favor. Although we cannot absolutely resolve the question of influence, we can push the analysis to include district variation by asking whether activist opinion in the district has a statistical effect on incumbent position-taking consistent with the claim that activists distort electoral outcomes from broader district opinion and behavior. I present two passes at this question: the first looks at the effect of activist opinion in districts on incumbent position-taking; the second explores the effect of activist mobilization on incumbent vote share.

Table 15.1 The effect of district and activist preferences on incumbent liberal—conservative positions

	District expert placements of incumbents		DW-NOMINATE scores of incumbents	
	b	*SE*	*b*	*SE*
District opinion	0.778[a]	0.268	0.196[a]	0.045
Activist opinion in district	0.179[b]	0.107	0.038[a]	0.018
Democratic incumbent	−2.378[a]	0.450	−.670[a]	0.074
Open/competitive district	0.258	0.205	−.028	0.034
Constant	1.10[a]	0.349	0.318[a]	0.058
F	82.93[a]		190.33[a]	
Adjusted R^2	0.756		0.880	
N	107		104	

Note: *b* = unstandardized regression coefficient; *SE* = standard error of the coefficient.
[a] *p* > .05; two-tailed test.
[b] *p* > .10; two-tailed test.
Source: 2006 Congressional Election Study, University of California, Davis.

The regression analysis in Table 15.1 presents two parallel sets of results to test for an effect of activist opinion on representatives' positions: the first column analyzes expert placements of incumbents on the 7-point scale; the second replicates the analysis using DW-NOMINATE scores computed from incumbents' roll call votes.[15] Replicating the analysis with a roll-call-based measure serves as a check on the possibility that district experts were influenced in placing incumbents by the positions and preferences they observe among party activists in the district.[16]

An extensive literature documents the correlation between district opinion and the positions of representatives (Ansolabehere, Snyder, and Stewart 2001b; W. Miller and Stokes 1963), but in an election such as 2006, characterized by national issues and partisan polarization, the impact of district opinion independently of party is striking. To be sure, party accounts for a huge effect—almost 2.5 units on the 7-point scale in Figure 15.1. Thus, Democrats in Congress were on average about 2.4 units to the left of Republicans, setting aside differences due to the preferences of the districts that elected them. In addition to party, however, district opinion has a strong effect.[17] For each unit more conservative a district is on the left–right scale in Figure 15.1, incumbents were 0.78 units more conservative, independent of party differences. As noted, this effect indicates a strong district basis of representation in the House, evident even in the context of a highly partisan election such as 2006.

Over and above district and partisan effects, however, the analysis shows that district activist opinion is associated with incumbent position taking. Democratic House members whose activist base is relatively moderate or conservative are tugged to the right by activist opinion in their district, whereas their fellow Democrats whose activist base is more liberal are nudged to the left. The results, combined with those in Figure 15.1, suggest an affinity between activists and representatives consistent with the idea that activists exert influence over the process of representation, distorting outcomes from what would be expected from mass constituency and party positions. As Verba et al. (1995) and others (Baron 1994; Moon 2004) contend, financial contributions, resources, and volunteer campaign activity may give activists access to their representatives and encourage responsiveness to their relatively extreme demands.

The second question we address is whether activist participation in House campaigns affects incumbent vote shares. The general hypothesis is that the more mobilization that occurs in district campaigns, the worse it is for the incumbent, primarily because mobilization against the incumbent begins with the entry of a

[15] NOMINATE scores on members of Congress are available from <http://voteview.com/dwnl.htm>.

[16] Scholars have speculated that one basis voters use for inferring party positions is the behavior and positions taken by activists in the parties (Aldrich 1983a; 1995; Carmines and Stimson 1989).

[17] District opinion measures are constructed from the CCES common-content survey, which included an average of about eighty-eight respondents per district.

Table 15.2 Explaining incumbent vote share, 2006

	Equation (1)		Equation (2)	
	b	SE	b	SE
Incumbent party's vote share, 2004	0.215[a]	0.038	0.215[a]	0.038
Democratic incumbent	10.357[a]	1.112	10.323[a]	1.124
Experienced challenger, 2006	−1.384	1.280	−1.402	1.287
Turnout, 2006	−11.871[a]	5.492	−11.868[a]	5.512
Mean activist participation, 2006	−5.199[a]	2.157	−	−
Mean activism for challenger	−	−	−2.816[a]	1.348
Mean activism for incumbent	−	−	−2.312	1.521
Open/competitive district subsample	−6.192[a]	1.340	−6.176[a]	1.347
Constant	50.721[a]	3.836	50.742[a]	3.850
F	51.09[a]		43.49[a]	
Adjusted R^2	0.690		0.688	
N	136		136	

Note: Analysis limited to districts in which incumbents where challenged. b = unstandardized regression coefficient; SE = standard error of the coefficient.
[a] $p > .05$; two-tailed test.
Source: 2006 Congressional Election Study, University of California, Davis.

strong challenger, who can marshal the skills, resources, and attention necessary to compete against the incumbent. The analysis in Table 15.2 takes account of the incumbent's vote share in 2004, the party of the incumbent, and whether the district is in the competitive subsample. The national swing to the Democrats in 2006 is evident in the table with a strong gain in vote share evident among Democratic incumbents; there is also a turnout effect consistent with the hypothesis that mobilization hurts incumbents. Controlling for these and the other variables in the analysis, however, there is also a strong negative effect of activist mobilization in the district. Equation 1 shows that the greater the overall level of activism in the district, the lower the incumbent's vote share; equation 2 shows that when we distinguish activism in the challenger's campaign from activism for the incumbent, it is activism for the challenger that significantly reduces the incumbent's vote share.[18]

In sum, the evidence is consistent with the expectation that activists distort electoral outcomes in US House elections by affecting the positions incumbents take on the left–right scale beyond what we would expect from party and district-wide opinion, and by their mobilization beyond voting turnout. Of course, the question of political influence is not so easily resolved, and there are other plausible

[18] The sign for the coefficient on incumbent campaign activism is also negative (and insignificant), which may reflect a tendency of activists on the incumbent's side to react to mobilization by and for the challenger.

explanations for our results. It may be that activists and representatives are closely aligned because activists disproportionately contribute needed funding resources to the candidates in their party, because they provide volunteer support for these candidacies, and because they are especially likely to participate in primary contests in their districts. On the other hand, other explanations for the results are possible. Candidates, including those who go on to win elections and become incumbents, frequently begin their political career as activists. That may be one way that activists in a district influence candidates by virtue of the social and political interactions that take place among them. And, since the distribution of preferences among activists differs from that of ordinary voters, randomly selecting incumbents from the activist pool would generate the patterns and correlations in our results, without any influence from activists on their representatives. It is also possible that activists are influenced by representatives and others in their party, rather than the other way around. This sort of influence may occur if activists are especially aware of or sensitive to their representatives' ideological positions. Likewise, the mobilization effects could result from strategic activism on the part of individuals who want to be associated with a winning candidate, rather than the mobilization itself increasing the vote share of challengers.

Conclusion

While the analysis cannot definitively demonstrate that activists distort electoral outcomes from what would occur based on broader electoral preferences and behavior, it does suggest one direction research on this question can take. The main point is to plead for more attention to activists in research on the electoral process. If parties have the potential their defenders emphasize, activists will be important to understanding how they achieve collective responsibility, integration, and electoral accountability. Much more work on the micro foundations of activist behavior is necessary, including tracking their links to interest groups, social movements, business interests, churches, and other interests external to the party. The permeability between the parties and other groups and organizations in society is doubtless a source of strength and durability for the parties, but it behooves us to increase our understanding of how activists' roots affect their behavior within the party.

The recognition that activists' interests and influence may shift the party away from outcomes in keeping with electoral equality does not necessarily mean that their involvement detracts from the performance of the party system. As noted throughout this chapter, there is an increasing realization among scholars of the electoral process that activists are essential to understanding the connections between the public and candidates, party images, and processes of change. Moreover, if activists recognize how to pursue their interests in the context of the institutional characteristics of the nomination process, it is likely they are sophisticated players in the multifaceted system that engages them. They are as likely to use the parties to pursue their interests as voters, candidates, or officeholders, and we need a much more complete picture of how and why they engage in politics as they do. As well, more research that can incorporate activists, voters, candidates, and officeholders in multilevel designs is likely to pay handsome dividends. It is possible that the participation of activists, despite the potential for distortion we have seen, contributes essentially to the health and functioning of the electoral system. The discipline has invested in studies of individual voters, made possible by national sample surveys, with salutary increases in our understanding of fundamental questions about American democracy. As many of the studies cited in this chapter attest, however, there is much to be learned from a more nuanced and comprehensive assessment of the political context, both as it shapes voter behavior, and for how it can add to our understanding about electoral processes and outcomes.

CHAPTER 16

POLITICAL PARTIES AND CONSULTANTS

DAVID B. MAGLEBY

POLITICAL consultants are one of the important means American political parties use to achieve their political ends. A primary objective of political parties is securing the election of party candidates. To that end, parties have become more professionalized and specialized. Political consultants are a primary manifestation of these developments.

THE BROADER PHENOMENON OF POLITICAL CONSULTANTS AND AMERICAN ELECTORAL DEMOCRACY

The use by political parties of political consultants is part of a broader phenomenon where candidates and interest groups also rely on consultants to foster their electoral goals. Electoral politics in the United States has increasingly come to be a team sport where the candidates, interest groups, and political party committees all seek to influence voters. They all draw from a pool of partisan political consultants who over time often work for all three types of participants (candidates, interest groups, and political party committees) and some for all three in different contests in the same election cycle.

The literature on elections correctly argues that US elections are candidate-centered (Wattenberg 1990). This is because in our single-member district, plurality winner system, the focus generally is on the major party candidates contending for a particular office. But the campaign efforts of the candidates in persuading voters to vote for themselves and against their opponents are not often distinguishable from the efforts of interest groups and political parties to persuade voters to vote against one candidate or for another. The same holds for other tasks related to electoral politics like candidate–opposition research, voter registration, and mobilization.

Because the focus of political parties is on winning elections and assembling legislative majorities, it is not surprising that these party committees focus dispro-portionate effort and resources on contests where investing resources may help secure at least 270 electoral votes or working majorities in the US House and US Senate. National party committees also understand the importance of winning governorships and are especially attuned to winning majorities in state legislatures so they control the redistricting process that follows the decennial census.

In any given cycle a single political consultant may be working for candidates in one set of contests, interest groups in others, and for the political party committees in still others. What consultants actually do while working for these different participants is substantially the same. To accomplish their goals, political parties and interest groups have long been in the business of communicating with the public. Take, for instance, the partisan press of the early years of US history. Many of the Founders recruited political thinkers to publish newspapers filled with partisan content (Magleby and Light 2009, 280). During Abraham Lincoln's 1860 presidential victory, partisan newspapers played a vital role in the campaign process (Goodwin 2005).

Similarly, candidates have long had advisers and confidants who provided assistance to them on political strategy, tactics, and organization. Early examples of individuals playing this role include Abigail Adams advising John Adams on politics and policy (McCullough 2002), Alexander Hamilton advising George Washington on many issues, and David Davis managing Lincoln's campaign (Goodwin 2005). Many point to Mark Hanna as an example of how to craft a modern political campaign. As William McKinley's campaign manager in the 1896 presidential election, he used a nationwide organization of volunteers, mass pub-licity, and an immense fundraising advantage to defeat William Jennings Bryan. Hanna regularly issued press releases, created millions of posters, buttons, and fliers, and raised almost $7 million for McKinley's campaign (Sussman 2005, 14).

Candidates, political party committees, and interest groups hiring political consultants to provide electioneering services are a more recent development. Most scholars trace the advent of campaign consultants to California in the 1930s when proponents of the Central Valley Project hired Clem Whitaker and Leone Baxter in an effort to prevent the Pacific Gas and Electric Company from blocking the project. Whitaker and Baxter, using newspaper and radio appeals, saved the project and subsequently notched the first victory for professional political consultants. Their victory led to the creation of the consulting firm Whitaker and Baxter Campaigns, which in turn spawned several rival California consulting firms (Sabato 1981, 13; Magleby 1984, 65). The widespread use of ballot initiatives in California created a political culture where political consultants could flourish. Moreover, "California, with no ancient political loyalties and only light party organizations, provided fertile ground for political marketing, a genre that is inherently anti-party and whose growth is intimately bound up with the demise of parties and which depends for its effectiveness on the absence of strong loyalties" (O'Shaughnessy 1998, 7).

The use of political consultants by the parties has expanded in recent years. This phenomenon has been simultaneous with the expanded use of consultants by candidates and interest groups. As I will argue, it is made possible by the political parties having sufficient funds to pay consultants but also by a strategic decision both political parties have made to invest their consultant money in competitive congressional contests and presidential battlegrounds.

Interestingly, one consulting specialization, fundraising, has helped the political parties expand their use of other consulting specializations. Without the money to pay consultants the parties would not have expanded their use of them.

IT STARTS WITH THE MONEY

The growing use of political consultants is in some ways a natural outgrowth of the capital-intensive, advertising-driven campaigns which have come to be typical of elections in the United States. Former California House Speaker Jesse Unruh famously said, "Money is the mother's milk of politics" (Keyes 2006). In the context of political parties, increased party fundraising has made possible the increased use of political consultants in recent decades.

The Campaign Finance Rules Matter

While there were prior efforts at banning some types of money as contributions to party committees and candidates such as the ban on corporate treasury funds for contributions imposed by the 1907 Tillman Act or the ban on union treasury funds set up by the 1947 Taft–Hartley Act, until the 1970s parties and candidates were relatively unconstrained in their fundraising (Magleby 2003b, 149). Most agree the reforms that were the most complete and significant were those enacted after the Watergate Scandal in 1974 in amendments to the Federal Election Campaign Act (FECA). This legislation was largely upheld as constitutional in *Buckley v. Valeo* (424 U.S. 1 (1976)).

The sections of FECA upheld by the courts required disclosure of receipts and expenditures by party committees, candidates, and political committees, and it limited the amounts individuals, political action committees (interest groups), and political party committees could contribute to candidates. While neither candidates nor party committees had aggregate contribution limits, the limitations on what individuals could give any one candidate or any combination of candidates and party committees in a two-year cycle created an impression of scarcity, which meant candidates became even more aggressive fundraisers. While the amounts the party committees could give to candidates came to be a small fraction of most competitive candidates' overall budgets, it was seen by both the parties and the candidates as important and meant the parties sought to "max-out" candidates where possible (Magleby and Nelson 1990).

Not long after FECA took effect, the political parties pressed for amendments to FECA to allow them to raise and spend money for generic party-building activities like voter registration drives or generic party advertising. In 1979, FECA was amended to allow this activity. Money raised in this way could include corporate and union general treasury money and, unlike other contributions to the parties, was not limited. Because it was seemingly easier to raise this new type of contribution it was labeled soft money; in contrast, the limited contributions were labeled hard money (Sorauf 1994).

In the wake of Watergate, the Republican Party is noted for having applied the lessons of direct mail fundraising in politics more broadly to build a large donor base of individuals who under FECA became even more important in funding political party activity. As one scholar has noted,

Because spending limitations and ceilings impose planning requirements and reward centralized efficiency, the long-dominant power flow from state and local parties to the national committee was reversed. FECA assisted the nationalization of the federal party structure by introducing economies of large-scale production. Concurrently, FECA also specifically allowed for parties to hire consultants on behalf of a candidate or to provide similar, in-kind services of their own design. (Sabato 1981)

Between 1980 and 1994, soft money was used in voter registration, get-out-the-vote drives, and more generic party activity. In 1996, the Clinton–Gore campaign used soft money for candidate-specific promotion and the Dole–Kemp campaign quickly followed suit. In the following election cycles party soft money fundraising increased, in part because candidates like Clinton and Gore hosted White House coffees and sleepovers to help raise the money. Party leaders in both parties, including congressional leaders, quickly followed suit and used events and access to themselves as a means to raise soft money (Magleby 2003a). Given the increased importance of soft money, both parties raised more soft money in 1996 and thereafter (see Table 16.1).

The surge in party soft money receipts was important for the relationship between the parties and political consultants because soft money gave the parties large amounts of additional money they could use to hire consultants to help defeat or elect particular candidates. Evidence that party soft money was used for this purpose is widespread (Magleby 2003a).

A second development that encouraged the political parties to use consultants working for them and not their candidates in competitive elections was the US Supreme Court ruling in *Colorado Republican Federal Campaign Committee Party v. FEC* (518 U.S. 604 (1996)). This decision allowed parties to spend unlimited amounts of hard money on elections independently of candidates, just as *Buckley v. Valeo* ruled individuals and interest groups could spend independently. The *Buckley v. Valeo* decision handed down in 1976 has come to be more important in the wake of the party soft money bans enacted in the Bipartisan Campaign Reform Act (BCRA) of 2002.

Among BCRA's most important provisions is a near complete ban of party soft money. In part to assist parties, BCRA increased the individual contribution limits and for individuals who wanted to give the maximum in an election cycle required them to give a fraction of their money to the political parties. In 2007–8, individuals wanting to give the maximum allowed to candidates could give up to $2,300. In addition they could give another $28,500 to party committees. For the first time, BCRA also indexed individual contributions to candidates and party committees to inflation.

The loss of the unlimited soft money contributions has no doubt had an effect on the parties, but to a remarkable extent the parties have substituted hard money for soft money. BCRA made fundraising consultants who can target appeals to individuals even more valuable. On the party expenditure side, the party committees continue to spend unlimited amounts independently. Table 16.2 provides the party independent expenditures for all six committees for the period 1996–2008.

Capital-Intensive Campaigns and the Rise of Political Consultants

Political campaigns need money to accomplish key organizing and communicating objectives. The political parties have come to play a more active role in the financing of our electoral politics, especially after the post-Watergate campaign finance reforms. Consultants have played central roles in assisting parties to raise

Table 16.1 Soft money receipts 1992–2002 ($)

	1992	1994	1996	1998	2000	2002
DNC	31,356,076	43,923,516	101,905,186	56,966,353	136,563,419	94,564,827
DSCC	566,111	372,448	14,176,392	25,880,538	63,717,982	95,049,520
DCCC	4,368,980	5,113,343	12,340,824	16,865,410	56,702,023	56,446,802
TOTAL	36,256,667	49,143,460	123,877,924	92,811,927	245,202,519	246,061,149
RNC	35,936,945	44,870,758	113,127,010	74,805,286	166,207,843	113,928,997
NRSC	9,064,167	5,582,013	29,395,329	37,866,845	44,652,709	66,426,117
NRCC	6,076,321	7,371,097	18,530,773	26,914,059	47,295,736	69,677,506
TOTAL	49,787,433	52,522,763	138,199,706	131,615,116	249,861,645	250,032,620

Note: Total receipts do not include transfers among the committees. DNC = Democratic National Committee; DSCC = Democratic Senatorial Campaign Committee; DCCC = Democratic Congressional Campaign Committee; RNC = Republican National Committee: NRSC = National Republican Senatorial Committee; NRCC = National Republican Congressional Committee.

Source: Federal Election Commission (2003).

Table 16.2 Independent expenditures by national party committee 1996–2008 ($)

	1996	1998	2000	2002	2004	2006	2008
DNC	0	0	0	0	120,333,466	−23,104	1,104,113
DSCC	1,386,022	1,329,000	133,000	0	18,725,520	42,627,470	73,028,432
DCCC	0	0	1,933,246	1,187,649	36,923,726	64,141,248	81,641,424
RNC	0	0	0	500,000	18,268,870	14,022,675	53,459,386
NRSC	9,734,445	216,874	267,600	0	19,383,692	19,159,901	110,886,286
NRCC	0	0	548,800	1,321,880	47,254,064	82,059,161	30,971,545

Note: For abbreviations, see Table 16.1.

Sources: 1996–2006 data: Federal Election Commission (2007). 2008 data: Bob Biersack, Deputy Press Officer, Federal Election Commission, email communication with Stephanie Curtis, Feb. 19, 2009.

money and in being the agents of the parties in spending money (Magleby, Patterson, and Thurber 2002).

Following the Watergate scandal and resignation of President Richard M. Nixon, the Republican Party turned to direct mail consultant Richard Viguerie to assist in raising money through an aggressive direct mail campaign (Shribman 1982). This early investment in targeted direct mail fundraising gave the GOP, until quite recently, a larger base of active small dollar donors. Democrats have also turned to consultants to assist the party with more recent uses of the Internet to raise contributions for the party from individual donors. Party fundraising is not the first time the parties have turned to the business world of consultants. But the parties also generate new expertise, "with many consultants being trained by the political parties and increasingly in specialist courses at universities across the United States" (Farrell, Kolodny, and Medvic 2001, 13).

As the parties have pushed for new ways to raise and spend money in support of their candidates, they have spent that money in ways often indistinguishable from the ways candidates spend money: on political broadcast and cable advertising, mail, phone banks, and get-out-the-vote efforts. Expenditures on television and radio advertising by the political parties came to be major priorities in the 1990s and since. Some also attribute the rising costs of campaigns to consultants: "The increased use of paid consultants, public opinion polls, direct mail, and professional television broadcasts, along with the extended duration of campaigns, led to rising costs and the shift from labor-intensive to more capital-intensive campaigns" (Norris 2005, 11–12).

Advertising-Driven Campaigns and the Rise of Political Consultants

A major element of campaign strategy is to increase the visibility or "name recognition" of your candidate. As the size of electoral constituencies has increased, candidates have sought efficient ways to communicate with voters. Such electioneering costs money and the most efficient of these media, television, costs a lot of money. All participants in the campaign process—candidates, party committees, and interest groups—invest in television advertising in competitive federal electoral settings. There has been a fundamental shifting of the campaign structure and methods where potential voters are now "less likely to encounter demanding, people-intensive forms of party communication, such as direct face-to-face discussions . . . and more likely to experience elections via more passive and indirect forms of involvement, such as simply watching television news" (Norris 2005, 12).

The party committees are most likely to mount their own television advertising campaigns in states or districts that are competitive. Such advertising supplements what the candidates spend. In some competitive contests the party committees equal or exceed the amount spent by the candidates. Consultants working for the party committees develop themes and messages for each contest rather than running the same message in all targeted races. They also develop communications strategies to fit the district or state, which may include different mixes of radio, broadcast television, and cable television (Magleby 2000, 2002; Magleby and Monson 2004; Magleby, Monson, and Patterson 2007a; Magleby and Patterson 2008).

Electoral communications are not limited to television. Party committees, candidates, and interest groups use radio, mail, phone calls, and personal contacts as approaches to persuade voters. Each of these different media constitutes a specialization in the consulting industry. Party committees retain several consultants in each cycle who produce political mail, often designed as large postcards, to be sent to targeted voters in competitive contests. Voters presumed to be undecided or persuadable may receive a dozen or more unique mail pieces from the party committees in addition to the mail they receive from the candidates or interest groups (2000, 2002; Magleby and Monson 2004; Magleby, Monson, and Patterson 2007a; Magleby and Patterson 2008).

An assumed division of labor has arisen in recent campaign cycles where election laws do not allow coordination between consultants working for the political party committees on independent expenditures or for interest groups to coordinate their messages and strategies with the candidates or their consultants. The advertising by the party committees and interest groups has often been more negative in tone than the advertising by the candidates (Magleby 2000, 2002; Magleby and Monson 2004; Magleby, Monson, and Patterson 2007a; Magleby and Patterson 2008).

In recent elections, the adoption of interactive technologies and social networking programs may represent a return to the old form of party communication, which emphasized person-to-person communication and interaction. Political consultants are now heavily involved in the development of technologies that emphasize the ability of volunteers to tap into their personal networks to gain supporters. The Barack Obama campaign in 2008 was innovative in this regard and their tools and strategies are likely to spread to the political party committees.

Political Consultants, "Voter Files," and the Party Ground Game

Past studies of political consultants and the political parties have identified voter registration and mobilization as functions presumed to be more the province of the party committees than television advertising or direct mail (Kolodny 2007). Although, as noted, in competitive contests the party committees duplicate the efforts of the candidates in their own expenditures on persuasion mail and television and radio advertising.

Party committees, often with the help of consultants, have long worked to build databases of voters. Enhanced voter lists include such variables as whether or not an individual has voted in party primaries and general elections in the past, states with partisan voter registration, and what the voter has indicated is her partisan prefer- ence; more recently, both parties have added consumer data and political contribu- tion history to build datasets that allow the candidate and party consultants to model political behavior. For example, both parties have developed propensity to vote models that are used to target more and less likely voters with different appeals. Merging data files from the states (and in some states, local jurisdictions) is a laborious and expensive process. States and localities vary in the extent to which they provide clean and consistent data. Categories for some variables are different in different jurisdictions and the data need constant updating.

The Republican dataset is called the "Voter Vault" and for the 2002 through 2006 elections was superior in terms of quality to the Democrats'. In these elections, the GOP and Bush 2004 campaign retained a political consulting firm named Target- Point to use the Voter Vault data to target individual voters with particular messages, a process called microtargeting.

The Democratic National Committee (DNC) also had a list in the 2000–6 period named "Demzilla." While similar to the Republican National Committee (RNC) list, it was widely perceived not to be as complete or current as the Voter Vault. Complicating things on the Democratic side was the fact that in 2004, Democratic Party allies had created their own massive list of voters with information on policy positions and vote history through a group called America Coming Together (ACT). Underwritten by a wealthy core of supporters, including Peter Lewis and George Soros, and labor unions like the Service Employees' International Union (SEIU), ACT played a significant role in the 2004 campaign. The former political director of the American Federation of Labor–Congress of Industrial Organizations (AFL–CIO) Steve Rosenthal led the organization, which became the largest 527 group of the 2004 cycle. ACT raised approximately $137 million for the 2004 campaign.

In the 2004 election cycle the Republican ability to microtarget voters, especially in exurban areas of states like Ohio, was seen as important to their retaining the White House (Bai 2007). Democrats emerged from the 2004 election with a greater commitment to voter files, voter registration, and voter mobilization. In both parties, a lot of this effort is done by consultants retained by the party, the candidate, or both.

In the 2008 cycle the Republicans continued to follow a strategy of having the database on voters within the party while retaining consultants to do much of the work of analyzing the data. TargetPoint has been joined by Grassroots Targeting LLC. The Democratic Party, under the leadership of Chair Howard Dean, continued to invest in its own list. In the 2006 and 2008 cycles, a new entity came into existence on the progressive side called Catalist. Under the leadership of Harold Ickes, many who had participated in ACT helped spearhead Catalist. The Catalist list in many ways rivals the RNC list for currency and a wide range of variables on the roughly 220 million individuals whose names and vote histories are in the dataset. Candidates like Hillary Clinton and Barack Obama and a wide array of groups including labor unions, the National Education Association, environmental groups, and pro-choice groups used Catalist in 2008.

PARTY STRATEGIES FOR THE USE OF CONSULTANTS

The two major parties, while being organized around the units of competition at the federal level, operate in some quite different ways. This is true not only for relationships between the three party committees for each party but also in how they interact with consultants.

Republicans: More Inclined to Bring Consultants In-House

The Republican Party committees are more hierarchical, at least in recent years, with the RNC clearly the predominant committee. Dennis Johnson explains, "During the 1980s and early 1990s, the Republican party developed superior campaign research capabilities. Hungry for victory and goaded on by their second-party status, Republican leaders raised and invested enormous sums of money in all facets of party developments" (Johnson 2007, 78). The RNC has taken the lead in developing the Voter Vault data file, and in organizing the voter mobilization activities (the "72 Hour Task Force") even in non-presidential battleground states.

The GOP has also tended to bring consultants into the party rather than retaining them, although as noted there are lots of examples of consultants on retainer. For example, Craig Bergman, a Republican consultant for the Robert Morris Group, is quoted as saying, "it's not this industry driving the endless election cycle; it's a matter of supply and demand. The market force is meeting demand and it has nothing to do with consultants engineering it" (Vlahos 2005).

Republican allied groups like the Chamber of Commerce, other business groups, the National Rifle Association, and conservative Christian groups have not employed consultants to the same extent in the aggregate as Democratic Party allied groups have.

Democrats: More Inclined to Outsource

The Democratic Congressional Campaign Committee and the Democratic Senatorial Campaign Committee operate more independently of the DNC than is the case with the Republicans. The Democratic candidates have long mounted their own get-out-the-vote efforts, for example. In 2008, these Democratic committees reversed a long pattern of GOP dominance in fundraising.

Perhaps because for many years the Democratic committees were more dependent on soft money, they developed a pattern of being more reliant on consultants for most phases of party activity. Another distinction between the parties is that Democratic-allied groups are more extensively involved in all forms of electioneering activity, including the use of consultants. This expands the pool of potential consultants open to the Democratic Party committees as consultants move freely from candidates to party committees to interest groups.

A Typology of Possible Consultant Roles
for Political Parties

Political consultants play a range of different roles for the political parties and their roles have changed with changes in campaigning. What follows is an effort to define the roles of some of the most important types of consultants employed by political party committees.

State Party Relationships and Shared Databases. In our federal system there are almost 100 state political parties and in some states there are also distinct local political party organizations. The DNC and RNC typically manage relationships with these state and local party organizations with their in-house staff. They also coordinate activity with their party's governor's association. One important overlapping of interests between the federal and state/local levels is voter files. The development, upkeep, and analysis of these voter files involves consultants, some of whom work inside the party and some who are retained.

Legal and accounting services. The professionals who provide legal and accounting services to the political parties can often be overlooked. Indeed, the National Republican Congressional Committee has been negligent in seeking external audits of its own accountants, a fact discovered when accountant Christopher J. Ward embezzled approximately $1 million between 2004 and 2008 (Kane 2008).

The party committees have some combination of in-house and retained legal counsel who consult with the party staff and leadership on a range of issues. Party committees take a lead in voting recounts like the protracted recount in the 2008 Minnesota US Senate race but also in disputes involving campaign finance laws, filing deadlines, etc.

Fundraising. Party committees "seek some form of professional assistance when it comes to fundraising" (Himes 1995). All of these activities require a large and experienced staff, a necessity that creates another expense for the campaign to meet (Magleby, Patterson, and Thurber 2002). The assistance of fundraising consultants ranges from designing direct mail campaigns to identifying target audiences for telemarketer fundraisers to, more recently, using online networking services to reach small-donor markets.

Media. For a time both parties have sought to bring more of the media production for candidates in-house, and both parties invested in broadcast studios and equipment. Much of the advertising run under the party banner is produced by consultants. The party has established relationships with media consultants and directs candidates to them. The party retains its own media consultants for its independent expenditures as it did in the era of soft money.

Polling. Both political parties make extensive use of public opinion polling. They use polling to try and encourage candidates to run for office or to dissuade others in an effort to clear the field for the stronger possible nominee. They rely on polls to prioritize how and where to spend independent expenditures and, before BCRA, soft dollars. Some polling is done as a coordinated expenditure between the party committee and the candidate in which the cost is shared. The cost to the candidate may be further reduced if the polling is turned over to the candidate sixteen days after the poll is completed and further reduced if not turned over until after sixty-one days. For early polls, sometimes called benchmark polls, such delays do not reduce the value to prospective candidates (Herrnson 2000, 299). Polling is generally contest-specific. The party of the incumbent president may do more generic policy polling, often at the behest of the president. During the presidencies of presidents Carter (Zeisel 1980) and Reagan (Aberbach and Peterson 2005, 180) the national party committee provided a substantial retainer to the president's pollster who did ongoing polling for the White House.

Candidate–opposition research. As with fundraising, candidate and opposition research is a function that the party committees have long staffed in-house. Increasingly, campaign consultants are assisting with the opposition research, but when they do it is usually the second tier of consultants, often called research specialists, who do the work. In early 2008, the RNC commissioned several polls and focus groups to determine how they could attack either Obama or Clinton (whichever was the eventual nominee) and not be labeled racists or sexists (Kuhn 2008). At the same time, candidates and incumbents are focusing increasing resources on "vulnerability research," which effectively turns the detectives and cameras on themselves to uncover as much revealing information about them in order to preempt attacks by opponents. Party committees also do this on their incumbents and on people they are thinking of recruiting for an important contest.

Persuasion. A major dimension of persuasion is television and radio, discussed above. Party committees also invest in mail, phone calls (both live and recorded which are sometimes called "robocalls"), and personal contacts, which are also part of voter mobilization efforts. Much of this activity is done by consultants on contract with the party committees. Much of it was previously funded with soft money but now is done as independent expenditures or as a coordinated expenditure between the party committee and the candidate.

Voter contact, registration, and mobilization. Voter mobilization involves the systematic identification of likely voters that the party committee would like to turn out. This has become a more complicated enterprise with early and no-excuse absentee voting. With the added complexity has come the need for better databases and a greater reliance on consultants. Political party committees have long been seen as taking a leading role in this activity. For the Republicans, the organization and management of voter mobilization has been more the province of the RNC, and in recent years that effort has been labeled the "72 Hour Task Force." For the Democrats, the process also involves consultants and is organized more around House, Senate, and presidential battleground states. In 2008, the Obama campaign took the lead in organizing the field–voter mobilization in the presidential battleground states.

As noted, much of the mobilization activity is driven by databases. While both parties manage the databases with in-house staff, they have relied on consultants to help build the files, in identifying key variables to add, and in the modeling, which creates additional data to help prioritize the voter mobilization efforts discussed above.

Voting process. This function is called different things by the parties but it involves legal and political consultants who track the voting process in terms of how local election officials manage voter registration, absentee ballots, early voting, identification requirements, the length of lines and delays in voting, and a range of possible legal challenges that may be made before the election or on election day itself. This function also manages recounts and disputed elections. A key component of this function is election lawyers who specialize in these matters.

THE INTERDEPENDENCE OF CONSULTANTS AND POLITICAL PARTIES

Political parties need consultants to achieve their electoral aims and consultants benefit from their association with political party committees. In several respects the parties and consultants are interdependent. One study of the topic concluded, "The evidence supports the thesis that election campaigns have outgrown the institutional limitations of political parties, requiring a role for campaign professionals to fill this increasing gap" (Farrell, Kolodny, and Medvic 2001, 11). Prior studies of political consultants have found that the party committees are often the training ground for political consultants and that "prior party employment favors party–consultant coordination" (Kolodny and Logan 1998, 157). The political parties are often important to the development of campaign tools and methods, but the parties also have benefited from insights provided them by consultants. Microtargeting and direct mail fundraising are examples of things consultants brought to the parties.

Facilitate coordination. The revolving door between consultants and party committees means that learning is passed along, at least after election cycles. Campaign finance rules prohibit coordination during election cycles but the constant back and forth between party committees and consulting shops means lessons learned in one area quickly move to the other.

While many consultants enjoy the direct contact to candidates and campaign staff that working on candidate campaigns involves, working with party committees also has advantages. As with working on initiative and referendum campaigns, consultants who work for parties are given wider latitude and do not have the challenges of sometimes difficult candidate personalities.

Advantages to the parties of using political consultants. Retaining consultants rather than giving more money to candidates is the result, in part, of campaign finance laws. For the party committees, using consultants may be more efficient as they can scale the activity to the resources available and ramp up if more resources become available. Using consultants also lowers infrastructure costs and allows parties to be more nimble and to shift from broadcast ads to mail to get-out-the-vote. Changes in the ways campaigns are conducted also allow parties to tap into new approaches quickly. The scale of party activity means that "parties simply could not provide sufficient personalized service, day-to-day advice, or regional experience. Consultants proved to be better equipped to deal with the unique circumstances of each race and district. Consultants also have a pecuniary interest in seeing their clients win and are therefore more likely to provide individual attention and service to those candidates" (Kolodny and Logan 1998, 156).

THE DISPUTED NEXUS BETWEEN POLITICAL CONSULTANTS AND WEAK PARTIES

A frequent debate in the literature is whether reliance on political consultants has weakened the political parties, is a marker of weak parties, and whether strong parties would not use consultants. There are three primary strands of argument in the debate; one school sees consultants as diminishing parties because consultants provide services parties could provide. A second strand sees the use by consultants as an accommodation to the reality of our candidate-centered politics where the party is an "intermediary" between the consultants and candidates. This view is more or less neutral on the question of whether the use of consultants weakens parties. Finally, there is a school of thought that the use of consultants by parties has not weakened them but rather is evidence of "adaptation" by the parties.

Several party scholars see the use of consultants as weakening parties, in part because the use of modern campaign techniques for communicating with voters and mobilizing them has been substituted for the more party-based approaches (Kelley 1956; Sorauf 1967; Agranoff 1972; Nimmo 2001; Sabato 1981). While some political machines for a time may have accomplished the mobilization and persuasion roles, the reforms of the Progressive era and since, like direct primaries, direct election of US senators, and non-partisan local elections, also elevated the candidate-centered reality of American elections. A second strand of argument in this school is the idea that consultants, operating independently of the party and employed directly by candidates, are "aloof to party politics and, although ideology played a role in client selections, many remained skeptical of party practices and avoided formal links to party leaders" (Lathrop 2003, 130, quoting Nimo 2001; Rosenbloom 1973; Sabato 1981).

As discussed previously, our candidate-centered system has been reinforced by the campaign finance laws. The use of consultants by candidates and party committees is mostly an artifact of our electoral and campaign finance rules. Because the focus of the US electoral system is on defeating or electing particular candidates in single-member districts, the focus of consultants working for candidates, party committees, and interest groups is the particular candidates running in each contest. Further evidence for this proposition is the way parties managed the surge in soft money in the 1990s and increasing hard money in the 2000s. They invest their money in competitive electoral contests hoping to win office.

More recent and more data-driven studies of consultants have found that the relationship between party committees and consultants, even consultants working occasionally for candidates, is characterized more as a cooperative effort (Farrell, Kolodny, and Medvic 2001; Herrnson 2000; Johnson 2000; Kolodny 2000; Kolodny and Logan 1998; Luntz 1988; Medvic and Lenart 1997; Thurber, Nelson, and Dulio 2000). Some scholars assert that political parties "accommodate" the current nature of candidate-centered politics rather than try to reassert any lost authority (Menefee-Libey 2000). Some making this argument of "accommodation" between parties, candidates, and consultants do not dispute the use of consultants as a sign of party weakness (Menefee-Libey 2000; Herrnson 2000).

Kolodny is the scholar most identified with the view that "consultant use by the political parties does not signal party decline, but party adaptation" (Kolodny and Dulio 2003, 729). Elsewhere she has argued that "modern campaigns demand specialized, technical services that are simply beyond the political parties' *institutional capacity* to deliver" (2000, 110). The need for technical services and the fact that consultants tend to work for candidates from only one party create a kind of "revolving door" for consultants who work for party committees, candidates, and allied interest groups. This makes less important who is paying them for their services as they have the common objective of electing the party's candidate.

Party committees even act as a "referral agency" for candidates in search of consultants. As David Dulio has stated, parties "recommend to a candidate who is interested in hiring a professional. Many times these consultants are ex-party staffers who have started their own consulting firm or are consultants the party has successfully worked with in the past. Instead of seeing consultants as the enemy, parties utilized their expertise and talents" (Dulio 2004, 27).

Some studies have found that more than half of the consultants surveyed had worked for political parties in some capacity (Thurber 1998; Kolodny 2000). Moreover, party committees tend to hire loyal consultants to work for them between election cycles (Thurber, Nelson, and Dulio 2000; Kolodny 2000; Kolodny and Logan 1998; Dennis Johnson 2000). Some have gone even further to contend that "the campaign techniques [consultants] provide have not destroyed the parties but have strengthened them" (Luntz 1988, 144).

In today's campaign environment for the voter the work of consultants working for party committees is indistinguishable from that of consultants working for candidates or interest groups. There are some slight variations in tone and message but all employ current techniques and tools. On some functions the party committees have an assumed lead role: candidate research and voter mobilization. But party committees are also involved in persuasion via the mail, television, radio, and email. The heightened partisanship of recent years has reinforced the sense that consultants work for one team or the other and exactly who on the team they work for is less important than which team they are on.

POLITICAL PARTIES AND CONSULTANTS:
A RESEARCH AGENDA

The study of political consultants and more broadly electioneering by political party committees has made major strides in recent years. But there are important topics needing further exploration and analysis. Party committees on both sides have become increasingly sophisticated about social science research and especially the work of Don Green and Alan Gerber on voter mobilization (2004). Social science modeling has also become very much a part of the microtargeting done by both party committees and on the Democratic side by outside vendors like Catalist and its underwriting groups.

What Impact Has Microtargeting Had on Voter Mobilization?

Given the close connection between fundraising and party committee electioneering, what have the parties done to substitute hard for soft money and could the parties learn from the candidacies of Barack Obama and Ron Paul in 2008 in more effectively using the Internet for fundraising? Another artifact of current campaign finance laws is that some consultants hired by the political party cannot talk with other consultants hired by the party to work on the same race. This oddity is the result of the parties arguing that they should be allowed to spend independently of their candidates. Consultants and party committees complain about this limitation on coordination but how consequential is it? In a world where there are few secrets, where monitoring services can tell one set of party consultants what the other set is running on television, then it is not clear this is a real limitation.

What are the implications of the growing specialization of political party consultants? How much does the party retain of the investment in consultants? Who builds the "memory bank" of lessons learned across campaigns and over time? Another way to look at this is to see consultants as the key part of the party operation with party committee staff and leaderships in a constant rotation. How much, then, of what the party does is driven by elected party committee leadership and how much of it is determined by the "permanent government" of consultants working for the party.

The increasing demand for specialized and technologically sophisticated expertise by candidates and party committees means political consultants are in high demand by all participants in our electoral process. Political parties have played an important coordinating function between the consultants they employ and those retained by candidates. The broader universe of consultants who work on election campaigns for interest groups also on occasion work for candidates and party committees. The unifying element in modern election campaigns is the need of all participants to influence the same set of voters. Instrumental to that end are political consultants and the services they provide.

PART VI

....

PARTY IN GOVERNMENT

....

....

CHAPTER 17

WHAT A DIFFERENCE TWENTY-FIVE YEARS MAKES

CHANGING PERSPECTIVES ON PARTIES AND LEADERS IN THE US HOUSE

....

DAVID W. ROHDE

In the early 1980s, there was a broad consensus in the research on American legislative politics that political parties in Congress were weak by historical standards, and getting weaker. For example, in an excellent and broad-ranging review essay, Brady and Bullock (1985, 159) said, "Anyone reviewing the literature on elections, congressional reforms, and congressional policy making cannot fail to be impressed by the extent to which they show party declining in the United States." Now, nearly a quarter of a century later, the picture is very different. The link between party identification and voting has grown stronger again (Bartels 2000), and the national parties have become central participants in candidate recruitment and campaign spending (Cann 2008; Currinder 2009). In Congress, and especially in the House, party organizations were visibly stronger, and majority party influence over the agenda, over member behavior, and over legislative outcomes had arguably increased markedly. In this chapter I will offer a critical overview of some major theoretical perspectives in the literature on party leadership, organization, and activity in the House from the 1970s on (although space constraints will permit discussion of only a fraction of this substantial body of work). I will then consider a few of the major issues raised in this work in more detail, and discuss some avenues for future research that can build on the solid foundation recent work has offered.

THE "TEXTBOOK CONGRESS" AND THE ELECTORAL CONNECTION

Kenneth Shepsle (1989) coined the term "textbook Congress" to describe the dominant collective understanding of the institution among scholars at a given point—a set of equilibrium practices and tendencies. The textbook House through the 1970s was a chamber in which legislative activity was dominated by the committee system, and where party leaders were usually just coordinators and cajolers. The root of this perspective was a widely shared view of the motivation of members and their linkages to their constituents and their parties, a view that received its most influential statement in the 1974 book by David Mayhew—*Congress: The Electoral Connection.*

Mayhew (1974, 13) sought to theorize about Congress by making a simple assumption about members' motivation: "congressmen are interested in getting reelected—indeed, in their role here as abstractions, interested in nothing else." Like all abstractions, this assumption admittedly glossed over some detail, but Mayhew made clear that, in his view, for the purposes of explanation this approximation did not result in significant violations of reality. Of particular interest to the current discussion, he argued (1974, 27) that congressional parties were not very consequential, and that "[the] fact is that no theoretical treatment of the United States Congress that posits parties as analytic units will go very far. So we are left with individual congressmen..." A number of reasons were offered for this atomistic perspective (1974, 25–7), including the facts that national parties had virtually no influence over nominations, that district parties were locally oriented, that candidates had to secure their own electoral resources, and that Congress's internal party organization did not engage the ambitions of members to induce cohesion.

As a consequence, Congress was organized instead to foster the reelection of members via the activities Mayhew famously identified and discussed: advertising, credit claiming, and position taking. Members needed to be free to support whatever positions would be most attractive to their constituents, and strong parties, it was argued, would only interfere with the pursuit of reelection. Thus, what congressmen wanted from their parties was "to leave them alone" (1974, 100). Among the institutional features that were seen as most consequential in this view was the seniority system, which Mayhew argued (1974, 96), served "to convert turf into property; it assures a congressman that once he initially occupies a piece of turf, no one can push him off." That is, the seniority system gave members independence from parties and leaders, and members wanted it to stay that way.

The perspective offered by Mayhew was reinforced by the influential book written a few years later by Morris Fiorina (1989).[1] Like Mayhew, his analysis focused on the relationship between the internal workings of Congress and the electoral arena, but with a somewhat different take on the matter. Fiorina concentrated in particular on the recently recognized increase in the incumbency advantage of representatives. His central argument was that one of the developments that fostered the incumbency advantage was members' increased role as ombudsmen for their constituents. The federal role had increased during the 1960s and 1970s, and the bureaucracy had increased correspondingly to implement that growth, and Congress had been responsible for both of those increases. When constituents had problems with the bureaucracy, they complained to their representatives, who in turn intervened on their behalf. Those efforts had electoral benefits; hence the link to the growing margins for incumbents. Fiorina did not argue explicitly against parties being influential in Congress, but as he noted (2001, 154), they simply did not figure in his argument, even in the second edition.[2] So the dominant textbook picture of Congress reflected the views expressed by Mayhew, Fiorina, and others. Members were independent entrepreneurs, pursuing legislative activities that brought them electoral security, and congressional parties were not consequential.

THE GROUND SHIFTS: IMAGES
FROM THE REFORM ERA

One of the characteristics of a textbook view is that it tends to be seen as immutable, or at least very stable. Yet during the decade in which Mayhew and

---

[1] Fiorina's first edition was published in 1977, and the second in 1989. The latter maintained the text of the first edition, and added a number of chapters that reflected on reactions to the book and how well the argument held up. A further reflection is presented in Fiorina (2001).

[2] Although it must be noted that he was among the earliest scholars to note the expanding role of national parties in congressional elections, and the possibilities this might have for fostering party cohesion. See Fiorina (1989, 112–15).

Fiorina published, vast changes took place in the Congress. Between 1970 and 1976, the Democratic majority in the House instituted a series of institutional reforms that substantially changed the landscape, and raised questions about the theoretical foundations of the textbook view. First, the inviolability of the seniority system was ended by rules that provided for automatic secret-ballot votes on committee chairmen at the beginning of every congress. Then, after the 1974 election, three southern chairs were deposed and replaced by northern Democrats. Second, the powers of committee chairs were substantially reduced, while those of subcommittees and their chairs were correspondingly strengthened. And third, the influence of the Democratic leadership was enhanced by changes that increased their role in committee assignments and that granted the Speaker direct control over Democratic appointments to the Rules Committee. Furthermore, these organizational changes were accompanied by substantial increases in levels of party voting in the House, and in members' party loyalty (Rohde 1991).

One of the maxims of science is that you cannot explain variation with a constant. Yet all of the main features that underlay the textbook view were stable before and during the reform era, including members' independence of party in nominations and in elections. Given that fact, analysts wondered, why did the reforms take place? Some scholars (Mayhew 1974; Davidson 1981; Hall and Evans 1990) saw the reforms primarily as evidence of further decentralization of the House, creating "subcommittee government" to replace committee government. Moreover, in one of the most instructive and widely cited analyses of party leadership in the post-reform period, Cooper and Brady (1981) argued that leadership power in the House was determined primarily by the institutional context and not by the leaders' personal style. Looking forward, they contended that Speaker O'Neill was likely to be less successful than Rayburn had been because both his formal powers and his resources based in the party system were even more fractionalized.[3]

One of the early leaders in trying to understand the causes and consequences of congressional change in this period was Barbara Sinclair. Her 1983 study of majority leadership in the House emphasized changes in rules, membership, norms, and the rise of new issues and voting alignments. Drawing on Fenno (1973) and in contrast to Mayhew, she contended that members had goals in addition to reelection, specifically power in the House and the enactment of good policy. Sinclair argued that leaders had little ability to influence members' achievement of their goals, and so the most important determinants of leader

---

[3] The view that weak parties would persist in the immediate post-reform era was widespread, but not unanimous. For example, Ornstein and Rohde (1978, 292) argued that "in the future, if the majority leadership *wants* to lead, the potential is there. If they are not successful, it will be because they lacked ability and the support of their fellow party members, and less because the character of the House and party rules blocked their way."

success would remain beyond their control. Shortly after Cooper and Brady and Sinclair wrote, however, further evidence of increasing party strength in Congress accumulated. House Democrats clashed repeatedly with President Reagan over domestic and foreign policy, and Speaker Jim Wright rallied his troops in 1987–8 to adopt an impressive party program.

In 1991, Rohde offered a theoretical argument called "conditional party government" (CPG), which was intended to account for both the reforms and the developments that accompanied them. (CPG was elaborated and extended by Aldrich 1995.) Like Mayhew's theory, the roots of CPG were in electoral politics, but with a broader focus than just the reelection motive, adopting Fenno's and Sinclair's triad of motives. The argument drew on work by Fiorina (1974) and Fenno (1978). Fiorina emphasized that constituencies could be homogeneous or heterogeneous regarding policy preferences, with differing implications for members' behavior. Fenno saw constituencies as having multiple levels—geographic, reelection, primary, and personal—with each level nested within the one preceding it. Moreover, CPG emphasized the role of party activists, for whom policy motives are often more salient than ordinary voters, and whose views on those policies are often more extreme.[4]

CPG agreed with the contextual perspectives of Cooper and Brady and Sinclair, arguing that the willingness of members to delegate strong powers to party leaders was dependent on the degree of preference homogeneity on policy among those members and the amount of interparty disagreement. However, the theory emphasized the relevance of members' *personal* policy preferences, not just those of their constituencies, noting that congressional candidates were often drawn from the ranks of policy-oriented party activists. Furthermore, CPG contended that the constituency bases within the parties had changed (particularly with regard to primary constituencies), so that the policy views of candidates nominated within each party became more similar over time, resulting in party contingents in Congress that were more homogeneous within parties and more divergent between them.

Thus, the CPG account of the reform era was that northern Democrats wanted to achieve more liberal policy outcomes, but believed that House institutional arrangements were biased against their interests. In order to improve the chances to achieve desired policies, they proposed changes in party rules that were designed to undermine the committee-based power of conservative southern Democrats, and to strengthen the power of party leaders. Then, in the reform and post-reform periods, the parties became more internally homogeneous (particularly the Democrats, as North–South differences became less pronounced), and members were more willing to delegate strong powers to leaders and to support the exercise of

---

[4] For more discussion of activist views and their consequences, see Aldrich (1995), Jacobson (2000), and Aldrich and Rohde (2001).

those powers to advance their parties' collective interests.[5] Thus, in direct contrast to Mayhew's perspective, central to CPG was the view that members cared about policy outcomes, not just position taking.[6] Indeed it seems impossible to explain the reforms that first made seniority conditional as a basis for committee leadership and then (under Republicans) almost an afterthought, or those reforms that granted substantial powers to party leaders, without recognizing the importance of this factor.

The conditional party government analysis and other work arguing that the impact of parties and leaders in the House had increased were not met with universal agreement. Certainly the most vigorous and persistent critic of this line of work was Keith Krehbiel. In his prizewinning work applying informational theory to Congress, Krehbiel (1991) simply omitted parties from his theory, arguing that predictions based on the preferences of the median member were at least as well supported by evidence as predictions that added party as explanatory element.[7] Krehbiel (1991, 16) argued that since both policy and procedural choices in the House were made by majorities (he called this the "majoritarian postulate"), then no result of the latter—by leaders or parties or anyone—could undermine "the fundamental principle of majoritarianism in democratic, collective choice institutions."

Then Krehbiel directly confronted partisan arguments in "Where's the Party?" (1993), a piece that set the agenda for a substantial amount of research over the next decade. Krehbiel noted that member behavior could be consistent with party policy objectives because it was the consequence of personal preferences or it could be independent of personal preferences. The latter would, presumably, be due to party pressure or some other kind of party action, and only that kind of behavior should be recognized as significant party behavior. Moreover, Krehbiel emphasized that the simple fact that party members were voting together more often was not by itself evidence of party effects (see also Krehbiel 2000). In support of these theoretical points, he presented empirical evidence on the representativeness of House committees and on the selection of conferees that he argued did not show evidence of party effects.

[5] The principal–agent perspective that underlies CPG's focus on delegation to leaders was pursued more explicitly by other scholars, particularly Sinclair (1995) and Maltzman (1997).

[6] As noted, CPG was formulated to explain the reform period and its aftermath in the 1980s and early 1990s. However, since intraparty homogeneity and interparty polarization (known as "the condition" in conditional party government) was almost universally recognized to have further increased with the GOP takeover in 1994 and afterward, the research community recognized that CPG had clear implications for these later periods. Aldrich and Rohde found support for the theory's applicability during the Gingrich years (1997–8, 2000a, 2000b) and the speakerships of Hastert and Pelosi (2009).

[7] Nor was he the only analyst to take this course. See, for example, the "distributive politics" perspective of Weingast and Marshall (1988).

Krehbiel's criterion for significant party behavior influenced the subsequent analysis of scholars who contended that parties were consequential in the House, although later work did not agree with the empirical claims in his article.[8] Many researchers accepted the idea that it made sense to look for consequences of party beyond merely the unfettered expression of members' preferences, although some thought that should not be the only criterion. We will consider some of that work below. Before that, however, it is important to note that in his later book, *Pivotal Politics* (1998), Krehbiel was much more explicit in his assumptions about parties. Specifically, in a discussion of CPG he contended that party activity was not ineffective, but rather that the two parties were about equally effective. That is (Krebiel 1998, 171), "the point is not that majority party organizations and their deployment of resources are inconsequential. Rather, it is to suggest that competing party organizations bidding for pivotal votes may roughly counterbalance one another, so final outcomes are not much different from what a simpler but completely specified nonpartisan theory predicts."

This more fully articulated characterization of the impact of parties is problematic in at least two significant respects. First, the discussion limits the conception of party effects to the situation of the parties bidding for marginal floor votes. While there are differing views among partisan theorists regarding the importance of parties' efforts to influence members' floor choices, the extant literature makes clear that in such theories (including CPG) that is neither the only, nor even the most important, party effect. Among more consequential effects are the ability to influence the composition of the legislative agenda, and actions that shape members' pre-floor activities and choices. I will consider some of these aspects in detail shortly.

Second, the assumption that the parties "roughly counterbalance one another" is remarkably strong. While it is true, as Krehbiel says, that whether his alternative view is correct is an empirical question (and so partisan theories must demonstrate effects on behavior and outcomes in specific instances), we can draw on the collective results of earlier research to assess the plausibility of an assumption and its logical consequences (see Fiorina 1995, 306). To accept that parties are consequential, and then assert that the parties counterbalance each other, is to assert that the majority and minority parties are equal in influence and impact in all important respects. Moreover (if we are to justify ignoring party effects theoretically), it is implicit that this equality exists not just on average, but also vote by vote, issue by issue, and over time (see Aldrich and Rohde 2000b, 35–6). The

---

[8] A number of published and as yet unpublished studies find solid evidence of majority party advantage in the selection on conferees and the operation of conference committees (see, for example, Lazarus and Monroe 2007; van Houweling 2007). Other studies challenged the view that strong party effects would imply only the kind of "outlier" committees Krehbiel said they should (Cox and McCubbins 1993; Aldrich and Rohde 2000b) or disagreed with the inferences from the way he measured preferences (Hall and Grofman 1990; Hurwitz, Moiles, and Rohde 2001).

contention that the power of the majority and minority parties is symmetric is very implausible in light of the literature on the House generally, and much of the post-reform research on parties marshals evidence that claims to demonstrate that it is false in fact. As we turn to consider some of that work, however, it must be recognized that much of that line of research exists in large measure because of the effort to respond to Krehbiel's conceptual challenges and the demanding standard for evidence that he set.

CARTEL THEORY

Shortly after the initial presentation of CPG and of Krehbiel's early work on this subject, Cox and McCubbins (1993) articulated another partisan perspective (termed "cartel theory"). They also confined their assumptions about member motivation to the desire for reelection, but unlike others with this starting point, they used that motive as leverage to reach the conclusion that the majority party would have disproportionate power. Specifically, they recognized that party labels and perceptions of the parties influenced voters' choices. As a consequence, they argued, members of the majority party are concerned about their party's reputation within the electorate and they are, therefore, willing to grant power over the chamber's agenda to party leaders that could be used to manage electoral externalities and protect that reputation. This grant of power creates the majority party as a species of "legislative cartel" that (Cox and McCubbins 1993, 2) "usurp[s] the power, theoretically resident in the House, to make rules governing the structure and process of legislation." This results in a legislative process stacked in favor of the majority party, and makes the members of the majority the usual key players in legislative deals.

In *Legislative Leviathan* Cox and McCubbins distinguished between parties as floor coalitions and as procedural coalitions, and they presented evidence related to both aspects. On the former they defined party leadership votes as roll calls on which the party leaderships take opposing stands and concluded that there was no secular decline in party support in the post-New Deal era among Democrats. Thus, the majority party was, on this score, not measurably weaker than it had been. On the procedural front, they demonstrated that loyalty to party was an important influence on whether members received desirable initial committee assignments as well as later transfers to better committees. Then, with regard to agenda setting, Cox and McCubbins argued that the majority promoted its advantage in two ways, by giving its members greater veto power over bills, and by granting them more power to push legislation. Based on all their analysis, they concluded that there had been a version of party government in the House throughout the postwar period.

Attention to the two aspects of agenda power became the central focus of Cox and McCubbins's later work, culminating in their second book, *Setting the Agenda* (2005). There they referred to the two aspects as positive and negative agenda power. With this focus they addressed similarities and differences between their theory and CPG. Cartel theory gave the greatest attention to negative agenda power, which Cox and McCubbins (2005, 20) defined as the ability to block bills from reaching a final passage vote on the floor. The ability of the majority to exercise negative power stemmed from the distribution of veto rights among offices held by "senior partners" of the majority, and the imposition of a fiduciary obligation on those officeholders to oppose unacceptable legislation. Their theory predicted that bills opposed by a majority of the majority party should be blocked from the floor, and the evidence they presented supported this expectation. Defining "rolls" as a situation in which a majority of a party votes against a bill but it passes anyway, they show that the incidence of majority party rolls is very low (e.g., only about two times a congress on average from 1953 to 1998; Cox and McCubbins 2005, 93). They also found that majority rolls were rare in votes on special rules for consideration of measures on the House floor, and in committee votes to report bills to the House.

Cox and McCubbins only focused on positive agenda power (the ability to bring measures to a final passage floor vote) in their penultimate chapter. There they asked what the differences are between cartel theory and CPG, and they inquired whether the majority party can, at least on occasion, use a mix of party discipline and side payments to secure passage of party bills that would not otherwise pass. On the second issue, they concluded, the answer is yes. Regarding CPG, they saw the difference between the two theories to be mainly a matter of focus; for CPG, positive agenda power is the core issue, while for cartel theory, negative power is at its core. Owing to this difference in focus, the theories tend to concentrate on different things.[9] Moreover, Cox and McCubbins stated that cartel theory expects that some features of legislative organization would vary with the homogeneity of preferences within the majority party, and some features would be invariant, and the existence of this constant minimum of party power is, in their view, the principal difference between the theories (2005, 203). Among the things that vary with homogeneity are the mix of positive and negative agenda powers, the size of the majority agenda, and the rate at which the minority party is rolled. Among the features claimed to be invariant were the existence of a rules "base" that empowers the majority party and persists over time, the minimum fiduciary standard imposed on party officials, and the majority roll rate (which would always be virtually zero).

[9] For a discussion of this relationship from the CGG perspective, see Finocchiaro and Rohde (2008).

What Course for the Future?

This brief account of theoretical perspectives on parties in the House is certainly not exhaustive. For example, Sarah Binder (1997) and Douglas Dion (1997) produced impressive long-term historical studies of the allocation of minority rights in the House, and Eric Schickler (2001) presented a multifaceted theory of institutional change (called "disjointed pluralism") that seeks to capture the varying impact of different coalitions with a range of collective interests in four major historical periods. The account is, however, sufficient to move us on to the next stage of the discussion to examine some of the issues raised by the theoretical arguments in more detail, and make a few suggestions about what future work would be fruitful.

The Centrality of Agenda Control

The work of Cox and McCubbins—and especially *Setting the Agenda*—has added substantially to our knowledge about the role of parties in Congress. To be sure, they were not the only ones to take this focus; the research by Sinclair, Aldrich and Rohde, and many others also saw matters related to agenda setting to be important. But Cox and McCubbins both chose this as their principal interest, and made the theoretical discussion more specific and more nuanced through the conceptual distinction between positive and negative agenda power. Yet there still seem to be important matters related to the Cox and McCubbins account (and the matter of agenda control more generally) that need further amplification or exploration.

For one thing, while the theoretical distinction between positive and negative agenda control is quite clear, the practical distinction may be less so. The findings about majority rolls on passage votes seem clearly to be very important evidence indicating, as Cox and McCubbins claim, that there is a continuing base of majority party power embedded in House rules that grant the majority persistent advantages in shaping legislation and the floor agenda. Moreover, their findings are reinforced by the results of related work. Aldrich and Rohde (2000b) found that both for final passage votes in general and for appropriations bills in particular, when the floor vote was partisan the winning coalition was more than ten times as likely to be dominated by the majority party than by the minority plus a defecting group of majority members. For "partyless" models such as the one proposed by Krehbiel, they argued, the incidence of these two types of coalitions should be expected to be equally likely. Lawrence, Maltzman, and Smith (2006) considered passage votes in more detail, assessing the explanatory power of four theories of legislative behavior. They concluded that the partyless theory receives little support, while a model based on majority party agenda control accounts well for the patterns in the data, with legislative outcomes usually being on the majority side of the chamber median.

Despite these strong results, it must be noted that they deal with votes on bills and not with details of the content of legislation. Yet that would seem to be the essence of negative agenda control, the idea that the majority party prevents policies it opposes from being written into law. Bills are often large aggregates of many policies (and even of many bills in the era of omnibus legislation; see Krutz 2001). If the minority party can succeed in getting a policy they want (and that the majority opposes) added to a bill via amendment, and that bill passes (even with the support of the majority party), then it would appear that negative agenda control by the majority has failed. Thus, it would seem that a more complete assessment of the majority party's success with respect to negative agenda power would need to include a broader range of data. This might include quantitative analysis of the legislators' actions in creating bills, both in committee and on the floor (e.g., the relationship between the patterns in amendment and passage votes). Alternatively, such analysis might involve qualitative analysis of the content of major legislation over time, assessing the relative success of efforts by the majority and minority to shape bill content.

Another consideration related to agenda control involves the recognition that the distinction between positive and negative power is not as clear in practice as the theoretical definitions would seem to imply. By that I mean that short of the majority party completely shutting down legislative activity (an impractical option to say the least), the essence of both of these matters must be dealt with simultaneously. As a practical matter, the House *must* deal with various legislative issues each congress. These virtually always include annual appropriations, the debt ceiling, and expiring legislation, and often include the budget and issues that are highly salient to the public, like the financial meltdown of 2008. In the case of legislation like this, determining the initial content of a bill and bringing it forward involves positive agenda power, while controlling the options to be considered leading to the decision on passage involves negative agenda power. I think there is still much to be learned about the interrelationship between the exercise of these two types of agenda power by the majority, both within a given congress and over time.

In addition to these general issues, there is much about the mechanisms of positive and negative agenda control that still needs to be considered. Cox and McCubbins (2005, 206), in discussing the differing conclusions of the work of Rohde (1991) and Schickler and Rich (1997), argued that we need a better theory of the effect of rules changes before we can be confident about conclusions from the timing of the adoption of such changes. In addition, there has been relatively little specific analysis of the decisions of House majorities about how to distribute positive and negative agenda power—in terms of both the balance between them and the particular institutional positions in which to vest them at any given time.

On the other hand, there has been more work on the exercise of agenda powers by certain institutional actors, and I turn now to one salient example.

Mechanisms of Agenda Power, the Rules Committee, and Related Matters

The House Rules Committee has probably been the focus of as much analysis as any other institutional feature in the body of work on congressional parties over the last thirty years. Both the institutional arrangements regarding Rules (especially the transfer of the power to appoint majority members from the Democrats' committee on committees to the Speaker in 1974), and the ways Rules crafted the "special rules" that governed floor debate, changed enormously during this period. Oppenheimer (1977) was among the first to recognize the nature and significance of the transformation of the role of Rules from an independent center of power to being a "new arm of the leadership," and a host of scholars followed in his wake.

Bach and Smith (1988) presented a detailed consideration of the evolution of the patterns of special rules, and of the ways complex special rules served various member interests. Rules and its altered role played major roles in the accounts of the changing impact of parties in the analyses by Sinclair (1983, 1995) and in the initial presentation of conditional party government theory (Rohde 1991), as well as in later work on that theory (Aldrich and Rohde 2000a, 2000b). Krehbiel argued for the majoritarian nature of restrictive special rules in his 1991 book, and he defended that position in a debate (1997a, 1997b) with Dion and Huber (1996, 1997), who concluded that restrictive rules were a device for securing non-centrist policy outcomes.

More recent work has grappled in various ways with the difficulty of demonstrating party effects related to special rules. Sinclair (2002a) offered a detailed analysis of the inferences that could be drawn from the special rules on bills, and concluded that, contrary to Krehbiel's theory, in at least some instances non-median outcomes were achieved by the majority party. More importantly, however, she contended that analysts of the consequences of procedures should take a broader focus than that imposed by responding to Krehbiel, and concentrate on ways in which members' preferences are themselves more contingent on context than Krehbiel's analysis allows. Young and Wilkins (2007) analyzed all bills with closed rules and final passage votes in five congresses, assessing whether the pattern of voting on the rule–passage pair for each bill could be governed by simple preference à la Krehbiel. They concluded that the patterns they observed were extremely unlikely to occur without significant party effects.

In a monograph that considered the politics of special rules in four Congresses under both Democrat and Republican control, Marshall (2005) followed the path of Sinclair's work and CPG with a principal–agent account. He examined in detail both the establishment of a strong principal–agent relationship between the majority leadership and the committee from the 1970s on, and changes in patterns related to the legislative process. These included a decline over time in majority support for floor amendments that sought to change committee bills, coupled with an increase in majority support for restrictive rules. Monroe and Robinson (2008) employed the cut points estimated via DW-NOMINATE scores to measure the character of the policy outcomes on final passage votes in eight congresses. Their analysis indicates that in congresses with Democratic majorities the cut points on bills with restrictive rules are significantly further to the left than those on bills with open rules. Under Republican majorities, on the other hand, bills under restrictive rules have cut points significantly further to the right.

All of this work indicates significant legislative consequences from majority party control of Rules and the agenda control it exerts, and these are among the most consequential results from the literature we have been discussing. There is still, however, a lot more we need to learn about this aspect of agenda control. Some matters relate to the interrelationship between positive and negative agenda control discussed in the previous section. Special rules set the procedural terms for positive action, but as the pre-reform accounts indicate, the committee can also exercise negative control by refusing to report a rule (or refusing the type of rule the leadership needs). The ability of the majority leadership to control the crafting of special rules (with respect to both the committee's action and the floor's) is essential to both types of control because inability to prevent an undesired policy that would pass from being offered as an amendment would be just as damaging as preventing it from being offered as a stand-alone bill.

Finocchiaro and Rohde (2008) sought to examine this interrelationship by focusing on the link between the vote to order the previous question on a special rule and the vote on the rule's passage. In a period when the majority leadership controls the Rules Committee, the minority party on the floor can block action by the majority by defeating passage of a rule, but it cannot seize positive agenda control that way. The only way that can be done is by defeating the previous question and then amending the rule on the floor. Thus, if a previous question motion on a rule failed, this could be interpreted as a potential failure of negative agenda control by the majority party. Finocchiaro and Rohde's analysis indicates that from the 100th Congress through the 107th (after leadership control had been solidified under Speaker Jim Wright), only a single defeat of the previous question occurred compared to eight in the preceding nine congresses. Similarly, during the earlier period there were seven majority rolls on special rules, while there was only one in the latter period. These results suggest that both the majority's positive and negative agenda powers may be conditional to a degree on the majority's homogeneity, in contrast to cartel theory's expectation of the unconditionality of negative power. However, more detailed research is necessary before firm conclusions can be drawn. Moreover, I should note that I do not think these results undermine Cox and McCubbins's central conclusion that there is an invariant minimal base of majority party power in the House regardless of variations in majority party homogeneity.

Another potentially fruitful focus for work is analysis of the Rules Committee before majority leadership control solidified. Not surprisingly, most of the attention has been on what effects leadership dominance has had, but an earlier temporal focus could provide us with a much better picture of how much and in what ways things have changed. One excellent effort along these lines is Schickler and Pearson (2008), a detailed study of the committee's activity between 1938 and 1952. They note that analysts can be misled by focusing only on roll call data, and so they include bills considered by other means. One of their important findings was that refusing to report special rules for majority-favored bills was not the only way the committee frustrated Democrats' preferred actions. Contrary to the expectations of cartel theory, Rules opened the gates for a number of bills that were opposed by a majority of Democrats.

Finally, it is desirable to continue the increasing attention being given to mechanisms of agenda control that can have implications for legislation analogous to special rules, such as the motion to recommit, discharge petitions, and conference reports. For example, Krehbiel and Meirowitz (2002) engaged the claims of party theorists that the majority party could use its procedural advantages to secure policy outcomes tilted in its direction compared to the preference of the median member. They argued that the motion to recommit with instructions permits the minority to effectively counter the majority's advantages because that device gave the minority the last move before final passage through which they could effectively amend the majority's proposed bill. However, Roberts (2005) challenged the theoretical argument offered by Krehbiel and Meirowitz, and he presented evidence that is contrary to their expectations as well as those of cartel theory, but which is generally consistent with CPG. (See also Cox and McCubbins 2005, 144–5.)

Regarding the discharge petition, Krehbiel (1995) claimed that this device would permit the minority to bypass majority efforts at (negative) agenda control by forcing blocked bills to the floor. Cox and McCubbins (2005, 61–2, 83–6), on the other hand, emphasized that discharge petitions are rarely undertaken and even more rarely successful. In recent analysis, Pearson and Schickler (forthcoming) considered all discharge petitions filed from 1929 through 1976, as well as public data on discharges from 1993 through 2006. Among a variety of important findings, they discovered that contrary to the expectations of cartel theory, northern Democrats were more likely than Republicans to sign discharge petitions during much of the 1940s–1960s.

Finally, more attention has been given recently to the conference committee process. Earlier theoretical work (Krehbiel 1987; Shepsle and Weingast 1987) focused mainly on whether conferences served as a device to augment and protect committee power for distributive purposes, but recent work has focused on the partisan implications of the process. For example, Lazarus and Monroe (2007) argued that the Speaker could anticipate when the routine appointment of senior committee members to conferences would be likely to produce outcomes contrary to the preferences of the majority party. In those instances, the Speaker could compensate for that problem by "packing" the conference with additional more loyal members. Their evidence supported this expectation. Moreover, van Houweling (2007) showed that conferences could be used by partisan majorities, in a manner similar to restrictive rules in the House, to provide cover for majority senators who personally favored extreme policy outcomes but could not afford politically to support them on open votes.

SOME OTHER CONSIDERATIONS

Had space permitted, much more could have been said about the topics considered above, and there are many other matters that deserve consideration. In closing, we can note a few of them. As Sinclair (2002a, 38) noted, her work and CPG focus much more on explaining changes in party influence and legislative organization over time than do cartel theory, Krehbiel's informational theory, or distributive theory. Indeed, CPG was originally formulated specifically for that purpose. I would argue that it is important for any theory of congressional parties to include within itself a dynamic perspective on organizational structure and member behavior. Yet whatever its merits, CPG is, to this point, surely incomplete in specifying the elements—in addition to variations in party homogeneity and interparty conflict—that are important in this dynamic perspective. Recent work by Rohde, Stiglitz, and Weingast (2009) sought to further specify and theorize about some of the additional elements by focusing on members' incentives regarding wanting to change or maintain policy status quos, and the relationship of those incentives to positive and negative agenda power. This included whether a new majority had taken control and the length of time since the last time it had such control, whether unified government was newly established and the time since that was last true, and the degree of uncertainty about future majority control.

A number of other authors have also recently sought explanations of legislative change related to congressional parties (e.g., Binder 1997; Schickler 2000, 2001; Lebo, McGlynn, and Koger 2007), but I think that much work is still needed to give us a more complete picture. In particular, it seems to me quite plausible that with a focus on a long time frame, we may find that different theories may do the best job in explaining patterns in different time periods, an argument that I think is consistent with Schickler (2001).

More work is also needed to flesh out the interaction among the multiple motives that representatives have. Smith (2007) was critical of much research on congressional parties for articulating an oversimplified picture of members' motives, particularly single-motive arguments. Now to be sure a reasonable defense of such work is that science should begin with simple theories for the sake of tractability and the feasibility of securing clear logical inferences. However, as research cumulates it becomes clearer where predictions from the simpler theories are insufficient, and what additional features must be built in. Smith (2007, 121) contended that CPG, despite its emphasis on multiple motives, fell short because it did not deal adequately with the collective electoral motive, getting party colleagues elected and securing or maintaining majority status.[10]

This is a fair complaint (although I would argue that it is truer of the early work than that which followed the shift to Republican control). Be that as it may, however, I think it is generally true that theories of congressional parties need to more fully assess the impact of the 1994 GOP landslide. This event separates two vastly different congressional worlds. For a long time preceding the 1994 election, congressional politics were shaped by a high degree of certainty about which party would be in the majority after the next election. Since 1994, majority control has been constantly at issue, and leaders of both parties have conditioned virtually every strategic decision partly on its possible effect on the parties' collective electoral fortunes. The full effects of this shift on all aspects of congressional politics are still not entirely clear, and analysts would profit by giving it diligent consideration.

In this chapter I have offered a brief discussion of changing theoretical perspectives on parties and leaders in the House, and some suggestions about desirable avenues for future research. In closing, I want to emphasize one point. When we conduct research, we properly cite earlier work on the subject at hand. What may be problematic, however, is that we often refer to findings regarding an earlier time without questioning whether they are still applicable to the current era. Unlike physicists who don't need to worry about protons and electrons joining together to change the laws of nature, students of the Congress are constantly faced with the efforts of strategic actors to alter the rules under which they operate and thereby to reshape the patterns of behavior and outcomes. One implication from the account above of the transition of the House away from the textbook view of the 1980s is that this analytical context calls for constant reassessment of the generalizations gleaned from earlier work. One happy consequence of this situation is that congressional analysts will have plenty of work to occupy them in coming decades.

---

[10] Another fertile ground for work related to variations in motives would be a greater appreciation of the impact of differing motives of party leaders and how those motives shape behavior and strategies. See Strahan (2007).

CHAPTER 18

....

PARTISAN MODELS AND THE SEARCH FOR PARTY EFFECTS IN THE US SENATE

....

BARBARA SINCLAIR

PARTISAN models and the search for party effects have dominated congressional research in recent years. Yet, after a book-length analytic discussion of the voluminous literature, Steve Smith concludes that "no persuasive treatment of the Senate exists in this recent literature" (2007, 214). In this chapter, I consider what we do know about party in the Senate and the questions that still need to be addressed.

Treating the Senate separately from the House of Representatives—or other democratic legislatures—is justified by its highly unusual, if not unique, rules. Cutting off debate, and thus bringing a matter to a final vote over the opposition of any senator, requires a supermajority, currently sixty votes, and, in general, amendments offered on the floor need not be germane. If, as Smith formulates it, the task is "identifying forms of party influence and their distinguishable consequences for legislators' behavior and policy outcomes" (2007, 5), the Senate offers challenges different from the House. Our prominent theories and much of the empirical literature focus on majority party agenda control as the central mechanism of party influence and, thus, the major producer of party effects. But, given Senate rules, it is unclear how much agenda control the majority party and its leadership have in the Senate. The first major question, then, concerns the extent and nature of agenda control in the Senate. Second, if agenda control is limited, what are the incentives, if any, for majority party senators to cooperate when it is not in their immediate interest to do so, that is, to, in some way, "take one for the party"? So, for example, what, if anything, induces senators to support the party on tough votes? What induces them to put in time on party endeavors of various sorts that produce collective goods when they could free-ride? Basically, are there endogenous party effects in the Senate?

Prominent contemporary theories of parties agree that parties arose in response to various collective action problems; purposive actors created and altered parties in their attempts to solve collective action problems confronting them. Aldrich, in his influential book *Why Parties?* (1995), argues that the "partisan impulse," the impulse to form and reform parties, stems from the "combination of goal-seeking behavior of politicians, channeling and nurturing their ambitions for long and successful political careers, providing access to office and control over its use" (1995, 296). The conditional party government (CPG) theory of congressional parties, developed by Aldrich and Rohde, sees intracongressional party organiza-tion and leadership as a means of handling the collective action problems asso-ciated with constructing floor majorities (Aldrich and Rohde 2000b; S. S. Smith 2007, 119); the strength and presumably the form of majority party organization and leadership are postulated to be a function of the party members' ideological homogeneity and their ideological distance from the opposing party. When mem-bers of a legislative party are like-minded, they are willing to give their party leaders more power and resources, and specifically control over the legislative agenda, in order to enable those leaders to deliver legislative outcomes that the members want. Cox and McCubbins's (1993, 2005) cartel theory similarly sees legislative parties as solutions to collective action problems within the legislature; in a recent essay on the organization of democratic legislatures, Cox argues that such legis-latures have universally created "offices endowed with special agenda-setting powers" and that "the lure of [such] office promotes the formation of legislative parties and coalitions" (2006, 142). As I elaborate more below, both theories posit that control over the legislative agenda is key to party influence.

ORIGINS AND EARLY DEVELOPMENT OF PARTY INSTITUTIONS AND OFFICES

What do we know about the origins and development of party institutions and offices in the Senate? How does it jibe with our theories? Specifically, can we explain their origins and development with a story about gaining agenda control? Doing so is, of course, not required to explain some party organization and party effects, crudely defined, in the Senate. Parties in the electoral process, whatever their origins, should carry over into the Senate in a number of ways. If senators get elected through a process that involves ideologically distinct partisan activists and somewhat like-minded party-identified voters, the electoral coalitions of Democrats and Republicans are likely to differ significantly. The influence of the preferences of electorally relevant constituents on member behavior is likely to produce what looks like partisan behavior to the extent that Democrats and Republicans do, in fact, represent constituencies that differ on the key issues of the day. Further, it is reasonable to assume that senators who represent similar constituencies may, in fact, also have similar personal legislative preferences given self-selection into the party might well organize informally for purposes of co-ordinating their actions in the legislative arena. In recent scholarship, however, the search for party effects has focused on influences over and above such exogenously generated impacts (Krehbiel 1993, 1998; but also Cox and McCubbins 1993, 2005; and CPG).

Until recently we knew remarkably little about the development of party institutions and offices in the Senate. Gamm and Smith's systematic research is not just filling lacunae but also revising previous claims (2002). This is rich work to which I cannot do full credit here, but there are several major findings that are especially noteworthy for my purposes. One is how late formal party leadership offices and organization developed in the Senate. Party caucuses existed and chose chairmen, but these men were not considered their party's leader; the caucus chairmanship was, in fact, largely ceremonial until the late nineteenth century. Various senators did begin informally and intermittently to perform some of the functions of modern party leaders in the 1890s, but "before the late 1890s, neither party elected its leader," Gamm and Smith find (2002, 221). The first newspaper account located by Gamm and Smith that refers to a caucus chairman as his party's elected leader did not appear until 1898. John Kern, elected Democratic caucus chair in 1913, was the first Senate leader consistently referred to as "majority leader" and, at the same time, his Republican counterpart was, also for the first time, regularly designated his party's "floor leader." Democrats in 1913 decided to establish the position of whip and Republicans followed in 1915. Certainly there were strong partisan divisions and some party leadership in the Senate long before these developments, but it was extremely informal; even after 1913, party leadership continued to display informal aspects.

Problems of agenda setting played a role in motivating these developments. In fact, the more or less formal recognition of Senate party leaders sketched above was preceded by the parties' experiments with steering committees to bring some order to floor agenda setting, among other tasks. Republicans began using an ad hoc steering committee in the 1860s, Smith and Gamm report; Democrats followed suit in the mid-1870s as their strength in the Senate grew (2002, 224). Nevertheless, the Senate floor often remained "a chaotic place," with members of the same party vying for agenda space (2002, 224). Not until the early 1890s did the parties regularly appoint steering committees. "By the middle 1890s," Gamm and Smith report, "party leaders like Aldrich and Gorman were using steering committees to direct party policy and strategy" (2002, 228). Floor agenda setting, via the steering committees, by informal but widely acknowledged party leaders such as Aldrich or, on the Democratic side, Gorman, the caucus chair and increasingly the acknowledged leader, probably contributed to the more formal recognition of Senate party leadership. Nevertheless, the party caucuses' delegation of agenda-setting authority to the steering committees was and remained highly informal. And, as the leaders become more central to agenda setting, they relied less and less on their steering committees.

The recognition and the formal election of leaders by the Senate parties was not accompanied by any delegation to them of special powers under Senate rules. The Senate's constitutional presiding officers (the president and the president pro tempore of the Senate) did not evolve into party leaders, as was the case with the House, nor did those presiding officers amass much parliamentary authority. Even now, the Senate majority leader is purely an officer of his or her party, not an officer of the chamber. The majority leader's only special parliamentary prerogative, the right of first recognition, is merely a precedent and dates only to the 1930s.

Majority Leadership and Agenda Setting in the Senate

The Senate majority leader is now the acknowledged chief agenda setter for the Senate floor. Using his prerogative of first recognition, he asks unanimous consent or moves to consider a measure (Sinclair 1997). Under the rules, any senator may make such a request (without having cleared it with the majority leader), but upholding the majority party leader's exclusive prerogative to do so is considered essential by the majority party and majority party senators are quick to back up their leader if necessary. Thus, in practice, other senators very seldom make the attempt to usurp the majority leader's role. Typically, the majority leader asks unanimous consent to consider a measure and, at that point or later in the process, may also ask unanimous consent to various provisions governing consideration. The offering of unanimous consent agreements—and certainly the granting of unanimous consent—has usually been preceded by an elaborate consultation process that, crucially, involves the minority party and specifically its leader.

Unanimous consent means that any one senator, including of course a minority party senator, can block agreement; and the minority party always has someone on the floor to assure that its rights are protected.

Smith reports that the Senate was using unanimous consent agreements with some frequency by 1870 (J. Roberts and Smith 2007, 194). In 1914, the Senate adopted a rule that made unanimous consent agreements (UCAs) orders of the Senate and thereby made them enforceable by the presiding officer; the rule also clarified that a unanimous consent agreement could be altered by unanimous consent. These changes made UCAs more useful for bringing order to the floor agenda. Bill managers had primarily negotiated UCAs but, over time, this became a responsibility of the majority leader. By the early 1920s, majority leaders were actively and regularly involved in doing so (J. Roberts and Smith 2007, 198). It seems reasonable to conclude that, as the Senate's workload expanded and demands on senators' time grew, owing in part to direct election, senators sought a more efficient use of floor time and more predictability. That required a coordinator, and who better, from the point of view of majority party senators, to take on the task than the majority leader? Yet, with the exception of acquiescing in the right of first recognition for the majority leader, senators did not give him any special powers under Senate rules.

The modern Senate majority leader does have substantial resources. He commands a sizeable staff. Under party rules and practices, he has considerable say in the awarding of desirable committee assignments. Party committees of various sorts have proliferated, as have leadership positions. The leader appoints or influences the appointment of party committees and of some of the subordinate leadership positions and these help him in carrying out his leadership duties. (In terms of staff and within-party influence over appointments, the minority leader's resources are similar to those of his majority party counterpart.) As the elected leader of the party with the largest number of Senate members, the majority leader presumably has the respect and confidence of his own members and, of course and crucially, the clout that comes from superior numbers. He does not, however, have much in the way of special parliamentary powers for agenda setting.

INHERITED RULES OR CONTEMPORARY PREFERENCES?

Why did the Senate majority party never give its leader much in the way of special agenda-setting powers in Senate rules? Scholars do not agree on the answer and, in fact, different takes on the Senate emerge when we examine how scholars have answered this question. Binder and Smith argue that inherited rules stymied majority party reform efforts (1997; J. Roberts and Smith 2007). In the House, organized and cohesive majorities—almost always partisan majorities—could change the rules to their benefit when the minority blocked their legislative efforts. Because the Senate lacked a previous question motion, there was no way—other than exhausting the participants—to cut off debate and bring a motion to a final vote over the objections of a determined minority. Rules changes in the Senate require a supermajority and that almost always means a bipartisan majority.

Gamm and Smith argue that the inability of normal-sized partisan majorities to change Senate rules so as to solve collective action problems and benefit the majority party acted as a constraint on empowering leaders through other means; thus, creating a highly centralized party apparatus might limit the freedom of action of individual senators but would not bring significant gains in terms of control over the Senate policymaking process, especially the Senate floor agenda (2002, 236). Still, senators' only means of handling collective action problems that are "structured by party" are intraparty innovations (not Senate rule-based innovations). They find that such innovations occur when the parties are near parity in strength—when, they argue, the majority feels itself vulnerable and the minority sees opportunities. The innovations they analyze—the use of steering committees, the development of formally designated party leadership—did not coincide with party polarization or with the development of careerism, as other, mostly House-based, theories have hypothesized (see below).

Other authors, notably Gregory Koger (2002, 2007) and Gregory Wawro and Eric Schickler (2006, 2007), have disputed the inherited rules argument. Koger contends that a simple majority of senators can always change the chambers' rules through precedents established by rulings of the chair and majority vote. Basically, a senator can raise a point of order from the floor—that only a majority vote is required to cut off debate on a presidential nomination, for example; a friendly chair can then rule in the senator's favor; that ruling can and would be appealed but only a simple majority is required to table the appeal, a non-debatable motion— and thereby uphold the ruling of the chair. Thus, the new interpretation becomes a precedent of the Senate. Senate rules have been changed by this route, not always advertently. The Republican majority in 2005 contemplated using what came to be called the "nuclear option" to change the rules on presidential nominations, but the attempt was preempted by a bipartisan deal.

Given the availability of this means of changing Senate rules by a simple majority, Koger argues that when majorities have not changed the rules or have failed in their attempts, it is because the costs outweigh the rewards (2007, 206–7). Koger's sophisticated explication of costs and benefits cannot be reviewed here in any detail; basically, he argues that although changing rules via unconventional tactics such as revising Senate precedents may entail high costs, it is an available strategy. Thus, when the majority chooses not to use it, it does so because the rewards, in terms of policy and/or external benefits from voters or other outside actors, are not sufficient to outweigh the costs, which may also include policy costs. Using this framework, Koger examines filibuster reform attempts from 1913 to 1917 and concludes that the cases "demonstrate the weak incentives to restrain obstructionism during the 1910s Senate" (2007, 224). Most importantly, he argues that the 1917 cloture rule (Rule 22), the first that the Senate ever adopted and which was adopted through bipartisan agreement, simply ratified the status quo. An exogenous shock, the public firestorm that President Woodrow Wilson instigated after the filibuster of the bill allowing the arming of merchant marine ships, increased the costs of inaction on the rules for both parties but even the majority Democrats did not favor majority cloture. "Legislators...designed the new rule to have minimal effects on policy outcomes" (2007, 224).

Wawro and Schickler argue that the threat of the nuclear option—of "a 'revolutionary' crackdown on obstruction by a determined floor majority" (2006, xi)—was a sufficient constraint on obstructive behavior that, on issues salient to both the majority and the minority, the pre-Rule 22 Senate was essentially majoritarian (2006, 28). One might assume that a legislative chamber without any means of cutting off debate, other than exhaustion of the obstructionists, would in effect operate under a near unanimity rule. They contend, in contradiction, that the small size and relatively light workload of the nineteenth-century Senate allowed the body to develop "shared, stable procedural expectations" that, although not institutionalized in rules or organization, nevertheless enabled the chamber to operate effectively (2006, 11). These norms were enforced by the threat of rules changes and by the physical costs of obstructionism in a chamber that, except at the end of the session, operated without severe time constraints.

Why, then, did the Senate adopt Rule 22, and did it have as little effect on outcomes as Kroger and many earlier scholars argue? Wawro and Schickler contend that, by the late nineteenth century, increases in the Senate's size and workload put this system under considerable stress, and senators began to act opportunistically, especially in the last days of the session; by 1917 senators were willing to institute a cloture rule. By adopting Rule 22, senators "trade[d] off a decrease in the uncertainty of passage for an increase in the size of coalitions necessary to pass legislation," they argue (2007, 229). Seemingly, the argument is that, with Rule 22 in place, a senator could be certain of passing his bill, even late in the session, so long as he amassed a two-thirds majority for it, so that is what risk-averse senators tended to do. Because everyone understood this, the rule would seldom actually have to be used, as was in fact the case. Wawro and Schickler claim to show that winning coalitions were, in fact, larger after Rule 22 than before and that variance was less, but Koger contests those findings. Furthermore, their interpretation of their findings is undercut by the similarity in the coalition size patterns in the House and the Senate.

In any case, Wawro and Schickler argue that obstruction in the Senate continued to be costly in time and energy for many years after the adoption of Rule 22. As many other scholars have contended as well, what is different about the modern Senate is that obstructionism is nearly costless; senators can place "holds" on bills and nominations, they can threaten to object to UCAs, they can threaten to engage in extended debate, but they almost never actually have to take to the floor and expend substantial time and energy to block a vote. Time constraints have become so severe that just a threat is often enough (Oppenheimer 1985; Sinclair 1989, 2005, 2006). The majority may simply capitulate, either never bringing the measure to the floor at all or making the substantive compromises the minority demands; or it may attempt to impose cloture and, if it cannot command a supermajority immediately pull the measure off the floor or compromise on substance. The majority almost never forces the minority to actually filibuster in the old sense of holding the floor for an extended period of time. Given the workload, floor time is simply considered too valuable to expend in that way. Yet both Wawro and Schickler and Koger argue that the majority could change the rules if it really wanted to and impose majority rule via the "nuclear option." That no majority has yet done so is taken to indicate that a determined majority for such a rules change has never existed.

Quite different understandings of the Senate seemingly emerge from Smith and his coauthors on the one hand and from Koger, Wawro, and Schickler on the other. The majority party's lack of true agenda control is due to inherited rules according to Smith; according to Koger, Wawro, and Schickler, it is because a majority of senators do not want that kind of Senate. According to Wawro and Schickler but not Koger, the majority, though not necessarily a partisan majority, in the past did have sufficient control of the Senate floor to pass measures about which it felt strongly, but increases in workload and size have eroded that—but not sufficiently to motivate a majority to change the Senate.

These accounts are not completely irreconcilable. Binder and Smith do mention the Senate's ability to change its rules through the alteration of precedents and Koger, Wawro, and Schickler all concede that the "nuclear option" entails signifi-cant and perhaps very high potential costs. What makes the nuclear option "nuclear," according to the Congressional Research Service, is that it depends on the presiding officer making a ruling that contravenes the accepted precedents of the Senate (Beth 2005). This is significant because it means that the new precedent could be just as easily overturned and other changes in rules so implemented. The use of the nuclear option thus opens the door to the very real potential for extraordinary instability in Senate rules and that, it seems reasonable to hypothe-size, raises costs hugely. I would argue that although Koger, Wawro, and Schickler are correct about the availability of the nuclear option, they tend to underestimate the price of employing it; therefore, Wawro and Schickler, in particular, are probably overly sanguine about the impact its availability has on restraining minority obstructionism. Smith and his coauthors sometimes discuss inherited rules as if they were truly immutable, but their emphasis on those rules' influence is nevertheless well placed; yes, a determined bare majority could change them, but the price of doing so might well be chaos and senators are aware of that.

Interestingly, the implications for party influence in the Senate of these two understandings of the Senate are not hugely different. Party plays a lesser role in the Senate than in the House, but a significant one nonetheless. These authors are not precise about the magnitude of the role; Gamm and Smith "postulate that party-based strategies [of internal reform] will be pursued when the collective action problems confronting senators are structured by party" (2002, 4); the implication is that whether such problems are structured by party is exogenously determined— by variables such as the strength of parties in the external political environment presumably. Their emphasis is on explaining why party-based rather than Senate-rule based strategies are used and on when such innovations occur. The why— inherited rules—does limit, in their view, the value of giving Senate party leaders great powers since those would of necessity only be powers over party members not powers in Senate rules and thus of limited policy value (2002, 31). The other authors do not focus on this question.

PARTISAN THEORIES, PARTY EFFECTS, AND NEGATIVE AGENDA CONTROL

The two most prominent party theories—conditional party government (CPG) theory and cartel theory—speak to the question of party effects—their nature and magnitude—directly. What do they have to say about the Senate? CPG has little to nothing to say about the Senate and does not claim to. It is a theory about parties in the House of Representatives and possibly is applicable to other legislatures governed by simple majority rule. In CPG ideological homogeneity within party and distance between the parties explains how much power members are willing to delegate to their party leaders. To be sure, we would expect that ideological homogeneity would lead to higher rates of party voting and quite possibly higher levels of intraparty cooperation of most sorts in the Senate. However, if even a totally cohesive majority party cannot necessarily prevail on the floor unless it is willing to employ the nuclear option and suffer the consequences, the incentives for delegation of less extreme sorts are diminished. In fact, Gamm and Smith show that the CPG variables do not explain party-based innovations in the Senate.

Cox and McCubbins, the developers of cartel theory, focus on the House but often imply that the majority party's control of the agenda is not much less in the

Senate. Agenda control is central to cartel theory; "legislative parties . . . specialize in controlling the agenda, rather than in controlling votes," they argue (2005, 6). Briefly summarized, cartel theory posits that modern political parties, facing mass electorates, have a strong incentive to fashion and maintain a favorable "brand name" because this reputation affects its members' individual probability of reelection and the party's probability of securing a chamber majority. The reputation depends in considerable part on the party's record of legislative accomplishment. The party's reputation is, however, a collective good with all the attendant problems of production. Legislative parties solve those problems by delegating agenda-setting powers to leaders who then use those powers to guard and burnish the party brand. Most importantly, leaders use the majority party's monopoly over agenda setting to keep off the floor measures that would split their party (2005, 18–24).

In their most recent major statement of cartel theory, Cox and McCubbins specifically disavow any claim to present a theory of agenda control for the Senate (2005, 95). In that work as well as in an earlier piece (Campbell, Cox, and McCubbins 2002), they do examine Senate "roll rates," the frequency with which a party is on the losing side on winning final passage roll calls. Their data show that little legislation passes the Senate that a majority of the Senate majority party opposes on a roll call vote. The mean roll rate for the Senate majority party for the post-Reconstruction congresses (45th–105th) is about 6 percent—higher than the House mean of 1.5 percent—but low nonetheless and considerably lower than the mean roll rate of about 28 percent of the Senate minority party (2005, 94). They interpret these data as showing that the Senate majority party has almost the same level of negative agenda control as the House majority party; that is, it is "remarkably good" at "keeping matters that may be offensive to a majority of its membership off the chamber floor for a final vote" (2005, 165). The observations Cox and McCubbins offer "as preliminary steps toward [a Senate] theory" are, by and large, ad hoc and do not go to the heart of the problem: if the Senate majority party exercises disproportionate agenda control, how does it do so? What are the mechanisms? They do mention changing the rules via precedent and several other procedural tactics but do not develop the argument.

Several other scholars have also examined roll rates and argued that the Senate is just not very different than the House. Two recent papers by Gailmard and Jenkins deserve special attention. In a 2007 *Journal of Politics* piece (2007b), they examine majority party roll rates in the House and the Senate over the period 1877–2000 to shed light on the extent of negative agenda control in the two bodies. Once they disaggregate roll call votes into passage votes on chamber-originated bills, conference report votes, and, for the Senate, votes on the confirmation of nominations, they find little difference in the roll rates in the two chambers for the two comparable types of votes. Further, they find that roll rates in the two chambers respond similarly to split control: roll rates in both chambers are higher when different parties control the House and Senate and roll rates on confirmation votes are considerably higher when the majority party in the Senate and the president are of different parties. In another paper, Gailmard and Jenkins (2007a) examine negative agenda control by the minority party in the House and Senate. Of course, most scholarship has argued that Senate minorities have much greater ability to block measures they oppose in the Senate than in the House (Sinclair 2006, 2008; Binder and Smith 1997; S. S. Smith 2007). If the majority party is incapable of monopolizing negative agenda-setting power, cartel theory is inapplicable to the Senate. Using the same roll data, Gailmard and Jenkins find that, in fact, on chamber-originated bills, the minority party is significantly less likely to get rolled in the Senate than in the House; however, on conference reports, the difference in the two chambers' roll rates is not statistically significant. They find, further, that more extreme minority parties (those for which the distance between the minority party and the chamber median is greatest) get rolled more frequently in both chambers and on both chamber-originated bills and conference reports; on the other hand, Senate minorities who share the president's party affiliation get rolled less on confirmation votes and conference reports. Finally, a variable for minority control of a filibuster pivot is never significant in their regressions; from that they conclude "the filibuster proves not to be a significant instrument of power across a range of legislative vehicles" (2007b, 1). That, however, is a rash conclusion since there is little variation in the variable; according to the coding of the variable, the minority always controlled a filibuster pivot before 1917; between 1917 and 1975, a minority of one-third plus one did so; since 1975, a minority of forty-one or greater did so. In other words, there are very few congresses in the dataset where the variable, a dummy, is zero.

Scholars using roll rates such as Cox and McCubbins and Gailmard and Jenkins have tended to emphasize how low the majority party's roll rate is in both chambers; Gailmard and Jenkins's data show that, on average, the Senate majority party is on the losing side on only 5.5 percent of Senate-originated bills that pass on the Senate floor; the comparable figure for the House majority is 4.2 percent (these are per-congress averages) (2007a, 691). As these authors also emphasize, roll rates for the minority parties are considerably higher. What is striking and not remarked upon by these scholars is how low minority roll rates are in both chambers and especially in the Senate. Thus, on a per-congress basis, the Senate minority gets rolled on 24.4 percent of Senate-originated bills and the House minority gets rolled on 34.4 percent of House-originated bills. This means that the minority party—or more accurately, a majority of the minority—is on the winning side on three-fourths of the Senate-originated bills that get to a final passage vote in the Senate; the House minority party is on the winning side on approximately two-thirds of House-originated bills. On the surface, this seems to indicate a remarkable level of consensus, especially considering that these figures are based only on measures subject to a roll call vote; in both chambers, many measures are passed by voice votes or unanimous consent. The very low roll rates for the majority party must thus be considered in light of the not very high roll rates for the minority.

In terms of the difference between the House and Senate, the matter of most concern here, not only is the roll rate for the minority party substantially lower in the Senate on chamber-originated bills, the number of roll calls on which the figure is based is also much lower; the Senate took 1,209 passage roll calls on Senate bills over the period 1877–2000 while the House took 3,804 roll calls on House bills— over three times as many. Is this because the Senate simply takes up fewer bills, and, if so, why? Is it because the Senate passes a larger proportion of its measures without a roll call, and does that mean a bipartisan consensus has been reached on those measures? The Senate does pass somewhat fewer bills than the House at least in the post-Second World War period, but the order of magnitude is not even close to being enough to account for the difference in the number of roll calls, so clearly the Senate also passes more bills without a roll call (Ornstein, Mann, and Malbin 2002, 146–7); however, we cannot answer these questions with any certainty for the entire period and we lack confirmed explanations for the differences.

The number of passage votes on conference reports also shows a considerable disparity between the House and the Senate; 1,417 versus 774. Here we can be more certain that most of the difference is due to the Senate less frequently taking roll call votes on conference reports; occasionally the Senate will not take up or will defeat a conference report approved by the House but this is rare. Thus, if we assume that most of the conference reports approved in the House were also approved in the Senate but by voice vote or unanimous consent, then the chambers' roll rates on conference reports that are quite similar, at a bit more than a third, are actually deceiving. If the lack of a recorded vote on a conference report can be interpreted as indicating minority party support, then 600 plus (1,417 minus 774) conference reports should go in the denominator—reducing the minority role rate on conference reports very considerably. (Of course, the same can be said about the Senate majority roll rate and, to a lesser extent, about the roll rate for both parties in the House where also sometimes conference reports or their equivalents are approved without a recorded vote.) In any case, we need to be suspicious of concluding that the minority party in the Senate lacks substantial blocking power (negative agenda control) based on these data.

RECONSIDERING AGENDA POWER

Neither of the most prominent theories of political parties, then, is readily applicable to the US Senate. Furthermore, the empirical studies of roll rates in the Senate leave us with less rather than more certainty about the minority party's blocking power (negative agenda control). In addition, these studies may focus on too narrow an operationalization of agenda control. A party is said to exercise negative agenda control if it can keep off the floor any measure that a majority of its members oppose, but this is indicated by whether measures that a majority of the party opposes actually do pass. Members of the Senate—and the House—think of agenda control more broadly: do measures that they do not want to debate and vote on get to the floor? It is hardly an original insight that members of Congress dislike taking "tough votes." And clearly, House majority party leaders are more capable than Senate majority party leaders of protecting their members from having to take such votes. In the House, majority party leaders can often—though certainly not always—spare their members from having to take tough votes by how they structure special rules that govern floor consideration. The much more open debate and amending process in the Senate makes it much harder for the Senate majority party leader to deny the minority an opportunity to get debate and some sort of vote on its issues.

In the 1990s exploiting Senate prerogatives to attempt to seize this sort of agenda control became a key minority party strategy (Sinclair 2006). Given the lack of a germaneness requirement for amendments, if the majority leader refuses to bring a bill to the floor, its supporters can offer it as an amendment to most legislation the leader does bring to the floor. The majority leader can make a motion to table the amendment, which is non-debatable. That does, however, require his members to vote on the issue, albeit in a procedural guise, and the leader—and his party members—may want to avoid that. The motion to table does not provide much of a fig leaf. Furthermore, even after the minority's amendment has been tabled, the minority can continue to offer other amendments, including even individual parts of the original amendment, and can block a vote on the underlying bill the majority party wants to pass. The leader can, of course, file a cloture petition and try to shut off debate, but he needs sixty votes to do so. The minority party can use this strategy to bring its agenda to the floor and, if accompanied by a sophisticated public relations campaign (which the Senate parties are increasingly capable of orchestrating), can gain favorable publicity and sometimes even pressure enough majority party members into supporting the bill to pass it. In 1996, during the first completely Republican-controlled Congress since the early 1950s, Senate Democrats used this strategy to enact a minimum wage increase; and since then, minority Democrats forced highly visible floor debate on tobacco regulation, campaign finance reform, gun control, and managed care reform, all issues the majority party would have preferred to avoid. In 2001, campaign finance legislation passed the Senate before the Democrats took control of the chamber. John McCain (Republican, Arizona) and the Democrats had threatened to use the add-it-as-an-amendment-to-everything strategy, which would have wreaked havoc with the consideration of President Bush's program. Furthermore, Republicans knew that the cost of trying to stop campaign finance from being considered would be terrible publicity. So the Senate Republican leadership capitulated and agreed to bring it to the floor.

Why should majority party senators care if the minority is able to force votes on measures of its choosing so long as the majority has the votes to defeat them? Why are "tough" votes tough? My account of party strategy in the paragraph above and many similar analyses posit, though often implicitly, multiple goals, and their answers to those questions are based on conflicts among members' goals. Thus, the most common example of a tough vote would be one pitting a member's notions of good public policy versus her reelection goal; for example, for many Democrats, the bill fixing the Foreign Intelligence Surveillance Act in the manner the Bush administration wanted, which came to a vote in August 2007, presented exactly this dilemma. Both CPG and cartel theory posit members of Congress with multiple goals (see Cox and McCubbins 2005, 21), but neither really grapples with the theoretical or empirical implications of that assumption (see S. S. Smith 2007). Yet, as I discuss further below, doing so is essential to making progress in a theoretical understanding of party and party effects in the Senate—and specifically for an understanding of agenda control in the Senate.

The emphasis on negative agenda control in the cartel model has unfortunately led to questions about positive agenda control being underemphasized. Given the centrality in cartel theory of a party's reputation or brand and its tight relationship to the party's legislative record, one would expect that legislative productivity in some form would be crucial to the theory. To be sure, the passage of legislation that a majority of the majority opposes is likely to damage the party's reputation; if that bill actually becomes law, the majority of the majority suffers policy losses and, even if it does not, the vote reveals splits in the party that, presumably, make it look bad. But surely, constituents, party activists, and members themselves expect positive accomplishments as well. Cox and McCubbins argue that the size of the majority party's agenda is related to intraparty ideological homogeneity, a proposition consistent with CPG theory, but they do not develop the theory much in this direction, and not at all for the Senate.

In the House, positive and negative agenda control are closely related. The majority party leadership with the aid of the Rules Committee can bring any measure it desires to the floor for consideration; it can also refuse to bring (almost) any measure to the floor. Furthermore, the House's strict germaneness rules and the now typical highly restrictive rules from the Rules Committee prevent the minority party from getting its measures to a floor vote through floor amendments (Sinclair 2007). Of course, the majority party leadership needs a floor majority to approve special rules, and the minority's right to offer a motion to recommit with instructions, as well as the majority's desire to appear reasonably fair, mean that the majority leadership cannot completely prevent the minority from having any shot at altering legislation on the floor. Still, the House majority party leadership can usually structure floor consideration in such a way as to substantially advantage the majority party position (Sinclair 2002a).

In the Senate, the majority party's positive floor agenda-setting power consists of the majority leader's right of first recognition; that, as Smith also argues, enables the majority leader to make a proposal as to what to consider (2007, 77). If a minority objects to the proposed agenda, a supermajority is required to proceed to the item; once the measure is under consideration, it is subject to unlimited amendments, including in most cases non-germane amendments; if a minority objects to going to a passage vote, a supermajority is required to do so. To be sure, the majority leader has available various procedural tactics to counter some minority tactics; he can move to table amendments and that is a non-debatable motion; using his right of first recognition, he can fill the amendment tree, that is, propose amendments in all the parliamentarily permissible slots, and thus block other amendments. However, as long as there is a senator seeking recognition, he cannot get a final vote without first getting a supermajority. And, even if the majority leader knows he has the sixty-vote supermajority necessary to cut off debate, he still faces a cumbersomeness and time-consuming process to invoke cloture. A few important measures, notably the budget resolution and reconciliation bills, are protected from a filibuster by statute. Otherwise, however, a minority of forty-one or greater has the parliamentary power to prevent the majority from acting. The Senate majority party thus has limited positive agenda control. To be sure, the majority may sometimes be able to use extralegislative strategies—publicizing the minority's obstruction of a salient and widely popular measure, particularly—to get the minority to relent. But, so long as the Senate majority party actually wants to accomplish something, it usually has to negotiate with some minority party members and that means its negative agenda control is also limited. In negotiations, the cost of acquiescence by the minority is almost always going to be some accommodation of those members' policy preferences (Sinclair 2002b, 2008).

The Value of Organizational Control

So what then is organizational control of the Senate worth intrinsically, over and above the fact that it derives from greater numbers? Given the great effort that goes into attempting to gain or maintain organizational control, it is incontestable that senators believe it is of substantial value. The 107th Congress (2001–2) provided a quasi-experimental situation for shedding light on that question. The 2000 elections resulted in a fifty-fifty split in the Senate; the Republicans organized the

Senate because the vice-president gave them the tie-breaking vote; when Jim Jeffords of Vermont left the Republican Party in May 2001 and began caucusing, for organizational purposes, with the Democrats, control switched. Unfortunately, our only real world experiment was cut short by the 9/11 attacks, which changed the political environment drastically. Chris Den Hartog (2005) compared roll rates in the period of Republican control before Jeffords's switch and the period of Democratic control after the switch up to 9/11 and found that organizational control made a difference; the Democrats' roll rate fell when they took organizational control and the Republicans' roll rate rose with their loss of control even though the membership of the Senate did not change. As Den Hartog points out, organizational control is far from the whole story; even after they lost control, Republicans did quite well and better than Democrats had done when they lacked organizational control; Republican control of the presidency and of the other chamber likely affected roll rates.

Den Hartog's study certainly bolsters the case for the value of organizational control of the Senate; it does not, however, tell us much about the sources thereof. One of the problems he faces is simply the relatively small number of final passage roll calls in the periods he studies—twenty-six before the switch and eighteen after. The entire Senate floor agenda during those periods is, however, considerably greater, and a careful analysis of what was brought to the floor and how this changed with the change in control might well shed more light on the question at issue. In any case, we need much more attention to a careful analysis of floor agendas with special attention to, first, the extent to which an item is discretionary and, second, the extent to which the majority has controlled the drafting of the legislative vehicle. Some matters have to be brought to the floor; if the Treasury requests it, the majority leader must bring up a debt limit increase eventually; a new president's cabinet nominations are usually politically non-discretionary. Appropriations bills are also non-discretionary (though there is some leeway in the way they are packaged); more importantly, however, the content of the bills is, to some important extent, discretionary, as I discuss below.

The value of organizational control, at least as it pertains to the floor agenda, is generally believed to reside in the majority leader's prerogative of first recognition, which gives him the power to propose a floor agenda. Den Hartog and Nathan Monroe, in their "asymmetric-costs theory of legislative agenda influence" in the Senate, argue that majority party agenda influence in the Senate largely stems from such advantages the majority possesses that make it considerably costlier for the minority to influence the agenda in a way that affects outcomes (2006). It is certainly the case that to bring up minority party agenda items via non-germane amendments is costlier in terms of the procedural barriers that the proponents are likely to face; amendments can be tabled without debate, for example. Yet, to a large extent, the majority party's advantages depend on customs not rules. It is the set of expectations concerning floor scheduling that developed around the prerogative of first recognition that gives the majority leadership the initiative in floor scheduling. The consensus expectation in the Senate is that the majority leader, after broad and bipartisan consultation, sets the floor agenda; the minority party may balk in the bargaining process and block some agenda items the majority wants to consider; but the default expectation for the minority as well as the majority is that the majority leader takes the initiative in determining what comes to the floor when. The Senate floor scheduling system seems to be maintained primarily, not by rules, but by tacit agreement. To be sure, the majority party's greater numbers back up the arrangement; they make it fruitless for the minority leader to move to consider a measure, for example. Still the arrangement seems to lack a real enforcement mechanism; much of the time it works because most senators, including most members of the minority, have an interest in a reasonably orderly process that makes possible some legislative productivity. But like any arrangement that depends on voluntary cooperation, it is fragile. The 110th Congress (2007–8) provides an example of a large minority party with great incentives to use its prerogatives for obstruction; and the result was a mutual veto (Sinclair 2008; S. S. Smith 2007).

So getting a better handle on the value of organizational control in the Senate and perhaps also formulating a more fruitful strategy in our search for party effects may require more fine-grained analysis. The simplifications necessary for model building may have led us to underestimate the real world value of proposal power of the sort that the party with organizational control possesses. At most stages of the legislative process, that party (or members of that party) proposes the legislative language that becomes the basis on which bargaining then takes place; for example, the committee chair puts forward a tentative chairman's mark that may then be subject to behind-the-scenes negotiations with other members of the committee, including perhaps the ranking member, or that may be the vehicle the committee marks up; alternatively, the committee may be bypassed and the majority leadership may negotiate a draft to take to the floor, but the bargaining will also almost always be based on language with majority party origins. Because the vehicle can be amended in committee and, if the chamber under discussion is the Senate, on the floor, proposal power seems relatively weak in our models, but, in fact, much legislation is complex, and, in practice, amendments are likely to be offered, much less accepted, to only parts of the bill; much of the language is likely to remain intact. Appropriations bills are particularly good examples of the advantages. To be sure, an entire substitute can be offered, but senators who have participated in the negotiations and others who consider the bill better than the status quo are unlikely to vote for an unvetted version—"a pig in a poke." I am arguing that, in the real legislative world of limited time and information, the drafting of the base proposal, even if it is subject to negotiation and amendments at many later stages of the process, is a greater advantage than our current models suggest. So we should consider whether the opportunity to participate in the drafting of the base proposal and/or having it drafted by someone whose legislative preferences are similar to yours may provide senators' with a considerable motive for maintaining party organizations and for sometimes "going along" to assure party victory. I would hypothesize that that motive will be stronger the more like-minded the party membership is, as CPG might suggest. In a general way, this argument is consonant with cartel theory, just more nuanced; the benefits of organizational control are considerable but not unconditional as cartel theory implies.

Taking the Multiple-Goals Assumption Seriously

To make progress in a theoretical understanding of party and party effects in the Senate, we really need to take the multiple-goals assumption seriously. Assuming multiple goals unquestionably complicates the enterprise. Yet without doing so, our understanding of the Senate will remain not only woefully incomplete but in some ways just wrong. As I discussed above, "tough votes" only exist in a world of multiple goals; and, in such a world, senators are concerned not just with what passes but also what they have to vote on. Thus, agenda control is multifaceted and both majority party and minority party strategies are concerned with both. Of course, this also, then, raises questions about the interpretation of roll call votes. For example, what can we infer about the preferences of minority members from their support of final passage votes or conference reports? Presumably, that, all things considered, the member prefers the likely consequences of being publicly recorded as voting for the bill to the consequences of being publicly recorded as voting against the bill; that is, if we take a multi-goal perspective seriously as both CPG and cartel theory contend they do, we cannot be sure that the member preferred the *policy* outcome to the status quo. A member may dislike the policy but dislike the potential electoral consequences of voting against the measure more. And, of course, that is potentially true for members of the majority party as well as members of the minority party. As many scholars have pointed out, the problem of inferring "true" policy preferences from roll call behavior is severe.

For the minority party especially the reverse is also the case. A vote against a bill may not necessarily mean that members prefer the status quo to the bill on policy grounds but rather that they prefer the status quo on electoral grounds and that, in that instance, electoral considerations trumped policy considerations. A cursory analysis of recent congresses, and perhaps especially of the 110th, suggests that the minority party has shown limited interest in passing major legislation and, in fact and presumably for electoral advantage, seemed intent on blocking action so as to make the majority look incompetent. If that is so, it implies that the Senate minority party has its greatest influence when it is least interested in legislative outputs and, furthermore, that the benefits of organizational control vary with political context. In brief, the multiple-goals assumption when taken seriously changes both the potential costs and potential benefits of party organization and party leadership to members.

I am arguing that, for the Senate particularly, we need more nuanced theories; those theories need to take into account the limited but varied sources of majority party advantage, including, of course, influence over the floor agenda; they need to deal more adequately with the problems and mechanisms of maintaining a system dependent, to a considerable extent, on voluntary cooperation; and they need to truly incorporate in their logic the multiple-goals assumption.

CHAPTER 19

PARTY COALITIONS IN THE US CONGRESS:

INTRA- V. INTERPARTY

DAVID W. BRADY

COALITIONS or factions in and across congressional parties might seem a historical topic to a newly minted Ph.D. because, as David Rohde points out (Chapter 17 in this volume), the last twenty-five years in political science have documented the resurgence of parties in Congress. Prior to the rise of party voting in the US Congress in the mid- to late 1970s, political scientists focused on the construction of minimum winning coalitions (Riker 1962), transient policy coalitions forged by presidents across policy areas (Mayhew 1966; Bond and Fleisher 1990; Edwards 1983, 1989), and on the all-important cross-party Conservative Coalition (Manley 1973; Shelley 1983). We as a profession were not far from V. O. Key's admonition that congressional leaders were constantly maneuvering to build quixotic majorities in one policy area and then move to the next majority in the next area.

The rise of party voting in Congress and the strengthening of the party leader hands in appointing committees and in the respective caucuses meant that from the 1980s on, students of party and Congress focused on the causes and consequences of increased party strength in the US Congress. There are, if one queries JSTOR or Google, few entries in regard to "party coalitions in Congress" over the last twenty years. The use of party strength and party voting in Congress caused scholars to focus on party, not coalition, and to theorize about parties (Aldrich 1995; Cox and McCubbins 1993, 2005; Rohde 1991). These theories are reviewed elsewhere in this volume, so I shall not duplicate those efforts. Rather, I shall show in this chapter that scholars' focus on the nature of coalitions within the parties and across parties in the US Congress has been and is that such coalitions are ultimately based on a left–right ideological space. In order to show the policy effects, at times specific policy areas are used as examples. The organization of this chapter is to present some data that document the rise of cross-party coalitions prior to the Second World War and their fall post-1970s, the argument being that in the Second World War era, a cross-party coalition of southern and border state Democrats with Republicans known as the Conservative Coalition dominated legislative politics and that political science literature follows the patterns observed in the Congress. In the period prior to the partisan era, the intracoalitional nature of American parties was crucial. In the era of parties post-1970s, intraparty coalitions are now studied within the framework of preference-based theories of Congress. I finish the chapter by showing how preferences within and across the parties are important for understanding policy outcomes. Along the way, I will fail to cite much of the rich literature that deserves to be cited and read; however, given length constraints, it is not possible to do justice to all.

Party Theories and Preference Theories: The Implications for Coalitions

I begin by showing how party theories of Congress are distinct from preference theories and the implications for coalition theory for two-party systems. Figure 19.1 shows two distributions of preferences over ideology, ranging from left to right. In the top figure, the preferences of the parties do not overlap; thus, over the normal range of policy issues there will be no overlapping voting. In the lower figure there is an overlapping of preferences such that some members of the party of the left are more conservative than some members of the party of the right and vice versa. The dimensional conflict could be other variables such as cases where race and religion as well as ideology divide the parties. In cases where there is no overlap of preferences between parties, the parties could still be coalitional in that the party preferences cover a range, i.e., they are not located at the same policy point. Thus, some in the left party are more left than others, and the party could be said to be a coalition of Wets and Dries, à la Conservative Party in England,

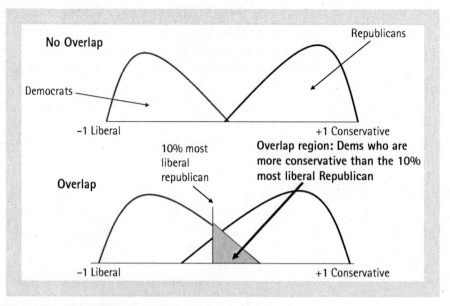

Figure 19.1 Determining partisan overlap in Congress

both pre- and post-Thatcher, or of moderate and liberal Democrats in the present Congress. Coalitions in this case would be intraparty. The same holds for the party of the right in the graphs.

Where party preferences overlap, it is clearly the case that there are intra- and interparty coalitions because the range of preferences within parties is sufficiently wide that some members of the conservative party are left of some members in the liberal party. The extent of the degree of overlap matters also in that the overlaps could be at the 10th, 25th, or 50th percentile and the number of cross-partisans matters. For example, it could be the case that 20 percent of the left party vote more conservatively than the 90th percentile of the right party and another 18 percent vote more conservatively than the 25th percentile of the party of the right. Surely this is more coalitional than a case in which there is no overlap or a case in which only 5 percent of the right party are more liberal than the 90th percentile of the left party. The point is that the larger the area of overlap and the more members overlapping, the greater the coalitional probabilities both within and across parties.

In this chapter, I will use a left–right ideological spectrum to describe coalitions in the US Congress, though I recognize that race, religion, and region all interact with ideology and in different ways over time.[1] Coalitions both within and between

---

[1] Pentecostals voted Democratic in the late nineteenth and early twentieth century, while blacks have voted Democratic since the 1960s. In each case, the religious and/or racial differences had important policy consequences for their time. I focus on the policy implications as expressed by a left—right continuum (Kleppner 1981).

parties in the United States are always present in US history. Given that in the US there are 100 state parties (fifty states × two parties in each) and that diversity exists both between states like Alabama and California and within states like California, American parties have always been relatively heterogeneous. In spite of this heterogeneity, I do not quarrel with Rohde's assertion that over time the parties have gotten stronger, and in voting behavior fewer, if any, bipartisan coalitions appear. Nevertheless, as the 2009 stimulus package showed, there was a necessary coalition of moderate Republicans and Democrats. Sixty to seventy years earlier, a coalition of southern and border state Democrats and northern Republicans could, and did, dominate the Congress. Thus, it is clear that coalitions matter across congressional history and that they wax and wane in composition and importance.

CONGRESSIONAL PARTY POLARIZATION IN HISTORICAL PERSPECTIVE

In this section, I focus on polarization over time, because the more polarized the Congress is (the more separate the parties), the less likely that scholars will study coalitional behavior in either voting behavior or public policy. The more that preferences between parties overlap, the greater the likelihood that coalitions affect behavior and policy. I believe this to be not inconsistent with both Rohde's (1991) and Aldrich's (1995) theory of parties and Cox and McCubbins's (1993) cartel theory of parties. That is to say, their theories allow for different policy positions within the congressional party. The question for both conditional party and cartel theory is how important are the decisions to party unity and thus to policy outputs. I begin with an analysis of overlapping voting behavior in Congress from 1870 to the present.

The origins and date of partisan voting in the US Congress are debated (Formisano 1969, 1974), but it seems clear by the time of Andrew Jackson and Martin Van Buren (1828–40) there was in place a two-party system that connected citizen votes with which party ran Congress and that members voted with their party often (Holt 1999). However, even in this highly competitive party system, there were coalitional aspects to the two parties: Whigs and Democrats. Each party had a southern and a northern wing that divided over the question of slavery, with northerners, to one degree or another, opposed to slavery in the North. The ultimate demise of the Whig Party came when Congress passed the Kansas–Nebraska Act, which dismantled the old slavery line and generated a new northern party, the Republicans (Holt 1978). In short, parties in the United States were diverse and coalitional at a very early period in US history.

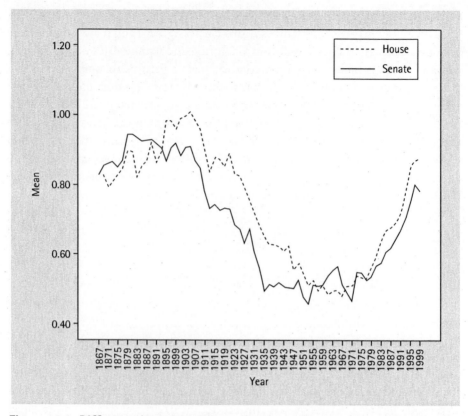

Figure 19.2 Difference in party medians, House and Senate, first-dimension DW-NOMINATE scores, 1867–1999

Throughout most of United States congressional history, parties in the House and Senate have been relatively polarized. Figure 19.2 plots the difference between Republican and Democratic party medians, as measured by first-dimension DW-NOMINATE scores in both the House and the Senate (Han and Brady 2007).[2] In both chambers, party polarization peaked in 1895 and plummeted to its lowest level in 1947 and the early 1950s.[3] The return to polarization in the final decades of the twentieth century does not look as unusual when placed in this historical context. The party differences during this era are lower than they were in the late nineteenth century. Instead, what becomes clear is that the era of bipartisanship in the immediate post-Second World War era is the unusual era in American history

[2] This graph is similar to one found in Shickler (2000) and measures ideological distance between the parties as measured by Poole–Rosenthal scores.

[3] It is worth noting that the difference between party medians in the Senate was consistently lower than the House from the late 1800s to the early 1950s. In addition, a relatively large decline in the difference between party medians in the Senate occurs in the early 1930s and persists through the 1950s.

and a period where you would expect scholars to study coalitions and bipartisanship.

The unique features of partisanship in the 1950s are highlighted by an alternative measure of polarization that examines the degree of overlap between the two parties. Parties can either be polarized, with high levels of internal cohesion and low levels of intraparty overlap, or they can be convergent, with low levels of internal cohesion (wider distributions) and high levels of intraparty overlap. Figure 19.1 presented two hypothetical models of partisanship. In the top figure, the two parties are relatively polarized, with very little overlap between them; there are very few Republicans who overlap with the more conservative Democrats and vice versa. In contrast, the bottom figure depicts considerable overlap between the two parties. Although the most liberal Democrats and the most conservative Republicans remain distinct from each other, partisanship in the middle of the two-party distribution is indistinct. The more conservative Democrats look quite similar to the more liberal Republicans, and the more liberal Republicans look like the more conservative Democrats.

I use two different measures of ideology: first-dimension DW-NOMINATE scores (1867–1999), and Americans for Democratic Action (ADA) scores (1947–99). Both ranking systems rate the liberalism (or conservatism) of elected officials based on their roll call voting records. Using these scores identifies how liberal or conservative members were relative to other members of their party, by identifying the cut points for the 10 percent, 25 percent, and 50 percent (the median value) most conservative Democrats, and the 10 percent, 25 percent, and 50 percent most liberal Republicans. The bottom of Figure 19.1 shows the hypothetical placement of the cut point for the 10 percent most liberal Republicans on a DW-NOMINATE scaling. In this case, the most conservative Democrats are more conservative (with higher ideological rankings) than the 10 percent most liberal Republicans. The shaded area shows the area of overlap. By identifying these cut points, one can observe the number of members from the opposite party who fall into the overlap region. In other words, how many Democrats are more conservative than the 10 percent most liberal Republicans? And how many Republicans are more liberal than the 10 percent most conservative Democrats?

As an example, in 1947 (80th Congress), the most conservative 10 percent of Democrats had DW-NOMINATE scores higher than 0.10. To identify the degree of overlap with Republicans, I counted the number of Republicans who had DW-NOMINATE scores lower than 0.10. Figures 19.3 and 19.4 show the degree of overlap for the House and Senate in each Congress from 1867 to 1999 for both DW-NOMINATE scores, while Figure 19.5 shows ADA scores for the 1947–95 time period.

These graphs demonstrate an unprecedented level of overlapping voting in both the House and the Senate in the immediate post-Second World War era. Looking at the distributions of DW-NOMINATE scores, it becomes clear that there was almost no House party overlap prior to the 1940s. In the Senate, there was some overlap in

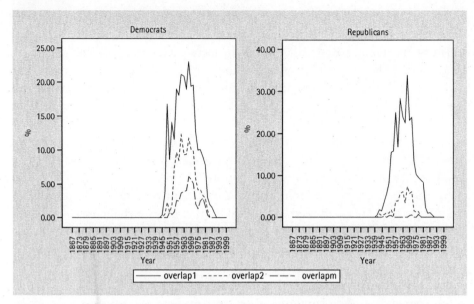

Figure 19.3 Partisan convergence in the House, DW-NOMINATE scores, 1867–1999

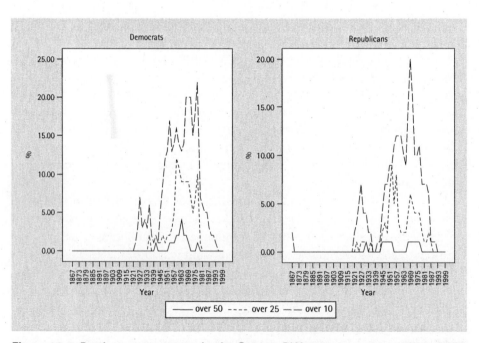

Figure 19.4 Partisan convergence in the Senate, DW-NOMINATE scores, 1867–1999

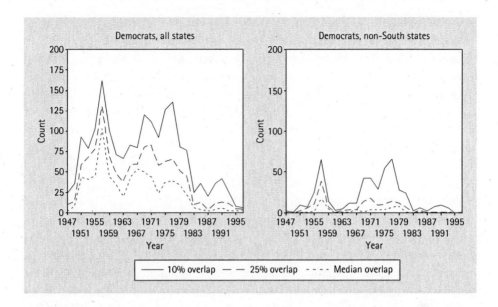

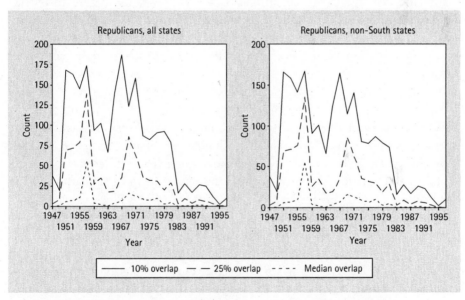

Figure 19.5 Partisan convergence in Congress, ADA scores, 1947–95

the 1920s and the 1930s, but it was relatively mild compared with the immediate post-Second World War era. By the 1940s and 1950s in both the House and the Senate, the degree of partisan overlap spiked upwards. By 1947, almost 45 percent of House Democrats were more conservative than the 10 percent most liberal Republicans. The numbers peaked around 1963, when over 55 percent of House Democrats were more conservative than the 10 percent most liberal House Republicans, and almost a third of Democrats were more conservative than the 25 percent most liberal Republicans. Ten percent of House Democrats were more conservative than even the median Republican member of the House. Among Republicans, levels of overlap grew sharply between 1947 and 1955, and persisted at high levels until the early 1970s when the number of members in the overlap region began to decline. In the Senate, the numbers were highest in the late 1960s. In 1969, 19 percent of Democrats were more conservative than the 10 percent most liberal Republicans, and 19 percent of Republicans were more liberal than the 10 percent most conservative Democrats. This level of overlap persisted through the late 1970s, when it began to decline in both chambers, and lasted in weaker form through the 1980s. This result confirms Roberts and Smith (2003), Rohde (1991), and others who find that for both parties in the House, polarization (or low levels of partisan overlap) reemerges in the 1980s. Using ADA scores shows the same general pattern of post-Second World War bipartisanship, with the rise of partisanship occurring in the 1970s and increasing thereafter. Looking only at non-southern states to see if the partisan overlap was merely an artifact of one-party politics dominant in the South before the civil rights movement shows that although the degree of overlap decreases among Democrats, the mid-twentieth century still emerges as a unique period of high partisan overlap. Among Republicans, the finding is that high levels of partisan overlap persist even when the southern states are taken out of the analysis.

Two important points emerge from this examination of historical patterns of polarization in Congress. First, the patterns of polarization in the House and the Senate have been markedly similar throughout most of history. This is true using several other measures of partisanship, including party voting scores (e.g., Rohde 1991; Hurley and Wilson 1989) and party unity scores (e.g., Hurley, Brady, Cooper 1979). By all measures, historical trends in the Senate are quite similar to those in the House.

During the period of cross-partisan voting, coalitions in Congress often crossed party lines, signaling that there was, especially within the Democratic congressional party, a heterogeneous set of interests over policy matters. On racial matters, from the 1880s to the late 1950s it was not possible to pass laws against segregation or even anti-lynching laws, because the congressional Democratic Party split along geographical lines (Shelley 1983). Legislation in regard to labor unions was hard to pass because, again, the Democratic Party was split between pro-union northern representatives and right-to-work southern states (D. Brady and Bullock 1980). The Conservative Coalition was widely viewed as having stopped the second part of the New Deal from becoming law; thus, civil rights, healthcare, union legislation, aid to secondary education, and other liberal legislation lay blocked. After the war, political scientists began to study Congress from a behavioral rather than a legal historical viewpoint. Part of the new set of studies focused on the nature of coalitions in Congress, both within and across parties. Manley (1973), Shelley

(1983), and others showed how the Conservative Coalition thwarted New Deal legislation (Polsby 2004). Stevens, Miller, and Mann (1974) and others documented the rise of the Democratic Study Group in Congress. This group was founded in 1958 after the northern Democrats gained seats in the 1958 congressional elections. Their purpose was to push liberal legislation through the US Congress; i.e., to have a majority sufficient to defeat the Conservative Coalition.

The political science profession began the post-Second World War era with the famous American Political Science Association Committee on Political Parties study (American Political Science Association 1950), which admonished the United States to create responsible parties. Subsequent work by Turner (1952) and Ranney (1962) among others showed that given the heterogeneity of American parties, we could not expect to have responsible political parties à la Great Britain. Burns (1963) and Clark (1964) among others viewed the Congress as having four-party politics, with each party having a presidential–progressive wing and a congressional–local-interest conservative wing. The result of all the interests in the US Congress, according to them, was a policy stalemate. In short, the empirical or behavioral study of Congress concluded that congressional parties were heterogeneous as coalitions within party, and thus not responsible in the British sense.

On the less ideological side of research, William Riker published his influential *The Theory of Political Coalitions* (1962), which advanced three propositions for political coalition. They are: first, the size principle (minimum winning coalition); second, the strategic principle, where representatives move toward minimum winning; and third, the selective elimination of participants to the coalition. This work generated a plethora of additional scholarship on whether or not there were minimum winning coalitions, and when they should appear.

The size principle was applied to the US Congress (Shepsle 1974; Hinckley 1972; Riker and Niemi 1962), showing how coalitions shift more than bloc-voting theory would predict. However, as late as the mid-1980s, political scientists were arguing about how to interpret congressional history in terms of the rise and fall of coalitions among the parties and factions. Hammond and Fraser (1983) analyzed various coalitions in Congress against the probability that such a coalition could occur by chance. In sum, post the Second World War, from 1945 to somewhere in the 1970s, was characterized by the cross-partisan Conservative Coalition and the study of coalitions, à la Riker, largely free of party. Sometimes the focus was on policy areas such as federal aid to education (Buchanan 1962), civil rights, and agriculture (Mayhew 1966), but in most cases the coalition was cross-party. When cross-party coalitions are dominant, it is clear that the within-party heterogeneity is significant; otherwise there would be no crossover voting.

In parliamentary systems like Japan and Britain, the intraparty differences between factions in the parties are worked out before the legislation is introduced. We cannot tell from voting where preferences lay, since all Labour votes one way and Tories the other. In short, there could be considerable differences within the party, as in the Wets and Dries in Margaret Thatcher's time, and we would never observe said differences in voting behavior. This point is important because as congressional parties began to cohere internally and separate spatially in voting, it became more difficult to identify coalitions or factions within parties.

THE IMPORTANCE OF INTRAPARTY DIFFERENCES IN A PARTISAN AGE

Rohde (in Chapter 17 in this volume) rightly shows that the last twenty-five years have changed our perception of whither party. Somewhere in the late 1970s, the tide began to turn and congressional voting became partisan and polarized, and this real-world shift, first documented by Rohde (1991) and Poole and Rosenthal (1987, 1991), gave rise to at least three major works on political parties in Congress. David Rohde's (1991) conditional party government, John Aldrich's *Why Parties?* (1995), and Cox and McCubbins's (1993) cartel theory of parties are summarized elsewhere in this volume so I will not duplicate that effort. Suffice it to say that the increased partisanship in Congress gave rise to studies documenting the rise and various causes of such partisanship. In spite of the rise in party voting in Congress, it seems clear that there is still a diversion of viewpoints within each congressional party. In the contemporary Congress, it is clear that senators Arlen Specter (Pennsylvania) and Susan Collins and Olympia Snowe (both Maine) do not hold the policy views of fellow Republican Senator Saxby Chambliss (Georgia). In the Democratic congressional party, the moderate Blue Dogs in the House of Representatives do not share all of Speaker Pelosi's policy positions. How should we interpret this diversity of opinion within parties in an era when party voting has dramatically increased?

Contemporary political science, unlike its forebears, does not see this phenomenon (or talk about it) as coalitional or factional in nature. Rather, the basic model began from the rational choice view that preferences are the basics and one summarizes the preferences. Since Arrow (1951), we have known that summarizing preferences into a majority or social welfare function is not easy, given reasonable conditions. Solving this problem in majority legislative bodies requires institutions (Shepsle 1979) and is beyond our scope herein, although it is clear that party strength affects how Congress is organized (Cooper and Brady 1981). Our purpose is to show how the ranking of preferences across legislators is how contemporary political science deals with the old issue of coalitions and factions in parties. Figure 19.1 showed the distribution of preferences to be spread across a party of the left and right. Figure 19.6 shows these preferences over two parties, where the preferences are over minimum wages. In Figure 19.6A, the parties don't overlap. In Figure 19.6B, the parties overlap. Suppose that the Democratic Party has members ranging from a preference of a minimum wage of $8 an hour (in A) to $16 an hour, whereas Republicans range from $2 to $6 an hour. If all of the Democrats in the $8–10 range come from southern and border states, while all of the Democrats in the $14–16 range are from New York, Massachusetts, and California, it is easy to see how factions might be described. It does not matter if the members' preferences are induced by the electorate or privately held; it only matters that they have preferences. In Figure 19.6A we could have strictly polarized party voting within a policy range from $8 to $16. That is, we would have to know members' preferences in order to know that the passage of a $12.50 minimum was a roughly median party vote. Since we do not have access to members' preferences in such detail, we do not know for certain that $12.50 is the median, only that it is greater than any Republican favors (no crossover vote).

Given the empirical data that since the 1980s we have returned to partisan, polarized voting, identifying preferences within party has been the main vehicle for identifying coalitions or factions in parties. Because we cannot know preferences as easily as in the minimum wage example, evidence for or against the exact nature of coalitions in parties is secondary, not direct. Krehbiel (1998) and Brady and Volden (1998, 2006) take up this issue of preferences. Krehbiel's positive analysis features supermajority institutions, the veto and Senate Rule 22, to show that policy can be shifted toward pivotal institutional players who by definition are not median voters. Implicitly, his analysis provides for factions or coalitions, in that preferences

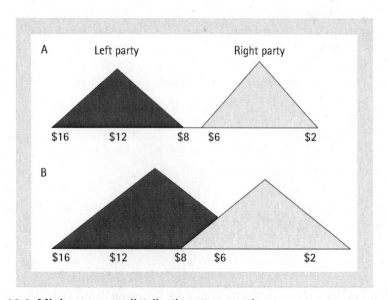

Figure 19.6 Minimum wage distributions over parties

dominate party. Specifically, it is the sorting process, where most liberals are Democrats and conservatives are Republicans, that leads us to attribute to party what is preference. Brady and Volden use roughly the same premise that representatives and senators are distributed across an ideological space, with most Democrats left and most Republicans right. Policy is the result of the status quo policy space relative to the median voter and the supermajority pivots, e.g., the sixtieth senator on a filibuster.

Coalitions or factions within parties as measured by preferences consist of putting together a majority based on members' preferred policy. Take Figure 19.6, for example. The Democrats could take any position from $8 to $16 on minimum wage policy. The range of preferences $8 to $16 defines the coalitional space but does not tell us what the number will be. The most obvious number to choose is somewhere around $12 because that is the median and theory tells us that policy should be there. However, policy could be at $16 or $8 with, say, presidential influence, e.g., the president converts representatives favoring $8 to $14 to vote for $16 by offering them side payments on other issues. If the coalition is, as was the old Southern Bloc in the US Congress, consistent over time on some basic issues like race, right-to-work laws, and federal aid to education, then the coalition exists over time and is called a coalition or faction.

Some coalitions are quite fleeting. Ferejohn (1974) showed the durability of pork barrel coalitions, and Hansen (1991) documents the declining influence of agriculture in Congress as the country turned urban and farms became bigger and more efficient. Subsidies to agriculture were under duress until the agriculture interests joined with urban districts needing food stamps. The rural–urban coalition had the votes to preserve subsidies and expand food stamps. This coalition, while covering only one policy area, is, nevertheless, a coalition that is identifiable over time.

Other coalitions, like the coalition favoring the North American Free Trade Agreement, exist only for a brief moment, are created out of necessity, and disappear after passage (D. Brady and Volden 2006, 126–8). Other potential coalitions do not form, and the legislation or policy around which the coalition forms does not pass. Universal healthcare coverage has been on the American agenda since 1948, yet it is still not national policy. In 1993, President Clinton came to power promising universal healthcare coverage. The failure to build a winning coalition on this issue has been widely written about (Broder and Johnson 1997; J. Hacker 1997; among others) and the causes for failure are described in widely varying ways.

Those who study Congress from a preferences position have a simple view. The legislation was simply too costly if universal coverage was included, which meant that moderate Democrats could not vote for it. The plan being drafted by a centrist coalition, including Moynihan (Democrat, New York) and Chafee (Republican,

Rhode Island), dropped universal coverage and was moving toward attaining a majority by increasing the numbers insured within budgetary limits (D. Brady and Buckley 1995) but ran out of time in 1994 and, with the new Republican majority, their compromise was not brought forward.

The examples of coalitions in and across parties have ranged from the relatively permanent through one-time coalitions, to coalitions not being majority and losing. In each case, the point is that the coalition's success (its size) depends upon the policy area and where the policy is located. The old Conservative Coalition blocked liberal legislation from 1938 to 1965 when, during the Great Society period, the second half of the New Deal was enacted over their objections. The Coalition fought on for a few years, but as electoral politics in the South changed, they disappeared (E. Black and Black 2002) because they could not turn the clock back on race and the other issues they had formed around. The agricultural interests lost power over time (J. Hansen 1991) and had to form a new coalition with urban interests to maintain subsidies. Likewise, President Clinton, who campaigned against NAFTA, had to work hard to bring enough Democrats to pass the bill. Health care failed because it cost too much and, thus, could not bring along moderate Democrats. Note that in each case, as the policy position shifts, new members are added or lost, depending upon the direction of the shift on a left–right dimension. Preferences of members as the basis for understanding coalitions within and between parties allow us to analyze how policy shifts determine coalition size and composition. What follows is a brief description of changes in coalitions from Reagan to the present, where I use examples to show the decline of cross-party coalitions over time.

CHANGING COALITIONS IN AN AGE OF PARTISANSHIP

The Reagan victory in 1980 brought a Republican Senate but maintained a Democratic House. Reagan proposed cuts in spending plus a 30 percent tax cut over three years and a $50 billion increase in defense spending. The House Democrats led by Dan Rostenkowski (Democrat, Illinois) proposed smaller cuts, a one-time tax cut of 10 percent, and a smaller military increase. Both sides turned to the Democratic Forum (the predecessor of today's Blue Dogs), led by Representative Kent Hance (Democrat, Texas), since they would determine the majority. In the end, Hance with Barber Conable (Republican, New York) carried a bill that cut taxes 25 percent and indexed them to inflation. Sixty-three southern and border Democrats voted for the tax cuts. On expenditures which are harder to defend, a smaller number went with Reagan, roughly forty-five, and he got neither the cuts he wanted nor the full defense buildup. Note that the southern-led Democratic Forum was crucial to passing Reagan's major proposals; note also that where the policy was located as well as the policy area determined success.

The victory of George H. W. Bush in 1988 came with a promise of no new taxes, yet given the deficit of $161 billion that Bush proposed in 1990, Democrats passed by 218 to 208 (without a single Republican vote) a budget resolution that increased taxes more than it cut spending. Given differences between Bush and the Democrats on the budget, the two sides came up with a compromise bill with taxes higher than Bush wanted and cuts in expenditures greater than the Democratic leadership wanted. This compromise was supported by the Republican and Democratic House leadership. Nevertheless, the legislation generated a new coalition, the Newt Gingrich (Republican, Georgia)–Ron Dellums (Democrat, California) coalition, a conservative–liberal coalition that defeated the compromise bill. Republican conservatives voted no because taxes were raised, and liberal Democrats voted no because expenditures were cut. In addition to policy causes for the bill's failure, Jacobson (1993) showed there was also an electoral connection; i.e., the closer your race, the greater the vote against the bill.

This interpretation of events from 1980 to 1993 is not unique. Charles Stewart (1991, 163–4) and Matthew McCubbins (1991) tell much the same story. Other work in regulatory policy (Romer and Weingast 1991) and welfare policy (Ferejohn 1991) share the same view that the tax and budget policies of this period were driven by first partisan and then cross-partisan (in the House) voting coalitions featuring conservative Democrats and pro-tax cut Republicans with liberal Democrats and conservative Republicans ready to join together if tax cuts were too high and expenditures too low. Finding a winning coalition depended on where the policy was set, and the balance was delicate.

The Clinton years were more of the same, with the first unified government in twelve years (1993–5) failing to generate the change hoped for, owing to a coalition of moderate to conservative Democrats and Republicans. The next six years produced divided government (1995–2001) in which the Republicans essentially failed to deliver on their Contract With America owing to the moderate Republicans in the Senate voting with the Democrats across a set of issues. The Clinton era gave the country welfare reform and a prosperous economy, but it did not yield universal health care, gays in the military, a renegotiated NAFTA, a China not in the World Trade Organization, and so on. Nor, after 1995, were any of the Republican promises fulfilled. One reason was that the differences between the parties had sharpened, and there were fewer centrists with whom to compromise.

Over time, the country was sorting out ideology and party electorally. Prior to the rise of partisanship in Congress there were liberal Republicans like Nelson Rockefeller (New York) and conservative Democrats like Richard Russell (Georgia). Reagan's victory began a sorting out whereby Democrat and liberal, on the one hand, and Republican and conservative, on the other, became more correlated. In short, over time the possibility for cross-partisan voting diminished because there were fewer conservative Democrats and liberal Republicans around. Black and Black (2002) and Han and Brady (2007) describe this process. The important point is that by the end of George W. Bush's presidency in 2008, there were very, very few districts represented by cross-party potential (see Fiorina and Levendusky 2006).

George H. W. Bush was not successful with his 1990 compromise budget, in which taxes were raised, and President Clinton lost or had to modify his positions in his first two years as president. The result of these policy failures was the Republicans controlling the Congress after the 1994 elections for the first time since 1954. The combination of sorting parties meant that the number of opposite party members with Democratic or Republican preferences declined. In the aftermath of the 1994 elections, the sorting continued with fewer Republicans in the northeast and fewer Democrats in the southern and border states. The result is that by the 111th Congress, the possibility of bipartisan coalitions comparable to the post-Second World War era was, for all practical purposes, non-existent. President Obama sought a $900 billion stimulus package and, true to his campaign promises, he sought bipartisan support, shooting for eighty Senate votes. However, given the sorting which results in polarization, he got only three of forty-one Republican votes. The increase in partisanship has now evolved into polarization, a situation where the parties are more internally consistent and spatially separated (see Nivola and Brady 2006). Obama's accomplishment of getting three moderate Republicans to support his stimulus plan cost him over $100 billion from the House proposal but was the best he could do, given the lack of moderates in the Republican party, because there were fewer conservative to moderate Democrats and moderate Republicans around. The 1994 election was the turning point in this process, as the Democrats who lost were largely from conservative districts (Canes-Wrone, Brady, and Cogan 2002), thus enhancing the sorting process. The sorting process has continued over time.

The sorting in electoral districts meant that there was less room for bipartisan coalitions in the Bush presidency. The Bush 2001 and 2003 tax cuts garnered far fewer Democratic votes than did Reagan's twenty years earlier. The original attempt by George W. Bush to transcend partisanship early in his presidency (e.g., recall No Child Left Behind) soon yielded to what Gary Jacobson described as the Great Divider (2008). During the 2008 election, candidate Barack Obama pledged to be a uniter also and, true to his word, in early 2009 he set about trying to woo Republicans to support his stimulus package. He met with congressional Republicans, invited them to the White House, and, in general, was serious in his attempt to garner cross-party support for his stimulus package. The effort was fruitless in the House of Representatives, as he failed to gather a single Republican vote. Some moderate Democrats (Blue Dog Democrats) voted against the package, and one from a moderate Chicago area district, Dan Lupinski, voted present. In the Senate, President Obama, as stated earlier, got three moderate Republicans to support the stimulus package, although at a cost of another $100 billion reduction from the House stimulus bill. In short, in spite of serious efforts to win broad support across parties for his policies, the rational prediction is that if he is successful on health care, cap and trade, and other significant policies, it will not be with broad-based congressional support. The rise of partisanship so richly documented elsewhere in this book allows a conclusion that there are fewer moderates and centrists with whom to coalesce. Thus, what passes will be mainly driven by partisan consider-ation, and the debate will occur largely within the Democratic Party between its liberal and moderate wings.

INTRAPARTY AND INTERPARTY COALITIONS IN THE FUTURE

The decline of bipartisan voting coalitions over time does not mean that biparti-sanship has disappeared; rather, it means that it has taken on new forms. First, as Francis Lee clearly shows, divisive roll calls have become more prominent over time (Lee 2008, 242). These ideological cleavages persist over time and are often brought up so as to show the parties as clear alternatives to each other. This is consistent with what Cox and McCubbins (1993) mean by party brands, i.e., the issues that distinguish one party from the other. The rise in the number of roll call votes featuring these brand issues automatically decreases the number of votes where bipartisanship is present.

There are, of course, other issues before Congress that are largely distributive in nature (Lee 2008). If we look at procedural and brand issues, it is the case that bipartisanship is not present. However, if we look at areas such as transportation and agriculture, we see significant bipartisan voting behavior (Brady, Ferejohn, and Harbridge 2008) on these geographic and distributional issues. Further proof of this point is given by looking beyond the Poole, Rosenthal, and/or Americans for Democratic Action scores, which are polarized by party. If we turn to look at voting scores such as those produced by the National Taxpayers' Union (NTU), the National Farmers' Union (NFU), the AFL–CIO Committee on Political Education (COPE), and the League of Conservation Voters (LCV), we find on NTU, COPE, and LCV concerns, which are brand issues, voting overlaps between parties have declined from the 1960s. Cross-partisan voting on the NFU issues shows no trend over time and frequently measures 50 percent overlap (Harbridge 2009). Thus, bipartisanship still exists in some areas for fairly obvious constituent-driven reasons. We as a profession should be clear what we mean by partisanship and polarization and recognize where cross-partisanship works and where it does not. Ultimately, I believe that the origins of coalitions lie in constituent preferences and that some distributions of party over preferences yield intraparty coalitions while other distributions yield interparty coalitions.

Partial proof for the assertion that coalitional possibilities reside in the electoral connection lies in the findings of Harbridge (2009). Over the 1973 to 2006 time period, safe seats in the Congress increased 50 percent, while bipartisan co-sponsorship of legislation declined at a similar rate. That is, members from competitive seats are far more likely to co-sponsor legislation with members of the other party than are members from safe seats. Members from districts where the parties are evenly divided have all but disappeared in the House. However, members from such districts, e.g., Lupinski (Democrat, Illinois), will vote differently (present on the stimulus package in 2009), sponsor more bipartisan legislation, and, in general, do what is necessary in a mixed district to be reelected. Other scholars have shown that district characteristics determine intra- and interparty coalitions (Kanthak and Crisp 2005). Here it is interesting to note that because senators represent more heterogeneous constituencies than the House, they continue to be the main source of bipartisan behavior. The Senate did not pass much of Clinton's early liberal policy, e.g., Clinton's proposal to integrate gays into the military, and they rejected the more liberal House reconciliation budget in 1993. When the Republicans took over in 1995, it was the Senate which scuttled the Republicans' Contract With America. In 2009, it was the Senate where President Obama got what little Republican support was needed for the stimulus, and it came from Republican senators representing Democratic states that voted Democratic in 2008.

The increase in partisanship and polarized voting in the Congress in the late 1970s and 1980s was recognized first by Rohde (1991), and the literature in political science turned to documenting the causes and rise of party rating in Congress, and to theorizing about political parties rather than coalitions. Present-day literature is starting to show that bipartisan coalitions still exist, albeit less in voting than in new forms, such as co-sponsorship. This mild corrective to the party movement should leave us as a profession with a clearer picture of the relationship between elections, the distribution of preferences over party, and the policy coalitions that can be formed, given the distribution. The focus on bipartisan coalitions and co-sponsorship should be continued and an emphasis on intraparty coalitions as faction should be encouraged in order to get a more complete picture. The nature of preferences within and across parties clearly affects how the majority party moves legislation to the floor and what subsequently passes. Much of the emphasis on rules and procedures in the Congress is the result of the distribution of preferences within parties, and scholars have begun to investigate these complex connections. There is no resolution at this point; however, Schickler and Pearson

(2008), Oppenheimer and Hetherington (2008) and Gailmard and Jenkins (2008) stand as very interesting attempts in this direction. Ultimately, the nature of preferences and the factions, coalitions, and parties they generate is to be found in the relations between elections and preferences in Congress. Until we have more definitive research in this area, the dispute over which is dominant, preferences or parties, will remain a central question.

CHAPTER 20

....

THE PRESIDENT, PARTY POLITICS, AND CONSTITUTIONAL DEVELOPMENT

....

SIDNEY M. MILKIS
JESSE H. RHODES

THE relationship between the president and the parties has never been easy, though its dynamics have varied over the course of American political history. The architects of the Constitution established a non-partisan president who, with the support of the judiciary and Senate, was intended to play the leading institutional role in checking and controlling "the violence of faction" that the framers feared would rend the fabric of representative government. Even after the presidency became a more partisan office, its authority continued to depend on an ability to remain independent of party politics, especially during national emergencies such as the Civil War and the Spanish–American War (Ketcham 1984). Indeed, the institutional imperatives of the executive appear at first glance to be inherently at odds with the character of political parties. Party organization seems better suited to legislative bodies, which have a collective action problem, than to an executive dedicated to vigorous and expeditious administration. Presidents can best display their personal qualities "above party," Wilson Carey McWilliams observed. By contrast, "Congress cannot be effective, let alone powerful, without the institution of party . . . A legislature can rival the executive's claim to public confidence only to the extent that it is accountable, which presumes a principle of *collective* responsibility" (McWilliams 1989, 35).

Nonetheless, presidents and parties need each other. By the 1790s, Thomas Jefferson and his Republican allies attacked the original constitutional presidency, which Alexander Hamilton and the Federalist Party championed, as an agent of "consolidation" that would create an unacceptable divide between the government and society. By enmeshing the president in a localized party system, those who adhered to Jeffersonian principles hoped to avoid the unified and energetic executive envisioned by Hamilton and thereby create a presidency "safe for democracy." A principal role for presidents in formulating policies and carrying them out would make the more decentralized and republican institutions—Congress and the states—subordinate, thus undermining popular sovereignty. Parties were formed during the first three decades of the nineteenth century to hold the constitutional presidency accountable to a highly decentralized and fiercely competitive party system that relentlessly organized and mobilized the American voter (Milkis 1999, ch. 2).

Presidents thus became dependent on parties, both in campaigning and governing, to shore up their electoral fortunes in a political culture highly resistant to centralized administration. Even presidential quests for independence have required the support of party. Throughout American history, but especially in the twentieth and twenty-first centuries, presidents have needed the support of their partisan brethren in Congress to establish institutions and programs that secured authority to exercise executive power autonomously. At the same time, parties have relied on presidential candidates and presidents to convey a coherent message and to infuse their organizations with energy. From the 1830s to the 1890s, the highly localized parties found their strength principally in the political combat of presidential elections—a battleground that encouraged Democrats and Whigs in the antebellum period and Democrats and Republicans after the Civil War to overlook their differences in the interest of victory. Parties became more dependent on presidents in the twentieth century as campaigns became more focused on national candidates. Even so, presidents continued to represent their parties' ideals and principles to the nation.

Although a combination of principle and strategy has created a degree of symbiosis between presidents and parties, the relationship has frequently been tense. Before the New Deal, presidents who sought to exercise executive power expansively, especially in the service of centralized administration, were thwarted "by the tenacity of [a] highly mobilized, highly competitive, and locally oriented democracy" (Skowronek 1982, 40). With the consolidation of executive power during the 1930s and 1940s, the president, rather than the Congress or the party organizations, became the leading instrument of popular rule—in Theodore Roosevelt's capacious phrase, "the steward of the public welfare." Many scholars thus viewed the rise of the modern presidency in the wake of the Great Depression and

Second World War as signaling the end of an old institutional order based on decentralized political control and the beginning of a permanent ascendance of national, non-partisan executive administration (see A. Schlesinger 1949). The birth of the modern presidency and the decline of traditional localized parties better equipped the federal government to carry out vital tasks at home and abroad; at the same time, this development appeared to portend an era of chronically low public engagement and voter turnout and an increasingly fractious national politics (Lowi 1985; Milkis 1993; Shea 1999).

The erosion of old-style partisan politics, however, allowed for a more national and issue-based party system to develop, forging new links between presidents and parties. Republican presidents, like Ronald Reagan and George W. Bush, dedicated themselves to building a national party organization that might mobilize popular support for, and devote governing institutions to, a new conservative political order. Allied to an assault on the liberal administrative state, the formation of a national Republican party seemed to provide a new presidential leadership synthesis and a "new" party system (Milkis and Rhodes 2007a). Although Bush's party leadership ultimately became an albatross for the Republican Party in the 2008 election, the experience suggests that vigorous presidential leadership in the present configuration of executive and party has the defects of its virtues. In the hands of an overweening executive, the party may simply become a means to the president's end, sapping the organization of both its autonomy and its ability to adapt to changing political circumstances.

The emergence of an executive-centered party system thus does not promise a return to pre-modern party politics; rather, it indicates a re-articulation of the relationship between the presidency and the party system. The traditional decentralized parties, nourished by the patronage system, acted as a gravitational pull on presidential ambition. The new national parties, sustained not only by the national party committees but also by advocacy groups, think tanks, the mass media, and use of the Internet to raise funds, recruit volunteers, and mobilize voters, encourage presidents to advance bold programs and policies. The "new party system" is prone to rancorous conflict, but partisan clashes over domestic and foreign policy have aroused the interest and increased the participation of the American people in elections. Without question, the rise of more national and programmatic parties deprives partisanship in the United States of some of the tolerance that hitherto has made party loyalty so compatible with the pluralistic traditions in American politics. It may be, however, "that a politics more clearly tied to principles and ideals is more appropriate to the current stage of our national life" (Reichley 1985b, 199).

Whatever its consequences, there is reason to suspect that the national structure of the party system—and a politics that privileges national issues and conflicts—will endure. Although the Democrats have renounced the fierce partisanship that the White House and Republican Congress practiced during the first six years of the Bush presidency, many liberal public officials and strategists have expressed more than grudging admiration for the effective party building that has buttressed partisan rancor in the nation's capital. The 2008 election made clear that Barack Obama and the Democrats learned a great deal from the political tactics employed by the Republicans, exceeding their fundraising and grassroots successes. More to the point, given the way national parties have abetted executive ambition, earnest presidential party leadership is likely to be an important feature of American politics for the foreseeable future.

PRESIDENTIAL LEADERSHIP AND THE RISE OF THE MASS PARTY SYSTEM

The critical and uneasy relationship between the American presidency and political parties sheds light on the central question of the American constitutional experiment: whether it is possible to realize self-government on a grand scale. This was the question that divided the Federalists and Anti-Federalists; and it was revisited in the constitutional struggles between the Jeffersonian Republicans and the Hamiltonian Federalists. As formed during the first three decades of the nineteenth century, political parties reflected the concern first expressed by Anti-Federalists, and later revised by Jefferson, that the Constitution provided inadequately for the cultivation of an active and competent citizenry. The Anti-Federalists were not fond of partisanship, but like their Jeffersonian descendants, they viewed political parties as the most practical remedy for the erosion of confidence between rulers and ruled. Localized political associations could provide a vital link between constitutional offices, especially the executive, and the citizenry, thereby balancing provincial liberties and the national government strengthened by the Constitution of 1787 (Storing 1981; Borowiak 2007).

Significantly, Madison, the principal architect of the "Constitution-against-Parties," became a defender of parties and local self-government during the critical battles between the Republicans and Federalists (Hofstadter 1969, 40–121). Alexander Hamilton's success as Washington's secretary of treasury in strengthening the executive led Madison to recognize that the Anti-Federalists might have been more correct in their criticisms of the Constitution than he previously had thought. By the early 1790s, he joined Jefferson in opposition to the Federalists, in the formulation of a party program of government decentralization, and, consequently, gave birth to the American party system (Joanne B. Freeman 2001; Ketcham 1984; Ferling 2004; Edling 2003).

"Out of this original clash" between the Federalists and the Republicans, James Piereson has written, "there developed in America the tension between party politics, on the one hand, and governmental centralization and bureaucracy, on the other" (Piereson 1982, 51). This tension contributed significantly to the fracturing of the Jeffersonian Republican Party and, eventually, to the welding of a formal two-party system to the Constitution. In the wake of the war of 1812, which dramatically exposed the limitations of Jeffersonian Republican principles, Madison recommended several measures to solidify the national resolve, including the chartering of the Second Bank of the United States. In fact, to facilitate the development of the domestic economy, the so-called National Republicans, led by the powerful Speaker of the House, Henry Clay, advanced an ambitious program later known as the "American System" that included a protective tariff, government supervision of public land distribution, and the construction of public works (Larson 2000; Jensen 2003). With the selection of the ardent nationalist John Quincy Adams to the presidency in the controversial election of 1824, an incipient administrative state began to take shape, a development which appeared to restore the non-partisan character of the executive branch. For these proto-state builders, "the founders' bold experiment in republican government was open-ended, and the central government a progressive, developmental force" (John 2003, 56).

The task of fending off the National Republicans' administrative ambitions fell after the 1824 election to more traditional Republicans, such as Martin Van Buren of New York. The outcome of this election, in which Adams was selected by the House of Representatives, even though Andrew Jackson had more popular and electoral votes, persuaded Jacksonian reformers that the Constitution's vulnerability to centralized administration had not been corrected by Jeffersonian democracy. Adams's selection of Clay, who orchestrated his victory in the House, as secretary of state, and the president's first State of the Union address, which proposed an active role for the federal government in the economy and society, further aroused the controversy. With the weakening of the national party structure, Van Buren lamented, a system of personal and local factions displaced the "common sentiment" that had upheld republican principles, thus favoring the champions of "consolidation" (Van Buren 1867, 4–6).

The Jacksonian ambition to revitalize partisanship gave rise to the Democratic Party. Styling themselves as "old Republicans," Democratic party leaders, as Van Buren put it, sought "to redraw anew and . . . reestablish the old party lines" (Van Buren 1827). The Federalists and National Republicans, dedicated to strengthening national power and proscribing popular rule, did not need a popular party rooted in the states and localities to advance their program. They sought to center government responsibility in the executive, which would cultivate and maintain the support of commercial interests through the disbursement of bounties, licenses, and tariffs. In this way, the executive would wed commercial interests to state power—and develop, in turn, a stable commercial republic. In contrast, Van Buren argued, the orthodox Republicans, and their heirs, the Democrats, stood in need of "an extraneous force to secure harmony in its ranks." The Jacksonian Democrats intended to organize public opinion in support of government decentralization. Dedicated to the tradition of local self-government, and to the provincial liberties that supported it, the Republicans would be successful, Van Buren counseled, as long as they had the prudence to "employ the [party] caucus system . . . and to use in good faith the influence it is capable of imparting to the popular cause" (Van Buren 1867, 4–6).

Jefferson and his supporters established a wall between the national government and the states; Jacksonian democracy fortified this barrier, which was breached by the National Republicans. The Jacksonian ambition to make partisanship part of the "living Constitution" was embodied by the Democratic Party, which organized voters on the basis of principles that were militantly decentralizing, as was the very process of party politics they established. The Jeffersonian emphasis on legislative supremacy comported with national parties, which rested on the nomination of presidential tickets by the congressional caucus. With the collapse of "King Caucus" after 1824, presidential tickets were soon nominated by national conventions, which were dominated by state party organizations. Moreover, although patronage appointments were not uncommon during the Jeffersonian era, the Jacksonians exalted the practice of "rotation in office" into a political creed and exploited positions in the widely scattered post offices and custom houses to recruit party footsoldiers and to raise campaign funds (McCormick 1986; Summers 1988).

Ostensibly, the national party organization gave presidents a source of political authority that was independent of the Congress. Indeed, scandalized by the way the legislative caucus and Congress rebuffed the popular Jackson in the notorious 1824 election, Democrats sought to make the president the "tribune of the people" (Korzi 2004; Laracey 2002). President Jackson is often credited with anticipating the modern presidency by establishing a direct relationship with the American people and by declaring, in his nullification proclamation, that secession was treason and the Union perpetual (Remini 1967; Stampp 1980, 33–5). Nonetheless, Jackson's powers were inextricably linked to a party dedicated to a program that "significantly weakened the organizational capacities of the central government" (John 2003, 65). After his election in 1828, Jackson withdrew the federal government from the realm of internal improvements, reduced the size of the military, held down government expenditures, dismantled the hated Bank of the United States, and reinvested its deposits in state banks. As such, the strengthening of the presidency during Jackson's stay in the White House "mobilized the powers of the government for what was essentially a dismantling operation" (Meyers 1957, 29).

By 1840, the Whigs, the political party committed to expanding the economic and social responsibilities of the national government, embraced the decentralizing practices of nomination by convention and the "spoils system" first championed by the Jacksonians. Although the Whigs' adoption of Jacksonian principles was in part a strategic effort to avoid the fate of the Federalists, they also had an appreciation for the critical role parties had come to play in maintaining the local democratic liberties of the nation's citizens. Indeed, Whigs claimed that as the party that championed legislative supremacy they, not the Democrats, were the true heirs of Jefferson.

Even the rise of the Republican Party during the 1850s as a result of the slavery controversy, and the subsequent demise of the Whigs, did not alter the essential characteristics of the party system in the United States, and these characteristics—decentralized organization and hostility to administrative centralization—restrained rather than facilitated executive power. The failure of Reconstruction was attributable in no small part to the Republicans' diffidence in the task of "state building," so much so that the self-styled modern reformers who emerged at the end of the nineteenth century overwhelmingly viewed party politics as an obstacle to their ambition to construct a modern state on American soil.

PROGRESSIVE DEMOCRACY AND THE DECLINE OF THE PARTY STATE

The decentralized party system did not always constrain presidential ambition. Indeed, Washington apart, all of America's "reconstructive leaders" have used parties to remake American politics in their own image, to "reset the very terms of constitutional government" (Skowronek 1997, 38–9). But political parties kept these presidents faithful to broader interests, even as they gave executives the political strength to embark on ambitious projects of national reform. More tellingly, presidents who have come to power during resilient political orders have been bounded by party organizations and practices that constrained presidential prerogative.

This was especially so following the upheaval of the Civil War. Since most Republicans were former Whigs, they stood for legislative supremacy. Fearful of what Lincoln accomplished during the Civil War in consolidating executive power, Republicans in Congress moved forcefully to constrain the executive after he was assassinated. Before the rise of the primary system and mass media in the twentieth century, parties controlled nominations of candidates for office as well as the general election contests. This party influence extended to Congress as party leaders—the Speaker of the House and the majority leader of the Senate—gained control over the committees, the real legislative policymaking bodies. Congress, therefore, strengthened itself as an institution and moderated the scuffle of local interests to which it was prone. So empowered by Republican principles and disciplined party organizations, Congress, as the political scientist Woodrow Wilson declared, was "unquestionably, the predominant and controlling force, the center and source of all motive and all regulative power" (Wilson 1956, 31).

Even at the height of party government, however, the late nineteenth-century polity witnessed the stirrings of new forms of presidential leadership and significant alterations in partisan practices that would eventually become institutionalized and regularized during the New Deal. Late nineteenth-century presidents, such as Hayes, Garfield, and Cleveland, struggled to rejuvenate executive independence, most notably on matters of staffing the departments and agencies, fighting bruising battles with Congress over appointments and using the Pendleton Act, enacted in 1883, to establish a foothold for a merit-based civil service. Moreover, beginning with the unsuccessful campaign of Samuel Tilden in 1876 and intensifying with William McKinley's successful effort in 1896, presidential candidates began to experiment with more candidate-centered, media-driven campaigns that denigrated traditional party labels and practices (McGerr 1986, 70; Troy 1996, 82–107; Klinghard 2005).

These presidential efforts to carve out greater autonomy were reinforced by broader political developments. Starting in the late 1880s, reforms in the states had resulted in the advance of the secret or official ballot; the adoption of registration requirements; the growth of civil service reforms; and the introduction of the direct primary in state, local, and congressional elections. These measures, combined with the emergence of mass circulation newspapers and magazines, independent of the traditional party press, had begun to weaken the grip of party organizations on candidates, government institutions, and the loyalties of voters (Reynolds 2006).

In an important sense, the late nineteenth century represented a way station between traditional partisan politics and the executive-centered polity of the twentieth century. Just as surely, this brief interregnum appeared to confirm the inherent tension between executive administration and the American party system. Indeed, the Progressive reformers who became prominent at the dawn of the twentieth century could not abide localized party democracy. Progressives perceived that the concentration of wealth brought on by industrialization—symbolized by the giant "Trusts"—threatened American democracy by undermining the right of individuals to earn a living. To Progressives, local party leaders, corrupted by big business, were complicit in this development. Progressives saw little possibility of converting the existing party machinery into an instrument for the realization of their national program. Like the National Republicans of the early nineteenth century, their goal was to restore the national character of the Constitution, to emancipate national administration from the constraints and corruption of localized parties. Many Progressives championed strengthening the federal bureaucracy to rein in the "Trusts" and advocated social welfare measures that would protect Americans from the tyranny of unbridled capitalism.

Progressive reformers elaborated the innovations that had begun to transform the relationship between the presidency and parties into a comprehensive program of political and constitutional reform. Viewing parties as the linchpin of corruption and injustice, Progressives advocated "direct democracy" in the form of women's suffrage and direct election of senators, as well as measures such as the direct primary, initiative, referendum, and recall that would forge direct ties between the government and public opinion. This commitment to national administration and direct democracy became the centerpiece of Theodore Roosevelt's Progressive Party campaign of 1912, which was sanctified as a "covenant" to make the people "masters of their Constitution."

The brief, but significant, experience of the Progressive Party underscores how progressive democracy could not be reconciled with the development of a strong party organization. With the celebrated TR as its candidate, the Bull Moose Party won 27.4 percent of the national popular vote and eighty-eight electoral votes from six states in 1912. This was extraordinary for a third party, the largest percentage of the popular vote ever achieved by a third party candidate for the presidency. Despite its remarkable showing in 1912, the Progressive Party was dead four years later, its fate inseparable from the charismatic leader who embodied its cause. Still, the Progressive Party lies at the very heart of fundamental changes in the relationship between the president and the parties. The personalistic quality of Roosevelt's campaign was part and parcel of these changes, but they went much deeper than his desire to regain past political mastery. The Progressive Party, with its leader-centered organization, accommodated and embodied an array of reformers—insurgent Republican office-holders, disaffected Democrats, crusading journalists, academics and social workers, and other activists—who hoped that the new party coalition would realize their common goal of expanding the responsibilities of the federal government and making it more responsive to popular economic, social, and political demands. Public opinion, Progressives argued, would reach its fulfillment with the formation of an independent executive power, freed from the provincial and corrupt influence of political parties (see Milkis and Tichenor 1994; Milkis 2009).

Many contemporary scholars point to the apparent contradiction between Progressives' celebration of direct democracy and their hope to achieve a more powerful, executive-oriented government (Rogers 1982; Wiebe 1995, ch. 7). But Progressives hoped to recast the constitutional presidency into an agent of social and economic reform. As Roosevelt described this concept of executive power, the president was "a steward of the people bound actively and affirmatively to do all he could for the people, and not content himself with the negative merit of keeping his talents undamaged in a napkin" (Roosevelt 1926, v. 20, 347). During his tenure as president, Roosevelt had made important efforts to fulfill this new understanding of executive power (see P. Arnold 2003). TR used his authority under the Pendleton Act to extend merit protection to approximately 60 percent of the civil service and thus establish a bulwark of administrative competence within the executive. Roosevelt also persuaded Congress to pass such measures as the Hepburn Act of 1906, which strengthened the Interstate Commerce Committee's authority to regulate the railroads in the public interest and set a major precedent for subsequent national state building. These policy ends were pursued through direct presidential appeals to public opinion and the mass media that heralded the emergence of the "rhetorical presidency" (Tulis 1987).

Woodrow Wilson, the victor of the 1912 election, would further extend Roosevelt's legacy. As the Democratic candidate in 1912, Wilson adhered to his party's commitment to decentralized administration, attacking the Progressive Party for proposing to create a bureaucratic agency to regulate unfair business practices. But Wilson's first term, the *New Republic* celebrated, "waxed increasingly paternalistic, centralizing, and bureaucratic" (*New Republic* 1916, 103). Wilson accepted the idea of a regulatory commission with broad responsibilities for overseeing business practices, resulting in the creation of the Federal Trade Commission in 1915. Wilson also persuaded the Democratic Congress to enact the Federal Reserve Act in 1913, which established a board to oversee the national banking and currency system. In each case, Wilson overcame the Democratic Party's traditional antipathy to national administrative power, suggesting that with the growing prominence of presidential candidates, party leaders in Congress were willing to sacrifice programmatic principles to win the White House (James 2000; Ware 2006).

Wilson also sought to further emancipate the presidency from party politics by strengthening the rhetorical presidency, most notably, reviving the practice, abandoned by Thomas Jefferson, of appearing before Congress to deliver important messages, including the State of the Union address. With the rise of the mass media, Wilson believed, such occasions would help concentrate public attention on the actions of the president and Congress. He recognized that the president now "stood at the intersection of party organization and national popular opinion and, if he was willing to assume the charge, could harness each to great national effect" (James 2005, 19).

To militant reformers, Wilson's full conversion to Progressive principles appeared to mark the triumph of a new political order. In his prosecution of the First World War, however, Wilson revealed that the promise of modern executive leadership also portended dangerous possibilities. Most Progressives believed that "the righteous use of superior force" in world affairs was even more critical than were battles for reform at home. Wilson's war message to Congress clearly linked the country's entry into the European fray as the fulfillment of progressive democracy. "The world must be made safe for democracy," the president stated in a famous phrase. Only total war would advance the cause of self-government, "achieve the ultimate peace for the world and for the liberation of its peoples, including the German peoples," who were suffering under the Prussian autocracy (Link 1984, xli. 519–27). Unmoored from the moderating effects of party, however, Wilson's idealistic rhetoric was joined to a plebiscitary politics that ultimately undermined civil liberties.

To convey his war aim—"to make the world safe for democracy"—to the American people, Wilson formed the Committee on Public Information (CPI), which enlisted 75,000 speakers, to "persuade" the American public that the war was a crusade for democracy against Germans, a barbarian people bent on world domination. The CPI and a number of self-styled patriotic groups sought to discourage and sometimes repress dissent. People who refused to buy war bonds were often ridiculed, and some were even assaulted. Those with German names, scorned as "hyphenate Americans," were persecuted indiscriminately. Wilson championed repressive legislation such as the Espionage Act of 1917, which imposed fines and jail sentences for persons convicted of aiding the enemy or obstructing military recruitment, and the Sedition Act of 1918, which made "saying anything" to discourage the purchase of war bonds, or "utter[ing], print[ing], writ[ing], or publish[ing] any disloyal, profane, scurrilous, or abusive language" about the government, the Constitution, or the uniforms worn by soldiers and sailors, crimes (Capozzola 2008). Socialist leader Eugene Debs, who received 6 percent of the popular vote in 1912, was sentenced to ten years in jail for making an antiwar speech. Ironically, a socialist, dedicated to nationalizing the means of production, he became the champion of natural rights. In his statement to the court, Debs scorned the Sedition Act, which he charged was in "flagrant conflict with democratic principles and the spirit of free institutions."[1]

The dire threat new nationalism posed to sacred freedoms—eventually led to a strong backlash against reformism, first in the defeat of Wilson's League of Nations Treaty, and then in the 1920 election. Republican Warren Harding was elected calling for a "return to normalcy." Riding the wave of his landslide victory, which in important respects marked a referendum on the modern presidency, the Republicans resumed power in March 1921, militantly determined to rehabilitate constitutional sobriety, rugged individualism, and party organization to their former stature. The 1920s did, in fact, revive certain features of the old order. But the Great Depression and the Second World War gave Franklin D. Roosevelt and a revamped Democratic Party the opportunity to resurrect Progressive democracy in a new, more familiar, suit of clothes.

THE FLOWERING OF THE MODERN PRESIDENCY AND THE TRANSFORMATION OF THE AMERICAN PARTY SYSTEM

The decisive break with the decentralized party system came with Franklin D. Roosevelt in the 1930s and his deft reinterpretation of the "liberal tradition" in the United States (Hartz 1955). Liberalism had always been associated with the natural rights tradition of limited government drawn from John Locke's *Second Treatise of Government* and the Declaration of Independence. Roosevelt pronounced a new

---

[1] Eugene Debs, Statement to the Court upon being convicted of violating the Sedition Act, Sept. 18, 1918, <http://www.wfu.edu/~zulick/341/Debs1918.html>.

liberalism in which constitutional government and the natural rights tradition were not abandoned but were linked to programmatic expansion and an activist federal government. This new liberalism presupposed a fundamental change in the relationship between the presidency and political parties, albeit one that seemed more consonant with traditional American values and institutions than had new nationalism.

Roosevelt first spoke about the need to modernize elements of the old faith in his Commonwealth Club address, delivered during the 1932 campaign and appropriately understood as the New Deal manifesto. The theme was that the time had come—indeed, had come three decades earlier—to recognize the "new terms of the old social contract." It was necessary to rewrite the social contract to take account of the national economy and the concentration of economic power. With the adoption of a new compact, the American people would establish a countervailing power—a stronger national state—lest the United States steer a "steady course toward economic oligarchy." Protection of the national welfare must shift from private citizens to the government; the guarantee of equal opportunity required that individual initiative be restrained and directed by national administration. As Roosevelt put it in a well-considered phrase, "The day of enlightened administration has come" (Roosevelt 1938–50, i. 751–2).

The task of modern government, FDR announced, was "to assist the development of an economic constitutional declaration of rights, an economic constitutional order." The traditional emphasis in American politics on individual self-reliance should therefore give way to a new understanding of individualism, in which the government acted as a regulating and unifying agency, guaranteeing individual men and women protection from the uncertainties of the marketplace. These new rights were never formally ratified as part of the Constitution, but Roosevelt's effective, well-timed use of the rhetorical presidency ensured they became the foundation of political dialogue. In the wake of the Roosevelt revolution, nearly every public policy was propounded as a right, attempting to confer constitutional status on programs like Social Security, Medicare, welfare, and food stamps. With the advent of the New Deal political order, an understanding of rights dedicated to limiting government gradually gave way to a more expansive understanding of rights, a transformation in the governing philosophy of the United States that required major changes in American political institutions (Melnick 1989).

The modern presidency thus became part of the living constitution, not as the steward of the people, but, rather, as the guardian of new rights. As became all too clear during Wilson's tempestuous second term, the Progressive dream of national responsibility portended an unvarnished majoritarianism that threatened the Constitution's promise to protect individual freedom from the vagaries of mass opinion. The New Deal understanding of reform, however, appealed more directly to the American constitutional tradition by asserting a connection between nationalism and "programmatic rights." Roosevelt gave legitimacy to Progressive principles by embedding them in the language of constitutionalism and interpreting them as an expansion of the natural rights tradition.

No less than the Progressive creed, however, the new understanding of the Declaration of Independence required an assault on the established party system, which had long been allied with constitutional arrangements that favored a decentralization of power. This effort to weaken traditional party organization, begun during the Progressive era, became an enduring part of American politics with the consolidation of the New Deal political order. Nonetheless, Roosevelt's attack on partisanship was more ambivalent than that of his Progressive predecessors. Indeed, Roosevelt and his New Deal political allies, many of whom experienced first-hand the short-lived Progressive Party, recognized that the Democratic Party was a critical means to the creation of the administrative constitution they envisioned.

In part, Roosevelt hoped to overcome the state and local orientation of the party system, which was suited to congressional primacy and was poorly organized for progressive action by the national government, and establish an executive-centered party, more suitably organized for the expansion of national purposes. Roosevelt's administration modified traditional partisan practices in an effort to make the Democratic Party, as FDR put it, one of "militant liberalism" (Roosevelt 1938–50, vii. xxxi). This, in turn, would bring about a structural transformation of the party system, pitting a reformed Democratic Party against a conservative Republican Party.

The most dramatic moment in Roosevelt's challenge to traditional party practices was the so-called purge campaign of 1938. This involved FDR directly in one gubernatorial and several congressional primary campaigns in a bold effort to replace conservative Democrats, particularly conservative southerners, with candidates who were "100 percent New Dealers" (Stokes 1940, 503).

This extraordinary effort to remake his party was anticipated and attended by other important initiatives. For example, FDR and his New Deal political allies won a hard-fought battle to eliminate the "two-thirds" rule, which required a candidate to receive two-thirds of the convention delegate votes in order to win the party's nomination. After 1936, Roosevelt used political patronage to reward New Dealers rather than Democrats associated with the traditional party machinery, thus deploying an "ideological patronage" that further abetted the party's national, programmatic character (Van Riper 1958, 327). The administration also worked to expand the Democratic coalition to incorporate new groups and social movements, especially labor, African Americans, and women (Milkis 1993, ch. 3).

The Roosevelt administration's challenge to traditional partisan practices initiated a process whereby the party system evolved from predominantly local to national and programmatic organizations. And yet by recasting and giving political effect to progressive principles, the New Deal also made partisanship less important. Roosevelt's partisan leadership, although it brought about important changes in the Democratic Party, envisioned a personal link with the public that would enable the president to govern from the position as leader of the nation, not just the party that governed the nation (Frisch 1975, 79). Following the example TR set at the Progressive Party convention, FDR accepted the 1932 Democratic nomination of his party in person, setting a precedent within the two-party system and signaling the emergence of presidential campaigns conducted less by parties than by individual candidates. Like Wilson, Roosevelt rejected the Jeffersonian tradition that prohibited presidents from delivering important messages before Congress. With Roosevelt's 1933 State of the Union address this practice became an enduring routine—an annual ritual that, with the rise of the mass media, encouraged presidents to make direct appeals to public opinion. Indeed, exploiting the growing importance of radio broadcasting, FDR used his famous "fireside chats" to speak more directly and frequently to the people than any previous occupant of the White House. Finally, as the "purge" campaign exemplified, Roosevelt frequently chose to make a direct appeal to public opinion rather than attempt to work through or to reform the regular party apparatus.

The "benign dictatorship" Roosevelt sought to impose on the Democratic Party was more conducive to corroding the American party system than to reforming it. The emphasis FDR placed on forging a direct link between himself and the public reflected the Progressives' lack of faith in party politics and a deliberate attempt to supplant collective responsibility (based on the give and take between the president and Congress) with executive responsibility. The immense failure of the purge campaign reinforced this view (Milkis 1993, ch. 4). More to the point, Roosevelt and his political allies did not view the welfare state as a partisan issue. The reform program of the 1930s was conceived as an "economic constitutional order" that should be established as much as possible in permanent programs, like Social Security, beyond the uncertainties of public opinion and elections. Unlike the Progressives, who sought to weaken the judiciary's institutional power, FDR's controversial "court-packing" plan and judicial appointments presumed to transform the way the federal courts interpreted the Constitution, to codify the development of an executive-centered administrative state (McMahon 2003).

Similarly, the most significant institutional reform of the New Deal did not promote party government but fostered a program that would establish the president as the guardian of an expanding national state. This program, as embodied in the 1937 executive reorganization bill, would have greatly extended presidential authority over the executive branch, including the independent regulatory commissions. The president and executive agencies would also be delegated extensive authority to govern, making unnecessary the constant cooperation of party members in Congress. Ironically, the administrative reform bill became, at Roosevelt's urging, a party government-style "vote of confidence" for the administration. Roosevelt initially lost this vote in 1938, when the reorganization bill was defeated in the House of Representatives, but he did manage to keep administrative reform sufficiently prominent in the party councils that a compromise version passed in 1939.

With the 1939 Executive Reorganization Act, Roosevelt's extraordinary crisis leadership was, in effect, institutionalized. This statute ratified a process whereby public expectations and institutional arrangements established the president, rather than Congress or political parties, as the center of government activity. The reorganization act represents the genesis of the "administrative presidency," which was equipped to govern independently of the constraints imposed by the regular political process (Nathan 1983). The Roosevelt administration's civil service reform solidified this program to replace partisan politics with executive administration. Through executive order and legislation, Roosevelt extended merit protection to thousands of New Deal loyalists, most of whom had been brought into government outside of merit channels (Milkis 1993, ch. 6).

The modern presidency's independence from party politics was greatly augmented by the Second World War and the Cold War. With the Great Depression giving way to war, another expansion of presidential power took place, further weakening the executive's ties with the party system. As the New Deal prepared for war, Roosevelt spoke not only of government's obligation to guarantee "freedom from want" but also of its responsibility to provide "freedom from fear"—to protect the American people, and the world, against foreign aggression. This obligation to uphold "human rights" became a new guarantee of security, which presupposed a further expansion of national administrative power (Roosevelt 1938–50, ix. 671–2). The forces of internationalism allowed Harry Truman to persuade Congress to carry out additional administrative reform in 1947, which increased the powers of, and centralized control over, the national security state. Dubbed the National Security Act, it created the National Security Council, the Central Intelligence Agency, and the Department of Defense (Shefter 2002, 123).

THE ADMINISTRATIVE STATE AND THE "NEW" PARTY SYSTEM

The consolidation of the modern presidency during the 1930s and 1940s transformed the executive office dramatically, with profound consequences for American democracy. Presidents no longer ran for office and governed as the head of a party; instead, they campaigned and sought to enact programs as the head of personal organizations they created in their own image. These institutions carried out tasks party leaders and organizations once performed, such as staffing the executive branch, connecting the president to interest groups, formulating public policy, and directing campaigns. Perhaps most importantly, the presidential staff played a critical part in enabling the president to communicate with the people. Roosevelt was not only the first president to make effective use of the radio, he also was the first to make extensive use of surveys and pollsters, thus giving the president information about what the people were thinking and how they were responding to his program (Milkis 2002; Eisinger and Brown 1998; on modern presidents' use of polling, see Jacobs 2005).

The emancipation of the presidency from the traditional constitutional order by anchored localized parties gave rise to "potentialities and pathologies" (James 2005, 25). On one hand, the modern executive allowed for a more expansive national state that responded effectively to domestic and international crises. Absent an independent executive, it is difficult to imagine the federal government possessing the national resolve to tackle disruptive economic insecurity and forced segregation at home or fascism and communism abroad. On the other hand, the rise of the modern presidency and the administrative state risked the recrudescence of the political diseases that reared their ugly head during the Progressive era: a plebiscitary politics in which effective and responsible leadership was dependent on the accident of personality; a tendency for presidents to rely extensively on unilateral executive action that denigrated Congress and encouraged corrosive interbranch conflict; and a serious decline in public interest, trust, and participation in government and politics. Indeed, the flowering of the modern presidency raised the fundamental question of whether a distant president, no matter how perspicacious, can forge meaningful links with the public.

The promise and the limitations of the modern presidency came into full relief when Lyndon Johnson assumed the office. Roosevelt's pronouncement of two new freedoms—Freedom from Want and Freedom from Fear—proclaimed and began the task of establishing the executive as the guardian of an administrative constitution, but it fell to Johnson to "codify the New Deal vision of a good society" (Rovere 1965, 118). This program entailed expanding the economic constitutional order with such policy innovations as Medicare, Medicaid, and, even more importantly, extending those benefits to African Americans. It also required upholding liberal internationalism's "containment" policy as the Cold War metastasized into a protracted struggle to control the development of Third World countries in Southeast Asia.

Johnson's attempt to fulfill the promise of the modern presidency accelerated the effort to transcend partisan politics. LBJ took Roosevelt's experience to be the best example of the generally ephemeral nature of party government in the United States, and he fully expected the cohesive Democratic support he received in Congress after the 1964 election to be temporary. Moreover, Johnson's greatest programmatic achievement, the enactment of the 1964 and 1965 civil rights bills, created considerable friction between the White House and local party organizations, especially in the South. Thus, Johnson, like Roosevelt, looked beyond the party system toward the politics of "enlightened administration."

The early years of the Johnson presidency marked the historic height of presidential government. Equally importantly, the civil rights acts enlisted the president and several executive agencies in an ongoing effort to ban racial discrimination. These laws empowered the federal bureaucracy—especially the Department of

Justice, the Department of Health, Education, and Welfare, and the newly formed Equal Employment Opportunity Commission—to assist the courts in successfully creating enforcement mechanisms for civil rights (see Milkis 1993, chs. 7 and 8; Milkis 2008). At its height, however, liberalism fractured. Since the 1930s, Democratic presidents had emphasized administrative politics that had reduced their dependence on traditional party organizations and practices. By the end of the 1960s, executive aggrandizement was giving way to a battle over how to use the national administrative power forged on the New Deal and the Great Society. With the enactment of the Voting Rights Act of 1965, Johnson ensured the transformation of southern Democracy that had eluded FDR. Civil rights reform emancipated the Democratic Party from its most conservative wing. But this gain in doctrinal consistency came at the price of weakening the Democratic coalition, ultimately driving a majority of southern white voters into the Republican Party and sharply reducing the size of the southern Democratic congressional delegation. Moreover, the Voting Rights Act substantially increased the number of black voters in the South, thus assuring that those seats that remained in Democratic hands would tend to be much more liberal than those representatives who balked at Roosevelt's "court-packing" and executive reorganization plans.

The transformation of Southern politics, fueled by deep division over race, was reinforced by the Johnson administration's decision to expand the American troop commitment in Vietnam. Not only did this action accentuate the isolation of the White House from Congress and the public, but it also further fractured the liberal coalition. The Vietnam War drove many younger middle-class liberals to oppose executive prerogative in foreign affairs. Meanwhile, southern whites, as well as other formerly strong Democratic constituencies such as northern Catholics, supported Republican presidents who were inclined to use US military power (Shefter 2002, 124–5). These developments dramatically changed the New Deal party system, preparing the ground for the rise of more national and programmatic parties. With the rise of a "new" party system, moreover, the modern executive became complicit in heated partisan conflicts that both renewed and dramatically transformed the relationship between presidents and parties.

RONALD REAGAN AND THE STIRRINGS OF A "NEW" PARTY SYSTEM

Ronald Reagan was the first modern president to pose fundamental challenges to received government arrangements, a stance that required the support of a national, programmatic Republican Party. Swept into office on principled opposition to the New Deal and Great Society, it was thus fitting that he would also initiate important changes to the relationship between the presidency and the political parties. In addition to reinvigorating the Republican Party's hostility to the liberal administrative state, Reagan would invest in the GOP's organizational and fundraising capacity, suggesting that modern presidential leadership was not inconsistent with party building. Nonetheless, conceiving of the modern presidency as a two-edged sword that could cut in a conservative as well as a liberal direction, the Reagan White House emphasized popular appeals and administrative politics that ultimately undermined collective responsibility.

Reagan's administrative partisanship was not created out of whole cloth; it resorted to some of the same tactics that Richard Nixon and his staff had first deployed. Like Nixon, Reagan centralized power in the White House, thus preempting the Republican Party organization's political responsibilities; like Nixon, too, Reagan pursued his programs with acts of administrative discretion that weakened efforts to carry out broad-based policy programs. Reagan's rhetoric and executive administration were more purposeful than Nixon's, and tended to please conservative stalwarts. Still, the centrality of presidential politics and policymaking highlighted the White House's failure to make a compelling public case for a *Republican* realignment or a fundamental reshaping of liberal programs. Reagan thus left an ambivalent legacy of presidential party leadership that would prefigure George W. Bush's subsequent experience.

Reagan's basic message was that centrally administered government demoralized and enervated its citizenry (Heclo 2003; McAlister 2003; Berman 1990; Muir 1988). In the context of the late 1970s and early 1980s Reagan's rhetorical assaults on the liberal administrative state and his paeans to individual responsibility were powerful party-building maneuvers. The president's forceful oratory altered the national political agenda, placing Republican issues such as tax and budget cuts, defense spending, and traditional morality at the center of American politics, and consolidated linkages between the Republican Party and constituencies such as southern whites, suburbanites, union workers, and Catholics (Beck 1988; Ginsberg and Shefter 1990; Busch 2001, ch. 5). These developments permitted Republicans to dominate presidential politics during the 1980s and early 1990s and forced the Democrats to accept fundamental departures from liberal orthodoxy. Bill Clinton, the Democrats' presidential standard bearer during the 1990s, recurrently sought the center during his presidency, championing welfare reform, free trade, government "reinvention", and accountability in education (see Skowronek 1997; Wilentz 2008).

Reagan's rhetorical leadership was coupled with unusual attention to the exigencies of party leadership. Building on efforts by Republican Party leaders in the 1960s and 1970s, Reagan encouraged the further improvement of the party's organizational and fundraising capacity (Klinkner 1994, 133–54). His efforts to ensconce allies in the Republican National Committee (RNC)—particularly his pick of Richard Richards for the RNC chairmanship—proved to be a boon for the party, strengthening its fundraising and improving coordination of campaign efforts and policy development between the RNC and the White House. The president's frequent speeches and fundraising appearances on behalf of the party's congressional candidates served to fortify the party's organizational base. These efforts contributed to the GOP's widening organizational advantage over the Democrats during the 1980s (Milkis and Rhodes 2007a; Mason 2008; Galvin forthcoming).

Still, Reagan's efforts to square the institution of the modern presidency with the demands of party leadership were only partially successful. While Reagan waged a rhetorical assault on modern liberalism, he failed at key moments to present his programs in the strongly partisan terms that would give voters a compelling reason to endorse enduring Republican leadership or a fundamental reshaping of liberal programs. Most importantly, in his reelection campaign of 1984, Reagan and his advisors decided to engage in personalistic, media-driven campaigns rather than make a strong case for conservative programs (Troy 2007; Mason 2008). This executive-centered campaign drained the election of the broad political meaning that might have boosted the fortunes of Republican congressional candidates. Moreover, flagging Republican strength in Congress denied Reagan the support necessary to pose a fundamental challenge to the institutional foundation of the New Deal–Great Society order.

Without a strong Republican congressional presence to reinforce and advance his reconstructive ambitions, Reagan was increasingly forced to retreat to administrative politics to achieve his policy objectives. Indeed, his campaign to master the bureaucracy was "more self-conscious in design and execution, and more comprehensive in scope, than that of any other administration in the modern era" (Benda and Levine 1988). The Reagan White House made extensive use of staffing authority, regulatory review, and executive orders to achieve its policy goals (Warshaw 2004, 2005; Stehr 1997). These moves were often supported by the president's congressional allies; at the same time, the emphasis on executive administration undermined collective responsibility for policy and threatened the stability of the Republican coalition. The scope of the administration's efforts to impose its will through the bureaucracy suggested that Reagan's ambitions substantially outstripped congressional support. The Reagan administration's political isolation was confirmed when the White House's most ambitious administrative maneuvers— its efforts to cut Social Security benefits and support Contra insurgents in Nicaragua—produced politically debilitating embarrassments for the president and his party (Derthick and Teles 2003; Barilleaux and Kelley 2005; Wilentz 2008, ch. 8; Ehrman 2005, ch. 4).

Reagan's ambiguous legacy of presidential party leadership illustrated the difficulty of reconciling partisanship with modern presidential power. There is a real sense in which Reagan's emphasis on presidential politics was a logical response to the liberal administrative state. The New Deal, like its successor the Great Society, was less a partisan program than an exercise in expanding the president's rhetorical and administrative powers. It is not surprising, then, that the challenge to liberal policies that culminated in the elevation of Reagan to the White House produced an effort to deploy the modern executive for conservative objectives. For a time, at least, this development retarded the revival of partisanship.

George W. Bush and the "New" American Party System

The challenge of remaking American politics *ex cathedra* would be cast in further relief during the presidency of George W. Bush. During his first six years in office, Bush elaborated on the partisan practices embraced by Ronald Reagan, prompting the further evolution of the "new" American party system. Indeed, Bush surpassed Reagan with his dramatic and unprecedented efforts to build his party at the congressional, grassroots, and organizational levels. Bush's presidency also revealed that the modern administrative state, so often anathema to party building, could be wielded to advance partisan objectives. Indeed, the Bush administration's party-building efforts were allied to an attempt to redefine Republican conservatism that envisioned exploiting rather than rolling back national administrative power. These efforts helped produce a remarkable string of electoral victories for Republicans at all levels of government. Until the 2006 elections, in fact, the party was as strong as at any point since the 1920s.

Nonetheless, Bush's presidency, which ended with record low approval ratings and Republican defeats in 2006 and 2008, demonstrates the enduring tension between the modern presidency and a vigorous party system. The president's enthusiasm for party building existed alongside a penchant for executive aggrandizement. But Bush's unilateralism, more deliberately attuned to partisan advantage than Reagan's, recurrently evoked controversy that brought the GOP brand into disrepute. Furthermore, Bush's vigorous party leadership tended to erode the distinctions between the presidency and the Republican Party and thereby threatened the capacity of the GOP to hold its leader to account. Because Republicans were so tightly tied to their president, they were unable to escape voters' retribution for Hurricane Katrina, the war in Iraq, and the financial crisis, which the administration had badly mismanaged.

Brought to the White House in the remarkably close and highly controversial 2000 election, Bush's sustained attention to party leadership stemmed from his realization that his ambitious domestic and foreign policy agendas would founder without vigorous popular and partisan support. His administration thus sought to reconcile presidential and party leadership with a comprehensive effort to form an executive-centered Republican organization. At the rhetorical level, Bush believed that building an enduring Republican majority would require redressing Reagan's "blind spot" to the important role government had come to play in people's lives (Heclo 2003; Riggs 2004; Milkis and Rhodes 2007b). Thus, rather than curtail New Deal and Great Society entitlements, as the Reagan administration and Gingrich-led 104th Congress attempted, the president and his Republican congressional allies sought to recast them in a more conservative image. Bush proposed to change federal and state regulations to permit private "faith-based" charitable organizations to play a larger role in providing government services to disadvantaged members of society. Instead of eliminating the Department of Education, as Reagan had proposed, Bush championed No Child Left Behind, which requires all states to set educational standards and hold schools accountable for results. To signal his concern for the elderly, he fought for a costly expansion of Medicare that would add coverage for prescription drugs, albeit with provisions that might set the program on the road to privatization (Mucciaroni and Quirk 2004; Fortier and Ornstein 2003; Beland and Waddan 2007). Even Bush's ill-fated proposal to permit Americans to invest portions of their Social Security savings presumed that the government would continue to require Americans to save for their retirements and control their investment strategies. To be sure, Bush would fight successfully for issues that appealed to the Republican base—most notably, massive tax cuts, punitive welfare reforms, class-action lawsuit reforms, and a ban on "partial birth" abortions—but his domestic agenda was clearly crafted to redirect, rather than retrench, national administrative power, and thereby appeal to a broader swath of the American public (Milkis and Rhodes 2007a, 2007b).

Bush's unprecedented efforts to strengthen the national Republican organization demonstrated the enormous potential of the modern presidency as an instrument of party building. In 2002, 2004, and 2006, Bush proved himself a committed party leader, raising funds for campaigns and stumping for candidates (Jacobson 2003; Busch 2005a; Beachler 2004; Bass 2004; Milkis and Rhodes 2007a). Significantly, attempting to meld executive prerogative and Republican advantage, the Bush White House sought to make the president's personal leadership of the war on terrorism a partisan issue, trumpeting Republicans' superiority over Democrats on matters of national and homeland security (J. Campbell 2008). Indeed, Bush became the first modern president since Franklin Roosevelt to win a second term while his party was gaining seats in the House and Senate.

The most innovative, and potentially consequential, component of Bush's party leadership was the administration's cultivation of a "national party machine." The "machine," which emerged from Bush–Cheney and GOP strategists' disappointment with Republican turnout in the 2000 presidential election, was an effort to systematically organize and mobilize the party's grassroots supporters. Relying on a combination of centralized hierarchy and decentralized volunteer effort, the GOP's grassroots campaign sought to develop personal lines of communication between the Bush campaign and local activists through email and the Internet. Campaign volunteers, recruited by professional staff on the ground and through the Internet, were charged with responsibilities for reaching specific goals developed by the Bush–Cheney headquarters: recruiting additional volunteers, organizing rallies and campaign events, writing letters to the editor, registering voters, or canvassing particular neighborhoods. Campaign officials in the states oversaw grassroots activity with tough love, holding volunteers accountable for meeting performance targets set by higher local officials. The campaign was highly successful in mobilizing supporters and voters: campaign officials estimate that between 1.2 and 1.4 million individuals volunteered for the campaign nationwide. Significantly, the grassroots machine was calibrated not only to bolster the president's reelection bid but to advance GOP prospects across the board. The Bush organization, coordinating with the RNC, emphasized reaching and turning out "lazy Republicans" who were predisposed to vote for Republicans at all levels but who were unreliable in their voting habits (Milkis and Rhodes 2007a).

Spurred by the Bush–Cheney mobilization, the 2004 election appeared to mark an important advance of a nationalized party system. The Republicans and, in a more defensive posture, the Democrats had made efforts since the 1970s to strengthen their discipline in Congress and to become a valuable source of campaign funds and other services for candidates. But the halting development of national, programmatic parties, overshadowed in important ways by Republican presidents' infatuation with the modern presidency, had failed to stir the passions and allegiances of the American people, as attested by the declining voter turnout from the 1970s to 2000. In contrast, the 2004 election was passionate, polarized, and participatory, redressing the long secular decline of voting turnout (MacDonald 2005; Abramowitz and Stone 2006). Beyond its immediate effectiveness in securing Bush's reelection, then, the Republicans' White House-inspired mobilization effort in 2004 provided a plausible blueprint for a revitalized party politics that draws more people into the political process and renews the linkages between citizens and their elected officials.

However, as Bush sought to advance the GOP's prospects, so his administrative presidency threatened to undermine the party's forward march. Reagan made extensive use of executive administration at a time when Congress was usually in the hands of Democrats. That Bush also made considerable use of administrative mechanisms to achieve his goals, even when his party controlled both houses of Congress, suggests that the administrative presidency might impede the emergence of a more collaborative, party-centered policy process under the most favorable circumstances. Indeed, subscribing to the "unitary executive" prescribed by Vice-President Cheney, Bush became a more zealous defender of presidential prerogatives than his Republican predecessor (C. Jones 2007; Pfiffner 2008; Rudalevige

2005). The president's staffing practices and aggressive use of the Office of Management and Budget's powers of regulatory review were gauged to maximize presidential control over the civil service. In domestic and foreign policy Bush made extensive use of executive orders, signing statements, and regulatory rule-making to achieve significant departures from past policy. The president also used executive orders to make headway on controversial social issues, launching "faith-based" initiatives, limiting funding for stem-cell research, and denying funds to family-planning organizations overseas that offered abortion counseling (Warshaw 2004; Aberbach 2005a, 2008; Rudalevige 2005). While these efforts often had the support of congressional Republicans, they also suggested that the Bush administration preferred to transcend institutions of collective responsibility rather than work through them to achieve compromise or consensus. Even when the administration sought to work with Congressional Republicans, it tended to do so in a heavy-handed manner as when Vice-President Cheney, sometimes with Bush's top political strategist, Karl Rove, in tow, intruded on senate Republicans' weekly strategy sessions to press the administration's views on its GOP leaders (Mahler 2008).

Bush's administrative strategy not only impeded the emergence of a more collaborative, party-centered policy process, it also contributed directly to the party's declining fortunes after 2004. The administration's ineffectual response to the Hurricane Katrina disaster undermined the claim to administrative competence that had previously bolstered the Republican Party. The negative consequences of Bush's administrative overreaching for the GOP were most evident in the fallout from the White House's imperious and insulated management of the war in Iraq and the broader war on terrorism (Woodward 2002, 2004, 2006). Determined to wage war on its own terms, the Bush administration made a series of unilateral decisions that departed from historic and legal convention: it would deny "enemy combatants" captured in the war on terrorism habeas corpus rights; abrogate the Geneva Conventions and sanction torture of detainees during interrogations; and engage in warrantless surveillance of American citizens suspected of communicating with alleged terrorists abroad (Pfiffner 2008). When these controversial decisions were revealed, they provoked widespread public condemnation and damaged the GOP's public support. The administration's insistence on a free hand to manage the war in Iraq resulted in the erosion of public confidence in the Republican Party as it became clear that the administration had badly botched reconstruction efforts (Jacobson 2008; Schier 2009, ch. 5). As the 2006 elections revealed, well before the 2008 economic crisis overwhelmed all other issues, the administration's and the party's prestige had been severely wounded.

Reagan might have erred on the side of insufficient attention to party building; Bush's experience illustrated the risks posed by overweening presidential partisanship. Ironically, the vigorousness of the Bush administration's party leadership—and the evident dependence of the GOP on Bush's stewardship—endangered the integrity of the Republican Party itself. Between 2001 and 2005, the GOP relied heavily on Bush's personal charisma and prestige as a wartime leader for its political sustenance (Jacobson 2003; J. Campbell 2005; Milkis and Rhodes 2007a; Abramson et al. 2007). Both the 2002 and the 2004 elections celebrated executive power, turning on the issues of international and domestic security that emphasized the modern presidency as the center of government. The White House also played a dominant role in organizing the massive grassroots efforts that characterized the 2004 election cycle and stimulating public participation in these efforts (Milkis and Rhodes 2007a). Although this approach reaped political dividends for GOP candidates in the short run, it threatened to make the party subservient to presidential authority and to enervate its capacity to hold the president accountable to broader principles. The modern GOP appeared to signal a political future in which the party "in effect [becomes] whatever the president needs it to be, and whatever capacity it had to hold its leaders to account would accordingly be lost" (Skowronek 2005). The ironic denouement of this development was revealed following the 2008 presidential election, in which many Republicans blamed Bush, whom they had previously followed with alacrity, for casting them into the political wilderness.

BARACK OBAMA, THE 2008 PRESIDENTIAL ELECTION, AND THE FUTURE OF THE "NEW" AMERICAN PARTY SYSTEM

Democratic Senator Barack Obama of Illinois promised "Change We Can Believe In" during the 2008 presidential campaign, but his organizational efforts were modeled after the techniques that Republicans had pioneered. Eschewing the Democrats' traditional reliance on organized labor and other auxiliary organizations to mobilize the party faithful, Obama vowed to wage a "fifty-state campaign" that would "build grassroots organizations" in every state, help "elect Democrats down the ballot," and register millions of new voters who would support his cause. Obama's organizational strategy, combining Internet-based recruiting of volunteers, the use of data files to carefully target potential loyalists, and old-fashioned door-to-door canvassing, elaborated on Bush tactics that had worked successfully in 2004 (Rutenberg 2008). The remarkable effectiveness of Obama's fundraising operation, which drew heavily on small, Internet-solicited donations, further reflected lessons learned from the Bush campaign. The Obama campaign developed an unprecedented capacity to raise funds, so much so that the Illinois senator became the first presidential candidate to refuse public funds for the general election.

Like the formidable Bush–Cheney machine of 2004, the Obama–Biden organization relied in part on the regular party apparatus. Democratic National Committee chairman Howard Dean's decision to extend the reach of his party's
campaign efforts beyond the battleground states laid a foundation that state and
local party leaders credited with abetting the party's impressive victories in 2006
and 2008. Just as the Bush–Cheney machine of 2004 resulted in a Republican
victory, so the Obama–Biden campaign of 2008 resulted not only in a decisive
triumph at the presidential level but also in substantial gains in House and Senate
races. Obama's sophisticated grassroots campaign conceived a victory that linked a
vast network of volunteers, elicited enormous enthusiasm among potential supporters, and mobilized the highest turnout since 1968. In light of increased turnout
in 2004, the 2008 campaign appeared to confirm the emergence of a national party
system that ameliorated the chronic voter apathy that had afflicted the presidency-
centered administrative state.

Nevertheless, the development of an executive-centered party system has not
eliminated the tension between presidential and party leadership. Following Obama's victory, campaign officials suggested that the Obama administration might
maintain its grassroots organization as a source of support for its policy agenda.
It is far from certain that the vaunted Obama machine can be transformed into
a durable organization that simultaneously strengthens the administration and
bolsters the Democratic Party. Like the Bush–Cheney machine, the Obama–Biden
campaign organization benefited Democratic congressional candidates and contenders for state and local office. At the same time, just as was the case with the
2004 Republican campaign, the grassroots effort was run out of the Obama–Biden
headquarters. The architects of the Obama campaign praised Dean's fifty-state
strategy, but they relied almost completely on their own staff, money, and organization, not only to compete in battleground states but also to make incursions into
traditional Republican territory. Moreover, just as the Bush–Cheney machine relied
on volunteers whose principal loyalty was to the presidential candidate, so the
extraordinary Obama–Biden grassroots organization rested in the volunteers' deep
admiration for the Democratic standard bearer (Nagourney 2008).

Beyond the 2008 election, then, the Democrats will be challenged to sustain a
collective commitment independent of their devotion to President Obama. The Bush
administration was split between those who wanted to meld the campaign organization and the GOP and presidential loyalists. The Obama administration, following a
campaign that promised to transcend the partisan rancor of the Bush years, is likely
to be even more divided between advisors who want to integrate the campaign into
the party structure and those who view the vast network of activists, neighborhood
organizers, and volunteers as a force that should remain "an independent entity—
organized around the 'Obama brand'" (Wallstein and Hamburger 2008).

It remains to be seen, therefore, whether the contest between conservatives and
liberals for national administrative power has brought a national party system to

fruition or continued the long-term development of a modern presidency that renders collective responsibility impractical. There is a real sense in which the "new" party system may be a creature of, and dependent on, the modern presidency. As the chief "architect" of the Bush administration's political strategy, Karl Rove, put it, the national parties that have emerged since the 1980s are "of great importance in the tactical and mechanical aspects of electing a president. But they are less important in developing a political and policy strategy for the White House." In effect, national parties serve as critical "means to the president's end" (Rove 2001). Similarly, when asked how his initial appointments to administrative positions, many of whom were old Washington hands, would carry out the campaign's promise to transform national politics, President-Elect Obama replied, "What we are going to do is combine experience with fresh thinking. But understand where vision for change comes from first and foremost. It comes from me" (Corn 2008).

Recent developments thus suggest that executive aggrandizement will likely continue to complicate efforts to achieve greater collective responsibility for policymaking. More significantly, the very vigor of strong party leaders such as George W. Bush and Barack Obama threatens the integrity of political parties as collective organizations with a past and a future. During the Progressive era, at the dawn of the modern presidency, Herbert Croly noted that Woodrow Wilson's effort to put his stamp on the Democratic Party suggested that aggressive executive partisanship might erode the integrity of collective responsibility, even as it strengthens party organization in the short term: "At the final test, the responsibility is his [the president's] rather than the party's. The party which submits to such a dictatorship, however benevolent, cannot play its own proper part in the system of government. It will either cease to have any independent life or its independence will eventually assume the form of revolt" (Croly 1914, 346). Croly's observation about the inherently antagonistic relationship between collective responsibility and executive dominion was made in a context when localized, decentralized parties prevailed. Yet it still may provide guidance for analyzing the dynamics of the relationship between the president and parties in an era of modern administration and nationalized, programmatic parties.

....

CHAPTER 21

STATE PARTIES RESEARCH

THE QUEST FOR STRONG, COMPETITIVE STATE PARTIES

....

GERALD C. WRIGHT

THE contours of political parties in the states, how they have changed, and how we study them are very much a function of two rather contrary reformist traditions. One is political: the Progressive movement which generated regulations, variously adopted across the states, and state laws and court decisions which at once constrain and limit the parties, while also institutionalizing them and almost guaranteeing some form of two-party competition across all the states. The second tradition is disciplinary: a reformist inclination within political science stemming from the mid-twentieth-century work which declared that many of America's political ills could and would be cured if only our weakly organized, poorly disciplined, and sometimes uncompetitive party systems could be greatly strengthened. The disciplinary movement set much of the normative and theoretical agenda for the study of parties in the states that followed.

To appreciate the journey of political scientists' study of state parties we need to appreciate some elemental truths which make the systematic study of state parties both vitally important and extremely challenging. The importance of parties is that they are so central; unlike the courts, for instance, which seem to sit off to the side of political battles much like the referees in a football game or boxing match, the parties, in the words of the authors of a major text, "permeate every aspect of state government" (Bibby and Holbrook 1996, 96). This is reflected in the commonly adopted framework that we use here, one that examines parties in the electorate, the party organizations, and the parties in government. Of course, as discussed below, the impact of parties in the political system can best be understood by focusing not just on these individual components, but on how they are interconnected.

The challenge in studying state parties stems from the complexity of the subject and the practical difficulty of gathering data across fifty states. First, obviously the states vary a lot—no one can confuse Alaska and New York or California and Mississippi. This means that the parties across the states also vary and operate in somewhat different ways. The full complexity of what is involved when we think about party activity in the states includes two compet-ing parties at three levels—in the electorate, as formal organizations, and in the branches of government across all the fifty states. Optimally, we would have analyses of the interrelationships of these components as well. As we will see, a lot of bright ideas have been floated and methods developed to make sense of this complexity.

Second, if we deal with the conceptual complexity, practical limitations in data gathering mean that we lack the good-quality measures that empirical research demands. While measures of a few aspects of party politics in the states have long been readily available, the field continues to suffer inadequate data on key features of the party system over time as well as across all or most of the states. The result is that too often scholars are left to make broad, imprecise generalizations ("some states do this, but most appear to do that"), or large differences are noted among the party systems—and they do vary a great deal in most respects—but we have not developed the theory or data resources to achieve convincing explanations. There is a lot left to do.

The plan for this chapter is as follows. In the next section I lay out the broad context for how the two reformist traditions have shaped the party systems of the states and how we study them. This helps to establish the broad evolution of the state parties over the last half-century or so and the main research trends that we have charted. Then the next three sections review the broad outlines of research on partisanship in the state electorates, state party organizations, and the role of the parties in state government. Each section contains some commentary on future directions for research. The concluding section briefly reviews these recommendations, focusing in partic-ular on what kinds of opportunities and challenges are presented for state parties research by the changes in the ideological polarization of the parties which are so evident at the national level.

Two Reformist Waves Shape State Parties and Parties Research

The Progressives Pushed Laws to Weaken Parties

The state parties have been shaped in good part by the reforms of the Progressive era around the beginning of the twentieth century. They sought to break the power of the traditional patronage-based parties, reflecting early beliefs that parties as "factions" worked against the public good and contributed to corruption and inefficiency in governing (Duncan 1913; L. Gould 1986; Hofstadter 1955). Their reforms sought to break the hold of the parties over electoral politics. The most pervasive in its adoption, and perhaps its impact, was the direct primary, which removed control of nominations—a key source of power for traditional party organizations—and gave that power to the citizenry. That change allowed the development of what in the latter half of the twentieth century became known as "candidate-centered" campaigns. The direct primary is the principal means of candidate selection in the country with only a handful of states either providing for or allowing nomination by state conventions. Within the realm of the direct primary the states vary in their permissiveness of who is allowed to participate (LaRaja, Chapter 9 in this volume) and whether the parties can endorse candidates (Morehouse and Jewell 2003b, 133–8). These provisions appear to have an effect on the ideological character of the primary and caucus participants (Carsey et al. 2006; G. Wright 2009).

The Progressives were less successful with other reforms, but these too have left lasting effects on the state parties. The institutions of direct democracy—the initiative, referendum, and recall—all sought to break the power of the parties and party-controlled state legislatures and were adopted in various combinations in about half the states. Although in recent years the parties have sometimes learned to use the initiative process to achieve policy ends, more generally it is accepted that initiative and referendum provide meaningful extraparty access to the policy process in the states where they are used (D. Smith 2006). Perhaps one of the least successful of the Progressive reforms in terms of adoptions in the states was the idea of non-partisan elections. Only Minnesota (until the early 1970s) and Nebraska have elected their state legislators without party labels, but the reform has gained much wider footing in local elections. Research on the effects of non-partisanship show that, indeed, the simple rule of removing party labels from general election ballots has major consequences for voting decisions (increasing the value of incumbency, decreasing voter turnout, weakening the policy ties between representatives and constituents) (Schaffner, Streb, and Wright 2001), and in the structure of political conflict in the legislatures (Aldrich and Battista 2002; G. Wright and Schaffner 2002).

At the same time that the Progressives' reforms weakened the political parties, other state laws and court decisions worked to ensure the survival of the basic two-party system. One such rule was the near universal adoption of single-member plurality elections for legislative office. This "first-past-the post" system presents a strong obstacle to the success of minor parties. In addition, the parties are propped up by favorable ballot access laws, making it much easier for the two major parties to put up candidates than it is for independents or third parties. As a result, the parties have become what some refer to as "quasi-public" entities (Bibby 2002, 21–2; Ware 2002, 89–90). The legal system lends a huge dose of stability in almost guaranteeing that the fundamental structure of political competition in the states will be between the Democratic and Republican parties. All of the incredible diversity of the states, and the conflicts that arise from this, must be accommodated within this relatively narrow competitive structure.

Political Scientists Back Reforms for Stronger Parties

As the Progressive reforms, the growth of civil service regulations, and Supreme Court rulings limiting patronage greatly weakened the parties, political scientists were arguing for change in the opposite direction. Beginning in the 1940s—and only sporadically challenged since—influential political scientists argued that stronger parties are better for democracy (Herring 1940; Key 1949; Schattschneider 1942). These scholars focused on the potential benefits of parties for providing voters with a clear choice, for bridging the problems inherent in a separation of powers system with powers divided even further by federalism, and for making the parties more responsive to citizens, particularly those denied participation in the existing one-party states of the South (Key 1949). Academic arguments were converted to reformist calls for change in the report of the Committee on Political Parties of the American Political Science Association (1950).

This general perspective on parties has structured a great deal of the research since.[1] The call for stronger parties came just at the dawn of the behavioral revolution with its goals of a more systematic and quantitative study of political processes. The assumption that stronger political parties are good is implicit through the great majority of research on state parties, although the efforts to demonstrate this position have been at best partially successful. What is remarkable is the virtual absence in the field of systematic efforts to demonstrate, or even test

---

[1] There were clearly dissenters from the advocacy of the responsible parties model, but as often because they were deemed unworkable in the US as that they were deemed undesirable (E. Kirkpatrick 1971; M. S. Steadman and Sonthoff 1951; Ranney 1951; Turner 1951).

for, any kinds of ill effects of strong political parties.[2] This perspective has certainly resulted in the illumination of some important aspects of party politics in the states, but it has also meant that some other, I believe increasingly important, aspects have not been as systematically incorporated into the ongoing research as they ought to be. My thesis is that research on parties, in the states as well as the nation, should attend at least equally to what the parties stand for as to their "strength" and competitiveness. For how else can we judge the impact of parties if we do not pay close attention to what they promise to do and what they actually do when in office?

MASS PARTISANSHIP

Since *The American Voter* (Angus Campbell et al. 1960) surveys have provided the bread and butter data for the study of mass partisanship. Unfortunately, the cost of gathering comparative data on anything like a full set of the state electorates has been prohibitive. This is because the cost of a single-state survey is not much less than that for a national survey. Such data collections would have allowed analyses of party in the electorate in the states to parallel the tremendous attention mass partisanship received for the national electorate.

Lacking survey-based estimates of partisan preferences, scholars relied on that which is easily measurable: voting returns and election outcomes. The most enduring measure was developed by Austin Ranney (Ranney 1976) and incorporated election returns for governor and the percentages of each house of the state legislatures controlled by the parties. This index (and a number of variations) is simple to compute and provides the basis for classifications of the states as ranging from one-party Democratic, through competitive, to one-party Republican.[3] The difficulty with the index for studying mass partisan tendencies is that it requires that we assume that which we often want to test, namely the relationship between party identification and voting outcomes. Indeed, it is often assumed that this is almost a one-to-one relationship in lower-level contests like those for the state legislature, seemingly on the assumption that citizens probably know next to nothing about candidates for these offices. But in fact, there have been virtually no systematic

---

[2] An exception to this statement are reactions of political scientists to the alarms of some observers concerning the heightened levels of party polarization. See, for example, the essays in Nivola and Brady (2008).

[3] This index is frequently "folded" to make a measure of interparty competition running from very competitive to safe for one of the parties.

studies of mass voting behavior for these contests, and certainly none done on a comparative basis.

By the 1980s enough national media polls had accumulated that researchers were able to patch together basic measures of partisanship in the states for comparative analyses. Erikson, Wright, and McIver (1993) used CBS–*New York Times* polls aggregated to the state level to achieve numbers of cases in the states that allow reliable estimates of state partisanship and ideology. Others have used the state-based samples of the Senate Election Studies of the American National Election series (Norrander 2001), or the General Social Survey (Brace et al. 2002), and media exit polls (R. Jackson and Carsey 1999; Stein 1990; G. Wright and Berkman 1986) to gauge the partisanship and issue preferences of state electorates. The findings, even from these secondary uses of data collected for other purposes, have been informative. For example, just the incidence of identifying oneself as a Democrat or Republican varies as much across the states as does the direction of partisan preferences (Norrander 1989a) and whether or not people identify themselves as partisans is significantly influenced by state voter registration requirements: there are more people who say they are Democrats or Republicans in states that have party registration, but interestingly, there is also more defection from party in these states (Finkel and Scarrow 1985).

We have never had the surveys that would allow in-depth comparative analyses of the processes of party identification and change in the states. However, exploiting the limited information available in media polls, Robert Brown's decomposition of the demographic characteristics of the state electorates showed that the social and economic compositions of the partisan coalitions in the states varied tremendously through the 1980s (R. Brown 1995). The state parties and their candidates seemed to adapt to their individual demographic terrains. Brown developed a typology of state party systems; it will be informative if future research will replicate those analyses to see if and how recent changes in partisanship in the states have altered the character of the demographic-based classifications.

New technologies including Internet-based surveys, and automated computer telephone interviews are collecting information on state-based samples at reasonable costs. These will expand our ability to do comparative analyses of the partisanship and electoral decision making of state electorates. See, for example, the results of Survey USA or the data being collected by Polimetrics for the Cooperative Congressional Election Studies.[4]

The big story in partisanship at the national level has been the transition from what looked in the 1970s and 1980s like a period of "dealignment," with the gradual disintegration of mass partisanship (Wattenberg 1994), to a period of partisan resurgence or reinvigoration (M. Brewer 2005; Hetherington 2001; Knuckey 2006). One aspect of the current system is the greater parity of the parties nationally.

---

[4] Survey USA (<http://www.surveyusa.com>) and the CCES (<http://web.mit.edu/polisci/portl/cces/index.html>).

Of course, much of this has been fueled by the decline of the one-party Democratic South. The overwhelming Democratic majority produced by the New Deal alignment is no more; rather we have a system of essential parity. Research drawing on media polls taken over a twenty-five-year period and aggregated into presidential administration time chunks at the state level allows us to chart changes in state partisanship and what moves it (Erikson, Wright, and McIver 2006). Looking at the individual states reinforces the general view based on regional analyses that most of the movement has been in relative growth of Republican identifications in the South. But these data also show a less dramatic but still significant growth in Democratic identifications in a number of northern states, adding to the images of the solid "blue" coastal voting we see in presidential elections.

The most important finding from the longitudinal analyses of state partisanship is that the causal agent driving changes in state party identifications is state ideology. At the aggregate level (as well as the individual level; Abramowitz and Saunders 2008; M. Brewer 2005; Hetherington 2001; Layman, Carsey, and Horowitz 2006) there has been a sharp increase over time in the correlations of partisanship and ideology. This means that today much more so than in earlier decades, party identification and ideological and policy preferences push voters in the same direction. This alignment of state partisanship and ideology has been a product of party identifications coming into alignment with relatively stable ideological orientations (Erikson, Wright, and McIver 2006).

At the foundational level of citizen political attachments, we see an important transformation of the state party systems. Whereas in the 1970 and early 1980s (and before) state partisanship and ideological preferences were virtually unrelated; today they are increasingly correlated, and thus reinforcing in their influence on most voters. This appears to be a good part of the explanation for perceptions of Americans dividing into sets of "red" and "blue" states. Ideology has been the driving force in these changes. The origins of this, of course, lie in the parties' efforts to win elections as well as changes in the motivations and preferences of the party elites (Carmines and Stimson 1989).

Transformed State Party Organizations: In Service of What?

Changes in the State Parties

There are few things that almost all researchers in an area agree upon, but the character of changes in state party organizations is one of them. The golden era of political parties has been dramatically changed. The strong party organizations of the Great Lakes, Middle Atlantic, and New England states which controlled nominations, elected officials, and had substantial patronage packages to dispense to supporters have largely vanished (Mayhew 1986). This led to the perception that the party organizations were all but dead, consistent with the growing consensus among party observers that the parties were dying; mass partisanship was declining and the state parties as forces in American politics had seen their day (Broder 1972; Wattenberg 1994).

The ideal of what Mayhew (1986) calls the "traditional party organizations" were clearly the exception rather than the rule by the time of his impressive survey of state party organizations of the late 1960s. Only a few of the states scored toward the top of his "TPO" scale, with the majority receiving the lowest score of a "1," indicating no evidence at all of the traditional, hierarchical, nomination-controlling, patronage-based organizations. It was something of a surprise for many scholars when Cotter et al. (1984) reported a major resurgence of party organizations based on their surveys of state and county party officials. In contrast to the expectations of many that state party organizations were moribund, Cotter et al. found healthy levels of professionalism and staffing, and extensive campaign activities, for many of the state and county organizations. The parties were providing financial support to gubernatorial, congressional, and state legislative candidates in the vast majority of states, as well as help in matching appropriate PAC donors with nominees (Aldrich 2000; Reichley 1992).

The party organizations were transformed. They no longer controlled nominations, although a handful still mustered the ability to make pre-primary endorsements, and the state parties made no pretense at controlling the actions of elected officials. Rather, their new activities earned them the label of "parties in service" of electing candidates who generally won election and re-election on their own, but now received assistance in increasing measure from the state parties. However, this help in the vast majority of cases is clearly supplemental; very few candidates for the state legislatures depend on the state parties for the bulk of their support (Francia et al. 2003b). In addition, the official state party organizations provide linkage with the increasingly well-funded national organizations which have provided a great deal of support for the state-level organizations, especially for party-building activities like registration and get-out-the-vote (Morehouse and Jewell 2003a). State party organizations are active in providing electoral support to candidates in the states, frequently with significant funding from the national party organizations.

At the very least the strengthened, more active, more professionalized state party organizations would seem to be an important ingredient in moving the parties toward the goal of a stronger, more responsible party system. However, if we reflect on the function of strong parties, a key factor is missing. The contemporary party organizations have little say in the nomination process. Although some state parties produce policy platforms (Coffey 2007; Paddock 1998), because these are not made by, nor binding on, those who make policy, the effective "platform" is arguably defined by the campaign promises of the candidates winning the primaries. Thus, in order to assess whether stronger parties are really helpful to democratic governance, it would seem prudent to focus on what it is the stronger and more able parties want to do. That is, the formal party organizations are impressively active and professional, even smartly strategic in supporting their candidates, but in support of what?

State Party Ideology

This is where the huge and increased role of ideology in the transformation of state parties comes into play. Contributors and activists in the parties are no longer motivated by prospects of a job but by issues that touch on deeply held values. Wilson (1962) was one of the first to identify the ideologically motivated activist in contrast to the older traditional job-seeking party regulars of the traditional party organizations. More generally, "pragmatists" who are primarily interested in winning elections have been replaced by "purists" (Wildavsky 1965) who are motivated by issues and ideology. The latter are more likely to be deeply committed and less willing to compromise in order to win (Layman, Carsey, and Horowitz 2006; Pomper 1999). Studies of campaign activists and convention delegates show the development of deep ideological polarization between the parties (Abramowitz, McGlennon, and Rapoport 1983; John S. Jackson, Brown, and Bositis 1982), mirroring that found in Congress (Poole and Rosenthal 1997).

One potentially fruitful avenue of research on state party organizations is to address the question of what determines the character of state party activists' preferences. Aldrich (1983a) developed an insightful model of how the ideological contours of party activists' communities may change. His model relies on the entrance and exit of activists with differing preferences. Some evidence of the processes he discusses can be seen in the "takeovers" of state party organizations. Wilson's (1962) depiction of the impact of the political clubs fits, as do more current efforts by the Christian Right in capturing the Republican Party apparatus in several states (J. Green, Rozell, and Wilcox 2000, 2003; Rozell and Wilcox 1995, 1997; Wilcox 1996, ch. 3). We know that state party activists have generally become more ideological, and a few efforts have been made to obtain descriptive information on the differing ideological or issue preferences of activists in the states. Some of these rely on surveys of convention delegates (Abramowitz and Stone 1984; John S. Jackson, Brown, and Bositis 1982; W. Miller, Jennings, and Farah 1986; W. Stone and Abramowitz 1983). Convention delegates have the advantage of providing a known universe for sampling and in some cases of getting that population together for the logistics of interviewing. However, they are limited because they are selected not as random samples of the states' party elites, but in presidential primaries and caucuses which, of course, are contests between alternative teams of activists within the parties committed to different candidates, frequently representing competing ideological camps within the parties. There is no guarantee that the state delegations attending the national conventions, are representative of the larger body of activists within the state parties. Biases are most likely to crop up on the Republican side, which still permits winner-take-all primaries and caucuses.

Others have used surveys of county or state party officials (Cotter et al. 1984; Uslaner and Weber 1979), while some have sought to use the readily available interest group ratings of members of Congress with various weights to measure "government ideology" (W. Berry et al. 1998). Erikson, Wright, and McIver (1993) used a combination of these as well as surveys of candidates to develop measures of state party elite ideology. Finally, another window into the ideological preferences of party activists is provided by the sometimes sporadic platforms of the state parties which can be content-analyzed to scale the state parties (Coffey 2007; Elling 1979; Paddock 1992, 1998).

Erikson et al. find a weak relationship between state party elite ideology and the ideological preferences of the mass electorate, while Coffey (2007), using party platform measures of elite preferences, finds absolutely no relationship between the preferences of elites and the mass public. This difference may be a function of timing. With greater polarization of elites the parties may have become internally more homogeneous across the states, thus losing an anchor to the values of the mass public. If so, then the parties have become detached ideologically from the mooring of local values. Indeed, that is exactly the relationship implied by a system of national responsible parties. A second possibility is that these are measurement–methods differences. Paddock (1998) uses both measures of party committee members' issue preferences and scales derived from state party platforms and produces an important finding. He relates the levels of polarization to several factors and finds that states with histories of strong traditional party organizations continued in the 1990s to have less ideological parties. He also found some relationship to ideological differences in the mass electorate.

The relationship between elite and mass polarization is causally problematic. Work on party changes which link party elites and the public find that elites are the independent movers, with the public responding to what they see elites and elected official do (Carmines and Stimson 1989). Among the states, elite ideology has had a clear impact on party identifications of the states' electorates. As state party elite opinion gets more extreme relative to state opinion, that party loses identifiers (Erikson, Wright, and McIver 1993, ch. 6). This *ought* to provide a brake on the ideological polarization of the parties: as they polarize, they shed more and more of their base. The interesting thing is that in the era of party "purists" seemingly fewer of these party activists care enough about winning to seriously compromise on the issues which motivated their participation in the first place (Carsey et al. 2006).

What we do not have a good handle on yet is the relative contributions of national versus state party elites (and here I include elected officials) to changes in state partisanship. Clearly the trend has been toward greater polarization and this has been documented repeatedly for the national scene. A good research question is whether individual states can stem this tide for their electorates and the extent to which ideologically motivated party elites even want to field electorally more attractive and less ideologically extreme candidates.

Based on simple spatial theories of elections, parties ought to face a trade-off in terms of ideological extremism and electoral success. Several have pointed out that the conservatism of the Republicans has provided a brake on their attaining a sustained majority (Hurley 1989; Stonecash, Brewer, and Mariani 2003). This tension, especially in an era where we see the parties polarizing, suggests what may be the prime question for scholars trying to discern the future of the parties and their role in American politics. What forces drive party elites (Carsey et al. 2006)? When does losing elections because of being out of touch with the median voter cause parties to moderate? We have fifty state party laboratories providing varying answers to these questions. What seems clear, however, is that the prospect of winning or losing alone is not enough; as we shall see below, systems with high levels of competition tend to be the most polarized, and it is clear that culture plays a substantial role. Systems that long ago were hierarchical, patronage-based systems continue to produce ideologically muted versions of political combat in their states. Will this historical brake continue? And can we identify other factors that influence levels of party elite polarization that have evolved?

The study of party organizations in the post-TPO era presents huge challenges. *The* party organization in the states is no longer performing all or even most of the roles of recruitment, nomination, electoral support, and party discipline of elected officials. The activities of the formal state party organizations are more supplemental than controlling. The effective "party" is now more accurately seen as a network of the formal party, allied interest groups, deep-pocketed donors, issue activists, and legislative leadership PACs. This picture of the presidential parties (M. Cohen et al. 2008) applies to the state parties as well. The glue for the individual and highly substitutable parts then becomes shared policy goals as much as any overarching loyalty to the parties. And as such, the shifting salience of different policies and the circulation of activists as the issue agendas of the states change should be a profitable area for future research.

This research agenda for state parties scholars should proceed arm in arm with the parallel search for the factors influencing change in the national parties. Indeed, if there is merit to the idea that party elites in the states at some point feel the pressures of a trade-off between ideological purity and winning, this in itself should provide a constraint on the national parties which continue to elect officials in contests defined in terms of local or state jurisdictions.

WHAT DOES STRONG PARTY GOVERNMENT ACHIEVE?

As mentioned above, the underlying and sometimes implicit theme of a great deal of the research on parties in the states is the familiar idea that strong, competitive parties are good both for getting politicians to attend to the interest of "have nots" (Key 1949) and for countering the power-splintering forces of federalism and separation of powers. In addition, stronger, responsible parties are supposed to increase both government's accountability to the public and policy coherence (American Political Science Association 1950).

Party Control

This general perspective on parties in the states has given rise to several lines of research. One of the most obvious has also been the most frustrating. This is the simple question of what difference it makes if Democrats or Republicans win office. The most frequently used measure of party control has been the Ranney index, discussed above, which provides an overall indicator of the extensiveness of party control of the governorship and state legislature. It would seem elementary that if parties are meaningful entities, and are fundamental to how voters control the broad contours of government policymaking (Angus Campbell et al. 1960; Erikson, MacKuen, and Stimson 2002), party control of government would have clear results for state policy. Initial forays to demonstrate this were not very successful. Thomas Dye (1966) used something of a shotgun approach in correlating party control and other factors across many measures of state spending, coming up, with few exceptions, with the message that party control did not matter. In another early but more focused effort, Winters (1976) found no impact of party control where it should have mattered the most, on redistributive policies. Several authors (R. Brown 1995; Dye 1984; Garand 1985; Jennings 1979) subsequently found modest support for the party control hypothesis by isolating those systems where the parties were especially polarized. Of course, this just backs up the question of why the parties were polarized in some states but not others. The diversity of state populations is part of the explanation (Aistrup 1993; Barrilleaux 1986; S. Patterson and Caldeira 1984), but the relationships have not been constant over time nor fully accounted for by combinations of environmental measures.

Interparty Competition

The frustration over the lack of party control effects was attributable in part to the odd situation of the southern states, which were at once solidly Democratic and also ideologically conservative. In fact, it was the observation of politics in the one-party states of the South that produced the most enduring hypothesis of parties in state politics. Key (1949) noted that in the non-ideological competition among party factions in these one-party states the "have-nots" were commonly left out. The fluidity of the factions prevented the disfranchised and poor from gaining any kind of electoral toehold in the system. Thus, Key hypothesized that if competition were organized around parties (presumably still non-programmatic), then the parties would have an incentive to develop policies that appealed to the (poor) non-voters who could supply the votes the parties' candidates would need to win. Thus, competition between organized parties was argued to benefit society's have-nots.

An early article by Dawson and Robinson (1963) set the stage for an explosion of work in the late 1960s and 1970s that became the field of comparative state policy. However, work in the field dropped off dramatically by the 1980s.[5] The early studies found that indeed states with greater interparty competition also had policies that favored the working class or poor, but this apparent relationship generally vanished when controls were brought into the analysis for such things as state income, urbanization, or industrialization. From a question focusing on Key's interparty competition hypothesis the field grew to address the more generic question of "does politics matter?" Repeatedly, the answer was "no" or, "maybe, just a bit under some circumstances." In short, whether party control matters or levels of party competition matter "depends," but in general, the conclusion was that the economic environment of the state political systems was a lot more important in explaining state policies.

For example, two important studies locate the impact of party control, but only after specifying both the liberal or conservative character of the parties and the condition of party competition. Plotnick and Winters (1990) show that the guarantees under the old Aid to Families with Dependent Children program were responsive to party control, but only when they tested for the statistical interaction of liberal–conservative party ideology and the competitiveness of the parties. Later, Barrilleaux and his collaborators (Barrilleaux 1997, 2000; Barrilleaux, Holbrook, and Langer 2002) used a measure of competition based on electoral competitiveness and reported that liberal parties in power do yield more generous

---

[5] This is a severely abbreviated account of the development of a rather substantial literature. Treadway (1985), for example, devotes an entire book to a review of the comparative state policy studies. See also the surveys by Brace and Jewett (1995) and Stonecash (1996). Throughout, the hypothesis of the effects of interparty competition on state policy is prominent.

policies for the poor when facing electoral competition. However, contrary to the Key hypothesis, their results indicate that Republican majorities faced with competition produce more conservative welfare policies.

These interactive effects do not appear to be consistent across studies, and more to the point, it is not clear why party elites would fall back to the values of their core supporters when they are in danger of losing office, but play to the median voter when they are electorally safe (Barrilleaux, Holbrook, and Langer 2002). Jackson (1992) did similar tests in looking at the interaction of public opinion and party competition (as well as several other "political" factors that might mediate how public opinion is translated into policy outcomes). He found very little evidence for such mediating effects, reinforcing the at best murky support to the long-running Key hypothesis about the policy effects of party competition.

One difficulty that researchers have had in nailing down the exact effects of party control and party competition lies with failure to take state electorates into account. When the ideological preferences of the state electorates are brought into the analysis, we find that electorates simply do not allow the "experiment" of having a legislature that is very liberal or very conservative, given state opinion (Erikson, Wright, and McIver 1993). When state party elites and the candidates they nominate get too liberal or too conservative, their numbers in the mass electorate shrink. The impact of party control has been hard to substantiate because in state policy research we are, for the most part, comparing policies made by relatively moderate Republican regimes with those made by relatively moderate Democratic regimes. The obvious question is how this pattern of electing more moderate governments stands up in an age of increasing party polarization. Are the ranks of party moderates in the states being decimated in the same way as appears to be the case in Congress? And is electoral—or even legislative—competition the factor to keep such polarization of party elites in check? Those are important questions for future work.

Strong Parties in Government

The interest in responsible parties was evident in much of the early behavioral work on state legislatures, where one of the principal questions was the character of party voting in the state legislatures (Buchanan 1963; Derge 1958; Flinn 1964; Keefe 1954; LeBlanc 1969; Sorauf 1963). They found remarkable variation in the levels of party voting. Party conflict tends to be higher in more urban states, but the striking feature even among these is the wide variation in the centrality of party in roll call voting (Dye 1965; Keefe 1956; Lockard 1959; Zeller 1954). One of the main findings of this early research was that party voting increases with the competitiveness of the parties (Broach 1972; Key 1956; S. Patterson 1962; S. Welch and Carlson 1973), although LeBlanc (1969) found little relationship between party voting and legislative competitiveness in the twenty-six chambers he studied. More recent work indicates that higher levels of party voting are associated with, if not causally connected to, levels of competitiveness of the parties in the state legislatures (Aldrich and Battista 2002; S. Jenkins 2006; G. Wright and Schaffner 2002).

There was a sharp drop-off in studies of state legislative roll call voting beginning in the 1970s. This coincided with the Inter-University Consortium for Political and Social Research making roll call votes of the US Congress available to scholars. Getting sets of roll calls already collected, coded, documented, and ready for analysis is much easier than traipsing to state capitols and copying roll calls from legislative journals and then getting them keypunched using the technology of the day. Many of the early efforts were generally motivated by behavioral assumptions about the importance of attitudes and group pressures (rather than institutions and rules) and concerns for responsible party government rather than state politics or parties per se. Hence, analyzing the more readily available congressional roll calls to deal with such concerns was an understandable choice and helps to explain the dramatic drop in party–roll call studies in the states.

In the congressional literature questions about the role of party in roll call voting decisions evolved from one of gauging degrees of loyalty and cohesion to the effects of leadership and rules in bringing about those patterns (see, for example, the discussions in McCarty, Poole, and Rosenthal 2001; Snyder and Groseclose 2001). The problem came to be framed as one of "partisanship," meaning party leaders' influence over members' votes, versus simple "preferenceship," in which levels of party loyalty reflect the coincidence of shared interests but no special efforts on the part of party leaders.[6] From the perspective of state politics or even that of advocates of responsible parties, the controversy is less central than its prominence in recent congressional scholarship. In fact, two studies have gone to the heart of the problem faced by congressional scholars, which is that roll call votes were used to measure both the preferences of members of Congress (ideal points) and the effects of party (measures of cohesion, party voting, or polarization). Using independent measures of attitudes toward the parties and members' ideological preferences, these studies showed that, not surprisingly, members' attitudes are important (Scully and Patterson 2001), as are the powers of the majority party leaders and some constituency factors (S. Jenkins 2008).

Two points should be remembered in thinking about this as a research question on the role of parties in state legislatures. First, the assumption that party matters

---

[6] This controversy pits Keith Krehbiel's (1993, 1998, 2000) position that a simple model of members pursuing their own preferences is able to account for most patterns of congressional behavior, including roll call voting. Seeking to demonstrate the importance of party in Congress, an array of scholars have used different datasets and methods (Ansolabehere, Snyder, and Stewart 2001a; Binder, Lawrence, and Maltzman 1999; McCarty, Poole, and Rosenthal 2001; S. Smith 2007).

only if it can be demonstrated that members are persuaded or influenced in their voting by party leaders is misleadingly narrow. In fact, comparing the non-partisan Nebraska legislature with the similar but partisan Kansas Senate shows that having partisan elections and organizing the chambers by party has a major influence on the structure of conflict. Parties, when in play as alternative governing teams, lead to the bundling of issues and reduce the dimensionality of conflict as evidenced in roll call voting (Aldrich and Battista 2002; G. Wright and Schaffner 2002).

Second, the advocates of the pro-party effects position are really positing that strong parties distort policy outcomes from the preferences of the median legislator (which presumably would be the optimally representative outcome for the polity). For example, Cox and McCubbins (1993) argue that strong majority parties will seek to pass legislation at the ideal point of the median majority party legislator. Thus, a hypothesis for further research is whether responsible party government increases the likelihood that policy will be unrepresentative of the preferences of the median citizen. When the parties are not so far apart, as in the 1950s and 1960s, this probably is not a great concern; it would entail movement a bit this way or that depending on the parties' recent electoral fates. However, when the parties are ideologically polarized, such majority power would appear to be a recipe for clearly unrepresentative policy outcomes.

Future work on party government in the state legislatures will be able to take advantage of significant new data resources that are becoming available.[7] These data collection efforts will enable significant expansion of questions about parties in the legislatures while adding crucial analytic leverage of comparative analysis across the states. These opportunities will hopefully prompt researchers to take a more complete accounting of the effects of party than simply whether legislative leaders influence their members' behavior. A full understanding and evaluation of party effects should look at the impact of party in the mass public, certainly among activists through the nomination processes as these filter who even gets into the legislatures. In terms of the controversy among congressional scholars, the comparative perspective of the states suggests if the nomination process is sufficiently efficient in yielding ideologically distinct sets of party nominees, there would be little need for arm twisting or major agenda manipulation by legislative leaders.

---

[7] These efforts include the Election Dynamic Project, which includes roll calls and interviews with legislators from five states over several sessions, 1992–6 (see S. Jenkins 2006 for a project description); Gerald Wright's Representation in America's Legislatures Project, which has collected comprehensive sets of roll calls for all the state legislatures for two sessions, 1999–2000 and 2003–4 (<http://www.indiana.edu/~ral>); and a parallel project by Nolan McCarty and his collaborators. They have collected roll calls over more sessions but include fewer states. The goal of their effort is to achieve a common scale for legislator ideal points across legislative chambers (<http://www.indiana.edu/~ral>) and a parallel project by Nolan McCarty and his collaborators. To date the major goal in that project has been to construct a common scale for legislator ideal points across legislative chambers (Shor 2009; Shor, Berry, and McCarty 2007).

Party effects may well be pervasive, as in the quote by Bibby and Holbrook at the outset, even in a legislative world of apparent pure preference voting.

Divided Government

We have had an interesting pair of contradictory trends in party control of the states governments—contradictory at least from the perspective of strong responsible parties. On the one hand, as we have noted, the parties appear to be more ideological today than was the case fifty or sixty years ago. That is clearly a step toward responsible party government. However, headed in the other direction over this period is the decline of unified government wherein one party clearly controls the executive and legislative branches, thus allowing the electorate to know which party to hold accountable for how things are going (Fiorina 1996). The trend toward divided government has been evident at both the state and national levels. We know that most of the instances of divided government stem from the success of minority party governors. This appears to be a reflection of the strong relationships between state partisanship and the partisan composition of the legislatures on the one hand, and the ability of governors to develop a "personal vote" less tied to state partisanship (Erikson, Wright, and McIver 1993, 128–30, 194–5).

An open research question is whether these patterns of divided government have continued. It would be reasonable to entertain the hypothesis that the growing polarization of American political parties reaches beyond Congress and the division of presidential voting patterns into "red" and "blue" state governments. This returns us to the basic question of what the parties stand for in an era of party polarization; how much homogenization has occurred, and do the centripetal forces pulling the parties apart from one another affect governors?[8]

One important question is whether it matters that government is unified. The answer is an unequivocal yes from the perspective of responsible party government, and indeed, Sundquist (1988) argued that the rise of divided government has created something of a theoretical crisis for parties scholars. In the states there is evidence that the governor clearly has more difficulty passing his or her legislation when the governor's party does not control the legislature, especially when the opposition has a majority in both chambers (Bowling and Ferguson 2001; Clarke 1998), and similarly, that changes in the expected directions of fiscal policy are more consistent with unified government in the states (Alt and Lowry 1994). Perhaps most surprising

---

[8] If the polarization of the parties has only a weak basis in the state publics, then we might find more divided government as voters confront party choices between too liberal and too conservative. On the other hand, if there is a strong mass basis to the polarization, the clearer brand labels would make it more difficult for minority party governors to win, as Fiorina pointed out happened with considerable frequency in places like Utah and South Dakota (Fiorina 1991).

concerning divided government in the states is Squire's (1993) discovery that citizens in states with divided government are significantly more content with their government than citizens living in states with unified government. One hypothesis, heretical from the responsible parties viewpoint, is that citizens prefer divided government because it produces policies offensive to fewer people than governments under unified control of parties that are clearly too liberal or too conservative for their average citizens. A similar challenge to the advocate of responsible parties comes from Daniel Shea (2003), who points out that the polarization of the current era has been accompanied by growing public alienation from government and high levels of disapproval of Congress in particular.

Policy gridlock is one of the problems parties scholars attribute to divided government, but this may not be much of a possibility for the important issues of state government: budgets have to be passed, and while much legislation no doubt faces rougher waters under divided control, we have few instances of government shutting down. In short, as Fiorina observed (1991), there is really no theoretical necessity that policies under divided governments will be inherently less desirable for the citizenry than those made by unified governments.

WHERE DO WE GO FROM HERE?

One of the challenges I mentioned was the complexity of state party systems. Much past research has sought to correlate variations in the "strength" of the parties in the electorate, the party organizations, and in government. An appropriate direction for future work may be to incorporate more systematically the ways in which ideological preferences tie the components of the parties together. Can strong ideological party networks successfully promote candidates without also winning over major portions of the mass electorate? And reflecting on the work on Congress, we should address the extent to which party polarization in government is endogenous, a function of rules and leadership powers, versus environmentally determined as a function of mass and party elite preferences, or even the cultural traditions of the states. Finally, can we find an equilibrium in the process of polarizing parties? Specifically, under what conditions do such factors as losing elections, or efforts to maintain majority status, lead to greater party moderation?

The second major challenge in studying the state party systems lies in the very heavy data demands for systematic comparative analyses. Fortunately, it appears that the future has some good news on this front. New polling technologies are likely to make increasing amounts of survey data with large state samples available to scholars. As these resources come on board, scholars will be able to delve deeper into the relationships between citizen partisan attachments on the one hand, and their values and how they perceive both the state and national parties (and their candidates) on the other. Ultimately, what happens to the state parties is rooted in the attachments of their mass electorates.

Party organizations are more diverse. As scholars, we should probably talk about state party networks and work to chart these rather than focus on the formal organizations. In doing so, we need to attend carefully to the currents of ideological change and cleavage, both within and between the parties. Extant work seems to establish that the main motors of change in American politics are the activists and contributors whose efforts frequently make or break candidates of different policy persuasions.

Policies are made by governments, and in responsible party systems these should reflect the preferences (and promises) of the majority party. Here too new resources should be available with much greater depth to legislative voting records, in committees and floor roll call votes, as well as better measures of state policy. These resources will allow scholars to gauge both what it is the parties want to do as well as whether they actually deliver responsibly.

The point is that to assess responsible party government in the states we need improved measures of party in the electorate, the party networks (as organization), and party in government and the policies they enact. At that point we should be able to provide a solid evaluation of the normative promise of strong competitive parties.

There are several reasons to expect that such conclusions might be mixed. Stronger competitive parties are clearly associated with some positive outcomes. One of the most consistent is voter turnout, which is consistently higher in more competitive contests (Grofman, Collet, and Griffin 1998; Hofstetter 1973; S. Patterson and Caldeira 1984). We also know that party voting is higher in chambers where there is near parity between the parties and that these systems are associated overall with more liberal policies. However, the analyses of the independent impact of the party system over and above the effects of state wealth, education, and particularly public opinion have been inconsistent and often non-existent across studies (Treadway 1985).

One of the remaining challenges is revisiting our thinking about how competition affects parties, candidates, and policymakers. The Key hypothesis presumed non-programmatic parties which were willing to adapt policy to the end of winning elections. That means making policy appeals to the non-voters who are disproportionately have-nots. But this logic needs to be amended in an era of highly programmatic parties where policy concerns are at least as much a driving force for activists and candidates as is winning. We have seen repeatedly that competition does not yield policy convergence; if anything as the parties have gotten more competitive we have seen polarization, although the causal connection here is far from established.

Another puzzle is the seeming contradiction between strong programmatic party policy platforms on the one hand and the fact that optimal policy should match well with the preferences of the great bulk of the population whose preferences are decidedly more moderate than the ideologues who define what the parties stand for on the other hand (Poole and Rosenthal 1984). In this situation voters have a clearer choice, but for the average citizen their ideal is not on the ballot. This by itself should form the basis for a strong argument that ever stronger, more cohesive parties are not an unmitigated good (John Coleman 1994).

The future for state parties research is bright with the promise of new data resources which will permit stronger and more definitive tests of theories of party and citizen behavior. But we are still dealing with concepts developed in reaction to the traditional party organizations of an earlier era. Either rethinking those or developing entirely new ideas is a necessary step to significantly improving our understanding of why the state party systems are what they are and what they are likely to become.

PART VII

....

INTEREST GROUPS

BIAS AND REPRESENTATION

....

....

WHO SINGS IN THE HEAVENLY CHORUS?

THE SHAPE OF THE ORGANIZED INTEREST SYSTEM*

....

KAY L. SCHLOZMAN

PERHAPS the most well-known comment upon the shape of the organized interest system was E. E. Schattschneider's remark that "the flaw in the pluralist heaven is that the heavenly chorus sings with a strong upper-class accent" (1960, 35). In this metaphor, he challenged the view, then dominant in political science, that organized groups of jointly concerned citizens will emerge more or less automatically in response to disturbances in the political environment that render them necessary. Instead, he argued that what he called the "pressure system" is biased in favor of groups representing the well-off, especially business, and against groups representing two other kinds of interests: the interests of broad publics and the interests of the disadvantaged.

---

* This chapter, which is part of a larger project about inequality of political voice being undertaken with Sidney Verba and Henry Brady, draws upon the intellectual framework in Schlozman and Tierney (1986, ch. 4). A fuller version of this argument and extensive elaboration regarding data collection and other technical matters can be found in Schlozman et al. (2008).

The nearly two generations since Schattschneider made his famous observation have witnessed a great deal of scholarly attention to the barriers to the emergence of interest groups, much of it a response to Mancur Olson's (1965) *Logic of Collective Action.* However, this literature sometimes neglects to specify why a student of democracy should be concerned about the difficulty of getting a nascent interest group off the ground and about the conditions under which the effort is likely to be successful. Perhaps the point is so obvious that is goes without saying. Still, it is critical to link the effort to model the circumstances under which interest groups emerge to an understanding of the significance of interest groups for politics in a democracy. Organized interests are such an essential part of the process by which policymakers in a democracy learn about the preferences and needs of citizens that barriers to entry into the political fray have potential consequences for the representation—and, in particular, for the equal representation—of citizen interests. Thus, political scientists should pay attention not only to explaining where groups come from but also to understanding the kinds of interests and concerns that have vigorous representation— and those that do not.[1] It is not simply the size but the shape of the organized interest system that counts.

Using a massive new dataset that enumerates and categorizes the organized interests active in Washington politics in the quarter-century between 1981 and 2006, this chapter takes an empirical look at the shape of the organized interest system in contemporary national politics. The discussion is predicated on two understandings that are sometimes overlooked in discussions of the mobilization of groups and the logic of collective action. The first is that interest *groups* are only a part—and, it turns out, only a small part—of the set of organizations that represent collective interests in politics. As will be shown, only a minority of such organizations are membership groups, and only a minority of such membership groups have individuals as members. Second, the shape of the organized interest system reflects not only processes by which organizations are created but also decisions to bring previously apolitical organizations into the political arena. A substantial literature focuses on the barriers to organizational formation; however, bringing an organization into existence is only the first step. Most existing organizations, even organizations that could be presumed to have a stake in political outcomes, are not active in politics, and the processes by which organizations come to take part politically are worthy of scrutiny. What we learn confirms the conclusions that Schattschneider drew on the basis, not of formal theory or statistical analysis, but of canny empirical observation.

---

[1] Further discussion of these issues and additional bibliography are contained in McFarland (1992); Baumgartner and Leech (1998, chs. 5 and 6).

ORGANIZED INTEREST REPRESENTATION: WHAT WOULD AN UNBIASED SYSTEM LOOK LIKE?

Schattschneider's discussion of "the scope and bias of the pressure system" seems based on the presumption that we could specify a set of organizations that would be both complete and representative. Questions of the representation of citizen interests, and in particular questions of the equal representation of interests, are among the most vexing for democracies. Alas, these questions become even more complicated when we move from consideration of the preferences of individuals to consideration of groups that are arrayed along a variety of dimensions of political cleavage and that have radically different numbers of members—and, sometimes, no members at all in the ordinary sense. With respect to norms of political equality, how do we compare the relative political weight of the AARP (formerly, the American Association of Retired Persons), which has more than 30 million members, and the American Beekeeping Federation, which has 1,200?[2]

A further dilemma for understanding the implications of collective representation for political equality is the ambiguity of knowing for whom the organization is speaking. The interests, needs, and preferences of the members of an association are rarely uniform on all relevant issues. Such divisions of opinion and interest are especially common when a voluntary association implicitly seeks to represent a constituency beyond its dues-paying members. The activists who join and run membership associations often have opinions that are, if not different in direction, more intensely held and more extreme than do the less vocal and active people the organization purports to represent. Thus, when an organization takes a stand in politics, there may be ambiguities as to whose voice is being heard.

Such ambiguities are multiplied when we move beyond associations of individuals. In fact, the majority of organizations in the pressure system are not associations of individuals. (On this point, which is often overlooked in discussions of organized interest politics, see Salisbury 1984; Lowery, Gray, Anderson, and Newmark 2004.) They may be associations of institutions like the Snack Food Association, which has firms as members, or the National Association of Children's Hospitals. Or they may—like General Motors, the Ford Foundation, or the American Ballet Theatre—have no members at all. The fact that many organizations in the pressure system have no members in the ordinary sense raises knotty questions for equal representation of citizens. When representation is by institutions like corporations or universities, whose concerns and preferences are being represented: the stockholders, executives, employees, or customers of a corporation?

---

[2] These figures were taken from the online version of *Encyclopedia of Associations*, <http://galenet. gale.com.proxy.bc.edu/a/acp/db/grr/extended-org.html>, accessed Nov. 27, 2006.

The administration, professors, staff, graduates, or students of a university? Surely, there are many occasions when the interests of these various stakeholders coincide. Still, evidence that ranges from the number of labor–management disputes before the National Labor Relations Board (NLRB) to student protests over tuition hikes suggests that what is good for one part of an institutional constituency is not necessarily good for all.

An additional complexity is that the set of organizations that take stands in politics is structured around multiple axes of cleavage. It is complicated enough to characterize equal political representation considering only the dimension around which the largest portion of organized interest representation takes place, economic interests associated with making a living. It becomes even more so when the framework includes the many other dimensions around which interests are organized. In an unbiased pressure system, how much of the space should be occupied by organizations based on race? On attitudes towards capital punishment or the rights of homeowners? On hobbies?

In short, organized interest politics poses an intractable problem with respect to equal representation of citizen interests. When it comes to voting, it is possible to specify as a baseline the eligible electorate and then to measure how much and in what ways the set of people who actually go to the polls departs from that baseline. An analogous assessment of the biases in the set of organized interests active in democratic politics is simply not feasible. However, even if it is impossible to generate indices of over- and underrepresentation for particular kinds of interests that are represented by organizations, we should not allow the perfect to become the enemy of the good. A careful and detailed description of the distribution of organizations in pressure politics yields important information about the accent of the singers in the organized interest chorus.

The Voices in the Chorus:
Some Expectations

Schattschneider's observation about the accent of the heavenly chorus was a response to the once-dominant analysis of American politics, interest group pluralism, which placed interest groups at the center of policymaking and emphasized the permeability and fluid nature of the organized interest system.[3] The interest group pluralist

---

[3] Discussions of the various explanations for the emergence of interest groups can be found in Nownes (2004, 49–58); McFarland (2007, 53–7); Schlozman et al. (2008). Among the most significant works from an interest group pluralist point of view are Bentley (1951); Truman (1971); Latham

argument about the absence of barriers to the emergence of political groups sustained its most formidable challenge from Mancur Olson (1965), who contended that the rational individual has an incentive not to spend scarce resources of money and time in support of favored causes but rather to free-ride on the efforts of others. Olson's model has elicited many efforts that meet it on its own terms and seek to specify the circumstances under which groups would, in fact, come into being.[4] Mancur Olson's analysis and the literature it has spawned suggest that large, diffuse groups lacking the capacity to coerce cooperation or to provide selective benefits often face severe collective action problems that prevent them from organizing on behalf of their joint political concerns.

In spite of the undoubted significance of Olson's analysis, the "free-rider problem" is not the whole story. One factor that is often lost in discussions of the costs of starting an organization or keeping one going is the consequences for the shape of the organized interest system of the disparities among groups in the capacity to assume those costs. What we might call the "resource problem" alerts us to the fact that not all potential constituencies are in a position to bear the costs of political organization and advocacy.[5] It is not simply that some potential constituencies have patrons who are willing to shoulder a disproportionate share of the costs. Even when there is no such patron on the scene, some sets of collectively concerned citizens not only are able to afford the financial costs of organizational support but are in a better position to command the skills, acquire the information, cultivate the media, and utilize the connections that are helpful in getting an organization off the ground or keeping it going. A group of jointly interested citizens that is reasonably well endowed with a variety of kinds of resources, for example, veterans,

(1952b); Dahl (1956). These authors differ from one another in important respects, and no single work serves as the definitive text for interest group pluralism.

[4] See, for example, Wilson (1974, esp. chs. 2 and 3), who points to a broader array of selective benefits that organizations can provide in place of material ones; Salisbury (1969) and Frolich, Oppenheimer, and Young (1971), who explore the role of entrepreneurs in founding and nurturing new organizations; Walker (1991, esp. ch. 5), who focuses on the significance of patrons that encourage and subsidize the founding of new organizations; and Nownes (1995), who emphasizes the importance of large donors among members.

[5] Although they focus more explicitly on social movements by drawing attention to basic resource requirements, resource mobilization theorists make a point that is directly applicable to the domain of political organizations. See, in particular, McCarthy and Zald (1977) and Zald and McCarthy (1987).

Gray and Lowery (1996a), who pioneered the application of population ecology theory to study various kinds of political organizations, shift the focus from micro-level processes that lead to the formation of individual organizations to macro-level consideration of organized interest communities. For a brief presentation and references to their many journal articles, see Lowery and Gray (2007b).

In his study of the relationship between the characteristics of individual members of social groups and the number of political organizations that represent those groups, Matt Grossmann (2006, 19) finds that "the mean socio-economic status of a constituency . . . is significantly correlated with the number of organizations and staff representing it."

is more likely to overcome the hurdle posed by the logic of collective action than is a group of similar size and similar intensity of concern that is resource-poor, say public housing tenants or nursing home residents. Similarly, among occupational groups, we would be more likely to find organized representation for building contractors, surgeons, or college deans than for baggage handlers, convenience store clerks, or gas station attendants.

Moreover, any perspective that focuses exclusively on group formation as the key to the shape of the pressure system misses two additional factors. First, as already mentioned, most of the organizations in pressure politics are not interest groups of individuals. Of the nearly 14,000 organizations listed in the 2006 *Washington Representatives* directory (Sheridan 2006), only a small fraction, 12.4 percent, are associations of individuals; 14.5 percent are associations of institutions such as trade and other business associations. A majority, 52.8 percent, are institutions like corporations, hospitals, or universities.[6] Second, the composition of the pressure community is affected not only by organizational births and deaths but also by decisions of previously apolitical organizations to enter the political fray and of politically active organizations to exit politics and revert to apolitical status. Olson's analysis provides no explanation for why an organization that is in a position to provide collective goods or coerce membership would take the step of devoting resources to political action. In fact, the logic of collective action obtains for decisions made by organizations—institutions as well as membership groups— at this stage as well. (Focusing on the motivations and actions of organization entrepreneurs, Robert Salisbury 1969 and James Q. Wilson 1974, 195–8, propose answers to this puzzle.) As we shall see, most of the organizations new to the pressure community are not organizations that have never existed, but rather are organizations that had been outside of politics and, for reasons that are less well studied, are activated into politics. Thus, the shape of the pressure community is influenced by a number of factors—of which an important one, but far from the only one, is the set of processes by which new political organizations come into being.

THE *WASHINGTON REPRESENTATIVES* DATABASE

In order to investigate the contours of the organized interest community, we have built an extensive data archive containing information about the characteristics, organizational histories, and political activity of organizations involved in national

---

[6] Governments or associations of governments make up 13.2 percent of them, and the remainder are mixed or unknown.

politics.[7] This newly compiled database covers the more than 27,000 organizations
listed in the 1981, 1991, 2001, or 2006 *Washington Representatives* directory as having
a presence in national politics—either by maintaining an office in the capital or by
hiring Washington-based consultants or counsel to manage their government
relations activities.[8]

The *Washington Representatives* directory is the single most nearly comprehensive
listing of politically active organizations in Washington.[9] The 1991 General Accounting Office Report that was used as justification for the 1995 Lobbying Disclosure Act
made the point that, of the 13,500 people named as lobbyists in the *Washington
Representatives* directory, fewer than 4,000 were registered with Congress (see Salant
1995a, 2239). That the GAO relied on the directory for its evidence about lobbyists
suggests its significance as a source of information. Still, we should note that even this
extensive listing is only partial. The *Washington Representatives* directory does not
include organizations active in state and local politics; organizations that drop in on
Washington politics on an occasional basis but do not maintain an ongoing presence;

[7] Collection of these data was supported by Boston College and Harvard University. This enterprise
has benefited from the industry, enthusiasm, and talents of an extraordinary group of research
assistants: Will Bacic, Jeremy Bailey, John Barry, Patrick Behrer, Traci Burch, Ageliki Christopher,
Lauren Daniel, Joshua Darr, Sarah Debbink, Lauren Escher, Glen Feder, John Gattman, Daniel Geary,
Heitor Gouvea, Gail Harmon, Caitlyn Jones, Philip Jones, Lora Krsulich, Samuel Lampert, Jeremy
Landau, Kate Letourneau, Miriam Mansury, Katie Marcot, Timothy Mooney, Rafael Munoz, Janice
Pardue, Michael Parker, Robert Porter, Nathaniel Probert, Karthick Ramakrishnan, Veronica Roberts,
Ganesh Sitaraman, Dorothy Smith, Kathryn Smith, Martin Steinwand, Emily Thorson, Clay Tousey,
and Jill Weidner.

[8] The directory *Washington Representatives* (Washington, DC: Columbia Books) is published
annually. According to an interview on Nov. 10, 2003, with Valerie Sheridan, the editor of the
Washington Representatives directory at Columbia Books, the directory includes organizations that are
active in Washington politics by virtue either of having an office in the DC area or hiring DC-area
consultants or counsel to represent them. The out-of-town organization—a union local in Seattle,
corporation in Dayton, or hospital in Phoenix—that sends a vice president on a day trip to
Washington to testify before a Senate committee is not listed. For details on the procedures used for
assembling the entries in the directory, see Schlozman et al. (2008).
   We are grateful to Ms Sheridan for her assistance and for her forthcoming answers to our questions.

[9] It has been suggested that we should have used the *Encyclopedia of Associations* rather than the
Washington Representatives directory. The *Encyclopedia* is an invaluable resource for those interested
in voluntary associations. We used it, and its Web-based counterpart, Associations Unlimited,
extensively in assembling background information about the associations in the directories.
Nevertheless, it has two disadvantages for our purposes. First, as we have mentioned, a majority of the
organizations in the *Washington Representatives* directories are not associations at all, whether
composed of institutional or individual members, but are instead institutions of some kind. These
institutions—corporations, universities, hospitals, and the like—are not listed in the *Encyclopedia of
Associations*. Furthermore, except when an organization category—for example, environmental
organizations—is inherently political, it is impossible to discern whether an organization is politically
active. Since, as we shall see, many organizations move in and out of politics, the failure to designate
organizations as politically active is a serious shortcoming for our purposes. It would, however, be
interesting to combine information from the *Encyclopedia* about the universe of membership
associations with information from our databases to predict which membership associations
eventually make their way into national politics.

or organizations whose participation is confined to writing checks to campaigns or filing amicus briefs.

Given our concern with organizational representation of varying interests, a crucial part of this data collection was to place each organization into one or more of ninety-eight organizational categories. These categories were designed to capture the nature of the interest being represented—business, an occupation, a foreign government, a group of universities, a religious or ethnic group, a conservative think tank, and so on—as well as something about its organizational structure. In contrast to most studies of organized interests that rely on highly aggregated categories, we deliberately proliferated the number of categories in order to capture fine distinctions. Thus, we can distinguish domestic from foreign corporations; public from private sector unions; organizations representing African Americans from those representing Latinos; private from public universities; consumer groups from environmental ones; and so on.[10]

The significance of the large number of categories is worth underlining. Observers of American politics have emphasized the significance of the emergence of large numbers of citizens' groups over the last generation. However, this aggregate category obscures important distinctions with theoretical importance for the understanding of American politics. Our classificatory scheme makes it possible to discriminate between organizations that seek benefits for more limited constituencies and those that seek public goods that are broadly beneficial to all in society. Among the former are a variety that advocate on behalf of the disadvantaged whether on the basis of economic need or of some non-economic identity such as race, religion, or gender. With respect to the latter, the categories differentiate among organizations pursuing a variety of kinds of public goods—objectives like safer streets or safer consumer products, cleaner water or cleaner government, enhanced domestic security or reduced government size—and allow us to distinguish between organizations that seek liberal and conservative public interests.

---

[10] When it was unclear how to classify an organization, we dug deeply—considering mission statements, FAQs, organizational histories, and the composition of the board or the staff. As a result, we were able to find information about all but 230, or 1.7 percent, of the nearly 14,000 organizations in the 2006 directory. Of course, in spite of repeated efforts to clean the database, the volume of the data coded means that, inevitably, mistakes were made.

Although the categories in this classification scheme accommodate many distinctions, there were, inevitably organizations that seemed to fit comfortably into more than one category. To accommodate such cases, we permit an organization to be coded into as many as three categories. Thus, the National Medical Association (NMA), a membership group of African American physicians, was coded as both a professional association and an African American organization. Appropriate weights have been applied to organizations that have been placed in more than one category. Thus, the NMA is considered to be 0.5 professional association and 0.5 African American racial or ethnic group.

The Contours of Organized Interest Representation

The range of politically active organizations contained in our database is nothing short of astonishing. For all the number and diversity of organizations, however, it turns out that both the free-rider problem and the resource-constraint problem have profound effects on whose voices are heard through the medium of collective representation. The data in Table 22.1, which summarizes the distribution of organizations that were listed in the *Washington Representatives* directory in 2006, make clear that the essential outlines of Schattschneider's analysis of the pressure system still pertain today and that the set of organized political interests continues to be organized principally around economic matters. In this domain— which includes large numbers of membership associations, for example, unions and professional associations, that join people on the basis of their shared occupations—the representation of business is dominant.[11]

Table 22.1 Organized interests in Washington politics[a]

Organized interest	%
Corporations[b]	36.1%
Trade and other business associations	10.7
Occupational associations	5.2
Unions	0.8
Education	5.4
Health	4.4
Public interest	4.1
Identity groups[c]	3.8
Social welfare or poor	0.9
State and local governments	11.8
Foreign	6.5
Other	8.6
Don't know	1.7
TOTAL	100.0%
N	13,776

[a] Distribution of organizations listed in the 2006 *Washington Representatives* directory.
[b] Includes US corporations, US subsidiaries of foreign corporations, and for-profit firms of professionals such as law and consulting firms.
[c] Includes organizations representing racial or ethnic groups, religious denominations, elderly, women, or LGBT.

[11] For a cogent critique of the possibility of drawing inferences from counts of organizations and extensive bibliographical citations, see Lowery and Gray (2004b). For all their criticisms, many of

Consistent with Schattschneider's analysis, the number of public interest groups is relatively small, accounting for less than 5 percent of the organizations active in Washington. In addition, those who are not economically advantaged—including those with ordinary jobs and middle-class incomes—are underrepresented in pressure politics. Organizations of the poor themselves are extremely rare, if not non-existent, and organizations that advocate on behalf of the poor are very scarce (see Imig 1996). In addition, Table 22.1 makes clear that a number of other kinds of organizations—in particular, state and local governments in the United States and a variety of kinds of foreign interests—that are less often featured in discussions of Washington pressure politics also have a substantial organizational presence.

Although this brief synopsis points to important features of the shape of the Washington pressure community, the highly aggregated nature of the categories in Table 22.1 obscures a great deal. Therefore, it seems useful to take a closer look at some of the more important categories of interest organizations.

Economic Organizations in Washington Politics

Over two-thirds of the organized interests in Washington are institutions or membership associations directly related to the joint political concerns attendant to making a living.[12] Among the thousands of organizations in this remarkably diverse sector, those representing business—domestic and foreign corporations, the multiple kinds of business associations, occupational associations of business executives, and business-oriented think tanks and research organizations—constitute the overwhelming share, more than three-quarters. Put another way, of all the organizations active in Washington, more than half, 51.6 percent, represent business in one way or another.[13] And, of these business groups, corporations are by far the most numerous. In fact, American corporations accounted for more than two-thirds of business organizations and more than a third of all the organizations with

---

which had been anticipated in earlier works (including Schlozman and Tierney 1986, ch. 4), it is interesting to note the following in their conclusion: "First, we are not suggesting that counts of interest organizations and their behaviors are uninteresting data, useless for understanding the nature of interest representation .... Second, and most emphatically, we are not arguing that business interests are under-represented within interest communities or that their predominance in numbers has declined over time" (2004b, 23).

[12] This figure includes corporations (both domestic and foreign), trade and other business associations (again, both domestic and foreign), farm organizations, occupational associations, labor unions, and institutions and organizations in the health and educational sectors.

[13] Using data coded from approximately 19,000 lobbying reports in 1996, Baumgartner and Leech (2001, tables 1–2) find a distribution of lobbying organizations quite similar to that described here. Echoing our findings, they conclude: "Unions, non-profits, and citizen groups will sometimes make their voices heard, but will often be absent. Rarely do these groups lobby alone. That may be the clearest statement of the privileged place of business" (2001, 1207).

Washington representation in 2006.[14] Although they are, by a factor of more than three, the most numerous of the organizations active in Washington, it is interesting to note that only a small proportion of American corporations are represented.[15] Moreover, we should make clear that our emphasis on the sheer number of organizations that represent business interests in national politics should not be interpreted as implying either that business speaks with one voice or that business interests always prevail when they are involved.[16]

The educational and health sectors contribute a much smaller, but still notable, set of organizations. In both cases, more than three-quarters of the organizations are individual institutions: for education, overwhelmingly universities; for health, hospitals, clinics, nursing homes, and other institutions that care for the ill or disabled. In both the education and health fields there are a variety of associations, the functional equivalent of trade and other business associations, that bring together institutions with joint concerns—for example, the Council of Graduate Schools, the National Association of Independent Schools, the Federation of American Hospitals, and the Eye Bank Association of America.

A much smaller, yet nonetheless highly important, set of organizations represent the agricultural sector. Farm organizations constitute little more than 1 percent of all organizations in the Washington pressure system.[17]

Labor Unions and Other Occupational Associations

The organizations in the economic sector are overwhelmingly either for-profit or non-profit institutions or associations of such institutions. Still, individuals gain significant representation through their memberships in various kinds of occupational associations. Labor unions are one category of occupational association that traditionally receives attention in discussions of Washington representation. Although they have larger memberships and enroll members from a broader array of occupations, as shown in Table 22.2A, unions are not especially numerous. Unions

[14] The umbrella category of "corporations" includes partnerships and sole proprietorships as well as corporations.

[15] This point is made by a number of analysts of the role of business in organized interest activity. Even Fortune 500 firms are not necessarily represented in Washington politics by lobbyists or PACs. See, for example, Boies (1989, 821); Lowery et al. (2004); Brasher and Lowery (2006); Drope and Hansen (2006, 7).

[16] Although they disagree among themselves about the aggregate weight of business interests in politics, scholars tend to agree that few controversies engage the entire business community speaking as one. For varying perspectives, see Lindblom (1977); Smith (2000); Baumgartner and Leech (2001); Baumgartner et al. (2009). A helpful review article is Hart (2004).

[17] Following the categorization used by the Census, fishing and forestry are included along with farming.

comprise only 13 percent of the occupational membership associations, or 1 percent of all organizations, in the Washington pressure community.

Most of the membership associations that represent individuals on the basis of their occupations do not bargain collectively. By far the most numerous—accounting for more than half—of such organizations are professional associations. These organizations unite people—for example, plant physiologists, landscape architects, historians, audiologists, transportation engineers, or thoracic surgeons—on the basis of a shared occupation that requires a prescribed course of educational training and at least a college degree.[18] Alone among the categories of occupational associations, professional associations include large numbers of organizations uniting members who share not only their profession but some other characteristic as well. There are, for example, associations of Hispanic journalists, black psychologists, women highway safety engineers, Jewish lawyers and judges, and gay and lesbian physicians.

Similar to professional associations is the much smaller number of occupational associations that represent executives, managers, and professionals working in the for-profit sector. There are organizations representing bank directors, lobbyists, investment managers, funeral directors, real estate executives, and home economists working in business. In addition are analogous organizations of managers and administrators in non-profit settings: healthcare administrators, academic deans, research administrators, art museum directors, and the like. Such non-union government employees as court reporters, planners, crime lab directors, circuit court judges, police officers, and postal supervisors are also organized.

Finally, 9 percent of the occupational associations, or less than 1 percent of all the organizations in the Washington pressure community, bring together those in non-professional and non-managerial occupations. Examples of such groups include associations of realtors, master printers, meeting planners, travel agents, medical sonographers, and pilots. Comparing the list of these organizations with the Census list of all occupations is instructive.[19] What is clear is the extent to which even the associations that enroll non-professional and non-managerial workers tend to represent those in occupations with relatively high levels of skill, pay, and status. Unless they are unionized, there are no associations representing many occupations: bellhops, telemarketers, hotel desk clerks, laundry workers, bus drivers, bartenders, custodians, bank tellers, or tool and die makers. A conservative estimate is that, except for unions, there are no associations representing the occupations held by seven-eighths of the more than 90 million American workers in non-professional

[18] In categorizing occupational associations as professional associations, we followed the Census definition of professional occupations, which includes certain occupations—for example, professional athlete—that do not conform fully to this criterion.

[19] The remainder of the paragraph is based on a comparison of the data about other occupational associations in our database with US Census data found at <http://www.census.gov/compendia/statab/labor_force_employment_earnings>, accessed June 5, 2009.

Table 22.2 Distributions of organizations within categories[a]
A. Occupational membership associations

Association	%
Union	
Blue-collar unions	5.8%
White-collar unions	3.3
Mixed and other unions	4.0
Non-union	
Associations of managers and professionals in business	10.1
Associations of administrators of non-profits	3.4
Professional associations	45.9
Associations of public employees[b]	18.6
Other occupational associations	8.9
TOTAL	100.0%
N	822

B. Identity groups

Identity group	%
Racial or ethnic	62.6%
Religious	20.2
Women	9.8
Elderly	5.3
LGBT	2.1
TOTAL	100.0%
N	526

C. Public interest groups

Public interest group	%
Consumer	6.4%
Environmental and wildlife	22.0
Government reform	4.5
Civil liberties	1.3
Citizen empowerment	3.5
Other liberal groups	18.8
Other conservative groups	14.2
Other	29.2
TOTAL	99.9%
N	567

[a] Distribution of organizations listed in the 2006 *Washington Representatives* directory.
[b] Includes associations of military employees.

and non-managerial occupations. Indeed, other than unions, there are *no occupational associations at all* to organize those who labor at low-skill jobs.

Representing the Less Privileged

We must entertain the possibility that, by focusing on how adults are represented in terms of their occupations or workforce status, we may have overlooked other forms of representation of the economic needs of those who are in the middle and lower rungs of the economic ladder, many of whom have experienced heightened economic insecurity over the past few decades. We live in an era when workers, even highly skilled ones, are squeezed by many trends designed to cut labor costs (see, for example, M. Katz 2001, chs. 7–8; J. Hacker 2006). These range from the export of jobs overseas to the outsourcing of service functions to the increased use of part-timers and independent contractors. Such developments create potential economic constituencies—for example, workers whose company pensions are in jeopardy or workers whose jobs provide neither healthcare benefits nor protection from disability or job loss. However, those who share such statuses have *no* Washington representation by groups organized around such joint non-occupationally defined economic interests.

Furthermore, like those who work in jobs requiring little in the way of skills and commanding little in the way of pay, those at the bottom of the economic ladder are also underrepresented in pressure politics. We saw in Table 22.1 that less than 1 percent of the organizations active in Washington in 2006 fell into the category we label as "social welfare or poor." The majority are providers of direct services like the Food Bank of Virginia Peninsula, Goodwill Industries, the Indianapolis Neighborhood Housing Partnership, Meals on Wheels, or the American Red Cross. The remainder are organizations that advocate on behalf of the poor in the United States or in favor of more comprehensive guarantees with respect to basic human needs in American politics. Such organizations, which may also attempt to organize the poor, include organizations like the Coalition on Human Needs, the Food Research and Action Project, and the Center on Budget and Policy Priorities.[20]

Finally, we looked for organizations of recipients of social welfare or tax benefits—for example, jobless workers, public housing tenants, or those who benefit from the Earned Income Tax Credit—advocating on their own behalf. These are needy constituencies with an obvious stake in policy outcomes. A very few such organizations—for example, the Full Employment Action Council and the Section 8 Housing Group—had appeared in earlier directories. However, of the nearly

---

[20] Many such organizations not only engage in advocacy but also provide direct services. Coders were instructed to consider the overall balance in organizational activities in placing an organization into one of the two categories.

14,000 organizations enumerated in the 2006 directory, *not one* was an association of beneficiaries of means-tested government benefits representing themselves. Furthermore, as Jeffrey Berry (Berry with Arons 2003, 65) points out, the health and human service non-profits that have as clients "constituencies that are too poor, unskilled, ignorant, incapacitated, or overwhelmed with their problems to organize on their own" are constrained by the 501(c)3 provisions in the tax code from undertaking significant lobbying.

Representing Identity Groups

The evidence about the representation of economic interests in pressure politics is compelling: the overwhelming share of organizations represent the well-off. We should, however, note an important qualification to this pattern. When it comes to the sets of groups constellated around non-economic axes of cleavage—for example, race, ethnicity, religion, age, sexual orientation, or gender—it is not the dominant groups in society that receive the lion's share of explicit organizational representation. In contrast to the circumstance that obtains for economic need, it is the less advantaged among the identity groups that have whatever organizational representation there is.[21] Of course, the interests of middle-aged white men are surely well represented in the mainstream economic organizations that form the bulk of the organized interest community. Still, numerous groups represent the interests of, for example, women, the elderly, Muslims, Asian Americans, or African Americans, and few, if any, are explicitly organized around the interests of men, the middle-aged, or WASPs.

While these organizations are remarkable for their diversity, they comprise less than 4 percent of all organizations in the pressure community. The distribution of such organizations is worthy of note. As shown in Table 22.2B, more than three-fifths of these organizations represent racial or ethnic groups. Interestingly, 65 percent of the organizations in this category (or 40 percent of all identity-based organizations) are organizations, usually tribes, representing Native Americans. By a factor of more than six, organizations representing Native Americans outnumber those representing African Americans, the group traditionally viewed as the vanguard with respect to minority politics.

---

[21] I am aware that the term "identity groups" is a contested one and use it to denote institutions and associations in which the organizing principle is some non-economic demographic characteristic. Note that, because they are staffed and supported by adults and only rarely have children or young people as members, we do not classify organizations that advocate for the young as identity groups.

Public Interest Groups

Earlier we discussed that the free-rider problem implies that public goods will receive less vigorous organized advocacy and noted that the number of public interest groups is relatively small, accounting for less than 5 percent of the organizations active in Washington. Although not especially numerous, the causes they advocate are remarkably diverse. Discussions of public interests often overlook how often, in any real political controversy, opposing conceptions of the public interest compete with each other: for example, wilderness preservation with economic growth, consumer product safety with low prices, or national security with low taxes (see McFarland 1976). Table 22.2C shows the distribution of such organizations and makes clear that, while in the aggregate public interest groups lean left, these broad public interests are not inevitably liberal, and that there is also considerable representation of such conservative public goods as low taxes or domestic security. Moreover, many of the public interest groups in various presumptively liberal categories are, in fact, either ideologically neutral or conservative. Examples would include consumer groups like the American Automobile Association and the American Motorcyclist Association; wildlife organizations like Pheasants Forever; or government reform organizations like Citizens against Government Waste.

State and Local Governments

Discussions of the pressure system do not usually focus on governments as advocates in federal politics. However, other than business interests, representatives of state and local governments are the most common organized interests. Given the extent to which the national government is a source of both financial largesse and regulatory headaches, subnational governments have incentives to establish a presence in Washington. More than two-thirds of the organizations in what is sometimes called the "intergovernmental lobby" are local and county governments and their affiliated departments and authorities: Lake County, Illinois; the city of Huntsville, Alabama; the Eugene Oregon Water and Electric Authority; and so on. Nearly all of the nation's most populous cities and most of the states either have an office in Washington or hire outside counsel to represent their interests.

Other Organizations

This review of the kinds of organizations that are represented in Washington politics has omitted a few categories that deserve mention. Given the global era in which we live and the impact that what happens in the United States has on other nations and their citizens, it is not unexpected that 6.5 percent of the organizations listed in the 2006 directory are foreign. Of these, 25 percent represent foreign governments from Albania to Zimbabwe and their ministries. The majority, 63 percent, represent foreign corporations and foreign business associations.

Table 22.1 lists 8.6 percent of the organizations in the 2006 directory as "Other." In fact, most of the organizations obscured under this rubric fall into small but significant categories. For example, a variety of kinds of organizations that are concerned with children and young people—ranging from the Boy Scouts to the Child Nutrition Forum to the National Center for Missing and Exploited Children—comprise less than 1 percent of all the organizations. Although their political clout is well known, veterans' organizations such as the American Legion and the Retired Officers' Association constitute an even smaller share, a mere 0.2 percent of the 2006 organizations. A residual group of 0.7 percent of the 2006 organizations—of which the Coin Coalition, a heterogeneous coalition that embraces advocates for the blind as well as vending machine manufacturers in support of the minting of a dollar coin, is an example—could be identified but not placed in one of the other categories.

THE EXPANDING PRESSURE COMMUNITY

This snapshot view of the composition of the organized interest community as of 2006 obscures its essential fluidity. In an era in which the costs of transportation and communications have fallen in relative terms and electronic technologies make it easier to stay in touch with both those at an organization's headquarters and the folks at the grassroots, organizations can move in and out of politics relatively easily. However, the entries and exits from Washington politics do not balance out. Overall, for the twenty-five-year period for which we have data, there has been substantial growth in the number of organizations that take part in Washington politics. Compared to the 1981 *Washington Representatives* directory, the 2006 directory lists more than twice the number of organizations, a rate of growth that far outpaces the increase in population, which has grown by less than one-third over the period.[22]

That the number of organizations in pressure politics has increased steadily over the past quarter-century would seem to contradict a widely documented trend in American society, the decline in affiliations with membership associations.

---

[22] The rate of increase has been somewhat uneven. The number of entries increased by 19 percent from 1981 to 1991 and by 47 percent from 1991 to 2001, a pattern that reflects, at least in part, the impact of the 1995 Lobbying Disclosure Act, which closed loopholes in the 1946 Federal Regulation of Lobbying Act, and led to an increase in the number of registered lobbyists. Note, however, that the number of entries in the 2006 directory was 18 percent higher than it had been in 2001, a rate of increase nearly twice that in the 1980s. On the Lobbying Disclosure Act, see Salant (1995b, 3632).

Although they make somewhat different arguments and use somewhat different kinds of evidence, both Robert Putnam (2000, especially ch. 3) and Theda Skocpol (2003, especially chs. 4–6) demonstrate an erosion in participation in voluntary associations. Putnam uses a variety of measures—ranging from the decrease in membership in organizations like PTAs to the dwindling of attendance at club meetings—to document a decrease in associational involvement. He considers the trend in organizational activity to be a crucial component of the deterioration of social capital, a wider phenomenon entailing a diminution of many kinds of formal and informal social connectedness as well as an erosion of social trust. Skocpol focuses on the increasing significance of staff-led, checkbook organizations at the expense of what she calls cross-class membership associations and discusses the consequences of these developments for the experience of democratic governance and cultivation of democratic habits. Although Skocpol and Putnam differ in the nature of their language and their data, they converge in a concern about the implications of their findings for the democratic capacities of citizens.

Skocpol also delineates the class implications of the trends she outlines: the increasing numbers of professionally managed national organizations, requiring little of their members other than financial support, draw their members very disproportionately from among the well-educated; the gap between the proportion of college-educated Americans who are members of a professional society and the proportion of non-college-educated Americans who are union members has grown substantially (see Skocpol 2003, 212–19 and fig. 5.10). Skocpol's concern with social class parallels issues that emerge later in this chapter where I document the decline in the relative weight of unions within the pressure system and the drastic erosion in the proportion of private sector workers who are union members. Where this approach departs from Skocpol's is in demonstrating that, in other ways, these citizen groups broaden the set of interests represented in the pressure system. In a pressure system dominated by economic organizations, most of them representing the interests of economic haves, these citizen groups bring into the political conversation perspectives that might otherwise go unvoiced—for example, advocates on behalf of public goods of both the left and the right or on behalf of groups organized around a shared identity, whether, race, ethnicity, gender, age, or sexual orientation.

With respect to the question of how to reconcile diminishing organizational involvement at the individual level with an ever increasing number of organizations active in pressure politics, there is no necessary contradiction. There is overlap, but not congruence, between two different sets of organizations. Both Putnam and Skocpol are discussing developments with respect to *voluntary associations of individuals*. The majority of membership associations are not active in politics on any level, especially nationally. And, as shown earlier, the vast majority of organizations that are active in Washington pressure politics are not associations with individuals as members.

Table 22.3 The changing Washington pressure community

	Share of DC organizations (%)				Relative increase (%)	Absolute increase (no.)
	1981	1991	2001	2006		
Corporations[a]	45.9%	33.8%	34.9%	36.1%	62%	1,898
Trade and other business associations	15.5	14.8	13.2	10.7	41%	429
Occupational associations	8.1	8.6	6.8	5.2	32%	172
Unions	1.6	1.5	1.0	0.8	0%	0
Education	1.6	3.0	4.2	5.4	612%	643
Health	0.9	2.4	3.5	4.4	883%	547
Public interest	3.8	4.8	4.6	4.1	123%	313
Identity groups[b]	2.7	3.5	3.8	3.8	192%	347
Social welfare or poor	0.5	0.7	0.8	0.9	291%	95
State and local governments	5.1	7.0	10.4	11.8	382%	1,292
Foreign	8.7	10.2	7.8	6.5	54%	315
Other	4.3	7.0	7.7	8.6	312%	896
Don't know	1.2	2.7	1.4	1.7	185%	148
TOTAL	99.0%	100.0%	100.1%	100.0%	106%	7,095
N	6,681	7,925	11,653	13,776		

[a] Includes US corporations, US subsidiaries of foreign corporations, and for-profit firms of professionals such as law and consulting firms.
[b] Includes organizations representing racial, ethnic, or religious groups, elderly, women, or LGBT.

As shown by Table 22.3, the expansion of the pressure system has been quite uneven across various categories of organizations. Not unexpectedly, the data show above average growth rates among the several kinds of citizens' organizations: identity groups, public interest groups, and organizations that provide social welfare services or that advocate on behalf of the poor. However, there are other striking changes that seem to have gone unnoticed by Washington watchers. One is the extraordinary growth rates both of organizations in the health and educational sectors and of state and local governments. Another is that growth in the kinds of organizations that have traditionally dominated in pressure politics—business organizations and occupational associations—has not kept pace with the overall rate of increase in the number of organizations in Washington politics. Especially striking is the fact that the number of labor unions is unchanged. Indeed, unions are the *only* one of the aggregated categories in Table 22.3 not to register an increase over the quarter-century period.

The right-hand column of Table 22.3, which shows the changes in the absolute number of organizations listed, tells a somewhat different story. A high rate of increase may not imply many new organizations and vice versa. For example, a fairly high rate of increase for organizations that provide social services and advocacy for the economically needy masks a quite small absolute increase. In contrast, although the relative rate of increase for organizations representing business lagged, the absolute increase was the most substantial. There were 1898 more corporations and 429 more trade and other business associations in the 2006 directory than in 1981. Taken together, these changes mean that, in absolute terms, the increases in the kinds of organizations traditionally well represented in pressure politics—corporations, trade and other business associations, occupational associations of professionals and managers, and the like—dwarf the increases in the kinds of organizations that we have seen to be less well represented—public interest groups and organizations representing the less advantaged.

The Changing Distribution of Organizations

Table 22.3 also presents data about the distribution of organizations in the pressure system for each of the years in the study. On balance, there is a great deal of continuity. Organizations representing broad publics and the disadvantaged continue to constitute only a small share of organized interest representation in Washington. The economic organizations that have traditionally dominated in the pressure system—corporations, trade and other business associations, occupational associations, and labor unions—continue to represent a majority of organizations active in national politics. Nevertheless, these traditionally dominant sectors command a somewhat smaller share of the pressure system than they did in 1981. As mentioned earlier, several categories of organizations represent the interests of the for-profit sector: corporations, both domestic and foreign; trade and other business associations, again both domestic and foreign, which have corporations as members; occupational associations of business executives and professionals; and business-related think tanks and research organizations. On one hand, these various kinds of organizations representing business constituted 69.3 percent of all organizations listed in 1981 but only 51.6 percent in 2006—a substantial drop. On the other hand, there were 2,486 more business-related organizations active in Washington politics than in 1981—a substantial increase. In fact, combining *all* the unions, public interest groups, identity groups, and organizations representing the economically needy listed in 2006 yields a total that is just about half the number of *additional* organizations representing the private sector.

The diminution of the share of the pressure system occupied by traditional business and professional organizations has not been accompanied by a corresponding enlargement in the share of the kinds of organizations that are traditionally underrepresented in pressure politics: organizations representing broad publics and the disadvantaged. Instead, there has been explosive growth of subnational governments, especially local governments, and institutions, especially in the health and education sectors. Taken together, the share of organizations accounted for by subnational governments and the health and educational sectors has nearly tripled from 7.6 percent to 21.6 percent over the twenty-five-year period.

With respect to the kinds of organizations that are traditionally underrepresented in national pressure politics, the share of both organizations representing public interests and organizations representing people in terms of their shared identities was a bit higher in 2006 than it had been in 1981. However, without the burst of growth in the number of organizations representing Native Americans, the share of identity organizations would actually have fallen.

Throughout the quarter-century period under discussion, the organizations that represent the economic interests of the less affluent—social welfare and poor people's organizations, occupational associations of non-professionals, and labor unions—have accounted for only a tiny fraction of the pressure system. However, between 1981 and 2006, that share decreased from 2.9 percent to 2.2 percent. (On this theme, see J. Berry 1999, 55–7, 157–8.) Decomposing that figure into its constituents, the minute share of organizations representing the poor and social welfare increased slightly. The share of organizations representing the occupational interests of the vast majority of American workers has diminished.

When it comes to union strength, what matters is not only the number of unions but also the number of members and the share of the workforce they enroll. Here, too, there has been unambiguous erosion. In 1981, 21.4 percent of all wage and salary workers were members of unions; by 2006, the figure had dropped to 12 percent. The decrease was sustained entirely by workers in the private sector. While the share of public sector workers who are union members fluctuated within a very narrow range and ended the period at a slightly higher level, 36.2 percent, than at the beginning, the proportion of private sector workers who are union members decreased steadily from 20.1 percent in 1981 to 7.8 percent in 2006. It is notable that, even as the size of the workforce expanded substantially, the absolute number of union members declined by nearly 4 million over the period.[23] To some it may seem counterintuitive to classify labor unions, which continue to enrol

---

[23] Data for 1981 taken from the Union Membership and Coverage Database, available at <http://www.unionstats.com>, constructed by Barry Hirsch and David Macpherson. Data for 2006 are taken from Greenhouse (2007, A11).

millions of workers, together with organizations that represent the economically disadvantaged. Still, by any measure—number of unions, share of the pressure system, proportion of workers in unions, the number of union members—labor unions, the most significant force in pressure politics for the advocacy of the economic interests of the less well-off, have lost out over the last generation.[24]

IN AND OUT: BIRTHS, DEATHS, AND CHANGES IN POLITICAL STATUS

The net increase in organizations active in Washington politics obscures complex processes by which organizations enter and leave the pressure community. The biological metaphors that are sometimes used to describe the population of politically active organized interests emphasize organizational births and deaths. However, in contrast to populations of plants and animals, the set of organizations that constitute the pressure system at any given moment represents the result of processes of organizational politicization as well as of organizational births and deaths. That is, new entrants into pressure politics can be either entirely new organizations or, more likely, existing organizations that have been outside politics. Similarly, organizations that exit from pressure politics may continue as organizations outside politics, or they may go out of business altogether.[25]

According to figures taken from the website of the Bureau of Labor Statistics (<http://www.bls.gov/news.release/union2.to3.htm>), accessed September 27, 2006, rates of unionization vary quite substantially across occupations and industries. Interestingly, because public-sector professional workers like teachers are relatively likely to be unionized, professionals have, overall, higher rates of union membership than do service, sales, or production workers. Within the private sector, workers in construction, transportation, or telecommunications have much higher rates than those in agriculture or financial services.

[24] See Goldfield (1987). The decline in union membership reflects a variety of political and economic trends ranging from increased sympathy to management at the NLRB to the decline in manufacturing jobs (itself a function of many factors ranging from globalization to productivity gains) to strategic errors by union leadership. On the economic factors, see Freeman and Katz (1994).

[25] In the work that makes the most extensive use of the biological model, Gray and Lowery (1996a) explicitly recognize that understanding the population of active organized interests requires tracing processes of organizational entries and exits as well as organizational births and deaths. Their work, which uses state-level data on the organizations active in state politics to explain the density and diversity of organized interests, is more theory-driven and less descriptive than the inquiry reported here and is animated by different intellectual concerns. To the extent that our analyses intersect, however, the findings are similar.

We reconstructed the histories back to 1981 of the organizations listed in 2006.[26] Of the organizations listed in the 2006 directory that were not included in 1981, fully 64 percent were alive in 1981—just not in politics. Only 36 percent of the organizations listed in 2006, but not in 1981, are new organizations that did not exist in 1981. These figures lend credence to the various theories contending that the costs of group organization imply that not all potential interests are mobilized into pressure politics. They also suggest that it is easier to move an existing organization into politics than it is to start a political organization from scratch. Table 22.4A elaborates by showing, for various categories of organizations, the 1981 status of those listed in 2006. There is considerable variation across categories of organizations. Of the organizations new to the 2006 list, those for which political objectives weigh especially heavily in the organizational mission are more likely to be newly hatched rather than existing but newly mobilized.

A parallel story can be told about the organizations listed in the 1981 directory. We were able to trace the subsequent histories of 83 percent of the organizations listed in 1981. Contrary to the received wisdom that "Once in politics, always in politics," a bare majority, 51 percent, were still listed in the 2006 directory. Moreover, only 34 percent of the organizations listed in 1981 were listed in all four directories. Table 22.4B elaborates these processes for the various categories of organizations. Surprisingly, there are no especially striking differences among organizational categories and no readily identifiable pattern as to which kinds of organizations stay in pressure politics from one decade to the next. What is striking is that when organizations exit the pressure system, they leave politics but are very unlikely to go out of business entirely. Of the no longer listed organizations about which we could find information, fully 86 percent were still alive, though not in politics; only 14 percent had gone out of business entirely. Of course, the 17 percent of the 1981 listings for which we were unable to trace subsequent history probably contain a disproportionate share that were no longer in existence. Still, it is noteworthy what a relatively high proportion of the 1981 organizations had exited the pressure system without going out of business.

---

[26] We were able to ascertain the 1981 status of 87 percent of the organizations listed in 2006. For several reasons, corporations are omitted from this discussion. The period covered by this study witnessed huge changes in corporate identities—mergers, acquisitions, spin-offs, and changes in names. While such organizational transformations are described for associations in sources like Associations Unlimited, this information is harder to locate for corporations. For the large number of listed corporations that are privately owned and not publicly traded, this information is even more difficult to find. Also, foreign organizations, just under half of which are corporations, are not included.

Table 22.4 In and out of the pressure community: births, deaths, and changes in political status

A. Status in 1981 of organizations listed in 2006

Organization	In existence (%)		Not yet in existence (%)	Total (%)	N
	Listed in 1981	Not listed			
Trade and other business associations	28%	32	39	99%	1,261
Occupational associations	36%	43	21	100%	677
Unions	56%	35	9	100%	102
Education	8%	76	16	100%	719
Health	5%	66	29	100%	532
Public interest	16%	30	54	100%	520
Identity groups	16%	57	28	101%	461
Social welfare or poor	14%	40	45	99%	119
State and local governments	9%	74	16	99%	1,417
Other	10%	48	42	100%	1,078
ALL 2006 ORGANIZATIONS	17%	53	30	100%	7,285

B. Status in 2006 of organizations listed in 1981

Organization	In existence (%)		No longer in existence (%)	Total (%)	N
	Listed in 2006	Not listed			
Trade and other business associations	51%	42	8	101%	813
Occupational associations	56%	42	2	100%	499
Unions	61%	32	7	100%	101
Education	56%	36	8	100%	101
Health	51%	45	4	100%	51
Public interest	48%	37	14	99%	207
Identity groups	51%	40	9	100%	164
Social welfare or poor	64%	32	4	100%	28
State and local governments	50%	48	2	100%	314
Other	56%	38	7	100%	232
ALL 1981 ORGANIZATIONS	51%	42	7	100%	2,728

CONCLUSION

Scholarly discussions of where organized interests come from sometimes proceed without explicit acknowledgment as to why students of American democracy might care about the question. At the risk of stating the obvious, since organized interests are so important in informing public officials about the preferences and needs of stakeholders in political controversies about how policies affect their lives and fortunes, the shape of the pressure community matters crucially for the equal protection of citizen interests.

Using an important new dataset about the organizations that represent citizen interests in national politics, this chapter has demonstrated that the shape of the organized interest community reflects both the free-rider problem and the re-source-constraint problem and confirmed Schattschneider's observations that the heavenly chorus underrepresents organizations advocating on behalf of either broad public interests or the resource-deprived.

The free-rider problem implies that public goods like wilderness preservation, an end to capital punishment, lower taxes, or crime reduction are less likely to receive organizational support unless the organizational advocates are very small or have the capacity to coerce support or to dispense selective benefits. When we considered the set of organizations that act on behalf of such public goods, we saw that, while a wide variety of such causes receive organized advocacy, as Olson would have predicted, public-goods-seeking organizations are less common than might be expected on the basis of the number of people who would potentially benefit from the conditions being sought.

While they take seriously the costs of founding and maintaining an organization, formal presentations of the free-rider problem often miss the differences among constituencies in the ability to bear those costs. The resources commanded by a potential constituency have powerful consequences for whether it achieves organiza-tional representation. Compared to those well endowed with resources, especially business interests, economically disadvantaged constituencies—including economi-cally disadvantaged groups defined by another characteristic such as race or gender—have limited representation in pressure politics if they are represented at all. In short, there are substantial barriers to entry into organized interest politics. Disturbances in the policy environment do not always elicit an organizational response by all who might be presumed to have a stake, and absence of organizational representation is not prima facie evidence of absence of collective concern.

Tracing organizations over time demonstrates that the overall expansion in the number of politically active organizations is accompanied by considerable fluidity. There is a great deal of turnover in the organized interest community. Organiza-tions listed in a single year are not necessarily in politics for the long haul, and only about a third of the organizations listed in 1981 appeared in all four directories.

When organizations are not listed in a later directory, they are relatively unlikely to have died. Instead, they are more likely to have gone into political hibernation—exiting Washington politics but continuing as organizations.

Organizations listed in 2006 but not in 1981 were much less likely to be newly formed organizations than to be existing, but politically inactive, organizations that were mobilized into politics, a finding that underlines the fact that political activation is a separate process often neglected by those who focus exclusively on organizational formation. That it seems much harder to get a new organization off the ground than to take an ongoing organization into politics reminds us, on the one hand, that organizational formation is, as Olson and his successors contend, a hurdle to organized representation in politics, and, on the other hand, that political action demands resources and is itself subject to the constraints of the logic of collective action. That is, a free-rider problem—analogous to that facing individuals considering joining an organization—arises for existing organizations that are contemplating collective political effort. Once again, an existing organization's resources become relevant, and affluent organizations seem to have less trouble becoming politically active than needy ones.

For all the churning of individual organizations and all the expansion in the number of organizations, the story is one of remarkable continuity in the kinds of interests that are represented. Indeed, as the heavenly chorus has gotten bigger, neither its accent nor the mix of voices has been transformed.

CHAPTER 23

....

THE MOBILIZATION AND INFLUENCE OF BUSINESS INTERESTS

....

MARK A. SMITH

JUST about every election cycle, a presidential candidate gains popularity by promising to confront the "special interests" that supposedly control political decisions in Washington, DC. Our political system is broken, we repeatedly hear from candidates, and we need to loosen the grip of the special interests to restore the responsiveness of government to the people. Candidates often leave the definition of the special interests vague, but when they do define them, the list typically includes trial lawyers along with the oil, insurance, banking, chemical, and pharmaceutical industries. In the version of how politics works held by many Americans, these industries exercise undue clout in Washington by giving large campaign contributions and hiring high-priced lobbyists who induce cynical politicians to do their bidding.

These concerns about special interests boast a long pedigree. The Populist and Progressive movements were built partly out of fear that corporate interests dominated the political scene. In the midst of the Populist agitation, Joseph Keppler in 1889 drew a famous cartoon for *Puck* magazine that captured commonly held beliefs about America's political system. With the caption "The Bosses of the Senate," the cartoon depicts bloated and self-indulgent men, described as "Coal," "Standard Oil Trust," "Sugar Trust," "Copper Trust," and the like, standing behind and lording over the minuscule senators working at their desks. A large doorway, over which hangs the sign "Entrance for Monopolists," allows easy movement for the designated favorites into the inner sanctuary of the Senate. Meanwhile, a tiny "People's Entrance" lies tucked away in a remote corner of the chamber, and it is locked shut and labeled "Closed."

Today's political climate lacks the intense fear of monopoly power, and the more general concern about corporate interests has morphed into a more specific criticism of campaign contributions, but in many respects the current public mood resembles that of the late nineteenth century. In capturing that mood, one artist from recent decades used imagery remarkably similar to Keppler's in making his points. The cartoon shows a large door to the halls of Congress for "Campaign Contributors" that swings wide open. The far smaller entrance for "The People" stands closed and abandoned. It is difficult to know whether this modern political cartoonist has self-consciously followed in Keppler's footsteps by adopting his imagery and critique. What can be said for certain is that the cartoons pack the same powerful punch and resonate with a skeptical and often cynical American public.

Given this public suspicion about the influence of "special interests," most of which are corporate, one might think that the study of business in politics would rank high on the agenda of political scientists. Studying the political activity of corporations, associations, and other business groups would not necessarily involve confirming the popular view of raw corporate power. Indeed, given the simplistic nature of the commonly held critique, which typically assumes a one-for-one trade of campaign contributions for political favors, serious investigations by political scientists might well challenge that view and replace it with an alternative one. Regardless of the particular conclusions that might be reached, however, business would represent a major area of research for political scientists.

As it turns out, the study of business remains a niche area in political science. Every discipline includes subjects of high priority, marked by new generations of scholars and a steady stream of informative articles and books, along with areas suffering from inattention. The study of business in political science clearly falls into the latter category. As a vivid illustration of this reality, I recall talking to the editor of a trade publication on business in 2000. After attending the annual meeting of the American Political Science Association, he lamented that he searched the program and found not a single study on corporations among the thousands of papers presented at the convention. The papers at that convention notwithstanding, political scientists have conducted some high-quality research on the subject, and this chapter attempts to identify the main themes and findings. Within the larger discipline of political science, though, investigations of business have never attracted the volume of scholarship that might match the presumed importance of the topic.

One reason for the paucity of available literature is that political scientists tend to research topics in which they have a personal connection or interest. Many of the policy issues important to parts of the business sector, such as narrow tax or regulatory provisions that no one but experts understand, make the eyes of most political scientists glaze over. Scholars might well recognize the collective importance of the full population of such matters, but when given the choice, they prefer to study something else. As a result, even within the study of interest groups, investigations of business do not constitute the main line of research. Most political scientists would find it far more interesting to investigate the behavior and influence of environmental groups or those working on hot-button issues like abortion, gun control, or gay rights.

A second reason why studies of business lie outside the beaten path in political science involves the difficulty of conducting thorough investigations. In many areas of political science, data can be acquired easily. Students of political behavior, for example, benefit from the regular holding of elections that generate immense amounts of individual-level and aggregate data. With the availability of large surveys like the National Election Studies and the General Social Survey, students of elections and public opinion often can simply download existing data and then begin their analyses. For scholars of legislatures, roll call votes and other publicly observable behaviors provide a wealth of data.

In studies of business and politics, the clear parallel comes in political action committee (PAC) contributions. Thanks to the disclosure provisions in the Federal Election Campaign Act of 1974 and parallel laws in many states, the contributions of PACs affiliated with corporations and trade associations are available to anyone with minimal proficiency in using a spreadsheet. This source of data proves to be a blessing in disguise, however. A methodological difficulty comes from the fact that PAC contributions are limited by law, thereby shrinking the variance and censoring the range at the high end. Those features of the law make it more difficult for statistical analyses to uncover robust relationships of PAC contributions with other variables. On a substantive level, the availability of PAC contributions may have crowded out the analysis of behaviors that are more difficult to observe, such as lobbying. Given that no business organization would simply give a contribution and then wait patiently for a favorable result, scholars need to study PAC contributions alongside other behaviors to determine the effectiveness of the strategies undertaken by business groups. Recent research moves in this direction (Ansolabehere, Snyder, and Tripathi 2002; Brasher and Lowery 2006), but the field as a whole still has a long way to go.

My discussion in this chapter of the mobilization and influence of business interests focuses on American domestic politics, a choice dictated by the limits of where I can claim expertise. Needless to say, this will lead to a different chapter than might be produced by scholars of international or comparative political economy, fields where business plays a major role as a subject of investigation. I will spend most of my attention on articles and books published by political scientists, but related work by sociologists, economists, and management scholars will also receive some attention here.

WHY AND WHEN DOES BUSINESS PARTICIPATE IN POLITICS?

One major area of research involves questions over why and when business participates in politics. Participation could involve several different kinds of behaviors. Besides the campaign contributions mentioned above, the conventional distinction between inside and outside lobbying is useful here. Inside lobbying refers to direct, normally face-to-face, contacts between policymakers and agents (i.e., lobbyists) for businesses either hired on a contract basis or employed full-time as part of a government relations department. Outside lobbying, commonly done by citizen-based or "public interest" groups such as the Sierra Club or the National Rifle Association, can also be employed by businesses. Those efforts seek to influence public opinion or build constituency pressures on legislators or bureaucrats.

When studying this political participation, scholars must define exactly what they mean by "business." That is, does business as a collective even exist as a meaningful entity? Debates in political science and sociology in the 1950s and 1960s attempted to determine who holds power in this and other societies. Pluralists portrayed a decentralized political system with different groups exercising power in different areas (Truman 1951; Dahl 1961; E. Epstein 1969). Competition among groups formed the linchpin of the system. Power elite theorists countered that elites in general, and businesses in particular, found ways to resolve differences of opinion such that on the large, encompassing issues, business approached politics as a unified whole (Mills 1956; Domhoff 1967).

Power elite research continued into the 1980s and 1990s. Some accounts held that policy-planning organizations, which include organizations such as think tanks, provide a forum through which elements of business create common views and preferences (Burris 1992; Peschek 1987; Domhoff 1978; Dye 1978). Much of the literature focused on interlocking directorates, the pattern whereby the directors of one corporation serve in a similar capacity for another corporation. By being uniquely situated as the eyes and ears of the entire business community, members of corporate boards gather information from many different corporations and mediate between them. Interlocking directorates thereby serve a coordinating function that builds the common ground on which business can stand (Mizruchi 1992; Useem 1984; Burris 2005). More generally, research in the class unity tradition attempts to show how various corporations coordinate their behavior at certain key moments when the larger interests of business are at stake (Burris 1987; Clawson and Neustadl 1989; Mizruchi 1989).

Other scholars of business and politics, however, doubt that one can gain analytical leverage by conceptualizing "business" as a coherent whole. Instead the economy is comprised of many different businesses, whose interests overlap at some times but not others. Even among large corporations, the extent to which they cooperate varies from issue to issue. In many cases, corporations desire under-the-radar policies that affect only them or possibly other firms in the same industry. Accordingly, political action can occur at the firm level, with each corporation acting on its own, at the industry level where firms join forces in a trade association, or across many sectors of business through peak associations such as the National Association of Manufacturers, Business Roundtable, or US Chamber of Commerce. The latter groups typically become involved only for large, broad-scale policies relevant to companies in many different sectors and industries.

Once one recognizes the need to distinguish between the political activity of corporations, trade associations, and peak associations, a complication arises. Namely, the same theories are unlikely to explain each of them successfully because a corporation can be considered a singular entity (at least for political purposes) and does not constitute a group at all (Hart 2004). Much of the theoretical apparatus from which political scientists draw, however, assumes that the object of study is a group. Indeed, the name of the field in question—"interest groups"— gives a label to the subject that is often inappropriate for analyzing the behavior of individual corporations. For example, Mancur Olson's (1965) logic of collective action has provided the most influential framework for studying the origins and maintenance of interest groups. Olson offers a useful starting point for examining any organization advocating for the collective interests of a certain population.

Olson focused on the economic domain in developing the evidence and examples to sustain his claims, and so organizations such as labor unions and trade associations received substantial amounts of attention in his book. Political scientists researching the determinants of business actions at an industry level therefore have often situated their work within the Olsonian tradition. Many of the policies governments enact carry similar effects throughout an entire industry, raising the possibility that collective action on behalf of the industry will be underprovided by the firms within it. Building on Olson's ways of conceptualizing political action, scholars have hypothesized that industries with a more concentrated market structure or a greater number of firms face the most intense collective action problems. The results of the research, however, reveal no clear patterns. Pittman's (1976) early work documented higher levels of campaign contributions in more concentrated industries, but follow-up studies by Esty and Caves (1983) and Zardkoohi (1985) found inconsistent relationships across different industries.

Grier, Munger, and Roberts (1994) studied a large number of industries and uncovered evidence for the presence of the collective action problems that Olson expected. Similarly, other research (Schuler 1996; Schuler, Rehbein, and Cramer 2002) showed that the costs of political participation were disproportionately borne by larger firms and by firms operating within concentrated industries.

Whatever one makes of the mixed set of results from studies of industries, the framework of collective action misses much of the action for single corporations. When a corporation acts politically on issues affecting only itself—say, obscure provisions of bills or unique decisions by regulatory agencies—then the concept of collective action does not apply. Lacking the guidance of the concept of collective action, scholars of the behaviors taken by individual corporations have pointed to several regularities that help explain which companies participate extensively in politics and which do not. Analyses often begin with the premise that political activity forms an extension of profit maximization through the regular provision of goods and services, meaning that corporate political behavior can be explained primarily with the economic characteristics of firms. One common finding is that companies whose profits depend heavily on government policies are more likely to give campaign contributions, hire lobbyists, and form a government affairs office (Hart 2001; N. Mitchell, Hansen, and Jepsen 1997; G. Wilson 1990). Public policy affects all corporations, of course, but some are implicated more heavily than others. Corporations that serve as contractors for government, most commonly in the area of defense, and those within heavily regulated industries like energy and chemicals are most likely to participate. They have the greatest incentive to do so, both to win favorable benefits—whether through lucrative contracts or regulatory exemptions—and to avoid the costs that come with certain forms of government regulation.

Similarly, the size of a corporation predicts its level of participation. The largest companies possess more resources that can be devoted to politics than do their smaller competitors (Andres 1985; Boies 1989; Keim and Baysinger 1988; Masters and Keim 1985). In addition, firm size serves as a proxy for other relevant characteristics of firms, such as visibility and prominence. Because larger firms are more likely to attract attention and hence become the target of government actions, they face greater incentives to become politically active. Recent work has also demonstrated the importance of the location of ownership. Whether out of uncertainty about the best strategy or a perception that participation would be seen as inappropriate, foreign-owned corporations undertake political activity at lower levels than do those with domestic ownership (W. Hansen and Mitchell 2000; W. Hansen, Mitchell, and Drope 2004).

Firms can also be driven to participate in politics by the actions of their competitors. In a competitive marketplace, profit-maximizing firms can be expected to pay close attention to both the market and non-market activities of their competitors. When one firm in an industry increases its political efforts, competitors may feel the need to follow suit in order to protect their interests. Similarly, among those already engaged in lobbying, competition for access to policymakers can lead companies to engage in additional activities such as giving campaign contributions. Data on PAC formation in the American states suggests the existence of an arms race of this kind (Gray and Lowery 1997). Among high-tech firms, interviews with industry insiders reveal that firms are aware of the potential for an arms race and take steps to keep it in check (Hart 2001). Within the automobile industry, domestic manufacturers appear to give more to House incumbents not only when they have employment ties to the members' district, but also when the same ties occur for their competitors (Hersch and McDougall 2000).

The pressures for entry into politics sometimes come not from competitors but from government officials. Scholars typically think of interest groups as the instigators and policymakers as the targets of action, but sometimes the relationship works the other way around. For example, the largest business group in America, the US Chamber of Commerce, was initially organized by government (Childs 1930). Desiring an organization that could speak for the unified interests of business, President William Taft helped convene a meeting of delegates from a diverse array of trade associations and local business groups. The initial conversations quickly led to the formation of a national organization that became the US Chamber of Commerce.

The formation of the US Chamber of Commerce is far from the only example of the phenomenon in question. Cathie Jo Martin (1989, 1994) points to more recent instances when government officials helped to organize and mobilize business groups. Martin observes that there is often conflict within government, where legislators or executive branch officials wanting to undertake a certain action face opposition from others who hold official positions of power. In such an instance, those pushing for new policies can help their cause by inviting assistance from supportive business groups, leading to a public–private coalition working on behalf of shared policy goals. In some instances the business groups might already exist, but in others government officials—as in the formation of the US Chamber of Commerce—actually help bring the groups into being. To push their tax policies through Congress, for example, presidents Kennedy and Johnson constructed coalitions of business supporters and encouraged them to use grassroots lobbying strategies to put pressure on Congress (Martin 1994).

Of course, the choice to participate in politics represents the beginning, not the end, of the decisions companies must make. Once they enter the political game, they must decide on the particular strategies to follow. Recent work (Vanden Bergh and Holburn 2007) depicts corporations as strategic actors in determining where to deploy their resources. Like other interest groups (Pralle 2003), corporations target their efforts to the governmental institutions most receptive to their interests and most pivotal to the policymaking process. Sandra Suárez (2000) shows that corporations also learn over time how best to translate their interests—assumed to be fixed—into specific political strategies. Because the best political strategies cannot be known with certainty, firms use their experiences from previous conflicts to guide their decisions. Political defeats encourage widespread reevaluations of strategies, whereas successes lead firms to repeat the strategies they used in the past (Suárez 2000).

Cathie Jo Martin (1995, 2000; see also Schuler 1999) offers a perspective broadly similar to Suárez's in stressing that the link from interests to preferences is not simple and straightforward. Yes, firms want to maximize profits and often see politics as a means to accomplish that end, but the precise political strategies that will allow them to attain their goal are not so obvious. For these reasons, factors internal to the organization of firms affect how general interests get translated into specific preferences on policies. Whereas Suárez emphasizes the asymmetric aspect of how learning differs according to whether past political efforts led to success or failure, Martin stresses the internal policy capacity of a firm, defined as its ability to interpret technical information about different policies. She uses case studies and quantitative data to highlight three important organizational features of companies: the presence of policy professionals in positions of responsibility, membership in larger business associations focused on an issue, and the outcomes of previous, largely private attempts within the company to address the policy in question.

The empirical components of Martin's book and related article center around social welfare policies, especially health care, job training, child care, and other "human capital" initiatives. With respect to health care, firms that had established government affairs offices in Washington, DC, or that had participated in business associations formed around the issue were more supportive of government man-dates for employers to provide health insurance to their employees. Child care, by comparison, did not benefit from policy expertise within the firm or national organizations devoted it, and so companies were more likely to see the provision of child care as a local rather than national issue. Overall, Martin depicts the population of large corporations as more supportive of government social welfare policies than the traditional image of a laissez-faire business community would suggest. The more progressive preferences of some firms do not become fully reflected in the positions taken by peak associations, though, because of what Martin calls "least common denominator" politics. Because the peak associations place a high premium on unity, they often end up taking weak or reactive positions, and often no position at all, to avoid offending the divergent elements of their membership.

The vast majority of the research on the political activity of business focuses on large corporations. In one sense, this makes for a logical choice, since concerns about the power of business focus far more often on major corporations with large lobbying operations than on the small businesses that tend to be disorganized. On the other hand, leaving small business out of the picture is problematic, for organizations such as the National Federation of Independent Business that represent small business commonly rank highly on insiders' lists of the most powerful organizations in Washington, DC. In fact, one of Martin's (2000) goals is to explain why the unified positions of small business against government involvement in human capital provision trump the more diffuse sentiments of large corporations that often favor such involvement.

McGee Young (2008) helps overcome this lacuna in the literature by addressing one important aspect of the political participation of small business, namely its divided and under-organized character in the period after the New Deal. Following Mancur Olson, most political scientists explaining that phenomenon would point to the collective action problems inherent to organizing many small firms. Other political scientists might take a pluralist approach and suggest that small business, as a group, is not a natural and functional division in society that could be organized for political action. Young challenges these views by arguing that the organization (and lack thereof) of small business during the period of his study reflects the legacy of state actions from the Populist era through the New Deal that connected it into politics in particular and factionalized ways. Rather than highlighting purely economic or functional forces, as in much of the literature on interest groups, Young creatively applies historical institutionalism to interest group formation and development.

The works of Cathie Jo Martin and McGee Young represent high points in the literature on business political activity. Future research will benefit by taking seriously their emphasis on studying not just whether business interests participate in politics, but also the ways they are organized and the strategies they undertake. In some instances, such investigations will need a strong historical component to demonstrate that current modes of organization were not inevitable and instead reflect political and social forces that unfolded over time. New studies will also need to reach well beyond campaign contributions and other easily available forms of data. Martin in particular has proven that systematic interviews with lobbyists, government affairs officials, and corporate managers can yield new insights. This is especially true for large corporations, institutions for which most political scientists have no direct experience "from the inside." Political scientists seeking to understand why and when corporations act as they do can benefit from a more thorough immersion—gained through interviews, archival records, and perhaps even participant observation—into the worlds that corporate decision makers inhabit.

Assessing Business Influence in American Politics

This chapter so far has focused on the questions of why and when corporations and other business groups participate in politics. These are important questions because the answers are linked to larger, more encompassing concerns of political scientists. Management and organizational scholars often care about corporations as corporations, and so breaking apart the "black box" to understand corporate behavior naturally forms a central point of research. Political scientists, however, are typically more interested in the consequences than the causes of business political activity.

Of course, understanding consequences requires some knowledge of causes, for any effects of business actions on public policy hinge on whatever determined the relevant behavior in the first place. In other words, for influence to be exerted— except in the case of "structural power" that comes through the threat of capital flight (Lindblom 1977, 1982)—business first needs to be organized for political activity. Therefore, it is important to understand both the factors that determine whether a corporation or business group becomes politically active and also the forms that activity takes. Still, it is understandable that the attention of political scientists most often lies with the consequences of corporate political behavior, for those consequences are intertwined with core concepts of political science such as power, democracy, representation, freedom, and equality. If corporate political behaviors did not create important consequences for outcomes of interest to political scientists, then few political scientists would bother to study the determinants of those behaviors.

The forms and magnitude of business influence in politics raise questions of interest not only to political scientists but also to the public at large. In 2006 the late comedian George Carlin performed a riff on the American dream that offers one common understanding of how business matters in American politics. Carlin's profanity-laced routine, which received nearly 600,000 hits on YouTube before it was removed for copyright violations, includes his widely quoted line that "it's called the American dream because you have to be asleep to believe it." He reaches that conclusion by pointing to "the big wealthy business interests that control things and make all the important decisions." Those interests "spend billions of dollars every year lobbying to get what they want. Well we know what they want, they want more for themselves and less for everyone else." Carlin doesn't specify the policies that exist because of those wealthy business interests, but he gives one hint of what he has in mind by stating that "now they're coming for your Social Security money."

Although it may seem unusual to use the words of a comedian as an entry point for a scholarly discussion, doing so demonstrates why we need rigorous political science research. At the time of Carlin's performance in 2006, President George W. Bush was still actively promoting the partial privatization of Social Security whereby younger workers would receive the option of placing some of their retirement money in various kinds of investment vehicles. When Carlin mentions Wall Street getting hold of people's Social Security money, he presumably refers to this partial privatization and the fees that financial services firms would charge for managing people's assets. Based on existing services that are provided for similar accounts through Individual Retirement Accounts (IRAs) and 401k or 403b plans, the annual fees average a couple of thousand dollars for basic startup costs or about 1 percent for the management of an entire portfolio, plus an additional 0.8 percent for bond funds, 1 percent for actively managed stock funds, and 0.3 percent for indexed stock funds.[1] Those fees seem sufficiently low to most investors who establish retirement plans that they willingly pay them. If we reached the point where financial services companies could charge fees of a similar magnitude on Social Security accounts, that would hardly indicate that wealthy business interests had seized control of American politics.

More importantly, the partial privatization of Social Security hasn't even oc-curred, and its prospects do not appear likely anytime in the near future. In fact, the idea proved so unpopular that President Bush, despite vigorously promoting it in 2005 and 2006, never formally introduced the relevant legislation in Congress. In other words, if greedy corporations want to implement private accounts within Social Security, then they have utterly failed to achieve their aims. Thus, the one policy area that Carlin explicitly mentioned served to undercut, rather than sustain, his claim about who really controls America. This episode tells us that something is seriously missing when one offers a mono-causal assertion that business controls American politics. In the case of Social Security, one must consider many other factors to reach an understanding of how the program is structured. That explanation would surely include public support for the program, which in turn reflects the fact that government provision of retirement security preceded the development of workplace-based private accounts (J. Hacker 2002). Most Americans envision the version of Social Security that has existed for several decades as the base of their retirement security, with any private accounts like a 401k adding to rather than replacing it.

Consider another area of public policy, taxes. If they could control the political system in America, wealthy business interests would surely pay considerable attention to taxes. They would design the tax system so that they paid as little as possible, with the burden of funding government resting on the passive and

---

[1] For data on the fees charged by financial services firms, see <http://www.icifactbook.org/fb_sec5.html>.

impotent citizenry. As it turns out, the corporate tax rate in America as of 2008 was the second highest among countries with a similar level of economic development. Based on that fact, it would be difficult to make the case that wealthy business interests dominate American politics. Of course, most corporations do not pay at the nominal tax rate, for the tax code is littered with exemptions and deductions that lower the tax bill for many companies and industries. As a result, the effective tax rate differs dramatically among corporations and small businesses, meaning that there is no such entity as "business" when it comes to taxes.

Coming to grips with tax policy requires understanding the broad array of complex and often technical provisions that make the effective tax rate of one company differ from that of another. No simple explanation of wealthy business interests controlling American politics will suffice. Political scientists have, in fact, conducted systematic research on taxation that sheds light on the varying provisions across companies and industries. The reasons for the complicated and particularistic tax code in America can be traced to the country's political institutions such as federalism, single-member legislative districts, and a decentralized committee structure in Congress that encourage individual businesses to act as narrow rent-seekers rather than a unified entity (Steinmo 1993).

Two implications flow from this brief consideration of Social Security and tax policy. First, any assessment of business influence in American politics must make due allowance for the diversity of interests within the business sector. Companies and industries sometimes work on their own and at other times cooperate, meaning that scholarly research must account for the full range of issues before reaching a conclusion about business influence. Second, business influence in American politics must be placed within the context of other forces that determine why one policy is chosen while another is not, and why still others never reach the agenda for consideration in the first place. Those factors include the design of American political institutions that steer policy in certain directions, along with the forces of public opinion and interests like labor unions, environmental organizations, and other citizen-based groups that compete with business.

Many works in political science recognize these implications. The notion that business interests control political decisions can be easily dismissed as, at best, an exaggeration, but one need not veer to the other extreme and take a Pollyannaish view of American politics that views the power of business as irrelevant. Various business interests surely matter a great deal in shaping the course of public policy; the challenge lies in determining where, when, and how. More specifically, the question can be best framed as the following: under what conditions do business interests influence political decisions? A considerable body of research in political science proves relevant to this question, with four books being especially noteworthy in taking this kind of conditional approach to examining business influence. Accordingly, the next section of this chapter will explore the contributions that these books have made.

THE CONDITIONAL NATURE OF BUSINESS INFLUENCE

David Vogel's *Fluctuating Fortunes: The Political Power of Business in America* (1989) set the tone for much of the work on business in politics over the following two decades. Vogel aims to understand the political success of business, and his signal contribution is to view that success as a variable, not a constant. In retrospect, this contribution might appear to be somewhat obvious, but given the state of the literature at the time, it was a major advance in our scholarly understanding. The previous three decades of debate in political science and sociology had contrasted pluralist and power elite schools of thought, with the latter being reinforced at certain points by neo-Marxists. The debate was often cast in stark terms of all or nothing, with one side insisting that class interests (of which business was a central component) dominated American politics, and the other claiming that power was decentralized among many different groups. Vogel broke free of that debate in a relentlessly empirical investigation of what happened in several policy areas from the beginning of the Kennedy presidency (1960) through the end of Reagan's (1988).

Noting that someone's work was not cast in theoretical terms is often a put-down; in Vogel's case, however, this is a compliment. By looking at what actually happens in American politics, without the distorting filter of a preconceived theoretical framework, Vogel was able to focus on the specific question of where and when business either wins or loses in politics. As his title would suggest, Vogel's central claim is that business sometimes wins major victories in Washington, DC, while at other times business finds itself on the losing end. More specifically, business was preeminent (much as power elitists might suggest) through the first half of the 1960s before facing a period where the regulatory arm of the state expanded from the mid-1960s to the mid-1970s. Business regained its footing thereafter and found itself much more frequently on the winning side until the late 1980s, when its position again eroded. Vogel fully recognizes that the label "business" is just a convenient summary; where policies affecting certain companies or industries deviate from the larger patterns, he takes note and explains why.

Vogel is not content merely to describe the fluctuating fortunes, for he also wants to explain why one period led to the next. He places considerable emphasis on the state of the economy. When the economy is performing poorly, the arguments of business to be relieved of tax or regulatory costs find a receptive audience among policymakers. Conversely, periods of economic prosperity lead politicians to ask businesses to act more vigorously to protect consumers, workers, and the environment. In other words, the success or failure of the policy agenda of business stands, to a large degree, outside the direct control of business. Given the hand it has been dealt, however, business can play its cards to improve its likelihood of policy success. Vogel thus documents the growth of the political activities of business beginning in the early 1970s, which included forming political action committees, establishing government affairs offices in Washington, DC, hiring more lobbyists, founding and strengthening cross-industry groups such as the Business Roundtable and US Chamber of Commerce, and funding think tanks to shape the climate of ideas. Those efforts bore fruit and contributed to the resurgence of business in the later part of the decade.

In *Agendas and Instability in American Politics* (1993), Frank Baumgartner and Bryan Jones share with Vogel an emphasis on the larger context within which business interests operate. It is now practically a truism in political science to recognize that the three foundational variables in politics are interests, ideas, and institutions. The challenge lies in carefully explaining how those variables interact to generate political outcomes, and arguably none have done so more successfully than Baumgartner and Jones. They begin by noting that American politics has often been marked by policy subsystems where narrow interests—typically involving particular industries—enjoy favorable public policy. At other times, broader publics become involved in politics and break up the previously cozy arrangements enjoyed by business interests. The contribution of Baumgartner and Jones is to construct a model of public policy that accounts for periods of both stability and change.

Narrow interests prevail when they enjoy a favorable climate of ideas and operate within a supportive set of institutions. Business groups are often involved in creating favorable policy images that will then be designed and implemented by a subsystem consisting of the interests, relevant congressional committees, bureaucratic agencies, and like-minded experts. Those arrangements can persist for decades without outside intervention by the political system. Through a process of punctuated equilibrium, however, those arrangements can be blown apart through the construction of new images of the policy in question and the entry of higher-level political actors, typically congressional leaders, presidents, and the larger public. Whereas previously the resolution of the issue through particular institutions protected narrow business interests, shifting the locus of institutional decision making—for example, from one congressional committee to another—both reinforces and contributes to the changing public image of the policies.

Baumgartner and Jones sustain their model of punctuated equilibrium through careful case studies of issues including nuclear power, smoking, urban issues, and pesticides. They bring together broad-ranging evidence for each case, including the amount and tone of media coverage, the attention in various institutional venues, the scope of interest mobilization, and policy outcomes. In 2001 the book won the Aaron Wildavsky award for a work of lasting impact on the field of public policy, and deservedly so. As the award would suggest, the book's scope ranges far beyond the study of business interests, and it is precisely that scope that makes it so informative for the study of business. Any attempt to investigate the influence of business in American politics without considering the public image of the issues at stake and the institutions that resolve them is bound to be incomplete at best and downright misguided at worst.

Mark Smith's *American Business and Political Power: Public Opinion, Elections, and Democracy* (2000) attempts to build on the insights of Baumgartner and Jones by examining how much and what kinds of influence private corporations wield over public policy; whether and in what ways the political power of corporations undermines the responsiveness of politicians to constituent sentiment; and how business groups can affect public opinion. Smith's book weds those concerns with other questions relating to democratic processes, including how elections affect the course of public policy and the conditions under which government officials either respond to or ignore public opinion. The book begins by noting a wide range of theoretical perspectives that, while differing in many other respects, share the assumption that business will be most powerful when it is internally unified. Smith challenges that assumption, finding that business unifies only on issues that also present strong incentives for officeholders to respond to constituent opinions and that make election outcomes central determinants of policy change. When business is unified on its preferred policies, its fortunes therefore depend more upon a favorable climate of public opinion than upon its own efforts to advance its interests, although it can gain noticeable returns from shaping public opinion.

The book and related article (M. Smith 1999) aim to make two contributions to our understanding of how masses and elites interact. First, Smith illuminates the circumstances under which public opinion does and does not affect how elected officials behave. He shows that unity among corporations, instead of undermining representation, actually coincides with forces that strengthen the public's voice in policymaking. This result arises because issues on which business unifies are marked by extensive attention from the mass media, high awareness among the public, divisions along ideological and partisan lines, and countermobilization by other interests. Paradoxically, the issues for which most scholars have expected corporations to wield their strongest influence and to be most problematic for democratic theory are actually those for which popular representation works best. At the same time, another class of issues exists—those important to a single company or one industry—with very different properties. Because these kinds of issues attract little media coverage, public knowledge, or differentiation among the parties, public input into the decision-making process is usually minimal and corporations can more easily prevail.

Smith's second contribution is to connect questions of business power in American politics with questions about representation. He shows that for issues that unify disparate corporations, the business community does not gain much leverage through the channels we ordinarily expect, such as lobbying, campaign contributions, and implicit threats to disinvest if policies are unfavorable. Instead, business gains power primarily by interceding when public opinion is being formed. The magnitude of business influence on public opinion indicates that business, while influential, does not control what people want from government; thus, the representation we later see is not hollow and beside the point. The book's evidence indicates that the relationships among the public, corporations, and politicians depend heavily upon the characteristics of the issue at stake. The political power of corporations and the responsiveness of politicians to constituents coexist in American politics, though with patterns that vary meaningfully across different categories of issues.

The line of research on business influence represented by Vogel (1989), Baumgartner and Jones (1993), and Smith (2000) carries through in Sheldon Kamieniecki's book *Corporate America and Environmental Policy: How Often Does Business Get its Way?* (2006). In one respect, Kamieniecki's work is more limited in scope than the others in that it examines only one policy area. Kamieniecki offsets that limitation, though, by carrying out a thorough analysis of the decisions made by all three branches of government. Like Smith, Kamieniecki finds that business is typically divided rather than unified, and the power of business can be countered by public opinion, environmental groups, and environmental advocates within government. Kamieniecki's theoretical discussion draws heavily from previous research, including Baumgartner and Jones's, on issue definition and agenda setting.

In the empirical parts of the book, Kamieniecki employs both quantitative data and six case studies of matters like coal mining and the management of old-growth forests. He demonstrates that business groups are selective in choosing the issues with which to become involved; often, they take no position at all. Business exerts the greatest amount of leverage at the earliest stages of the political process, before a matter becomes a prominent issue for public discussion. For example, in the area of global warming, business groups have cast doubt on the science and thereby prevented serious attempts to address the problem. The larger argument of the book is that business carries a strong but often challenged position in the formation of environmental policy.

CONCLUSIONS ABOUT BUSINESS INFLUENCE IN AMERICAN POLITICS

The four books by Vogel (1989), Baumgartner and Jones (1993), Smith (2000), and Kamieniecki (2006) offer two lasting lessons for future research on business influence. First, the political power of business must be studied alongside other forces that shape American politics. Political science, like other academic disciplines, becomes more and more specialized with each passing year. Scholars learn the theories and methodologies deemed appropriate to their subjects of study while ignoring research conducted in other areas. Some of this specialization is inevitable, for keeping up with new articles and books in one's own area is difficult enough by itself, let alone reading widely across fields and subfields. The gain from doing so, however, can be immense. The books under review here show that any robust understanding of business influence needs to grapple with public opinion, elections, and political parties, the workings of institutions such as Congress, the presidency, and the bureaucracy, and the policy process more generally. Future research on business will benefit from explicitly linking to the best work in these other areas.

A second lasting lesson that the books provide is the need for a well-grounded empirical approach. Much—perhaps most—of what corporations and other business groups do in politics is observable, whether it be lobbying, forming organizations, giving campaign contributions, or using the mass media to shape the climate of ideas. All four books take advantage of the available observations such that one can judge the conclusions reached by the quality of the evidence rather than one's a priori expectations about what such research will find. These books certainly do not definitively resolve debates over corporate power, popular representation, and the workings of American democracy, for those questions are more encompassing than can be answered within any single study—or even four of them. In addition, because questions about the place of business in American politics can be studied with many different methodologies, the books under review here may not yield the last word. These books nevertheless provide an important perspective for future research on business and politics to consider.

CHAPTER 24

SOCIAL AND ECONOMIC JUSTICE MOVEMENTS AND ORGANIZATIONS

DARA Z. STROLOVITCH

M. DAVID FORREST

SOCIAL and economic justice advocacy organizations have long been a crucial conduit for the articulation and representation of the interests of groups such as women, racial minorities, and low-income people—populations that have traditionally been ill-served by the two major political parties and underrepresented by the electoral system (Costain 2005; Frymer 1999; Heaney 2008). Long before women won the right to vote in 1920, for example, organizations such as the National American Woman Suffrage Association (formed in 1890) and the National Woman's Party (formed in 1913) mobilized women and lobbied legislators on their behalf. Similarly, the National Association for the Advancement of Colored People (NAACP, formed in 1909) provided political and legal representation for African Americans in the South, who, after a brief period of voting following Reconstruction and the passage of the Fifteenth Amendment, were largely disfranchised and denied formal representation until the passage and enforcement of the Voting Rights Act of 1965.

While advocacy organizations were often the only voice for marginalized groups, they were nonetheless at a severe disadvantage for much of the twentieth century. Scholars such as Robert Dahl (1967) had been optimistic that organizations would form to represent groups when their interests were at stake in the policy process. However, organizations advocating on behalf of groups such as women, racial minorities, and low-income people were greatly outnumbered and outresourced by business, financial, and professional interest groups that spoke for more powerful and anti-egalitarian interests. "The flaw in the pluralist heaven," Schattschneider wrote famously in his 1960 classic *The Semisovereign People*, "is that the heavenly chorus sings with a strong upper-class accent." He estimated that approximately 90 percent of the population simply had no access to what he called "the pressure system" and that interest groups consequently exacerbated rather than eased inequalities in political access (Schattschneider 1975, 35).[1]

True as it was when he wrote it, Schattschneider's well-known rejoinder to the optimism of earlier scholars such as Dahl was soon challenged by an explosion in the number of organizations representing marginalized groups, many of which had grown out of the social and economic justice movements of the "long 1960s." By the beginning of the twenty-first century, more than 700 organizations represented women, racial minorities, and low-income people in national politics, including more than forty African American organizations, more than thirty Asian Pacific American organizations, and well over 100 women's organizations (Strolovitch 2007). Social and economic justice organizations continue to make up only a small portion of the broader interest group universe that counts more than 17,000 national organizations and that encompasses organizations representing much wealthier and more powerful interests such as business, professional, financial, ideologically conservative, and foreign policy organizations. Nonetheless, organizations such as the NAACP, the National Organization for Women, the Center for Law and Social Policy, the National Council of La Raza, and the National Asian Pacific American Law Center have become a significant and visible presence in Washington politics. Organizations such as these promise to provide a measure of "insider" access to "outsider" groups by opening up the policymaking process and offering them an institutionalized voice and compensatory representation for their concerns.

---

[1] In addition, rational choice theorists such as Mancur Olson (1965) argued that rational actors would decline the costs of participation in pursuing "public goods" unless selective incentives were made available only to participants. Subsequent research has identified benefits other than selective incentives (such as purposive and solidary incentives) and narrow economic self-interest as well as conditions under which collective action problems can be overcome, but the inevitability of organization and mobilization on behalf of marginalized groups is no longer taken for granted.

The extent to which this promise has been fulfilled, however, is the source of much debate. Guided by overarching questions about the role of advocacy groups as compensatory representatives for marginalized groups, this chapter examines these debates about organizations that represent and activate populations that were mobilized by social movements during the 1950s, 1960s, and 1970s. To do so, we address four interrelated questions: (1) How do social and economic justice advocacy organizations compare with other organizations in the broader universe of interest groups, and how has this changed over time? (2) Are advocacy organizations better able to act as compensatory representatives for marginalized groups than they were when Schattschneider initially critiqued the interest group system? (3) What are the implications of formalized, professionalized, and institutionalized organizations for the participatory, democratic, and radical social movements to which many of them are related? (4) What are the effects of social and economic advocacy organizations on politics and public policy, and how might these effects be assessed?

These topics do not, by any means, represent an exhaustive list of the many important questions about social and economic justice advocacy organizations in American politics. Taken together, however, they draw attention to several constellations of research that both illuminate the contours of contemporary social and economic justice advocacy while also suggesting some areas that stand to benefit from further inquiry. Because organizations that represent groups such as women, racial minorities, and low-income people straddle boundaries both politically and disciplinarily—simultaneously outsiders and insiders, the object of inquiry by sociologists, political scientists, and scholars of public policy—our ability to understand them consequently depends on an expansive and interdisciplinary engagement with wide-ranging scholarship.

We argue that, much like interest groups and social movements themselves, scholarship on organizations that advocate on behalf of marginalized groups exists in productive tension with research about social movements and with work in related and overlapping fields such as public policy, state and local politics, political participation, and the politics of race, gender, and class. Scholarship investigating advocacy on behalf of marginalized groups is also in preliminary but productive conversation with policy feedback and social constructionist theories that challenge the idea that groups based on identities such as race, class, gender, and sexuality exist prior to politics. Scholars interested in the role of economic and social justice organizations should more thoroughly incorporate such understandings of interests, identities, and constituencies as simultaneously politically constructed and politically salient. They should also integrate the insights of scholarship that foregrounds the political consequences of intersecting axes of privilege and disadvantage by, for example, examining the varying abilities of organizations to reframe negative constructions of the groups they represent, to make appeals to popular majorities, and to press claims for resources and fuller citizenship during times of national crisis.

COMPARISONS WITH THE BROADER UNIVERSE OF INTEREST GROUPS

Organizations that represent women, racial minorities, and low-income people straddle the boundary between "insider" interest groups and "outsider" social movements (see, for example, Costain 1992; Geron, de la Cruz, and Singh 2001; Marquez and Jennings 2000; Rimmerman 2002).[2] In spite of their origins in and continued connections to outsider movements, many of the organizations that advocate for marginalized groups have come to look a lot like political insiders. For example, Dara Strolovitch (2007) found that a majority of the organizations that represent women, racial minorities, and low-income people in national politics are located in the greater District of Columbia area, and many have offices on or near K Street, home to some of the most powerful lobbying firms and interest groups in the country.

While they may look similar on the surface, organizations advocating on behalf of marginalized groups remain different from other interest groups in fundamental ways. Not only do they remain outmoneyed by corporate, business, and professional organizations, they are also far less likely to employ lobbyists or a legal staff or to have affiliated political action committees (PACs) (Strolovitch 2006, 2007). In addition to these disparities in resources and political tools, the increase in the number of social and economic justice organizations has been outpaced by increases among business and professional organizations. Kay Schlozman and Traci Burch (2009) found recently that, of the nearly 12,000 organizations listed in the 2001 edition of *Washington Representatives*, less than 5 percent are public interest groups, less than 4 percent represent groups such as women, racial minorities, and lesbian, gay, bisexual, or transgender (LGBT) people, and a mere 1 percent are labor unions. Only a fraction of 1 percent of the organizations are social welfare organizations or organizations that represent poor and low-income people, a proportion that remains almost identical to the proportion that Schlozman found in her 1986 study with John Tierney. Such disparities in presence and resources lead to large and consequential disparities in activity as well. Frank Baumgartner and Beth Leech (2001), for example, show that business groups, trade associations, and

---

[2] For recent explorations of the study of social movements within political science, see Costain (2005) and Meyer and Lupo (2007).

intergovernmental lobbies are the most active organizations and that they are also able to lobby across a much wider spectrum of issues than groups like social and economic advocacy organizations (see also Heaney 2004b).

The foregoing research would seem to confirm that business and professional organizations remain at an inevitable advantage within the broader interest group system. There are, however, some important exceptions to this general tendency. These exceptions, however, have mixed implications for organizations that advocate on behalf of weak and marginalized groups. In particular, work by scholars such as Elizabeth Gerber and Mark Smith shows that the power of business organizations is often constrained by political processes and institutions in which popular majorities are necessary for policy change. Laws that pass by initiative, for example, are more likely to reflect the interests of citizen groups than they are to reflect those of business organizations (E. Gerber 1999). Smith (2001) finds that business lobbies prevail mainly on issues that have public backing or that are important to only a single company or industry because these attract little media coverage and generate little countermobilization.

Research demonstrating the limitations of business power suggests that there are circumstances under which public interest groups can prevail against powerful lobbies in spite of vastly unequal material resources. However, the circumstances under which such victories are possible underscore tensions between and questions about the possibilities of populist victories against entrenched and powerful interests as well as longstanding concerns about majority tyranny over weak, unpopular, stigmatized, and minority groups. Specifically, this work draws attention to the additional hurdles faced by unpopular, stigmatized, or minority groups for whom appeals to populist impulses are typically less effective or even counterproductive. Populist appeals can, under the right conditions, mobilize broad coalitions to oppose unpopular business goals. However, the need for this same electoral majority can work against weak, unpopular, stigmatized, and minority groups, as exemplified by the 2008 passage of California's Proposition 8, the ballot initiative that eliminated same-sex couples' right to marry in that state (other significant examples include previous initiatives such as Proposition 209, which ended affirmative action for women and minorities, and Proposition 187, which would have denied health care, public education, and public assistance benefits to undocumented immigrants had it not subsequently been ruled unconstitutional). A key direction for future work, therefore, should be to explore in more depth the conditions under which advocacy organizations representing groups such as women, racial minorities, and LGBT people succeed in blocking ballot initiatives and referenda or in mobilizing popular majorities in spite of their negative social constructions or minority status (Schneider and Ingram 1997).

ADVOCACY ORGANIZATIONS AS COMPENSATORY REPRESENTATIVES

As Anne Costain has noted, part of what makes social and economic justice advocacy "unique and worthy of study" is its "demonstrated capability to deliver access to the excluded" (Costain 2005, 111). Much of the research reviewed thus far suggests that, while organizations that represent marginalized groups have delivered a measure of access to the excluded and a modicum of diversity to the interest group system, biases and inequalities within the broader pressure group system continue to make it difficult for them to deliver this access, even as their numbers have grown and they have become a more entrenched and forceful presence in national politics. The fact of this entrenchment has raised its own questions about how effectively these "insider" organizations act as compensatory representatives for the "outsider" groups that comprise their constituencies. In response to such questions, a growing body of research has begun to examine the extent and effects of biases *within* the organizations that claim to remedy the inequities lamented by Schattschneider.

One line of research takes as its starting point a set of debates about whether movements for more equitable redistribution have been displaced and disarmed by a "politics of recognition" that is overly concerned with identity-based struggles and that has led to a middle-class bias in the agendas of organizations representing formerly excluded groups (N. Fraser 1997). Berry (1999), for example, finds that liberal advocacy groups have abandoned the pursuit of economic justice in favor of activity on post-materialist issues such as the environment, which, he argues, are of interest mainly to middle-class people. Theda Skocpol argues that "[p]rivileged and well-educated citizens" have withdrawn from cross-class membership federations, "redirecting leadership and support to staff-led organizations" and abandoning low-income and working-class people as well as their policy concerns (Skocpol 1999, 462). Others allege the opposite, arguing that organizations concerned with class and economic issues marginalize issues of race, gender, and sexuality such as affirmative action, abortion, and LGBT rights (Duberman 2002; Frymer 1999).

Recent work has tried to move beyond an "either/or" debate in which recognition is pitted against redistribution by examining advocacy organizations through what scholars have termed an *intersectional* lens. Theories of intersectionality were introduced by women of color who were frustrated with a feminist movement that privileged the experiences and positions of white women, representing these experiences as those of "all women," and also with a civil rights movement that similarly privileged the experiences and positions of black men (Patricia Collins 1990; Crenshaw 1989; A. Davis 1981; hooks 1981). As such, intersectional frameworks reject the notion that economic and social injustices are mutually exclusive and that one particular form of domination or social relation—be it race, class, patriarchy, or heteronormativity—is the primary source of oppression (Kurtz 2002, 38).[3] While recognizing that important inequalities persist *among* racial, gender, or economic groups, intersectional approaches highlight the ways in which social and political forces manipulate the overlapping and intersecting inequalities *within* marginal groups. They also emphasize the consequent unevenness in the effects of the political, economic, and social gains made by marginalized groups since, and as a result of, the social movements and policy gains of the 1960s and 1970s (McCall 2005).

From an intersectional perspective, advocacy organizations do not represent commonalities or unitary constituencies with clearly defined and bounded interests that are givens in nature—assumptions that can mask the privileges associated with differences within constituencies (M. Warren 2001). Instead, intersectional frameworks view identities and the interests with which they are associated as constructions that result from social and political processes and experiences, including those related to the actions of social movements and advocacy organizations themselves (see, for example, Fausto-Sterling 1993; J. Katz 1995; Omi and Winant 1994). From this perspective, the broad constituencies spoken for by advocacy organizations are coalitions of intersecting and overlapping groups that are organized around one particular axis that is *constructed* or *framed* as what they have in common.

Interest group research that employs an intersectional framework has found that rather than a zero-sum trade-off between economic and social issues, the problems facing marginalized groups stem from the fact that advocacy organizations are traditionally organized around single axes of discrimination. Organizations consequently erase and fail to address issues that affect subgroups of their constituencies whose marginalized positions are constituted by the intersections of different forms of disadvantage.

In her research about the politics of HIV/AIDS, for example, Cathy Cohen (1999) shows that understanding that HIV/AIDS engages multiple axes of marginalization—including sexuality, race, class, and intravenous drug use—helps to explain why African American organizations were largely inactive on this issue in the early years of the epidemic in spite of the disproportionate impact of the disease on black communities. Strolovitch (2007) demonstrates that organizations representing women, racial minorities, and low-income people apply double standards when it comes to the levels of energy and resources that they devote to issues affecting differently positioned subgroups of their constituencies, devoting disproportionately high levels of attention and politically and financially more costly tactics to advantaged subgroups and disproportionately low levels of activity and

---

[3] Examples of intersectionally marginalized groups include, for example, low-income women, whose disadvantage is constituted by the intersection of economic and gender-based marginalization.

less costly tactics when it comes to disadvantaged subgroups. Her analyses show that these double standards cannot be explained as trade-offs between attention to economic issues on the one hand and attention to social issues on the other, but rather that they are caused by failures to address issues that intersect multiple disadvantages. While Strolovitch's work focuses on the implications of these failures for processes of representation, Sharon Kurtz's (2002) research shows that such elisions can severely impede advocacy outcomes as well. Examining several union campaigns, she finds that the failure to employ "multiple identity politics" that engage several axes of marginalization severely hampers labor organizations' ability to achieve their goals (see also Frymer 2008; Cohen and Warren 2000; D. Warren 2005).

The results of studies such as Cohen's, Kurtz's, and Strolovitch's are not necessarily at odds with the argument that identity-based and quality-of-life-oriented organizations pay insufficient attention to issues of economic justice for low-income people (indeed, Strolovitch finds relatively low levels of activity on welfare reform on the part of organizations representing women, suggesting that very phenomenon). However, their findings suggest that scholars who find less attention devoted to economic issues on the part of some organizations are capturing one side of a multifaceted problem in which economic disadvantage is one of many possible manifestations of intersectional disadvantage. Because low-income people are, by definition, less advantaged economically than middle-class people, one manifestation of intersectional disadvantage is a lack of attention to issues affecting low-income constituents in favor of ones that are of interest to middle-class constituents. However, this is not the only manifestation of the problem; issues affecting intersectionally disadvantaged subgroups of all kinds are given short shrift.

Although the mobilization of bias against advocacy on behalf of intersectionally disadvantaged groups is widespread, it is not ubiquitous, and research about social and economic justice advocacy is also beginning to detail some of the ways in which organizations can better serve their full constituencies. Strolovitch (2007), for example, finds that many organization officers are genuinely committed to the goal of advocacy for their multiply disadvantaged constituents and that many do speak extensively and effectively on behalf of intersectionally disadvantaged subgroups. Based on the best practices of these organizations, she provides empirically grounded suggestions about remedial measures for improving the representation of marginalized groups. Similarly, while Kurtz (2002) documents many challenges facing internally diverse movements, she also uncovers conditions under which movements can overcome the impediments of intersectional marginalization, showing that inclusive solidarity based upon practices that address multiple injustices better reflect the experiences of their constituencies and are key to movement successes.

Jeffrey Berry and David Arons (2003) suggest a very important way in which organizations can better represent disadvantaged populations. Focusing in particular on 501(c)3 non-profit service providers, they note that while non-profit status can attract government resources, this same status also limits how much groups can lobby, thereby limiting their ability to politicize their work. Rather than lobby as much as they can within the limits, non-profits instead minimize the political nature of their work, refrain from lobbying, and, consequently, miss important opportunities to represent the marginalized groups they serve. The authors conclude, however, that this situation is easily remedied through the "H election." Whereas the rules for lobbying under 501(c)3 status are vague and discourage political engagement, H election rules are clear and allow for exceptions to the definition of lobbying. For example, under some circumstances, the H election exempts the drafting of statutes from being considered lobbying.

In addition to highlighting some ways in which organizations can improve representation for women, racial minorities, and low-income people, much of the preceding research underscores the value of scholarship that examines state and local advocacy on behalf of marginalized groups. As Berry notes in Chapter 26 in this volume, the barriers faced by organizations representing weak groups are often lower at the local level than they are at the national level. Research about local-level organizations has illuminated a great deal about advocacy on behalf of groups such as women, racial minorities, and low-income people. Janelle Wong (2007), for example, has found that local-level community-based groups such as labor organizations, workers' centers, advocacy and social service organizations, ethnic voluntary associations, and religious organizations have been critical in mobilizing groups such as Asian American and Latino immigrants, reaching out to non-citizens and others who are often ignored by elected officials (see also Fung 2004; Swarts 2008). Combined with research showing that national organizations with strong ties to state and local associations are more likely to address issues that affect disadvantaged subgroups of their constituencies (Strolovitch 2007), there is much to suggest that scholars interested in assessing the role of advocacy organizations as compensatory representatives for marginalized groups should train their lenses on state and local organizations and on the "federalism" of advocacy as it is manifested in relationships among state, local, and national groups.

THE EFFECTS OF INSTITUTIONALIZATION

If outsider movements, in Schattschneider's words, "expand the scope of conflict," what happens to the terrain of political contestation when some of the vehicles for these movements are incorporated into policy processes and political institutions (Piven and Cloward 1977; see also Lipsky 1968; Lowi 1971)? As the movements of the "long 1960s" declined and the number of interest groups representing women, racial minorities, and low-income people grew, scholars began to devote increased attention to the effects of this transformation. Echoing Robert Michels's (1911) concern about the "iron law of oligarchy," much of this scholarship explores the implications of the rise in formalized, professionalized, and institutionalized organizations for the participatory, democratic, and radical social movements to which many of them are related.

Like work addressing the relationship between social and economic justice organizations and the broader interest group universe, investigations of the effects of institutionalization reflect the location occupied by these organizations at the boundary of insider and outsider status. On the one hand, formalized organizations that use "insider" tactics play crucial roles in politicizing previously unrecognized group interests, in maintaining movements during periods of low mobilization (Staggenborg 1986), in following up on movements' victories through lobbying, litigation, and monitoring government agencies (J. Jenkins and Eckert 1986; Tarrow 1994), and in buffering organizations from having to revert to less overtly political forms of activity such as service provision when political conditions change (Minkoff 1995). On the other hand, however, institutionalization can also enable the creation of "abeyance structures" through which organizations shift attention to activities such as research during periods when they are unlikely to succeed politically (Spalter-Roth and Schreiber 1995; Taylor 1989; Whittier 1995). While such practices can preserve a group's identity and core values in hostile political climates, they also lead organizations to disengage from direct political action and to miss opportunities to intervene in the policy process on behalf of the groups they represent. For example, Traci Sawyers and David Meyer find that abeyance strategies such as organizational maintenance and sustainability prevented women's organizations from vigorously opposing the fetal protection policies that undermined legal prohibitions on sex discrimination in the 1980s (Sawyers and Meyer 1999, 199).[4]

Another set of concerns about institutionalization is related to longstanding questions about alleged trade-offs between participatory and representative democracy and about the effects of the shift from mass movements to formal organizations on the possibilities for citizen political engagement. The central concern is that while mass movements are *participatory*, allowing for direct citizen participation and face-to-face political deliberation, advocacy groups are *representative*, mediating the voices and demands of potential movement participants by

---

[4] Fetal Protection Policies deny women access to jobs involving exposure to chemical or radiation "based on the premise that women are always potentially pregnant, and thus must be protected" (Sawyers and Meyer 1999, 199).

instead advocating *on their behalf.* Advocacy organizations may well offer compensatory representation to weak groups, but this may come at too high a cost if doing so also has the effect of depressing the political participation of members of these populations by making it seem unnecessary. Moreover, by relying on hierarchical and bureaucratized organizational structures, formalized advocacy organizations may risk perpetuating professionalist and hierarchical forms of politics rather than using their organizations as prefigurative models of the democratic values that many movements seek to instill in both citizens and the state. In her study of large national membership organizations, for example, Theda Skocpol (1999) finds that advocacy organizations rarely mobilize their members to participate in organizational or direct political activity. Instead, she argues, their members prefer "giving money to giving time." This form of engagement nurtures a weak form of participation and encourages organizations to be more engaged in "doing for" than in "doing with" (1999, 462).

Participatory movements and organizations are undoubtedly associated with beneficial outcomes including strong group consciousness and the development of political skills and new activists among members of the general population. However, while checkbook activism may be prevalent among members of Washington DC-based organizations that target the federal government, it may be less widespread among national, state, and local groups that target their advocacy efforts at actors and institutions outside the beltway. Among these latter organizations, participatory membership seems to be more the norm (Foley and Edwards 2002). In addition, Francesca Polletta's (2002) in-depth study of civil rights, new left, and women's liberation organizations in the 1960s and 1970s demonstrates that many of the benefits of participatory organizations can be achieved or at least facilitated through representative ones as well.

There are unavoidable pitfalls associated with institutionalization and inevitable trade-offs between participation and representation. However, as political theorist David Plotke (1997) has argued, there is an equally important trade-off between representation and exclusion from politics. Rather than preventing participation and engagement, formalized representative organizations seem instead to enable some aspects of participatory democracy by cultivating constituencies and facilitating their engagement in other, more participatory political activities. New research detailing the processes through which advocacy organizations help representation and participation to operate in tandem and in ways that enhance the connections between them for the members of marginalized groups can continue to illuminate the key role of social and economic justice organizations in leveling the playing fields of American politics and public policy.[5]

---

[5] Research has also found that participation in unconventional political activity such as protests tends to be "an addition to, rather than a substitution for, more conventional political participation"

EFFECTS ON POLITICS AND PUBLIC POLICY

The ultimate goals of advocacy on behalf of marginalized groups are, of course, to generate changes that improve the social, economic, and political conditions of group members or to prevent changes which have the potential to worsen these conditions. In light of these goals, it is not surprising that a perennial focus of studies of economic and social justice advocacy organizations is whether and how their activities influence politics and public policy. There is broad agreement that these organizations have opened up the policy process by breaking down "sub-governments" and expanding issue networks (J. Berry 1993). Measuring and demonstrating the direct and systematic effects of social movement and advocacy group activity on political and public policy outcomes has proven more difficult, however, in part because of a lack of readily available data on policy influence and the absence of consensual definitions of concepts such as policy impact and policy success (F. Baumgartner and Leech 1998). Such difficulties are evidenced by the fact that studies examining the effects of advocacy on public policy have reached widely ranging and conflicting conclusions, with some finding substantial effects on policy (J. Berry 1999), others judging the effects to be negligible or contingent (Burstein and Linton 2002), and still others arguing that the evidence is largely inconclusive (F. Baumgartner and Leech 1998). While the array of forces and many complex stages involved in policymaking and implementation may make isolating the direct impact of advocacy organizations elusive (see, for example, Kingdon 1984; D. Stone 2002), recent work offers some potentially fruitful frameworks and useful tools for isolating the mediating role of organizations in achieving the political and policy goals of organizations that represent marginalized groups. These frameworks and tools incorporate insights from social constructionist theories of interests and identities as being simultaneously politically constructed and politically salient.

Crises, Catastrophes, and Political Change

One avenue for examining the effects of advocacy brings together insights from American political development and international relations scholarship, focusing on the effects of catastrophic events such as wars and economic crises on the ability of advocacy organizations to achieve their policy goals. Philip Klinkner and Rogers Smith, for example, contend that wars often enable progress for marginalized

and that "challenging movements and unrest" can be positively related "to the stability of established political institutions" (see Meyer and Lupo 2007, 112, for an overview).

groups, arguing that equality and justice for African Americans have advanced only when wars have required the mobilization of African Americans, when the nature of the enemies being fought has required that egalitarian and democratic traditions be emphasized, or when domestic political protest has demanded that national leaders live up to the justificatory rhetoric by instituting reforms (Klinkner and Smith 1999, 3–4). Others argue similarly that movements successfully advanced redistributive policies and labor rights during the economic crisis of the Great Depression (Goldfield 1989). While civil rights for African Americans and the New Deal demonstrate the kind of opportunities that wars and economic crises present to advocates for marginalized groups, other examples suggest some of the constraints that can emerge in such contexts. For example, during the Civil War and the First World War, women's suffrage activists were attacked as selfish and unpatriotic for not focusing solely on the war effort (Banaszak 1996).

The period following 9/11 provides more recent illustrations of the double-edged challenges to and opportunities for social and economic justice advocacy that result from national crises and political instability. Sidney Tarrow (2005), for example, has described the situation faced by "Mobilization for Global Justice" (MGJ), a coalition that had planned mass protests during the meetings of the World Bank and International Monetary Fund that were scheduled to take place in Washington, DC, in late September 2001. Following the events of 9/11, however, most of the MGJ events were derailed: ten of the eighteen scheduled events—particularly those that would likely have been disruptive—were cancelled, and four were significantly revised.

While the MGJ demonstrates the limitations imposed by crises such as terrorist attacks, the movement to allow gays and lesbians to serve openly in the military illustrates the possibilities presented by crises to advocates for marginalized groups. After a 2006 General Accounting Office report found that over 300 language experts, including over fifty who speak Arabic, were discharged under the "don't ask, don't tell" (DADT) policy that forbids gay men and lesbians to serve openly in the US military, the Department of Defense issued a statement making the unprecedented suggestion "that lesbian and gay service personnel should continue to use their skills in support of national security efforts, even after facing dismissal under the law" (PRNewswire 2007). While the policy remains in effect at the time of publication, in his 2008 commencement address at the US Military Academy, Joint Chiefs of Staff chair Admiral Mike Mullen told graduating cadets that the military would accept gay service members if Congress repealed DADT (Terkel 2008). President Barack Obama has expressed some support for repealing the policy as well.

Taken together, the foregoing examples suggest that systematic comparisons between the activities and achievements of social and economic justice organziations during periods of war and economic crisis and their activities during periods of relative "peace and prosperity" can illuminate the conditions under which organizations are constrained as well as those that present opportunities for advancement. Such investigations can also shed light on some of the conditions under which groups might more effectively lobby from the inside or exert pressure from the outside and on the relative effects of institutional and environmental factors such as public opinion and partisan control of Congress or the executive branch. By comparing organizations that represent a range of marginalized groups and examining the intersections between enduring racial, gender, and economic inequalities on the one hand and punctuated crises and catastrophes on the other hand (F. Baumgartner and Jones 1993), such examinations promise to reveal the possibilities for advocacy organizations to address the ongoing issues that affect their constituents as these vary over time and among groups and issues.

For example, because crises tighten connections between "citizenship" and the "national interest," whether the goals of advocacy organizations are constrained or enabled by national crises is likely to vary based on factors such as the perceived moral worthiness of the constituents they represent or on the extent to which organizations are able to frame their claims as extending fuller citizenship rights to groups so that they might better serve the national interest. While organizations and movements that are able to frame their claims in such ways may be able to make gains during times of crisis, organizations seeking changes that are themselves destabilizing of existing racial, gender, or class orders are likely to face increased resistance unless they are able to reframe the negative or stigmatized constructions of the groups they represent (Schneider and Ingram 1993). Understanding the varying abilities of organizations to reframe their constituencies and to make claims to citizenship will provide a deeper account of the intersections among but also the differences between the ways in which race, class, and gender structure the political opportunities available to social and economic justice advocacy groups. In these ways, work investigating the comparative effects of catastrophic events can illuminate the ways in which notions of citizenship are tied to race, class, and gender structure and structured by American political processes, institutions, and public policies.

Feedback Effects

Another promising avenue for assessing the effects of movements and advocacy borrows from a framework known as "policy feedback." At its most basic level, policy feedback captures Schattschneider's idea that "new policies create a new politics" and that particular policy forms "set particular political forces in motion" (Soss and Schram 2007), shaping future directions of the policy by "influencing patterns of mobilization" (Amenta, Bonastia, and Caren 2001) and mediating the potential impact of future movements and advocacy organizations (Bonastia 2000). As Joe Soss and Sanford Schram explain, feedback theorists argue that policies can set political agendas, shape identities and interests, influence beliefs about what is possible, desirable, and normal, alter conceptions of citizenship and status, channel or constrain agency, define incentives, redistribute resources, and convey cues that define, arouse, or pacify constituencies (Soss and Schram 2007, 113). Most important for our purposes, policy designs can "influence the mobilization of organized interests and their interactions with elected officials" (Soss and Schram 2007, 113; see also Lowi 1964; J. Wilson 1995).

Policy feedback approaches deemphasize direct causal outcomes of movement and organization actions. Instead, they suggest that scholars might best capture the effects of social movements and advocacy organizations holistically and over time. "Putting the needle on the record" earlier in the political process and examining the interactions among political organizations, institutions, and the public illuminates the role of policies in the formation of movement and advocacy constituencies. Such a longitudinal and interactive approach also highlights the ability of advocacy organizations to indirectly support change by helping to *create the conditions* that alter the course of future events. In these ways, feedback frameworks push us to consider advocacy organizations as both cause and effect of policy changes and state formation, simultaneously organizing mass activity while also working within and challenging the constraints created by political institutions and policy processes (Diani 1997, 143). Operating as both expressions and framers of mass activity, advocacy organizations are both products and causes of constituency formation.

Andrea Campbell (2003), for example, demonstrates that the enactment of Social Security in 1935 not only provided more resources to individuals over the age of sixty-five but also had the important effect of politicizing them and leading them to become a constituency with potential interests and preferences that policy entrepreneurs, interest groups, and political parties subsequently attempted to represent and claim as their own. Along similar lines, Suzanne Mettler (2002) demonstrates that policies build capacity for civic engagement by distributing resources and creating interpretive conditions that shift people's perceptions of their relationships to other citizens and to the government, thereby prompting or facilitating organization formation and increased demands on the state. The educational and training benefits provided to Second World War veterans through the GI Bill, for example, helped create the conditions that led returning black veterans to mobilize for civil rights, which led, in turn, to the creation of additional civil rights organizations and eventually to policy changes such as the Civil Rights Act of 1964 (Mettler 2002).

From a policy feedback perspective, advocacy organizations influence policy outcomes by creating incentives for beneficiaries to "mobilize in favor of programmatic expansion," for the creation of organizational niches that are ripe for lobbying activity, and for the granting of group access to policymakers (Pierson 1993, 599). Through the process that Paul Pierson terms "policy learning," organizations learn over time about policy consequences and this knowledge allows them to strategically shift and focus their efforts. By creating a "sense of political crisis" among elites, advocacy groups also create space for the realignment of various groups around new issues, thereby opening contested political space in which previously uncrystallized and unrecognized political interests can be made present and mobilized (Jenkins and Brents 1989). Through this politicization of issues, advocacy contributes to the formation of new political interests and the creation of political opportunities. In this light, advocacy organizations representing marginalized groups might be described as sites in which two "feedback loops" meet and interact. The first "loop" connects government institutions, processes, and policies to the advocacy organizations (see, for example, Amenta and Young 1999; Meyer 2005; Skocpol 1992). In the second loop, advocacy organizations connect the state to a range of political constituencies (see, for example, Diani 1997; Polletta and Jasper 2001; M. McCann 1994), expressing their grievances and mobilizing new constituencies that make demands on the state.

Policy feedback approaches are not unique to the study of social and economic advocacy, of course, but their insights are particularly useful for work in this area. In particular, such approaches provide a rich framework and useful tools for analyzing the complicated interplay among political interests, identities, and institutions and between interest groups, social movements, and policy outcomes that benefit or disadvantage marginalized groups. Work that brings together intersectional and policy feedback frameworks is particularly promising. Synthesizing insights about the discursive roles of advocacy organizations in processes such as framing, identity construction, and the constitution of political interests with insights about the functioning of political institutions and opportunity structures also has the potential to illuminate answers to wide-ranging questions about the role of social and economic justice advocacy organizations in constituency formation, policy change, and state formation.

CONCLUSION

Straddling the boundaries between "insider" interest groups and "outsider" movements politically, and among several disciplines and subfields intellectually, advocacy organizations that represent marginalized groups such as women, racial minorities, and low-income people continue to play a vital role in American politics and to be an important focus of inquiry within political science and sociology. Guided by overarching questions about how these organizations represent and activate populations that were mobilized by social movements during the

1950s, 1960s, and 1970s, scholars have advanced important arguments about the evolving contours and composition of this community of organizations, about the costs, benefits, and trade-offs associated with their institutionalization, and about the ways in which these organizations affect politics and public policy. Scholars should continue to investigate the circumstances under which organizations representing marginalized groups best represent their constituencies, the conditions under which they are able to achieve their goals, and the conditions under which they prevail against stronger opponents, as well as to explore the differences between and connections among possibilities and the local, state, and national levels. They should also continue to mine the productive tension between advocacy groups and the social movements out of which many organizations have grown, particularly as this tension is manifested within and in conjunction with contemporary religious, immigrants', LGBT, antiwar, and transnational movements. They should also examine the ways in which new technologies are further muddying distinctions among forms of participation, mobilization, and representation (Chadwick 2007).

Scholarship investigating advocacy on behalf of marginalized groups should also continue its preliminary but productive conversation with the work of political theorists who challenge the idea that groups based on identities such as race, class, gender, and sexuality exist prior to politics. Social constructionist ideas about interests and identities might seem at first to be incompatible with empirical social science's reliance on such categories of analysis. However, at the nexus of intersectional and policy feedback frameworks is an emerging—and potentially fruitful— approach to understanding the "groupness" of constituencies as being simultaneously politically constructed and politically salient. Scholars should continue to grapple with the intersections of multiple forms of privilege and disadvantage and with the implications of the consequent contingent and constructed nature of interests and identities.

CHAPTER 25

....

THE COMPARATIVE ADVANTAGE OF STATE INTEREST ORGANIZATION RESEARCH

....

DAVID LOWERY

VIRGINIA GRAY

WHAT role do studies of interest organizations in the American states play in the larger literature on interest group politics? Indeed, do the literatures on state and national interest representation have anything to say to each other? In "State Interest Group Research and the Mixed Legacy of Belle Zeller" (2002), Gray and Lowery answered this question by identifying a broad range of landmark studies conducted at both levels of government and found remarkably little cross-fertilization between them. Rather, the landmark state studies were often more descriptive, and focused on a trade-off between group and party power, reflecting the legacy of Belle Zeller (1954), while the national-level studies were embedded in broad-range theories about democratic politics used in the discipline at large and, therefore, focused on quite different processes. One consequence of this is that the national literature did not cite state-level studies very often, while the converse was far from true. Thus, decades of research on state interest organizations seem to have had rather little impact on the larger literature.

Gray and Lowery (2002) offered a number of recommendations for enhancing the relevance, impact, and theoretical contribution of the state literature on the more general literature on the politics of interest representation. These entailed greater engagement with more fundamental theories about interest representation, greater reliance on analyses of all fifty states rather than single-state studies so as to take advantage of the empirical leverage provided by comparison, and greater attention to the interactions among organized interests across national and state levels. Starting with this general framework, we examine how the state interest group research program has responded to these recommendations. More polemically, we take Gray and Lowery's (2002) argument further by highlighting the rather paradoxical character of the dominance of descriptive studies of state interest organizations and the greater attention to theory in national-level research. Simply put, we argue that national-level studies—as opposed to those focusing on the states—are highly constrained in terms of their ability to actually test more recently developed theories about interest representation that emphasize the importance of context. Indeed, the states as a locus of research provide considerable advantages in developing our collective research program on the politics of organized interests.

We develop our argument in three steps. First, as a foundation for our argument, we examine the recent dialogue between theory and empirical analysis on the politics of interest representation. We suggest that recent attention to mid-range theories based on a logic of segmentation has allowed us to sidestep some of the traditional barriers to developing a progressive research program on interest representation.[1] Second, however, the logic of segmentation itself raises, or has at least made more evident, a number of new barriers to research progress. In addressing these newer barriers, we argue that examination of the states offers critical advantages over studying the interest system of the US or other national governments. We examine the comparative advantages of the states in some detail, arguing that the institutional variation found in the states can enhance research of several topics of importance at the national level, especially the study of how institutions condition interest organization influence. We illustrate these by discussing several leading research themes uniquely originating in contemporary state politics research and examine how these have influenced or should influence interest group scholarship more generally. Especially important here will be a discussion of the formation of interest group communities, the role of direct democracy and term limits, the influence of campaign contributions by organized interests, and interactions among organized interests *across* levels of government. We conclude our analysis by summarizing both how the state literature has responded to the three recommendations noted above, considering how the

---

[1] By progressive, we mean in Lakatos's (1970) sense of continually generating new test implications and research hypotheses.

broader interest group literature should view research on state interest systems, and how the latter should proceed in better understanding the complex role of organized interests in politics and public policy.

THE THEORY–DATA DIALOGUE

In understanding the differences between the state and national research programs on interest organizations, their imbalanced influence on each other, and their collective capacity to promote a progressive dialogue between theory and data, we need first to dismiss a couple of false trails that might mislead us.[2] It is, for example, sometimes claimed there are not sufficient data at the state and/or national level to conduct truly comparable kinds of studies. It is certainly true that some types of data were once more readily available in some political systems than others. For example, the national government only adopted lobby registration rules of sufficient strength to provide a reasonable census of the national interest community with the adoption of the Lobby Disclosure Act of 1995 (F. Baumgartner and Leech 2001) when such data had been routinely available at the state level for three decades (Gray and Lowery 1996a). And broadly comprehensive information on such critical data as comparable measures of public ideology and public opinion (Erikson, Wright, and McIver 1993; W. Berry et al. 1998; Brace et al. 2002), issues of critical importance to the study of organized interests, have only recently become available when such data have been a staple of national political analyses for decades. But as indicated by these citations, many of these disparities across the two levels of government have now greatly diminished. Thus, the longstanding complaint that research on interest groups is theory-rich and data-poor (D. Arnold 1982, 97)—at whatever level of analysis—has far less validity today than in the past.

Indeed, several scholars have more recently dismissed the positive element of this conventional complaint—the claim that the study of organized interests was "theory-rich." Baumgartner and Leech (1998), for example, argued that the literature's emphasis on small-n studies of the influence of lobbying and campaign contributions on individual issues provided a poor foundation for generalization and an inadequate prod toward theory development because such studies were

---

[2] Another and likely still serious problem precluding a closer interaction between state and national research on interest representation noted by Gray and Lowery (2002) is the existence of rather hard subdisciplinary lines that, for example, lead state scholars to present papers at conferences on panels for state politics scholars while students of the national interest group system rarely stray from panels organized to address issues having to do with Congress or political behavior at the national level.

inherently inattentive to context. They argued instead that we needed large-*n* studies that would more validly assess old theories and encourage the development of new theories of the politics of organized interests (F. Baumgartner and Leech 1998, 168–88). One of the most important advantages of these large-*n* studies is that they must inevitably be attentive to contextual forces that are, by their nature, constants in small-*n* studies. And understanding such contextual forces compels us in turn to develop hypotheses and theories that account for variation across cases. Recent years have indeed seen an explosion of large-*n* studies that are grounded on new theories of context and, thereby, provide a foundation for a progressive dialogue between theory and data (Gray and Lowery 1996a; F. Baumgartner and Jones 1993). Even more broadly, the other chapters in this volume attest to the rapid evolution of both theory and data in the domain of interest group research, developments that studies of interest representation in the states have fully participated in.

Importantly, these new context-based theories of interest representation rely relatively little on some of the traditional or classic theories of interest representation harkening back to Bentley's (1908) group theory of politics and including both Truman's (1951) pluralist model and corporatism in the European context (Lehmbruch and Schmitter 1982). As noted above, successful research programs entail a dialogue between theory construction and theory probing that generates and then answers new questions (Lakatos 1970).[3] Such a dialogue can be difficult if our theories are overly abstract because they lack a direct empirical referent (Dogan and Pelassy 1990). Overly abstract theories tend to be vague and are, therefore, difficulty to falsify. More useful are "theories intermediate to the minor working hypotheses evolved in abundance during the day-by-day routines of research and the all-inclusive speculations comprising a master conceptual scheme from which it is hoped to derive a very large number of empirically observed uniformities of social behavior" (Robert Merton 1968, 5). That is, as suggested by King, Keohane, and Verba (1994, 20), theories need to be "as concrete as possible" in order that they "could be wrong" and yet have "as many observable implications as possible." Thus, the cutting edge of research programs is typically evident not in kinds of hypotheses driving either context-less small-*n* analyses or overly abstract paradigms, but in research using middle-range theories that are rigorously tested via comparative research designs in which contexts vary.

In the study of the politics of interest representation, we have constructed these mid-range theories using a logic of segmentation. That is, we now routinely divide the domain of research on organized interests into distinct topics, one construction of which is evident in Lowery and Gray's (2004a) characterization of the influence

---

[3] Parts of this and the following section of this chapter are in part based on the discussion—with specific reference to the European Union and national European interest systems—of the evolution of comparative interest group research in Lowery, Poppelaars, and Berkhout (2008).

Table 25.1 Three perspectives on the influence production process

Perspective	Mobilization and maintenance stage	Interest community stage	Exercise of influence stage	Political and policy outcome stage
Pluralist perspective	Mobilization is natural product of shared concerns	All salient interests are represented in community	Organizations provide only information	Pluralist heaven
	Truman (1951)	Truman (1951)	Bauer, Pool, and Dexter (1963)	Dahl (1961)
		Morehouse (1981)	Zeigler and Baer (1969)	Hrebenar and Thomas (1987, 1992, 1993a, 1993b)
Transactions perspective	Mobilization is biased by collective action problems	The interest community is biased in favor of elites	Public policy is bought and sold like any commodity	Pluralist hell
	M. Olson (1965)	Schattschneider (1960)	McChesney (1997)	M. Olson (1982)
			Best and Teske (2002)	
Neopluralist perspective	Collective action problems can be solved	Community is a complex organization ecology	Influence is contingent and most often limited	Pluralist purgatory
	Walker (1991)		Heinz et al. (1993)	F. Baumgartner and Jones (1993)
	Haider-Markel (1997); Crowley and Skocpol (2001)	Gray and Lowery (1996a); Boehmke (2008)	Lowery et al. (2009)	Bowling and Ferguson (2001)

Note: Initial citation is a canonical example of argument, with subsequent citations in some cells a more recent state-based analysis. This table was partially adapted from Lowery and Brasher (2004, 18) and Gray and Lowery (2002, 398).

production process, as seen in Table 25.1.[4] The table is comprised of four columns segmenting or separating the various stages of the influence production process. These are the topics on which research on the politics of organized interests is now routinely conducted, running from the mobilization and maintenance of interest organizations, their interactions among each other within interest communities,

---

[4] For a more detailed discussion of the national literature cited in Table 25.1, see Lowery and Brasher (2003, 16–24). For a further discussion of the state cites, see Gray and Lowery (2002).

their lobbying practices, and the ultimate consequences of these for public policy. The row categories represent three broad conceptions about the role of organized interests in democracies, ranging from the optimistic evaluations of pluralists through the pessimistic assessments of transactions theorists to the more contingent expectations of neopluralist scholars. The first citations in the cells refer to canonical examples of research work from a given stage of and perspective on the influence production process, followed by work (often more recent and less canonical) on state interests representing the respective themes of some cells.[5] As is obvious from the patterns of citations, the state literature has at least recently evolved from its more introspective ghetto into analyses on and debates over the same core issues as observed in the national literature on interest representation.

More to the point, however, the three broad evaluative perspectives along the rows of the table are not themselves falsifiable. Instead, the key locus of research typically concerns either the comparing of competing mid-range theories within the columns defined by the influence production process or, if research is focused on the rows, examining how changes at one stage of the influence production process feed forward or feed back to the other stages of the process. On the first, for example, a Trumanesque (1951) model of mobilization can be directly tested against an Olsonian (1965) model of mobilization. Similarly, Olson's (1982) institutional sclerosis model and/or Schattschneider's (1960) explanation of origins of bias in interest communities can be directly tested against the population ecology model of Gray and Lowery (1996a). Thus, each pair of mid-range theories point to specific test implications that can be used to assess their truth status. On the latter, we are interested in knowing, for example, how the characteristics of the population an organized interest enters alter both its strategy of survival as an organization and the repertoire of influence tools it employs.

Progressive research programs in the Lakatosian sense (1970) are significantly more likely to be found *within* the topics defined by the columns in Table 25.1 or *within* the rows of the table rather than doing both types of research together at the same time. We think that the former are especially important. That is, alternative mid-range theories are found down the columns of the table, competing mid-range theories that provide the kinds of specific and contrasting test implications that allow for meaningful empirical evaluation. Indeed, most of the interesting progress in our collective research program since the more pessimistic assessment of Baumgartner and Leech (1998) is occurring at this mid-range level of theory. This is a direct consequence of dividing the domain of topics on the organized interests into theoretically and empirically manageable segments. As Dogan and Pelassy (1990, 113) noted, there is "need to segment before comparing."

---

[5] This categorization of research on organized interests is very loose. That is, research in different domains might in the end support a neopluralist view of mobilization while also supporting a transactions perspective on the influence activities of organized interests.

This does not mean, however, that the strategy of segmentation can or has solved all of our research problems even given the notable renaissance in scholarship on interest organizations since the early 1990s. Indeed, we will see that segmentation itself can at times raise barriers to progress within a research program by making the comparative testing of mid-range theories more complicated. But before considering these, the key thing to note for now is that the problems that seemed to so impede more integrative scholarship on interest representation in the not so distant past have now receded to a considerable degree. By eschewing both small-n analyses and overly abstract "theories" about interest representation regimes, and by instead concentrating our attention on mid-range theories with sharply contrasting hypotheses, clear test implications have pointed to large-n studies needed to advance the dialogue between theory and empirical analyses of interest representation.

THE COMPARATIVE ADVANTAGE OF STATES

This broad shift in the character of interest group scholarship has, we believe, not only brought state interest group research into the mainstream of scholarship on interest representation; it has also inadvertently enhanced the role of the states as a locus of research of value to the larger research program. In developing this argument, we need to assess the relative merits of different research loci for this kind of research. The key issues we need to consider concern not the availability of theory and/or data per se since large-n analyses of mid-range theories have become the norm since the early 1990s. Rather, the question is one of empirical leverage over the kinds of contextual forces the mid-range theories draw our attention to. That is, do the cases we study—whether the US national government, other national governments, transnational governments such as the European Union, the states, or cities—provide for sufficient controlled variation to allow us to rule out rival explanations of any observed associations between dependent and independent variables of interest? And especially importantly, how do the research designs applicable to these different loci allow us to address issues of context, which have become so important in the new literature on the politics of interest representation?

Answering this question depends, of course, on the nature of the theoretical question being asked. And many of the theoretical questions we ask can be answered with the kinds of empirical variation provided within any number of these loci. For example, Robert Dahl's initial analysis of pluralism in *Who Governs?* was founded on an empirical analysis of interest representation in one local government—New Haven, Connecticut. Similarly, important analyses of organizational mobilization and maintenance, which focus on variations across members and/or organizations, have been successfully conducted on both state (Moe 1980; Haider-Markel 1997; Gray and Lowery 1996b) and national (Rothenberg 1992) organizations. The same is true—if less fully so as seen below—when comparing the behaviors of individual interest organizations, such as their joining in coalitions with other organized interests in lobbying or working on their own, a topic that has been usefully explored at both the state (Heaney 2004a; Gray and Lowery 1998) and national (Hojnacki 1997; Hula 2007) levels. On such theoretical questions, the covariation we are interested in occurs across organizations or members or even issues within any given government. These questions can be studied at any level, with research on the states having neither an advantage nor a disadvantage as a locus of research.

The advantages of the states really develop when we look at phenomena that are constants within any one government, whether that is the national government or the government of a single state. And fortunately or unfortunately, many of the theoretical questions we are interested in address such issues. The most important of these concern how political institutions influence a variety of characteristics of organized interests running from the construction of populations of organized interests and the lobbying strategies and tactics they employ. To a large extent, such institutions are constants—at least at any one point in time—within any one locus of analysis. But the problem extends beyond the obvious cases of political institutions to include any variable of potential interest in understanding the behaviors of organized interests that are constants, including simply the potential number of organized interests that might be mobilized to engage in political activity, the laws that regulate lobbying activity, or the state of the economy at any one time or place. Studying such contextual forces requires variation for comparison. The literature on national interest organizations has addressed this need for comparison in a number of ways, all of which, at least on their own, do not fully satisfy.[6]

Avoiding Comparison

The first and perhaps least satisfactory way is simply to limit our generalizations to the cases at hand, accepting the constants demarking any one case as rather absolute limits on the scope of our theories. Indeed, to a significant degree, the national literature simply ignores many important questions about interest representation. Theories on interest representation in Washington are often framed in

---

[6] Many of the limitations apply, of course, to studies of interest representation focusing on a single state.

strikingly narrow terms with little effort to express their concepts in a manner that is capable of speaking to a broader appreciation of the politics of interest representation. This parochialism is fully evident in the titles of many research monographs and texts on the politics of organized interests, including Browne's *Cultivating Congress: Constituents, Issues, and Interest in Agricultural Policy* (1995), Wright's *Interest Groups and Congress: Lobbying Contributions and Influence* (1996), Dwyre and Farrar-Myers's *Legislative Labyrinth: Congress and Campaign Finance Reform* (2001), and Mahood's *Interest Groups in American National Politics* (2000). We would not suggest that such an exclusive focus on the national interest system is unimportant. Rather, by adopting such a focus, hypotheses will be inevitably framed in a narrower manner than is conducive to developing broader theory about interest organizations.

This approach carries with it, however, an even more severe cost than simple parochialism. Indeed, the national literature largely eschews examining what are on their face critical issues about interest representation. One such issue concerns the relative balance of political parties and organized interests in influencing public policy, a topic that was addressed in the state politics literature going back to Zeller (1954) and continuing to be a major theme in the state literature in the work of Morehouse (1981) and Thomas and Hrebenar (1991, 1999). Simply put, the literature on Washington interest representation is essentially silent on this obviously important issue, necessarily so, of course, given the lack of variation in the national political party and national interest group systems at any given point in time. Similarly, Berkman (2001) found that the level of legislative professionalization in the states influences mobilization, with more professional legislatures attracting fewer organized interests given the former's capacities to develop independent sources of information. This hypothesis about the influence of legislative institutions on the contours of the interest system has never been examined in the national literature, not because it is unimportant, but because there simply is no variation in the level of congressional professionalization.

Another issue that is examined only in a highly limited manner in the national literature concerns the relationship between public opinion and organized interests. This claim might strike some as odd given the deserved prominence of Kollman's *Outside Lobbying: Public Opinion and Interest Group Strategies* (1998) and Smith's *American Business and Political Power: Public Opinion, Elections, and Democracy* (2000). The former addresses how public opinion critically shapes lobbying strategies in Washington while the latter examines how public opinion determines how successful those strategies might be. But in such national-level scholarship, public opinion only indirectly influences public policy. The states—or even more usefully, some of the states—provide an answer from direct decision making on the part of citizens through the instruments of direct democracy. Thus, state scholars have amply examined how the availability of the initiative stimulates mobilization among citizens' organizations (Boehmke 2002, 2008) as well as how and how effectively interest organizations lobby the public in referendum voting (E. Gerber 1999). More generally still, the significant variation in public opinion and interest group systems as a whole has allowed state scholars to address their linkage at a more encompassing or system-level characteristic of the kinds of broad summative assessments reported in the last column of Table 25.1 (Gray et al. 2004), something that is more difficult to do at the national level. In short, national-level studies are often limited even when specific hypotheses are addressed given the limited variance in key variables provided by any one government.

And last in terms of this approach, attention to only the national level—or for that matter, to only a single state—misses considerable opportunities to study how different interest systems are linked to each other. A number of longstanding theoretical issues are at stake here, including how interest groups might facilitate a system of policy diffusion and might themselves diffuse across the states or move to and from different levels of government. Understanding the nature of federalism is also a relevant concern given Grodzins's (1966) observation that the federal systems can be viewed as a structure with many cracks through which influence may be exercised. Organizations impeded at one level may find opportunities at another. But none of these issues can be examined from the perspective of a single government. Nevertheless, few have bothered to assess the role of interest organizations in these vertical and horizontal diffusion processes. The limited evidence now available suggests that national policy has a significant impact on the mobilization of interest organizations in the states (F. Baumgartner, Gray, and Lowery forthcoming), but that interest communities of the states develop largely independently of each other (Wolak et al. 2002). The more general point, though, is that attention to only one government precludes asking such questions.

Comparisons with Other Nations

A second solution, one that until very recently has been far less employed, is to look for covariation across national governments. If the states are seen as a bit too small potatoes from someone steeped in the self-importance of the beltway, perhaps we can usefully compare the Washington interest system to those of other nations or the European Union. One notably ambitious recent example is Christine Mahoney's comparison of interest representation in the US and the European Union in *Brussels versus the Beltway* (2008).[7] Still, it is quite difficult to formulate compara-

---

[7] We should note that Mahoney is exceedingly cautious in her comparisons of these two systems, restricting her analysis largely to separate analyses of the models with only soft comparisons across the cases.

tive theories capable of coping with the hard fact that variables that are meaningful in one political system are not always meaningful in another very different one. This problem was identified by Sartori (1970, 1033) as the "traveling problem." That is, to cope with comparisons across widely distinct systems, scholars must define concepts at a higher level of abstraction, a process labeled "concept stretching." But doing so often leaves us with concepts that are too vague and broad and are, as a consequence, no longer falsifiable (Sartori 1970, 1034). Sartori certainly did not oppose such concept stretching per se. But he noted that it often went too far so as to enter the realm of the unfalsifiable.

This problem is especially severe, however, for the study of interest representation given the strategy of segmentation and attention to mid-range theories about interest representation noted earlier. That is, segmentation itself raises barriers to cross-national comparative analysis. Lowery, Poppelaars, and Berkhout (2008) note that while employing a strategy of segmentation has proven to be useful for isolating competing theories with more precise test implications, segmentation is rarely complete. Indeed, one of the key findings of recent work on both US and EU interest systems is that the mobilization of individual interest organizations, their interactions with populations of organized interests, their selection of lobbying strategies, and the policy consequences arising from those efforts are connected in complex ways (Lowery, Gray, and Monogan 2008; Beyers and Kerremans 2007). These linkages are likely to be potent sources of specification error under any condition. Still, they can be ignored when we focus on one stage of the influence production process *within* one political system. Behaviors at the other stages of the influence production process are then constants by design. These linkages might also pose no great threat if we restrict our comparisons of rival hypotheses at a given stage of the influence production process across relatively similar types of political systems, such as across counties that are relatively corporatist in the sense of openness or across countries that are relatively pluralist in terms of access (Sairoff 1999). But the potential for specification error arising from linkages across the stages of the influence production process is likely to be more problematic when comparing across quite different kinds of political systems.

For this reason, Lowery, Poppelaars, and Berkhout (2008) conclude that a truly cross-national analysis of the politics of interest representation may yet be a bridge too far. To make such an approach viable without concept stretching to the point of obfuscation, we would need a true multilevel theory about how the several steps in the influence production process are linked within separate national governments as a necessary precursor to accounting for variation across polities in causal relationships within each of the segments. Failure to do so would either lead to specification error through exclusion of relevant explanatory variables or non-useful recourse to dummy variables indicating, for example, that lobbying in the EU and the US differ because mobilization processes vary across the two cases. The constructing of a multilevel theory, however, is likely to be difficult given the kinds of variables that are likely to account for how patterns of mobilization *or* processes governing the construction of interest communities *or* variations in influence strategies *or* their policy consequences vary across very different kinds of political systems. These variables involved are likely to go far beyond those addressing organized interests per se. Dogan and Pelassy (1990, 116), based on the pessimistic analyses of Macridis (1961) and Ehrmann (1958) on the possibilities of comparative work on interest systems, observed that such models may stretch to "a point beyond which the explanation of the differences moves outside the framework of any 'theory of groups'; the contrasts must then be attributed to some element buried in the cultures, social structures, or political systems considered in their entirety." This seems a challenge that we are not yet fully prepared to accept.

Time Series Analyses

The remaining solution typical in research on national interest systems is, given the limited variation on a number of variables of obvious significance at any one point in time within the national interest system, to look for alternative sources of variation *within* systems. There is, of course, considerable variation to employ if we focus our attention on issues or decisions. Indeed, there are many opportunities to study covariation of important concepts across issues or decisions within the single-interest system provided by the federal government or by any one state. The range of such studies is notable, running from Hojnacki's (1997) work on the formation of lobbying coalitions, Wright's (2004) analysis of the impact of political action committee (PAC) contributions on roll call voting in Congress on tobacco legislation, Smith's (2000) analysis of lobbying on bills of interest to business interests more generally, to, most recently, Baumgartner, Berry, Hojnacki, Kimball, and Leech's analysis (2009) of issue reframing. But the better versions of these analyses, of which these are outstanding examples, search for variation within selective substantive topics and focus on the end stage of the influence production process by examining the impact of lobbying on political decisions. They are able to find useful variation across multiple, if relatively similar, types of legislative decisions. Thus, we certainly would not suggest that the study of the states is inherently superior in all cases. But this approach is far less useful for testing theories addressing the earlier stages of the influence production process focusing on the mobilization of lobbying activity and the formation of communities of interest organizations.

An alternative approach, then, is to look for variation in variables of interest *over time* within any one political system. Unfortunately, what is perhaps most notable about both the literatures on national and state interest systems is the sheer paucity of time series analyses of hypotheses about interest representation. This is certainly true of state research, where most of the analyses have been cross-state at a given point in time with only the occasional effort to compare across two or three time points (Gray and Lowery 1996a). Indeed, more complete time series of lobbying registrations have been conducted for only a handful of states (Wolak, Lowery, and Gray 2001; Brasher, Lowery, and Gray 1999), and these were largely limited to exploring the potential influence of outliers in the more dominant cross-state analyses. But it is even more shocking, given the lack of readily available comparisons, that there have been few time series analyses of lobbying the national government. Again, the issue is not one of lack of data. The national PAC regulatory regime was established by the Federal Election Campaign Act, with the first registration of PACs in 1978. The Lobby Disclosure Act of 1995 provided the first comprehensive registration of lobbyists starting in 1996. But when the latter are examined by Grier, Munger, and Roberts (1991, 1994), as just one example of many such studies, the analysis is limited to a single year's cross-section. And since Baumgartner and Leech (2001) analyzed the first year of lobby registrations from 1996, no attempt has been made to take advantage of the subsequent decade's worth of data. The incredibly rich lobby registration data has been employed from time to time, but largely only in a single-year, cross-section manner (Tripathi, Ansolabehere, and Snyder 2002; W. Hansen, Mitchell, and Drope 2005; Brasher and Lowery 2006).

Two very important exceptions to this lack of attention to time series analysis that must be noted are Nownes (2004) and Nownes and Lipinski's (2005) analysis of the development of the population of national gay and lesbian organizations and Bosso's (2005) more qualitative analysis of the national environmental interest community. These studies test several of the core hypotheses of the population ecology model of interest system density, including how the size of a lobbying community develops over time in a density-dependent manner and how this in turn influences the birth and death rates of organized interests. This theory was most prominently developed in cross-sectional analyses of the sizes of state interest systems (Gray and Lowery 1996a). But such analyses cannot easily distinguish between the population ecology interpretation of interest system density and Olson's (1965) explanation based on the problem of collective action (Lowery, Gray, and Monogan 2008). But while Olson would lead us to expect that interest communities grow in a simple linear fashion as organizations slowly solve collective action problems using selective incentives, Nownes (2004) and Nownes and Lipinski's (2005) analyses show clear evidence of slow growth with few births and many deaths in the legitimation phase of an interest guild, rapid growth with many births and few deaths following initial legitimation, and little growth with many deaths and few births during the mature density-dependent stage of population development. This s-shaped pattern is a hallmark of environmentally constrained population growth (Hannan and Freeman 1989). And Bosso (2005) provides a detailed analysis of the evolution of issue niches over time among the environmental interests, again, a key expectation of the population ecology theory of interest organizations. Thus, close time series analyses of national organizations provide an important source of validation of cross-section state studies that on their own generate results that might be interpreted as supportive of more than one of the several available theories of the development of interest communities.

Greater recourse to time series analysis, while certainly merited, still would not solve all of the problems associated with limited empirical leverage given that some variables of considerable import would remain essentially constants over a reasonable period of time. Consider, for example, the question of whether lobby or PACs registration influences the population of lobby organizations represented in Washington, a question raised by both supporters and critics of the present lobby regulatory regime (Hamm, Weber, and Anderson 1994; Brinig, Holcombe, and Schwartzstein 1993; Gais 1996) and one of considerable practical import. As noted above, the national PAC regulatory regime was established by the Federal Election Campaign Act, with the first registration of PACs in 1978, and the Lobby Disclosure Act of 1995 required the first comprehensive registration of lobbyists starting in 1996. With only relatively minor modifications,[8] these laws have remained in force, with, for example, the population of PACs rapidly stabilizing within a decade and remaining a near constant. Thus, any analysis of the impacts of these laws on numbers of either PACs or lobby organizations would constitute, in Campbell and Stanley's (1963) terms, a one-shot case study, with all of the attendant threats to valid inference. There were none and then, following an intervention, there were some. Beyond that, analysis at the national level of the impact of regulation of lobbyists or the role of interest groups in campaign finance can tell us essentially nothing. State studies, in contrast, allow us to examine considerable variation in both lobby registration laws and campaign finance regulations. Indeed, these studies have failed to find that such rules matter to any great extent (Gross and Goidel 2001; Ramsden 2002; Malbin and Gais 1998; K. Mayer 1998; Donnay and Ramsden 1995; Lowery and Gray 1994, 1997),[9] suggesting perhaps that the long, overly speculative, and unproductive debate at the national level between those favoring stronger or weaker regulatory requirements on lobbying and/or campaign finance has been largely unnecessary.

Similarly, we have already seen that there are good theoretical reasons to believe that legislative institutions influence the manner in which legislators interact with lobbyists and are influenced by them (Berkman 2001). Yet, institutional variations in Washington are relatively few and far between, and rather limited in scope in terms of the range of changes that might be considered. Obviously, the states provided considerably more institutional variations. Perhaps the most important of these in terms of interest organizations is the natural comparative interrupted

---

[8] We say minor in terms of the broad changes that might be considered when addressing the range of variation in both available at the state level.

[9] Except, of course, the important exception of social scientists needing data.

time series quasi-experiment in legislative incentives provided by recently adopted term limits in a number of states (Lazarus 2006; Mooney forthcoming). Changes in these incentives will have potentially important implications for legislators' interactions with interest groups and, thus, the latter's influence on public policy. To date, the evidence for such effects is mixed (Alt and Lassen 2003; Mooney 2003; Sarbaugh-Thompson et al. 2003) and more work is being done. More to the point, however, the states provide through these changes in institutions opportunities to test any number of rather fundamental propositions about legislators and interest group influence.

Cross-Sector Analyses

Here, the literature on interest representation in Washington has sought to find tractable variation in a second manner, by focusing on comparisons *across interest sectors*. These studies test a variety of theories from Olson's (1965) collective action hypotheses to the role of federal activity in creating a demand for lobbying by comparing the rates of PAC formation and/or lobbying activity across different types of business interests (McKeown 1994; Grier, Munger, and Roberts 1991, 1994; N. Mitchell, Hansen, and Jepsen 1997; W. Hansen, Mitchell, and Drope 2005). The problem with this creatively manufactured variation is that it carries with it the rather large assumption that the theoretical processes under examination work in the same manner across very different types of organized interests. This approach assumes, for example, that collective action problems or the influence of federal legislation on mobilization operate in the same manner across health, manufacturing, and many other interests in essentially the same manner. Yet, we know from studies within these many different types of interest sectors across the states that the economies of scale of interest representation, and thus their responsiveness to the incentive for and constraints on mobilization, vary markedly across very different types of interests (Lowery, Gray, and Fellowes 2005) and even within relatively different subsets of interests, such as those addressing health issues (Lowery and Gray 2007a). Given this variation, extracting valid conclusions from comparisons within systems across economic sectors risks serious errors of inference. Indeed, the economies of scale of interest representation in the US national health and manufacturing interest subsystems may differ more than do the health interest subsystems found in Richmond, Virginia and in Brussels. We simply do not know.

This does not mean, however, that all such comparisons are useless. Underpinning their validity, however, requires additional argumentation. Importantly, secondary studies of state interest organizations can be used to validate relatively weak research designs used at the national level. Indeed, this mutual support that the state and national literatures might provide each other is the counterpart of the earlier example of how Nownes (2004) and Nownes and Lipinski's (2005) time series analysis of national gay and lesbian organizations validates key elements of the population ecology model of interest system density developed initially in cross-sectional analyses of state interest populations. A good example of how this pattern of mutual support can work in the opposite manner is provided by Leech, Baumgartner, La Pira, and Semanko's (2005) analysis of how congressional activity influences the demand for lobbying. While an important step toward better understanding how legislators stimulate lobbying, the cross-sector research design assumed that quite different interests reacted to congressional activity in the same way. Thus, potential sector-level variations in determinants of lobbying activity *across* guilds might have introduced considerable unaccounted-for heterogeneity into the model. To assess the severity of this problem, Gray, Lowery, Fellowes, and Anderson (2005) replicated Leech et al.'s analysis at the state level using both their cross-sector design within states and an alternative across-state, within-sector design to control for unobserved heterogeneity across the interest sectors. Fortunately, both designs generated essentially the same empirical results, albeit somewhat weaker for the former, a result that surely strengthens the credibility of the national-level findings.

Not all such replications have been so supportive, however. For example, within-sector analyses of PAC mobilization in the states have not provided strong support for many of the findings of the national PAC literature cited earlier, in large part because cross-sector heterogeneity easily confounds findings drawn from the single population of interests lobbying any one government (Lowery, Gray, and Monogan 2008). In either case, though, it should be clear that replications at the state level can be usefully employed both to probe the veracity of results generated at the national level and sometimes to bolster their relatively weak research designs. This important validation function of state studies is certainly underemployed at present given the paucity of attention to state studies within the broader literature.[10]

CONCLUSION

Given these research findings, what can we conclude about the recent developments of the literature on state interest representation? In our review of 2002, we

---

[10] We should note, however, that the severity of this problem of inattention, which was central to Gray and Lowery's (2002) analysis of the limited role of the state literature in the larger domain of studies of interest representation, has, if the citations in the other chapters in this volume are any evidence, considerably diminished over the last decade.

noted a one-way pattern of influence running from national to state research on organized interests (Gray and Lowery 2002). To better balance this pattern by making the state literature relevant to national-level research, we recommended that the state literature better engage the fundamental theories about interest representation addressed in the larger literature, rely more fully on analyses of all fifty states rather than single-state studies so as to take advantage of the empirical leverage provided by comparison, and begin to study how organized interests interact across levels of government. Does the more recent research examined reflect these recommendations? The answer is clearly yes. In even the short time since we offered our assessment of the state literature in 2002, much has changed. As seen in Table 25.1, the range of research on state interest organizations in terms of theory and methods now more completely matches the range traditionally found at the national level. Research has also begun, if slowly, on looking at interest groups' horizontal and vertical interactions within the federal system. Taken together with the more frequent citation of state research in the other chapters in this volume, it is clear that the state literature is no longer so isolated from the more general research program on interest organizations.

More importantly for the other purpose of this chapter, we have argued that declining isolation is a rather minimal goal. Indeed, we have argued that the states provide a Goldilocks-like option between all too parochial theories framed at only one level of government and the traveling problems associated with concept stretching when we attempt to compare across fundamentally different interest systems. The states provide the kind of constrained variation that is essential to developing and then testing core propositions about organized interests. Indeed, if we wish to compare the US national interest system, it should best be viewed as that of a fifty-first state. In the end, comparison is essential to probing theories by ruling out rival explanations. For many topics of concern to interest group scholars, of course, the interest system of any single city, state, or nation might provide us the variation needed for comparison. This is certainly true if our unit of analysis is the decision or the issue. But on many other topics, especially those concerning the population dynamics of interest systems and political institutions, the values of key variables are constants within any one system. This limits the theoretical questions we can ask or even imagine. Just as bad, it compels us to often manufacture tractable variation—such as by within-system cross-sectoral analysis as a substitute for cross-system, within-sectoral designs—using research designs that are highly vulnerable in terms of threats to internal validity. More attention to the states, then, should lead to better theory and better empirical analysis. At a minimum, consistent replications of analyses across multiple systems should allow us to account for the weakness of our research designs in any one interest community.

....

CHAPTER 26

URBAN INTEREST GROUPS

....

JEFFREY M. BERRY

THE relationship between the scholarship on urban interest groups and national interest groups is uneven at best. Research on national politics continues to influence the study of local groups, but the work on national groups in Washington seems little affected by urban research.

The divide between these two research subspecialties lies in part in the long debate over pluralism. The urban research of the 1950s and 1960s had its roots in an earlier generation of sociological and anthropological studies of communities, for example the Lynds' (1929, 1937) two studies of Middletown (Muncie, Indiana). These community power studies asked what makes cities tick? What is their social structure? And how does their government operate in light of that social structure? A later generation of political scientists, led by Robert Dahl (1961), began asking about city government but focused more precisely on the relationship between social structure and the governmental process in cities. Dahl's conclusion that cities are democratic suggested the same was true of our nation.

The early empirical scholars who went to Washington to study groups concentrated on different questions (Bauer, Pool, and Dexter 1963; Milbrath 1963). Asking if America was a democracy and then trying to answer that question by studying the behavior of interest groups lobbying Congress or agencies was too far a reach. Intellectually and pragmatically, it was certainly a case of the ocean is so wide and my boat is so small. Linking together local society, business, and politics may have been tractable for a modest-sized city but undertaking such a study for America writ large was daunting. Although radical critics of American society, like C. Wright Mills (1959), tried to weave together an all-encompassing portrait of America, mainstream interest group scholars gravitated toward narrower, more practical studies of Washington politics.

Unfortunately, this broad intellectual divide widened over time as interest group scholars of all stripes began to develop sophisticated quantitative databases. As Baumgartner and Leech (1998) argue in their indictment of the interest group subfield, scholars increasingly posed narrow questions that could be answered with concrete measurements. Many of the more impressive works used surveys of various types, yet scholars didn't carefully build on each other's work. A great deal has been learned about interest groups but the field has not developed around a set of common questions or theoretical perspectives.

Thus, for a variety of reasons, it is not easy to connect local interest group politics with national interest group politics. And as Gray and Lowery (1996a) have demonstrated, state interest group politics is different still. (I leave this subject in their capable hands in the previous chapter in this volume.) In many ways interest group politics in urban America is different from what goes on at the national level. Among the most basic of differences is that the population of groups at the local level is quite different from what we find in Washington. Changes in the nature of the American economy and the country's demographics have been felt more sharply at the urban level, and that in turn has affected interest group politics. Business, long the most powerful of interest group sectors, plays a much different role in cities today than its contemporary counterparts in national politics.

This chapter analyzes the changing nature of urban interest group politics and contrasts trends and developments at the urban level with what we know about lobbies in Washington. The higher status and greater visibility of research on national groups has created vivid, clear images of how interest groups are organized and how they exert influence. Even if it was never the national politics scholars' intent to suggest a commonality between national and local groups, it is all too easy to assume that while the details may be different, the basic dynamics of lobbying and public policymaking are the same at both levels. The argument here is just the opposite: that there are fundamental differences between national and local interest group politics.

The next section examines the barriers to entry for interest group politics and finds strikingly low barriers at the local level. Analysis then turns to the politics of location, maintaining that the traditional image of downtown business groups dominating local politics while neighborhoods are politically feeble is outdated and misleading. The subsequent section describes the revival of citizen participation programs in urban politics and finds that it gives neighborhoods leverage that they would not otherwise possess. The arguments developed in these three sections are linked together in a fourth, which examines the implications of the much smaller scale of advocacy organizations in urban politics and policymaking. The high density of non-profits leads to a question about the effectiveness of citizen advocacy in cities. In the conclusion discussion returns to the possible common-alities in future research on national and local interest groups.

LOW BARRIERS TO ENTRY

A basic structural difference divides national and urban interest group systems. In national politics the barriers to entry for lobbies are rather high. Washington-based interest groups compete against large numbers of other groups, both in the aggregate and within their policy niche. Even the most prominent national groups must struggle to be noticed and gaining space on a government institution's agenda may be the most difficult task they face. Consequently, an enormous amount of their resources are devoted to agenda building. Fundraising, recruitment, public relations, and other organizational maintenance tasks are also central and heavily demanding of available resources.

In contrast, low barriers to entry characterize urban interest group politics. Policymakers are much more accessible than their national counterparts and competition among groups to be noticed is not nearly as pronounced. The geographical basis of interest group politics (discussed in the following section) ties city councilors to virtually any and all organizations in their home neighbor-hood. The more limited competition for the attention of policymakers has pro-found implications for interest group politics. If phone calls to policymakers are routinely returned, there is less pressure on organizational maintenance. That allows for more of the limited resources of groups to be allocated directly to advocacy. Scarce resources—and they are especially scarce for neighborhood groups and other voluntary organizations—are not consumed by the efforts to gather such resources.

The differences in access to government by groups at different levels in our federal system is vividly demonstrated by Lisa Miller's research on political partici-pation and policy debate on crime. She notes that "Groups representing black victims of routine crime are virtually absent from the national discourse" (L. Miller 2007, 308). Yet groups representing African Americans on crime issues are highly active in local policymaking. "Scaling up" to the state or federal level works against this constituency as the collective action problem becomes a prohibitive barrier to entry. In observing policymaking in Philadelphia, Miller found no significant barrier to entry in lobbying the city council.

When advocacy organizations try to extend beyond the neighborhood, attempt-ing to mobilize large numbers of citizens, the mission becomes more difficult. The barriers to entry rise considerably with the greater demands for resources for organizational maintenance. Social movement organizations, which unfortunately cannot be adequately covered here, thus face a more challenging task.

Information-based advocacy is also rather different in city politics. In Washington every interest group has its own set of facts, often including research it has conducted or commissioned. Overlaying the enormous universe of lobbying groups in Washington are the ubiquitous think tanks, collectively channeling a continuing flow of research reports to policymakers, staffers, and reporters. Washington policymakers are information-rich and attention-poor while local policymakers are neither information-rich nor attention-poor. There may be a local think tank on budgetary matters and maybe a research institute at a local university, but those organizations with the ability to generate or contract for research, namely business, are competitively advantaged by the more shallow information base in city politics. Given that they have no professional staff and few dollars in their coffers, neighborhood groups are the most disadvantaged in this realm. Neighborhood groups can sometimes benefit by the work of community development corporations, which do have a professional staff and a technical capacity.

One great difference in the policy arguments over evidence is that in local politics the "data" are often experiential. The arguments that advocates make are frequently stated in the form of "this is what will happen to my home," "my neighborhood," "my business." Stories and anecdotes are popular means of argumentation in Washington, too, but they are typically expressed under an umbrella of dueling research studies (Esterling 2007). In local politics, fights are often over what is going to happen to a particular place and these experiential facts are forcefully articulated by those who live or work in that particular place.

Relatedly, local bureaucracies tend to be lean. Over time fiscal pressures on the cities have mounted while the states and federal government have cut back on various forms of local aid. Many local bureaucracies have found that their responsibilities increased just as their overall resources declined. Coupled with this general trend is nothing short of a revolution in the American welfare state. Beginning with congressional legislation in 1962 to fund social service grants to the states and culminating with the 1996 law to end "welfare as we know it," federal policy has moved away from income maintenance and toward a new welfare framework. The goal of social policy today is to provide the services, training, and education necessary to help people off welfare. Under Temporary Assistance for Needy Families, the successor to Aid to Families with Dependent Children, income maintenance is time-limited while the programmatic emphasis has shifted to a structure that is highly labor-intensive. Training an individual for the work world is a complex task and requires professional instruction in small group settings. Offering support services to families requires skilled assistance and, thus, the modern welfare state is more expensive to administer than one centered around the dispersal of checks. In short, the modern welfare state requires lots of social workers and other experts.

Neither the federal, state, nor local governments employs anywhere near the number of professionals and para-professionals to provide those services. Instead, the administration of welfare has been devolved onto non-profits (Smith 2002; Grønbjerg and Salamon 2002; S. Smith and Lipsky 1993). And these non-profits are collaborators—they are not merely awarded grants and contracts and then instructed to submit periodic reports. Rather, many local non-profits have a close, ongoing relationship with state and local officials. Since state and local policy-makers must operate with limited staffs, they are typically dependent on non-profit service providers for basic information about program performance. David Arons and I demonstrated that non-profits with a high information capacity were most likely to be consulted by government (Berry and Arons 2003, 132–45). Such organizations are frequently at the conference table with bureaucrats, discussing program design, performance, and means of evaluation.

Research allowing a direct comparison of the degree of group–agency collaboration at the local, state, and federal levels is not available. But what is clear is that whatever the level of collaboration in Washington, it is a function of far different norms and motivations. Whereas state and local agencies are dependent on social service and health-related non-profits to administer programs, federal agencies looking to collaborate with interest groups are generally searching for political support. Working out an agreement with client groups can reduce the likelihood of White House or congressional intervention into rule making.

The low barriers to entry are also illustrated by the most common source of urban interest group conflict: large-scale real estate development projects. Cities have an enormous stake in nurturing a continuing stream of new development projects. As scholars such as Harvey Molotch (1976), Paul Peterson (1981) and Stephen Elkin (1987) have argued, cities are preoccupied with promoting development as tax revenues cannot significantly expand without large-scale private sector projects. Yet the era when plans could be formulated by developers and bureaucrats and implemented without concern for inconveniently placed small businesses and residences is long gone. Today elaborate planning, consultation, and negotiation with all affected parties define urban politics (Altshuler and Luberoff 2003).

As will be explored more fully in the section on citizen participation below, even the poorest of cities must incorporate neighborhood groups into development politics. It is politically infeasible to try to exclude neighborhoods from the planning of projects that will significantly affect them. A crucial difference, though, is that developers initiate and neighborhoods react. Those who come to city hall with development projects may not have exclusive access to policymakers but their access is unparalleled. Not only does real estate development represent enhanced tax revenues; the office buildings and condominiums are tangible manifestations of progress. In their own way, they represent each mayor's legacy, visible evidence of their efficacy. The door at city hall is always open, wide open, to those who want to build.

LOCATION, LOCATION, LOCATION

Urban politics is the politics of place. Most urban interest group advocacy springs from proposals or complaints about a condition or problem in a specific place where people live or where businesses are located.

With our understanding of interest group politics based on congressional lobbying, national-level interest aggregation is generally viewed in a different way. Of course, ties to home matter in Congress, though most directly they matter in relation to earmarks. Within Congress earmarks are exceptionally popular since each member gets a share of grants and projects and has a great deal of autonomy in deciding which of the supplicants from one's district or state will be awarded these lucrative prizes. However, most policymaking by Congress is not directly connected to geography: defense, science and technology, health care, education, welfare, and most other policies are debated on the basis of ideology and national goals. While some policies are regional in nature (agriculture, for example), it is generally true that the aggregation of interests on the national level is strikingly different than the neighborhood-based advocacy that fuels city politics.

Traditionally, urban analysts discounted the neighborhoods as strong political entities. The passivity of Boston's West Enders to the urban renewal that destroyed their neighborhood has long been the iconic image of the politics of place (Gans 1962). Clarence Stone's (1989) influential study of Atlanta testified to the weakness of neighborhoods as well. His findings were no anomaly. Atlanta did possess a strong and active downtown business establishment. The relationship between these business leaders and mayors, what Stone called a "regime," was a marriage of necessity as each needed the other to accomplish their goals. Business leaders not only lobbied for policies beneficial to their own companies, but they were also motivated by *noblesse oblige*. They wanted their cities to thrive because of civic pride and a general belief that a strong city makes for a strong business climate. Paul Peterson's *City Limits* acknowledged the power of business but otherwise called local politics "groupless politics" (1981, 116).

The politics of place, however, has changed dramatically. Although cities vary considerably, it is generally the case that today downtown business establishments are smaller and less concerned with city politics, while the neighborhoods have become more empowered and more influential. For a variety of reasons neighborhood advocacy has expanded and neighborhoods have become more widely incorporated in policymaking affecting them. The explosion in the number of community development corporations, now over 4,500 across the country, with their independent income stream, professional staffs, and important role in development projects, has emboldened and empowered neighborhoods (Stoutland 1999; Democracy Collaborative 2007). Many city councilors get their start in politics from working with neighborhood associations or other neighborhood-based non-profits.

Despite city councils' general weakness within the larger operation of city government, councilors cannot be ignored on issues relating to their neighborhoods. Citizen participation programs are also a tool for neighborhood groups. Finally, with most cities growing in population, neighborhood revitalization can be found in many areas of a city. The influx of professionals back into cities works to the benefit of all city neighborhoods. As programs, facilities, and processes are put into place to please reviving middle-class neighborhoods, there is a spillover effect onto other neighborhoods that demand the same benefits.

The decline of downtown business establishments comes not from a conscious decision by corporate executives to withdraw from city politics and large-scale urban development planning, but from a transformation in the nature of business. The face of contemporary city politics has been altered by the growth of the service economy, corporate mergers and acquisitions, suburbanization, and globalization. By way of example, the city of Boston was dominated for years by an elite, semi-secret business group known as the "Vault." (Its formal name was the Boston Coordinating Committee but the nickname came from the group's meeting room at the Boston Safe Deposit and Trust Company, which was adjacent to the bank's safe.) Composed of the leaders of more than two dozen Boston-based firms, the Vault met regularly with the mayors of the city to plan Boston's future. Only a handful of the companies that were members of the Vault still remain today in Boston. None of the six banks that were members of the group exist in the same form as all have been swallowed up by mergers or acquisitions by banks headquartered elsewhere. Four eventually wound up as part of the Bank of America, which is now the city's largest bank. But headquartered in North Carolina, the company has played virtually no role in city politics and is only a modest presence in the civic fabric of the city (J. Berry et al. 2006).

The Vault formally disbanded in 1997 though its influence had begun to wane years earlier. Of course, new and vibrant corporations have emerged in the Boston area but few of the large companies that have recently developed have made their headquarters in the city. Instead the relatively new and successful high-tech and biotech corporations have made their homes in the suburbs and exurbs. Not only is the world flat, as Thomas Friedman has argued (2005), but so are the metropolitan areas of cities. The handful of mega-firms that remain in Boston, such as Fidelity Investments and State Street Bank, are good citizens of the city with their philanthropy while just a modest presence in city politics.

Part of the political vacuum created by businesses' exit in Boston and other large cities is filled by neighborhood groups, large non-profits like universities and hospital systems, and the executive branch of city government itself. In our study of five metropolitan Boston area cities, three-quarters of the interest groups active on the issues we observed were either neighborhood groups (20 percent), citywide citizens' groups (24 percent), or other non-profits (31 percent). Business constituted 18 percent and labor just 6 percent (J. Berry et al. 2006, 9). The number of advocacy organizations participating does not equate with influence but these figures do tell us about the mobilization of interests and that is no small matter.

The changes in the demography and economy of cities challenge interest group theory. As noted above, classic democratic theory on interest groups was built around the study of groups in cities. The decades-long argument over pluralism, stratification, and elitism revolved around the centrality and dominance of a city's big-business sector (Dahl 1961; F. Hunter 1963; Mills 1959; Polsby 1980; C. Stone 1989). The analysis here may seem to suggest that pluralism, rather than elitism, is more descriptive of contemporary cities. Aside from being a tired theoretical dispute that lasted for decades, this framework doesn't adequately capture the dynamics of modern city politics. The prevalence of non-profits, for example, is unaccounted for in any of the earlier theorizing. Neighborhood mobilization was not so much discounted as it was ignored. The waning presence of big business in cities is difficult to square with any of the prominent theories of city politics. As will be discussed below, theory needs to turn toward collaborative policymaking. Already a staple in public administration and public policy literature, this melding of participation patterns and policymaking processes holds promise as a means of better understanding how groups function in the modern American city.

CITIZEN PARTICIPATION

A striking difference in the role of interest groups in policymaking at the national and local levels is the more participatory nature of local politics. At first glance this may not seem terribly surprising: lobbyists represent our interests in Washington because it is not practical for us to go there to speak for ourselves. But springing from this basic reality of location are some important structural and procedural differences. The most important is that depending on the issue area, city politics is often characterized by some type of citizen participation requirements. Alone or in combination, local, state, and federal processes may require open meetings, hearings, or advisory panels. On the federal level there are, of course, some opportunities for public participation, such as notice-and-comment procedures for proposed regulations. Yet these are largely opportunities for lobbyists to participate and not for rank-and-file citizens.

Political scientists have long rendered a decidedly negative verdict on the efficacy of citizen participation. The initial impetus for public involvement came from the War on Poverty and the directive in the Community Action Program for "maximum feasible participation." Conflict ensued over control of resources between city hall and neighborhood agencies, primarily in low-income African American communities (Moynihan 1969). Over time the number of federal public involve-ment programs grew rapidly as once the idea of participatory democracy escaped from the political genie's lantern, it was hard to put it back in (N. Roberts 2008). By 1977 there were 226 federal public participation programs in operation, but as Walter Rosenbaum concluded, this was a "counterfeit prosperity" because few programs worked well. In Rosenbaum's words, "Some are rituals; many are mori-bund" (1978, 81).

The federal government's enthusiasm for direct public involvement programs waned and the Reagan administration dismantled or emasculated many of them. In contrast local and state mandates continued to expand. A small number of cities, such as St Paul, Minnesota, and Portland, Oregon, have gone as far as to implement a system of neighborhood government. Volunteer-led neighborhood councils exert considerable control over zoning and are allowed a great deal of autonomy by city hall (J. Berry, Portney, and Thomson 1993). Yet this model has not caught on, surely because it requires mayors and city councilors to give up just too much power to the neighborhoods. Los Angeles is one of the few cities in recent years to try to establish neighborhood government, but an evaluation noted that "the neighborhood councils have no formal powers" (Musso, Weare, and Cooper 2004, 3).

Even though neighborhood government has not become a popular option in city politics, other meaningful forms of public involvement have become com-mon. By and large these are tied to specific programs, especially in the areas of environment, housing, and urban development. There are many reasons why citizen participation requirements are so common in city politics. Having a well-defined process with stated procedures is vital to keeping development projects out of court, or if litigation is pursued, protecting developers and the city from an adverse decision in favor of neighborhood plaintiffs. In some cases public in-volvement at the city level is a response to a requirement of a state or federal program. Citizen participation also provides bureaucrats with a way to navigate conflicting pressures from opposing sides. Public involvement channels activism into processes and formats that city planners find constructive. Critics contend that citizen participation co-opts opposition and there is surely some truth to this. The flip side of this coin, however, is that public involvement programs help neighborhood residents find a means of participating in useful and non-symbolic ways. In some formats these programs may serve to facilitate negotiations when opposing sides need to reconcile. Overall, citizen participation programs are popular with city administrators because they help them to move the process forward.

When a developer purchased the dilapidated Dainty Dot Hosiery factory at the edge of Boston's Chinatown, there was a great deal of concern about the proposed 341-foot height of the 180-unit condominium project. At the same time some community groups approved of the project in general because the developer was going to comply with a linkage requirement to build forty-seven affordable housing units at another Chinatown site. Three administrative agencies began processing the proposal and a host of community groups, some against, some for, began working the process. These neighborhood groups included the Chinese Progressive Association, the Chinatown/Leather District Park Community Task Force, the Chinese Consolidated Benevolent Association, the Chinatown Neighborhood Association, Chinatown Main Street, the Mayor's Central Artery Completion Task Force, the Seaport Alliance for Neighborhood Design, the Chinese Economic Development Council, and the Impact Advisory Group. By the time the final approvals came, the developer had twice agreed to scale back the building and the new structure will be 265 feet with 147 units. The final compromise was brokered by the mayor's office. There is no comparing the power of these small neighborhood groups with that of Mayor Thomas Menino, but it was pressure from these groups and the long-drawn-out citizen participation process that pushed him to respond to neighborhood concerns.

Public involvement programs range from working wonderfully to not working at all. What are the keys to success? More broadly, what makes them contribute to the democratic process rather than making neighborhood residents feel they've been gamed? Archon Fung argues persuasively that there are design elements that are critical and he argues for "empowered participation" built around "accountable autonomy" (2004). In his study of the Chicago police department and the city's schools, Fung shows how neighborhood residents acted responsibly and conscientiously within a well-designed participation process. In the cities cited above, a crucial difference between the successful programs in St Paul and Portland and the citywide program in Los Angeles is, in fact, the much greater autonomy of the St Paul and Portland neighborhood councils. This is not to suggest that autonomy over certain kinds of large-scale economic development projects (like the Dainty Dot building in Boston) is likely to be given over to neighborhood groups. Surely it is also the case that administrative designs for meaningful participation must be coupled with norms of cooperation and collaboration.

This realm of urban interest group politics is, again, foreign to the basic literature on interest groups. Developed around the behavior of Washington lobbies, the scholarly literature focuses on representation: how paid professionals in Washington represent our interests before government. Although some lobbies develop warm relations with agencies or congressional committees, it would be a stretch to call most interest group–government relationships in Washington "collaborative policymaking." In cities, though, it is common for neighborhood residents to become directly involved in government. Citizen participation requirements greatly facilitate this involvement.

ORGANIZATIONS AND ADVOCACY

When one thinks of lobbies in Washington, images of their physical presence quickly come to mind: a trade association with its own multistory building across the river in Arlington; a citizens' group operating out of a town house on Capitol Hill; lawyer–lobbyists for hire in stark boxy office buildings along "K" Street. For groups lobbying in a city, the visuals are murkier. Many local groups have no office and no paid employees, and are organizations only in the loosest sense of the word. Neighborhood associations and citywide citizens' groups typically operate out of leaders' homes by volunteers who dominate the "organizations."

Even when we turn to those local lobbies that do have an office and a professional staff, we still find that local interest groups are not smaller versions of national lobbies. As already discussed, most advocacy organizations in local politics are non-profits of one type or another. Although there are non-profits in Washington, they tend to be trade or professional associations rather than service providers. In a large city local unions may have an office, and a local chamber of commerce may have a headquarters as well. More similar to national politics are the local businesses which lobby for contracts, and on development projects in particular. At the same time they are far less organized by industry ties than is the case in Washington and few business trade groups are active in cities. One commonality to national groups among non-profit service providers, labor, and business is that their lobbying is a byproduct of other organizational purposes (M. Olson 1965).

To draw out the national–local differences beyond organizational size, let us examine each of these sectors more in depth. Above it was noted that 44 percent of groups identified as lobbying in one study of urban politics in Massachusetts were either neighborhood associations or citywide citizens' groups. Most were free-standing civic or political organizations and had no other purpose. Owing to the low barriers to entry, it is relatively easy to start a local group, especially a neighborhood group. As discussed earlier, the barrier to entry is low precisely because an organization does not need an office or a paid staff to be regarded as credible. No one in city politics believes a neighborhood association should be able to attract such resources. Even though they are fragile organizations with no professional staffs, they are perceived by policymakers as legitimate representatives of their neighborhood. What is truly remarkable about local politics is that just a handful of people can constitute an interest group. However, there's little accountability or transparency in how internally democratic they are or how they arrive at decisions.

Consider again the example of Boston's Chinatown and the long and involved permitting process concerning redevelopment of the Dainty Dot site. Six of the groups mentioned are rooted solely in that neighborhood and they are by no means the only neighborhood organizations operating there. Yet Boston's China-town consists of just 42 acres and the total population of the neighborhood is only 5,100 residents (including children). It is disproportionately populated by recent immigrants as 40 percent of residents have lived in Boston five years or less (Asian Community Development Corporation 2008). But despite its tiny size and low-income immigrant population, Chinatown appears to be fertile ground for neigh-borhood organizations. And these organizations have a voice at City Hall, a voice amplified by a sympathetic city councilor. No one would describe these organiza-tions as a powerhouse in Boston politics, but in the same vein no one could accurately describe government decision making involving Chinatown without taking into account the role these organizations play.

Are such groups really effective? Isn't it possible that they're being patronized by policymakers who include them in meetings as a means of co-opting them? Don't those meetings deal with ancillary matters of small consequence rather than the central issues at hand? And once a builder has both financing and city hall's blessing, isn't the basic decision, whether to build, essentially made already? That does not, however, make the related decisions trivial. To force a developer to redesign a major project can alter the fundamental business plan. It is not unusual in Boston for large projects to be forced to scale down because of neighborhood advocacy. Also, the presence of active neighborhood groups in a city that is participatory is a serious constraint on developers as they understand that many locations are simply untenable because of the outcry that would emerge and the mobilization that would follow.

Neighborhood groups are also empowered by the friends-and-neighbors scale of local elections. City councilors are often elected by district and that nurtures a very strong tie between councilors and neighborhood groups, even in the largest of cities. Business is generally uninvolved in city council elections and neighborhood groups can easily signal who their "friends" are in an election. Even non-profits, whose tax status forbids them from endorsing or working for candidates, can help to generate support for city council or mayoralty candidates (Marwell 2004).

The density of interest groups in cities reflects the growing role of non-profits in American society. There are over a million 501(c)(3) non-profits in the United States and this underestimates the true number as small non-profits often don't bother to register with the IRS or their state authorities (G. Williams 2008). The preference of government to subcontract service delivery to non-profits rather than hiring the necessary workers itself not only has resulted in the sharp growth of non-profits but brings non-profits into the governmental process.

In exchange for their tax-deductible status, 501(c)(3) non-profits are saddled with an ambiguous restriction on their lobbying. Non-profits may lobby but by law they cannot do so to a "substantial" degree. The IRS refuses to define what level or type of lobbying constitutes a substantial amount and non-profit directors often misinterpret the law to mean that they shouldn't be involved in public policymaking lest their organization loses its tax-deductible status (J. Berry and Arons 2003). The restriction only applies to legislative lobbying, though, and there is no comparable legal restraint on administrative lobbying. Non-profits do fear that aggressive lobbying that runs against the preferences of agencies can result in lost contracts and grants and, thus, there is caution related to administrative advocacy too. Overall, though, non-profits are a large part of local economies and they are embedded in the economic and governmental fabric of the city. Local governments are particularly sensitive to the needs of the largest non-profits, notably hospitals and universities, which are so critical to their economies.

Business advocacy on the local level is quite distinct from the patterns found in national politics. Local governments do little in the way of industry regulation and that, in turn, weakens the incentives for companies within a business area to formally ally in a local trade association. More commonly, critical business-related decisions by local governments involve land use. When it comes to possible sites for development, individual companies will engage in advocacy that may stretch out over years because of lengthy zoning, siting, and permitting processes. Since city hall is so interested in the addition of new jobs and new taxable buildings, bureaucrats and developers will often work collaboratively to get projects off the ground. Like business, local labor unions lobby on matters somewhat different from their national counterparts. Since local governments do little in the way of regulation, unions have a limited orientation toward policy. Rather, their focus is on contracts with fire, police, and school departments and other city agencies.

In terms of the organizational dimension of interest group behavior, the lobbying literature prepares us poorly for understanding urban groups. When a legitimate "group" can be a handful of activists who give themselves a formal name, organizational maintenance is not a major focus, as it can be for national organizations. The volunteers who run neighborhood groups run counter to our image of highly skilled professionals in Washington who have turned lobbying into a highly lucrative and highly sophisticated occupation. Non-profit service providers are a core of the local lobbying universe but have no analog in Washington politics except for the byproduct nature of their advocacy. Business lobbying by individual corporations at the national and local levels offers more similarities, though businesses within a city are poorly organized along industry lines. In the end what is most striking is how different local groups are from their national counterparts.

NEW DIRECTIONS

Despite the many reasons for these distinctive research approaches, one hopes that new thinking will emerge as to how to integrate interest group scholarship, recognizing both the differences and commonalities among local, state, and national advocacy organizations. Some work will remain uniquely situated at a particular level of government, but there are questions central to any study of interest groups: who is represented and who is represented well? How are organizational resources converted into effective advocacy? What are the characteristics of effective advocacy and effective advocates?

Some work may be comparative, directly examining local, state, and national groups. For example, little has been done in recent years on internal decision making and democracy within interest groups (Barakso 2004). Most such organizations tend toward oligarchy but there are surely degrees of difference and the variety of decision frameworks and the degree they involve rank and file are significant. In short, what does it mean for an advocacy organization to be more or less democratic?

Careful consideration of urban political processes may also help American government scholars think more rigorously about ongoing relationships between interest groups and governmental institutions. Ironically, the theory of subgovernments that long defined such relationships at the national level now more closely fits local government. The rise of citizens' groups and the broader advocacy explosion broke what subgovernments existed at the national level (Heclo 1978). At the local level "collaborative policymaking" is a more descriptive term than "subgovernments" as policymaking communities in urban systems are far more fluid and open than those at the national level during earlier times (Cater 1964). On the national level, however, network theory is a promising approach to the large groups of participants in individual policy areas (Heinz et al. 1993; Heaney 2006). How well it applies to the smaller sets of actors in local policymaking is unclear.

Another approach from urban politics springs from the classification of regime type. Among urbanists Clarence Stone's framework categorizing cities by their orientation toward economic development has been highly influential (C. Stone 1993). There is only one national government, of course, but comparisons can be made across time. The impact of partisan change on interest group behavior in Washington has been documented, but are there other kinds of differences over time (M. Peterson and Walker 1986; Walker 1991)? And how do the states compare?

This is hardly an exhaustive list of promising research avenues and there are many other approaches and topics that could yield important advances. Hopefully the interest group subfield will reorient itself, with research crossing boundaries set by tradition. It is not a field short on imaginative and important research projects but, unfortunately, it is characterized by a narrowness of vision.

PART VIII

INTEREST GROUPS

DIMENSIONS OF BEHAVIOR

CHAPTER 27

INTEREST GROUPS
AND AGENDAS

FRANK R. BAUMGARTNER

SCHATTSCHNEIDER'S DUAL CONTRIBUTIONS

E. E. SCHATTSCHNEIDER's (1960) slim but lasting volume made two points that remain central to the study of agenda setting and interest groups: the salience of a political issue is often the result of a political process, not a simple result of objective conditions; and the interest group system harbors tremendous bias. Whereas democracies are defined by the concept of "one person one vote," he pointed out that certain segments of society are virtually excluded from participation in the "pressure system" while others speak with voices amplified by their access to many decision makers and their ability to mobilize vast resources. In comparing groups to political parties, which in his view ultimately rest on their ability to appeal to ever larger groups of voters, Schattschneider shows a sense that the group system was clearly unfair.

The Power of Conflict

Schattschneider is often the first citation in reviews on the topic of agenda setting and among the first in those analyzing the structure of the nation's interest group system. He virtually invented the modern field of agenda setting with his simple point that participants in any conflict consist of a winner and a loser and that these actors have different incentives with regard to the scope of their fight. Losers may want to "expand" the conflict while winners logically should be content with the current scope of the issue, wanting no "outsiders" to become involved. His point was that the number of participants in a conflict, its public salience, or the range of actors (especially government agencies) considered legitimately involved in the issue were not a given based on decisions made by neutral outside observers, but indeed were the fundamental determinants of the outcome of the battle, and were therefore the object of the political struggle itself. Labor unions demanded government involvement in establishing working conditions and labor–management conflict resolution procedures whereas business resisted these efforts, seeing them as unwelcome "outside interference." Of course, what is unwelcome to the powerful may be welcome indeed to the powerless. Scholars have often taken the idea that the scope of a conflict is the result of interest group strategies to mean that scope is determined by the strategies of individual interest groups. It is rare that a single actor can determine the scope or salience of the conflict in which they are engaged; it is a collective process, not an individual choice. Scope is partially but not fully endogenous to the strategies of groups.

Class Bias in the "Pressure System"

The second reason scholars refer to Schattschneider is his emphasis on an aspect of the group system that was not so widely acknowledged at the time he wrote, during the heyday of pluralism: most Americans have no chance of participating. For Schattschneider, the flaw in the pluralist "heaven" that scholars such as Bentley (1908), Truman (1951), and Dahl (1961) described was that the "heavenly chorus sings with a strong upper-class accent. Probably about 90 per cent of the people cannot get into the pressure system" (1960, 35). Later empirical studies suggest that he may have exaggerated, as many Americans participate in the group system through such organizations as labor unions. None of these empirical studies refute his general point, however; the interest group system does not reach down to all levels of society, and it has a very strong professional or occupational character. In their recent large-scale study of the Washington interest group universe, Schlozman et al. (2008) found, for example, that *not a single* group in DC was organized with the primary focus of representing the interests of such low-wage workers as janitors, cleaners, or fast-food workers. Whereas bankers, lawyers, firefighters, teachers, and others are well represented through the group system because of its occupational bias, many others are virtually excluded. The normative implications of Schattschneider's dual theses were clear. First, one should view with suspicion arguments tending to limit the role of government, as these are logically the arguments that the powerful will use against the weak. Rather, arguments about the scope of legitimate government activity define the political struggle, reflecting rather than determining the distribution of power in society. Second, political parties act as the ultimate mechanism for the expansion of social conflict, and they should be stronger. (Schattschneider, of course, had been the chair of the American Political Science Association's committee on responsible parties, which issued a report suggesting just this; American Political Science Association 1950.)

INTEREST GROUPS AND AGENDA SETTING

The idea that the scope of conflict was in fact a part of the political process, rather than something imposed by outside forces, stimulated political scientists as few ideas ever have. It took some time, however, before scholars translated the general idea into empirical research projects.

Subsystems. The first book-length study was by Roger Cobb and Charles Elder (1983; originally published in 1972). They noted, as had many scholars of public policy and interest groups before them, that many public policies are surrounded by what they called "systems of limited participation" (1983, ch. 1). This idea was, of course, a staple of interest group studies going back at least to Bentley's (1908) and Griffith's (1939) review of the roles of groups in government or the more contemporary studies such as Milbrath's (1963) review of the power of interest groups, Bauer, Pool, and Dexter's (1963) findings that groups often worked as mere "service bureaus" to those legislators who already agreed with them, or Cater's (1964) analysis of the sugar price protection program. The point was simple but important: most public policies, most of the time, are debated and discussed within relatively small communities of experts. Whether these are called "whirlpools," "subsystems," "iron triangles," or "systems of limited participation," they all have in common that experts dominate (see McFarland 2004). But in many cases, the experts all had certain interests in common, as in the expansion and continuation of favorable government policies toward the industry in question. If political debate stems from conflicts within these professional communities, then we need to be concerned about issues that are *not* on the agenda, and the abilities of tightly knit communities of like-minded professionals to keep their issues out of the public spotlight. The study of interest groups, which had long focused on the functioning of these communities, was to meet the study of agenda setting.

Non-decisions. Peter Bachrach and Morton Baratz (1962) came into this debate with a critique of previous studies of pluralism focusing on the problem that some interests in society were simply not represented and therefore not part of the public discussion. Their article was recognized recently as the single most highly cited study in the history of the *American Political Science Review* (Sigelman 2006). Two book-length studies (Crenson 1971; Gaventa 1980) took seriously the authors' proposal that non-decisions should be studied as well as those issues that are the object of manifest public debate. Few, however, have followed up with empirical studies of how or why issues remain off the agenda (the biggest exception to this is Cobb and Ross 1997). However, the field was set for a consistent concern about what happens when communities of specialists interact with the broader political system.

Agenda setting. John Kingdon (1984) was the next author to devote a book-length study to the process of agenda setting. Kingdon did not stress the role of groups, but he certainly focused on the distinction between those actors in the policy process who are experts on the subject matter and those who are not. He noted that interest groups were often "outside" government but it was inaccurate to describe them as "just looking in." Just as had a long string of interest group scholars dating back to Bentley, he stressed the integration between those outside and inside government who share a concern about a particular policy, industry, or social problem.

Frank Baumgartner and Bryan Jones (1993) suggested an important role for interest groups in their study of agenda setting, noting how "Schattschneider mobilizations" could occur in which disgruntled policymakers from within a specialized community make alliances with outsiders in order to upend an established policy monopoly. Nuclear scientists concerned about inadequate attention to safety issues in the 1960s are the simplest example: just as Schattschneider discussed, these "losers" in the debate about how to allocate resources appealed to expand the scope of the conflict, and outsiders did indeed become involved on their side of the debate, ultimately leading to the demise of the nuclear power industry.

Framing. This last example raises issues that few authors had addressed up to this point: to what extent do individual interest groups or other policymakers control or manipulate the process? The concept of conflict expansion (or its corollary, the privatization of conflict) suggests that the eventual scope of the conflict is the result of the strategic behaviors of the original protagonists. But to say this is not the same as to suggest that the final outcome is easily controlled by any single actor. Schattschneider gave little indication of how, or by what process, groups would appeal to the audience (and even less about how their rivals would attempt to justify audience deference to "the experts"). We have come to understand that this is through the process of framing, a point discussed below. But who can frame? What of the opponents who have an interest in framing the issue in a different way?

William Riker (1984, 1986) made clear that strategically minded politicians could indeed induce major policy change and affect the political agenda by shifting the terms of the debate. This could be done by choosing new dimensions of evaluation, to shift a debate from being "about" topic X to describing it in terms of topic Y. For example, when faced with the possible introduction of dangerous nerve gas to be shipped from an overseas military base to his home state, one clever senator convinced his colleagues that the debate was not "really" about where the gas would go, but rather about the Senate's power to ratify treaties. As few senators want to give up power to the executive branch, the motion carried. "Heresthetics," the word he used to describe this process of manipulating decision-making procedures or the dimensions of debate, became an important part of the literature on agenda setting.

The Stability of Frames

But how common is it to reframe a debate? Riker's book gave a number of examples, but then again he covered over 2,000 years of human history in compiling his interesting stories. The literature developed no sense of what the denominator might be: for every hundred times that framing is attempted, how many times does it succeed, and what increases the chances of success? James Druckman (2001, 2004) has provided the best recent analyses of framing, though his focus is not on interest groups or even on agenda setting (he looked at how individuals respond to different arguments or frames when they read them in newspaper articles in an experimental setting). Still, he notes the peculiarities in a literature where scholars have found framing virtually each time they have looked for it. Baumgartner and Jones, for example, stressed the importance of "policy images" and how these can shift quickly from positive to negative as collective attention shifts from one aspect of a complicated issue to another. Riker gave examples of successful strategic politicians actually causing these changes. But few have studied a random sample of issues or discussed the degree to which any single actor could successfully manipulate the collective framing associated with an issue. Cobb and Ross (1997) compiled the only book-length study of efforts to keep issues off the agenda. This is clearly the next step in the literature, to explain the relative capacities of interest groups, government officials, and others to affect how issues are understood. Baumgartner and others (2009) studied ninety-eight cases of lobbying activity representing a random sample of the objects of lobbying in Washington, DC, and followed the issues for four years; they found that only about 5 percent of the issues were significantly reframed during the period of their study. This gives some idea of the power of the status quo. Reframing may be important when it occurs, but interest groups typically are working to protect, not to upset, the status quo, and the collective efforts of groups contribute mightily to the maintenance of existing policies as well as the frames that undergird them.

There is strong evidence from throughout the literature going back decades to make clear that policy definitions are strongly related to policy outcomes (see, for example, the literature reviewed immediately above, or D. Stone 1988, 1989; Schneider and Ingram 1993; Bosso 1987). So lobbyists have a strong incentive to reframe issues and when they succeed the direction of policy often changes. But perhaps the shifts in policy images are due to broader factors such as new evidence and not only to the clever rhetorical tactics of individual lobbyists or policy entrepreneurs. To this point, the literature has failed to pinpoint exactly the causes of shifts in frames, though it has clearly established that such things are fundamental to explaining policy outcomes and the impact of agenda setting.

Venue Shopping

Since Schattschneider's original insights about conflict expansion, two complications have arisen. First, venue shopping by protagonists is strategic: they do not put out a general appeal for help from an undifferentiated audience, but rather seek out particular allies, especially institutional venues or locations in government where they hope that they may have a better chance at success. Second, as in the question of framing, success by the aggrieved party is anything but assured, as the dominant party in the original dispute will naturally fight back, justifying their control over the dispute by denying the legitimacy of any "outside interference."

Baumgartner and Jones (1993) developed the idea of venue shopping, arguing that a peculiarity of US institutional design is that single institutions rarely have monopolistic control over given policy issues. Through separation of powers and federalism, we see "separated institutions sharing power" (Neustadt 1964, 42), or even more than this a series of shared and overlapping jurisdictions where states, localities, and various federal agencies often vie for control or have control over different parts of a given issue. Policy actors seek to push their issues to one or another institutional venue depending on their estimate of their likely success; many policy changes have been related to shifts in institutional control or the emergence of a new institutional player rather than to an established institutional player shifting its position. The Department of Agriculture, after all, did not suddenly shift position on the health effects of smoking and tobacco; rather, policy change came when those with jurisdiction over health issues exerted greater influence. Explaining the policy change requires looking at many policy venues.

Sarah Pralle (2003, 2006) has provided the most in-depth analysis of venue shopping as a strategy, and she notes that lobbyists are often ineffective or only boundedly rational in their search for the most favorable venue. Groups establish comfort levels with certain venues, or develop staff with expertise in dealing with the legal, regulatory, or other types of analyses demanded in a particular venue, and these sunk costs or organizational routines inhibit their abilities to operate in new venues. So the process is far from perfect, far from fully rational. Further, institutional leaders themselves often seek out issues on which they can exert their influence: the venues seek out the issues, in other words. In any case, scholars have noted the importance of lobbying strategies that focus not only on "expanding" a conflict to a broader audience, but on much more specific strategies of targeting specific institutional audiences. Mazey and Richardson (1993) similarly noted that the relative competencies of Brussels-based regulatory agencies, the European Court of Justice, and the traditional national political systems have recently become the object of considerable jurisdictional ambiguity as the European Union has developed its policy apparatus in more policy areas (see also Guiraudon 2000; Hooghe and Marks 2001; Keating and Hooghe 2001; Beyers 2002; Eising 2004, 2007; Woll 2006; Coen 2007; Mahoney 2004, 2007a, 2007b, 2008; Mahoney and Baumgartner 2008).

Salience

The literature on venue shopping and institutional control is strongly related to the efforts of groups to gain (or to avoid) greater public salience for their dispute. Ken Kollman's (1998) work remains the best systematic treatment of efforts of groups to "go public" and he notes that they do so systematically on those issues where public opinion is in line with their preferences, other things equal (such as the resource capacity to follow this expensive strategy of lobbying). For every lobbyist who seeks to expand a conflict or shift it to a new institutional venue, or onto the front pages of the national newspapers, there is at least another who has the opposite interest: maintain control right where it was in the past. And considering that these actors are typically more powerful than their adversaries, it is not at all clear why they would fail to protect themselves and their institutions from unwanted "outside interference." Some institutions, to be sure, are more successful in this than others. No one contests in modern times the authority of the Federal Reserve Board to fix interest rates or to control monetary policy. No one contests that the US Census Bureau should conduct the decennial census. No other public agency competes with the Postal Service. So all public policies are not subject to jurisdictional ambiguity; for some issues the jurisdictions are quite firmly set. To date, little research has focused on the ability of those in positions of power to limit efforts by rivals to move an issue away from their institutional control or to limit efforts by competing institutions to encroach on those issues that have traditionally fallen within their jurisdiction. Venue shopping is certainly a common occurrence, but so is boundary maintenance. We know little about what causes success in either.

Individual versus Collective Behaviors

The simplest way to think of why we know so much about strategies of agenda setting, venue shopping, and framing from the perspective of the individual lobbyist but so little about the determinants of their success is that scholars have not designed projects to study the process at two levels. Schattschneider focused on the actions of the two original protagonists in a dispute, but he clearly stated that the outcome in the dispute would be determined by the behavior of the audience. This implies that understanding crowd behavior is more important than understanding individual strategies of lobbying and agenda setting. Few scholars have shifted their attention to this question, however, because of its complexity, though attention to these issues appears to be growing.

The salience, issue definitions, and agenda status of any policy issue are determined by the collective behaviors of all those involved in the policy debate. Any individual actor may attempt to influence the collective outcome, but none determines it singlehandedly (see F. Baumgartner and Mahoney 2008). The idea of many actors competing to control the outcome of a policy process is, of course, central to any kind of democratic decision making, but it creates methodological issues with which political scientists concerned about interest group strategies have not yet grappled sufficiently. The problems are well known in other disciplines, however, including such closely related ones as the study of collective action in sociology. For example, is salience the result of interest group strategies? Yes, since groups clearly seek to manipulate the level of attention to their issues (see Kollman 1998). However, what if there are hundreds of lobbyists working on a given issue? From the perspective of any single actor, none singlehandedly created the observed level of salience, but all must react to it. So in this view salience is imposed from the outside, not the result of lobbying strategy. Similarly, if Riker gives examples of issue definitions being the result of clever speeches by influential senators, this does not mean that frames are on average completely endogenous to the actions of lobbyists or policymakers. In fact, they are exogenous for the vast bulk of lobbyists. In other words, even if individual policymakers might like to affect such collective outcomes as salience, venue, agenda status, or framing, they typically have no control over these things. Rather, for any given lobbyist, these characteristics of the issue are imposed from the outside and the lobbyist must react to them. Collective outcomes are *partially* affected by the actions of individual policymakers, but for the most part it is the individual who responds to the system, not the system which responds to the individual.

Cascades and Power Laws

One reason scholars have been slow to integrate the individual and collective behaviors of groups of lobbyists and other policymakers as they attempt to affect such issues as salience, agenda status, and framing may be that the collective outcomes of these processes are subject to cascades, threshold effects, and other characteristics that make them very difficult to model. Assume simply that policy actors with many potential concerns are likely to spend their time on those issues that are currently the object of attention by others in their environment. When a lobbyist sees that an issue is "moving" or has some chance of passage, then, like it or not, it may be necessary to get involved. If entire communities of lobbyists behave this way, their collective behavior will be subject to cascade effects where tremendous surges occur occasionally, mobilizing large numbers of lobbyists on a small number of issues. This is exactly what Baumgartner and Leech (2001) found; they looked at a random sample of 137 issues that were mentioned in thousands of lobby disclosure reports filed at the end of 1996 and found that the top two issues accounted for half of all the lobby reports filed while those issues that fell below the median level of lobbying activity generated just 2.27 percent of all the reports (2001, 1202).

Such "power laws" are found in many social and physical processes such as the distribution of income, and certain aspects of what can lead to them are well understood (see Barabasi 2005; Watts and Strogatz 1998; Watts 1999a, 1999b). For example, economic bubbles and crashes can be caused by "herd behavior" where individuals base their behaviors on what they see their colleagues around them doing rather than on their own independent judgment (see Lux 1995). In the field of social movements, such cascade and threshold models have been used to explain such things as why social movements can suddenly "catch on" even if for many years participation is relatively stagnant (see Chong 1991). Thomas Schelling used such a model to explain how neighborhoods can suddenly "tip" in one direction or another in his model of racial segregation (1971), and threshold effects have become common in studies of collective action in general (see, for example, Granovetter 1978; Granovetter and Soong 1983; Macy 1991; Kuran 1991; or Lohmann 1994). These models have in common some form of mimicking, where individuals base their actions on the actions they observe those around them engaging in rather than on their own independent assessment. The simplest examples of such herdlike behaviors may be such things as fashion trends or the sudden popularity of restaurants or movies (see Granovetter and Soong 1988; Becker 1991).

The difficulty with studying power laws is that political scientists have been accustomed to studying the behaviors of individuals much more than the collective actions of crowds. Of course, where the issue of interest groups and agenda setting is concerned, we are interested in both. Can individual lobbyists or groups affect the agenda status of an issue? We know they do sometimes and we can point to examples throughout the literature of where successful lobbying campaigns have indeed changed issue definitions or salience. But from another perspective it is clear that the true determinant of these collective outcomes lies, as Schattschneider suggested, in the behavior of the crowd, not the original disputants. Lohmann's (1994) analysis of who participated in the collective demonstrations leading eventually to the collapse of the East German government in 1991 makes clear that the dynamics of collective action concerns the contagion of the conflict more than the strategies of individual actors.

Subsystems Redux

Baumgartner and others (2009) emphasized the importance of the collective actions of entire communities of experts. We found that specialized communities surrounded virtually every issue we studied, typically including government officials administering relevant programs, corporate or other clients or beneficiaries, local governments, trade associations, unions, and other actors with a professional interest in the issue. Whereas scholars often stress the informational value of specialized knowledge, we find that specialized knowledge was widely available within these communities of experts. While individual advocates certainly attempt to shift attention to one dimension of the issue rather than another, or to build up or avoid public salience for their issue, they do not control these processes singlehandedly. Outcomes were determined by the collective actions of the entire community of experts, and proponents and opponents of policy change engaged in highly structured conflicts where neither side typically mobilized strongly without a counteraction from the other side. The study brings our attention to the need to understand individual lobbying behavior, but also to return to Schattschneider's original suggestion that "when a fight breaks out, watch the crowd" because the outcome of the fight will largely be determined by how many members of the audience get involved. A future challenge in the study of interest groups and agenda setting is clearly to address these issues of the embeddedness of individual lobbying strategies within larger structures, including allies and opponents working on the same issue and often responding to the same contextual factors.

BIASES IN INTEREST GROUP MOBILIZATION

From the beginnings of the modern literature on interest groups (e.g., Bentley 1908; Griffith 1939) scholars have focused on two related items: the close connections among professionals inside and out of government (the so-called "policy whirlpools" or subsystems), and the social class bias associated with representation through the "pressure system" rather than through parties and elections. The system is nothing if not elitist. Then again, it is not limited to social elites, but rather to corporations, occupations, and professions, and there can be great diversity of views associated with those coming from different professional backgrounds. Tobacco farmer trade group representatives and those representing hospitals and public health authorities certainly have different perspectives on appropriate regulation of the tobacco industry, so the fact that the pressure system has a strong occupational, professional, and corporate bias does not mean it is unified. Pluralists, of course, focused on this diversity but none have argued that the pressure system was representative of average Americans. There is little evidence that the system's elitist character is due to harsh boundary setting or active efforts to exclude; rather, the bias comes from the fact that some segments of society mobilize powerfully and speak with amplified voices and others mobilize little or not at all. This in turn has great consequences for the types of issues that are brought up.

Social Class Bias in Participation

Scholars of public opinion and mass political behavior have long documented the social class biases in who participates in various political activities (see Angus Campbell et al. 1960; Verba and Nie 1972 for classic treatments). Verba and Nie (1972) showed that these biases were not limited to such activities as voting and contacting government officials, but also were apparent in such things as joining voluntary associations (see also F. Baumgartner and Walker 1988; Putnam 2000). Mancur Olson (1965), of course, explained theoretically why many potentially relevant interest groups would be unlikely to mobilize to their full potential (e.g., groups such as consumers or clients of government programs or others whose goals focus on protecting or maintaining something which will be available to all citizens if granted to any, such as clean air, lower consumer prices, or universalistic government policies). The free-rider problem and the collective action dilemma fundamentally limit the possibilities that David Truman (1951) and Robert Dahl (1961) saw for interest groups to mobilize wherever there might be social need. Some mobilize more easily than others. Jack Walker (1983, 1991) and Robert Salisbury (1984) added fundamental new insights into this process, but the importance of their work for the types of issues that are likely to be addressed in government has not been widely recognized.

The Occupational Nature of the Group System

Walker noted that three-quarters of the groups he identified in his survey of Washington interest groups had an occupational basis; just one-quarter were what he called "citizens' groups." This last category would include such interest group behemoths as the National Rifle Association and the AARP, as well as most groups associated with the environment, gun control, or abortion—much of what people often think of as "single interest groups." In fact, he showed that these are the exception; the rule is that groups active in Washington generally have an occupational basis—they are groups of lawyers, bankers, architects, store owners, nurses, or labor unions, where the membership basis of the group has to do with a person's job, not their ideology. Salisbury showed that many groups are not only occupational, but they are institutional—their members are not individual citizens or professionals at all, but rather such organizations as cities, hospitals, corporations, or universities. The professional, rather than ideological, motivation to mobilize has many implications.

Bias

The bias in the interest group system has been repeatedly found in study after study (in addition to the studies above, see also Schlozman 1984; Heinz et al. 1993; Verba, Schlozman, and Brady 1995; F. Baumgartner and Leech 1998 and 2001; Schlozman et al. 2008). This justifies the concerns brought forward by Bachrach and Baratz (1962) and Crenson (1971) concerning the possibility of certain issues being held permanently "off the agenda" because no one in the "pressure system" has an interest in addressing those concerns. Charles Lindblom's (1977) discussion of the "privileged position of business" in the political system certainly has resonance here. The issue is even more severe than most scholars have recognized, because the interest group system not only ignores many, such as low-wage workers, the unemployed, or those with diffuse social, ideological, or economic interests, but it also provides others the opportunity to speak with huge amplification. Whereas no one can vote more than once, nothing stops a wealthy interest or corporation from lobbying on its own behalf, joining related interest or trade associations, mobilizing allies, hiring PR and consulting firms, and purchasing as much television time or lobbying access as it can afford. Many industries have trade associations with hundreds of staff members permanently monitoring government actions that may affect their members, and individual corporations or professional groups often have government relations departments that dwarf the operations of well-known interest groups.

The Interest Group Policy Agenda

Since Bachrach and Baratz (1962) pointed to the issue of agenda control, scholars have made little progress in investigating the possible implications of bias in the group system for what issues hit the agenda; it is much easier simply to count the number of groups of different types. Since they worked from a random sample of issues in Washington, Baumgartner and colleagues (2009) were able to compare the issues on which the lobbyists were active with data from the Policy Agendas Project[1] which include responses to Gallup Poll questions asking samples of Americans about what they consider to be the most important problem facing the nation today. Thus, one can easily compare the "lobbying agenda" with the concerns of the public. The results

---

[1] <http://www.policyagendas.org>.

were very troubling indeed. During the period when their study was done, the most important problem, according to the public, was crime, with 26 percent of the public selecting this issue. Second was unemployment (or the state of the economy more generally), with 19 percent, followed by international affairs (e.g., terrorism, war) at 10 percent, and education (also 10 percent). Lobbyists had different priorities: 21 percent worked on health care, followed by the environment (13 percent), transportation (8 percent), communications (7 percent), and banking (7 percent) (2009, table 1.4). The disjuncture between the concerns of Americans and the priorities of the lobbyists could hardly be clearer. Looking more closely at the issue priorities of the lobbyists, the differences are even starker. Healthcare lobbyists are more likely to be working on such issues as ensuring higher reimbursement rates for their medical specialty than they are to be working toward greater insurance availability or more attention to patient needs. Lobbying in Washington is largely about issues relating to professions.

The Importance of Investing in a Washington Policy Presence

Few scholars have addressed these issues directly, but Jeffrey Berry did so in his book *The New Liberalism* (1999). He noted the greater effectiveness of citizen groups of the political left compared to those of the right in affecting the national agenda, and he attributed this to their efforts to build a Washington research infrastructure rather than relying only on grassroots efforts. Berry also noted the heavily post-material issue concerns of the liberal groups he studied, and this is reflected in the data presented above as well. Environmental groups deviate from the heavy predominance of occupational groups in Washington in general, and they have been quite effective in pushing many environmental issues to the forefront of the national agenda. It is clear therefore that the political agenda is not immune to pressure if the groups can mobilize. We see little movement to push for issues relating to low-wage workers or those in poverty, or even to relieve homeowners struggling with crushing mortgages during the financial and mortgage crisis of 2008, partly because there are so few interest groups in Washington speaking out in favor of those constituencies. Bankers, mortgage insurance companies, and large corporations like General Motors certainly are present, however, and speaking with voices amplified by the number of lobbyists they can recruit.

The Unintended Biases of Federalism

Lisa Miller (2008) raised troubling issues of agenda control in her study of the politics of crime control at three levels of the federal system. An unintended consequence of the increased "federalization" of the issue of crime over the past several decades is that neighborhood groups, which typically have found ways to participate at the local level (e.g., in public hearings, city council meetings, and directly with police authorities), are virtually excluded from policy debates at the state and national levels. Looking at lists of witnesses involved on crime issues at the national level, she notes a predominance of law enforcement and public authorities. At the local level, participation is much broader, and includes many who live in neighborhoods where crime and poverty is a serious problem. These groups typically are based locally, however, and do not coalesce into national- or state-level organizations with the organizational resources needed to play the lobbying game. Venue shifting, biases in mobilization, and policy agendas all come together in Miller's study.

Journalists and politicians often raise issues about improper access of interest groups. The accumulated literature about the social class and occupational bias in the mobilization of interests that the literature has continually documented over the past several decades suggests that these are real concerns for the strength of democracy. However, the issue is not so much about the access and right of organized interests to develop relations with government officials; of course, they must be able to trade information with them—government often depends on the information provided from within various professional communities. The real issues relate to the inability or unwillingness of members of the general public to mobilize into groups themselves, and that of elected officials to recognize that when they listen to what is being said in Washington there are tremendous distortions in what voices are massively amplified and what voices are not heard at all.

FUTURE AGENDAS OF AGENDA STUDIES

Schattschneider's dual observations about groups and agendas have been at the core of our subfield for almost fifty years now and there is no reason to abandon these important questions. One might suggest abandonment after such a time period if it were apparent that rigorous empirical work could not be done, as some argued about the "agenda denial" idea so prominent in the 1960s. Studies of agenda setting have gained from the creation of large infrastructure projects that have allowed us now to enumerate the items that are on various agendas: congressional, presidential, media, state, and judicial agendas can be studied through established databases or through simple electronic searches.

This review of where we stand has made clear a number of points of interest in the literature but also items obviously needing further detailed work. Who can frame? What determines movements or shifts in collective framing, and what roles do lobbyists play in that? How effective are lobbyists, and under what conditions, in venue shopping? What is the impact of bias in the mobilization of interests in the composition of the public agenda? To what extent do political parties and elected officials raise issues that are of concern to diffuse publics even if they do not have powerful interest group sponsors? How do groups work with government allies in advocating for positions in the policy process that both share (see Hall and Deardorff 2006)? To what degree do elected officials accurately judge the biases in the group system?

One generation ago the literature on interest groups in comparative politics was largely disconnected from that in the United States, and the US literature focused largely on the federal government only (and even more specifically on Congress). Today there is less of an intellectual divide and there are fewer logistical justifica-tions for such divisions so we can look forward to much more ambitious projects as well as the development of a theoretically coherent comparative literature. No matter what the points of comparison (e.g., across time, across countries, across issue domains, across levels of the federal system, or across different institutional agendas), scholars are much more likely to take seriously the problem of studying both the individual actions of lobbyists and interest groups and the collective patterns that can be studied only by looking at entire policy issues or issue communities.

Assessing the roles of groups in affecting what policymakers in Washington hear about is sobering because it is so apparent that the group system amplifies the voices of many corporate actors and virtually shuts out millions of Americans, as Schattschneider noted so forcefully. The massive mobilization of resources to save "Wall Street" but which ignored "Main Street" in the 2008 financial bail-out is a case in point. However, the political system is not made up only of interest groups, and politicians must reflect broader interests as well. There is certainly nothing in the interest group system to suggest accurate representation of the views and concerns of all Americans. Thus, understanding the processes described here has theoretical and great practical importance as well.

CHAPTER 28

....

LOBBYING AND INFLUENCE

....

BETH L. LEECH

No simple, categorical statement can be made about the effect of pressure groups on American democracy. Only one thing is certain: the difficulty of determining the effect.

(Donald Blaisdell, *American Democracy under Pressure*)

POLITICAL observers have long decried the unhealthy influence of "special interests" on government. For nearly as long, political researchers have struggled to measure that influence, with contradictory results. The search for a definitive statement about the power of lobbyists has become the Holy Grail of interest group studies. All seek it, but are forever being led astray. For those writers who simply assert the power of interest groups, that power is clearly very great. For those who try to quantify and systematically measure that influence, however, it has proved illusive. Why, when politicians, the public, and most other political scientists all are convinced that interest groups are so powerful, is it so hard for interest group scholars to pin down this relationship? Almost everyone believes that interest groups are influential, and yet systematic studies have as often pointed to the limits on interest group influence as have concluded that strong influence exists.

This is by no means a new observation. Bernard Cohen, in his 1963 book about agendas and foreign policy, noted that "a 'legend' of pressure group potency in foreign policy appears to be accepted and passed on without evidence to new generations of students and researchers" (1963, 2). When evidence is presented, it is most often anecdotal rather than systematic. And yet no one believes that interests without lobbyists are better off than those that have them. Nearly $3 billion is spent each year on lobbying and political action committee (PAC) campaign contributions in apparent attempts to influence public policy. Hundreds of thousands of people mobilize for hundreds of different causes—demonstrating, writing letters, and making phone calls to officials. If all of these efforts are so lacking in influence, why does anyone bother?

In this chapter, I will give an overview of the scholarly efforts to document the influence of interest groups and suggest some reasons why there is such a great disconnect between popular belief and scholarly evidence. The problems are both substantive and methodological: we have been measuring the wrong things in the wrong ways. That is not to suggest, however, that there is not a good deal of truth and good scholarship to be found in the existing literature on interest group influence—there certainly is. But that often contradictory scholarship must be viewed with a wide lens to capture and fully understand what we know about interest group power in politics.

DEFINING THE TERMS

To understand the influence of lobbying, we first must define what we mean by "lobbying" and what we mean by "influence." Definitions of lobbying vary greatly from user to user. The most narrow definitions focus on direct contacts of legislators by interest group representatives, and sometimes count those contacts only when they are aimed at persuasion, at changing the mind of a given legislator (see, for example, Austen-Smith and Wright 1994). It is more helpful, however, not to truncate the meaning of lobbying in this way and to instead use the word interchangeably with "advocacy." If the phenomenon we wish to understand is the influence of interest groups in the political arena, and not simply the effects of one tactic used by those groups, then we should define lobbying quite broadly. Interest groups do many, many things in their efforts to influence public policy and work in many political arenas. So, rather than investigating the impact just of words said to a legislator in an office, we should investigate all actions of interest groups that are aimed at influencing public policy. Almost all activities that interest groups engage in could be included as long as they are aimed at changing a public policy. Direct contacts of legislators, as in the narrow view of lobbying, would certainly be included, but so would policy research, many grassroots efforts at mobilizing constituents, public relations campaigns, and lawsuits that try to change the way existing law is interpreted or enforced.

To define lobbying is relatively easy; influence itself is almost as hard to define as it is to measure. At the most basic level, influence over public policy is often defined to mean the power to determine outcomes—either to change a public policy or to defeat efforts to have the policy changed. As a result, most studies of lobbying influence have looked at floor votes in Congress, final decisions in bureaucratic rule making, or court rulings. This, certainly, is the gold standard of influence: actually changing an outcome from no to yes or yes to no, or preventing that change from taking place. One of the problems with this way of measuring influence is that it lacks variability—influence tends to then be conceptualized as a yes–no, up-or-down proposition. We could instead measure interim interest group success; for example, interest group success in changing the way an issue is talked about, interest group success in gaining access to members of government, interest group success in getting an issue on the agenda, or interest group success in getting members of government active on an issue. The assumption is, of course, that interest group success at these stages makes success at the end stage possible.

CONTRADICTORY CONCLUSIONS

One of the best-known examples of contradictory findings about the influence of interest groups comes from the classic studies of US trade policy conducted by E. E. Schattschneider (1935) and, three decades later, Bauer, Pool, and Dexter (1963). Schattschneider's searing description of lobbyists dictating the wording of the Smoot–Hawley trade bill to members of Congress is the quintessential depiction of interest groups as "pressure" groups whose influence and power is greater than that held by the elected officials themselves. When Bauer, Pool, and Dexter conducted their decade-long study of the politics behind the renewal of that same legislation in the 1950s, they came to the surprisingly opposite conclusion, as evidenced by the most cited line from their book: 'It...came as a surprise to discover that the lobbies were on the whole poorly financed, ill-managed, out of contact with Congress, and at best only marginally effective in supporting tendencies and measures which already had behind them considerable Congressional impetus from other sources' (1963, 324).

Many political scientists have struggled to explain why Schattschneider found power and Bauer, Pool, and Dexter found impotence. Theodore Lowi's attempt to explain why the two analyses of trade policy seemed to differ so much resulted in a book review (Lowi 1964) of Bauer, Pool, and Dexter's work that contained an early version of his famous policy typology. Lowi argued that while trade policy during Schattschneider's time was primarily viewed by members of Congress as a distributive issue (making it a simple matter to hand out pork because there was enough to go around), thirty years later trade had become a regulatory issue on which members of Congress were much more reluctant to yield to interest group pressure. Of course, this explanation begs the question why it was that members of Congress shifted in the way they talked about trade over time. Why did trade become regulatory? We have thus given a name to a situation in which interest groups had power and a situation in which they had little power, but we are no closer to knowing why the issue was defined one way at one time and another way at another time and what it takes to make such a definition shift.

Other scholars have tried to explain the differences between the two cases as well. Hayes (1978) compared the two cases and proposed a somewhat different typology of costs and benefits that he thought might better account for the disparate findings. Nelson (1989) suggested that interest groups lost power over time because trade policy came to be more integrated into foreign policy (an arena in which both interest groups and public opinion have traditionally had less influence than in other issue areas). Hansen (1991) compared the same two cases and suggested that the difference might be the result of differing levels of access granted to organized interests in the two cases, and argued in his book about farm policy that access on that issue waxed and waned according to how important farm interests were to electoral politics at any given point in time. Baumgartner and Leech (1996) suggested that variation in how conflictual and publicly salient the issues were at the two times might explain the contradictory findings.

Or perhaps it could be that the two studies are not so different after all. Cupitt and Elliot (1994) undertook a quantitative analysis of eleven votes from Schattsch-neider's case and concluded that actually there was no discrepancy between his case and Bauer, Pool, and Dexter's case—the quantitative reanalysis showed very little interest group impact in Schattschneider's time. Along the same lines, Baumgart-ner and Leech (1998) suggested that a closer reading of Schattschneider and Bauer, Pool, and Dexter would show that the two cases actually agreed with one another much more than the popular one-sentence summaries of the books usually allowed. Schattschneider documented many limitations on group influence and Bauer, Pool, and Dexter documented many instances in which the close relation-ships interest groups had with their allies led to advantageous outcomes.

Continuing Contradictions

Modern-day quantitative studies of the influence of lobbying and PACs are as contradictory as the classic cases were. Smith (1995) reviewed thirty-seven studies of PAC contributions and roll call votes in the House and Senate. Eight of those studies found that contributions were not related to congressional voting decisions, twelve found mixed results, and seventeen found that contributions did influence congressional voting decisions. Especially given the bias against publishing null findings that many journals adhere to (and, thus, the actual number of mixed findings and findings of no relationship might well be larger in the unpublished literature and in real life), this is a pattern that indicates that the relationship between campaign contributions and vote outcomes is essentially random.

Baumgartner and Leech (1998) built on Smith's analysis, considering fifteen quantitative studies of lobbying influence and thirty-three studies of PAC influence to identify some of the reasons why contradictory findings might be so common. Null findings were nearly as common as findings of influence, and the majority of studies found only marginal influence that was strongly limited by other variables such as constituency, ideology, or visibility. The difficulty, according to Baumgartner and Leech, was that each of the studies focused on different sets of these variables, measuring them differently and omitting and adding without clear reference to the past studies, making reasoned comparison across the studies difficult. Most looked at only a single issue, making even a seemingly quantitative analysis the practical equivalent of a case study. Burstein and Linton (2002) made the best of these difficulties in a meta-analysis of all studies of interest group influence published in major political science and sociology journals from 1990 to 2000. The fifty-three articles analyzed showed interest groups as being influential less than half the time. Burstein and Linton point out that given that the studies virtually never controlled for public opinion and given that most journals have a publication bias against null findings, the actual effects of interest group influence are likely even weaker.

To address some of these criticisms and possible reasons for a lack of findings, Frank Baumgartner, Jeffrey Berry, Marie Hojnacki, David Kimball, and I studied more than 1,000 organizations active on a random sample of ninety-eight issues over the course of two congressional sessions (F. Baumgartner et al. 2009). Making use of more than 300 interviews and a vast array of publicly available information, we created more than a dozen different measures of monetary resources available to interest groups. None of them were correlated with wished-for outcomes for the groups studied. PAC contributions, in fact, were *negatively* correlated with success (although the result was not statistically significant). More lobbying or more campaign donations did not equal more influence.

There are some indications that looking at the system as a whole, rather than trying to measure influence issue by issue, might lead to less contradiction and to more interest group influence. Quinn and Shapiro (1991), for example, conducted a time series analysis with corporate tax rates as the dependent variable and the proportion of PACs and proportion of registered lobbyists that represented corporations as two of the independent variables. PACs did seem to make a difference. As the proportion of corporate PACs rose, corporate tax rates went down: each additional percentage point in the proportion of corporate PACs decreased the tax rates about 0.1 percent in most of their model specifications. But the proportion of lobbyists did not make any difference and neither the proportion of PACs nor the proportion of lobbyists was as influential as a change in party control (under the Democrats tax rates went up between 1.5 and 2.5 percent). And a somewhat similar research design—albeit on a very different set of issues—by Fellowes, Gray, and Lowery (2006) found that the relative number of interest organizations involved in "post-material" issues did not increase the agenda space for such issues in state legislatures. So the contradictions remain.

Studies of interest group influence before courts and within the bureaucracy in the past decade or so have been fewer (in part because the data are harder to compile since PAC contribution records are not of use) and somewhat less contradictory. Still, there is far from a unanimous verdict about interest groups' influence. Golden (1998) studied eleven proposed rules within three agencies, comparing the comments submitted by interest groups and the resulting rules from the agencies. She found that only one of the rules changed "a great deal" and that when there was change, it was most often when the commentators showed consensus about the need for a change. More extensive influence was found, however, in a series of analyses by Susan Webb Yackee and others (e.g. J. Yackee and Yackee 2006; McKay and Yackee 2007), based on a much larger sample of 1,700 comments on forty rules. The studies considered whether there was a shift toward more or less regulation as a result of the comments, and found, among other things, that more comments lead to more changes.

Before the courts, interest groups can affect outcomes by filing suit or filing amicus briefs that put forth their arguments on the issue. Studies here have most often looked to a particular case or policy area and then analyzed the role of interest groups in those legal decisions. A few studies have tried to look more systematically at how successful interest groups are before the courts. One of the best of these studies, by Epstein and Rowland (1991), compared twenty cases in which interest groups were involved as a litigant to twenty cases in which interest groups were not involved. The cases were matched by judge, year, and issue. The results? Well, the title of the article is "Debunking the Myth of Interest Group Invincibility in the Courts." Interest groups were no more likely than non-groups to win their cases. So while studies of specific policy areas (which have a tendency to select on the dependent variable) often find interest group influence over the courts, one of the few broader studies disagrees. These findings were replicated by Songer and Sheehan (1993) in a study of 132 matched cases in which amicus briefs had been filed in one of the cases but not in the other. Cases with amicus briefs were no more likely to win on the merits. The issue is far from settled, however. Collins (2007) analyzed all Supreme Court cases between 1946 and 1995 and concluded that if the ideology of the justices were controlled for, amicus briefs did have an impact on the merits. More conservative briefs increased the chance of a conservative ruling, while more liberal briefs increased the chance of a liberal ruling, as long as one first controlled for the ideological predispositions of justices to vote one way or the other.

Why So Much Disagreement?

There are almost as many ideas about why studies of interest group influence disagree as there are studies that disagree. Smith (1995, 94–5) listed twelve explanations from the interest group literature, including differences in the visibility, technicality, partisanship, and salience of the issue, how costs and benefits were distributed, the degree of organized opposition, several electoral variables, and public opinion. Baumgartner and Leech (1998) pointed to a series of methodological problems, including a tendency to study one or a handful of issues, failure to include relevant variables, modeling influence as dichotomous, as well as a lack of attention to the political context of the issues in question. Here I will step back, away from specific variables, to view the most important big-picture reasons behind contradictory findings regarding interest group influence: a tendency to select on the dependent variable, a tendency to focus on the end stage of the policy process, misconceptions about what it is that interest groups actually do, and misconceptions about how the policy process actually works.

Selecting on the Dependent Variable

When an observer of politics—whether a citizen, journalist, or political scientist—views a political issue, sees that an organized interest is getting the outcome that it prefers, and then concludes that the organized interest has been successful, the observer is committing an all too common error of inference: selecting on the dependent variable. The observer has, in essence, sought out examples in which organized interests were successful and, based on this biased sample, concluded that influence exists. But what if there is an equally resource-rich interest group that does not like the way that issue turned out? Or what if there are an equal number of issues for which a seemingly powerful interest group did *not* get its way?

Many political scientists have made a parallel error by selecting issues that were prominent, that were known to have a lot of interest group activity, and that reached the final stage of the vote. All of these factors increase the interest group's chance of success, since the hardest hurdle for any issue to overcome is simply to get on the agenda in the first place. If the goal is to measure whether interest groups are influential, selecting a prominent issue is thus a form of selecting on the dependent variable.

Jordan (2001) clearly sees this trap of inference in his case study of a series of protests by the environmental group Greenpeace against Shell Oil Company's proposed disposal of a North Sea oil storage buoy called the Brent Spar. Greenpeace occupied the 14,500-ton buoy and its protests helped change the terms of the debate. Rather than focusing on whether it was safer and more practical to dispose of the buoy on land or in the Atlantic Ocean, the debate came to be understood in the media and by the public as whether to allow the ocean to become "the great sewer of the world." Public pressure led the company to rescind its plans to sink the buoy in the Atlantic. But Jordan warns us against concluding that the reason Greenpeace prevailed in this case is because of the great influence the group wields:

The first explanation of the policy change that is at the heart of this book is that Greenpeace "forced" Shell to back down. The book assumes that that is too simple. If pressure group power "explains" the Brent Spar then why was the same organization using very similar tactics against similar opponents far less immediately successful in 1997 in trying to stop the exploration and exploitation in the Atlantic margins? (Jordan 2001, 21)

Interest group power is contingent. The Brent Spar certainly would have been sunk in the Atlantic if not for Greenpeace, and yet just because Greenpeace seeks an outcome is not enough to bring that outcome about. Interest group influence is an *important* (I will not say *necessary*) but by no means *sufficient* cause. In the case of the Brent Spar, preexisting support for environmentalist causes in Europe and the success in the media of a catchy phrase ("the great sewer of the world") were among the additional conditions that helped to bring about the change in policy.

The error of selecting only issues in which interest groups are known to have been influential or selecting only prominent cases is perhaps the most important reason why journalists and political commentators have such a different view of interest group influence compared to the political scientists who actually try to measure that influence.

Focusing on a Single Stage of the Process

If interest group influence is conceived of as yes–no, there are going to be a lot of nos. That alone will lead to contradictory findings if most work is focusing on policy case studies. But focusing only on policy outcomes also is problematic because it turns our attention away from the earlier stages of the policy process in which interest groups may have the most influence. Looking only at outcomes may also lead us to make errors in causal inference. By looking only at the end stage of the process, we risk assuming that the conditions present at that end stage are the conditions that result in interest group influence. If we see, for example, interest groups making the rounds of members of Congress, encouraging a vote one way or another, we might assume these last pressure-filled rounds of persuasion are the main source of interest group influence. We are liable to forget that simply reaching that end stage—where a vote or a decision on a rule is imminent—is itself a measure of success. We may forget that the long years of research, issue framing, and building alliances were necessary to that success.

Efforts to change the terms of the debate and the details of a policy proposal are critical to interest group influence. The classic policy studies and descriptive studies of lobbying saw the importance of these early stages most clearly, as evidenced in Schattschneider's famous descriptions of lobbyists dictating the wording of the trade bill. The "iron triangle" policy studies of the 1950s and 1960s, which investigated the symbiotic relationships among interest groups, congressional committees, and agency officials, also documented much influence that took place in the policy formation stages rather than in the decision-making stages (e.g. Maass 1951; J. L. Freeman 1955; Fritschler 1975).

A few recent studies have systematically and quantitatively documented the importance of these earlier stages in Congress. Hansen's study of the influence of US farm interests (1991) defined success not through outcomes, but through how much access they had to members of Congress. Access was measured by how often interest groups testified and how positively that testimony was reacted to in hearings. His study concluded that interest groups were influential during time periods when they could be of greater electoral help. An entire chapter in this volume is devoted to agenda setting and interest groups, so I will not say much more about that here, except to note that while noticing and bringing a potential problem to the attention of policymakers is known to be a critically important tactic for interest groups (McCubbins and Schwartz 1984; Heinz et al. 1993), agenda status itself is too seldom used as a measure of interest group influence.

Once an issue has been introduced in Congress, it is shaped in committee and here an interest group may have great influence. An interest group may ultimately "lose" on the floor when a bill it opposes passes, but may have succeeded in an earlier stage in ensuring that the enforcement measures in a bill were watered down or contained loopholes. Although most interest group scholars would agree with this characterization—and while this is what most descriptive studies of interest groups in the policymaking process have documented—there are relatively few systematic studies of interest group influence at the committee stage. Exceptions include Wright (1990), Hall and Wayman (1990), and Hojnacki and Kimball (1998, 2001). This influence is sometimes hypothesized to be the result of PAC donations leading to greater access, but Hojnacki and Kimball (2001) do not find evidence to support that theory. While the approximately one-third of all interest groups who give campaign donations do tend to make more contacts in committee, Hojnacki and Kimball conclude that this is because of their on-average greater resources and greater ties to the legislators' districts. Wright (1990) likewise found that PAC donations did not seem to matter but that the number of lobbying contacts did. The only way in which PAC donations do seem to have an independent effect on interest group influence in committee is through a tendency to increase how much members of Congress participate in committee hearings (Hall and Wayman 1990). These studies of interest group influence in committee indicate that while interest groups have a role to play in these early stages, even here it is not an image of dictatorial power by groups. Organized interests and their lobbyists are influential at the margins, after ideological predispositions and other variables affecting voting decisions have been taken into consideration.

The limited agenda of the Supreme Court—it accepts only 1 or 2 percent of the thousands of petitions filed before it each year—has made the examination of interest group influence on that agenda a central research topic and one of the few areas in the study of interest group influence that has consistently found positive results. Because the list of all possible cases from which the Supreme Court could choose is a public list, it then becomes a relatively straightforward (albeit time-consuming) task to compare those cases that are chosen to those that are not. Studies have repeatedly shown that the presence of amicus briefs makes it more likely that the Supreme Court will consider the case, and more amicus briefs make it more likely (Caldeira and Wright 1988, 1990; Lee Epstein 1992; McGuire and Caldeira 1993). These friends of the court briefs are theorized to serve as a signal to justices about the importance and potential impact of the case. Briefs that try to discourage the Supreme Court from considering the case do not have an impact (Caldeira and Wright 1988), and the briefs do not seem to serve as primary sources of information. Although justices often cite the amicus briefs (Lee Epstein 1992), the amicus briefs themselves tend to repeat the same arguments as the briefs from the original parties in the case and even when there are new arguments, the justices do not tend to cite those new arguments (Spriggs and Wahlbeck 1997). But the briefs do seem to signal salience and importance. The more amicus briefs filed, the more likely the Supreme Court is to hear the case.

Recent quantitative studies of interest group influence in bureaucratic processes have, as noted earlier, focused on agency rule making, in particular on notice and comment procedures. Here, too, there are earlier stages in the process, when agencies must decide which topics are in need of additional rules and how initial proposals will be formulated. This area of agenda setting in the bureaucracy is ripe for additional research. Yackee (2008) calls it the "least understood stage of the American policymaking process," and that certainly is true in terms of the role of interest groups in that stage. Data collection here is difficult, however, because unlike studies of formal notice and comment proceedings, at the agenda-setting stage and the rule formulation stage there is no public record to turn to. Researchers must turn to interviews, surveys, or ethnographic work within an agency. Yackee takes a first step into this area with a survey of 133 interest groups combined with content analysis of proposed rules and finds that interest groups that reported *ex parte* communications with agency officials were more likely to have influenced the content of proposed rules. Interest group involvement in agencies also takes place outside formal rule-making processes, in procurement and decisions about how rules will be applied in particular instances. Godwin and Seldon (2002) argue that interest groups often succeed in gaining private (rather than collective) benefits in these venues and that this important realm of influence remains vastly understudied.

Thousands of bills are introduced each year in Congress, thousands of petitioners appeal to the court system, and there is a virtually unlimited range of issues on which an agency might decide to create a rule. With the exception of studies of agenda setting in the Supreme Court, however, too little work has been done on interest group efforts to affect the agendas of these decision-making bodies or on interest group efforts in the early stages of the policymaking process. Researchers often shy away from studying committee and agenda-setting processes and prefer the study of role call votes both because roll call data are easier to compile and analyze and because, when the study is done, all anyone outside of the interest group subfield ever wants to know is how those processes track onto final outcomes. Studies that show why an interest group chose this tactic rather than that one, or studies that show interest groups succeeding in getting issues on the agenda or shifting the way an issue was framed, are still likely to be greeted with the question "OK, but what was the outcome?" And yet surveys of interest group behavior repeatedly find that organizations spend a vast amount of time on these earlier tactics; it is unwise for scholars to ignore their possible effects.

WRONG ASSUMPTIONS ABOUT WHAT IT IS INTEREST GROUPS DO

Bauer, Pool, and Dexter attributed the lack of influence they found in part to poor financing and in part to reticence and fear among the lobbyists they studied—they assumed that the reason lobbyists spoke mostly to members of Congress who already agreed with them was that they wanted to avoid uncomfortable confrontations. These problems are far less evident today: the professionalized world of lobbying is not for the timid, and business organizations, at least, tend to be extremely well financed. Nonetheless, the patterns that were observed more than a half-century ago remain today: interest group lobbyists spend far more time talking with policymakers who agree with them than those who disagree with them (Leech and Baumgartner 1998; Hojnacki and Kimball 1998). One of the most important roles for interest groups is their role as allies to government officials in the policymaking process, providing information, strategy, and public support (see, for example, Browne and Paik 1993; Ainsworth 1997; Heaney 2006; F.

Baumgartner et al. 2009). Studies that define lobbying only as attempts to pressure legislators to change their votes are liable to measure influence incorrectly because they overlook the tactics that interest groups use that are most likely to bring success: working together with like-minded allies within government, monitoring the policymaking environment, and working to build momentum for an issue to get it onto the policymaking agenda.

In the age of Bauer, Pool, and Dexter, interest groups were effective in part because of the information they supplied.

These associations became nodes in the communications process. What they knew or failed to learn, what they heard or did not hear, what they said or failed to say, had a profound effect on what other people learned, heard, or said. These other people were not merely the general public, but more importantly, their own members, the press, the administration, and congressmen.... Thus, although lobbying by any given pressure group was relatively limited in effectiveness, the presence of pressure associations astride the communications process was important indeed. (1963, 325)

Provision of information remains a central component of interest group influence today, whether that information is supplied directly or indirectly through the media. While systematic examinations of interest group provision of information tend to focus on its role as a tactic, rather than linking it explicitly to policy outcomes (see, for example, Danielian and Page 1998; Esterling 2007; J. Berry 1999), the assumption generally is that more and better provision of information will lead to preferred outcomes for an interest group. Burstein and Hirsh (2007) argue that one of the main reasons there may be so much contradiction in the interest group subfield is that while theory suggests that groups are influential because of the information they provide, most studies of interest group influence before Congress fail to consider the role of information. Most studies have either focused on the dollar amount donated in campaign contributions or simply use a measure of whether the interest group was present and lobbying.

Burstein and Hirsh examined interest group information provided during hearings held on twenty-seven randomly selected policy proposals and found that information provided by supporters about the expected effectiveness of a policy area greatly increased the probability of passage, while information regarding why the proposal would not work decreased the probability of passage. Information about the importance of the issue and attempts to reframe the issue did not consistently change the outcomes; perhaps because by the time an issue is at the hearing stage, importance and frames have already been settled. Interestingly enough, and contrary to some interest group theory about why members of Congress should listen to interest groups, information about electoral concerns did not factor prominently in the testimony. A parallel finding comes from Baumgartner et al. (2009), who asked lobbyists on ninety-eight different issues to list all of the arguments they were making about their issues, both publicly and behind the scenes. Only about 3 percent of the cases in both studies included lobbying arguments that were electoral in nature. The information that interest groups typically provide to legislators about their issues and the arguments that they make tend to focus on policy substance rather than on how the issue is likely to play out electorally. This may be because electoral concerns are so all-pervasive that they become the elephant in the room that nobody talks about. That still leaves us with the conclusion, however, that interest groups' role is not primarily to provide *information* about those electoral concerns. The presence of lobbyists may signal salience of an issue among an electoral group, but the actual content of interest group lobbying is clearly not primarily aimed at transmitting further electoral knowledge.

Working together with governmental allies as described by Bauer, Pool, and Dexter involves more than mere provision of information, however. Bauer, Pool, and Dexter called the interest group allies "service bureaus" to the allied members of Congress because the roles the groups undertook were like those of adjunct staff members. Hall and Deardorff (2006) update this concept as "interest group subsidy," formalizing the reasons why lobbyists would be motivated to act in this way and deriving hypotheses about the patterns of behavior we should find if this theory is true. When interest groups work with their allies, it is the organization best able to provide what politicians need—information, facts, supporters, media coverage, or strategic expertise—that will be the most influential interest group. Every member of Congress has many different causes and issues that he or she supports, and each has numerous possible venues in which to become involved. One way that interest groups can be influential is by lowering the cost to government officials of working on the issue that the interest group cares about, by making it easier to take up that cause rather than another.

The provision of information and the subsidization of agenda setting on an issue do not only take place in governmental offices, but through public channels as well. That means that one measure of interest group success is the amount and type of news coverage an interest group garners on the issues it cares about. This arena of interest group influence contains a perfectly parallel case of contradiction about interest group influence: Danielian and Page (1994) and Berry (1999). Danielian and Page analyzed nearly 800 television stories about eighty prominent issues during the period 1969 to 1982. They concluded that unions and citizen groups were vastly underrepresented in television news compared with corporations and government officials, and that when citizen groups were used as sources, it was in protest stories that portrayed them in an unflattering light. Berry updated their study and found that liberal citizen groups had moved from being an afterthought in the 1970s to a central news source by the 1990s. These two studies, however, provide an example of contradiction gone right. Because of the effort Berry took to consider and replicate the important aspects of what Danielian and Page had done, he is able to assess why his findings were so different from theirs. In this case the contradiction is not an anomaly but evidence that the strategic position of liberal citizen groups had shifted over the decades. Berry showed that the liberal citizen groups had spent a great deal of time and effort building the capacity to conduct research and disseminate that research, and argued that it was those efforts that helped lead to the change in climate.

WRONG ASSUMPTIONS ABOUT HOW POLICY WORKS

One reason why scholarly attempts to measure interest group influence seldom result in findings that mirror the "big bad lobbyist" images of the popular press is that policymaking is a lot more complicated than the big bad lobbyist view allows. If we define interest group influence as the ability to determine outcomes, we are very seldom going to find any interest group influence. There are always other political actors involved and who wins and loses depends on party power, dominant issue frames, and political mood, not simply lobbying resources. Popular depictions of interest group influence suffer greatly from omitted variable bias.

Heterogeneous Sides

One reason why interest group lobbying and other forms of advocacy may often fail to lead to the outcomes the interest groups prefer is that in many cases there is an opposing group of interests that *did* get what it wanted. Although pluralist approaches to policymaking from decades past have been criticized for assuming that interest organizations would arise naturally as they were needed to protect their interests, these older studies were not just imagining the patterns of opposing interests that they saw. Indeed, for most issues, there are opposing interest groups active and the two sides tend to be fairly equally balanced in terms of resources. Baumgartner et al. (2009) found that only seventeen of their ninety-eight issues had only a single side, and having only a single side did not guarantee success. In fact, in many of those seventeen cases the reason why there was no opposing organized interest was that the issue was not high on the agenda and opposing groups saw no reason to mobilize.

For the eighty-two issues with at least two sides, Baumgartner et al. found sides that were relatively equally balanced. While corporate interests and unions tend to have far more resources than citizen groups, for example, in most of the issues each side was a mix of different types of groups. If the richest group won, so would the poorest group, since they shared the same side. If the group that donated the most in campaign donations won, so would a group that did not have a PAC at all, since they shared the same side. Policy sides were heterogeneous, with any given group's resources correlating only weakly with the total resources of its side. The lesson from this is to note the importance of assessing all interest groups active on a given side together and to remember that the weakest of groups may have powerful allies.

The Power of the Status Quo

Many interest group scholars have noted the truism that it is easier for an interest group to protect an existing policy than it is to change that policy. What is less seldom noted is that means that interest group influence over policy change will not be incremental and linear, but substantial and punctuated. Baumgartner et al. found that about two-thirds of the issues exhibited no policy change whatsoever over the four years that we studied them. We also found, however, that when change did occur it tended to be substantial rather than incremental. The power of the status quo means that the status quo has great staying power in the face of interest groups that would prefer to change it. Analyses that controlled for whether a side was fighting to change the status quo or preserve it showed that level of resources did indeed change the probability of a side achieving its goal. Baumgartner et al. argue that it is also important to remember that any status quo policy already reflects the equilibrium power of actors in the system at that point in time. Given that, we should be most likely to see interest group influence as the result of *changes* in mobilization and resources, not as the result of the *level* of those factors as it is usually measured in most studies, including that of Baumgartner et al.

Throughout our study, Baumgartner et al. found that policy advocacy was a long-term enterprise lasting years, thanks to the power of the status quo. Getting an issue on the political agenda, lining up support, and working for passage are not done quickly for most interest groups. This means that before interest group success is observed, there will be many years of lack of success, and it means that any study that considers only small numbers of issues in the cross-section is likely to add to the pattern of contradictory findings.

The Contingent Nature of Influence

Scholars who look at interest group influence in the policy process qualitatively, after time spent in Washington interviewing and observing, often come to mixed conclusions of another sort. Especially if they have studied more than a single issue and followed a policy area over time, their findings tend to portray interest group influence not as black or white but as partial, conditional, and intrinsically bound up in the wants and goals of powerful members of Congress and agency officials or judges with ideas of their own. Christine DeGregorio (1997), for example, in her book documenting the passage of six prominent bills in the 1980s, found that while interest groups did have influence, corporate interests were the most likely to report dissatisfaction with those outcomes. Why? DeGregorio attributes the dissatisfaction of the corporate interests and the relative satisfaction of the citizen groups, church groups, and unions to the Democratically controlled Congress at the time of her study. In Andrew Rich's study of think tanks, influence was contingent despite the fact that his issue areas were chosen explicitly because they were areas in which think tanks had been active and seemed to have had some success. Whether the message of any given think tank carried through into policy outcomes was "subject to the constraints . . . that are typically out of control of the experts, whatever their talents" (2004, 138).

It may well be that interest groups are most influential when there is no countervailing pressure. But countervailing pressure comes from many sources and not just other interest groups, as traditional pluralist theory would have it. The desires of elected officials, the policy beliefs of bureaucrats and judges, the expected reaction of the general public (even if at the moment the public is not attentive to the issue), all are potential constraints. Many of the contradictory findings throughout the interest group literature may be attributable to this contingent nature of influence.

How Does Interest Group Influence Occur?

For the average student of politics, the $64,000 question, the issue it all boils down to, is: does lobbying make a difference? That is, are interest groups influential? This, to a student of interest groups, is an extraordinarily frustrating question. It is frustrating both because it is so difficult to answer and because it is a question that is almost never asked of scholars who study the formal branches of government, as Robert Salisbury has noted:

Think of it this way. Does it make much sense to ask who is the most influential member of the U.S. Senate? Or . . . is it a high priority to determine the influence rank among the Supreme Court Justices? It is not that influence is irrelevant; it is simply not the best way to frame the central questions. (1994, 18)

What most observers mean when they ask about interest group influence is "Can interest groups dictate outcomes?" That is almost never true. Studies that are designed to show that PAC contributions caused an outcome are doomed to failure; the real picture is much more complex and contingent than that.

Why and how are interest groups influential? The studies surveyed above suggest that they may be influential in three basic ways. First, it may be a simple case of bribery or bought votes. That is what the many PAC studies would seem to suggest. Second, it may be that interest groups are influential because they help members get re-elected, by providing information (signals) about constituency preferences and by their potential to mobilize constituencies in support or opposition to a candidate. Third, it may be that interest groups help make policymaking itself easier by serving as service bureaus, working with allied members of Congress, providing information, mobilizing publics, attracting media attention, and generally subsidizing the activities of government officials.

Clearly the first case is most normatively troublesome and it is little wonder that so much effort has gone into assessing whether it is indeed possible for money to buy votes. Fortunately, the conflicting results of these studies suggest that there does not seem to be any clear evidence that this is common or easy to do. Limits on amounts that may be given and cross-pressures from ideological and electoral concerns make outright vote buying unlikely to be common. And yet, there are worrisome indications from some of these studies that suggest that donations may indeed have some effects at the margins, especially on elected officials who are not already strongly predisposed one way or the other. Donations may also affect the amount of effort a public official is willing to put into pushing a bill forward (Hall and Wayman 1990). Campaign finance contributions (and electoral pressure, for that matter) are only a factor for legislative lobbying, however. How then do we explain interest group influence in non-legislative settings or interest group influence in countries with publicly financed elections?

The second case would be somewhat less normatively problematic, as it certainly is reasonable to expect and hope that elected officials would be influenced by constituency concerns, although there is limited evidence that providing electoral information is a central tactic for interest group lobbyists. Both Burstein and Hirsh (2007) and Baumgartner et al. (2009) found little evidence of constituency or electoral arguments as being central in hearings testimony or in the lobbying messages that groups use.

The evidence is strongest that the third case—provision of information and other policy-related aid—is a source of interest group influence, at least under some circumstances. Should we be worried about this? Many of the activities that fall under the category of interest group subsidization of policymaking are routine political activities covered by First Amendment rights, including the rights to free assembly and speech. The trouble arises if some types of interest groups and some types of interests are better able to take advantage of this ability to subsidize than others. If, for example, what money buys is the ability to mobilize constituencies and the ability to provide information to government officials and poorer groups and poorer interests are shut out of this process, then a democratic problem remains.

Fortunately for the health of US democracy, there is little evidence of the outright buying of votes and outcomes. If the power to dictate outcomes, with that power stemming from economic might, is what we mean by interest group influence, then the evidence that such influence exists is shaky at best. But if what we mean by interest group influence is a conditional power that relies in large part on alliance making and provision of information, then it is clear that interest group influence permeates American politics. It is difficult to see, however, how such influence could be avoided in any democratic system that allows individuals to petition their government. So in one sense, influence that stems from providing information and finding elected officials who have similar goals is natural and unavoidable. If the ability to petition government were equal regardless of means, we would have no worries about the effect of interest groups on the health of our democracy. But where alliances are forged in part because of abilities to raise campaign funds and where some interests have a much greater capacity to create and compile information, then the finding of friends and the provision of information become not wholly benign. It is for this reason that research agendas that look at the *composition* of the group population and the *tactics* that different sets of groups are able to use are as important as those agendas that consider lobbying influence and policy outcomes. Who the groups in the system are and what they are able to do is critical to understanding how equal or unequal the playing field has become.

CHAPTER 29

INTEREST GROUPS IN AMERICAN ELECTIONS

CLYDE WILCOX

RENTARO IIDA

INTEREST groups are involved in elections in myriad ways. Some groups give money to a single candidate; others contribute to many national, state, and local candidates and to other interest groups and parties. Some recruit and train candidates, trying to change the ideological balance within a party; others prefer to avoid primary elections entirely. Some endorse candidates; others help candidates without endorsing them. Some try to increase turnout among targeted constituencies by registering voters, canvassing neighborhoods, and by phoning, emailing, or mailing packets to prospective voters; others run advertisements on television, radio, or the Internet, sometimes explicitly endorsing candidates, and in other cases implicitly doing so. Some groups focus exclusively on one of these activities, others do them all.

Political scientists, sociologists, and economists have studied interest group activity in elections for more than seventy years (Overacker and West 1932; Heard 1956; Sorauf 1992; Rozell and Wilcox 1999). Studies have used a variety of methods, including formal models (Morton and Cameron 1992; Bailey 2004), statistical models of which groups contribute and how much they give (Hart 2001; Appolonio and La Raja 2004), and comparative case studies of interest group activities (Biersack, Herrnson, and Wilcox 1999; Malbin et al. 2002).

Yet there remains fundamental disagreement among scholars on most of the key questions about interest groups and elections. Why do groups become active in elections, and how do they make this decision? How do groups choose strategies and tactics, and what causes these to change over time? Finally, how do groups benefit from their electoral involvement? Before reviewing scholarship on these specific topics, it is important to consider the general problems faced by scholars who study interest groups in elections.

General Problems in the Study of Interest Groups and Elections

Like all political science problems, the study of interest groups in elections raises problems of conceptualization, measurement, and estimation. And like all problem areas, the specific manifestation of these problems affects what is studied, how it is studied, and the conclusions that can be drawn.

Conceptual Issues

Most research on interest groups begins with a broad definition, such as "any organization or institution that makes policy-related appeals to government" (F. Baumgartner and Leech 1998, xxii). Because of the diversity in types of organizations that meet this definition, scholars then frequently limit their discussion to particular types of groups, such as corporations, oil companies, or groups with members who meet face to face (D. Evans 1988; M. Warren 2001; Handler and Mulkern 1992). But the study of interest groups in elections poses special conceptual problems, because tax and campaign finance law create incentives for interests to organize in particular ways.

Interest groups that contribute money in national elections must form political action committees (PACs), but not all PACs represent interest groups. Some PACs are clearly party groups, others represent party leaders, presidential aspirants, or other policymakers, and still others are the former campaign committees of incumbents who have retired and now use surplus campaign funds to contribute to other candidates. Most but not all scholarly work screens these PACs from analysis.

During the last decade, groups have been allowed to spend money that does not explicitly advocate the election or defeat of a candidate in ways that are outside of normal disclosure processes. Some of the "groups" are clearly conduits for at most a handful of individuals, such as the Republicans for Clean Air, who spent money attacking John McCain's environmental record in the New York presidential primary of 2000. When an organization exists for a single election cycle and represents one or a handful of donors, is it an interest group, or a conduit for individuals?

The fluidity of the 527 committees that formed and often disbanded in the 2000s has raised additional questions. Are these committees best conceived as a party network, are they coalitions of groups that have formed bonds to divide labor and limit shirking, or are they also conduits for communities of donors (Boatright 2007; Skinner 2005)? Many of these organizations were formed by the leaders of existing interest groups, using money from a handful of large donors (Weissman and Hassan 2006). These 527 committees represented a significant percentage of campaign activity by interest groups in recent elections, but they are difficult to fit into interest group theories. We will return to the question of 527 committees and to networks of groups more generally below.

Data Issues

The availability of reliable data on PACs in national elections has prompted a host of studies of PAC formation, PAC contribution strategies, and the effects of contributions on policy (Witko 2006; Ansolabehere, de Figueiredo, and Snyder 2003; Hojnacki and Kimball 2001; Fleisher 1993; J. Wright 1989; Eismeier and Pollock 1986; Wilcox 1989b).[1] Most statistical analysis of interest group participation in elections focuses on contributions from PACs to candidates in national elections. But PACs are not the only way that interest groups give to candidates and parties during elections.

Some interest groups have given directly from their treasuries to party commit-tees, and to 527 and 501(c) organizations (Appolonio and La Raja 2004; Weissman and Ryan 2006).[2] Soft money contributions to national parties and to 527 com-mittees can be traced, although there are difficulties in deciding whether contribu-tions by corporate executives are made on behalf of the company. Other types of giving are far harder to trace. Groups can give to state and local party committees, and to state 527 committees. They can also bundle contributions formally, or arrange to "buy tables" at fundraising events. Coordinated giving by corporations can be traced (with some error) since donors are required in national and many

---

[1] The availability of these data owes much to Robert Biersack, who managed the data division of the Federal Election Commission for many years.

[2] Soft money contributions to parties were banned by the Bipartisan Campaign Reform Act in 2002, but groups can still give contributions directly to state parties for use in state elections.

state elections to list their employer,[3] but coordination by other types of groups cannot be tracked using Federal Election Commission (FEC) or state disclosure data. Surveys of donors have shown that many coordinate with ideological groups (Francia et al. 2003a), and that a majority of individual donors in some state elections give in coordination with interests (T. Marshall 1999).

More importantly, groups can do more than simply give to candidates and parties; they also spend their own money to help them win. Membership organizations share their endorsements with their members with minimal disclosure, and may coordinate volunteer activities by their members with no disclosure. They can work to get out the vote, often in coordination with other groups. The total effort of large membership organizations and unions on behalf of candidates is far greater than the value of their PAC contributions (Magleby 2004; Francia 2006; Boatright et al. 2006; Magleby and Patterson 2007). Organizations that are broadly involved in elections may have PACs, 527 committees, and 501(c) committees that are active in national elections, and other structures that are active in state elections. Some of this activity is disclosed to the FEC, some of it is partially disclosed to the IRS, but a growing portion is simply not disclosed. Thus, the relatively clean database of PAC contributions represents often only a fraction of total activity by specific groups.

Scholars have sought to develop databases to supplement FEC disclosure of PAC contributions. The Wisconsin Advertising Project tracks advertising by interest groups, candidates, and parties. To date, most published research has focused on candidate or party spending (Freedman, Franz, and Goldstein 2004), but data exist on group advertisements. Other scholars have begun to measure direct mail packages received by voters in key races (Monson and Oliphant 2007). The total spent on these packages is more difficult to trace, since mailing lists are typically developed by 501(c)3 non-profits that may be affiliates of interest groups and are not required to disclose their spending.

Data on state and local elections is even more difficult to obtain, for disclosure standards and enforcement vary considerably across the states (Malbin and Gais 1998; Wilcox 2005). Moreover, different regulations may lead groups to be active in different ways in different states, although the activity may be similar. This is unfortunate, because many interest groups establish relationships with state legislators that persist into the US Congress (Mutch 1999). The absence of good data on state interest group activity is especially troubling because variations in state laws provide an opportunity to see how interest groups behave under various regulatory constraints (see Hogan 2005 for an example of comparative state studies).

---

[3] The Center for Responsive Politics tracks contributions by employees of corporations and their families, although it is difficult to be certain which of these gifts are made in coordination with the company. Federal contribution records frequently do not include the principal place of business, and the same company may be listed many different ways in the database.

Endogeneity Issues

Estimating the effects of contributions on election outcomes or on policymaking is complicated because contributions are not exogenous to election outcomes or policy. The likelihood that a candidate will win influences contributions, but these contributions also influence the probability that the candidate will win. Groups may give to policymakers who they think are likely to advance their agenda, but these contributions may influence the probability that the policymaker will work on the group's issues. These endogeneity problems plague the study of political science more generally, but are especially troublesome in the study of groups in elections.

It might seem that endogeneity problems could be solved, since we have panel data on at least some group activity (PAC contributions) and panel data on election outcomes and congressional roll call voting (e.g., DW-NOMINATE scores) (Wawro 2001). But the interactions between candidates and interest groups can change rapidly over the course of an election cycle, and interactions between incumbents and interest groups can change over the course of a legislative session, involving multiple and ongoing signals (Magleby and Patterson 2007).

Moreover, the changing nature of national, state, and local regulations poses challenges to using longitudinal data. For example, during the 1980s contributions from a corporate PAC would probably represent much of the overall activity of the company. In the 1990s, however, many companies gave far more soft money to parties than they gave through their PACs, and many also began to bundle contributions more effectively. In the last decade, some company executives have given to 527 committees and especially to 501(c) groups, which have run extensive issue advocacy campaigns. Thus, comparing a contribution from the same PAC over thirty years might represent a varying portion of the company's total electoral involvement.[4]

THE DECISION TO BE ACTIVE IN ELECTIONS

Surveys of interest groups show that only 20–30 percent report being involved in elections (Schlozman and Tierney 1986; Heinz et al. 1993; Walker 1991; Nownes and Freeman 1998). These surveys may understate the level of activity, since tax-exempt

---

[4] For many companies, the PAC contribution may consistently represent most or all of their activity, but this will vary from company to company.

groups may be reluctant to admit electoral involvement. Nonetheless, it is clear that involvement in elections is the exception for interest groups.

Some groups are formed explicitly for the purpose of influencing elections. EMILY's List and the Christian Coalition did not choose to become involved in elections: they were formed to mobilize money and voters for candidates. The formation of election-oriented groups is theoretically similar to the formation of any group that seeks collective goods. But groups that focus primarily on elections are especially likely to receive support from networks of interest groups and party activists who subsidize collective action costs.

But why do existing groups decide to become involved in elections? Most scholars posit that the decision is a rational choice by group leaders, who consider the organization's policy goals and the likelihood that electoral activity would increase the chance of policy success. Changes in the political environment, in group resources, and in legal regulations may affect this decision. Case studies of the National Rifle Association, Sierra Club, and Microsoft show that changes in the political environment were central to their decision to be involved in elections (Cantor 1999; Shaiko 2005; K. Patterson and Singer 2007).

But there have been few quantitative studies of group decisions to enter elections. None of the surveys discussed above are panel surveys, allowing us to trace changing decisions over time. It is more generally difficult to define the universe of possible groups who might decide to be involved in elections, especially if this must include latent groups that form specifically for electoral activity.

Special attention has been focused on the decision by corporations to become involved in elections, and especially the decision to form a PAC (Andres 1985). The proliferation of studies on business PAC formation occurs because the universe of potential groups can be defined, and business decisions to contribute to candidates are generally assumed to be investments, either by individual companies or by industries in coalition (Snyder 1992). Most studies show that companies with Washington offices, with active lobbying presence, and in regulated industries are more likely to form PACs (Handler and Mulkern 1992; Hart 2001). Some corporate PACs are formed because rival companies have formed them (Gray and Lowery 1997).

The focus on corporate PAC formation has achieved perhaps more attention than it deserves, because corporate PACs vary considerably in size. In the 2006 election cycle, fourteen corporate PACs gave more than $1 million apiece to federal candidates, but one in five gave $5,000 or less.[5] The largest corporate and trade PACs clearly are significant electoral actors, but the formation of the smaller committees seems to defy conventional wisdom about collective action costs (Lowery et al. 2004.)

---

[5] Calculated among only those corporate PACs which made contributions in the 2006 election cycle. Nearly 20 percent of corporate PACs made no contributions during this cycle.

It must be remembered that PACs cost the parent company only limited resources, since they are primarily funded by contributions from employees. Internal company dynamics may help explain the formation of a PAC: an executive who works to launch a PAC might benefit within the company, and running a small corporate PAC does not require great effort, for a corporate culture that encourages executives to give to the PAC may assure a stable, if limited, flow of resources (Hart 2004). Moreover, broad business groups such as the Chamber of Commerce and especially BIPAC have urged companies to form PACs, as have Republican party leaders.

Choosing Electoral Strategies

Groups that choose to become involved in elections can choose from a variety of strategies and tactics. In this decision, groups consider their policy goals, resources that can be used in elections and constraints on the use of those resources, and the political environment, as well as other factors (Malbin et al. 2002).

Some organizations seek particularistic benefits that may be championed by Republicans or Democrats, and these types of organizations typically concentrate on building bridges to powerful incumbents. Corporations and trade associations are especially likely to seek rents from policymakers. Other groups need for one party or ideological coalition to have control of Congress in order to prevail, so they concentrate their resources on close elections where they can help a sympathetic candidate win. Still other groups seek to move the ideological center of their preferred party by working in intraparty nomination contests.

Group resources include money—from treasury funds, from wealthy members willing to make large contributions and from other members willing to give smaller sums to a PAC or candidate. They include size of the group's membership, and the willingness of those members to take cues from group leaders and perhaps to volunteer for candidates. They can include the group's reputation both in the general public and among the Washington, DC, political community.

Legal regulations help channel the use of these resources. Tax law forbids some types of non-profits from endorsing candidates, thus limiting the use of reputation. Any group that can raise money from its members can form a PAC and contribute to candidates, but large contributions from affluent members cannot be used to finance direct contributions or independent expenditures. In the 1990s, large contributions from enthusiastic members could be used to contribute soft money directly to political parties, and in the 2000s they have been allowed in the funding of issue advocacy campaigns. There are no limits on the ability of a group to communicate with its members, or mobilize volunteers for campaigns (Rozell and Wilcox 1999).

Groups face other types of restraints in using their resources. Corporations and trade associations are reluctant to do direct broadcast advertising for candidates, both because it might be counterproductive, and because they hope to sell products to members of both parties. Membership groups often have Democratic and Republican members, and overtly partisan activities might reduce membership.

But these constraints are conditioned by the political environment. Growing party unity and polarization affect the ability of groups with broad social agendas to be bipartisan, because every member votes to organize the chamber. Party leaders aggressively solicit contributions from groups, and frequently seek to deter their contributions to candidates of the other party (J. Berry and Wilcox 2007).

Group strategies are also affected by their organizational structure. Federated trade associations, membership associations, and unions frequently consider senti-ments of state and local affiliates in endorsements and contributions, thus limiting the ability of Washington staff to link contributing and lobbying (John Wright 1985; Bedlington 1999). Some groups have institutionalized decision-making struc-tures, while others leave these decisions to the group's leaders (Biersack, Herrnson, and Wilcox 1994). And the type of the group greatly affects strategic decisions.

Corporations and Trade Associations

Corporations and trade associations have concentrated primarily on contributing to candidates and parties. Collectively these groups have been the source of a majority of PAC contributions, and were the source of most soft money contribu-tions to parties as well. Most corporate and trade PAC giving is "service-induced," aimed at incumbent politicians with agenda power, regardless of whether they face close elections. In the 2006 election cycle, corporate PACs directed more than 80 percent of their contributions to Senate candidates and nearly 95 percent of their contributions to House candidates to incumbents. The concentration of contribu-tions to committee chairs and party leaders who face no serious electoral opposi-tion suggests that these donations are lobbying expenditures rather than an attempt to influence electoral outcomes.

Corporations also give through bundling, and lobbyists may host fundraisers for candidates or even chair a policymaker's personal PAC (J. Berry and Wilcox 2007). When companies were permitted to contribute to national political parties, some gave far more than their PAC totals. Studies have shown that the largest companies gave the most, although some smaller companies gave soft money even if they did not have a PAC (Appolonio and La Raja 2004).

Corporations and trade associations give to important policymakers in both parties, although many prefer GOP control of Congress. Between 1995 and 2006 these partisan and access considerations coincided, but many companies greatly increased their Democratic contributions when party control shifted. A few corporate PACs have invested more aggressively in pro-business challengers, but this has been mainly confined to private companies, companies whose agenda requires changing the ideological balance in Congress, and those where the lobbyist is not part of the decision-making process (Ferrara 1994; Wilcox 1989b).

Corporations and executives provided the majority of soft money contributions to national parties in the 1980s and 1990s. Some smaller companies gave soft money without sponsoring a PAC, but larger companies gave more overall. When soft money was banned, some executives (especially of privately held companies) gave to national 527 committees, but companies gave directly to state 527 committees (Franz 2008a). To date there has been little research seeking to predict which companies made these contributions.

Some companies have engaged in electioneering by contributing to 527 and 501(c)(6) organizations that run the ads. During the late 1990s, a group called Citizens for Better Medicare ran television ads defending the records of Republican incumbents on health care. The organization was funded primarily by drug companies, who understandably did not want the ads' tag line to say "This advertisement is brought to you by Pharma." Companies and executives in the 2008 campaign helped fund ads by the Chamber of Commerce and many other business groups. In the 2008 campaign, the Chamber's PAC gave less than $150,000 but its 501(c)(6) committee reported spending more than $35 million. There is no disclosure of who contributed to this latter effort.

Labor Unions

Unions fare considerably better under Democratic majorities than when the GOP has control of Congress, so they use all available tools to help maximize Democratic seat strength in Congress. This leads them to focus their efforts on close races, and to strategically shift their efforts from incumbents to challengers with the prevailing partisan winds (Eismeier and Pollock 1986). Unions PACs contribute primarily to Democratic candidates, although the amount contributed may depend on the member's support on key legislative votes such as free trade (D. Jackson and Engel 2003). When soft money was legal, they gave significant sums to national, state, and local party committees—often insisting that state and local committees prepare a plan of action to use the money effectively (Francia 2006). Unions continue to make soft money contributions to state and local parties in states that permit them, although there has been little research on this.

Unions endorse candidates, and communicate those endorsements to members. They coordinate voter mobilization efforts by their members. In 2006, more than 200,000 union members reportedly knocked on more than 8 million doors and made more than 30 million phone calls, and contacted "drop-off" voters as many as twenty-five times. They have engaged in substantial broadcast campaigns, including more than $35 million in 1994 targeting newly elected Republicans. They have sponsored their own 527 committees and helped to coordinate others (Weissman and Hassan 2006).

Membership Associations and Ideological Groups

Some membership organizations have PACs, 527 committees, and/or 501(c) organizations. They face two constraints on their political activities—most have members of both parties and thus seek to be at least somewhat bipartisan, and many are federated structures where endorsements may come from local or state chapters. These constraints have led most membership associations to support candidates of both parties, but with partisan polarization and tight margins in Congress, national staffs have gravitated toward one or the other party (Malbin et al. 2002).

Organizations such as the Sierra Club, the NRA, and National Right to Life endorse candidates of both parties, but increasingly their PAC contributions and especially their additional electoral mobilization has been focused on helping one party win control of the legislature (K. Patterson and Singer 2007; Cantor 1999). In the 2000s, many membership organizations have launched substantial issue advocacy campaigns on television, radio, and through mail and phone, and have also sought to register and mobilize voters. Often groups have worked together to coordinate advertising or mobilization efforts, in unofficial or official coalitions. They have also frequently been coordinated with party efforts.

Ideological groups generally seek to maximize the number of legislators who share their views. This leads to involvement in party primaries, where groups frequently recruit and train candidates, and/or spend substantial resources on helping candidates win. Club for Growth spent millions of dollars in the 2004 Pennsylvania Republican Senate primary, seeking to defeat moderate incumbent Arlen Specter. Specter survived that race, but just barely, and the Club for Growth continues to try to unseat Republican moderates. In general elections, ideological groups generally seek to maximize the seats of the party that is closest to their policy agenda. In the 1990s, the Christian Coalition distributed tens of millions of voter guides in conservative churches the Sunday before the election, and concentrated these heavily in competitive states or districts. Occasionally ideological groups will make contributions to candidates who are certain to lose, signaling stronger potential candidates of the availability of their support.

Changing Interest Group Strategies

Although much of the literature treats interest group strategies and tactics as standing decisions, over the past decade many groups have dramatically changed their strategies and tactics (Franz 2008a; Malbin et al. 2002). Existing research has consisted primarily of qualitative studies, for much of this activity is at best partially disclosed (Magleby and Patterson 2007; Magleby, Monson, and Patterson 2007b). But these studies provide enough cases of significant change to allow generalizations.

First, when changes in regulations permit new campaign activities by groups, some are "early adopters," others adopt after a few election cycles, and many groups are content to continue their current strategies. It therefore takes several election cycles after a regulatory change for the pattern of group activity to become clear. The gradual adoption of various strategies—forming PACs, giving soft money, or engaging in issue advocacy, might be conceived as the diffusion of innovation, but candidates, parties, and other groups frequently ask interest groups to adopt new strategies.

Second, the political environment has given groups an incentive to innovate in strategies and tactics. When the GOP took control of Congress in 1994, lobbyists for unions, environmental groups, feminist organizations, and other liberal cause groups had little access to policy negotiations. After the Democrats took control of Congress in 2006, many business groups became more active, especially as the possibility of a filibuster-proof Senate became possible.

Third, networks of activists have coordinated their efforts, allowing both for more rapid diffusion of innovation and also for specialization. These networks include partisans and large donors who have provided resources for new strategies. For example, the National Association for the Advancement of Colored People (NAACP) established a 501(c)4 in the 2000 campaign which sought to mobilize African American turnout. The effort was headed by an activist from the Women's Campaign Fund, and headquartered down the hall from Handgun Control, which gave frequent advice. The field effort received logistic help from the National Association of Letter Carriers, and the media campaign was coordinated with the Sierra Club. A single donor provided most of the funding.

Fourth, many organizations have begun to systematically assess the effectiveness of their efforts, often with sophisticated research designs. The American Federation of Labor–Congress of Industrial Organizations (AFL–CIO), Chamber of Commerce, and other large groups have commissioned surveys and focus groups to test the effectiveness of various campaign efforts. The NAACP asked Yale University political scientist Donald Green to evaluate their voter mobilization efforts (D. Green 2004). In 2005, a network of groups created a complicated experiment in microtargeting in Virginia's gubernatorial race. In some cases these evaluations are required by donors, but they also represent a sincere effort on the part of groups to develop the most effective strategies.

Finally, large changes in interest group strategies often occur at the time of changes in organizational leadership. The AFL–CIO, Sierra Club, Planned Parenthood, Handgun Control, BIPAC, and many other organizations adopted new strategies around the time that new leaders took control. Yet while leadership change may appear to explain new strategies, it may also be that new leaders are selected as organizations decide to adopt new strategies. Groups that select leaders more committed to electoral action may change as a result of that leadership in other ways, but little research has been done on this.

Do Interest Group Efforts Affect Elections or Policy?

Although interest groups have invested increasing amounts in electoral activities in recent years, scholars remain divided on whether and how these efforts influence elections or policies. Candidates, parties, and interest groups behave as if these efforts matter, but activists can be mistaken in assessing the efficacy of their actions. Moreover, the large stakes in control of government mean that groups may contribute or spend money even if the odds that it will make an impact are modest.

Impact on Elections

Although there have been many efforts to assess the impact of candidate spending on election outcomes, consensus remains elusive. Among incumbents, increased spending is associated with decreased vote share, because incumbents who face little competition do not bother to spend large sums. Among non-incumbents, spending is associated with increased vote share, but when polls show that these candidates might win it is far easier to raise money.

Scholars have used a variety of techniques to sort out causality, including efforts to control for challenger quality and spending in prior elections, and focusing on repeat challengers (where candidate quality could be considered constant) or close races (where the marginality of the race would be constant). These studies have produced mixed results, with most showing a positive effect of spending by both incumbents and challengers (A. Gerber 1998; Erikson and Palfrey 1998), but others finding smaller effects (Levitt 1994).

Studies may find mixed results because of differences in the way money is spent, because of varying costs across states and districts, and because other contextual factors matter (Imai 2005; Stratmann 2005; Ansolabehere and Gerber 1994; A. Gerber and Green 2000). But they also may get mixed results because they do not include spending by parties and interest groups in the campaign. In many Senate elections, interest group spending is vastly greater than candidate spending.

There have been a few quantitative studies of interest group efforts in campaigns. The AFL–CIO's effort to unseat newly elected House Republicans in 1996 was instrumental in the defeat of several targeted candidates and in reducing the vote share of others (Jacobson 1999). The limited studies of independent expenditure efforts have generally concluded that they do affect outcomes (Engstrom and Kenny 2002). But all quantitative efforts have been limited by the inability to measure most interest group activity. For example, Jacobson's study is unable to control for voter guide distribution by the Christian Coalition, or efforts by other groups in these elections. The inability to fully measure interest group efforts means that most studies of candidate spending are misspecified. This extends to other questions, such as whether spending educates voters (John Coleman and Manna 2000).

Qualitative studies have frequently concluded that interest group efforts have had a substantial impact on outcomes. The best of this work has done careful comparisons of several key races, and used the best available comparable measures of group activity (Magleby 2004). The large body of research conducted by the interest groups themselves might prove to be a useful source in future work, along with data from the Wisconsin Advertising project.

Impact on Policy

Despite the large body of research on the impact of PAC contributions on roll call voting, the results are decidedly mixed. A number of studies show modest effects (Stratmann 2005), but others find no effect (Ansolabehere, de Figueiredo, and Snyder 2003). Untangling endogeneity questions in the relationship between PAC contributions and roll call votes is difficult (Grenzke 1989). It may be that context matters, for most studies ignore competing PAC contributions and other factors. But these negative results should be reassuring, for the Federal Electoral Campaign Act limited the size of PAC contributions precisely to limit the impact of contributions on policymaking.

Many PAC directors publicly admit that they give to facilitate access by lobbyists, but studies have again shown mixed results. Interest groups allocate their contributions in a manner that is consistent with access seeking (Stratmann 1992). But although some have found that contributions do lead to increased access and attention from lawmakers (Langbein 1986; Hall and Wayman 1990; J. Wright 1989), others report that once organizational strength in the district is controlled, contributions do little to increase lobbying access (Hojnacki and Kimball 2001).

But studies of PAC contributions on roll call votes suffer from measurement issues on both sides of the equation. The limited contributions from a business PAC may be far less important than the various other ways that companies can give. It is impossible to trace all of the money flowing from a company into elections, but journalists who focus on single cases often show large sums flowing through diverse channels. In the Keating Five scandal, the Senate reprimanded California Democrat Alan Cranston for linking a contribution to a 501(c)3 organization that mounted a turnout campaign on behalf of his campaign (D. Thompson 1993). The real variation in total contributions is far greater than variation in PAC contributions, which are limited by law.

Moreover, final votes on legislation are not the only way that legislators can reward donors. A good deal of lobbying is aimed at determining which provisions are contained in legislation, and some members intervene at this stage while still voting against the final package. Groups may well care as much about which bills do not reach the floor as about voting on those that do advance (Bachrach and Baratz 1962). Contributions may be intended to induce legislators to intervene with the bureaucracy, as in the case of Charles Keating. We do not mean to assert that contributions *do* matter in these matters, only that studies of roll call votes ignore many other ways that money could influence policy.

Scholars who report that contributing does not influence policy must then explain why groups continue to give if it does not directly benefit them. Some suggest that contributions are merely consumption—an effort by a group to participate in the democratic process, although recent studies have contested this interpretation (Ansolabehere, de Figueiredo, and Snyder 2003; Sanford Gordon, Hafer, and Landa 2007). Others have argued that contributions represent a signal to policymakers of organizational strength (J. Wright 1990). Still other scholars have suggested that contributions may be intended to satisfy an organization's members (Hojnacki and Kimball 2001). Finally, some have suggested that PAC contributions are merely social niceties, like bringing a bottle of wine to dinner (Milyo 2002).

Small PAC contributions may well constitute consumption or social lubricants, but it is difficult to conceive of a corporate soft money contribution of more than $1 million as a fruit basket, or of 12 million phone calls as a signal. Sometimes a contribution is just a contribution, and in at least some cases these contributions are intended to increase access and to influence legislation, or to influence election outcomes to create a more sympathetic legislative environment.

THE FUTURE OF STUDIES OF INTEREST GROUPS
IN ELECTIONS

Changes in the activities of interest groups, donors, and political parties over the past several elections pose difficult conceptual issues. It might be useful to focus on coalitions of groups rather than on specific organizations. Over the past decade, interest groups have increasingly shared political intelligence and divided responsibilities. Recent studies using social network analysis have focused on shared contribution strategies or other formal ties (Robbins and Tsvetovat 2009; Mizruchi 1990). Of course, not all groups that support the same candidates are actively cooperating, even if they share a common issue agenda. The League of Conservation Voters has continued to do independent expenditures targeted against the "Dirty Dozen" legislators least friendly to environmental issues, and has not joined in larger collaborative efforts launched by the Sierra Club in part to keep their spending independent.

But the cooperation among unions and environmental, feminist, and other liberal groups has been extensive in the 2000s. Weissman and Hassan (2006) report that party leaders and heads of these organizations met to plan a strategy to offset Republican financial advantages in the 2004 election. They formed groups like America Coming Together, the Media Fund, and America Votes. Large donors (especially George Soros) helped to fund these efforts, which constituted a substantial portion of interest group activity in the 2004 campaign. Many of these 527 committees had disappeared by 2006.

The 527 committees could be conceived of as partisan networks, for they were organized at the explicit request of the Democratic National Committee chair, and similar organizations were formed by Republican activists after a signal from the Republican National Committee. But they are also networks of organizations, using their own best resources more effectively in coalition. And finally they are networks of donors, who have increasingly insisted on cooperation before writing large checks.

Recent studies have argued that interest groups have increasingly formed into party coalitions linked by donors (Koger, Masket, and Noel forthcoming). These may not be symmetrical, for the Democrats have long relied on interest groups to mobilize voters while Republicans performed the same activities through party committees. But thinking about donors may be a useful lens to understanding interest group activity. In 1994, Republican activists directed donors to the Christian Coalition as a mechanism to mobilize evangelical voters; in 2004, many of the same donors were asked to give to party efforts with frequently used direct mail packages virtually identical to those used by the Coalition. A small number of large donors financed the NAACP voter mobilization effort and Planned Parenthood's media campaign in 2000, as well as the 527 committees in 2004.

This suggests the utility of exploring more fully the party–group connection (Heaney, Chapter 30 in this volume). Party leaders have worked hard to encourage and shape interest group activities in elections, and have frequently pressured groups to alter their strategies. The interactions between candidates and groups have been modeled formally, but the relationships between parties and groups have game-theoretic aspects as well. But these relationships may be theoretically complex and difficult to untangle (Wilcox 2009).

More generally, to understand interest group activity in elections, it is important to move beyond studies of PAC contributions, although these remain useful for some questions. But with increasing portions of interest group campaign activity done outside the disclosure system, it becomes more difficult to answer the most basic questions. This makes it even more important for political scientists to more fully mine data from available studies that measure advertising and direct mail communications, and develop new measures of group activity.

Much of the best qualitative work has drawn on interviews with interest group activists and even on good journalistic studies, but there are reasons to sometimes doubt such accounts. The Christian Coalition claimed to mail electoral communications to 2 million members in the 1990s, but purchased postal permits for only 40,000 mailings. But without solid data, it is difficult to know whether and how much to discount their claims.

There is a need for Congress and the FEC to require full disclosure of all electoral activity, regardless of the type of committee that the interest group uses to conduct the activity. Better disclosure is critically important for scholars, for the media and civil society, and for democratic governance. Without better disclosure, it will be nearly impossible to answer the central questions about interest groups in elections.

CHAPTER 30

....

LINKING POLITICAL PARTIES AND INTEREST GROUPS

....

MICHAEL T. HEANEY

THE ongoing contest between political parties and interest groups is one of the epic struggles of American politics. Political parties strive to craft platforms that will draw the support of majorities of voters, while interest groups pressure the government to enact policies that advance the substantive agendas or ideological perspectives of narrower constituencies. In negotiating these tensions, parties and groups may work cooperatively or they may find themselves at cross-purposes. Groups sometimes prop up parties by supplying them with essential volunteers and financial resources, thus enabling a group to dictate key parts of a party's agenda. At other times, a group may find itself "captured" by a party such that the group must accept a party's weak efforts on its behalf because the other major party refuses (or is unable) to bargain for its loyalty. Occasionally, groups find themselves wedged between the parties in such a way that they become decisive on selected policy matters. On the other hand, groups may be on the sidelines sometimes as the major parties clash on the great issues of the day.

A substantial body of political science research explores the linkage between political parties and interest groups. However, the perspective that parties and groups are inextricably bound has not been a part of the dominant paradigm either in the study of parties or in the study of groups in recent years. Instead, scholars tend to divide the subjects according to scale, seeing parties as concerned primarily with the large-scale endeavor of winning elections and seeing interest groups as concentrating on the small-scale task of organizing narrower constituencies. For example, party scholars give scant attention to interest groups in their effort to understand how parties' electoral coalitions form and evolve over time. Similarly, interest group scholars generally ignore the role of parties in examining the logic of collective action among citizens or interest groups. Indeed, the study of interest groups and parties has not been unified under a common paradigm since the heyday of pluralism in the mid-twentieth century.

This chapter argues that political parties and interest groups are intricately and inextricably linked to one another for at least four reasons. First, parties and groups *co-evolve* with one another. Both entities emerged out of the protean factions that existed at the nation's founding. Since that time, parties and groups have grown, declined, and changed form in tandem and in response to one another. Second, parties and groups have attempted to *discipline* each other. Groups weigh into the electoral process to influence which kinds of candidates represent parties. Parties pressure groups to become the kinds of organizations that naturally support a party's cause. Third, interest groups and parties are key *brokers* within one another's networks and between other actors in the policy process. Interest groups may serve to bring actors in competing parties together or drive them apart. Parties may help to put some interest groups into key positions of influence or exclude others from decision making. Parties and groups cooperate and compete to intervene between citizens and lawmakers. Fourth, parties and groups serve to fashion interlinked political *identities* for individuals and organizations. Political loyalties are forged out of both ideological, partisan alignments and committed membership in groups. The bonds between organized labor and the Democratic Party, for example, or between Christian conservatives and the Republican Party, create, reinforce, and potentially break down group and party loyalties. Thus, the study of parties necessitates the study of groups, and vice versa; the political dynamics and behavior of both kinds of organizations ought to be part of a common research program.

This chapter begins by exploring *co-evolution, discipline, brokerage,* and *identity* as mechanisms that link parties and groups. It explains the theoretical perspective behind each of these mechanisms in the context of empirical research that documents their relevance to organizational strategies and behaviors. The chapter then considers how a research program that more explicitly addresses the party–group linkage might revise our understanding of parties and groups, and the nature of their dynamic interaction.

CO-EVOLUTION

At the time the Constitution was ratified in 1789, parties and interest groups did not exist in the United States in a form that we would recognize today (Hofstadter 1969). Americans were aware of parties and other factional groupings from their experience with the British system. Rather than embracing parties and groups, however, they sought to stymie these entities. Indeed, as James Madison (1982, 45) argued in *The Federalist,* No. 10, the Constitution itself was designed to root out the mischiefs of faction. In Madison's day, factions were loosely formed groupings of citizens, business leaders, politicians, and others, but not the well-organized machines that we encounter today (Yoho 1995). As a result, Americans were left to invent a system of parties and groups over time as political situations demanded them.

Just as species evolve, parties and interest groups change form over time. Parties and groups grow and contract in size, adopt and shed tasks, and serve different roles in the political system. For example, the presidencies of Andrew Jackson and Martin Van Buren helped to transform the Democratic Party from a disorganized faction into a mass organization designed to mobilize the electorate to win elections, thus imbuing the party with a new set of institutions and functions (Aldrich 1995). Interest groups similarly metamorphose as political conditions change. For example, between the 1950s and the 2000s, many interest groups transitioned from chapter-based, member-oriented federations to centralized organizations run by professional managers out of Washington, DC (Skocpol 2003). This move from membership to management fundamentally changed the nature of representation performed by groups. Thus, the basic form and function of parties and groups is contingent on the historical era in which they exist.

As parties and groups evolved over time, they adapted to one another. Parties sprung up to routinize electoral competition, groups developed to compensate for the deficits of parties, and then parties demanded new services from groups. The biological metaphor of co-evolution is apt to describe this process. In biology, co-evolution occurs when the development of one species influences the evolution of another species (J. Thompson 1994). For example, bees and flowers co-evolved as pollination by bees facilitated the sexual reproduction of flowers and as bees' morphology adapted to improve the transfer of pollen. Co-evolution may involve a variety of types of dynamics. One species may consume the resources of another species, driving it out of existence. Or, a species may enable the growth of another by performing a task it cannot accomplish alone. Regardless of how species impinge on one another, their mutual presence alters the evolutionary path taken by both species. Analogously, parties and interest groups co-evolve over time, continuously redefining the political roles played by one another.

The co-evolution of parties and groups is fostered by both competition and cooperation. Parties and groups compete with one another because they are alternative ways to represent interests. Citizens care about what the government does or does not do, but not necessarily about who pressures it to do so. If political parties represent citizens' interests, then citizens may be willing to give their loyalty and support to parties. But if political parties fail to deliver, then citizens may look elsewhere to get what they want from government. This process of searching for better representation leads to new organizations—and new types of organizations—that seek to mobilize interests.

An example of the co-evolution of parties and groups through competition for representation is provided by Elisabeth Clemens (1997) in *The People's Lobby*. Clemens argues that what we understand today as the modern "interest group" was created during the Progressive era by political entrepreneurs who were frustrated with party politics. These entrepreneurs sought to organize politics on the basis of issue—rather than on party, class, or some other factor—and struggled to realign political identities with key issues. They adopted the reviled model of corporate lobbying, but adapted it to promote its organizational legitimacy using preexisting political structures, such as labor unions, agricultural associations, and women's groups.

Clemens's argument has three parts. First, she notes that the major parties of the late nineteenth century had failed to address issues facing several well-organized constituencies. The subsequent failure of third parties (such as the Greenback Party and the Populist Party) to win control of government left issue activists increasingly doubtful of parties as an effective mechanism to achieve policy change. Second, Clemens argues that issue advocates resolved to create a new organizational form to pressure government directly on specific policies, rather than indirectly, through the party system. The "invention" of interest group politics came when the methods of corporate lobbying were adopted by grassroots organizations, such as the American Federation of Labor, the American Farm Bureau Federation, and the Women's Christian Temperance Union. Third, Clemens posits that nascent interest groups demonstrated their legitimacy by combining lobbying with other organizational models that were widely perceived as legitimate. Once their legitimacy was secured, these citizens' groups exploited opportunities to become directly involved in the politics of state legislatures and displaced some of the activities of political parties. Interest groups thus became a direct competitor to political parties for citizens' loyalties.

Clemens's analysis demonstrates that the interest group arose as a new "species" of political organization because of strategic responses to the party system. Interest groups evolved to compete with parties over policy. Alternatively, co-evolution may be driven by a desire for party–group cooperation. For example, parties and groups co-evolved as they mutually adapted to changes in campaign finance laws. The Federal Election Campaign Act (FECA) of 1971, its 1974 amendments, and the

Supreme Court's 1976 ruling in *Buckley v. Valeo* established a regime in which interest groups created Political Action Committees (PACs) and political parties came to rely on PAC contributions to finance electoral campaigns (Rozell, Wilcox, and Madland 2006, 80–112). As the campaign finance system evolved in the 1980s, 1990s, and 2000s, parties and groups responded by altering their strategies and structures.

The emergence of 527 organizations in the wake of the Bipartisan Campaign Reform Act (BCRA) of 2002 is an example of cooperatively driven co-evolution. 527s are a type of tax-exempt organization designed to influence the selection of candidates for public office. They are known for the section of the Internal Revenue Code that gives them their name (specifically, title 26, subtitle A, chapter 1, subchapter F, part VI, section 527). Section 527 is a longstanding provision of the tax code, but it became politically relevant only once soft money became controversial in the 1990s.

By the 1990s, the system of campaign finance established by FECA and *Buckley* had begun to break down (Malbin 2003, 7). Rather than directing their contributions exclusively through PACs, a norm developed of giving unregulated donations—known as "soft money"—directly to parties, thus creating an "unparalleled linkage between interest groups and parties" (Franz 2008b, 4). One of the major goals of BCRA was to place strict limitations on donations of soft money to parties. These limitations posed a problem for parties in the 2004 election because they had learned to rely on this source of financing (Ansolabehere and Snyder 2000). Consequently, their repertoire of electoral tactics catered to the peculiarities of soft money requirements (e.g., advertisements that do not explicitly advocate the election or defeat of a particular candidate). Funding through 527 organizations—which could still raise and spend soft money—became a method for the parties to adjust to BCRA's soft money limits. Parties thus required the creation of new 527 organizations to implement their campaign strategies, concomitantly requiring interest groups that would support these new organizations.

Seeking to jump on the 527 bandwagon in the 2000s, a number of prominent interest groups (such as the Service Employees' International Union (SEIU), the Sierra Club, and MoveOn.org) modified their organizational structures to add (or expand) an affiliated 527 (Boatright 2007, 5). While many 527s are affiliated with an established interest group, others were created as freestanding organizations intended to advance the overall fortunes of a specific party, such as America Coming Together (Democratic Party) and Progress for America (Republican Party). Still other 527s were designed with more specific missions. Swift Boat Veterans and POWs for Truth, for example, infamously was created in 2004 to debunk Democratic presidential nominee John Kerry's wartime record in Vietnam (Rutenberg 2004).

527 organizations differ significantly from preexisting political organizations. They are not party organizations in the sense that they do not nominate candidates

for public office. However, in some ways, they do appear to act collectively *as if* they are parties. Boatright (2007) notes that there are no bipartisan 527s and argues that within-party 527s cooperatively divide tasks into functional niches—advertising, voter mobilization, network brokerage, and candidate recruitment—much as would likely be done by a unified party organization. Skinner (2005) goes so far as to argue that 527s form "shadow parties" that "subcontract" services from parties. From the interest group perspective, freestanding 527s (e.g., the Media Fund, the November Fund) differ from typical groups in that they do not advocate for a specific policy agenda and are more ephemeral, often existing only for a single election cycle. Yet 527s are often attached to well-established interest groups with specific legislative goals in mind. So, are 527s parties, interest groups, or what?

The emergence of 527 organizations reflects a genuine hybridization of typical party and group forms (Chadwick 2007). Some 527s bear a strong resemblance to parties (e.g., America Coming Together, Progress for America), while others share a greater likeness with interest groups (e.g., SEIU Political Education and Action Fund, MoveOn.org Voter Fund). Within the framework of co-evolution, 527s can be viewed as a new species that has resulted from cooperation between parties and groups. Understanding 527s systematically ought to involve some combination of party and group theories.

The birth of a new species is no guarantee of its survival. Republicans found that 527s were less appealing to start with than did Democrats, with the majority of large 527s favoring Democratic interests (Boatright 2007). 527s were viewed by Democrats as a way to catch up with Republicans' money advantage in 2004. However, John Kerry's loss in the presidential election led many Democrats to question whether the reduced control suffered by outsourcing key party functions to 527s was a fair trade-off for their greater fundraising potential. Further, Barack Obama's fundraising prowess and robust grassroots campaign reduced the Democrats' need to rely heavily on 527s in 2008. As a result, 527s were considerably less visible players in the 2008 election than they were in 2004, with spending by the top ten 527s falling from $216 million to $73 million (Center for Responsive Politics 2008). Several influential organizations, such as MoveOn.org, severed their 527s altogether in 2008 (J. Jones and Rosado 2008).

Whether or not 527s will retain a strong presence in American elections remains to be seen. They may shortly become extinct. Or, they may remain abeyant in the toolkits of parties and groups, waiting for the right opportunity to arise. Republicans may seek to counter President Obama's expected fundraising advantage in 2012 by turning to 527s. Regardless of whether 527s ultimately flower or decay in the coming years, the case of 527 organizations provides insight on the nature of party–group co-evolution. This case might provide clues to whether the Democratic and Republican parties co-evolve differently with interest groups. Further, it may suggest how core activities of parties and groups—such as getting out the vote and lobbying—are changed by becoming more or less intertwined with a particular 527.

DISCIPLINE

Parties and interest groups tend to see each other as a means to an end. Each seeks to use the other to fulfill its own goals. Interest groups would like parties to install group agendas as part of their platforms and to carry out the group's wishes when in control of government (Clifton 2004). Parties would like interest groups to give money to support the party in the next election and to lend other resources to keep the party in power.

The effort of parties and groups each to get the other to do its bidding is an intense power struggle that has several faces. The so-called "first face of power" may show itself through threats or coercion (Bachrach and Baratz 1962). For example, a party may tell a group that it must support a party's presidential candidate or it will not be included in the set of groups consulted when the party controls the government. The second face of power is about setting the agenda so that some issues are actively considered and others are avoided (Bachrach and Baratz 1962, 1963). For example, if members of a particular interest group hold the balance of power on a party's platform committee, they may force the consideration of a controversial abortion provision that party leaders would prefer to avoid. The third face of power—sometimes called "hegemony"—is about influencing the language, preferences, and basic assumptions of politics such that challenging certain positions is seen as outside the rules of politics (Gaventa 1980; Gramsci 1992). For example, the American Medical Association may engender the belief that only medical doctors have the legitimate authority to make medical judgments about patient care, thus making a wide range of policy reform options unimaginable (Starr 1982).

The fourth face of power—sometimes called "discipline"—is the ability to influence what kinds of agents participate in politics (Digeser 1992; Foucault 1978). Discipline is about gaining control by putting agents into place that act in a certain way without having to be asked. For example, if the elected representatives of a party are all predisposed to support a group's point of view, then the need to influence the party to do the group's bidding is reduced—the party is inclined to do so anyway. Consider that Christian conservatives would not need to pressure the Republican Party to oppose abortion and same-sex marriage if all Republicans were already born-again Christians. Of course, this type of control is extraordinarily difficult to achieve. Parties and groups attempt to discipline each other, though their degree of success is highly limited.

Interest groups may attempt to discipline parties by trying to control who receives party nominations for key elected positions. Murakami (2008) points out that some interest groups form explicitly with the goal of selecting party nominees, with some groups operating as "party purity groups" and others serving as "big tent groups." Party purity groups work to make sure that a party's nominees satisfy an ideological or issue-based litmus test. The Club for Growth is the most prominent group of this type. Founded by Stephen Moore in 1999, the Club for Growth is a fiscally conservative interest group that helps to mount primary challenges against Republicans that it perceives to be too moderate, nicknaming them RINOs (Republicans In Name Only). EMILY's List and MoveOn.org are Democratic-leaning organizations that play a similar role on the political left. Big tent groups, on the other hand, press to keep a party closer to the ideological center. The Main Street Partnership is an example of a group that works to keep the Republican Party closer to the ideological center. It gives money to pragmatic, business-oriented candidates, often supporting the very candidates attacked by the purity groups.

The extent to which party purity groups and big tent groups are able to discipline the parties is not entirely clear. The Club for Growth gained attention through its efforts in a handful of House and Senate races. It unsuccessfully sought the ouster of moderate Senator Arlen Specter (Republican, Pennsylvania) when it supported Pat Toomey in the 2004 primary against him. However, the Club ultimately prevailed when Specter left the Republican Party in 2009 due to an anticipated Club-sponsored primary challenge in 2010. The Club helped to weaken moderate Senator Lincoln Chafee (Republican, Rhode Island) in the 2006 Republican primary, setting the stage for his defeat in the general election by Sheldon Whitehouse (Democrat, Rhode Island). Andy Harris, the Club's candidate for Congress from the first district of Maryland, defeated incumbent Congressman Wayne Gilchrist (Republican, Maryland) in the 2008 primary. Thus, the Club has demonstrated some success in knocking Republican moderates out of their seats. By posing a potential threat to incumbents who do not follow the party line, then, the existence of the Club may inspire some prospective and sitting Republican officeholders to stick more closely to "true conservative" principles. The Club may also make some legitimate claims to helping a much larger group of candidates for open seats win their primary races (Horrigan 2006). Because of these electoral practices, the Club and other party purity groups may be partly responsible for hastening the polarization of parties within Congress (Murakami 2008).

Interest group discipline over parties may take place less overtly through the conscious efforts of groups to select one nominee rather than another, but more subtly through the influence of institutions on how groups factor into the nominating process. Masket's (2007) study of partisanship in the California state legislature suggests that the existence of partisanship itself among officeholders may be partially dependent on how interest groups' participation in nominations is moderated by institutional rules. California's adoption of rules in 1914 that allowed candidates to cross-file their candidacies with multiple parties undermined the ability of interest groups to influence the nominating process. When cross-filing was banned in 1952, the role of groups—and partisanship—returned to the legislature.

Masket's (2007) work demonstrates that groups influence the selection of nominees, not only through their support of any one particular nominee, but through their very presence in the system. The case of California suggests that the behavior of parties is quite different when institutions permit interest groups a role in nominations than when they do not. While Masket's empirical study is specific to California, his approach could be applied to other states or to the American party system more generally. For example, the McGovern–Fraser reforms of the 1970s changed Democratic Party nominations to make them more open to interest groups (Atkeson and Maestas 2009; M. Cohen et al. 2008; Shafer 1983). These considerations suggest that groups play a more extensive role in disciplining parties than may be gleaned from their direct involvement in the specific elections.

Political parties may attempt to discipline interest groups by trying to control who holds key positions of leadership within groups. Since the selection of group leaders resembles a closed oligarchy more than an open democracy (Michels 1949; Truman 1951), parties have only limited means to shape group choices. One avenue of control is through the norm that lobbyists generally require experience working for (or serving as) members of Congress or the administration before they go to work for interest groups. Individual lobbyists usually identify as members of either the Democratic or the Republican Party, depending on the politician for which they served (Kersh 2002). Thus, in selecting their candidates and their staffs, the parties are selecting the universe of future lobbyists. The fact that lobbyists have to pass through the party's hands in this informal training process provides an opportunity to define the kind of lobbyists that they will eventually become. Surely, the nature of lobbying is much different than it would be if there were no expectations that lobbyists have previous congressional or administrative experience.

Parties could take a more direct approach and attempt to encourage interest groups to select certain kinds of people to work for them. The Republican Party undertook just such an effort during the late 1990s and early 2000s with its so-called "K Street Project," named after the street in downtown Washington, DC, where many large lobbying firms have their offices. When the Republican Party gained control of both houses of Congress in the 1994 election, it inherited a community of lobbyists that had grown up under forty continuous years of Democratic domination of the House of Representatives and thirty-four years of intermittent Democratic control of the Senate since 1954. Confessore (2003) reported that high-level officials within the Republican Party began to work strategically to change the composition of lobbyists on Capitol Hill. They worried that the Democratic-leaning pool of lobbyists would stymie their agenda. Instead, a more supportive cohort—chosen with the encouragement of Republican leaders—was thought to be necessary.

The idea that a new congressional and administrative majority demands a different cadre of lobbyists is not unusual. The notable feature of the K Street Project, however, was the effort by Republican leaders to exert *centralized* control over the shift to a Republican-leaning bias (J. Hacker and Pierson 2005; Loomis 2007). The efforts were coordinated on the K Street side by Republican lobbyist Grover Norquist, president of the interest group Americans for Tax Reform. On the Capitol Hill side, Majority Leader Tom DeLay (Republican, Texas) took the lead for the House and Republican Conference Chairman Rick Santorum (Republican, Pennsylvania) weighed in for the Senate. Together they set out to cajole interest groups to turn more reliably to Republican lobbyists.

Norquist, DeLay, and Santorum developed an array of tactics to promote an increased Republican presence on K Street. First, they created and published a database of lobbyists for interest groups that were supposed to favor Republicans, especially those in the business community (Chaddock 2003; Hamburger and Wallstein 2006). The database added some transparency to the lobbying process so that Republicans could see which groups had "properly" hired Republican lobbyists and which had not. The implication was that those groups out of compliance might not receive equal treatment from Republican officeholders. Second, they formed a coalition-like structure to coordinate lobbying and legislative activity. This coalition generally met once a week on Capitol Hill or K Street while Congress was in session (Confessore 2003; Loomis 2007). Coalition forces were marshaled more actively when must-pass legislative items were on the agenda. For example, when the party sought the passage of a new prescription drug benefit under Medicare, the group employed former Tom DeLay staff member Susan Hirschman to help round up support for the bill (Heaney 2006). This army of Republican lobbyists was summoned to lobby wavering legislators, thus creating an unusually circular chain: a congressional party actively pressured interest groups to, in turn, lobby Congress. Interest groups had become an informal part of the Republican Party's congressional whipping operation. Third, DeLay and others associated with the K Street Project are alleged to have put direct pressure on interest groups to choose specific leaders. For example, DeLay prodded the Electronics Industry Alliance to name a Republican president if it expected favorable treatment in the provisions of the Digital Millennium Copyright Act (Dubose and Reid 2004, 163–8). These efforts were aimed at cementing Republican congressional majorities, along with their control of the presidency and the Supreme Court, into an unchallengeable political machine (Confessore 2003; Hamburger and Wallstein 2006).

With a new Democratically dominant government having taken power in Washington in 2009, and with DeLay and Santorum having left Congress, the K Street Project quickly faded into political history. Projects that intentionally and centrally seek to dictate which agents join any system are problematic, as the power that creates such discipline is defused widely throughout society, rather than being concentrated in any one place (Foucault 1978). Nonetheless, the very attempt by Republicans to achieve such discipline is especially revealing of the way in which parties and interest groups think about each other, even if it is an extreme example. The K Street experiment demonstrates that parties see the leaders of groups as tools that they can use—and potentially manipulate—to achieve specific political ends.

BROKERAGE

Information and trust are scarce commodities in politics. For information to be valuable, it must be timely, relevant, and, sometimes, kept in confidence. For politicians to trust each other, they have to know that today's agreement will not be exploited tomorrow for political gain. Brokers are actors that stand between others who have difficulty sharing information and/or trusting one another (R. Gould and Fernandez 1989). Therefore, brokers are vital to passing on sensitive information. They may help to negotiate agreements between those who lack trust in one another. In essence, brokers help to grease the wheels of politics.

Brokerage is a key function of political parties and interest groups—one that assures that they remain closely linked to one another. Parties and groups engage in at least four different types of brokerage relationships. First, interest groups may act as brokers within party coalitions. Second, interest groups may act as brokers between parties, or between parties and other actors. Third, parties may act as brokers among interest groups, or between interest groups and other actors. Fourth, parties and interest groups may compete with one another to act as brokers among other actors. This section explores these four relational types and then considers the notion of "network" on which they are premised.

A first type of brokerage relationship exists when interest groups act as brokers within party coalitions. These relationships may manifest themselves over shorter or longer time horizons. For example, over a relatively short time, interest groups may broker within a party's factions to promote a particular piece of legislation. Heaney (2006) details how the Archer Medical Savings Account (MSA) Coalition—composed of a swath of socially and fiscally conservative interest groups— was vital to bringing conservative Republicans on board to support the passage of the Medicare Modernization Act (MMA) of 2003. The coalition brokered discussions of the Bush administration and big business conservatives who were pushing the MMA with the small business conservatives who objected to the Act's broad expansion of the Medicare entitlement. The coalition's strategy was to persuade small business conservatives that the victory, produced by adding Health Savings Accounts (HSAs—the name that replaced the original "MSAs") to the healthcare system more broadly, vastly outweighed any damage to conservatism caused by entitlement expansion. The coalition largely achieved its goal, almost singlehandedly persuading enough conservative members of the House to vote for the measure to ensure its passage.

Over the longer term, interest group brokerage within a party may lead to the creation of permanent structures and enduring relationships. Greenstone's (1969) analysis of the place of organized labor within the Democratic Party of the 1960s exemplifies such a long-term relationship. Organized labor—as represented by the AFL–CIO (American Federation of Labor–Congress of Industrial Organizations)– worked closely with the Democratic caucus during these years. The AFL–CIO aided Democratic campaigns through its Committee on Political Education. It helped to mobilize Democratic sympathizers at the local level by working through district-level organizations. Working within Congress, the AFL–CIO undertook a whipping function to aid the party in overcoming its collective action problems and in passing landmark social welfare legislation, including the creation of Medicare in 1965.

The extensive involvement of the AFL–CIO in Democratic Party affairs permitted "the labor movement [to] act as a disinterested broker among some of the Democrats' competing or suspicious leadership factions" (Greenstone 1969, 356). In recognizing labor's expanded role, Greenstone concurred with Schattschneider, who saw a breakdown in the delineation between parties and groups:

a shift in the locus of power or a revision of party functions may leave the formal structure untouched, or new structures may arise without being recognized as parts of the party system. Thus, pressure groups may become so partisan that they might properly be described as ancillary organizations of one or the other major parties. (Schattschneider 1956, 213)

Thus, groups' brokerage roles within parties extend from occasional, episodic interventions to a sustained integration between party and group functions.

A second type of brokerage relationship exists when interest groups act as brokers between the parties, or between parties and other actors. If interest groups are able to manage these relationships successfully, the parties may benefit greatly, since their high level of distrust with one another makes negotiations necessarily difficult. Simultaneously, interest groups may exploit this brokerage position to their own gain because they are uniquely able to play the parties off against one another (Burt 1992; Simmel 1955). The AARP (formerly the American Association of Retired Persons) seized exactly this opportunity when negotiating between the

Democratic and Republican parties during the debate over the MMA (Heaney 2006). AARP traditionally has aligned closely with the Democratic Party, which has been the party of the elderly in the United States since the New Deal. In recent years, AARP's membership has grown younger (into the fifties, rather than the sixties and seventies) and more affluent. This changing base is consistent with AARP becoming closer with the Republican Party. During the MMA debate, AARP played both sides of the aisle and helped to ensure passage of the measure in exchange for the key items that it wanted in the legislation.

While AARP found itself uniquely wedged between the parties during the MMA debate, this brokerage position is not a common one in which interest groups find themselves. Securing the genuine trust of both parties is a delicate balancing act in an era of polarized parties. Indeed, there are strong indications that AARP may have irreparably damaged its reputation among Democrats in supporting the Republican-sponsored Medicare law (Heaney 2007; Sinclair 2006). As AARP watched its brokerage position dissolve, it found itself as part of a trend. As Roof (2008, 85) points out, "there are few organizations with ties to both parties to help broker compromise and more groups trying to pull away from the center." A brokerage position of groups between the parties is highly desirable for both entities, but became more fleeting in the 1990s and 2000s.

A third type of brokerage relationship exists when parties act as brokers among interest groups, or between interest groups and other actors. Cohen et al. (2008, 34) argue that parties are, in their essence, coalitions of groups that have chosen to use parties as brokers between themselves and government. From this perspective, parties are often the best means for groups to extract the gains that they seek. To be good brokers, then, parties need to select the nominees that best balance the interests of members of the coalition. Changes in the nature of a party's nominees and the behavior of its officeholders may be explained in part by the evolution of the groups in the party's coalition. For example, the inclusion of the Christian Right in the Republican Party coalition in the late 1970s and early 1980s partially accounts for why nominees and officeholders—such as presidents Ronald W. Reagan and George H. W. Bush—advanced policies on abortion and school prayer that previously had not been a part of the Republican Party platform.

Parties may act as brokers between groups and candidates for elected office. For example, McCarty and Rothenberg (2000) maintain that the system of campaign finance through soft money contributions relied on the party to act as brokers between groups and candidates. The existence of a soft money regime allowed groups which had maxed out their hard money limits in contributions directly to candidates to instead donate soft money to parties. The implicit assumption of such donations was that parties would use these funds to the benefit of the candidates favored by the groups, thus making the party a conduit between the candidate and the group (Franz 2008b, 4).

A fourth type of brokerage relationship exists when parties and interest groups compete with one another to act as brokers among other actors. Hansen (1991) recounts the rise and fall of the farm lobby's access to Congress between 1919 and 1981 to illustrate this competition. Hansen explains that both groups and parties sought to provide Congress with the information that it needed to represent its constituents on agricultural policy. The political question at hand was whether member–constituent relations would be brokered by groups or parties. Hansen argues that Congress chose to rely on the broker that could provide information with a competitive advantage (e.g., greater efficiency and electoral value) that recurs over time. Hansen shows how groups snatched the brokerage role from parties by the early 1930s, but then began to lose it in the 1950s as agricultural interest groups gradually became more fragmented. When farm groups were trusted brokers, they were given access to key leaders and decision processes within Congress. However, as their brokerage value faded, farm groups were marginalized relative to other interests and parties were trusted to a greater extent to judge the political winds in agriculture. This study illuminates not only the competition between parties and groups for brokerage opportunities, but also how the advantages in carrying out brokerage evolve over time with economic, political, and organizational change.

The four types of brokerage relationships discussed here all presuppose the existence of a common political network shared by parties and groups. A map of this network would reveal what opportunities for brokerage are present and absent in the political system. Who is connected to whom? Who is disconnected from whom? What are the determinants of these connections and disconnections, such as alliances, ideology, and issues?

A number of scholars have investigated the "extended party networks" that unify parties and groups. These scholars assume that interest groups are integral parts of the network:

An interest group can be treated as part of a party network when its political actions are directed solely or largely on behalf of a given party. . . . We can expect a bias toward a single party to be true of many . . . organized interest groups whose lobbying efforts generally are spent disproportionately with one party. (M. Schwartz 1990, 5)

Working through informal networks—rather than as formal, hierarchical organizations—allows parties to adapt swiftly to local conditions in a decentralized system and to change as circumstances require it (J. Monroe 2001). Recent studies have used social network analysis to map the structure of these networks and to compare them with other kinds of alliance networks (M. Grossman and Dominguez 2009; Koger, Masket, and Noel 2009).

Moving toward a broader definition of parties and party networks—as has been done in the extended party network studies—significantly advances the understanding of the brokerage relations between parties and groups. Terming these networks "extended party networks," however, presupposes a dominant role for parties in these interactions and draws artificial boundaries along the lines of party affiliation. Much could be learned from instead treating network dominance and network boundaries as empirical questions: under what conditions are these networks dominated by parties or by groups? Are the networks split between the Democratic and Republican parties, or are there significant bipartisan (or third party) ties that define these relationships? Richer accounts of party–group brokerage would likely result from developing more nuanced and complete mappings of political networks structures.

IDENTITY

Individuals often have multiple political identities. They may strongly identify with a political party and orient their political life around that attachment (D. Green, Palmquist, and Schickler 2002). They may strongly identify with a group or groups (Truman 1951), potentially relating to their sex or gender, race or ethnicity, sexual orientation, occupation, class, religion, issue concerns, or some other basis. These identities may occasionally clash with one another. African American and homosexual identities may sometimes be incompatible within black associations (C. Cohen 1999). The poor may find themselves marginalized within an organization created to represent women (Strolovitch 2007). Or, identities may mutually reinforce one another, as labor union membership promotes loyalty to the Democratic Party, and vice versa (Finifter 1974).

When individuals show up to participate in group or party politics, they bring their other political identities with them. The organizational structures of parties and groups may even encourage them do to so. For example, the Democratic Party institutionalized special-interest caucuses for women, blacks, Hispanics, Asians, gays, liberals, and business at its 1980 national nominating convention (Jo Freeman 1986, 330). These caucuses developed institutional structures that prompt party activists to raise interest group considerations at the conventions and in their other dealings with the party. The Republican Party, in contrast, does not give special-interest groupings as prominent a place in its rules, diminishing the importance of its caucus-like structures, even though its ideological groupings are critical to its party politics (Jo Freeman 1986, 331). Thus, group and party identities have the potential to interact in ways that are consequential to both organized entities, while the nature of this interaction may vary from party to party and from group to group.

This section explores four types of interaction between partisan and group identities. First, parties' identities may be a source of conflict within groups, as was the case for many antiwar organizations opposed to the US–Iraq War of 2003 on. Second, group identities may be a source of conflict within parties, as with the experience of the Log Cabin Republicans within the Republican Party and African Americans within the Democratic Party. Third, partisan identities may strengthen groups, as Democratic affiliations did for the National Organization for Women. Fourth, group identities may facilitate the success of a party, as the Republican Party benefited from the insurgency of Christian Right activists in its ranks in the early to mid-1990s. While these four types of interaction by no means exhaust the range of possibilities, they provide clues to the major implications of interacting identities.

When individuals bring their partisan identifications to group politics, conflicts may erupt. Heaney and Rojas (2007) consider the antiwar movement as an instance of this kind of conflict. Antiwar activists disagree fervently about whether there is a place for Democratic partisanship within the peace movement. Some movement partisans attempt to use the antiwar cause to advantage the Democratic Party and to use the party to end the Iraq War. These actors form a kind of "party in the street." In contrast, other activists are concerned that partisan commitments lead to an unending series of compromises that dilute group goals. A principal division within the antiwar movement, then, is over the degree to which it should connect with the Democratic Party. This division is managed to some degree by segregating activists into organizations that favor one philosophy on party politics or another (e.g., the Democratic-leaning activists may join MoveOn.org, while non-partisans join World Can't Wait). Yet, peak antiwar interest groups, such as United for Peace and Justice, find that their ranks are split among the partisans and the non-partisans. These splits potentially complicate intra-organizational decision making, such as the degree to which the organization should engage in lobbying versus civil disobedience.

When individuals bring their group identifications to party politics, they may disagree with the party's goals or believe that their interests are insufficiently represented within the party. The Log Cabin Republicans, for instance, have struggled to fit within the Republican Party, though the fit has been incongruous. Founded locally in California in 1978 and established nationally in 1993, Log Cabin exists to represent gay and lesbian Republicans (Rimmerman 2000). While members of the organization are firmly supportive of Republican causes, such as lower taxes and strong national defense, they come into conflict with the party line on same-sex marriage. At times, Log Cabin's disagreements with the national party were strong enough that the organization withheld its endorsement of the party's presidential nominee (Kuhr 2005).

African American organizations, in contrast, may believe that they are not in a strong position to deny their endorsement to the Democratic Party even when they disagree with the party. The structure of national politics is such that African American interests feel "captured" by the party, since the Republican Party is an untenable alternative representative (Frymer 1999). Democratic leaders have, at times, attacked blacks as a way to court white support, as was the case in 1992 when Democratic presidential candidate Bill Clinton famously rebuked rap artist Sister Soulja during a Rainbow Coalition-sponsored event. These kinds of incidents occur because the electorally incentivized "party system exacerbates rather than diminishes the marginalized position of a historically disadvantaged minority group" (Frymer 1999, 6). It remains to be seen whether (and, if so, how) the election of Democrat Barack Obama as the first African American president of the United States will fundamentally and permanently alter the relationship between black interest groups and the Democratic Party.

Party and group identities need not be in conflict but, instead, strengthen and reinforce each other. For example, a close identification of many women with the Democratic Party contributed to the institutionalization of the National Organization for Women (NOW) from a social-movement-like entity to a traditional interest group. The Democratic Party's adoption in 1980 of a rule guaranteeing equal representation for women and men at all levels within the party's organization—a provision championed by NOW leaders—helped NOW to grow in strength (Barakso 2004, 78). By 1988, leaders of NOW and other women's interest groups could claim to be "insiders" within the party, even if tensions remained with the party's mainstream (Hershey 1993; Jo Freeman 1988). NOW's victories within the Democratic Party demonstrated the efficacy of the organization and emboldened its supporters at a time when the Equal Rights Amendment had been derailed and abortion rights were widely under attack.

Group identifications of a party's members at times may prove to be enormously beneficial to a party. The 1994 congressional elections are a case where the activities of Christian Right interest groups (such as the Christian Coalition of America) are widely believed to have contributed significantly to the Republican takeover of Congress. In a comparison of Christian Right activism in four states (Virginia, Minnesota, Washington, and Texas), Green, Rozell, and Wilcox (2001) uncover a conditional relationship between the Christian Right and Republican success. They find that when the Christian Right was able to generate general support in the electorate, it was helpful to Republican fortunes. However, when the Christian Right sparked divisions within the party, it tended to undercut Republican candidates. The potential benefits of Christian Right involvement were contingent on tactics: "confrontation among party activists was harmful while consolidation was helpful to the party" (J. Green, Rozell, and Wilcox 2001, 418). Thus, while parties are not uniformly boosted by strong group identification within their ranks, under the right conditions, a party may be able to harness a group's enthusiasm to promote its cause.

The intersection of partisan and group identities, in general, has the potential to alter party and group politics in unexpected ways. Parties and groups are competing objects of loyalty for individuals. They may motivate a party's members to act against the interests of the party, as when the Log Cabin Republicans failed to endorse George W. Bush's reelection in 2004 (Kuhr 2005). Or, groups may motivate people to promote the fortunes of a party, as when antiwar interest groups and their supporters worked to elect a Democratic Congress in 2006 (Heaney and Rojas 2007). Party and group identities spark new organizational dynamics by altering constituencies, raising new issues, and motivating members to act out in instances where they might have otherwise remained quiescent. Party and group scholarship, therefore, could benefit from expanded investigations of activist attachments to a wider range of organizations in the political system.

DIRECTIONS FOR FUTURE RESEARCH

The broad range of scholarship referenced in this chapter indicates that party–group linkages certainly have not been ignored by political scientists. At the same time, however, this topic has not been a well-defined subject of inquiry by either party scholars or group scholars, as has been the case for subjects such as interest group coalitions and party primaries. The topic has been investigated almost entirely as a series of case studies, often designed with another question in mind. However, if parties and groups are essentially and systematically linked, as I have argued here, then this subject is worthy of more focused attention by party and group scholars alike. Scholars should conduct research that moves toward the creation of general theories about how groups and parties relate. In this concluding section, I suggest a number of avenues for future inquiry that would help to build more systematic knowledge about the ties between parties and groups.

A first direction for research would be more attention to historical interactions between parties and groups. One approach would be to search for co-evolution in places where evolution has already been observed. For example, Skocpol (2003) describes the evolution of interest group structures from a membership orientation to a management orientation, but does not highlight how this shift related to the party system. It is reasonable to suspect that some of the evolution observed by Skocpol was caused by, or had effects on, evolving party structures. Another approach would be to devote closer scrutiny to seemingly banal modifications in party and group organizational structures. While changing structures may, at first glance, appear to be organizational minutia, they may be signals of important adjustments of organizations to other political actors in their environments.

A second research direction would be greater attention to the personal biographies of party and group activists. Such research would be revealing both for how parties and groups discipline each other and for how partisan and group identities become interconnected. While an activist may have a relatively small set of organizational affiliations or responsibilities at any one point in time—for example, she may hold only one office at a time—her entire career may reflect a broader range of affiliations. This history may suggest deeper linkages between partisan and group identities and how each entity shapes other's agents. One-time party officials become the presidents of interest groups. Yesterday's grassroots activists are tomorrow's political candidates. Systematic investigations of these career paths and vacancy chains would illuminate further the origins of party–group connections.

A third area where more research is needed is on party–group networks. Both party and group scholars began to follow this path more aggressively in the mid- to late 2000s, but the current state of work on this topic has only begun to scratch the surface of what is possible. More care should be given to the measurement of network ties, specification of network boundaries, and analysis of multiplex relationships. While much work to date has focused on networks generated through campaign contributions and spending, the wider range of party–group ties—among lobbyists and activists, for example—would be revealing of the subtle and profound connections between parties and groups.

A final suggestion is to seek greater unification between the analysis of party and group coalitions. Studies of interest group coalitions almost entirely ignore the role that parties play in encouraging or blocking collective action within these entities (cf. Hojnacki 1997; Hula 1999), though recent events sparked by the K Street Project hint that such interventions may be very important. Research on party coalitions pays greater attention to the place of groups (cf. M. Cohen et al. 2008), but more often as "groupings" within parties (e.g., women, fiscal conservatives) than as formal organizations (e.g., NOW, Americans for Tax Reform). Perhaps it is time to move beyond thinking about "interest group coalitions" and "party coalitions" toward the analysis of "political coalitions," which, no doubt, must include both group and partisan elements in order to be viable.

In conclusion, a new agenda for party–group linkages should recognize that the subject requires more than merely "more research." Instead, a reorientation to the topic is required. The study of parties and groups has become unnecessarily polarized, with most scholars in these fields identifying either with parties or with groups, but rarely with both. Many of the seminal works in the field—such as Key (1942), Truman (1951), and Schattschneider (1960)—did not draw the bright lines that are often drawn today. Much of the division may be attributed to academic specialization and professional institutionalization. The cost has been to leave systematic lacunae in the theories of parties and groups. A first corrective step would be for every investigation on parties to address "What is the group angle to this question?" and vice versa. A second corrective step would be to envision the boundaries between parties and groups to be more porous than is currently assumed. Parties and groups are not so radically different from one another. Rather, they are marginally variant institutions that set out to accomplish similar ends for the citizens that constitute them. Embracing these steps would move scholarship productively toward a more dynamic view of parties and groups, thus creating new explanations for organizational change, the shifting structure of party–group networks, and the evolution of personal political identities.

References

ABERBACH, JOEL. 2005a. The Political Significance of the George W. Bush Administration. *Social Policy and Administration*, 39/2: 130–49.

—— 2005b. Transforming the Presidency: The Administration of Ronald Reagan. In *The Reagan Presidency: Assessing the Man and his Legacy*, ed. Paul Kengor and Peter Schweizer. Lanham, Md.: Rowman & Littlefield.

—— 2008. Supplying the Defect of Better Motives? The Bush II Administration and the Constitutional System. In *The George W. Bush Legacy*, ed. Colin Campbell, Bert A. Rockman, and Andrew Rudalevige. Washington, DC: CQ Press.

—— and PETERSON, MARK A. 2005. *The Executive Branch*. New York: Oxford University Press.

ABRAMOWITZ, ALAN. 1988. Explaining Senate Election Outcomes. *American Political Science Review*, 82/2: 385–403.

—— 2008. Don't Blame Primary Voters for Polarization. *The Forum*, 5/4.

—— McGLENNON, JOHN, and RAPOPORT, RONALD. 1983. Party Activists in the United States: A Comparative State Analysis. *International Political Science Review/Revue Internationale de Science Politique*, 4: 13–20.

—— and SAUNDERS, KYLE L. 1998. Ideological Realignment in the U.S. Electorate. *Journal of Politics*, 60 (Aug.), 634–52.

—— —— 2005. Why Can't We All Just Get Along? The Reality of a Polarized America. *The Forum*, 3/2.

—— —— 2008. Is Polarization a Myth? *Journal of Politics*, 70: 542–55.

—— and STONE, WALTER J. 1984. *Nomination Politics: Party Activists and Presidential Choice*. New York: Praeger.

—— —— 2006. The Bush Effect: Polarization, Turnout, and Activism in the 2004 Presidential Election. *Presidential Studies Quarterly*, 36/2: 141–54.

ABRAMSON, J. 1998. Political Parties Channel Millions to "Issue" Attacks. *New York Times*, Oct. 14, A1.

ABRAMSON, PAUL R., ALDRICH, JOHN H., BLAIS, ANDRÉ, DIAMOND, MATHEW, ABRAHAM DISKIN, INDRIDASON, INDRIDI, LEE, DANIEL, and LEVINE, RENAN. Forthcoming. Comparing Strategic Voting under FPTP and PR. *Comparative Political Studies*.

—— —— PAOLINO, PHIL, and ROHDE, DAVID W. 1995. Third-Party and Independent Candidates in American Politics: Wallace, Anderson, and Perot. *Political Science Quarterly*, 53: 495–522.

—— —— RICKERSHAUER, JILL, and ROHDE, DAVID W. 2007. Fear in the Voting Booth: The 2004 Presidential Election. *Political Behavior*, 29: 197–220.

—— —— and ROHDE, DAVID W. 1987. Progressive Ambition among United States Senators: 1972–1988. *Journal of Politics*, 49/1: 3.

ACHEN, CHRIS. 1992. Social Psychology, Demographic Variables and Linear Regression: Breaking the Iron Triangle in Voting Research. *Political Behavior*, 14: 195–211.

ADAMANY, DAVID. 1984. Political Parties in the 1980s. In *Money and Politics in the United States*, ed. Michael J. Malbin. Chatham, NJ: Chatham House.

ADAMS, JAMES and EZROW, LAWRENCE. 2009. Why Do European Parties Represent? How Western European Parties Represent the Policy Preferences of Opinion Leaders. *Journal of Politics*, 71/1: 1–18.

—— MERRILL, SAMUEL, III, and GROFMAN, BERNARD. 2005. *A Unified Theory of Party Competition*. New York: Cambridge University Press.

AGRANOFF, ROBERT. 1972. Introduction: The New Style Campaigning. In *The New Style in Election Campaigns*, ed. Robert Agranoff. Boston: Holbrook.

AINSWORTH, SCOTT H. 1993. Regulating Lobbyists and Interest Group Influence. *Journal of Politics*, 55: 41–56.

—— 1997. The Role of Legislators in the Determination of Interest Group Influence. *Legislative Studies Quarterly*, 22: 517–33.

—— 2002. *Analyzing Interest Groups: Group Influence on People and Policies*. New York: W. W. Norton.

—— and SENED, ITAI. 1993. Interest Group Entrepreneurs: Entrepreneurs with Two Audiences. *American Journal of Political Science*, 37: 834–66.

AISTRUP, JOSEPH A. 1993. State Legislative Party Competition: A County-Level Measure. *Political Research Quarterly*, 46: 433–46.

AKARD, PATRICK J. 1992. Corporate Mobilization and Political Power: The Transformation of U.S. Economic Policy in the 1970s. *American Sociological Review*, 57: 597–615.

AKERLOF, GEORGE A. 1997. Social Distance and Social Decisions. *Econometrica*, 65: 1005–27.

ALDRICH, JOHN H. 1983a. A Downsian Spatial Model with Party Activism. *American Political Science Review*, 77 (Dec.), 974–90.

—— 1983b. A Spatial Model with Party Activists: Implications for Electoral Dynamics. *Public Choice*, 41: 63–100.

—— 1993. Rational Choice and Turnout. *American Journal of Political Science*, 37 (Feb.), 246–78.

—— 1995. *Why Parties? The Origins and Transformation of Political Parties in America*. Chicago: University of Chicago Press.

—— 1999. Political Parties in a Critical Era. *American Politics Quarterly*, 27 (Jan.), 9–32.

—— 2000. Southern Parties in State and Nation. *Journal of Politics*, 62: 643–70.

—— 2003. Electoral Democracy during Politics as Usual—and Unusual. In *Electoral Democracy*, ed. Michael B. MacKuen and George Rabinowitz. Ann Arbor: University of Michigan Press.

—— and BATTISTA, JAMES S. COLEMAN 2002. Conditional Party Government in the States. *American Journal of Political Science*, 46: 164–72.

—— BERGER, MARK M., and ROHDE, DAVID W. 2002. The Historical Variability in Conditional Party Government, 1877–1994. In *Party, Process, and Political Change in Congress: New Perspectives on the History of Congress*, ed. David Brady and Matthew D. McCubbins. Palo Alto, Calif.: Stanford Press.

—— and BIANCO, WILLIAM. 1992. A Game-Theoretic Model of Party Affiliation of Candidates and Office-Holders. *Mathematical and Computer Modeling*, 16: 103–16.

—— and LEE, DANIEL. n.d. A Multi-dimensional Model That Implies Duverger's Law. Unpub. paper. Duke University.

—— and McGinnis, Michael D. 1989. A Model of Party Constraints on Optimal Candidate Positions. *Mathematical and Computer Modelling*, 12: 437–50.

—— and Rohde, David W. 1997–8. The Transition to Republican Rule in the House: Implications for Theories of Congressional Politics. *Political Science Quarterly*, 112 (Winter), 541–67.

—— —— 2000a. The Republican Revolution and the House Appropriations Committee. *Journal of Politics*, 62 (Feb.), 1–33.

—— —— 2000b. The Consequences of Party Organization in the House: The Role of the Majority and Minority Parties in Conditional Party Government. In *Polarized Politics: Congress and the President in a Partisan Era*, ed. Jon Bond and Richard Fleisher. Washington, DC: CQ Press.

—— —— 2001. The Logic of Conditional Party Government: Revisiting the Electoral Connection. In *Congress Reconsidered*, ed. Lawrence C. Dodd and Bruce I. Oppenheimer. 7th edn. Washington, DC: CQ Press.

—— —— 2009. Congressional Committees in a Continuing Partisan Era. In *Congress Reconsidered*, ed. Lawrence C. Dodd and Bruce I. Oppenheimer. 9th edn. Washington, DC: CQ Press.

—— —— and Tofias, Michael W. 2008. One D is Not Enough: Measuring Conditional Party Government, 1887–2002. In *Party, Process, and Political Change in Congress: Further New Perspectives on the History of Congress*, ed. David Brady and Matthew D. McCubbins. Palo Alto, Calif.: Stanford Press.

—— et al. Forthcoming. Comparing Strategic Voting under FPTP and PR. *Comparative Political Studies*.

Alesina, Alberto. 1988. Credibility and Policy Convergence in a Two-Party System with Rational Voters. *American Economic Review*, 78: 796–806.

—— and Rosenthal, Howard. 1995. *Partisan Politics, Divided Government, and the Economy*. New York: Cambridge University Press.

—— and Spear, Stephen. 1988. An Overlapping Generations Model of Electoral Competition. *Journal of Public Economics*, 37: 359–79.

Alexander, Herbert E. 1984. *Financing Politics*. Washington, DC: CQ Press.

Allen, Michael Patrick. 1992. Elite Social Movement Organizations and the State: The Rise of the Conservative Policy-Planning Network. *Research in Politics and Society*, 4: 87–109.

—— and Campbell, John L. 1994. State Revenue Extraction from Different Income Groups: Variations in Tax Progressivity in the United States, 1916 to 1986. *American Sociological Review*, 59: 169–86.

Alt, James and Lassen, David Dreyer. 2003. The Political Economy of Institutions and Corruption in American States. *Journal of Theoretical Politics*, 15/3: 341–65.

—— and Lowry, Robert C. 1994. Divided Government, Fiscal Institutions, and Budget Deficits: Evidence from the States. *American Political Science Review*, 88: 811–28.

Altshuler, Alan and Luberoff, David. 2003. *Mega-Projects*. Washington, DC: Brookings Institution.

Altschuler, Glenn C. and Blumin, Stuart M. 2000. *The Rude Republic: Americans and their Politics in the Nineteenth Century*. Princeton: Princeton University Press.

Alvarez, Michael R., Canon, David T., and Sellers, Patrick. 1995. *The Impact of Primaries on General Election Outcomes in the U.S. House and Senate*. Social Science Working Paper 932. California Institute of Technology.

AMENTA, EDWIN, BONASTIA, CHRIS, and CAREN, NEAL. 2001. US Social Policy in Comparative and Historical Perspective: Concepts, Images, Arguments, and Research Strategies. *Annual Review of Sociology*, 27: 213–34.

—— and YOUNG, MICHAEL P. 1999. Democratic States and Social Movements. *Social Problems*, 57: 153–68.

AMERICAN NATIONAL ELECTION STUDIES. 2005. *The 1948–2004 ANES Cumulative Data File.* Dataset. Stanford University and the University of Michigan.

AMERICAN POLITICAL SCIENCE ASSOCIATION. 1950. *Toward a More Responsible Two-Party System: A Report of the Committee on Political Parties. American Political Science Review*, 44/3, pt. 2, Suppl.

American Whig Review. 1852. The Pittsburg Platform. 94: 366–74.

ANBINDER, TYLER. 1992. *Nativism and Slavery: The Northern Know Nothings and the Politics of the 1850s.* New York: Oxford University Press.

ANDERSON, KRISTI. 1979. *The Creation of a Democratic Majority, 1928–1936.* Chicago: University of Chicago Press.

ANDRES, GARY. 1985. Business Involvement in Campaign Finance: Factors Influencing the Decision to Form a Corporate PAC. *PS: Political Science & Politics*, 18 (Spring), 215–19.

ANNEN, KURT. 2003. Social Capital, Inclusive Networks, and Economic Performance. *Journal of Economic Behavior and Organization*, 50: 449–63.

ANSOLABEHERE, STEPHEN, DE FIGUEIREDO, JOHN M., and SNYDER, JAMES M., JR. 2003. Why Is There So Little Money in U.S. Politics? *Journal of Economic Perspectives*, 17/1: 105–30.

—— and GERBER, ALAN. 1994. The Mismeasure of Campaign Spending: Evidence from the 1990 U.S. House Elections. *Journal of Politics*, 56/4: 1106–18.

—— HANSEN, JOHN MARK, HIRANO, SHIGEO, and SNYDER, JAMES M., JR. 2007a. The Incumbency Advantage in U.S. Primary Elections. *Electoral Studies*, 26/3: 660–8.

—— HIRANO, SHIGEO, and SNYDER, JAMES M., JR. 2007b. What Did the Direct Primary Do to Party Loyalty in Congress? In *Party, Process, and Political Change in Congress*, ed. David W. Brady and Matthew D. McCubbins, ii. Stanford, Calif.: Stanford University Press.

—— —— —— and UEDA, MICHIKO. 2006. Party and Incumbency Cues in Voting: Are They Substitutes? *Quarterly Journal of Political Science*, 1: 119–37.

—— and IYENGAR, SHANTO. 1995. *Going Negative: How Political Advertisements Shrink and Polarize the Electorate.* New York: Free Press.

—— and SNYDER, JAMES M., JR. 2000. Soft Money, Hard Money, Strong Parties. *Columbia Law Review*, 100/3: 598–619.

—— —— and STEWART, CHARLES, III. 2001a. The Effects of Party and Preferences on Congressional Roll-Call Voting. *Legislative Studies Quarterly*, 26: 533–72.

—— —— —— 2001b. Candidate Positioning in U.S. House Elections. *American Journal of Political Science*, 45/1: 136–59.

—— —— and TRIPATHI, MICKY. 2002. Are PAC Contributions and Lobbying Linked? New Evidence from the 1995 Lobby Disclosure Act. *Business and Politics*, 4/2: 131–55.

APPOLONIO, D. E. and LA RAJA, RAYMOND J. 2004. Who Gave Soft Money? The Effects of Interest Group Resources on Political Contributions. *Journal of Politics*, 66/4: 1134–54.

ARANSON, PETER H. and ORDESHOOK, PETER C. 1972. Spatial Strategies for Sequential Elections. In *Probability Models of Collective Decision Making*, ed. Richard G. Niemi and Herbert F. Weisberg. Columbus, Ohio: Charles E. Merrill.

ARGERSINGER, PETER. 1992. *Structure, Process and Party: Essays in American Political History.* Armonk, NY: M. E. Sharpe.

—— 2001. The Transformation of American Politics: Political Institutions and Public Policy, 1865–1910. In *Contesting Democracy: Substance and Structure in American Political History, 1775–2000*, ed. Byron E. Shafer and Anthony J. Badger. Lawrence: University Press of Kansas.

ARNOLD, DOUGLAS R. 1982. Overtilled and Undertilled Fields in American Politics. *Political Science Quarterly*, 97: 91–103.

ARNOLD, PERI E. 2003. Effecting a Progressive Presidency: Roosevelt, Taft, and the Pursuit of Strategic Resources. *Studies in American Political Development* (Spring), 61–81.

ARROW, KENNETH J. 1951. *Social Choice and Individual Values*. New York: Wiley.

ARTERTON, CHRISTOPHER F. 1982. Political Money and Party Strength. In *The Future of American Political Parties: The Challenge of Governance*, ed. Joel L. Fleishman. New York: American Assembly.

ASHWORTH, JOHN. 1983. *"Agrarians" and "Aristocrats": Party Political Ideology in the United States, 1837–1845*. Cambridge: Cambridge University Press.

ASIAN COMMUNITY DEVELOPMENT CORPORATION. 2008. Target Population: Chinatown Neighborhood and Community. <http://www.asiancdc.org/>. Accessed Aug. 5, 2008.

ATKESON, LONNA RAE. 1998. Divisive Primaries and General Election Outcomes: Another Look at Presidential Campaigns. *American Journal of Political Science*, 42/1: 257.

—— McCANN, JAY A., RAPOPORT, RONALD B., and STONE, WALTER J. 1996. Citizens for Perot: Activists and Voters in the 1992 Presidential Campaign. In *Broken Contract? Changing Relationships between Citizens and the Government in the United States*, ed. Stephen C. Craig. Boulder, Colo.: Westview Press.

—— and MAESTAS, CHERIE D. 2009. Meaningful Participation and the Evolution of the Reformed Presidential Nominating System. *PS: Political Science and Politics*, 42/1: 59–64.

AUSTEN-SMITH, DAVID. 1993. Information and Influence. *American Journal of Political Science*, 37: 799–833.

—— and WRIGHT, JOHN R. 1994. Counteractive Lobbying. *American Journal of Political Science*, 38: 25–44.

BACH, STANLEY and SMITH, STEVEN S. 1988. *Managing Uncertainty in the House of Representatives*. Washington, DC: Brookings Institution.

BACHRACH, PETER. 1967. *The Theory of Democratic Elitism: A Critique*. Boston: Little, Brown.

—— and BARATZ, MORTON S. 1962. Two Faces of Power. *American Political Science Review*, 56/4: 947–52.

—— —— 1963. Decisions and Nondecisions. *American Political Science Review*, 57: 632–42.

BAI, MATT. 2007. *The Argument: Billionaires, Bloggers, and the Battle to Remake Democratic Politics*. New York: Penguin Press.

BAILEY, MICHAEL. 2004. The (Sometimes Surprising) Consequences of Societally Unrepresentative Contributors on Legislative Responsiveness. *Business and Politics*, 6/3, art. 2.

—— 2005. Bridging Institutions and Time: Creating Comparable Preference Estimates for Presidents, Senators, and Justices, 1946–2002. Paper presented at the Annual Meeting of the American Political Science Association, Washington, DC.

BAIN, YANJIE. 1997. Bringing Strong Ties Back In: Indirect Ties, Network Bridges, and Job Searches in China. *American Sociological Review*, 62: 366–85.

BAKER, JEAN. 1998. *Affairs of Party: The Political Culture of Northern Democrats in the Mid-Nineteenth Century*. New York: Fordham University Press.

BALLA, STEVEN J. and WRIGHT, JOHN R. 2001. Interest Groups, Advisory Committees, and Congressional Control of the Bureaucracy. *American Journal of Political Science*, 45: 799–812.

BANASZAK, LEE ANN. 1996. *Why Movements Succeed or Fail*. Princeton: Princeton University Press.

BANNER, JAMES. 1970. *To the Hartford Convention: The Federalists and the Origins of Party Politics in Massachusetts*. New York: Alfred A. Knopf.

BANNING, LANCE. 1978. *The Jeffersonian Persuasion: Evolution of a Party Ideology*. Ithaca, NY: Cornell University Press.

BARABASI, ALBERT-LASZLO. 2005. *Linked*. New York: Penguin.

BARAKSO, MARYANN. 2004. *Governing NOW*. Ithaca, NY: Cornell University Press.

BARBER, BENJAMIN R. 1984. *Strong Democracy: Participatory Politics for a New Age*. Berkeley: University of California Press.

BARDWELL, KEDRON. 2002. Money and Challenger Emergence in Gubernatorial Primaries. *Political Research Quarterly*, 55/3: 653–67.

BARILLEAUX, RYAN and KELLEY, CHRISTOPHER. 2005. Ronald Reagan, Iran-Contra, and Presidential Power. In *The Reagan Presidency: Assessing the Man and his Legacy*, ed. Paul Kengor and Peter Schweizer. Lanham, Md.: Rowman & Littlefield.

BARON, DAVID. 1994. Electoral Competition with Informed and Uninformed Voters. *American Political Science Review*, 88/1: 33–47.

BARONE, MICHAEL. 1990. *Our Country*. New York: Free Press.

BARRILLEAUX, CHARLES J. 1986. A Dynamic Model of Partisan Competition in the American States. *American Journal of Political Science*, 30: 822–40.

—— 1997. A Test of the Independent Influences of Electoral Competition and Party Strength in a Model of State Policy-Making. *American Journal of Political Science*, 41: 1462–6.

—— 2000. Party Strength, Party Change and Policy-Making in the American States. *Party Politics*, 6: 61–73.

—— HOLBROOK, THOMAS, and LANGER, LAURA. 2002. Electoral Competition, Legislative Balance, and American State Welfare Policy. *American Journal of Political Science*, 46: 415–27.

BARTA, CAROLYN. 1993. *Perot and his People*. Fort Worth, Tex.: Summit Group.

BARTELS, LARRY M. 1988. *Presidential Primaries and the Dynamics of Public Choice*. Princeton: Princeton University Press.

—— 2000. Partisanship and Voting Behavior, 1952–1996. *American Journal of Political Science*, 44 (Jan.), 35–50.

—— 2002. Beyond the Running Tally. *Political Behavior*, 24/2: 117–50.

—— 2006. What's the Matter with What's the Matter with Kansas? *Quarterly Journal of Political Science*, 1/2: 201–26.

BASS, HAROLD F. 2004. George W. Bush, Presidential Party Leadership Extraordinaire? *The Forum*, 2/4, art. 6.

BAUER, RAYMOND A., POOL, ITHIEL DE SOLA, and DEXTER, LEWIS A. 1963. *American Business and Public Policy: The Politics of Foreign Trade*. New York: Atherton Press.

BAUMGARTNER, FRANK R., BERRY, JEFFREY M., HOJNACKI, MARIE, KIMBALL, DAVID C., and LEECH, BETH L. 2009. *Lobbying and Policy Change: Who Wins, Who Loses, and Why*. Chicago: University of Chicago Press.

—— GRAY, VIRGINIA, and LOWERY, DAVID. Forthcoming. Congressional Influence on State Lobbying Activity. *Political Research Quarterly*.

—— and JONES, BRYAN D. 1993. *Agendas and Instability in American Politics.* Chicago: University of Chicago Press.

—— and LEECH, BETH L. 1996. The Multiple Ambiguities of "Counteractive Lobbying." *American Journal of Political Science,* 40: 521–42.

—— —— 1998. *Basic Interests: The Importance of Groups in Politics and in Political Science.* Princeton: Princeton University Press.

—— —— 2001. Issue Niches and Policy Bandwagons: Patterns of Interest Group Involvement in National Politics. *Journal of Politics,* 63: 1191–213.

—— and MAHONEY, CHRISTINE. 2008. The Two Faces of Framing: Individual-Level Framing and Collective Issue-Definition in the EU. *European Union Politics,* 9/3: 435–49.

—— and WALKER, JACK L., JR. 1988. Survey Research and Membership in Voluntary Associations. *American Journal of Political Science,* 32: 908–28.

BAUMGARTNER, JODY. 2000. *Modern Presidential Electioneering: An Organizational and Comparative Approach.* Westport, Conn.: Praeger.

BEACHLER, DONALD. 2004. Ordinary Events and Extraordinary Times: The 2002 Congressional Elections. In *Transformed by Crisis: The Presidency of George W. Bush and American Politics,* ed. Jon Kraus, Kevin J. McMahon, and David M. Rankin. New York: Palgrave Macmillan.

BEARD, CHARLES A. 1929. *The American Party Battle.* New York: Macmillan.

BECK, PAUL A. 1977. Partisan Dealignment in the Postwar South. *American Political Science Review,* 71 (June), 477–96.

—— 1979. The Electoral Cycle and Patterns of American Politics. *British Journal of Political Science,* 9 (Apr.), 129–56.

—— 1984. The Electoral Cycle and Patterns of American Politics. In *Controversies in American Voting Behavior,* in Richard G. Niemi and Herbert F. Weisberg. Washington, DC: CQ Press.

—— 1988. Incomplete Realignment: The Regan Legacy for Parties and Elections. In *The Reagan Legacy: Promise and Performance,* ed. Charles O. Jones. Chatham, NJ: Chatham House.

BECKER, GARY S. 1991. A Note on Restaurant Pricing and Other Examples of Social Influence on Price. *Journal of Political Economy,* 99: 1109–16.

BEDLINGTON, ANNE H. 1999. The Realtors Political Action Committee: Covering All Contingencies. In *After the Revolution: PACs, Lobbies and the Republican Congress,* ed. Robert Biersack, Paul S. Herrnson, and Clyde Wilcox. New York: Allyn and Bacon.

BELAND, DANIEL and WADDAN, ALEX. 2007. Conservative Ideas and Social Policy in the United States. *Social Policy and Administration,* 41/7: 768–86.

BENDA, PETER M. and CHARLES H. LEVINE. 1988. Reagan and the Bureaucracy: The Bequest, the Promise, and the Legacy. In *The Reagan Legacy: Promise and Performance,* ed. Charles O. Jones. Chatham, NJ: Chatham House.

BENNEDSEN, MORTEN and FELDMANN, SVEN E. 2006. Informational Lobbying and Political Contributions. *Journal of Public Economics,* 90: 631–56.

BENSON, LEE. 1961. *The Concept of Jacksonian Democracy: New York as a Test Case.* Princeton: Princeton University Press.

BENTLEY, ARTHUR F. 1908. *The Process of Government.* First edn. Chicago: University of Chicago Press.

—— 1951. *The Process of Government.* Chicago: University of Chicago Press.

—— 1967. *The Process of Government.* New edn. Cambridge, Mass.: Harvard University Press.

BERKMAN, MICHAEL. 2001. Legislative Professionalism and the Demand for Groups: The Institutional Context of Interest Population Density. *Legislative Studies Quarterly*, 26/4: 661–79.

BERMAN, LARRY. 1990. Looking Back on the Reagan Presidency. In *Looking Back on the Reagan Presidency*, ed. Larry Berman. Baltimore: Johns Hopkins University Press.

BERNHARDT, DANIEL and INGBERMAN, DANIEL. 1985. Candidate Reputations and the Incumbency Effect. *Journal of Public Economics*, 27: 47–67.

BERNSTEIN, JONATHAN. 1999. The Expanded Party in American Politics. Ph.D. dissertation, University of California, Berkeley.

BERNSTEIN, ROBERT A. 1977. Divisive Primaries Do Hurt: U.S. Senate Races, 1956–1972. *American Political Science Review*, 71/2: 540–5.

BERRY, JEFFREY M. 1977. *Lobbying for the People*. Princeton: Princeton University Press.

—— 1978. On the Origins of Public Interest Groups: A Test of Two Theories. *Polity*, 10: 379–97.

—— 1985. *Feeding Hungry People: Rulemaking in the Food Stamp Program*. New Brunswick, NJ: Rutgers University Press.

—— 1993. Citizen Groups and the Changing Nature of Interest Group Politics in America. *Annals of the American Academy of Political and Social Science*, 528: 30–41.

—— 1997. *The Interest Group Society*, 3rd edn. New York: Longman.

—— 1999. *The New Liberalism: The Rising Power of Citizen Groups*. Washington, DC: Brookings Institution.

—— with ARONS, DAVID F. 2003. *A Voice for Nonprofits*. Washington, DC: Brookings Institution.

—— PORTNEY, KENT E., LISS, ROBIN, SIMONCELLI, JESSICA, and BERGER, LISA. 2006. *Power and Interest Groups in City Politics*. Cambridge, Mass.: Rappaport Institute for Greater Boston, Kennedy School of Government, Harvard University.

—— —— and THOMSON, KEN. 1993. *The Rebirth of Urban Democracy*. Washington, DC: Brookings Institution.

—— and WILCOX, CLYDE. 2007. *The Interest Group Society*, 4th edn. New York: Pearson Longman.

BERRY, WILLIAM D. and CANON, BRADLEY C. 1993. Explaining the Competitiveness of Gubernatorial Primaries. *Journal of Politics* 55/2: 454.

—— RINGQUIST, EVAN J., FORDING, RICHARD C., and HANSON, RUSSELL L. 1998. Measuring Citizen and Government Ideology in the American States, 1960–93. *American Journal of Political Science*, 42: 327–48.

BERTELLI, ANTHONY MICHAEL and WENGER, JEFFREY. Forthcoming. Demanding Information: Think Tanks and the U.S. Congress. *British Journal of Political Science*.

BEST, SAMUEL J. and TESKE, PAUL. 2002. Explaining State Internet Sales Taxation: New Economy, Old-Fashioned Interest Group Politics. *State Politics and Policy Quarterly*, 2/1: 37–51.

BETH, RICHARD. 2005. "Entrenchment" of Senate Procedure and the "Nuclear Option" for Change: Possible Proceedings and the Implications. CRS Report RL32843. Washington, DC: United States Congressional Research Service.

BEYERS, JAN. 2002. Gaining and Seeking Access: The European Adaptation of Domestic Interest Associations. *European Journal of Political Research*, 41: 585–612.

—— and KERREMANS, BART. 2007. Critical Resource Dependencies and the Europeanization of Domestic Interest Groups. *Journal of European Public Policy*, 14/3: 460–81.

BIBBY, JOHN F. 1980. Party Renewal in the National Republican Party. In *Party Renewal in America*, ed. Gerald M. Pomper. New York: Praeger.

—— 1990. Party Organization at the State Level. In *The Parties Respond: Changes in the American Party System*, ed. L. Sandy Maisel. Boulder, Colo.: Westview Press.

—— 2002. State Party Organizations: Strengthened and Adapting to Candidate-Centered Politics and Nationalization. In *The Parties Respond: Changes in American Parties and Campaigns*, ed. L. Sandy Maisel. Boulder, Colo.: Westview Press.

—— and HOLBROOK, THOMAS. 1996. Parties and Elections. In *Politics in the American States: A Comparative Analysis*, ed. Virginia Gray and Herbert Jacob. Washington, DC: CQ Press.

—— and MAISEL, LOUIS SANDY. 2003. *Two Parties—or More? The American Party System*. 2nd edn. Boulder, Colo.: Westview Press.

BIERSACK, ROBERT, HERRNSON, PAUL S., and WILCOX, CLYDE. 1994. *Risky Business? PAC Decisionmaking in Congressional Elections*. Armonk, NY: M. E. Sharpe.

—— —— —— 1999. *After the Revolution: PACs, Lobbies, and the Republican Congress*. Boston: Allyn and Bacon.

BINDER, SARAH A. 1997. *Minority Rights, Majority Rule: Partisanship and the Development of Congress*. New York: Cambridge University Press.

—— LAWRENCE, ERIC D., and MALTZMAN, FORREST. 1999. Uncovering the Hidden Effect of Party. *Journal of Politics*, 61: 815–31.

—— and SMITH, STEVEN S. 1997. *Politics or Principle? Filibustering in the United States Senate*. Washington, DC: Brookings Institution.

BINKLEY, WILFRED. 1943. *American Political Parties: Their Natural History*. New York: Alfred A. Knopf.

BLACK, DUNCAN. 1958. *The Theory of Committees and Elections*. New York: Cambridge University Press.

BLACK, EARL and BLACK, MERLE. 2002. *The Rise of Southern Republicans*. Cambridge, Mass.: Harvard University Press.

BLACK, GORDON S. 1972. A Theory of Political Ambition: Career Choices and the Role of Structural Incentives. *American Political Science Review*, 66/1: 144–59.

BLACK, MERLE. 2004. The Transformation of the Southern Democratic Party. *Journal of Politics*, 66: 1001–17.

BLAISDELL, DONALD C. 1957. *American Democracy under Pressure*. New York: Ronald Press Co.

BOATRIGHT, ROBERT G. 2007. Situating the New 527 Organizations in Interest Group Theory. *The Forum*, 5/2, art. 5.

—— MALBIN, MICHAEL J., ROZELL, MARK J., and WILCOX, CLYDE. 2006. Interest Groups and Advocacy Organizations after BCRA. In *The Election After Reform: Money, Politics, and the Bipartisan Campaign Reform Act*, ed. Michael J. Malbin. Lanham, Md.: Rowman & Littlefield.

BOEHMKE, FREDERICK J. 2002. The Effect of Direct Democracy on the Size and Diversity of State Interest Group Populations. *Journal of Politics*, 64: 827–44.

—— 2008. The Initiative Process and the Dynamics of State Interest Populations. *State Politics and Policy Quarterly*, 8/4: 362–83.

BOGDANOR, VERNON. 1995. *The Monarchy and the Constitution*. Oxford: Oxford University Press.

BOIES, JOHN L. 1989. Money, Business, and the State: Material Interests, Fortune 500 Corporations, and the Size of Political Action Committees. *American Sociological Review*, 54 (Oct.), 821–33.

BONASTIA, CHRIS. 2000. Why Did Affirmative Action in Housing Fail during the Nixon Era? *Social Problems*, 47: 523–42.

BOND, JON R., COVINGTON, CARY, and FLEISHER, RICHARD. 1985. Explaining Challenger Quality in Congressional Elections. *Journal of Politics*, 47/2: 510.

—— and FLEISHER, RICHARD. 1990. *The President in the Legislative Arena*. Chicago: University of Chicago Press.

BORN, RICHARD. 1981. The Influence of House Primary Election Divisiveness on General Election Margins, 1962–76. *Journal of Politics*, 43/3: 640.

BOROWIAK, CRAIG. 2007. Accountability Debates: The Federalists, the Anti-Federalists, and Democratic Deficits. *Journal of Politics*, 69/4: 998–1014.

BOSSO, CHRISTOPHER. 1987. *Pesticides and Politics*. Pittsburgh: University of Pittsburgh Press.

—— 2005. *Environment, Inc.: From Grassroots to Beltway*. Lawrence: University Press of Kansas.

BOWLING, CYNTHIA J. and FERGUSON, MARGARET R. 2001. Divided Government, Interest Representation, and Policy Differences: Competing Explanations of Gridlock in the Fifty States. *Journal of Politics*, 63: 182–206.

BOX-STEFFENSMEIER, JANET M. and JONES, BRADFORD S. 2004. *Event History Modeling: A Guide for Social Scientists*. New York: Cambridge University Press.

—— DE BOEF, SUZANNA, and LIN, TSE-ᵐIN. 2004. The Dynamics of the Partisan Gender Gap. *American Political Science Review*, 98 (Aug.), 515–28.

BRACE, PAUL and JEWETT, AUBREY. 1995. The State of State Politics Research. *Political Research Quarterly*, 48: 643–81.

—— SIMS-BUTLER, KELLIE, ARCENEAUX, KEVIN, and JOHNSON, MARTIN. 2002. Public Opinion in the American States: New Perspectives Using National Survey Data. *American Journal of Political Science*, 46: 173–89.

BRADY, DAVID W. and BUCKLEY, KARA. 1995. Health Care Reform in the 103rd Congress: A Predictable Failure. *Journal of Health Politics, Policy, and Law*, 2: 447–57.

—— and BULLOCK, CHARLES S., III. 1980. Is there a Conservative Coalition in the House? *Journal of Politics*, 42: 549–59.

—— —— 1985. Party and Factions within Legislatures. In *Handbook of Legislative Research*, ed. Gerhard Loewenberg, Samuel C. Patterson, and Malcolm E. Jewell. Cambridge, Mass.: Harvard University Press.

—— FEREJOHN, JOHN, and HARBRIDGE, LAUREL. 2008. Polarization and Public Policy: A General Assessment. In *Red and Blue Nation?* ed. Pietro Nivola and David Brady, ii. Washington, DC: Brookings Institution; Stanford, Calif.: Hoover Press.

—— and HAN, HAHRIE. 2006. Polarization Then and Now: A Historical Perspective. In *Red and Blue Nation?* ed. Pietro Nivola and David Brady, i. Washington, DC: Brookings Institution; Stanford, Calif.: Hoover Press.

—— and VOLDEN, CRAIG. 1998. *Revolving Gridlock: Politics from Carter to Clinton*. Boulder, Colo.: Westview Press.

—— —— 2006. *Revolving Gridlock: Politics from Carter to George W. Bush*. Boulder, Colo.: Westview Press.

BRADY, HENRY E. and JOHNSTON, RICHARD. 1987. What's the Primary Message: Horse Race or Issue Journalism? In *Media and Momentum: The New Hampshire Primary and Nomination Politics*, ed. Gary R. Orren and Nelson W. Polsby. Chatham, NJ: Chatham House.

BRAMS, STEVEN J. 1978. *The Presidential Election Game*. New Haven: Yale University Press.

BRANTON, REGINA P. 2008. The Importance of Race and Ethnicity in Congressional Primary Elections. *Political Research Quarterly*, 20/10.

BRASHER, HOLLY and LOWERY, DAVID. 2006. The Corporate Context of Lobbying Activity. *Business and Politics*, 8: 1–23.

—— —— and GRAY, VIRGINIA. 1999. State Lobby Registration Data: The Anomalous Case of Florida (and Minnesota Too!). *Legislative Studies Quarterly*, 4/2: 303–14.

BREWER, MARK D. 2005. The Rise of Partisanship and the Expansion of Partisan Conflict within the American Electorate. *Political Research Quarterly*, 58 (June), 219–29.

—— and STONECASH, JEFFREY M. 2007. *Split: Class and Cultural Divides in American Politics*. Washington, DC: CQ Press.

—— —— 2009. *The Dynamics of American Political Parties*. New York: Cambridge University Press.

BREWER, PAUL R. and DEERING, CHRISTOPHER J. 2005. Interest Groups, Campaign Fundraising, and Committee Chair Selection: House Republicans Play "Musical Chairs." In *The Interest Group Connection: Electioneering, Lobbying, and Policymaking in Washington*, ed. Paul S. Herrnson, Ronald G. Shaiko, and Clyde Wilcox. Washington, DC: CQ Press.

BRINIG, MARGARET F., HOLCOMBE, RANDALL G., and SCHWARTZSTEIN, LINDA. 1993. The Regulation of Lobbyists. *Public Choice*, 77: 377–84.

BROACH, GLEN T. 1972. A Comparative Dimensional Analysis of Partisan and Urban–Rural Voting in State Legislatures. *Journal of Politics*, 34: 905–21.

BRODER, DAVID S. 1972. *The Party's Over: The Failure of Politics in America*. New York: Harper & Row.

—— and JOHNSON, HAYNES. 1997. *The System: The Death of Health Care Reform in 1993–1994*. Boston: Little, Brown.

BROUSSARD, JAMES. 1978. *The Southern Federalists, 1800–1816*. Baton Rouge: Louisiana State University Press.

BROWN, CLIFFORD W., POWELL, LYNDA W., and WILCOX, CLYDE. 1995. *Serious Money*. New York: Cambridge University Press.

BROWN, ROBERT D. 1995. Party Cleavages and Welfare Effort in the American States. *American Political Science Review*, 89: 23–33.

BROWNE, WILLIAM P. 1990. Organized Interests and their Issue Niches: A Search for Pluralism in a Policy Domain. *Journal of Politics*, 52: 477–509.

—— 1995. *Cultivating Congress: Constituents, Issues, and Interests in Agricultural Policymaking*. Lawrence: University Press of Kansas.

—— and PAIK, WON K. 1993. Beyond the Domain: Recasting Network Politics in the Postreform Congress. *American Journal of Political Science*, 37: 1054–78.

BRUCE, HAROLD R. 1927. *American Parties and Politics*. New York: Henry Holt.

BUCHANAN, WILLIAM. 1962. Federal Aid to Education on the Conservative–Liberal Scale. *Annals of the American Academy of Political and Social Science*, 344: *Conservatism, Liberalism, and National Issues* (Nov.), 55–64.

—— 1963. *Legislative Partisanship: The Deviant Case of California*. Berkeley: University of California Press.

Buckley v. Valeo, 424 U.S. 1 (1976).

BUDGE, IAN, KLINGEMANN, HANS-DIETER, VOLKENS, ANDREA, BARA, JUDITH, and TANENBAUM, ERIC. 2001. *Mapping Policy Preferences: Estimates for Parties, Electors, and Governments 1945–1998*. Oxford: Oxford University Press.

—— ROBERTSON, DAVID, and HEARL, DEREK. 1987. *Ideology, Strategy, and Party Change: Spatial Analyses of Post-War Election Programmes in 19 Democracies*. Cambridge: Cambridge University Press.

BUELL, EMMETT H., JR. 2000. The Changing Face of the New Hampshire Primary. In *In Pursuit of the White House 2000: How We Choose Our Presidential Nominees*, ed. William G. Mayer. New York: Chatham House.

BUENKER, JOHN. 1973. *Urban Liberalism and Progressive Reform.* New York: Scribner.

BURDEN, BARRY C. 2001. The Polarizing Effects of Congressional Primaries. In *Congressional Primaries and the Politics of Representation*, ed. Peter F. Galderisi, Marni Ezra, and Michael Lyons. Lanham, Md.: Rowman & Littlefield Publishers.

—— 2004. Candidate Positioning in U.S. Congressional Elections. *British Journal of Political Science*, 34/2: 211–27.

—— 2005. Minor Parties and Strategic Voting in Recent U.S. Presidential Elections. *Electoral Studies*, 23: 603–18.

—— 2007. Ballot Regulations and Multiparty Politics in the States. *PS: Political Science and Politics*, 40: 669–73.

BURNHAM, WALTER DEAN. 1965. The Changing Shape of the American Political Universe. *American Political Science Review*, 59 (Mar.), 7–28.

—— 1969. The End of American Party Politics. *Trans-Action*, 7(Dec.), 12–22.

—— 1970. *Critical Elections and the Mainsprings of American Politics.* New York: W. W. Norton.

—— 1982. *The Current Crisis in American Politics.* New York: Oxford University Press.

—— 1986. Periodization Schemes and "Party Systems": The "System of 1896" as a Case in Point. *Social Science History*, 10 (Fall), 263–74.

—— 1996. Realignment Lives: The 1994 Earthquake and its Implications. In *The Clinton Presidency: First Appraisals*, ed. Colin Campbell and Bert A. Rockman. Chatham, NJ: Chatham House.

BURNS, JAMES MACREGOR. 1963. *The Deadlock of Democracy: Four Party Politics in America.* Englewood, Cliffs, NJ: Prentice-Hall.

BURRELL, BARBARA C. 1994. *A Woman's Place Is in the House: Campaigning for Congress in the Feminist Era.* Ann Arbor: University of Michigan Press.

BURRIS, VAL. 1987. The Political Partisanship of American Business: A Study of Corporate Political Action Committees. *American Sociological Review*, 52: 732–44.

—— 1992. Elite Policy-Planning Networks in the United States. *Research in Politics and Society*, 4: 111–34.

—— 2005. Interlocking Directorates and Political Cohesion among Corporate Elites. *American Journal of Sociology*, 111 (July), 249–83.

BURSTEIN, PAUL and HIRSH, C. ELIZABETH. 2007. Interest Organizations, Information, and Policy Innovation in the U.S. Congress. *Sociological Forum*, 22/2: 174–99.

—— and LINTON, APRIL. 2002. The Impact of Political Parties, Interest Groups, and Social Movement Organizations on Public Policy: Some Recent Evidence and Theoretical Concerns. *Social Forces*, 81/2: 381–408.

BURT, RONALD S. 1992. *Structural Holes.* Cambridge, Mass.: Harvard University Press.

BUSCH, ANDREW E. 2001. *Ronald Reagan and the Politics of Freedom.* Lanham, Md.: Rowman & Littlefield.

—— 2005a. National Security and the Midterm Elections of 2002. In *Transforming the American Polity: The Presidency of George W. Bush and the War on Terrorism*, ed. Richard S. Conley. Upper Saddle River, NJ: Pearson Prentice Hall.

—— 2005b. *Reagan's Victory: The Presidential Election of 1980 and the Rise of the Right.* Lawrence: University Press of Kansas.

—— 2008. The Reemergence of the Iowa Caucuses: A New Trend, an Aberration, or a Useful Reminder. In *The Making of the Presidential Candidates 2008*, ed. William G. Mayer. Lanham, Md.: Rowman & Littlefield.

CAIN, BRUCE. 1978. Strategic Voting in Britain. *American Journal of Political Science*, 22/3: 639–55.

—— FEREJOHN, JOHN A., and FIORINA, MORRIS P. 1987. *The Personal Vote: Constituency Service and Electoral Independence*. Cambridge, Mass.: Harvard University Press.

CALDEIRA, GREGORY A. and WRIGHT, JOHN R. 1988. Organized Interests and Agenda Setting in the U.S. Supreme Court. *American Political Science Review*, 82: 1109–27.

—— —— 1990. Amici Curiae before the Supreme Court: Who Participates, When, and How Much? *Journal of Politics*, 52: 782–806.

CALLOW, ALEXANDER B., JR. 1966. *The Tweed Ring*. New York: Oxford University Press.

CALVERT, RANDALL L. 1980. The Role of Imperfect Information in Electoral Politics. Ph.D. dissertation, California Institute of Technology, Pasadena.

—— 1985. Robustness of the Multidimensional Voting Model: Candidate Motivations, Uncertainty, and Convergence. *American Journal of Political Science*, 29/1 (Feb.), 69–95.

CAMPBELL, ANDREA L. 2003. *How Policies Make Citizens*. Princeton: Princeton University Press.

—— COX, GARY, and McCUBBINS, MATTHEW. 2002. Agenda Power in the U.S. Senate, 1877–1986. In *Party, Process, and Political Change in Congress*, ed. David Brady and Matthew McCubbins. Stanford, Calif.: Stanford University Press.

CAMPBELL, ANGUS, CONVERSE, PHILIP E., MILLER, WARREN E., and STOKES, DONALD E. 1960. *The American Voter*. New York: Wiley.

—— MILLER, WARREN E., STOKES, DONALD E., and CONVERSE, PHILIP. 1966. *Elections and the Political Order*. New York: Wiley.

CAMPBELL, BALLARD. 1995. *The Growth of the American Government: Governance from the Cleveland Era to the Present*. Bloomington: Indiana University Press.

CAMPBELL, BRUCE A. and TRILLING, RICHARD J. (eds.) 1979. *Realignment in American Politics: Towards a Theory*. Austin: University of Texas Press.

CAMPBELL, DONALD T. and STANLEY, JULIAN C. 1963. *Experimental and Quasi-Experimental Design for Research*. Boston: Houghton Mifflin.

CAMPBELL, JAMES E. 2005. Why Bush Won the Presidential Election of 2004: Incumbency, Ideology, Terrorism, and Turnout. *Political Science Quarterly*, 120/2: 219–41.

—— 2006. Party Systems and Realignments in the United States, 1868–2004. *Social Science History*, 30 (Fall), 359–86.

—— 2008. Presidential Politics in a Polarized Nation: The Reelection of George W. Bush. In *The George W. Bush Legacy*, ed. Colin Campbell, Bert A. Rockman, and Andrew Rudalevige. Washington, DC: CQ Press.

CAMPBELL, JOHN L. and ALLEN, MICHAEL PATRICK. 1994. The Political Economy of Revenue Extraction in the Modern State: A Time-Series Analysis of U.S. Income Taxes, 1916–1986. *Social Forces*, 72: 643–69.

CANES-WRONE, BRANDICE, BRADY, DAVID W., and COGAN, JOHN F. 2002. Out of Step, Out of Office: Electoral Accountability and House Members' Voting. *American Political Science Review*, 96: 127–40.

CANFIELD, JAMES L. 1984. *A Case of Third Party Activism: The George Wallace Campaign Worker and the American Independent Party*. Lanham, Md.: University Press of America.

CANN, DAMON M. 2008. *Sharing the Wealth*. Albany: State University of New York Press.

CANON, BRADLEY C. 1978. Factionalism in the South: A Test of Theory and a Revisitation of V. O. Key. *American Journal of Political Science*, 22/4: 833.

CANON, DAVID T. 1990. *Actors, Athletes, and Astronauts: Political Amateurs in the United States Congress*. Chicago: University of Chicago Press.

CANTOR, DAVID. 1999. The Sierra Club Political Committee. In *After the Revolution: PACs, Lobbies, and the Republican Congress*, ed. Robert Biersack, Paul S. Herrnson, and Clyde Wilcox. New York: Allyn and Bacon.

CAPOZZOLA, CHRISTOPHER. 2008. *Uncle Sam Wants You: World War I and the Making of the Modern American Citizen*. Oxford: Oxford University Press.

CAREY, JOHN M., NIEMI, RICHARD G., and POWELL, LYNDA W. 1998. Are Women State Legislators Different? In *Women and Elective Office: Past, Present, & Future*, ed. Sue Thomas and Clyde Wilcox. New York: Oxford University Press.

CARMINES, EDWARD G., RENTEN, STEVEN H., and STIMSON, JAMES A. 1984. Events and Alignments: The Party Image Link. In *Controversies in American Voting Behavior*, ed. Richard G. Niemi and Herbert F. Weisberg. Washington, DC: CQ Press.

—— and STANLEY, HAROLD W. 1992. The Transformation of the New Deal Party System: Social Groups, Political Ideology, and Changing Partisanship among Northern Whites, 1972–1988. *Political Behavior*, 14: 213–37.

—— and STIMSON, JAMES A. 1989. *Issue Evolution: Race and the Transformation of American Politics*. Princeton: Princeton University Press.

—— and WAGNER, MICHAEL W. 2006. Political Issues and Party Alignments: Assessing the Issue Evolution Perspective. *Annual Review of Political Science*, 9: 67–81.

—— and WOODS, JAMES. 2002. The Role of Party Activists in the Evolution of the Abortion Issue. *Political Behavior*, 24/4: 361–77.

CARPENTER, DANIEL P. 2002. Groups, the Media, Agency Waiting Costs and FDA Drug Approval. *American Journal of Political Science*, 46: 490–505.

—— ESTERLING, KEVIN M., and LAZER, DAVID M. J. 2004. Friends, Brokers, and Transitivity: Who Informs Whom in Washington Politics? *Journal of Politics*, 66: 224–46.

CARSEY, THOMAS M., GREEN, JOHN C., HERRERA, RICHARD, and LAYMAN, GEOFFREY C. 2006. State Party Context and Norms among Delegates to the 2000 National Party Conventions. *State Politics and Policy Quarterly*, 6: 247–71.

CARSON, JAMIE L. 2005. Strategy, Selection, and Candidate Competition in U.S. House and Senate Elections. *Journal of Politics*, 67: 1–28.

—— and ROBERTS, JASON M. 2005. Strategic Politicians and U.S. House Elections, 1874–1914. *Journal of Politics*, 67/2: 474–96.

CARTER, DAN T. 1996. *From George Wallace to Newt Gingrich: Race in the Conservative Counterrevolution*. Baton Rouge: Louisiana State University Press.

—— 2000. *The Politics of Rage*. 2nd edn. Baton Rouge: Louisiana State University Press.

CARTY, R. KENNETH. 2004. Parties as Franchise Systems: The Stratarchical Organizational Imperative. *Party Politics*, 10/1: 5–24.

CATER, DOUGLASS. 1964. *Power in Washington*. New York: Random House.

CEASER, JAMES W. 1979. *Presidential Selection: Theory and Development*. Princeton: Princeton University Press.

CENSUS, UNITED STATES BUREAU OF THE. 1975. *Historical Statistics of the United States, Colonial Times to 1970*. Washington, DC: Government Printing Office.

CENTER FOR RESPONSIVE POLITICS. 2008. *Top Contributors to 527 Committees*. <http://www.opensecrets.org/527s/527contribs.php?cycle=2004>. Accessed Dec. 31, 2008.

CHADDOCK, GAIL RUSSELL. 2003. Republicans Take Over K Street. *Christian Science Monitor* (Aug. 29).

CHADWICK, ANDREW. 2007. Digital Network Repertoires and Organizational Hybridity. *Political Communication,* 24/3: 283–301.

CHAMBERS, WILLIAM N. 1963. *Political Parties in a New Nation, 1776–1809.* New York: Oxford University Press.

—— and BURNHAM, WALTER DEAN. 1967. *The American Party Systems.* New York: Oxford University Press.

—— —— 1975. *The American Party Systems.* 2nd edn. New York: Oxford University Press.

CHARLES, JOSEPH. 1956. *The Origins of the American Party System.* Williamsburg, Va.: Institute of Early American History and Culture.

CHASE, JAMES S. 1973. *Emergence of the Presidential Nominating Convention 1789–1832.* Urbana: University of Illinois Press.

CHESTER, LEWIS, HODGSON, GODFREY, and PAGE, BRUCE. 1969. *An American Melodrama.* London: André Deutsch.

CHHIBBAR, PRADEEP and KOLLMAN, KEN. 2004. *The Formation of National Party Systems: Federalism and Party Competition in Canada, Great Britain, India, and the United States.* Princeton: Princeton University Press.

CHILDS, LAWRENCE. 1930. *Labor and Capital in National Politics.* Columbus: Ohio State University Press.

CHIOU, FANG-YI and ROTHENBERG, LAWRENCE. 2003. When Pivotal Politics Meets Partisan Politics. *American Journal of Political Science,* 47: 503–22.

CHONG, DENNIS. 1991. *Collective Action and the Civil Rights Movement.* Chicago: University of Chicago Press.

CHWE, MICHAEL SUK-YOUNG. 2000. Communication and Coordination in Social Networks. *Review of Economic Studies,* 67: 1–16.

CLAASSEN, RYAN L. 2007. Floating Voters and Floating Activists. *Political Research Quarterly,* 60/1: 124–34.

—— 2008. Testing the Reciprocal Effects of Campaign Participation. *Political Behavior,* 30/3: 277–96.

CLARK, JOSEPH. 1964. *Congress: The Sapless Branch.* New York: Harper & Row.

CLARKE, WES. 1998. Divided Government and Budget Conflict in the U.S. States. *Legislative Studies Quarterly,* 23: 5–22.

CLAWSON, DAN and NEUSTADTL, ALAN. 1989. Interlocks, PACs, and Corporate Conservatism. *American Journal of Sociology,* 94: 749–73.

CLEMENS, ELISABETH S. 1997. *The People's Lobby.* Chicago: University of Chicago Press.

CLIFTON, BRETT M. 2004. Romancing the GOP. *Party Politics,* 10/5: 475–98.

CLINTON, JOSHUA, JACKMAN, SIMON, and RIVERS, DOUGLAS. 2004. The Statistical Analysis of Roll-Call Data. *American Political Science Review,* 98/2: 355–70.

CLUBB, JEROME, FLANIGAN, WILLIAM, and ZINGALE, NANCY. 1980. *Partisan Realignment: Voters, Parties and Government in American History.* Beverly Hills, Calif.: Sage Publications.

COBB, ROGER W. and ELDER, CHARLES D. 1983. *Participation in American Politics: The Dynamics of Agenda-Building* (1972). 2nd edn. Baltimore: Johns Hopkins University Press.

—— ROSS, MARC HOWARD (eds.) 1997. *Cultural Strategies of Agenda Denial.* Lawrence: University Press of Kansas.

COEN, DAVID (ed.) 2007. *Empirical and Theoretical Studies in EU Lobbying. Journal of European Public Policy*, Special Issue, 14/3.

COFFEY, DANIEL J. 2007. State Party Activists and State Party Polarization. In *The State of the Parties*, ed. John C. Green and Daniel J. Coffey. Lanham, Md.: Rowman & Littlefield.

COHEN, BERNARD C. 1963. *The Press and Foreign Policy*. Princeton: Princeton University Press.

COHEN, CATHY J. 1999. *The Boundaries of Blackness*. Chicago: University of Chicago Press.

—— and WARREN, DORIAN T. 2000. Organizing at the Intersection of Labor and Civil Rights. *University of Pennsylvania Journal of Labor and Employment Law*, 2/4: 629–55.

COHEN, JOSH and ROGERS, JOEL (eds.) 1995. *Associations and Democracy*. London: Verso.

COHEN, MARTY, KAROL, DAVID, NOEL, HANS, and ZALLER, JOHN. 2008. *The Party Decides: Presidential Nominations Before and After Reform*. Chicago: University of Chicago Press.

COLEMAN, JAMES S. 1971. Internal Processes Governing Party Positions in Elections. *Public Choice*, 11: 35–60.

—— 1972. The Positions of Political Parties in Elections. In *Probability Models of Collective Decision Making*, ed. Richard G. Niemi and Herbert F. Weisberg. Columbus, Ohio. Charles E. Merrill.

COLEMAN, JOHN L. 1994. The Resurgence of Party Organizations? A Dissent from the New Orthodoxy. In *The State of the Parties: The Changing Role of Contemporary American Parties*, ed. Daniel M. Shea and John C. Green. Lanham, Md: Rowman & Littlefield.

—— 1996. *Party Decline in America: Policy, Politics, and the Fiscal State*. Princeton: Princeton University Press.

—— and MANNA, PAUL F. 2000. Congressional Campaign Spending and the Quality of Democracy. *Journal of Politics*, 62/3: 757–89.

COLLETT, CHRISTIAN and WATTENBERG, MARTIN. 1999. Strategically Unambitious: Minor Party and Independent Candidates in the 1996 Congressional Elections. In *The State of the Parties*, ed. Daniel Shea and John C. Green. 3rd edn. Lanham, Md.: Rowman & Littlefield.

COLLINS, PATRICIA HILL. 1990. *Black Feminist Thought*. Boston: Unwin Hyman.

COLLINS, PAUL M., JR. 2007. Lobbyists before the U.S. Supreme Court: Investigating the Influence of Amicus Curiae Briefs. *Political Research Quarterly*, 60/1: 55–70.

Colorado Republican Federal Campaign Committee v. Federal Election Commission et al., 518 U.S. 604 (1996).

COMER, JOHN. 1976. Another Look at the Effects of the Divisive Primary: A Research Note. *American Politics Research*, 4/1: 121–8.

COMMISSION ON PARTY STRUCTURE AND DELEGATE SELECTION. 1970. *Mandate for Reform*. Washington, DC: Democratic National Committee.

CONFESSORE, NICHOLAS. 2003. Welcome to the Machine. *Washington Monthly*. July–Aug. <http://www.washingtonmonthly.com/features/2003/0307.confessore.html>. Accessed Jan. 4, 2009.

Congressional Quarterly 1997. *National Party Conventions 1831–1996*. Washington, DC: CQ Press.

CONVERSE, PHILIP E., MILLER, WARREN E., RUSK, JEROLD G., and WOLFE, ARTHUR C. 1969. Continuity and Change in American Politics: Parties and Issues in the 1968 Election. *American Political Science Review*, 73: 1083–1105.

CONWAY, M. MARGARET. 1983. Republican Party Nationalization, Campaign Activities, and their Implications for the Political System. *Publius*, 13: 1–17.

COOPER, JOSEPH and BRADY, DAVID W. 1981. Institutional Context and Leadership Style: The House from Cannon to Rayburn. *American Political Science Review*, 75: 411–25.

CORN, DAVID. 2008. This Wasn't Quite the Change We Pictured. *Washington Post*, Dec. 7. <http://www.washingtonpost.com/wp-dyn/content/article/2008/12/05/AR2008120502602.htm>. Accessed Apr. 26, 2009.

CORNWELL, CHRISTOPHER and MUSTARD, DAVID B. 2007. Merit-Based College Scholarships and Car Sales. *Education Finance and Policy*, 2: 133–51.

CORRADO, ANTHONY. 1996. The Changing Environment of Presidential Campaign Finance. In *In Pursuit of the White House 2000: How We Choose Our Presidential Nominees*, ed. William G. Mayer. New York: Chatham House.

—— 2006. Party Finance in the Wake of BCRA. In *The Election after Reform*, ed. Michael J. Malbin. Lanham, Md.: Rowman & Littlefield.

—— and GOUVEA, HEITOR. 2004. Financing Presidential Nominations under the BCRA. In *The Making of the Presidential Candidates 2004*, ed. William G. Mayer. Lanham, Md.: Rowman & Littlefield.

COSTAIN, ANNE N. 1992. *Inviting Women's Rebellion*. Baltimore: Johns Hopkins University Press.

—— 2005. Social Movements as Mechanisms for Political Inclusion. In *The Politics of Democratic Inclusion*, ed. Christina Wolbrecht and Rodney E. Hero. Philadelphia: Temple University Press.

—— and McFARLAND, ANDREW S. (eds.) 1998. *Social Movements and American Political Institutions*. Lanham, Md.: Rowman & Littlefield.

COTTER, CORNELIUS P. 1989. *Party Organizations in American Politics*. Pittsburgh: University of Pittsburgh Press.

—— and BIBBY, JOHN F. 1980. Institutional Development of the Parties and the Thesis of Party Decline. *Political Science Quarterly*, 95: 1–27.

—— GIBSON, JAMES L., BIBBY, JOHN F., and HUCKSHORN, ROBERT J. 1984. *Party Organizations in American Politics*. New York: Praeger.

—— —— —— —— 1989. *Party Organizations in American Politics*. Pittsburgh: University of Pittsburgh Press.

—— and HENNESSY, BERNARD C. 1964. *Politics without Power: The National Party Committees*. New York: Atherton Press.

COX, GARY W. 1997. *Making Votes Count: Strategic Coordination in the World's Electoral Systems*. New York: Cambridge University Press.

—— 2006. The Organization of Democratic Legislatures. In *Handbook of Political Science*. Oxford: Oxford University Press.

—— and KATZ, JONATHAN N. 1996. Why Did the Incumbency Advantage in U.S. House Elections Grow? *American Journal of Political Science*, 40/2: 478.

—— and McCUBBINS, MATHEW D. 1993. *Legislative Leviathan*. Berkeley: University of California Press.

—— —— 2005. *Setting the Agenda*. New York: Cambridge University Press.

CRAIG, STEPHEN C. 2006. *The Electoral Challenge: Theory Meets Practice*. Washington, DC: CQ Press.

CRAMER, RICHARD BEN. 1992. *What it Takes: The Way to the White House*. New York: Random House.

CRENSHAW, KIMBERLÉ. 1989. Demarginalizing the Intersection of Race and Sex. *University of Chicago Legal Forum*, 39: 139–67.

CRENSON, MATTHEW A. 1971. *The Unpolitics of Air Pollution*. Baltimore: Johns Hopkins University Press.

CRESPIN, MICHAEL H. 2004. Direct Primaries and the Openness of the Two Party System, 1904–1920. Manuscript, Michigan State University.

CROLY, HERBERT. 1914. *Progressive Democracy*. New York: Macmillan.

CROSS, WILLIAM. 2008. Democratic Norms and Party Candidate Selection: Taking Contextual Factors into Account. *Party Politics*, 14/5: 596–619.

CROTTY, WILLIAM J. 1983. *Party Reform*. New York: Longman.

—— 1984. *American Parties in Decline*. Boston: Little, Brown.

CROUSE, TIMOTHY. 1973. *The Boys on the Bus: Riding with the Campaign Press Corps*. New York: Ballantine Books.

CROWLEY, JOCELYN ELISE and SKOCPOL, THEDA. 2001. The Rush to Organize: Explaining Associational Formation in the United States, 1860s–1920s. *American Journal of Political Science*, 45 (Oct.), 813–29.

CUNNINGHAM, NOBLE, JR. 1957. *The Jeffersonian Republicans: The Formation of Party Organization, 1789–1801*. Chapel Hill: University of North Carolina Press.

CUPITT, RICHARD T. and ELLIOTT, EUEL. 1994. Schattschneider Revisited: Senate Voting on the Smoot–Hawley Tariff Act of 1930. *Economics and Politics*, 6/3: 188–99.

CURRINDER, MARIAN L. 2003. Leadership PAC Contribution Strategies and House Member Ambitions. *Legislative Studies Quarterly*, 28: 551–77.

—— 2009. *Money in the House*. Boulder, Colo.: Westview Press.

CURTIS, GEORGE T. 1884. How Shall We Elect Our Presidents? *The Century*, 29: 124–35.

DAHL, ROBERT A. 1956. *A Preface to Democratic Theory*. Chicago: University of Chicago Press.

—— 1961. *Who Governs?* New Haven: Yale University Press.

—— 1967. *Pluralist Democracy in the United States*. Chicago: Rand McNally.

—— 1989. *Democracy and its Critics*. New Haven: Yale University Press.

—— 1994. *The New American Political (Dis)Order*. Berkeley: Institute of Governmental.

DALTON, RUSSELL J. and WATTENBERG, MARTIN P. 2000. *Parties without Partisans: Political Change in Advanced Industrial Democracies*. New York: Oxford University Press.

DANIELIAN, LUCIG H. and PAGE, BENJAMIN I. 1994. The Heavenly Chorus: Interest Group Voices on TV News. *American Journal of Political Science*, 38: 1056–78.

DARCY, R., WELCH, SUSAN, and CLARK, JANET. 1987. *Women, Elections, and Representation*. New York: Longman.

DAVID, PAUL T., GOLDMAN, RALPH M., and BAIN, RICHARD C. 1960. *The Politics of National Party Conventions*. Washington, DC: Brookings Institution.

DAVIDSON, ROGER H. 1981. Subcommittee Government: New Channels for Policy Making. In *The New Congress*, ed. Thomas E. Mann and Norman J. Ornstein. Washington, DC: American Enterprise Institute.

DAVIS, ANGELA Y. 1981. *Women, Race, and Class*. New York: Random House.

DAVIS, JAMES W. 1967. *Presidential Primaries: Road to the White House*. New York: Thomas Y. Crowell.

DAWSON, RICHARD E. and ROBINSON, JAMES A. 1963. Inter-Party Competition, Economic Variables, and Welfare Policies in the American States. *Journal of Politics*, 25: 265–89.

DE LA GARZA, RODOLFO O. 2004. Latino Politics. *Annual Review of Political Science*, 7: 91–123.

DECKARD, BARBARA SINCLAIR. 1976. Political Upheaval and Congressional Voting. *Journal of Politics*, 38: 326–45.

DeGREGORIO, CHRISTINE A. 1997. *Networks of Champions: Leadership, Access, and Advocacy in the U.S. House of Representatives*. Ann Arbor: University of Michigan Press.

DEMOCRACY COLLABORATIVE. 2007. Community Development Corporations. <http://www.community-wealth.org/strategies/panel/cdcs/index.html>. Accessed July 16, 2008.

DEMSETZ, HAROLD. 1990. Amenity Potential, Indivisibilities, and Political Competition. In *Perspectives on Positive Political Economy*, ed. Kenneth Shepsle and James Alt. New York: Cambridge University Press.

DEN HARTOG, CHRIS. 2005. The Jeffords Switch and Party Members' Success in the U.S. Senate. Paper presented at the Annual Meeting of the American Political Science Association, Washington, DC, Sept. 1–4.

—— and MONROE, NATHAN. 2006. Home Field Advantage: An Asymmetric-Costs Theory of Legislative Agenda Influence in the U.S. Senate. Paper presented at the Conference on Party Effects in the United States Senate, Duke University, Apr. 7–8.

DENZAU, ARTHUR T. and MUNGER, MICHAEL C. 1986. Legislators and Interest Groups: How Unorganized Interests Get Represented. *American Political Science Review*, 80: 86–106.

DERGE, DAVID R. 1958. Metropolitan and Outstate Alignments in Illinois and Missouri Legislative Delegations. *American Political Science Review*, 52: 1051–65.

DERTHICK, MARTHA and TELES, STEVEN. 2003. Riding the Third Rail: Social Security Reform. In *The Reagan Presidency: Pragmatic Conservatism and its Legacies*, ed. W. Elliot Brownlee and Hugh Davis Graham. Lawrence: University Press of Kansas.

DEXTER, LOUIS ANTHONY. 1969. *How Organizations Are Represented in Washington*. Indianapolis: Bobbs-Merrill.

DIANI, MARIO. 1997. Social Movements and Social Capital. *Mobilization*, 2: 129–47.

DÍAZ-CAYEROS, ALBERTO and MAGALONI, BEATRIZ. 1996. Dominancia de partido y dilemas Duvergerianos en las elecciones federales de 1994. (Party Dominance and Duvergerian Dilemmas in the 1994 Federal Elections.) *Política y Gobierno*, 3/2: 281–326.

DICKINSON, TIM. 2008. The Machinery of Hope. *Rolling Stone Online*. Mar. 20. <http://www.rollingstone.com/news/coverstory/19106326>.

DIERMEIER, DANIEL. 2006. Coalition Government. In *The Oxford Handbook of Political Economy*, ed. Barry Weingast and Donald Wittman. New York: Oxford University Press.

—— and FEDDERSEN, TIMOTHY. 1998. Cohesion in Legislatures and the Vote of Confidence Procedure. *American Political Science Review*, 92: 611–22.

DIGESER, PETER. 1992. The Fourth Face of Power. *Journal of Politics*, 54/4: 977–1007.

DION, DOUGLAS. 1997. *Turning the Legislative Thumbscrew*. Ann Arbor: University of Michigan Press.

—— and HUBER, JOHN. 1996. Procedural Choice and the House Committee on Rules. *Journal of Politics*, 58: 25–53.

—— —— 1997. Sense and Sensibility: The Role of Rules. *American Journal of Political Science*, 41: 945–57.

DIONNE, E. J. 1991. *Why Americans Hate Politics*. New York: Simon & Schuster.

—— 1992. Anger at the Economy Was the Glue Binding Supporters to Perot. *Washington Post*, Nov. 12, A10.

—— 2006. Polarized by God? American Politics and the Religious Divide. In *Red and Blue Nation?* ed. Pietro Nivola and David Brady. Washington, DC: Brookings Institution Press; Stanford, Calif.: Hoover Press.

DOGAN, MATTEI and PELASSY, DOMINIQUE. 1990. *How to Compare Nations: Strategies in Comparative politics*. 2nd edn. Chatham, NJ: Chatham House.

DOHERTY, JOSEPH. 2006a. The Candidate–Consultant Network in California Legislative Campaigns: A Social Network Analysis of Informal Party Organization. Ph.D. dissertation, University of California, Los Angeles.

—— 2006b. The Congressional Campaign Network: Candidate–Consultant Linkages in House Races, 1996–2004. Paper presented at the Annual Meeting of the American Political Science Association, Philadelphia, Aug. 31–Sept. 3.

DOMHOFF, G. WILLIAM. 1967. *Who Rules America?* Englewood Cliffs, NJ: Prentice Hall.

—— 1978. *The Powers that Be: Processes of Ruling Class Domination in America*. New York: Random House.

DOMINGUEZ, CASEY. 2005. Before the Primary: Party Participation in Congressional Nominating Processes. Ph.D. dissertation, University of California, Berkeley.

—— and BERNSTEIN, JONATHAN. 2003. Candidates and Candidacies in the Expanded Party. *PS: Political Science and Politics*, 36: 165–9.

DONNAY, PATRICK D. and RAMSDEN, GRAHAM P. 1995. Public Financing of Legislative Elections: Lessons from Minnesota. *Legislative Studies Quarterly*, 20: 351–64.

DOPPELT, JACK C. and SHEARER, ELLEN. 1999. *Nonvoters: America's No-Shows*. Thousand Oaks, Calif.: Sage Publications.

DORSETT, LYLE. 1977. *FDR and the City Bosses*. Port Washington, NY: Kennikat Press.

DOWNS, ANTHONY. 1957. *An Economic Theory of Democracy*. New York: HarperCollins.

DROPE, JEFFREY M. and HANSEN, WENDY L. 2006. Does Firm Size Matter? Analyzing Business Lobbying in the United States. *Business and Politics*, 8/2, art. 4.

DRUCKMAN, JAMES N. 2001. On the Limits of Framing Effects: Who Can Frame? *Journal of Politics*, 63/4: 1041–66.

—— 2004. Political Preference Formation: Competition, Deliberation, and the (Ir)Relevance of Framing Effects. *American Political Science Review*, 98/4: 761–86.

DUBERMAN, MARTIN. 2002. *Left Out*. Boston: South End Press.

DUBOSE, LOU and REID, JAN. 2004. *The Hammer*. New York: Public Affairs.

DULIO, DAVID A. 2004. *For Better or Worse? How Professional Political Consultants Are Changing Elections in the United States*. Albany: State University of New York Press.

DUNCAN, SAMUEL JOHN. 1913. *The Progressive Movement's Principles and its Programme*. Boston: Small, Maynard.

DUVERGER, MAURICE. 1954. *Political Parties: Their Organization and Activities in the Modern State*. London: Methuen; New York: Wiley.

—— 1963. *Political Parties*. Trans. B. North and R. North. New York: Wiley.

DWYRE, DIANA and FARRAR-MYERS, VICTORIA A. 2001. *Legislative Labyrinth: Congress and Campaign Finance Reform*. Washington, DC: CQ Press.

DYE, THOMAS R. 1965. State Legislative Politics. In *Politics in the American States*, ed. Herbert Jacob and Kenneth Vines. Boston: Little, Brown.

—— 1966. *Politics, Economics, and the Public: Policy Outcomes in the American States*. Chicago: Rand McNally.

—— 1978. Oligarchic Tendencies in National Policy-Making: The Role of Private Policy-Planning Organizations. *Journal of Politics*, 40: 309–31.

—— 1984. Party and Policy in the States. *Journal of Politics*, 46: 1097–1116.

EDELMAN, MURRAY. 1964. *The Symbolic Uses of Politics*. Urbana: University of Illinois Press.

EDLING, MAX. 2003. *A Revolution in Favor of Government: Origins of the U.S. Constitution and the Making of the American State.* Oxford: Oxford University Press.

EDSALL, THOMAS B. 2006. *Building Red America: The New Conservative Coalition and the Drive for Permanent Power.* New York: Basic Books.

EDWARDS, GEORGE. 1983. *The Public Presidency.* St Martin's Press.

—— 1989. *At the Margins: Presidential Leadership of Congress.* New Haven: Yale University Press.

EHRMAN, JOHN. 2005. *The Eighties: America in the Age of Reagan.* New Haven: Yale University Press.

EHRMANN, HENRY W. 1958. *Interest Groups in Four Continents.* Pittsburgh: University of Pittsburgh Press.

EISING, RAINER. 2004. Multilevel Governance and Business Interests in the European Union. *Governance,* 17/2: 211–45.

—— 2007. Institutional Context, Organizational Resources, and Strategic Choices: Explaining Interest Group Access in the European Union. *European Union Politics,* 11/3: 329–62.

EISINGER, ROBERT and BROWN, JEREMY. 1998. Polling as a Means Toward Presidential Autonomy: Emil Hurja, Hadley Cantril, and the Roosevelt Administration. *International Journal of Public Opinion,* 10: 239–56.

EISMEIER, THEODORE J. and POLLOCK, PHILIP H. 1986. Strategy and Choice in Congressional Elections: The Role of Political Action Committees. *American Journal of Political Science,* 30/1: 197–213.

ELDER, LAUREL. 2008. Whither Republican Women: The Growing Partisan Gap among Women in Congress. *The Forum,* 6/1. <http://www.bepress.com/forum/vol6/iss1/art13>. Accessed Apr. 26, 2009.

ELDERSVELD, SAMUEL JAMES. 1964. *Political Parties: A Behavioral Analysis.* Chicago: Rand McNally.

—— 1982. *Political Parties in American Society.* New York: Basic Books.

ELKIN, STEPHEN L. 1987. *City and Regime in the American Republic.* Chicago: University of Chicago Press.

ELKINS, STANLEY and McKITRICK, ERIC. 1993. *The Age of Federalism: The Early American Republic, 1790–1800.* New York: Oxford University Press.

ELLING, RICHARD C. 1979. State Party Platforms and State Legislative Performance: A Comparative Analysis. *American Journal of Political Science,* 23: 383–405.

ENELOW, JAMES and HINICH, MELVIN. 1981. A New Approach to Voter Uncertainty in the Downsian Spatial Model. *American Journal of Political Science,* 25: 483–93.

—— —— 1982. Nonspatial Candidate Characteristics and Electoral Competition. *Journal of Politics,* 44/1 (Feb.), 115–30.

—— and MUNGER MICHAEL C. 1993. The Elements of Candidate Reputation: The Effect of Record and Credibility on Optimal Spatial Location. *Public Choice,* 77: 757–72.

ENGSTROM, RICHARD L. and ENGSTROM, RICHARD N. 2008. The Majority Vote Rule and Runoff Primaries in the United States. *Electoral Studies,* 27/3: 407–16.

ENGSTROM, RICHARD N. and KENNY, CHRISTOPHER. 2002. The Effects of Independent Expenditures in Senate Elections. *Political Research Quarterly,* 55/4: 885–905.

EPSTEIN, EDWIN M. 1969. *The Corporation in American Politics.* Englewood Cliffs, NJ: Prentice-Hall.

EPSTEIN, LEE. 1992. Interest Group Litigation during the Rehnquist Court Era. *Journal of Law and Politics,* 9: 639–718.

EPSTEIN, LEE and ROWLAND, C. K. 1991. Debunking the Myth of Interest Group Invincibility in the Courts. *American Political Science Review*, 85: 205–17.

EPSTEIN, LEON D. 1967. *Political Parties in Western Democracies*. New York: Praeger.

—— 1986. *Political Parties in the American Mold*. Madison: University of Wisconsin Press.

ERIKSON, ROBERT S., MACUEN, MICHAEL, and STIMSON, JAMES A. 2002. *The Macro Polity*. New York: Cambridge University Press.

—— and PALFREY, THOMAS R. 1998. Campaign Spending and Incumbency: An Alternative Simultaneous Equations Approach. *Journal of Politics*, 60/2: 355–73.

—— WRIGHT, GERALD C., and McIVER, JOHN P. 1993. *Statehouse Democracy: Public Opinion and Policy in the American States*. New York: Cambridge University Press.

—— —— —— 2006. Public Opinion in the States: A Quarter Century of Change and Stability. In *Public Opinion in the States*, ed. Jeffrey E. Cohen. Stanford, Calif.: Stanford University Press.

ESPINOSA, GASTON (ed.) 2009. *Religion, Race and the American Presidency*. Lanham, Md.: Rowman & Littlefield.

ESTERLING, KEVIN M. 2007. Buying Expertise: Campaign Contributions and Attention to Policy Analysis in Congressional Committees. *American Political Science Review*, 101: 93–109.

ESTY, DANIEL C. and CAVES, RICHARD E. 1983. Market Structure and Political Influence: New Data on Political Expenditures, Activity, and Success. *Economic Inquiry*, 21: 24–38.

EVANS, DIANA. 1988. Oil PACs and Aggressive Contribution Strategies. *Journal of Politics*, 50/4: 1047–56.

EVANS, PETER B., RUESCHEMEYER, DIETRICH, and SCOCPOL, THEDA (eds.) 1985. *Bringing the State Back In*. Cambridge: Cambridge University Press.

EXLEY, ZACK. 2008. The New Organizers: What's Really behind Obama's Ground Game. *Huffington Post* (Oct. 8).

FARRA-MYERS, VICTORIA A. and DWYRE, DIANA. 2008. *Limits and Loopholes: The Quest for Money, Free Speech, and Fair Elections*. Washington, DC: CQ Press.

FARRAND, MAX (ed.) 1937. *The Records of the Federal Convention of 1787*, ii. New Haven: Yale University Press.

FARRAR-MYERS, VICTORIA A. and DWYRE, DIANA. 2008. *Limits and Loopholes: The Quest for Money, Free Speech and Fair Elections*. Washington, DC: Congressional Quarterly.

FARRELL, DAVID M., KOLODNY, ROBIN, and MEDVIC, STEPHEN. 2001. Parties and Campaign Professionals in a Digital Age: Political Consultants in the United States and their Counterparts Overseas. *Harvard International Journal of Press/Politics*, 6/4: 11–30.

FAUSTO-STERLING, ANNE. 1993. The Five Sexes. *Sciences*, 33: 20–5.

FEDDERSEN, TIMOTHY. 1992. A Voting Model Implying Duverger's Law and Positive Turnout. *American Journal of Political Science*, 36: 938–62.

—— SENED, ITAI, and WRIGHT, STEPHEN G. 1990. Rational Voting and Candidate Entry under Plurality Rule. *American Journal of Political Science*, 34: 1005–16.

FEDERAL ELECTION COMMISSION. 1992. Candidate Report Filings, Jan.–July 1992.

—— 2003. Party Committees Raise more than $1 Billion in 2001–2002. Press release, Mar. 20. <http://www.fec.gov/press/press2003/20030320party/20030103party.html>. Accessed Feb. 18, 2009.

—— 2007. Party Financial Activity Summarized for the 2006 Election Cycle. Press release, Mar. 7. <http://www.fec.gov/press/press2007/partyfinal2006/20070307party.shtml>. Accessed June 4, 2007.

—— 2008. FEC Releases Summary of National Party Financial Activity. <http://www.fec. gov/press/press2008/20081029party/20081029party.shtml>. Accessed Apr. 26, 2009.

FEINSTEIN, BRIAN and SCHICKLER, ERIC. 2008. Platforms and Partners: The Civil Rights Realignment Reconsidered. *Studies in American Political Development*, 22: 1–31.

FELLOWES, MATTHEW, GRAY, VIRGINIA, and LOWERY, DAVID. 2006. What's on the Table? The Content of State Policy Agendas. *Party Politics*, 12/1: 35–55.

FENNO, RICHARD F. 1973. *Congressmen in Committees*. Boston: Little, Brown.

—— 1978. *Home Style: House Members in their Districts*. Boston: Little, Brown.

FEREJOHN, JOHN. 1974. *Pork Barrel Politics*. Palo Alto, Calif.: Stanford University Press.

—— 1991. Changes in Welfare Policy in the 1980s. In *Politics and Economics in the Eighties*, ed. Alberto Alesina and Geoffrey Carliner. Chicago: University of Chicago Press.

FERLING, JOHN. 2004. *Adams vs. Jefferson: The Tumultuous Election of 1800*. New York: Oxford University Press.

FERRARA, JOE 1994. The Eaton Corporation Public Policy Association: Ideology, Pragmatism, and Big Business. In *Decisionmaking in Congressional Elections*, ed. Robert Biersack, Paul S. Herrnson, and Clyde Wilcox. Armonk, NY: M. E. Sharpe.

FINIFTER, ADA. 1974. The Friendship Group as a Protective Environment for Political Deviants. *American Political Science Review*, 68/2: 112–75.

FINKE, ROGER and STARK, RODNEY. 2006. *The Churching of America, 1776–2005: Winners and Losers in Our Religious Economy*. New Brunswick, NJ: Rutgers University Press.

FINKEL, STEVEN E. and SCARROW, HOWARD A. 1985. Party Identification and Party Enrollment: The Difference and the Consequences. *Journal of Politics*, 47: 620–42.

FINOCCHIARO, CHARLES J. and ROHDE, DAVID W. 2008. War for the Floor: Partisan Theory and Agenda Control in the U.S. House of Representatives. *Legislative Studies Quarterly*, 33 (Feb.), 35–61.

FIORINA, MORRIS P. 1974. *Representative, Roll Calls, and Constituencies*. Lexington, Mass.: Lexington Books.

—— 1977. An Outline for a Model of Party Choice. *American Journal of Political Science*, 21/ 3: 601–25.

—— 1980. The Decline of Collective Responsibility in American Politics. *Daedalus*, 109: 25–45.

—— 1981. *Retrospective Voting in American Elections*. New Haven: Yale University Press.

—— 1989. *Congress: Keystone of the Washington Establishment*, 2nd edn. New Haven: Yale University Press.

—— 1991. Divided Government in the States. *PS: Political Science and Politics*, 24: 646–50.

—— 1995. Afterword (But Undoubtedly Not the Last Word). In *Positive Theories of Legislative Institutions*, ed. Kenneth A. Shepsle and Barry R. Weingast. Ann Arbor: University of Michigan Press.

—— 1996. *Divided Government*. 2nd edn. Boston, Mass: Allyn and Bacon.

—— 2001. Keystone Reconsidered. In *Congress Reconsidered*, ed. Lawrence C. Dodd and Bruce I. Oppenheimer. 7th edn. Washington, DC: CQ Press.

—— 2006. *Culture War? The Myth of a Polarized America*. 2nd edn. New York: Pearson Longman.

—— ABRAMS, SAMUEL J., and POPE, JEREMY. 2005. *Culture War? The Myth of a Polarized America*. New York: Pearson Longman.

—— and LEVENDUSKY, MATTHEW S. 2006. Disconnected: Political Class vs. the People. In *Red and Blue Nation?*, ed. Pietro Nivola and David Brady, i. Washington, DC: Brookings Institution; Stanford, Calif.: Hoover Press.

FISCHER, DAVID HACKETT. 1965. *The Revolution of American Conservatism: The Federalist Party in the Era of Jeffersonian Democracy*. New York: Harper & Row.

—— 1970. *Historians' Fallacies: Toward a Logic of Historical Thought*. New York: Harper & Row.

FLEISHER, RICHARD. 1993. PAC Contributions and Congressional Voting on National Defense. *Legislative Studies Quarterly*, 18/3: 391–409.

—— and BOND, JON R. 2001. Evidence of Increasing Polarization among Ordinary Citizens. In *American Political Parties: Decline or Resurgence?* ed. Jeffrey E. Cohen, Richard Fleisher, and Paul Kantor. Washington, DC: CQ Press.

FLINN, THOMAS A. 1964. Party Responsibility in the States: Some Causal Factors. *American Political Science Review*, 58: 60–71.

FOLEY, MICHAEL W. and EDWARDS, BOB. 2002. How do Members Count? In *Exploring Organizations and Advocacy*, ed. Elizabeth J. Reid and Maria D. Montilla. Washington, DC: Urban Institute.

FONER, ERIC. 1988. *Reconstruction: America's Unfinished Revolution, 1863–1877*. New York: Harper & Row.

FORBES, ROBERT PIERCE. 2007. *The Missouri Compromise and its Aftermath: Slavery and the Meaning of America*. Chapel Hill: University of North Carolina Press.

FORMISANO, RONALD P. 1969. Political Character, Antipartyism, and the Second Party System. *American Quarterly*, 21 (Winter), 683–709.

—— 1974. Deferential-Participant Politics: The Early Republic's Political Culture, 1790–1840. *American Political Science Review*, 68 (June), 473–87.

—— 1981. Federalists and Republicans: Parties, Yes—System, No. In *The Evolution of American Electoral Systems*, ed. Paul Kleppner et al. Westport, Conn.: Greenwood Press.

—— 1983. *The Transformation of Political Culture: Massachusetts Parties, 1790s–1840s*. New York: Oxford University Press.

—— 1999. The Party Period Revisited. *Journal of American History*, 86 (June), 93–120.

—— 2001. State Development in the Early Republic: Substance and Structure, 1780–1840. In *Contesting Democracy: Substance and Structure in American Political History, 1775–2000*, ed. Byron E. Shafer and Anthony J. Badger. Lawrence: University Press of Kansas.

FORTIER, JOHN C. and ORNSTEIN, NORMAN J. 2003. President Bush: Legislative Strategist. In *The George W. Bush Presidency: An Early Assessment*, ed. Fred I. Greenstein. Baltimore: Johns Hopkins University Press.

FOUCAULT, MICHEL. 1978. *Discipline and Punish*. New York: Pantheon Books.

FOX, RICHARD L. and LAWLESS, JENNIFER L. 2004. Entering the Arena? Gender and the Decision to Run for Office. *American Journal of Political Science*, 48/2: 264–80.

—— —— 2005. To Run or Not to Run for Office: Explaining Nascent Political Ambition. *American Journal of Political Science*, 49/3: 642–59.

FRANCIA, PETER L. 2006. *The Future of Organized Labor in American Politics*. New York: Columbia University Press.

—— GREEN, JOHN C., HERRNSON, PAUL S., POWELL, LYNDA W., and WILCOX, CLYDE. 2003a. *The Financiers of Congressional Elections: Investors, Ideologues, and Intimates*. New York: Columbia University Press.

—— HERRNSON, PAUL S., FRENDREIS, JOHN P., and GITELSON, ALAN R. 2003b. The Battle for the Legislature: Party Campaigning in State House and State Senate Elections. In *The State of the Parties: The Changing Role of Contemporary American Parties*, ed. John C. Green and Rick Farmer. 4th edn. Lanham, Md.: Rowman & Littlefield.

FRANK, KENNETH A. and YASUMOTO, JEFFREY Y. 1998. Linking Action to Social Structure within a System: Social Capital within and between Subgroups. *American Journal of Sociology*, 104: 642–86.

FRANTZICH, STEPHEN E. 1989. *Political Parties in the Technological Age*. New York: Longman.

FRANZ, MICHAEL M. 2008a. *Choices and Changes: Interest Groups in the Electoral Process*. Philadelphia: Temple University Press.

—— 2008b. The Interest Group Response to Campaign Finance Reform. *The Forum*, 6/1, art. 10.

FRASER, NANCY. 1997. *Justice Interruptus*. New York: Routledge.

FRASER, STEVE and GERSTLE, GARY (eds.) 1989. *The Rise and Fall of the New Deal Order, 1930–1980*. Princeton: Princeton University Press.

FREEDMAN, PAUL, FRANZ, MICHAEL, and GOLDSTEIN, KENNETH. 2004. Campaign Advertising and Democratic Citizenship. *American Journal of Political Science*, 48/4: 723–41.

—— and GOLDSTEIN, KEN. 1999. Measuring Media Exposure and the Effects of Negative Campaign Ads. *American Journal of Political Science*, 43: 1189–208.

FREEMAN, J. LEIPER. 1955. *The Political Process*. Garden City, NJ: Doubleday.

FREEMAN, JO. 1975. *The Politics of Women's Liberation*. New York: McKay.

—— 1986. The Political Culture of the Democratic and Republican Parties. *Political Science Quarterly*, 101/3: 327–56.

—— 1988. Women at the 1988 Democratic Convention. *PS: Political Science and Politics*, 21/4: 875–81.

FREEMAN, J. B. 2001. *Affairs of Honor: National Politics in the New Republic*. New Haven: Yale University Press.

FREEMAN, RICHARD B. and KATZ, LAWRENCE. 1994. Rising Wage Inequality: The United States vs. Other Advanced Countries. In *Working under Different Rules*, ed. Richard B. Freeman. New York: Russell Sage.

FRENDREIS, JOHN P. 1996. Voters, Government Officials, and Party Organizations: Connections and Distinctions. In *The State of the Parties*, ed. John C. Green and Daniel M. Shea. 2nd edn. (Lanham, Md.: Rowman & Littlefield).

—— GIBSON, JAMES L., and VERTZ, LAURA L. 1990. The Electoral Relevance of Local Party Organizations. *American Political Science Review*, 84/1: 225–35.

—— and GITELSON, ALAN R. 1999. Local Parties in the 1990s: Spokes in a Candidate-Centered Wheel. In *The State of the Parties*, ed. John C. Green and Daniel M. Shea. 3rd edn. Lanham, Md.: Rowman & Littlefield.

—— —— FLEMING, GREGORY, and LAYZELL, ANNE. 2004. Local Political Parties and the 1992 Campaign for the State Legislature. In *The State of the Parties*, ed. Daniel M. Shea and John C. Green. Lanham, Md.: Rowman & Littlefield.

FRIEDENBERG, ROBERT V. 1997. *Communications Consultants in Political Campaigns: The Ballot Box Warriors*. Westport, Conn.: Praeger.

FRIEDMAN, MILTON. 1962. *Capitalism and Freedom*. Chicago: University of Chicago Press.

FRIEDMAN, THOMAS L. 2005. *The World Is Flat*. New York: Farrar, Straus, and Giroux.

FRISCH, MORTON J. 1975. *Franklin D. Roosevelt: The Contribution to the New Deal to American Political Thought and Practice*. Boston: St Wayne.

FRITSCHLER, A. LEE. 1975. *Smoking and Politics*. 2nd edn. Englewood Cliffs, NJ: Prentice-Hall.

FROHLICH, NORMAN, OPPENHEIMER, JOE A., and YOUNG, ORAN R. 1971. *Political Leadership and Collective Goods*. Princeton: Princeton University Press.

FRYMER, PAUL. 1999. *Uneasy Alliances*. Princeton: Princeton University Press.

—— 2008. *Black and Blue*. Princeton: Princeton University Press.

FUNG, ARCHON. 2004. *Empowered Participation*. Princeton: Princeton University Press.

GAILMARD, SEAN and JENKINS, JEFFERY A. 2007a. Examining Minority Party Power in the House and Senate. Revision of paper presented at the Conference on Party Effects in the US Senate, University of Minnesota, Sept. 29–30, 2006.

—— —— 2007b. Negative Agenda Control in the Senate and House: Fingerprints of Majority Party Power. *Journal of Politics*, 69: 689–700.

—— —— 2008. Minority-Power in the Senate and House of Representatives. In *Why Not Parties: Party Effects in the United States Senate*, ed. Nathan Monroe, Jason Roberts, and David Rohde. Chicago: University of Chicago Press.

GAIS, THOMAS. 1996. *Improper Influence: Campaign Finance Law, Political Interest Groups, and the Problem of Equality*. Ann Arbor: University of Michigan Press.

GALDERISI, PETER F., EZRA, MARNI, and LYONS, MICHAEL. 2001. *Congressional Primaries and the Politics of Representation*. Lanham, Md.: Rowman & Littlefield.

GALVIN, DANIEL J. 2008. Changing Course: Reversing the Organizational Trajectory of the Democratic Party from Bill Clinton to Barack Obama. *The Forum*, 6/2.

—— Forthcoming. *Presidential Party Building*. Princeton: Princeton University Press.

GAMM, GERALD and SMITH, STEVEN S. 2002. Emergence of Senate Party Leadership. In *U.S. Senate Exceptionalism*, ed. Bruce Oppenheimer. Columbus: Ohio State University Press.

GANS, HERBERT. 1962. *The Urban Villagers*. New York: Free Press.

GARAND, JAMES C. 1985. Partisan Change and Shifting Expenditure Priorities in the American-States, 1945–1978. *American Politics Quarterly*, 13: 355–91.

GARSON, G. DAVID. 1978. *Group Theories of Politics*. Beverly Hills, Calif.: Sage Publications.

GARTNER, SCOTT S. and SEGURA, GARY M. 1997. Appearances Can Be Deceptive: Self-Selection, Social Group Identification, and Political Mobilization. *Rationality and Society*, 9: 131–61.

GAVENTA, JOHN. 1980. *Power and Powerlessness: Quiescence and Rebellion in an Appalachian Valley*. Urbana: University of Illinois Press.

—— 1982. *Power and Powerlessness: Quiescence and Rebellion in an Appalachian Valley*. Urbana: University of Illinois Press.

GEER, JOHN G. 1988. Assessing the Representativeness of Electorates in Presidential Primaries. *American Journal of Political Science*, 32/4: 927.

—— 1989. *Nominating Presidents: An Evaluation of Voters and Primaries*. New York: Greenwood Press.

—— and SHERE, MARK E. 1992. Party Competition and the Prisoner's Dilemma: An Argument for the Direct Primary. *Journal of Politics*, 54/3: 741.

GELMAN, ANDREW, PARK, DAVID, SHOR, BORIS, BAFUMI, JOSEPH, and CORTINA, JERONIMO. 2008. *Red State, Blue State, Rich State, Poor State: Why Americans Vote the Way They Do*. Princeton: Princeton University Press.

GERBER, ALAN S. 1998. Estimating the Effect of Campaign Spending on Senate Election Outcomes Using Instrumental Variables. *American Political Science Review*, 92/2: 401–11.

—— and GREEN, DONALD P. 1998. Rational Learning and Partisan Attitudes. *American Journal of Political Science*, 42: 794–818.

—— —— 1999. Misperceptions about Perceptual Bias. *Annual Review of Political Science*, 2: 189–210.

—— —— 2000. The Effects of Canvassing, Telephone Calls, and Direct Mail on Voter Turnout: A Field Experiment. *American Political Science Review,* 94/3: 653–63.

GERBER, ELISABETH R. 1999. *The Populist Paradox: Interest Group Influence and the Promise of Direct Legislation.* Princeton: Princeton University Press.

—— and MORTON, REBECCA B. 1998. Primary Election Systems and Representation. *Journal of Law and Economic Organizations,* 14/2: 304–24.

GERMOND, JACK and WITCOVER, JULES. 1981. *Blue Smoke and Mirrors: How Reagan Won and Why Carter Lost the Election of 1980.* New York: Viking.

—— —— 1993. *Mad as Hell: Revolt at the Ballot Box, 1992.* New York: Warner Books.

GERON, KIM, DE LA CRUZ, ENRIQUE, and SINGH, JAIDEEP. 2001. Asian Pacific American Social Movements and Interest Groups. *PS: Political Science and Politics,* 34: 619–24.

GERRING, JOHN. 1998. *Party Ideologies in America: 1828–1996.* Cambridge: Cambridge University Press.

GIBBARD, ALLAN. 1973. Manipulation of Voting Schemes: A General Result. *Econometrica,* 41/4 (July), 587–601.

GIBSON, JAMES, et al. (1983). Assessing Party Organizational Strength. *American Journal of Political Science,* 27/2 (May), 193–222.

GIBSON, RACHEL and ROMMELE, ANDREA. 2001. Changing Campaign Communications: A Party-Centered Theory of Professionalized Campaigning. *Harvard International Journal of Press/Politics,* 6/4: 31–43.

GIDLOW, LIETTE. 2004. *The Big Vote: Gender, Consumer Culture, and the Politics of Exclusion, 1890s–1920s.* Baltimore: Johns Hopkins University Press.

GIENAPP, WILLIAM. 1982. "Politics Seems to Enter into Everything": Political Culture in the North, 1840–1860. In *Essays on American Antebellum Politics, 1840–1860,* ed. Steven Maizlish and John Kushma. College Station: Texas A&M University Press.

—— 1987. *The Origins of the Republican Party, 1852–1856.* New York: Oxford University Press.

GIERZYNSKI, ANTHONY. 1992. *Legislative Party Campaign Committees in the American States.* Lexington, Mass.: University Press of Kentucky.

GILLESPIE, J. DAVID. 1993. *Politics at the Periphery: Third Parties in Two-Party America.* Columbia: University of South Carolina Press.

GIMPEL, JAMES. 1996. *National Elections and the Autonomy of American State Party Systems.* Pittsburgh: University of Pittsburgh Press.

GINSBERG, BENJAMIN and MARTIN SHEFTER. 1990. The Presidency, Interest Groups, and Social Forces: Creating a Republican Coalition. In *The Presidency and the Political System,* ed. Michael Nelson. 3rd edn. Washington, DC: CQ Press.

GLASER, JAMES M. 2005. *The Hand of the Past in Contemporary Southern Politics.* New Haven: Yale University Press.

—— 2006. The Primary Runoff as a Remnant of the Old South. *Electoral Studies,* 25/4: 776–90.

GODWIN, R. KENNETH and SELDON, BARRY J. 2002. What Corporations Really Want from Government. In *Interest Group Politics,* ed. Allan Cigler and Burdett Loomis. 6th edn. Washington: CQ Press.

GOFFMAN, ERVING. 1974. *Frame Analysis.* Cambridge, Mass.: Harvard University Press.

GOLD, HOWARD J. 1995. Third Party Voting in Presidential Elections: A Study of Perot, Anderson, and Wallace. *Political Research Quarterly,* 48: 775–94.

GOLDEN, MARISSA MARTINO. 1998. Interest Groups in the Rule-Making Process: Who Participates? Whose Voices Get Heard? *Journal of Public Administration Research and Theory,* 8/2: 245–70.

GOLDFIELD, MICHAEL. 1987. *The Decline of Organized Labor in the United States.* Chicago: University of Chicago Press.

—— 1989. Worker Insurgency, Radical Organization, and New Deal Labor Legislation. *American Political Science Review,* 83: 1257–82.

GOLDSTEIN, KENNETH M. 2004. What Did They See and When Did They See It? Measuring the Volume, Tone, and Targeting of Television Advertising in the 2000 Presidential Elections. In *Television Advertising and American Elections,* ed. Kenneth M. Goldstein and Patricia Strach. Upper Saddle River, NJ: Prentice-Hall.

—— and FREEDMAN, PAUL. 2002. Campaign Advertising and Voter Turnout. *Journal of Politics,* 46: 721–40.

GOLDWATER, BARRY. 1960. *The Conscience of a Conservative.* New York: Hillman Books.

GOODLIFFE, JAY and MAGLEBY, DAVID B. 2001. Campaign Finance in U.S. House Primary and General Elections. In *Congressional Primaries and the Politics of Representation,* ed. Peter F. Galderisi, Marni Ezra, and Michael Lyons. Lanham, Md.: Rowman & Littlefield.

GOODMAN, PAUL. 1975. The First American Party System. In *The American Party Systems: Stages of Party Development,* ed. William D. Chambers and Walter Dean Burnham. New York: Oxford University Press.

GOODWIN, DORIS KEARNS. 2005. *Team of Rivals: The Political Genius of Abraham Lincoln.* New York: Simon & Schuster.

GOODWYN, LAWRENCE. 1976. *Democratic Promise: The Populist Movement in America.* New York: Oxford University Press.

GORDON, SANFORD C. and HAFER, CATHERINE. 2005. Flexing Muscle: Corporate Political Expenditures as Signals to the Bureaucracy. *American Political Science Review,* 99: 245–61.

—— —— 2007. Corporate Influence and the Regulatory Mandate. *Journal of Politics,* 69: 300–19.

—— —— and LANDA, DIMITRI. 2007. Consumption or Investment? On Motivations for Political Giving. *Journal of Politics,* 69/4: 1057–72.

GORDON, STACY B. 2005. *Campaign Contributions and Legislative Voting: A New Approach.* New York: Routledge.

GOULD, LEWIS. 1986. *Reform and Regulation: American Politics from Roosevelt to Wilson.* 2nd edn. New York: Alfred A. Knopf.

—— 2003. *Grand Old Party: A history of the Republicans.* New York: Random House.

GOULD, ROGER V. and FERNANDEZ, ROBERTO M. 1989. Structures of Mediation. *Sociological Methodology,* 19: 89–126.

GRAMSCI, ANTONIO. 1992. *Prison Notebooks.* New York: Columbia University Press.

GRANOVETTER, MARK S. 1973. The Strength of Weak Ties. *American Journal of Sociology,* 78: 1360–80.

—— 1974. *Getting a Job: A Study of Contacts and Careers.* Cambridge, Mass.: Harvard University Press.

—— 1978. Threshold Models of Collective Behavior. *American Journal of Sociology,* 83: 1420–43.

—— and SOONG, ROLAND. 1983. Threshold Models of Diffusion and Collective Behavior. *Journal of Mathematical Sociology,* 9: 165–79.

—— —— 1988. Threshold Models of Diversity: Chinese Restaurants, Residential Segregation, and the Spiral of Silence. *Sociological Methodology,* 18: 69–104.

GRAY, VIRGINIA and LOWERY, DAVID. 1996a. *The Population Ecology of Interest Representation: Lobbying Communities in the American States.* Ann Arbor: University of Michigan Press.

—— —— 1996b. A Niche Theory of Interest Representation. *Journal of Politics*, 59 (Mar.), 91–111.

—— —— 1997. Reconceptualizing PAC Formation: It's Not a Collective Action Problem, and It May Be an Arms Race. *American Politics Quarterly*, 25/3: 319–46.

—— —— 1998. To Lobby Alone or in a Flock: Foraging Behavior among Organized Interests. *American Politics Quarterly*, 26/1: 5–34.

—— —— 2002. State Interest Group Research and the Mixed Legacy of Belle Zeller. *State Politics and Policy Quarterly*, 2/4: 388–410.

—— —— Fellowes, Matthew, and Anderson, Jennifer. 2005. Understanding the Demand-Side of Lobbying: Interest System Energy in the American States. *American Politics Research*, 33/1: 404–34.

—— —— —— and McAtee, Andrea. 2004. Public Opinion, Public Policy, and Organized Interests in the American States. *Political Research Quarterly*, 57/3: 411–20.

Green, Donald P. 2004. Mobilizing African-American Voters Using Direct Mail and Commercial Phone Banks: A Field Experiment. *Political Research Quarterly*, 57/2: 245–55.

—— and Gerber, Alan S., 2004. *Get Out the Vote! How to Increase Voter Turnout*. Washington, DC: Brookings Institution.

—— and Palmquist, Bradley. 1994. How Stable Is Party Identification? *Political Behavior*, 16: 437–66.

—— —— and Schickler, Eric. 2002. *Partisan Hearts and Minds: Political Parties and the Social Identities of Voters*. New Haven: Yale University Press.

Green, John C. 2007. *The Faith Factor: How Religion Influences the Vote*. Westport, Conn.: Praeger.

—— and Dionne, E. J. 2008. Religion and American Politics: More Secular, More Evangelical or Both? In *Red, Blue and Purple American: The Future of Election Demographics*, ed. Ruy Teixeira. Washington, DC: Brookings Institution Press.

—— and Jackson, John S. 2007. Faithful Divides: Party Elites and Religion in 2004. In *A Matter of Faith: Religion in the 2004 Presidential Election*, ed. David E. Campbell. Washington, DC: Brookings Institution Press.

—— Kellstedt, Lyman A., Smidt, Corwin E., and Guth, James L. 2007. How the Faithful Voted: Religious Communities and the Presidential Vote. In *A Matter of Faith: Religion in the 2004 Presidential Election*, ed. David E. Campbell. Washington, DC: Brookings Institution Press.

—— Rozell, Mark J., and Wilcox, Clyde. 2000. *Prayers in the Precincts: The Christian Right in the 1998 Elections*. Washington, DC: Georgetown University Press.

—— —— —— 2001. Social Movements and Party Politics. *Journal for the Scientific Study of Religion*, 40/3: 413–26.

—— —— —— 2003. *The Christian Right in American Politics: Marching to the Millennium*. Washington, DC: Georgetown University Press.

Greenberg, Joseph and Shepsle, Kenneth. 1987. The Effect of Electoral Rewards in Multiparty Competition with Entry. *American Political Science Review*, 81/2 (June), 525–37.

Greenberg, Stan and Carville, James. 2005a. Re: Defining the Choice: A Strategy for Going Outside and Reaching New Ground. Washington, DC: Democracy Corps.

—— —— 2005b. Battle Plan for Democrats in 2006—Go After Perot Voters as Reformers. Washington, DC: Greenberg, Quinlan, Rosner.

Greenhouse, Steven. 2007. Sharp Decline in Union Members in '06. *New York Times*, Jan. 26, A11.

GREENSTEIN, FRED I. and POLSBY, NELSON W. 1975. *Governmental Institutions and Processes*, vol. v of *The Handbook of Political Science*. Reading, Mass.: Addison-Wesley.

GREENSTONE, J. DAVID. 1969. *Labor in American Politics*. New York: Alfred A. Knopf.

GRENZKE, JANET M. 1989. PACs and the Congressional Supermarket: The Currency Is Complex. *American Journal of Political Science*, 33/1: 1–24.

GRIER, KEVIN B., MUNGER, MICHAEL C., and ROBERTS, BRIAN E. 1991. The Industrial Organization of Corporate Political Participation. *Southern Economic Journal*, 57/3: 727–38.

—— —— —— 1994. The Determinants of Industry: Political Activity, 1978–1986. *American Political Science Review*, 88/4: 911–26.

GRIFTH, ERNEST S. 1939. *The Impasse of Democracy*. New York: Harrison-Hilton.

GRODZINS, MORTON. 1966. *The American System: A New View of Government in the United States*. Chicago: Rand McNally.

GROFMAN, BERNARD. 2004. Downs and Two-Party Convergence. *Annual Review of Political Science*, 7: 25–46.

—— and BRUNELL, THOMAS L. 2001. Explaining the Ideological Differences between the Two U.S. Senators Elected from the Same State: An Institutional Effects Model. In *Congressional Primaries and the Politics of Representation*, ed. Peter F. Galderisi, Marni Ezra, and Michael Lyons. Lanham, Md.: Rowman & Littlefield.

—— COLLET, CHRISTIAN, and GRIFN, ROBERT. 1998. Analyzing the Turnout–Competition Link with Aggregate Cross-Sectional Data. *Public Choice*, 95: 233–46.

GRØNBJERG, KIRSTEN A. and SALAMON, LESTER M. 2002. Devolution, Marketization, and the Changing Shape of Government–Nonprofit Relations. In *The State of Nonprofit America*, ed. Lester Salamon. Washington, DC: Brookings Institution.

GROSECLOSE, TIM and SNYDER, JAMES M. 1996. Buying Supermajorities. *American Political Science Review*, 90: 303–15.

GROSS, DONALD A. and GOIDEL, ROBERT K. 2001. The Impact of State Campaign Finance Laws. *State Politics and Policy Quarterly*, 1/2: 180–95.

GROSSMAN, LAWRENCE. 1976. *The Democratic Party and the Negro: Northern and National Politics, 1868–1892*. Urbana: University of Illinois Press.

GROSSMAN, MATTHEW. 2006. One Person, One Lobbyist? American Public Constituencies and Organized Representation. MS, Department of Political Science, University of California, Berkeley.

—— and DOMINGUEZ, CASEY B. K. 2009. Party Coalitions and Interest Group Networks. *American Politics Research*, 37/5: 767–800.

GRYNAVISKI, JEFFREY. 2006. A Bayesian Learning Model with Implications for Party Identification. *Journal of Theoretical Politics*, 18: 323–46.

—— 2009. *Partisan Bonds*. Cambridge: Cambridge University Press.

GUIRAUDON, VIRGINIE. 2000. European Integration and Migration Policy: Vertical Policy-Making as Venue Shopping. *Journal of Common Market Studies*, 38/2: 251–71.

GUNDERSON, ROBERT. 1957. *The Log Cabin Campaign*. Lexington: University Press of Kentucky.

GUTH, JAMES L. and GREEN, JOHN C. 1993. Salience: The Core Concept? In *Rediscovering the Religious Factor in American Politics*, ed. David C. Leege and Lyman A. Kellstedt. Armonk, NY: M. E. Sharpe.

—— and KELLSTEDT, LYMAN A. 2001. Religion and Congress. In *In God We Trust?* ed. Corwin E. Smidt. Grand Rapids, Mich.: Baker Press.

HACKER, ANDREW. 1965. Does a Divisive Primary Harm a Candidate's Election Chances? *American Political Science Review*, 59/1: 105–10.

HACKER, JACOB S. 1997. *The Road to Nowhere: The Genesis of President Clinton's Plan for Health Security*. Princeton: Princeton University Press.

—— 2002. *The Divided Welfare State: The Battle over Public and Private Social Benefits in the United States*. Cambridge: Cambridge University Press.

—— 2006. *The Great Risk Shift*. New York: Oxford University Press.

—— and PIERSON, PAUL. 2005. *Off Center*. New Haven: Yale University Press.

HADLEY, ARTHUR T. 1976. *The Invisible Primary*. Englewood Cliffs, NJ: Prentice-Hall.

HAEBERLE, STEVEN H. 1985. Closed Primaries and Party Support in Congress. *American Politics Quarterly*, 13: 341–52.

HAGEN, MICHAEL G. and MAYER, WILLIAM G. 2000. The Modern Politics of Presidential Selection: How Changing the Rules Really Did Change the Game. In *In Pursuit of the White House 2000: How We Choose Our Presidential Nominees*, ed. William G. Mayer. New York: Chatham House.

HAIDER-MARKEL, DONALD P. 1997. Interest Group Survival: Shared Interests versus Competition for Resources. *Journal of Politics*, 59/3: 903–12.

HALL, RICHARD L. and DEARDORFF, ALAN V. 2006. Lobbying as Legislative Subsidy. *American Political Science Review*, 100: 69–84.

—— and EVANS, C. LAWRENCE. 1990. The Power of Subcommittees. *Journal of Politics*, 52: 335–55.

—— and GROFMAN, BERNARD. 1990. The Committee Assignment Process and the Conditional Nature of Committee Bias. *American Political Science Review*, 84: 1149–66.

—— and MILER, KRISTINA C. 2008. What Happens after the Alarm? Interest Group Subsidies to Legislative Overseers. *Journal of Politics*, 70: 990–1005.

—— and WAYMAN, FRANK. 1990. Buying Time: Moneyed Interests and the Mobilization of Bias in Congressional Committees. *American Political Science Review*, 84: 797–820.

HAMBURGER, TOM and WALLSTEIN, PETER. 2006. *One Party Country*. Hoboken, NJ: Wiley.

HAMM, KEITH E. and HOGAN, ROBERT E. 2008. Campaign Finance Laws and Candidacy Decisions in State Legislative Elections. *Political Research Quarterly*, 61/3: 458–67.

—— WEBER, ANDREW R., and ANDERSON, R. BRUCE. 1994. The Impact of Lobbying Laws and their Enforcement: A Contrasting View. *Social Science Quarterly*, 75: 378–91.

HAMMOND, THOMAS and FRASER, JANE. 1983. Baselines for Evaluating Explanations of Coalition Behavior in Congress. *Journal of Politics*, 45: 635–56.

HAN, HAHRIE and BRADY, DAVID. 2007. A Delayed Return to Historical Norms: Congressional Party Polarization after the Second World War. *British Journal of Political Science*, 37/03 (July), 505–31.

HANDLER, EDWARD and MULKERN, JOHN R. 1992. *Business in Politics: Strategies of Corporate Political Action Committees*. Lexington, Mass.: Lexington Books.

HANNAN, MICHAEL T. and FREEMAN, JOHN. 1989. *Organizational Ecology*. Cambridge, Mass.: Harvard University Press.

HANSEN, JOHN MARK. 1991. *Gaining Access: Congress and the Farm Lobby, 1919–1981*. Chicago: University of Chicago Press.

HANSEN, WENDY L. and MITCHELL, NEIL J. 2000. Disaggregating and Explaining Corporate Political Activity: Domestic and Foreign Contributions in National Politics. *American Political Science Review*, 94 (Dec.), 891–903.

HANSEN, WENDY L. and DROPE, JEFFREY M. 2004. Collective Action, Pluralism, and the Legitimacy Tariff: Corporate Activity or Inactivity in Politics. *Political Research Quarterly*, 57 (Sept.–Oct.), 421–9.

————— 2005. The Logic of Private and Collective Action. *American Journal of Political Science*, 49: 150–67.

HARBAUGH, WILLIAM. 1961. *Power and Responsibility: The Life and Times of Theodore Roosevelt.* New York: Farrar, Straus, and Cudahay.

HARBRIDGE, LAUREL. 2009. Bipartisanship in a Polarized Congress. Ph.D. dissertation, Stanford University.

HARMEL, ROBERT and ROBERTSON, JOHN D. 1985. Formation and Success of New Parties: A Cross-National Analysis. *International Political Science Review*, 6: 501–23.

HARRINGTON, JOSEPH, JR. 1992. The Role of Party Reputation in the Formation of Policy. *Journal of Public Economics*, 49: 107–21.

HART, DAVID M. 2001. Why Do Some Firms Give? Why Do Some Firms Give a Lot? High-Tech PACs, 1977–1996. *Journal of Politics*, 63: 1230–49.

—— 2004. "Business" Is Not an Interest Group: On the Study of Companies in American National Politics. *Annual Review of Political Science*, 7: 47–69.

HARTZ, LOUIS. 1955. *The Liberal Tradition in America.* New York: Harcourt Brace.

HARVEY, ANNA and MUKHERJEE, BUMBA. 2006. Electoral Institutions and the Evolution of Partisan Conventions, 1880–1940. *American Politics Research*, 34/3: 368–98.

HAWLEY, ELLIS. 1966. *The New Deal and the Problem of Monopoly: A Study in Economic Ambivalence.* Princeton: Princeton University Press.

HAYES, MICHAEL T. 1978. The Semi-Sovereign Pressure Groups. *Journal of Politics*, 40: 134–61.

HEALE, MICHAEL J. 1982. *The Presidential Quest: Candidates and Images in American Political Culture, 1787–1852.* London: Longman.

HEANEY, MICHAEL T. 2004a. Issue Networks, Information, and Interest Group Alliances: The Case of Wisconsin Welfare Politics, 1993–99. *State Politics and Policy Quarterly*, 4 (Fall), 237–70.

—— 2004b. Outside the Issue Niche. *American Politics Research*, 32/6: 611–51.

—— 2006. Brokering Health Policy. *Journal of Health Politics, Policy and Law*, 31/5: 887–944.

—— 2007. Identity Crisis. In *Interest Group Politics*, ed. Allan J. Cigler and Burdett A. Loomis. 7th edn. Washington, DC: CQ Press.

—— 2008. Public Interest Advocacy. In *International Encyclopedia of the Social Sciences*, ed. William A. Darity, Jr. 2nd edn. Farmington Hills, Mich.: Gale Publishing.

—— and ROJAS, FABIO. 2007. Partisans, Nonpartisans, and the Antiwar Movement in the United States. *American Politics Research*, 35/4: 431–64.

HEARD, ALEXANDER. 1956. *Money and Politics.* New York: Public Affairs Committee.

HEBERLIG, ERIC S. 2003. Congressional Parties, Fundraising, and Committee Ambition. *Political Research Quarterly*, 56/2: 151–62.

—— HETHERINGTON, MARC, and LARSON, BRUCE. 2006. The Price of Leadership: Campaign Money and the Polarization of Congressional Parties. *Journal of Politics*, 68: 992–1005.

HECKMAN, JAMES and SNYDER, JAMES. 1997. *Linear Probability Models of the Demand for Attributes with an Empirical Application to Estimating the Preferences of Legislators. Rand Journal of Economics*, Special Issue, S142–89.

HECLO, HUGH. 1978. Issue Networks and the Executive Establishment. In *The New American Political System*, ed. Anthony King. Washington, DC: American Enterprise Institute.

—— 2003. Ronald Reagan and the American Public Philosophy. In *The Reagan Presidency: Pragmatic Conservatism and its Legacies*, ed. W. Elliot Brownlee and Hugh Davis Graham. Lawrence: University Press of Kansas.

HEINZ, JOHN P., LAUMANN, EDWARD O., NELSON, ROBERT L., and SALISBURY, ROBERT H. 1993. *The Hollow Core: Private Interests in National Policy Making*. Cambridge, Mass.: Harvard University Press.

HERRERA, RICHARD. 1995. The Crosswinds of Change: Sources of Change in the Democratic and Republican Parties. *Political Research Quarterly*, 48 (June), 291–312.

HERRING, PENDLETON. 1940. *The Politics of Democracy: American Parties in Action*. New York: W. W. Norton.

HERRNSON, PAUL S. 1988. *Party Campaigning in the 1980s*. Cambridge, Mass.: Harvard University Press.

—— 1989. National Party Decision Making, Strategies, and Resource Distribution in Congressional Elections. *Western Political Quarterly*, 42: 301–23.

—— 1990. Reemergent National Party Organizations. In *The Parties Respond: Changes in the American Party System*, ed. L. Sandy Maisel. Boulder, Colo.: Westview Press.

—— 1994. The Revitalization of National Party Organizations. In *The Parties Respond: Changes in the American Party System*, ed. L. Sandy Maisel. 2nd edn. Boulder, Colo.: Westview Press.

—— 1998. *Congressional Elections: Campaigning at Home and in Washington*. 2nd edn. Washington, DC: CQ Press.

—— 2000. *Congressional Elections: Campaigning at Home and in Washington*. 3rd edn. Washington, DC: CQ Press.

—— 2002. National Party Organizations at the Dawn of the Twenty-First Century. In *The Parties Respond*, ed. L. Sandy Maisel. 4th edn. Boulder, Colo.: Westview Press.

—— 2004. *Congressional Elections: Campaigning at Home and in Washington*. 4th edn. Washington, DC: CQ Press.

—— 2008. *Congressional Elections: Campaigning at Home and in Washington*. 5th edn. Washington, DC: CQ Press.

—— and DWYRE, DIANA. 1999. Party Issue Advocacy in Congressional Elections. In *The State of the Parties*, ed. John C. Green and Daniel M. Shea. 3rd edn. Lanham, Md.: Rowman & Littlefield.

—— and MENEFEE-LIBEY, DAVID. 1990. The Dynamics of Party Organizational Development. *Midsouth Political Science Journal*, 11: 3–30.

HERSCH, PHILIP L. and McDOUGALL, GERALD S. 2000. Determinants of Automobile PAC Contributions to House Incumbents: Own Versus Rival Effects. *Public Choice*, 104 (Sept.), 329–43.

HERSHEY, MAJORIE RANDON. 1993. Citizens' Groups and Political Parties in the United States. *Annals of the American Academy of Political and Social Science*, 528/2: 142–56.

HETHERINGTON, MARC J. 2001. Resurgent Mass Partisanship: The Role of Elite Polarization. *American Political Science Review*, 95 (Sept.), 619–31.

—— LARSON, BRUCE, and GLOBETTI, SUZANNE. 2003. The Redistricting Cycle and Strategic Candidate Decisions in U.S. House Races. *Journal of Politics*, 65/4: 1221–34.

HILL, DAVID. 1981. Political Culture and Female Political Representation. *Journal of Politics*, 43/1: 159.

—— 2006. *American Voter Turnout: An Institutional Perspective*. Boulder, Colo.: Westview Press.

HIMES, D. 1995. Strategy and Tactics for Campaign Fundraising. In *Campaigns and Elections: American Style*, ed. James A. Thurber and Candice J. Nelson. Boulder, Colo.: Westview Press.

HINCKLEY, BARBARA. 1972. Coalitions in Congress: Size and Ideological Distance. *Midwest Journal of Political Science*, 16: 197–207.

HINDMAN, MATTHEW. 2008. *The Myth of Digital Democracy*. Princeton: Princeton University Press.

HINICH, MELVIN H. 1977. Equilibrium in Spatial Voting: The Median Voter Result Is an Artifact. *Journal of Economic Theory*, 16/2 (Dec.), 208–19.

—— LEDYARD, JOHN, and ORDESHOOK, PETER. 1972. Nonvoting and Existence of Equilibrium under Majority Rule. *Journal of Economic Theory*, 4: 144–53.

—— and MUNGER, MICHAEL C. 1997. *Analytical Politics*. Cambridge: Cambridge University Press.

—— and ORDESHOOK, PETER. 1969. Abstentions and Equilibrium in the Electoral Process. *Public Choice*, 7: 81–106.

HIRANO, SHIGEO and SNYDER, JAMES M., JR. 2007. The Decline of Third-Party Voting in the United States. *Journal of Politics*, 69/1: 1–16.

HIRSCHMAN, ALBERT O. 1970. *Exit, Voice, and Loyalty*. Cambridge, Mass.: Harvard University Press.

HOFSTADTER, RICHARD. 1955. *The Age of Reform: From Bryan to FDR*. New York: Vintage Books.

—— 1969. *The Idea of a Party System: The Rise of Legitimate Opposition in the United States, 1780–1840*. Berkeley: University of California Press.

HOFSTETTER, C. RICHARD. 1973. Inter-Party Competition and Electoral Turnout: The Case of Indiana. *American Journal of Political Science*, 17: 351–66.

HOGAN, ROBERT E. 2003a. The Effects of Primary Divisiveness on General Election Outcomes in State Legislative Elections. *American Politics Research*, 31/1: 27–47.

—— 2003b. Institutional and District-Level Sources of Competition in State Legislative Elections. *Social Science Quarterly*, 84/3: 543–60.

—— 2005. State Campaign Finance Laws and Interest Group Electioneering Activities. *Journal of Politics*, 67/3: 887–906.

HOJNACKI, MARIE. 1997. Interest Groups' Decisions to Join Alliances or Work Alone. *American Journal of Political Science*, 41/1: 61–87.

—— and KIMBALL, DAVID C. 1998. Organized Interests and the Decision of Whom to Lobby in Congress. *American Political Science Review*, 92: 775–90.

—— —— 1999. The Who and How of Organizations' Lobbying Strategies in Committee. *Journal of Politics*, 61: 999–1024.

—— —— 2001. PAC Contributions and Lobbying Contacts in Congressional Committees. *Political Research Quarterly*, 54: 161–80.

HOLT, MICHAEL F. 1978. *The Political Crisis of the 1850s*. New York: Wiley.

—— 1999. *The Rise and Fall of the American Whig Party: Jacksonian Politics and the Onset of the Civil War*. New York: Oxford University Press.

—— 2001. Change and Continuity in the Party Period: The Substance and Structure of American Politics, 1835–1885. In *Contesting Democracy: Substance and Structure in American Political History, 1775–2000*, ed. Byron E. Shafer and Anthony J. Badger. Lawrence: University Press of Kansas.

HOOGENBOOM, ARI. 1961. *Outlawing the Spoils: A History of the Civil Service Reform Movement, 1865–1883*. Urbana: University of Illinois Press.

HOOGHE, LISBET, and MARKS, GARY. 2001. *Multi-Level Governance and European Integration.* Lanham, Md.: Rowman & Littlefield.

HOOKS, BELL. 1981. *Ain't I a Woman?* Boston: South End Press.

HOPKINS, JAMES F. 1973. Election of 1824. In *History of US Political Parties.* 4 vols., ed. Arthur M. Schlesinger Jr. New York: Chelsea House.

HORRIGAN, MARIE. 2006. Conservative "Club" Wins with a Broader Battle Plan. *CQ Politics* (July 31).

HOTELLING, HAROLD. 1929. Stability in Competition, *Economic Journal*, 39: 41–57.

HOWE, DANIEL WALKER. 1979. *The Political Culture of the American Whigs.* Chicago: University of Chicago Press.

HREBENAR, RONALD J. and THOMAS, CLIVE S. (eds.) 1987. *Interest Group Politics in the American West.* Salt Lake City: University of Utah Press.

—— —— (eds.) 1992. *Interest Group Politics in the Southern States.* Tuscaloosa: University of Alabama Press.

—— —— (eds.) 1993a. *Interest Group Politics in the Midwestern States.* Ames: Iowa State University Press.

—— —— (eds.) 1993b. *Interest Group Politics in the Northeastern States.* University Park: Pennsylvania State University Press.

HUBER, JOHN D. 1996. The Vote of Confidence in Parliamentary Democracies. *American Political Science Review*, 90: 269–82.

HUCKFELDT, ROBERT and KOHFELD, CAROL WEITZEL. 1989. *Race and the Decline of Class in American Politics.* Urbana: University of Illinois Press.

HUG, SIMON. 2000. Studying the Electoral Success of New Political Parties. *Party Politics*, 6: 187–97.

HULA, KEVIN W. 1999. *Lobbying Together: Interest Group Coalitions in Legislative Politics.* Washington, DC: Georgetown University Press.

—— 2007. *Lobbying Together: Interest Group Coalitions in Legislative Politics.* Washington, DC: Georgetown University Press.

HUNTER, FLOYD. 1953. *Community Power Structure.* Chapel Hill: University of North Carolina Press.

—— 1963. *Community Power Structure.* Garden City, NY: Anchor Books.

HUNTER, JAMES DAVISON. 1991. *Culture Wars: The Struggle to Define America.* New York: Basic Books.

HURLEY, PATRICIA A. 1989. Partisan Representation and the Failure of Realignment in the 1980s. *American Journal of Political Science*, 33: 240–61.

—— BRADY, DAVID, and COOPER, JOSEPH. 1979. The Decline of Party in the U.S. House of Representatives, 1887–1968. *Legislative Studies Quarterly*, 4: 381–407.

—— and WILSON, RICK. 1989. Partisan Voting Patterns in the U.S. Senate, 1877–1986. *Legislative Studies Quarterly*, 14: 225–50.

HURWITZ, MARK S., MOILES, ROGER J., and ROHDE, DAVID W. 2001. Distributive and Partisan Issues in Agriculture Policy in the 104th House. *American Political Science Review*, 95 (Dec.), 911–22.

IMAI, KOSUKE. 2005. Do Get-Out-the-Vote Calls Reduce Turnout? The Importance of Statistical Methods for Field Experiments. *American Political Science Review*, 99: 283–300.

IMIG, DOUGLAS R. 1996. *Poverty and Power: The Political Representation of Poor Americans.* Lincoln: University of Nebraska Press.

INGBERMAN, DANIEL and VILLANI, JOHN. 1993. An Institutional Theory of Divided Government and Policy Polarization. *American Journal of Political Science*, 37: 429–71.

IYENGAR, SHANTO. 2002. The Effects of Media-Based Campaigns on Candidate and Voter Behavior: Implications for Judicial Elections. *Indiana Law Review*, 35: 691–700.

JACKMAN, MARY R. and JACKMAN, ROBERT W. 1983. *Class Awareness in the United States*. Berkeley: University of California Press.

JACKSON, DAVID J. and ENGEL, STEVEN T. 2003. Friends Don't Let Friends Vote for Free Trade: The Dynamics of the Labor PAC Punishment Strategy over PNTR. *Political Research Quarterly*, 56/4: 441–8.

JACKSON, JOHN E. 1975. Issues, Party Choices, and Presidential Votes. *American Journal of Political Science*, 19/2: 161–85.

JACKSON, JOHN S., BROWN, BARBARA L., and BOSITIS, DAVID. 1982. Herbert McClosky and Friends Revisited: 1980 Democratic and Republican Elites Compared to the Mass Public. *American Politics Quarterly*, 10: 58–80.

JACKSON, ROBERT A. 1992. Effects of Public Opinion and Political System Characteristics on State Policy Outputs. *Publius*, 22: 31–46.

——— and CARSEY, THOMAS M. 1999. Presidential Voting across the American States. *American Politics Research*, 27: 379–402.

JACOBS, LAWRENCE R. 2005. Communicating from the White House: Narrowcasting and the National Interest. In *The Executive Branch*, ed. Joel D. Aberbach and Mark A. Peterson. New York: Oxford University Press.

JACOBSON, GARY C. 1985–6. Party Organization and Campaign Resources in 1982. *Political Science Quarterly*, 100: 604–25.

——— 1989. Strategic Politicians and the Dynamics of U.S. House Elections, 1946–86. *American Political Science Review*, 83/3: 773–93.

——— 1993. Deficit-Cutting Politics and Congressional Elections. *Political Science Quarterly*, 108: 375–402.

——— 1999. The Effect of the AFL–CIO's "Voter Education" Campaigns on the 1996 House Elections. *Journal of Politics*, 61/1: 185–94.

——— 2000. Party Polarization in National Politics: The Electoral Connection. In *Polarized Politics: Congress and the President in a Partisan Era*, ed. Jon Bond and Richard Fleisher. Washington, DC: CQ Press.

——— 2003. Terror, Terrain, and Turnout: Explaining the 2002 Midterm Elections. *Political Science Quarterly*, 118/1: 1–22.

——— 2008. *A Divider, Not a Uniter: George W. Bush and the American People*. New York: Pearson Longman.

——— and KERNELL, SAMUEL. 1981. *Strategy and Choice in Congressional Elections*. New Haven: Yale University Press.

JAMES, SCOTT. 2000. *Presidents, Parties, and the State: A Party System Perspective on Democratic Regulatory Choice, 1884–1936*. New York. Cambridge University Press.

——— 2005. The Evolution of the Presidency: Between the Promise and the Fear. In *The Executive Branch*, ed. Joel D. Aberbach and Mark A. Peterson. New York: Oxford University Press.

JELEN, TED G. (ed.) 2002. *Sacred Markets, Sacred Canopies*. Lanham, Md.: Rowman & Littlefield.

——— and WILCOX, CLYDE. 1995. *Public Attitudes toward Church and State*. Armonk, NY: M. E. Sharpe.

JENKINS, J. CRAIG and BRENTS, BARBARA. 1989. Social Protest, Hegemonic Competition and Social Reform: The Political Origins of the American Welfare State. *American Sociological Review*, 54: 891–909.

—— ECKERT, CRAIG M. 1986. Channeling Black Insurgency. *American Sociological Review*, 51/6: 812–29.

JENKINS, SHANNON. 2006. The Impact of Party and Ideology on Roll-Call Voting in State Legislatures. *Legislative Studies Quarterly*, 31: 235–57.

—— 2008. Party Influence on Roll Call Voting: A View from the States. *State Politics and Policy Quarterly*, 8: 239–62.

JENNINGS, EDWARD T., JR. 1979. Competition, Constituencies, and Welfare Policies in American States. *American Political Science Review*, 73: 414–29.

JENSEN, LAURA. 2003. *Patriots, Settlers, and the Origins of American Social Policy*. Cambridge: Cambridge University Press.

JENSEN, RICHARD. 1969. American Election Analysis. In *Politics and the Social Sciences*, ed. Seymour Martin Lipset. New York: Oxford University Press.

—— 1971. *The Winning of the Midwest: Social and Political Conflict, 1888–1896*. Chicago: University of Chicago Press.

—— 2001. Democracy, Republicanism, and Efficiency: The Values of American Politics, 1885–1930. In *Contesting Democracy: Substance and Structure in American Political History, 1775–2000*, ed. Byron E. Shafer and Anthony J. Badger. Lawrence: University Press of Kansas.

JEWELL, MALCOLM E. 1984. *Parties and Primaries: Nominating State Governors*. New York: Praeger.

—— and MOREHOUSE, SARAH McCALLY. 2001. *Political Parties and Elections in American States*. 4th edn. Washington, DC: CQ Press.

—— and WHICKER, MARCIA LYNN. 1994. *Legislative Leadership in the American States*. Ann Arbor: University of Michigan Press.

JOHN, RICHARD. 2003. Affairs of Office: The Executive Departments, the Election of 1828, and the Making of the Democratic Party. In *The Democratic Experiment: New Directions in American Political History*, ed. Meg Jacobs, William J. Novak, and Julian Zelizer. Princeton: Princeton University Press.

JOHNSON, DENNIS. 2000. Business of Political Consulting. In *Campaign Warriors: Political Consultants in Elections*, ed. James A. Thurber and Candice J. Nelson. Washington, DC: Brookings Institution.

—— 2007. *No Place for Amateurs: How Political Consultants Are Reshaping American Democracy*. New York: Routledge.

JOHNSON, DONALD B. 1960. *The Republican Party and Wendell Willkie*. Urbana: University of Illinois Press.

—— and GIBSON, JAMES R. 1974. The Divisive Primary Revisited: Activists in Iowa. *American Political Science Review*, 68 (Mar.), 67–77.

JOHNSON, PAUL E. 1990. Unraveling in Democratically Governed Groups. *Rationality and Society*, 2: 4–34.

—— 1996. Unraveling in a Variety of Institutional Settings. *Journal of Theoretical Politics*, 8: 299–331.

JONES, BRYAN D. and BAUMGARTNER, FRANK R. 2005. *The Politics of Attention*. Chicago: University of Chicago Press.

JONES, CHARLES O. 1975. *Clean Air: The Policies and Politics of Pollution Control*. Pittsburgh: University of Pittsburgh Press.

JONES, CHARLES O. 2007. Governing Executively: Bush's Paradoxical Style. In *Second Term Blues: How George W. Bush Has Governed*, ed. John C. Fortier and Norman J. Ornstein. Washington, DC: American Enterprise Institute and Brookings Institution.

JONES, JAYSON K. and ROSADO, ANA C. 2008. MoveOn Terminates its 527. *New York Times*, June 20. <http://thecaucus.blogs.nytimes.com/2008/06/20/moveon-terminates-its-527/?scp=1&sq=obama%20527&st=cse>. Accessed Dec. 31, 2008.

JORDAN, GRANT. 2001. *Shell, Greenpeace, and the Brent Spar*. New York: Palgrave.

KAMIENIECKI, SHELDON. 2006. *Corporate America and Environmental Policy: How Often Does Business Get its Way?* Stanford, Calif.: Stanford University Press.

KANDORI, MICHIHIRO. 1992. Social Norms and Community Enforcement. *Review of Economic Studies*, 59: 63–80.

KANE, PAUL. 2008. NRCC Says Ex-Treasurer Diverted up to $1 Million. *Washington Post*, Mar. 14.

KANTHAK, KRISTIN and CRISP, BRIAN. 2005. Partisans, Collaborators, Loners and Compromisers: Co-sponsorship Patterns as a Means of Challenger Deterrence. Paper presented at Annual Meeting of the Midwest Political Science Association, Chicago.

——and MORTON, REBECCA. 2001. The Effects of Electoral Rules on Congressional Primaries. In *Congressional Primaries and the Politics of Representation*, ed. Peter F. Galderisi, Marni Ezra, and Michael Lyons. Lanham, Md.: Rowman & Littlefield.

KAROL, DAVID. 2009. *Party Position Change in American Politics: Coalition Management*. New York: Cambridge University Press.

KATZ, JONATHAN NED. 1995. *The Invention of Heterosexuality*. New York: Dutton.

KATZ, MICHAEL B. 2001. *The Price of Citizenship*. New York: Henry Holt.

KATZ, RICHARD S. and MAIR, PETER. 1994 *How Parties Organize: Change and Adaptation in Party Organizations in Western Democracies*. Thousand Oaks, Calif.: Sage Publications.

—— —— 1995. Changing Models of Party Organization and Party Democracy: The Emergence of the Cartel Party. *Party Politics*, 1/1: 5–28.

KATZENSTEIN, PETER J. 1985. *Small States in World Markets*. Ithaca, NY: Cornell University Press.

KAUFMANN, KAREN M., GIMPEL, JAMES G., and HOFFMAN, ADAM H. 2003. A Promise Fulfilled? Open Primaries and Representation. *Journal of Politics*, 65/2: 457–76.

——and PETROCIK, JOHN R. 1999. The Changing Politics of American Men: Understanding the Sources of the Gender Gap. *American Journal of Political Science*, 43 (July), 864–87.

KAYDEN, XANDRA and MAHE, EDDIE, JR. 1985. *The Party Goes On: The Persistence of the Two-Party System*. New York: Basic Books.

KAZEE, THOMAS A. and THORNBERRY, MARY C. 1990. Where's the Party? Congressional Candidate Recruitment and American Party Organizations. *Western Political Quarterly*, 43/1: 61–80.

KEATING, MICHAEL and HOOGHE, LIESBET. 2001. By-passing the Nation State? Regions and the EU Policy Process. In *European Union: Power and Policy-Making*, ed. Jeremy J. Richardson. 2nd edn. New York: Routledge.

KECK, MARGARET E. and SIKKINK, KATHRYN. 1998. *Activists beyond Borders: Advocacy Networks in International Politics*. Ithaca, NY: Cornell University Press.

KEEFE, WILLIAM J. 1954. Parties, Partisanship, and Public Policy in the Pennsylvania Legislature. *American Political Science Review*, 48: 450–64.

—— 1956. Comparative Study of the Role of Political Parties in State Legislatures. *Western Political Quarterly*, 9: 726–42.

—— 1976. *Parties, Politics, and Public Policy in America*. Hinsdale, Ill.: Dryden Press.

KEIM, GERALD and BAYSINGER, BARRY. 1988. The Efficacy of Business Political Activity: Competitive Considerations in a Principal Agent Context. *Journal of Management*, 14: 163–80.

KELLER, MORTON. 1977. *Affairs of State: Public Life in Late Nineteenth Century America*. Cambridge, Mass.: Harvard University Press.

—— 2007. *America's Three Regimes: A New Political History*. New York: Oxford University Press.

KELLEY, STANLEY, JR. 1956. *Professional Public Relations and Political Power*. Baltimore: Johns Hopkins University Press.

KELLSTEDT, LYMAN A., GREEN, JOHN C., GUTH, JAMES L., and SMIDT, CORWIN E. 2007. Faith Transformed: Religion and American Politics from FDR to George W. Bush. In *Religion and American Politics: From the Colonial Period to the Present*, ed. Mark A. Noll and Luke E. Harlow. 2nd edn. Oxford: Oxford University Press.

KENNEY, PATRICK J. 1988. Sorting Out the Effects of Primary Divisiveness in Congressional and Senatorial Elections. *Western Political Quarterly*, 41/4: 765–77.

—— and RICE, TOM W. 1984. The Effect of Primary Divisiveness in Gubernatorial and Senatorial Elections. *Journal of Politics*, 46/3: 904.

—— —— 1987. The Relationship between Divisive Primaries and General Election Outcomes. *American Journal of Political Science*, 31/1: 31.

KENT, FRANK R. 1923. *The Great Game of Politics*. New York: Doubleday, Page.

KERSH, ROGAN. 2002. Corporate Lobbyists as Political Actors: A View from the Field. In *Interest Group Politics*, ed. Allan J. Cigler and Burdett A. Loomis. 6th edn. Washington, DC: CQ Press.

KETCHAM, RALPH. 1984. *Presidents above Party*. Chapel Hill: University of North Carolina Press.

KEY, V. O. 1942. *Politics, Parties, and Pressure Groups*. New York: Thomas Y. Crowell.

—— 1949. *Southern Politics in State and Nation*. New York: Alfred A. Knopf.

—— 1952. *Politics, Parties, and Pressure Groups*. 3rd edn. New York: Thomas Y. Crowell.

—— 1954. The Direct Primary and Party Structure: A Study of State Legislative Nominations. *American Political Science Review*, 48/1: 1–26.

—— 1955. A Theory of Critical Elections. *Journal of Politics*, 17 (Feb.), 3–18.

—— 1956. *American State Politics: An Introduction*. 1st edn. New York: Alfred A. Knopf.

—— 1958. *Politics, Parties, and Pressure Groups*. 4th edn. New York: Thomas Y. Crowell.

—— 1959. Secular Realignment and the Party System. *Journal of Politics*, 21 (May), 198–210.

—— 1964. *Politics, Parties, and Pressure Groups*. 5th edn. New York: Thomas Y. Crowell.

KEYES, R. 2006. *The Quote Verifier: Who Said What, Where, When*. New York: St Martin's Griffin.

KEYSSAR, ALEXANDER. 2000. *The Right to Vote: The Contested History of Democracy in the United States*. New York: Basic Books.

KING, DAVID C. 1997. The Polarization of American Parties and Mistrust of Government. In *Why People Don't Trust Government*, ed. Joseph S. Nye, Philip D. Zelikow, and David C. King. Cambridge, Mass.: Harvard University Press.

KING, GARY. 1989. *Unifying Political Methodology: The Likelihood Theory of Statistical Inference*. New York: Cambridge University Press.

—— KEOHANE, ROBERT O., and VERBA, SIDNEY. 1994. *Designing Social Inquiry: Scientific Inference in Qualitative Research*. Princeton: Princeton University Press.

KINGDON, JOHN W. 1984. *Agendas, Alternatives, and Public Policy.* Boston: Little, Brown.

—— 1995. *Agendas, Alternatives, and Public Policies.* 2nd edn. New York: HarperCollins.

KIRBY, EMILY HOBAN and GINSBERT, KEI KAWASHIMA. 2009. The Youth Vote in 2008. Fact sheet. The Center for Information and Research on Civic Learning and Engagement (June 22). <http://www.civicyouth.org/PopUps/FactSheets/FS_youth_Voting_2008_updated_6.22.pdf>. Accessed July 2, 2009.

KIRCHHEIMER, OTTO. 1966. The Transformation of the Western European Party Systems. In *Political Parties and Political Development,* ed. Joseph LaPalombara and Myron Weiner. Princeton: Princeton University Press.

KIRKPATRICK, EVRON M. 1971. Toward a More Responsible Two-Party System: Political Science, Policy Science, or Pseudo-Science? *American Political Science Review,* 65: 965–90.

KIRKPATRICK, JEANNE. 1976. *The New Presidential Elite: Men and Women in National Politics.* New York: Russell Sage.

KLEPPNER, PAUL 1979. *The Third Electoral System: Parties, Voters and Political Cultures.* Chapel Hill: University of North Carolina Press.

—— 1981. Partisanship and Ethnoreligious Conflict: The Third Electoral System, 1853–1892. In *The Evolution of American Electoral Systems,* ed. Paul Kleppner. Westport, Conn.: Greenwood Press.

—— 1982. *Who Voted: The Dynamics of Electoral Turnout, 1870–1980.* New York: Praeger.

—— 1987. *Continuity and Change in Electoral Politics, 1893–1928.* Westport, Conn.: Greenwood Press.

—— et al. 1981. *The Evolution of American Electoral Systems.* Westport, Conn.: Greenwood Press.

KLINGHARD, DANIEL P. 2005. Grover Cleveland, William McKinley, and the Emergence of the President as Party Leader. *Presidential Studies Quarterly,* 35/4 (Dec.), 736–60.

KLINKNER, PHILIP A. 1994. *The Losing Parties: Out-Party National Committees, 1956–1993.* New Haven: Yale University Press.

—— and SMITH, ROGERS M. 1999. *The Unsteady March.* Chicago: University of Chicago Press.

KNUCKEY, JONATHAN. 2006. Explaining Recent Changes in the Partisan Identifications of Southern Whites. *Political Research Quarterly,* 59: 57–70.

KOCH, JEFFREY. 1998. The Perot Candidacy and Attitudes toward Government and Politics. *Political Research Quarterly,* 51: 141–54.

KOGER, GREGORY. 2002. Obstructionism in the House and Senate: A Comparative Analysis of Institutional Choice. Ph.D. dissertation, University of California, Los Angeles.

—— 2007. Filibuster Reform in the Senate. In *Party, Process, and Political Change in Congress,* ed. David Brady and Matthew McCubbins, ii. Stanford, Calif.: Stanford University Press.

—— MASKET, SETH, and NOEL, HANS. 2009. Partisan Webs: Information Exchange and Party Networks. *British Journal of Political Science,* 39/3: 609–31.

—— —— Forthcoming. Cooperative Party Factions in American Politics. *American Politics Research.*

KOHUT, ANDREW, GREEN, JOHN C., KEETER, SCOTT, and TOTH, ROBERT. 2000. *The Diminishing Divide: Religion's Changing Role in American Politics.* Washington, DC: Brookings Institution Press.

KOLLMAN, KEN. 1998. *Outside Lobbying: Public Opinion and Interest Group Strategies.* Princeton: Princeton University Press.

KOLODNY, ROBIN. 1998. *Pursuing Majorities: Congressional Campaign Committees in American Politics*. Norman: University of Oklahoma Press.

—— 2000. Electoral Partnerships: Political Consultants and Political Parties. In *Campaign Warriors: The Role of Political Consultants in Elections*, ed. James A. Thurber and Candice J. Nelson. Washington, DC: Brookings Institution.

—— 2007. One Agent—Multiple Principles: A Theory of the Role of Political Consultants in the American Political System. Paper prepared for presentation at the Annual Meeting of the Midwest Political Science Association, Chicago, April 12–15.

—— and DULIO, DAVID. 2003. Political Party Adaptation in U.S. Congressional Campaigns: Why Political Parties Use Coordinated Expenditures to Hire Political Consultants. *Party Politics*, 9/6: 729–46.

—— and LOGAN, ANGELA. 1998. Political Consultants and the Extension of Party Goals. *PS: Political Science and Politics*, 31: 155–9.

KOOPMAN, DOUG. 2001. Religion and American Political Parties. In *In God We Trust?* ed. Corwin E. Smidt. Grand Rapids, Mich.: Baker Press.

KORNHAUSER, WILLIAM. 1959. *The Politics of Mass Society*. Glencoe, Ill.: Free Press.

KORZI, MICHAEL. 2004. *A Seat of Popular Leadership: The Presidency, Political Parties, and Democratic Government*. Amherst: University of Massachusetts Press.

KOUSSER, J. MORGAN. 1974. *The Shaping of Southern Politics: Suffrage Restriction and the Establishment of the One-Party South, 1880–1910*. New Haven: Yale University Press.

KRASNER, STEPHEN D. 1984. Approaches to the State: Alternative Conceptions and Historical Dynamics. *Comparative Politics*, 16: 223–46.

KRASNO, JONATHAN. 2004. The Electoral Impact of "Issue Advocacy" in 1998 and 2000 House Races. In *The Medium and the Message: Television Advertising and American Elections*, ed. Kenneth M. Goldstein and Patricia Strach. Upper Saddle River, NJ: Prentice-Hall.

—— and GREEN, DONALD PHILIP. 1988. Preempting Quality Challengers in House Elections. *Journal of Politics*, 50/4: 920.

KREHBIEL, KEITH. 1987. Why Are Congressional Committees Powerful? *American Political Science Review*, 81: 929–35.

—— 1991. *Information and Legislative Organization*. Ann Arbor: University of Michigan Press.

—— 1993. Where's the Party? *British Journal of Political Science*, 23: 235–66.

—— 1995. Cosponsors and Wafflers from A to Z. *American Journal of Political Science*, 39: 906–23.

—— 1997a. Restrictive Rules Reconsidered. *American Journal of Political Science*, 41: 919–44.

—— 1997b. Rejoinder to "Sense and Sensibility." *American Journal of Political Science*, 41: 958–64.

—— 1998. *Pivotal Politics: A Theory of U.S. Lawmaking*. Chicago: University of Chicago Press.

—— 2000. Party Discipline and Measures of Partisanship. *American Journal of Political Science*, 44: 212–27.

—— and MEIROWITZ, ADAM. 2002. Minority Rights and Majority Power: Theoretical Consequences of the Motion to Recommit. *Legislative Studies Quarterly*, 27 (May), 191–217.

—— —— and WOON, JONATHAN. 2005. Testing Theories of Lawmaking. In *Social Choice and Strategic Decisions: Essays in Honor of Jeffrey S. Banks*, ed. David Austen-Smith and John Duggan. Berlin: Springer.

KRUTZ, GLEN S. 2001. *Hitching a Ride: Omnibus Legislation in the U.S. Congress.* Columbus: Ohio State University Press.

KSELMAN, DANIEL. Forthcoming. Four Factions or Four Parties? Party System Concentration and Ideological Polarization. Ph.D. dissertation, Duke University.

KUHN, DAVID PAUL. 2008. GOP Fears Charges of Racism, Sexism. *Politico.* <http://www.politico.com/news/stories/0208/8659.html>. Accessed Jan. 30, 2009.

KUHR, FRED. 2005. Growing a Gay Old Party. *Advocate,* 952: 44–6.

KURAN, TIMUR. 1991. The East European Revolution of 1989: Is it Surprising that We Were Surprised? *American Economic Review,* 81/2: 121–5.

KURTZ, SHARON. 2002. *Workplace Justice.* Minneapolis: University of Minnesota Press.

LA RAJA, RAYMOND J. 2004. Clean Elections: An Evaluation of Public Funding for Maine Legislative Election Contests. Amherst: Center for Public Policy and Administration, University of Massachusetts.

—— 2006. State Political Parties after BCRA. In *Life after Reform: When Bipartisan Campaign Reform Act Meets Politics,* ed. Michael Malbin. Lanham, Md.: Rowman & Littlefield.

—— 2008. *Small Change: Money, Political Parties, and Campaign Finance Reform.* Ann Arbor: University of Michigan Press.

—— Forthcoming. Redistricting: Reading between the Lines. *Annual Review of Political Science,* 12.

LADD, EVERETT CARLL, JR. 1970. *American Political Parties: Social Change and Political Response.* New York: W. W. Norton.

—— 1978. *Where Have All the Voters Gone? The Fracturing of America's Political Parties.* New York: W. W. Norton.

—— 1980. A Rebuttal: Realignment No, Dealignment Yes. *Public Opinion,* 3 (Oct.–Nov.), 13–15, 54–5.

—— 1991. Like Waiting for Godot: The Uselessness of "Realignment" for Understanding Change in Contemporary American Politics. In *The End of Realignment: Interpreting American Electoral Eras,* ed. Byron E. Shafer. Madison: University of Wisconsin Press.

—— with HADLEY, CHARLES D. 1975. *Transformations of the American Party System.* New York: W. W. Norton.

LAKATOS, IMRE. 1970. Falsification and the Methodology of Scientific Research Program. In *Criticism and the Growth of Knowledge,* ed. Imre Lakatos and Alan Musgrave. Cambridge: Cambridge University Press.

LANGBEIN, LAURA I. 1986. Money and Access: Some Empirical Evidence. *Journal of Politics,* 48/4: 1052–62.

LAPPÉ, FRANCES MOORE. 1989. *Rediscovering America's Values.* New York: Ballantine Books.

LARACEY, MEL. 2002. *Presidents and the People: The Partisan Story of Going Public.* College Station: Texas A&M University Press.

LARSON, JOHN. 2000. *Internal Improvements: National Public Works and the Promise of Popular Government in the Early United States.* Chapel Hill: University of North Carolina.

LASSITER, MATTHEW D. 2006. *The Silent Majority: Suburban Politics in the Sunbelt South.* Princeton: Princeton University Press.

LASSWELL, HAROLD D. 1936. *Politics: Who Gets What, When, How.* New York: Whittlesey House McGraw-Hill.

LATHAM, EARL. 1952a. The Group Basis of Politics: Notes for a Theory. *American Political Science Review,* 46: 376–96.

—— 1952b. *The Group Basis of Politics.* Ithaca, NY: Cornell University Press.

LATHROP, DOUGLAS A. 2003. *The Campaign Continues: How Political Consultants and Campaign Tactics Affect Public Policy.* Westport, Conn.: Praeger.

LAVER, MICHAEL. 2006. Legislatures and Parliaments in Comparative Perspective. In *The Oxford Handbook of Political Economy*, ed. Barry Weingast and Donald Wittman. New York: Oxford University Press.

—— BENOIT, KENNETH, and GARRY, JOHN. 2003. Extracting Policy Positions from Political Texts Using Words as Data. *American Political Science Review*, 97/2: 311–32.

—— and BUDGE, IAN (eds.) 1992. *Party Policy and Government Coalitions.* London: Macmillan.

—— and HUNT, W. BEN. 1992. *Policy and Party Competition.* New York: Routledge.

—— and SCHOFIELD, NORMAN. 1990. *Multiparty Government: The Politics of Coalition in Europe.* Oxford: Oxford University Press.

LAWLESS, JENNIFER L. and FOX, RICHARD LOGAN. 2005. *It Takes a Candidate: Why Women Don't Run for Office.* New York: Cambridge University Press.

—— and PEARSON, KATHRYN. 2008. The Primary Reason for Women's Underrepresentation? Reevaluating the Conventional Wisdom. *Journal of Politics*, 70/1: 67–82.

LAWRENCE, ERIC D., MALTZMAN, FORREST, and SMITH, STEVEN S. 2006. Who Wins? Party Effects in Legislative Voting. *Legislative Studies Quarterly*, 31 (Feb.), 33–69.

LAWRENCE, JILL. 2009. New DNC Chair Will Rally Millions of Obama Backers. *USA Today.* Jan. 21. <http://www.usatoday.com/news/politics/2009-01-21-Kaine_N.htm>.

LAYMAN, GEOFFREY C. 2001. *The Great Divide: Religious and Cultural Conflict in American Party Politics.* New York: Columbia University Press.

—— and CARSEY, THOMAS M. 2002a. Party Polarization and Party Structuring of Policy Attitudes: A Comparison of Three NES Panel Studies. *Political Behavior*, 24 (Sept.), 199–236.

—— —— 2002b. Party Polarization and Conflict Extension in the American Electorate. *American Journal of Political Science*, 46/4: 786–802.

—— —— and HOROWITZ, JULIANA MENASCE. 2006. Party Polarization in American Politics: Characteristics, Causes, and Consequences. *Annual Review of Political Science*, 9: 83–110.

—— and GREEN, JOHN C. 2005. Wars and Rumors of Wars: The Contexts of Cultural Conflict in American Political Behavior. *British Journal of Political Science*, 36: 61–89.

LAZARUS, JEFFREY. 2005. Unintended Consequences: Anticipation of General Election Outcomes and Primary Election Divisiveness. *Legislative Studies Quarterly*, 30: 435–61.

—— 2006. Term Limit's Multiple Effects on State Legislators' Career Decisions. *State Politics and Policy Quarterly*, 6/4: 357–83.

—— 2008. Incumbent Vulnerability and Challenger Entry in Statewide Elections. *American Politics Research*, 36/1: 108–29.

—— and MONROE, NATHAN W. 2007. The Speaker's Discretion: Conference Committee Appointments in the 96th through 106th Congresses. *Political Research Quarterly*, 60 (Dec.), 593–606.

LEBLANC, HUGH L. 1969. Voting in State Senates: Party and Constituency Influences. *Midwest Journal of Political Science*, 13: 33–57.

LEBO, MATTHEW J., McGLYNN, ADAM J., and KOGER, GREGORY. 2007. Strategic Party Government: Party Influence in Congress. *American Journal of Political Science*, 51 (July), 464–81.

LEE, FRANCES. 2005. Interests, Constituencies and Policymaking. In *Institutions of American Democracy: The Legislative Branch*, ed. Paul J. Quirk and Sarah A. Binder. Oxford: Oxford University Press.

—— 2008. Beyond Ideology: Politics, Principles, and Partisanship in the U.S. Senate. MS.

LEECH, BETH L. and BAUMGARTNER, FRANK R. 1998. Lobbying Friends and Foes in Washington. In *Interest Group Politics*, ed. Allan J. Cigler and Burdett A. Loomis. 5th edn. Washington, DC: CQ Press.

—— —— LA PIRA, TIMOTHY, and SEMANKO, NICHOLAS A. 2005. Drawing Lobbyists to Washington: Government Activity and Interest-Group Mobilization. *Political Research Quarterly*, 58/1: 19–30.

LEEGE, DAVID C., WALD, KENNETH D., KRUEGER, BRIAN S., and MUELLER, PAUL D. 2002. *The Politics of Cultural Differences: Social Change and Voter Mobilization Strategies in the Post-New Deal Period*. Princeton: Princeton University Press.

LEHMANN, CHRIS. 1997. In the End: Cynical and Proud. *New York Times*, May 12, 40.

LEHMBRUCH, GERHARD and SCHMITTER, PHILIPPE C. 1982. *Patterns of Corporatist Policy-Making*. Beverly Hills, Calif.: Sage Publications.

LEIGHLEY, JAN E. 1995. Attitudes, Opportunities and Incentives: A Field Essay on Political Participation. *Political Research Quarterly*, 48/1: 181–209.

LEONARD, GERALD. 2002. *The Invention of Party Politics: Federalism, Popular Sovereignty, and Constitutional Development in Jacksonian Illinois*. Chapel Hill: University of North Carolina Press.

LEUCHTENBURG, WILLIAM. 1963. *Franklin D. Roosevelt and the New Deal, 1932–1940*. New York: Harper & Row.

—— 1983. *In the Shadow of FDR: From Harry Truman to Ronald Reagan*. Ithaca, NY: Cornell University Press.

—— 2005. *The White House Looks South: Franklin D. Roosevelt, Harry S. Truman, Lyndon B. Johnson*. Baton Rouge, La.: State University Press.

LEVINE, JEFFREY, CARMINES, EDWARD G., and HUCKFELDT, ROBERT. 1997. The Rise of Ideology in the Post-New Deal Party System, 1972–1992. *American Politics Quarterly*, 25: 19–34.

LEVITT, STEVEN D. 1994. Using Repeat Challengers to Estimate the Effect of Campaign Spending on Election Outcomes in the U.S. House. *Journal of Political Economy*, 102/4: 777–98.

LEVY, GILAT. 2004. A Model of Political Parties. *Journal of Economic Theory*, 155: 250–77.

LEWIS-BECK, MICHAEL, et al. 2008. *The American Voter Revisited*. Ann Arbor: University of Michigan Press.

LICHTMAN, ALLAN. 1976. Critical Election Theory and the Reality of American Presidential Politics, 1916–1940. *American Historical Review*, 82 (Apr.), 317–51.

—— 1982. The End of Realignment Theory? *Historical Methods*, 15 (Fall), 170–88.

LIJPHART, AREND. 1969. Consociational Democracy. *World Politics*, 21: 207–25.

LIN, NAN. 2001. *Social Capital: A Theory of Social Structure and Action*. Cambridge: Cambridge University Press.

LINDBLOM, CHARLES E. 1977. *Politics and Markets: The World's Political-Economic Systems*. New York: Basic Books.

—— 1982. The Market as Prison. *Journal of Politics*, 44: 324–36.

LINK, ARTHUR S. 1984. *The Papers of Woodrow Wilson*. 69 vols. Princeton: Princeton University Press.

—— and MCCORMICK, RICHARD L. 1983. *Progressivism*. Arlington Heights, Ill.: Harlan Davidson.

LIPSET, SEYMOUR MARTIN. 1963. *Political Man*. Garden City, NY: Doubleday.

—— TROW, MARTIN A., and COLEMAN, JAMES S. 1956. *Union Democracy*. Glencoe, Ill.: Free Press.

LIPSKY, MICHAEL. 1968. Protest as a Political Resource. *American Political Science Review*, 62: 1144–58.

LOCKARD, DUANE. 1959. *New England State Politics*. Princeton: Princeton University Press.

LOHMANN, SUSANNE. 1994. The Dynamics of Informational Cascades: The Monday Demonstrations in Leipzig, East Germany, 1989–1991. *World Politics*, 47: 42–101.

LOOMIS, BURDETT A. 2007. Does K Street Run through Capitol Hill? In *Interest Group Politics*, ed. Allan J. Cigler and Burdett A. Loomis. 7th edn. Washington, DC: CQ Press.

LOTT, JOHN R., JR. 1986. Brand Names and Barriers to Entry in Political Markets. *Public Choice*, 51: 87–92.

LOWELL, LAWRENCE. 1913. *Public Opinion and Popular Government*. London: Longmans, Green.

LOWENSTEIN, DANIEL H. 1993. Associational Rights of Major Political Parties: A Skeptical Inquiry. *Texas Law Review*, 71: 1741.

LOWERY, DAVID and BRASHER, HOLLY. 2004. *Organized Interests and American Government*. Boston, Mass.: McGraw-Hill.

—— and GRAY, VIRGINIA. 1994. Do Lobbying Regulations Influence Lobbying Registrations? *Social Science Quarterly*, 75/2: 382–4.

—— —— 1997. How Some Rules Just Don't Matter: The Regulation of Lobbyists. *Public Choice*, 91: 139–47.

—— —— 2004a. A Neopluralist Perspective on Research on Organized Interests. *Political Research Quarterly*, 57/1: 163–75.

—— —— 2004b. Bias in the Heavenly Chorus: Interests in Society and before Government. *Journal of Theoretical Politics*, 16: 5–30.

—— —— 2007a. Understanding Interest System Diversity: Health Interest Communities in the American States. *Business and Politics*, 9/2: 1–38.

—— —— 2007b. Interest Organization Communities: Their Assembly and Consequences. In *Interest Groups Politics*, ed. Allan J. Cigler and Burdett A. Loomis. 7th edn. Washington, DC: CQ Press.

—— —— ANDERSON, JENNIFER, and NEWMARK, ADAM J. 2004. Collective Action and the Mobilization of Institutions. *Journal of Politics*, 66: 684–705.

—— —— BENZ, JENNIFER, DEASON, MARY, KIRKLAND, JUSTIN, and SYKES, JENNIFER. 2009. Understanding the Relationship between Health PACs and Health Lobbying in the American States. *Publius*, 39 (Winter), 70–94.

—— —— and FELLOWES, MATTHEW. 2005. Sisyphus Meets the Borg: Economic Scale and the Inequalities in Interest Representation. *Journal of Theoretical Politics*, 17/1: 41–74.

—— —— and MONOGAN, JAMES. 2008. The Construction of Interest Communities: Distinguishing Bottom-Up and Top-Down Models. *Journal of Politics*, 70/4: 1160–76.

—— POPPELAARS, CAELESTA, and BERKHOUT, JOOST. 2008. The European Union Interest System in Comparative Perspective: A Bridge Too Far? *West European Politics*, 31/6: 1231–52.

LOWI, THEODORE J., JR. 1964. American Business, Public Policy, Case Studies and Political Theory. *World Politics*, 16: 677–715.

—— 1969. *The End of Liberalism*. New York: W. W. Norton.

—— 1971. *The Politics of Disorder*. New York: Basic Books.

—— 1979. *The End of Liberalism: The Second Republic of the United States*. Rev. edn. New York: W. W. Norton.

—— 1985. *The Personal President: Power Invested, Promise Unfulfilled*. Ithaca, NY: Cornell University Press.

LOWI, THEODORE J., JR. 1996. Towards a Responsible Three-Party System: Prospects and Obstacles. In *The State of the Parties*, ed. John C. Green and Daniel M. Shea. 2nd edn. Lanham, Md.: Rowman & Littlefield.

LOWRY, ROBERT C. 1999. Foundation Patronage toward Citizen Groups and Think Tanks: Who Get Grants? *Journal of Politics*, 61: 758–76.

LUBELL, SAMUEL. 1956. *The Future of American Politics*. Rev. edn. Garden City, NY: Doubleday Anchor.

LUBLIN, DAVID. 2004. *The Republican South: Democratization and Partisan Change*. Princeton: Princeton University Press.

LUNTZ, FRANK I. 1988. *Candidates, Consultants, and Campaigns: The Style and Substance of American Electioneering*. New York: Basil Blackwell.

LUX, THOMAS. 1995. Herd Behavior, Bubbles, and Crashes. *Economic Journal*, 105: 881–96.

LYND, ROBERT S. and LYND, HELEN MERRILL. 1929. *Middletown*. New York: Harcourt Brace.

—— —— 1937. *Middletown in Transition*. New York: Harcourt Brace.

MAASS, ARTHUR. 1951. *Muddy Waters: Army Engineers and the Nation's Rivers*. Cambridge, Mass.: Harvard University Press.

McADAM, DOUG. 1982. *Political Process and the Development of Black Insurgency, 1930–1970*. Chicago: University of Chicago Press.

—— 1999. Introduction to *Political Process and the Development of Black Insurgency, 1930–1970*. 2nd edn. Chicago: University of Chicago Press.

McALLISTER, TED V. 2003. Reagan and the Transformation of American Conservatism. In *The Reagan Presidency: Pragmatic Conservatism and its Legacies*, ed. W. Elliot Brownlee and Hugh Davis Graham. Lawrence: University Press of Kansas.

McCALL, LESLIE. 2005. The Complexity of Intersectionality. *Signs: Journal of Women in Culture and Society*, 30/3: 1771–1800.

McCANN, JAMES A. 1995. Nomination Politics and Ideological Polarization: Assessing the Attitudinal Effects of Campaign Involvement. *Journal of Politics*, 57 (Feb.), 101–20.

—— PARTIN, RANDALL, RAPOPORT, RONALD B., and STONE, WALTER J. 1996. Presidential Nomination Campaign Participation and Party Mobilization: An Assessment of Spillover Effects. *American Journal of Political Science*, 40/3: 756–67.

—— RONALD B. RAPOPORT, and WALTER J. STONE. 1999. Heeding the Call: An Assessment of Mobilization into Ross Perot's 1992 Presidential Campaign. *American Journal of Political Science*, 43: 1–28.

McCANN, MICHAEL W. 1994. *Rights at Work*. Chicago: University of Chicago Press.

McCARTHY, JOHN D. and ZALD, MAYER N. 1977. Resource Mobilization and Social Movements: A Partial Theory. *American Journal of Sociology*, 82: 1212–41.

McCARTY, NOLAN, POOLE, KEITH, and ROSENTHAL, HOWARD. 2001. The Hunt for Party Discipline in Congress. *American Political Science Review*, 95/3: 673–87.

—— and ROTHENBERG, LAWRENCE. 2000. Coalitional Maintenance. *American Politics Quarterly*, 28/3: 291–308.

McCHESNEY, FRED S. 1997. *Money for Nothing: Politicians, Rent Extraction, and Political Extortion*. Cambridge, Mass.: Harvard University Press.

McCLOSKY, HERBERT, HOFFMAN, PAUL J., and O'ARA, ROSEMARY. 1960. Issue Conflict and Consensus among Party Leaders and Followers. *American Political Science Review*, 54/4: 406–27.

McCONNELL, GRANT. 1966. *Private Power and American Democracy*. New York: Alfred A. Knopf.

McCormick, Richard L. 1967. *The Second American Party System: Party Formation in the Jacksonian Era*. Chapel Hill: University of North Carolina Press.

—— 1974. Ethno-Cultural Interpretations of Nineteen-Century American Voting Behavior. *Political Science Quarterly*, 89: 351–77.

—— 1981. *From Realignment to Reform: Political Change in New York State, 1893–1910*. Ithaca, NY: Cornell University Press.

—— 1982. *The Presidential Game: The Origins of American Presidential Politics*. New York: Oxford University Press.

—— 1986. *The Party Period and Public Policy: American Politics from the Age of Jackson to the Progressive Era*. Oxford: Oxford University Press.

McCubbins, Matthew. 1991. Party Government and U.S. Budget Deficits: Divided Government and Fiscal Stalemate. In *Politics and Economics in the Eighties*, ed. Alberto Alesina and Geoffrey Carliner. Chicago: University of Chicago Press.

—— and Schwartz, Thomas. 1984. Congressional Oversight Overlooked: Police Patrols versus Fire Alarms. *American Journal of Political Science*, 28: 165–79.

McCullough, David. 2002. *John Adams*. New York: Simon & Schuster.

McDonald, Michael P. 2004. Up, Up and Away! Voter Participation in the 2004 Presidential Election. *The Forum*, 2/4, art. 4.

—— 2005. Voter Turnout. *United States Election Project*. <http://elections.gmu.edu/voter_turnout.htm>.

McFarland, Andrew S. 1976. *Public Interest Lobbies*. Washington, DC: American Enterprise Institute.

—— 1984. *Common Cause: Lobbying in the Public Interest*. Chatham, NJ: Chatham House.

—— 1992. Interest Groups and the Policymaking Process: Sources of Countervailing Power in America. In *The Politics of Interests*, ed. Mark P. Petracca. Boulder, Colo.: Westview Press.

—— 1993. *Cooperative Pluralism: The National Coal Policy Experiment*. Lawrence: University Press of Kansas.

—— 2004. *Neopluralism: The Evolution of Political Process Theory*. Lawrence: University Press of Kansas.

—— 2007. Neopluralism. *Annual Review of Political Science*, 10: 45–66.

McFarland, Gerald N. 1975. *Mugwumps, Morals, and Politics, 1884–1920*. Amherst: University of Massachusetts Press.

McGerr, Michael. 1986. *The Decline of Popular Politics: The American North, 1865–1928*. New York: Oxford University Press.

McGirr, Lisa. 2001. *Suburban Warriors: The Origins of the New American Right*. Princeton: Princeton University Press.

McGuire, Kevin T. and Caldeira, Gregory A. 1993. Lawyers, Organized Interests, and the Law of Obscenity: Agenda Setting in the Supreme Court. *American Political Science Review*, 87/3: 715–26.

McKay, Amy and Yackee, Susan Webb. 2007. Interest Group Competition on Federal Agency Rules. *American Politics Research*, 35/3: 336–57.

McKelvey, Richard D. 1976. Intransitives in Multidimensional Voting Models and Some Implications for Agenda Control. *Journal of Economic Theory*, 18/3: 472–82.

—— and Palfrey, Thomas R. 1995. Quantal Response Equilibria in Normal Form Games. *Games and Economic Behavior*, 7: 6–38.

—— —— 1998. Quantal Response Equilibria for Extensive Form Games. *Experimental Economics*, 1: 9–41.

MACKENZIE, G. CALVIN and WEISBROT, ROBERT. 2008. *The Liberal Hour: Washington and the Politics of Change in the 1960s*. New York: Penguin.

McKEOWN, TIMOTHY J. 1994. The Epidemiology of Corporate PAC Formation, 1975–84. *Journal of Economic Behavior and Organization*, 24/2: 153–68.

McKITRICK, ERIC L. 1975. Party Politics and the Union and Confederate War Efforts. In *The American Party Systems: Stage of Political Development*, ed. William N. Chambers and Walter Dean Burnham. New York: Oxford University Press.

McLOUGHLIN, WILLIAM G. 1978. *Revivals, Awakenings, and Reform*. Chicago: University of Chicago Press.

McMAHON, KEVIN. 2003. *Reconsidering Roosevelt on Race: How the Presidency Paved the Road to Brown*. Chicago: University of Chicago Press.

MACRIDIS, ROY C. 1961. Interest Groups in Comparative Analysis. *Journal of Politics*, 23/1: 25–45.

McSEVENEY, SAMUEL T. 1972. *The Politics of Depression: Political Behavior in the Northeast, 1893–1896*. New York: Oxford University Press.

McWILLIAMS, WILSON CAREY. 1989. The Anti-Federalists, Representation, and Party. *Northwestern University Law Review*, 84/1: 12–38.

—— 2000. *Beyond the Politics of Disappointment: American Elections, 1980–1998*. Chatham, NJ: Chatham House.

MACY, MICHAEL W. 1991. Chains of Cooperation: Threshold Effects in Collective Action. *American Sociological Review*, 56/6: 730–47.

MADISON, JAMES. 1982. *The Federalist*, No. 10 (1787). In *The Federalist Papers*, ed. Gary Wills. New York: Bantam Books.

MAESTAS, CHERIE D., FULTON, SARAH, MAISEL, L. SANDY, and STONE, WALTER J. 2006. When to Risk It? Institutions, Ambitions, and the Decision to Run for the U.S. House. *American Political Science Review*, 100/2: 195–208.

MAGLEBY, DAVID B. 1984. *Direct Legislation: Voting on Ballot Propositions in the United States*. Baltimore: Johns Hopkins University Press.

—— 2000. *Outside Money: Soft Money and Issue Advocacy in the 1998 Congressional Elections*. New York: Rowman & Littlefield.

—— 2002. *Financing the 2000 Election*. Washington, DC: Brookings Institution.

—— 2003a. *The Other Campaign: Soft Money and Issue Advocacy in the 2000 Congressional Elections*. New York: Rowman & Littlefield.

—— 2003b. Party and Interest Group Electioneering in the Federal Elections. In *Inside the Campaign Finance Battle: Court Testimony on the New Reforms*, ed. Anthony Corrado, Thomas E. Mann, and Trevor Potter. Washington, DC: Brookings Institution.

—— 2004. The Importance of Outside Money in the 2002 Congressional Elections. In *The Last Hurrah? Soft Money and Issue Advocacy in the 2002 Congressional Elections*, ed. David B. Magleby and J. Quin Monson. Washington, DC: Brookings Institution.

—— and LIGHT, PAUL C. 2009. *Government by the People*. New York: Longman.

—— and MAYER, WILLIAM G. 2008. Presidential Nomination Finance in the post-BCRA Era. In *The Making of the Presidential Candidates 2008*, ed. William G. Mayer. Lanham, Md.: Rowman & Littlefield.

—— and MONSON, J. QUIN. 2004. *The Last Hurrah? Soft Money and Issue Advocacy in the 2002 Congressional Elections*. Washington, DC: Brookings Institution.

—— —— and PATTERSON, KELLY. 2007a. *Dancing without Partners: How Candidates, Parties, and Interest Groups Interact in the Presidential Campaign*. Lanham, Md.: Rowman & Littlefield.

—— —— —— 2007b. The Morning After: The Lingering Effects of a Night Spent Dancing. In *Dancing without Partners: How Candidates, Parties, and Interest Groups Interact in the Presidential Campaign*, ed. David B. Magleby, J. Quin Monson, and Kelly Patterson. Lanham, Md.: Rowman & Littlefield.

—— and NELSON, CANDICE J. 1990. *The Money Chase: Congressional Campaign Finance and Proposals for Reform*. Washington, DC: Brookings Institution.

—— and PATTERSON, KELLY D. 2007. War Games: Issues and Resources in the Battle for Control of Congress. In *Center for the Study of Elections and Democracy Report*. Salt Lake City, Ut.

—— —— 2008. *The Battle for Congress: Iraq, Scandal, and Campaign Finance in the 2006 Election*. Boulder, Colo.: Paradigm.

—— —— and THURBER, JAMES A. 2002. Campaign Consultants and Responsible Party Government. In *Responsible Partisanship? The Evolution of American Political Parties since 1950*, ed. John C. Green and Paul S. Herrnson. Lawrence: University Press of Kansas.

MAHLER, JONATHAN. 2008. After the Imperial Presidency. *New York Times Magazine* (Nov. 9).

MAHONEY, CHRISTINE. 2004. The Power of Institutions: State and Interest Group Activity in the European Union. *European Union Politics*, 5/4: 441–66.

—— 2007a. Networking versus Allying: The Decision of Interest Groups to Join Coalitions in the US and the EU. *Journal of European Public Policy*, 14/2: 366–83.

—— 2007b. Lobbying Success in the United States and the European Union. *Journal of Public Policy*, 27/2: 35–56.

—— 2008. *Brussels versus the Beltway: Advocacy in the United States and the European Union*. Washington, DC: Georgetown University Press.

—— and BAUMGARTNER, FRANK R. 2008. Converging Perspectives on Interest-Group Research in Europe and America. *West European Politics*, 31/6: 1251–71.

MAHOOD, H. R. 2000. *Interest Groups in American National Politics*. Upper Saddle River, NJ: Prentice-Hall.

MAISEL, L. SANDY (ed.) 1990. *The Parties Respond: Changes in the American Party System*. Boulder, Colo.: Westview Press.

—— 1994. *The Parties Respond: Changes in American Parties and Campaigns*. 2nd edn. Boulder, Colo.: Westview Press.

—— and STONE, WALTER J. 1997. Determinants of Candidate Emergence in U.S. House Elections: An Exploratory Study. *Legislative Studies Quarterly*, 22/1: 79–96.

—— —— and MAESTAS, CHERIE. 2001. Quality Challengers to Congressional Incumbents: Can Better Candidates Be Found? In *Playing Hardball: Campaigning for the U.S. Congress*, ed. Paul S. Herrnson. Upper Saddle River, NJ: Prentice-Hall.

MALBIN, MICHAEL J. 2003. Thinking about Reform. In *Life after Reform*, ed. Michael J. Malbin. Lanham, Md.: Rowman & Littlefield.

—— and GAIS, THOMAS L. 1998. *The Day after Reform: Sobering Campaign Finance Lessons from the American States*. Albany, NY: Rockefeller Institute Press.

—— WILCOX, CLYDE, ROZELL, MARK, and SKINNER, RICHARD. 2002. New Interest Group Strategies: A Preview of Post McCain–Feingold Politics? *Election Law Journal*, 1/4: 541–55.

MALTZMAN, FORREST. 1997. *Competing Principals: Committees, Parties, and the Organization of Congress*. Ann Arbor: University of Michigan Press.

MANLEY, JOHN. 1973. The Conservative Coalition in Congress. *American Behavioral Scientist*, 17: 223–47.

MANSBRIDGE, JANE. 1992. A Deliberative Theory of Interest Representation. In *The Politics of Interests*, ed. Mark P. Petracca. Boulder, Colo.: Westview Press.

MARCUS, ROBERT. 1971. *Grand Old Party: Political Structure in the Gilded Age, 1880–1896.* New York: Oxford University Press.

MARIANI, MACK D. 2008. A Gendered Pipeline? The Advancement of State Legislators to Congress in Five States. *Politics and Gender,* 4/2: 285–308.

MARKUS, GREGORY B. and CONVERSE, PHILIP. 1979. A Dynamic Simultaneous Equation Model of Electoral Choice. *American Political Science Review,* 73/4: 1055–70.

MARQUEZ, BENJAMIN and JENNINGS, JAMES. 2000. Representation by Other Means. *PS: Political Science and Politics,* 33: 541–6.

MARSDEN, GEORGE M. 1990. *Religion and American Culture.* Washington, DC: Harcourt Brace Jovanovich.

MARSHALL, BRYAN W. 2005. *Rules for War.* Aldershot: Ashgate.

MARSHALL, THOMAS R. 1999. Why PAC, Why Bundle? Patterns of Interest Group Donations. *American Review of Politics,* 20 (Fall), 245–60.

MARTIN, ANDREW D. and SPANG, BRIAN E. 2001. A Case Study of a Third Presidential Campaign Organization: Virginians for Perot. In *Ross for Boss,* ed. Ted Jelen. Albany: State University of New York Press.

MARTIN, CATHIE J. 1989. Business Influence and State Power: The Case of U.S. Corporate Tax Policy. *Politics and Society,* 17/2: 189–223.

—— 1994. Business and the New Economic Activism: The Growth of Corporate Lobbies in the Sixties. *Polity,* 27 (Fall), 49–76.

—— 1995. Nature or Nurture? Sources of Firm Preference for National Health Reform. *American Political Science Review,* 89: 898–913.

—— 2000. *Stuck in Neutral: Business and the Politics of Human Investment Capital Policy.* Princeton: Princeton University Press.

MARWELL, NICOLE P. 2004. Privatizing the Welfare State: Nonprofit Community-Based Organizations as Political Actors. *American Sociological Review,* 69 (Apr.), 265–91.

MASKET, SETH E. 2007. It Takes an Outsider: Extralegislative Organization and Partisanship in the California Assembly, 1849–2006. *American Journal of Political Science,* 51/3: 482–97.

—— 2009. *No Middle Ground: How Informal Party Organizations Control Nominations and Polarize Legislatures.* Ann Arbor: University of Michigan Press.

MASON, ROBERT. 2008. Ronald Reagan and the Republican Party: Responses to Realignment. In *Ronald Reagan and the 1980s: Perceptions, Policies, Legacies,* ed. Cheryl Hudson and Gareth Davies. New York: Palgrave-Macmillan.

MASTERS, MARICK F. and KEIM, GERALD D. 1985. Determinants of PAC Participation among Large Corporations. *Journal of Politics,* 47 (Nov.), 1158–73.

MAYER, KENNETH R. 1998. *Public Financing and Electoral Competition in Minnesota and Wisconsin.* Los Angeles: Citizens' Research Foundation, University of Southern California.

—— WERNER, TIMOTHY, and WILLIAMS, AMANDA. 2006. Do Public Funding Programs Enhance Electoral Competition? In *The Marketplace of Democracy: Electoral Competition and American Politics,* ed. Michael McDonald and John C. Samples. Washington, DC: Cato Institute and Brookings Institution.

MAYER, WILLIAM G. 1987. The New Hampshire Primary: A Historical Overview. In *Media and Momentum: The New Hampshire Primary and Nomination Politics,* ed. Gary R. Orren and Nelson W. Polsby. Chatham, NJ: Chatham House.

—— 1996. Caucuses: How They Work, What Difference They Make. In *In Pursuit of the White House: How We Choose Our Presidential Nominees,* ed. William G. Mayer. Chatham, NJ: Chatham House.

—— 2004. The Basic Dynamics of the Contemporary Nomination Process: An Expanded View. In *The Making of the Presidential Candidates 2004*, ed. William G. Mayer. Lanham, Md.: Rowman & Littlefield.

—— 2008a. Voting in Presidential Primaries: What We Can Learn from Three Decades of Exit Polling. In *The Making of the Presidential Candidates 2008*, ed. William G. Mayer. Lanham, Md.: Rowman & Littlefield.

—— 2008b. What the Founders Intended: Another Look at the Origins of the American Presidential Selection Process. In *The Making of the Presidential Candidates 2008*, ed. William G. Mayer. Lanham, Md.: Rowman & Littlefield.

—— 2009. Superdelegates: Reforming the Reforms Revisited. In *Reforming the Presidential Nomination Process*, ed. Steven S. Smith and Melanie J. Springer. Washington, DC: Brookings Institution.

—— and BUSCH, ANDREW E. 2004. *The Front-Loading Process in Presidential Nominations.* Washington, DC: Brookings Institution.

MAYHEW, DAVID R. 1966. *Party Loyalty among Congressmen: The Difference between Democrats and Republicans, 1947–1962.* Cambridge, Mass.: Harvard University Press.

—— 1974. *Congress: The Electoral Connection.* New Haven: Yale University Press.

—— 1986. *Placing Parties in American Politics: Organization, Electoral Settings, and Government Activity in the Twentieth Century.* Princeton: Princeton University Press.

—— 1991. *Divided We Govern: Party Control, Lawmaking, and Investigations, 1946–1990.* New Haven: Yale University Press.

—— 2002. *Electoral Realignments: A Critique of an American Genre.* New Haven: Yale University Press.

MAZEY, SONIA and RICHARDSON, JEREMY (eds.) 1993. *Lobbying in the European Community.* Oxford: Oxford University Press.

MAZMANIAN, DANIEL A. 1974. *Third Parties in Presidential Elections.* Washington, DC: Brookings Institution.

MEDVIC, STEPHEN K. and LENART, SILVO. 1997. The Influence of Political Consultants in the 1992 Congressional Elections. *Legislative Studies Quarterly,* 22/1: 61–77.

MELNICK, R. SHEP. 1989. The Congress, Courts, and Programmatic Rights. In *Remaking American Politics,* ed. Richard A. Harris and Sidney M. Milkis. Boulder, Colo.: Westview Press.

MENEFEE-LIBEY, DAVID B. 2000. *The Triumph of Campaign-Centered Politics.* New York: Chatham House.

MERCURIO, JOHN and VAN DONGEN, RACHEL. 1999. Robb, Davis Have a Lot Riding on Off-Year Races. *Roll Call* (Nov. 1).

MERRIAM, CHARLES E. 1923. *The American Party System.* New York: Macmillan.

MERTON, ROBERT. 1968. *Social Theory and Social Structure.* 2nd edn. New York: Free Press.

METTLER, SUZANNE. 2002. Bringing the State Back in to Civic Engagement. *American Political Science Review,* 96/2: 351–65.

MEYER, DAVID S. 2005. Social Movements and Public Policy. In *Routing the Opposition,* ed. David S. Meyer, Valerie Jenness, and Helen Ingram. Minneapolis: University of Minnesota Press.

—— and LUPO, LINDSEY. 2007. Assessing the Politics of Protest: Political Science and the Study of Social Movements. In *Handbook of Social Movements across Disciplines,* ed. Bert Klandermans and Conny Roggband. New York: Springer.

MEYERS, MARVIN. 1957. *The Jacksonian Persuasion: Politics and Belief.* Stanford, Calif.: Stanford University Press.

MEYERS, MARVIN. 1960. *The Jacksonian Persuasion: Politics and Belief.* New edn. Stanford, Calif.: Stanford University Press.

MICHELETTI, MICHELE and McFARLAND, ANDREW (eds.) 2009. *Creative Participation: Responsibility-Taking in a Political World.* Boulder, Colo.: Paradigm.

—— FØLLESDAL, ANDREAS, and STOLLE, DIETLIND (eds.) 2003. *Politics, Products, and Markets: Exploring Political Consumerism Past and Present.* New Brunswick, NJ: Transaction Publishers.

MICHELS, ROBERT. 1911. *Political Parties.* New York: Free Press.

—— 1949. *Political Parties,* trans. Eden and Cedar Paul. Glencoe, Ill.: Free Press.

—— 1959. *Political Parties.* New York: Dover.

MICKEY, ROBERT W. 2008. The Beginning of the End for Authoritarian Rule in America: *Smith v. Allwright* and the Abolition of the White Primary in the Deep South, 1944–1948. *Studies in American Political Development,* 22/2: 143–82.

MILBRATH, LESTER W. 1963. *The Washington Lobbyists.* Chicago: Rand McNally.

MILCHTAICH, IGAL and WINTER, EYAL. 2002. Stability and Segregation in Group Formation. *Games and Economic Behavior,* 38: 318–46.

MILKIS, SIDNEY M. 1993. *The Presidents and the Parties: The Transformation of the American Party System since the New Deal.* Oxford: Oxford University Press.

—— 1999. *Political Parties and Constitutional Government: Remaking American Democracy.* Baltimore: Johns Hopkins University Press.

—— 2002. Franklin Roosevelt, the Economic Constitutional Order, and the New Politics of Presidential Leadership. In *The New Deal and the Triumph of Liberalism,* ed. Sidney M. Milkis and Jerome Mileur. Amherst: University of Massachusetts Press.

—— 2008. The Modern Presidency, Social Movements and the Administrative State: Lyndon Johnson and the Civil Rights Movement. In *Race and American Political Development,* ed. Joseph Lowndes, Julie Novkov, and Dorian Warren. New York: Routledge.

—— 2009. *Theodore Roosevelt, the Progressive Party, and the Transformation of American Democracy.* Lawrence: University Press of Kansas.

—— and RHODES, JESSE H. 2007a. George W. Bush, the Republican Party, and the New American Party System. *Perspectives on Politics,* 5/3 (Sept.), 461–88.

—— —— 2007b. George W. Bush, the Republican Party, and American Federalism. *Publius,* 37/3: 478–503.

—— and TICHENOR, DANIEL J. 1994. "Direct Democracy" and Social Justice: The Progressive Party Campaign of 1912. *Studies in American Political Development,* 8/2 (Fall), 282–340.

MILLER, ARTHUR H., WATTENBERG, MARTIN P., and MALANCHUK, OKSANA. 1986. Schematic Assessments of Presidential Candidates. *American Political Science Review,* 80: 521–40.

MILLER, LISA L. 2007. The Representational Biases of Federalism. *Perspectives on Politics,* 5 (June), 305–21.

—— 2008. *The Perils of Federalism: Poor People and the Politics of Crime Control.* New York: Oxford University Press.

MILLER, NICHOLAS R. 1983. Pluralism and Social Choice. *American Political Science Review,* 77: 734–47.

MILLER, WARREN E. 2000. Temporal Order and Causal Inference. *Political Analysis,* 8/2: 119–39.

—— and JENNINGS, M. KENT. 1986. *Parties in Transition.* New York: Russell Sage.

—— —— and FARAH, BARBARA G. 1986. *Parties in Transition: A Longitudinal Study of Party Elites and Party Supporters.* New York: Russell Sage.

—— and SHANKS, J. MERRILL. 1996. *The New American Voter.* Cambridge, Mass.: Harvard University Press.

—— and STOKES, DONALD E. 1963. Constituency Influence in Congress. *American Political Science Review,* 57/1: 45–57.

MILLS, C. WRIGHT. 1956. *The Power Elite.* New York: Oxford University Press.

—— 1959. *The Power Elite.* 2nd imp. New York: Oxford University Press.

MILYO, JEFFREY. 2002. Bribes and Fruit Baskets: What Does the Link between PAC Contributions and Lobbying Mean? *Business and Politics,* 4/2: 157–60.

MINKOFF, DEBRA. 1995. *Organizing for Equality.* New Brunswick, NJ: Rutgers University Press.

MITCHELL, ALISON. 1998. House G.O.P. Content to Make Ripples. *New York Times,* Mar. 11, A14.

MITCHELL, NEIL J., HANSEN, WENDY L., and JEPSEN, ERIC M. 1997. The Determinants of Domestic and Foreign Corporate Political Activity. *Journal of Politics,* 59: 1096–1113.

MIZRUCHI, MARK S. 1989. Similarity of Political Behavior among Large American Corporations. *American Journal of Sociology,* 95: 401–24.

—— 1990. Similarity of Ideology and Party Preference among Large American Corporations: A Study of Political Action Committee Contributions. *Sociological Forum,* 5/2: 213–40.

—— 1992. *The Structure of Corporate Political Action: Interfirm Relations and their Consequences.* Cambridge, Mass.: Harvard University Press.

MOE, TERRY M. 1980. *The Organization of Interests: Incentives and the Internal Dynamics of Political Interest Groups.* Chicago: University of Chicago Press.

MOLOTCH, HARVEY. 1976. The City as a Growth Machine: Toward a Political Economy of Place. *American Journal of Sociology,* 82 (Sept.), 309–332.

MONCRIEF, GARY F., SQUIRE, PEVERILL, and JEWELL, MALCOLM E. 2001. *Who Runs for the Legislature?* Upper Saddle River, NJ: Prentice-Hall.

MONDAK, JEFFERY J. 1995. Competence, Integrity, and the Electoral Success of Congressional Incumbents. *Journal of Politics,* 57/4: 1043.

MONROE, BURT, COLARESI, MICHAEL, and QUINN, KEVIN M. Forthcoming. Fightin' Words: Lexical Feature Selection and Evaluation for Identifying the Content of Political Conflict. *Political Analysis.*

MONROE, J. P. 2001. *The Political Party Matrix: The Persistence of Organization.* Ithaca, NY: State University of New York Press.

MONROE, NATHAN W. and ROBINSON, GREGORY. 2008. Do Restrictive Rules Produce Nonmedian Outcomes? A Theory with Evidence from the 101st–108th Congresses. *Journal of Politics,* 70 (Jan.), 217–31.

MONSON, J. QUIN. 2004. Polling in Congressional Election Campaigns. Ph.D. dissertation, Ohio State University.

—— and OLIPHANT, J. BAXTER. 2007. Microtargeting and the Instrumental Mobilization of Religious Conservatives. In *A Matter of Faith: Religion in the 2004 Presidential Election,* ed. David E. Campbell. Washington, DC: Brookings Institution.

MOON, WOOJIN. 2004. Party Activists, Campaign Resources and Candidate Position Taking: Theory, Tests and Applications. *British Journal of Political Science,* 34: 611–33.

MOONEY, CHRISTOPHER Z. 2003. The Impact of State Legislative Term Limits on Lobbyists and Interest Groups. Paper presented at the 5th Annual State Politics and Policy Conference, East Lansing, Michigan, May.

—— Forthcoming. Term Limits as a Boon to Legislative Scholarship: A Review Essay. *State Politics and Policy Quarterly,* 9.

MOREHOUSE, SARAH M. 1981. *State Politics, Parties and Policy.* New York: Holt, Rinehart, Winston.

—— and JEWELL, MALCOLM E. 2003a. State Parties: Independent Partners In the Money Relationship. In *The State of the Parties: The Changing Role of Contemporary American Parties,* ed. John C. Green and Rick Farmer. Lanham, Md.: Rowman & Littlefield.

—— —— 2003b. *State Politics, Parties, and Policy.* 2nd edn. Lanham, Md.: Rowman & Littlefield.

MORGAN, H. WAYNE. 1963. *William McKinley and his America.* Syracuse, NY: Syracuse University Press.

MORGAN, WILLIAM G. 1969. The Origin and Development of the Congressional Nominating Caucus. *Proceedings of the American Philosophical Society,* 113: 184–96.

MORTON, REBECCA B. 1999. *Methods and Models: A Guide to the Empirical Analysis of Formal Models in Political Science.* New York: Cambridge University Press.

—— and CAMERON, CHARLES. 1992. Elections and the Theory of Campaign Contributions: A Survey and Critical Analysis. *Economics and Politics,* 4/1: 79–108.

MOYNIHAN, DANIEL P. 1969. *Maximum Feasible Misunderstanding.* New York: Free Press.

MUCCIARONI, GARY and QUIRK, PAUL J. 2004. Deliberations of a Compassionate Conservative: George W. Bush's Domestic Policy. In *The George W. Bush Presidency: Appraisals and Prospects,* ed. Colin Campbell and Bert A. Rockman. Washington, DC: CQ Press.

MUIR, WILLIAM K. 1988. Ronald Reagan: The Primacy of Rhetoric. In *Leadership in the Modern Presidency,* ed. Fred I. Greenstein. Cambridge, Mass.: Harvard University Press.

MURAKAMI, MICHAEL H. 2008. Divisive Primaries. *PS: Political Science and Politics,* 41/4: 918–23.

MUSSO, JULIET A., WEARE, CHRISTOPHER, and COOPER, TERRY L. 2004. *Neighborhood Councils in Los Angeles.* University of Southern California, Neighborhood Participation Project.

MUTCH, ROBERT E. 1999. AT&T PAC: The Perils of Pragmatism. In *After the Revolution: PACs, Lobbies, and the Republican Congress,* ed. Robert S. Biersack, Paul S. Herrnson, and Clyde Wilcos. New York: Allyn and Bacon.

MUTZ, DIANA C. 1997. Mechanisms of Momentum: Does Thinking Make It So? *Journal of Politics,* 59: 104–25.

—— 2002. The Consequences of Cross-Cutting Networks for Political Participation. *American Journal of Political Science,* 46: 838–55.

NAGOURNEY, ADAM. 2008. Dean Argues his 50-State Strategy Helped Obama Win. *International Herald Tribune* (Nov. 12).

NATHAN, RICHARD. 1983. *The Administrative Presidency.* New York: Wiley.

NEELY, MARK. 2002. *The Union Divided: Party Conflict in the Civil War North.* Cambridge, Mass.: Harvard University Press.

NELSON, ALBERT J. 1991. *Emerging Influentials in State Legislatures: Women, Blacks, and Hispanics.* New York: Praeger.

NELSON, DOUGLAS. 1989. Domestic Political Preconditions of US Trade Policy: Liberal Structure and Protectionist Dynamics. *Journal of Public Policy,* 9/1: 83–108.

NEUSTADT, RICHARD E. 1964. *Presidential Power.* New York: Wiley.

New Republic. 1916. Editorial, The Democrats as Legislators. Sept. 2.

New York Times/CBS News. 2008a. Democratic National Delegate Survey, July 16–Aug. 17, 2008.

—— —— 2008b. Republican National Delegate Survey, July 23–Aug. 26, 2008.

NEXON, DAVID. 1971. Asymmetry in the Political System: Occasional Activists in the Republican and Democratic Parties, 1956–1964. *American Political Science Review*, 65/3: 716–30.

NICHOLS, ROY F. 1948. *This Disruption of American Democracy*. New York: Macmillan.

—— 1967. *The Invention of American Political Parties: A Study of Political Improvisation*. New York: Macmillan.

NIE, NORMAN H., VERBA, SIDNEY, and PETROCIK, JOHN R. 1970. *The Changing American Voter*. Cambridge, Mass.: Harvard University Press.

—— —— —— 1976. *The Changing American Voter*. Cambridge, Mass.: Harvard University Press.

—— —— —— 1979. *The Changing American Voter*. Enlarged edn. Cambridge, Mass.: Harvard University Press.

NIMMO, DAN. 2001. *The Political Persuaders: The Techniques of Modern Election Campaigns*, 2nd edn. New Brunswick, NJ: Transaction Publishers.

NIVOLA, PIETRO and BRADY, DAVID. 2006. *Red and Blue Nation?*, i. Washington, DC: Brookings Institution; Stanford, Calif.: Hoover Press.

—— 2008. *Red and Blue Nation?*, ii. Washington, DC: Brookings Institution; Stanford, Calif.: Hoover Press.

NOEL, HANS. 2007. Listening to the Coalition Merchants: Measuring the Intellectual Influence of Academic Scribblers. *The Forum*, 5/3.

NOLL, MARK A. and HARLOW, LUKE E. (eds.) 2007. *Religion and American Politics: From the Colonial Period to the Present*, 2nd edn. Oxford: Oxford University Press.

NORRANDER, BARBARA. 1989a. Explaining Cross-State Variation in Independent Identification. *American Journal of Political Science*, 33/2: 516–36.

—— 1989b. Ideological Representativeness of Presidential Primary Voters. *American Journal of Political Science*, 33/3: 570–87.

—— 1992. *Super Tuesday: Regional Politics and Presidential Primaries*. Lexington: University Press of Kentucky.

—— 1996. Field Essay: Presidential Nomination Politics in the Post-Reform Era. *Political Research Quarterly*, 49: 875–915.

—— 2001. Measuring State Public Opinion with the Senate National Election Study. *State Politics and Policy Quarterly*, 1: 113–27.

—— and WILCOX, CLYDE. 1998. The Geography of Gender Power: Women in State Legislatures. In *Women and Elective Office: Past, Present, and Future*, ed. Sue Thomas and Clyde Wilcox. New York: Oxford University Press.

NORRIS, PIPPA. 1997. *Passages to Power: Legislative Recruitment in Advanced Democracies*. New York: Cambridge University Press.

—— 2004. *Electoral Engineering: Voting Rules and Political Behavior*. New York: Cambridge University Press.

—— 2005. Political Parties and Democracy in Theoretical and Practical Perspectives: Developments in Party Communications. *National Democratic Institute for International Affairs*, 11–13.

—— and INGLEHART, RONALD. 2004. *Sacred and Secular: Religion and Politics Worldwide*. New York: Cambridge University Press.

NOWNES, ANTHONY J. 1995. Patronage and Citizen Groups: A Reevaluation. *Political Behavior*, 17: 203–21.

NOWNES, ANTHONY J. 2004. The Population Ecology of Interest Group Formation: Mobilizing for Gay and Lesbian Rights in the United States, 1950–1998. *British Journal of Political Science*, 34: 49–67.

—— 2006. *Total Lobbying: What Lobbyists Want (and How They Try to Get It)*. Cambridge: Cambridge University Press.

—— and CIGLER, ALLAN J. 2007. Large Donor Patrons: What They Give and What They Get. In *Interest Group Politics*, ed. Allan J. Cigler and Burdett A. Loomis. 7th edn. Washington, DC: CQ Press.

—— and FREEMAN, PATRICIA. 1998. Interest Group Activity in the States. *Journal of Politics*, 60/1: 86–112.

—— and LIPINSKI, DANIEL. 2005. The Population Ecology of Interest Death Formation: Mobilizing for Gay and Lesbian Rights in the United States, 1945–1998. *British Journal of Political Science*, 29: 303–19.

OLSON, LAURA R. and GREEN, JOHN C. (eds.) 2008a. *Beyond Red State, Blue State: Electoral Gaps in the Twenty-First Century American Electorate*. Upper Saddle River, NJ: Prentice Hall.

—— —— 2008b. The Worship Attendance Gap. In *Beyond Red State, Blue State*, ed. Laura R. Olson and John C. Green. Upper Saddle River, NJ: Prentice Hall.

OLSON, MANCUR. 1965. *The Logic of Collective Action*. Cambridge, Mass.: Harvard University Press.

—— 1982. *The Rise and Decline of Nations*. New Haven: Yale University Press.

OMI, MICHAEL and WINANT, HOWARD. 1994. *Racial Formation in the United States*. New York: Routledge.

OPPENHEIMER, BRUCE. 1977. The Rules Committee: New Arm of Leadership in a Decentralized House. In *Congress Reconsidered*, ed. Lawrence C. Dodd and Bruce I. Oppenheimer. New York: Praeger.

—— 1985. Changing Time Constraints on Congress: Historical Perspectives on the Use of Cloture. In *Congress Reconsidered*, ed. Lawrence C. Dodd and Bruce I. Oppenheimer. 3rd edn. Washington, DC: CQ Press.

—— and HETHERINGTON, MARC. 2008. Catch-22: Cloture, Energy Policy, and the Limits of Conditional Party Government. In *Why Not Parties: Party Effects in the United States Senate*, ed. Nathan Monroe, Jason Roberts, and David Rohde. Chicago: University of Chicago Press.

ORNSTEIN, NORMAN J., MANN, THOMAS E., and MALBIN, MICHAEL J. 2002. *Vital Statistics on Congress 2001–2002*. Washington, DC: American Enterprise Institute.

—— and ROHDE, DAVID W. 1978. Congressional Reform and Political Parties in the U.S. House of Representatives. In *Parties and Elections in an Anti-Party Age*, ed. Jeff Fishel. Bloomington: Indiana University Press.

ORREN, GARY R. and POLSBY, NELSON W. (eds.) 1987. *Media and Momentum: The New Hampshire Primary and Nomination Politics*. Chatham, NJ: Chatham House.

O'SHAUGHNESSY, NICHOLAS J. 1988. High Priesthood, Low Priestcraft: The Role of Political Consultants. *European Journal of Marketing*, 24/1: 7–11.

OSTROGORSKI, MOISEI. 1964. *Democracy and the Organization of Political Parties*, 2 vols (1902), ii: *The United States*, ed. Seymour Martin Lipset. Garden City, NY: Anchor Books.

—— 1982. *Democracy and the Organization of Political Parties*, 2 vols (1902), ii: *The United States*, ed. Seymour Martin Lipset. New Brunswick, NJ: Transaction Books.

OVERACKER, LOUISE. 1926. *The Presidential Primary*. New York: Macmillan.

—— and WEST, VICTOR J. 1932. *Money in Elections*. New York: Macmillan.

PADDOCK, JOEL. 1992. Inter-Party Ideological Differences in Eleven State Parties: 1956–1980. *Western Political Quarterly*, 45: 751–60.

—— 1998. Explaining State Variation in Interparty Ideological Differences. *Political Research Quarterly*, 51: 765–80.

PAGE, BENJAMIN I. and JONES, CALVIN C. 1979. Reciprocal Effects of Policy Preferences, Party Loyalties and the Vote. *American Political Science Review*, 73/4: 1071–89.

PALFREY, THOMAS R. 1984. Spatial Equilibrium with Entry. *Review of Economic Studies*, 51: 139–56.

—— 1989. A Mathematical Proof of Duverger's Law. In *Models of Strategic Choice in Politics*, ed. Peter C. Ordeshook. Ann Arbor: University of Michigan Press.

PANAGOPOULOS, COSTAS (ed.) 2007. *Rewiring Politics: Presidential Nominating Convention in the Media Age*. Baton Rouge, La.: LSU Press.

PANEBIANCO, ANGELO. 1988. *Political Parties: Organization and Power*. New York: Cambridge University Press.

PASTOR, GREGORY S., STONE, WALTER J., and RAPOPORT, RONALD B. 1999. Candidate-Centered Sources of Party Change: The Case of Pat Robertson, 1968. *Journal of Politics*, 61 (May), 423–44.

PATTERSON JAMES T. 1972. *Mr. Republican: A Biography of Robert A. Taft*. Boston: Houghton Mifflin.

—— 2001. The Rise of Rights and Rights Consciousness in American Politics, 1930s–1970s. In *Contesting Democracy: Substance and Structure in American Political History, 1775–2000*, ed. Byron E. Shafer and Anthony J. Badger. Lawrence: University Press of Kansas.

PATTERSON, KELLY D. 1996. *Political Parties and Maintenance of Liberal Democracy*. New York: Columbia University Press.

—— and SINGER, MATTHEW M. 2007. Targeting Success: The Enduring Power of the NRA. In *Interest Group Politics*, ed. Alan J. Cigler and Burdett A. Loomis. 7th edn. Washington, DC: CQ Press.

PATTERSON, SAMUEL C. 1962. Dimensions of Voting Behavior in a One-Party State Legislature. *Public Opinion Quarterly*, 26: 185–200.

—— and CALDEIRA, GREGORY A. 1984. The Etiology of Partisan Competition. *American Political Science Review*, 78: 691–707.

PATTERSON, THOMAS E. 1980. *The Mass Media Election: How Americans Choose their President*. New York: Praeger.

—— 2008. Voter Turnout Approaches Some Records, Breaks Others. *Harvard University Gazette Online* (Nov. 6).

PEARSON, KATHRYN and SCHICKLER, ERIC. Forthcoming. Discharge Petitions, Agenda Control, and the Congressional Committee System, 1929–1976. *Journal of Politics*.

PESCHEK, JOSEPH G. 1987. *Policy-Planning Organizations: Elite Agendas and America's Rightward Turn*. Philadelphia: Temple University Press.

PETERSON, GEOFF D. and WRIGHTON, J. MARK. 1998. Expressions of Distrust: Third-Party Voting and Cynicism in Government. *Political Behavior*, 20: 17–34.

PETERSON, MARK A. and WALKER, JACK L. 1986. Interest Group Responses to Partisan Change. In *Interest Group Politics*, ed. Allan J. Cigler and Burdett A. Loomis. Washington, DC: CQ Press.

PETERSON, PAUL E. 1981. *City Limits*. Chicago: University of Chicago Press.

PETROCIK, JOHN. 1981. *Party Coalitions: Realignments and the Decline of the New Deal Party System*. Chicago: University of Chicago Press.

—— 1996. Issue Ownership in Presidential Elections, with a 1980 Case Study. *American Journal of Political Science*, 40: 825–50.

—— 2006. Party Coalitions in the American Public: Morality Politics, Issue Agendas, and the 2004 Election. In *The State of the Parties*, ed. John C. Green and Daniel Coffey. 5th edn. Lanham, Md.: Rowman & Littlefield.

PEW FORUM ON RELIGION AND PUBLIC LIFE. 2008. How the Faithful Voted. <http://pewforum.org/docs/?DocID=367#1>. Accessed Nov. 2008.

PEW INTERNET AND POLITICAL LIFE PROJECT. 2005. *The Internet and Campaign 2004*. Mar. 6. <http://www.pewinternet.org/Search.aspx?q=the%20internet%20and%20campaign%202004>. Accessed July 2, 2009.

PFFNER, JAMES P. 2008. *Power Play: The Bush Presidency and the Constitution*. Washington, DC: Brookings Institution.

PIERESON, JAMES. 1982. Party Government. *Political Science Reviewer*, 12/1 (Fall), 2–52.

PIERSON, PAUL. 1993. When Effect Becomes Cause. *World Politics* 45: 595–628.

PITTMAN, RUSSELL. 1976. The Effects of Industry Concentration and Regulation in Three 1972 U.S. Senate Campaigns. *Public Choice*, 27: 71–80.

PIVEN, FRANCES FOX and CLOWARD, RICHARD A. 1977. *Poor People's Movements*. New York: Vintage Books.

—— —— 2000. *Why Americans Don't Vote and Why Politicians Want it That Way*. Boston: Beacon Press.

PLASSER, FRITZ. 2001. Parties' Diminishing Relevance for Campaign Professionals. *Harvard International Journal of Press/Politics*, 6/4: 44–59.

PLOTKE, DAVID. 1996. *Building a Democratic Political Order: Reshaping American Liberalism in the 1930s and 1940s*. New York: Cambridge University Press.

—— 1997. Representation is Democracy. *Constellations*, 4: 19–34.

PLOTNICK, ROBERT D. and WINTERS, RICHARD F. 1990. Party, Political Liberalism, and Redistribution: An Application to the American States. *American Politics Research*, 18: 430–58.

POLAKOFF, KEITH. 1981. *Political Parties in American History*. New York: Wiley.

POLLETTA, FRANCESCA. 2002. *Freedom Is an Endless Meeting*. Chicago: University of Chicago Press.

—— and JASPER, JAMES M. 2001. Collective Identity and Social Movements. *Annual Review of Sociology*, 27: 283–305.

—— —— 2002. *Freedom Is an Endless Meeting*. Chicago: University of Chicago Press.

POLSBY, NELSON W. 1963. *Community Power and Political Theory*. New Haven: Yale University Press.

—— 1975. Legislatures. In *Handbook of Political Science*, ed. Fred I. Greenstein and Nelson W. Polsby. Reading, Mass.: Addison-Wesley.

—— 1980. *Community Power and Political Theory*. 2nd edn. New Haven: Yale University Press.

—— 1983. *The Consequences of Party Reform*. New York: Oxford University Press.

—— 2004. *How Congress Evolves*. New York: Oxford University Press.

—— and WILDAVSKY, AARON. 1968. *Presidential Elections: Strategies of American Electoral Politics*. 2nd edn. New York: Scribner.

—— —— 1984. *Presidential Elections*. New York: Scribner.

POMPER, GERALD. 1966. *Nominating the President: The Politics of Convention Choice*. New York: W. W. Norton.

—— 1967a. "If Elected, I Promise": American Party Platforms. *Midwest Journal of Political Science*, 11/3: 318–52.

—— 1967b. The Classification of Presidential Elections. *Journal of Politics*, 29: 535–66.

—— 1972. From Confusion to Clarity: Issues and American Voters, 1956–1968. *American Political Science Review*, 66 (June), 425–8.

—— 1977. The Decline of Party in American Elections. *Political Science Quarterly*, 92 (Spring), 21–41.

—— 1999. Parliamentary Government in the United States. In *The State of the States*, ed. John C. Green and Daniel M. Shea. Lanham, Md.: Rowman & Littlefield.

POOLE, KEITH T. and ROSENTHAL, HOWARD. 1984. The Polarization of American Politics. *Journal of Politics*, 46: 1061–79.

—— —— 1987. Analysis of Congressional Coalition Patterns: A Unidimensional Spatial Model. *Legislative Studies Quarterly*, 12: 55–75.

—— —— 1991. Patterns of Congressional Voting. *American Journal of Political Science*, 35/1: 228–78.

—— —— 1997. *Congress: A Political-Economic History of Roll Call Voting*. Oxford: Oxford University Press.

POTTER, DAVID. 1976. *The Impending Crisis, 1848–1861*. Completed and ed. Don E. Fehrenbacher. New York: Harper & Row.

POTTER, TREVOR. 1997. Issue Advocacy and Express Advocacy. In *Campaign Finance: A Sourcebook*, ed. Anthony Corrado et al. Washington, DC: Brookings Institution.

PRALLE, SARAH. 2003. Venue Shopping, Political Strategy, and Policy Change: The Internationalization of Canadian Forestry Advocacy. *Journal of Public Policy*, 23 (Sept.), 233–60.

—— 2006. *Branching Out and Digging In: Environmental Advocacy and Agenda Setting*. Washington, DC: Georgetown University Press.

PRATT, HENRY J. 1976. *The Gray Lobby*. Chicago: University of Chicago Press.

PRICE, DAVID E. 1984. *Bringing Back the Parties*. Washington, DC: CQ Press.

PRICE, H. DOUGLAS. 1976. Critical Elections and Party History: A Critical View. *Polity*, 4: 236–42.

PRNEWSWIRE. 2007. Department of Defense Issues Revised Statement about "Don't Ask, Don't Tell." June 26.

PROKSCH, SVEN-OLIVER and SLAPIN, JONATHAN B. Forthcoming. Position Taking in European Parliament Speeches. *British Journal of Political Science*.

PUTNAM, ROBERT D. 2000. *Bowling Alone: The Collapse and Revival of American Community*. New York: Simon & Schuster.

QUINN, DENNIS P. and SHAPIRO, ROBERT Y. 1991. Business Political Power: The Case of Taxation. *American Political Science Review*, 85: 851–74.

RAE, DOUGLAS W. 1967. *The Political Consequences of Electoral Laws*. New Haven: Yale University Press.

—— and TAYLOR, MICHAEL. 1970. *The Analysis of Political Cleavages*. New Haven: Yale University Press.

RAE, NICOL C. 1989. *The Decline and Fall of the Liberal Republicans from 1952 to the Present*. New York: Oxford University Press.

—— 1992. Class and Culture: American Political Cleavages in the Twentieth Century. *Western Political Quarterly*, 45: 629–50.

RAHAT, GIDEON, HAZAN, REUVEN Y., and KATZ, RICHARD S. 2008. Democracy and Political Parties: On the Uneasy Relationships between Participation, Competition and Representation. *Party Politics*, 14/6: 663–83.

RAMSDEN, GRAHAM P. 2002. State Legislative Campaign Finance Research: A Review Essay. *State Politics and Policy Quarterly*, 2/2: 176–98.

RANNEY, AUSTIN. 1951. Toward a More Responsible Party System: A Commentary. *American Political Science Review*, 45: 488–99.

—— 1962. *Doctrines of Responsible Party Government: Its Origins and Present State.* Urbana: University of Illinois Press.

—— 1965. *Pathways to Parliament: Candidate Selection in Britain.* Madison: University of Wisconsin Press.

—— 1968. The Representativeness of Primary Electorates. *Midwest Journal of Political Science*, 12/2: 224–38.

—— 1975. *Curing the Mischiefs of Faction: Party Reform in America.* Berkeley: University of California Press.

—— 1976. Parties in State Politics. In *Politics in the American States: A Comparative Analysis*, ed. Herbert Jacob and Kenneth Vines. Boston: Little, Brown.

RAPOPORT, RONALD B. and STONE, WALTER J. 1994. A Model for Disaggregating Political Change. *Political Behavior*, 16 (Dec.), 505–32.

—— —— 2005. *Three's a Crowd: The Dynamic of Third Parties, Ross Perot and Republican Resurgence.* Ann Arbor: University of Michigan Press.

REDPATH, BILL. 1995. Ballot Access: The View from the Street: A Conversation with Bill Redpath. <http://www.hks.harvard.edu/case/3pt/redpath.html>. Accessed July 2, 2009.

REICHLEY, A. JAMES. 1985a. *Religion in American Public Life.* Washington, DC: Brookings Institution Press.

—— 1985b. The Rise of National Parties. In *The New Direction in American Politics*, ed. John E. Chubb and Paul E. Peterson. Washington, DC: Brookings Institution.

—— 1992. *The Life of the Parties: A History of American Political Parties.* New York: Free Press.

—— 2007. The Future of the American Two Party System in the Twenty-First Century. In *The State of the Parties*, ed. John C. Green and Daniel J. Coffey. 5th edn (Lanham, Md.: Rowman & Littlefield).

REITER, HOWARD L. 1985. *Selecting the President: The Nominating Process in Transition.* Philadelphia: University of Pennsylvania Press.

REMINI, ROBERT V. 1959. *Martin Van Buren and the Making of the Democratic Party.* New York: Columbia University Press.

—— 1967. *Andrew Jackson and the Bank War: A Study in the Growth of Presidential Power.* New York: W. W. Norton.

REYNOLDS, JOHN F. 2006. *The Demise of the American Convention System.* Cambridge: Cambridge University Press.

RICE, TOM W. 1985. Gubernatorial and Senatorial Primary Elections: Determinants of Competition. *American Politics Research*, 13/4: 427–46.

RICH, ANDREW. 2004. *Think Tanks, Public Policy, and the Politics of Expertise.* New York: Cambridge University Press.

RICHARDSON, HEATHER COX. 1997. *The Greatest Nation of the Earth: Republican Economic Policy during the Civil War.* Cambridge, Mass.: Harvard University Press.

RIGGS, WILLIAM W. 2004. Compassionate Conservatism Meets Communitarianism. In *George W. Bush: Evaluating the President at Midterm*, ed. Bryan Hilliard, Tom Lansford, and Robert P. Watson. Albany: State University of New York Press.

RIKER, WILLIAM H. 1962. *The Theory of Political Coalitions*. New Haven: Yale University Press.

—— 1980. Implications from the Disequilibrium of Majority Rule for the Study of Institutions. *American Political Science Review*, 74/2: 432–46.

—— 1982. The Two Party System and Duverger's Law: An Essay on the History of Political Science. *American Political Science Review*, 76/4: 753–66.

—— 1984. The Heresthetics of Constitution-Making: The Presidency in 1787, with Comments on Determinism and Rational Choice. *American Political Science Review*, 78/1: 1–16.

—— 1986. *The Art of Political Manipulation*. New Haven: Yale University Press.

—— and NIEMI, RICHARD G. 1962. The Stability of Coalitions on Roll Calls in the House of Representatives. *American Political Science Review*, 56: 58–65.

RIMMERMAN, CRAIG A. 2000. Beyond Political Mainstreaming. In *The Politics of Gay Rights*, ed. Craig A. Rimmerman, Kenneth D. Wald, and Clyde Wilcox. Chicago: University of Chicago Press.

—— 2002. *From Identity to Politics*. Philadelphia: Temple University Press.

ROBBINS, SUZANNE M. and TSVETOVAT, MAKSIM. 2009. Follow the Money: The Network of Political Organizations and Candidates in 2000. In *Interest Groups and Lobbying*, ed. Conor McGrath, i: *The United States, and Comparative Studies*. Lewiston, NY: Edwin Mellen Press.

ROBERTS, JASON M. 2005. Minority Rights and Majority Power: Conditional Party Government and the Motion to Recommit in the House. *Legislative Studies Quarterly*, 30 (May), 219–34.

—— and SMITH, STEVEN S. 2003. Procedural Contexts, Party Strategy, and Conditional Party Voting in the U.S. House of Representatives, 1971–2000. *American Journal of Political Science*, 47: 305–17.

—— —— 2007. The Evolution of Agenda-Setting Institutions in Congress: Path Dependency in House and Senate Institutional Development. In *Party, Process, and Political Change in Congress*, ed. David Brady and Matthew McCubbins, ii. Stanford, Calif.: Stanford University Press.

ROBERTS, NANCY (ed.) 2008. *The Age of Direct Citizen Participation*. Armonk, NY: M. E. Sharpe.

ROEMER, JOHN. 2001. *Political Competition*. New York: Cambridge University Press.

ROETTGER, WALTER B. 1978. Strata and Stability: Reputations of American Political Scientists. *PS: Political Science and Politics*, 11: 6–13.

ROGERS, DANIEL. 1982. In Search of Progressivism. *Review of American History*, 10 (Dec.), 114–23.

ROHDE, DAVID W. 1979. Risk-Bearing and Progressive Ambition: The Case of Members of the United States House of Representatives. *American Journal of Political Science*, 23/1: 1–26.

—— 1991. *Parties and Leaders in the Postreform House*. Chicago: University of Chicago Press.

—— STIGLITZ, EDWARD H., and WEINGAST, BARRY R. 2009. Dynamic Congressional Organization: A Theory of Institutional Stability and Reform. Unpub.

ROMASCO, ALBERT U. 1983. *The Politics of Recovery: Roosevelt's New Deal*. New York: Oxford University Press.

ROMER, THOMAS and WEINGAST, BARRY. 1991. Political Foundations of the Thrift Debate. In *Politics and Economics in the Eighties*, ed. Alberto Alesina and Geoffrey Carliner. Chicago: University of Chicago Press.

ROOF, TRACY. 2008. Can the Democrats Deliver for the Base? *PS: Political Science and Politics*, 41/1: 83–7.

ROOSEVELT, FRANKLIN D. 1926. *The Works of Theodore Roosevelt*. 20 vols. New York: Scribner.

—— 1938–50. *The Public Papers and Addresses of Franklin D. Roosevelt*, ed. Samuel Rosenman. 13 vols. New York: Random House.

ROSEBOOM, EUGENE H. 1970. *A History of Presidential Elections*. New York: Macmillan.

ROSENBAUM, WALTER A. 1978. Public Involvement as Reform and Ritual: The Development of Federal Participation Programs. In *Citizen Participation in America*, ed. Stuart Langton. Lexington, Mass.: Lexington Books.

ROSENBLOOM, DAVID. 1973. *The Election Men: Professional Campaign Managers and American Democracy*. New York: Quadrangle Books.

ROSENOF, THEODORE. 2003. *Realignment: The Theory that Changed the Way We Think about American Politics*. Lanham, Md.: Rowman & Littlefield.

ROSENSTONE, STEVEN J., BEHR, ROY L., and LAZARUS, EDWARD H. 1996. *Third Parties in America: Citizen Response to Major Party Failure*. 2nd edn. Princeton: Princeton University Press.

—— and HANSEN, JOHN MARK. 1993. *Mobilization, Participation and Democracy in America*. New York: Macmillan.

ROSENTHAL, CINDY SIMON. 1995. New Party or Campaign Bank Account? Explaining the Rise of State Legislative Campaign Committees. *Legislative Studies Quarterly*, 20/2: 249–68.

ROSSITER, CLINTON. 1960. *Parties and Politics in America*. Ithaca, NY: Cornell University Press.

ROTHBARD, MURRAY N. 1962. *The Panic of 1819: Reactions and Policies*. New York: Columbia University Press.

ROTHENBERG, LAWRENCE S. 1992. *Linking Citizens to Government: Interest Group Politics at Common Cause*. Cambridge: Cambridge University Press.

ROVE, KARL. 2001. Personal interview with Sidney M. Milkis (Nov. 15).

ROVERE, RICHARD A. 1965. A Man for this Age Too. *New York Times Magazine* (Apr. 11).

ROZELL, MARK J. and WILCOX, CLYDE. 1995. *God at the Grass Roots: The Christian Right in the 1994 Elections*. Lanham, Md.: Rowman & Littlefield.

—— —— 1997. *God at the Grass Roots: The Christian Right in the 1996 Elections*. Lanham, Md.: Rowman & Littlefield.

—— —— 1999. *Interest Groups in American Campaigns: The New Face of Electioneering*. Washington, DC: CQ Press.

—— —— and MADLAND, DAVID. 2006. *Interest Groups in American Campaigns*. 2nd edn. Washington, DC: CQ Press.

RUDALEVIGE, ANDREW. 2005. *The New Imperial Presidency: Renewing Presidential Power after Watergate*. Ann Arbor: University of Michigan Press.

RULE, WILMA. 1981. Why Women Don't Run: The Critical Contextual Factors in Women's Legislative Recruitment. *Western Political Quarterly*, 34/1: 60–77.

—— 1990. Why More Women Are State Legislators. A Research Note. *Western Political Quarterly*, 43/2: 437–48.

RUTENBERG, JIM. 2004. Anti-Kerry Ad Is Condemned by McCain. *New York Times*, Aug. 6, A13.

—— 2008. Obama Plans to Take Campaign to Republican Bastions. *International Herald Tribune*, June 23.

SABATIER, PAUL A. 1999. The Advocacy Coalition Framework: An Assessment. In *Theories of the Policy Process*, ed. Paul A. Sabatier. Boulder, Colo.: Westview Press.

—— and JENKINS-SMITH, HANK C. (eds.) 1993. *Policy Change and Learning: An Advocacy Coalition Approach*. Boulder, Colo.: Westview Press.

SABATO, LARRY J. 1981. *The Rise of Political Consultants: New Ways of Winning Elections*. New York: Basic Books.

—— 1988. *The Party's Just Begun*. Glenview, Ill.: Scott, Foresman; Little, Brown.

SAIROFF, ALAN. 1999. Corporatism in 24 Industrial Democracies: Meaning and Measurement. *European Journal of Political Research*, 36/2: 175–205.

SAIT, EDWARD M. 1927. *American Political Parties and Elections*. New York: Century.

SALANT, JONATHAN D. 1995a. Senate Passes Tighter Rules on Registration, Disclosure. *Congressional Quarterly Weekly Report* (July 29), 2239.

—— 1995b. Highlights of Lobby Bill. *Congressional Quarterly Weekly Report* (Dec. 2), 3632.

SALISBURY, ROBERT H. 1969. An Exchange Theory of Interest Groups. *Midwest Journal of Political Science*, 13 (Feb.), 1–32.

—— 1984. Interest Representation: The Dominance of Institutions. *American Political Science Review*, 78: 64–76.

—— 1994. Interest Structures and Policy Domains: A Focus for Research. In *Representing Interests and Interest Group Representation*, ed. William Crotty, Mildred A. Schwartz, and John C. Green. Washington, DC: University Press of America.

SALMORE, BARBARA G. and SALMORE, STEPHEN A. 1989. *Candidates, Parties, and Campaigns: Electoral Politics in America*. 2nd edn. Washington, DC: CQ Press.

SANBONMATSU, KIRA. 2002a. *Democrats, Republicans, and the Politics of Women's Place*. Ann Arbor: University of Michigan Press.

—— 2002b. Political Parties and the Recruitment of Women to State Legislatures. *Journal of Politics*, 64/3: 791–809.

—— 2006a. *Where Women Run: Gender and Party in the American States*. Ann Arbor: University of Michigan Press.

—— 2006b. The Legislative Party and Candidate Recruitment in the American States. *Party Politics*, 12/2: 233–56.

SANDERS, M. ELIZABETH. 1999. *Roots of Reform: Farmers, Workers and the American State, 1877–1917*. Chicago: University of Chicago Press.

SARBAUGH-THOMPSON, MARJORIE, THOMPSON, LYKE, ELDER, CHARLES P., COMIN, MEG, ELLING, RICHARD C., and STRATE, JOHN. 2003. Democracy among Strangers: Term Limits' Effects on Relationships between State Legislators in Michigan. *State Politics and Policy Quarterly*, 6/4: 384–409.

SARTORI, GIOVANNI. 1970. Concept Misformation in Comparative Politics. *American Political Science Review*, 64/4: 1033–53.

—— 1976. *Parties and Party Systems: A Framework for Analysis*. New York: Cambridge University Press.

SATTERTHWAITE, MARK. 1975. Strategy Proofness and Arrow's Conditions. *Journal of Economic Theory*, 10/2: 187–217.

SAUNDERS, KYLE L. and ABRAMOWITZ, ALAN I. 2004. Ideological Realignment and Active Partisans in the American Electorate. *American Politics Research*, 32 (May), 285–309.

SAWYERS, TRACI M. and MEYER, DAVID S. 1999. Missed Opportunities. *Social Problems*, 46: 187–206.

SCAMMON, RICHARD M. and WATTENBERG, BEN J. 1970. New York: Conrad McCann.

SCHAFFNER, BRIAN F., STREB, MATTHEW, and WRIGHT, GERALD. 2001. Teams without Uniforms: The Nonpartisan Ballot in State and Local Elections. *Political Research Quarterly*, 54/1: 7–30.

SCHATTSCHNEIDER, E. E. 1935. *Politics, Pressures, and the Tariff*. New York: Prentice Hall.

SCHATTSCHNEIDER, E. E. 1942. *Party Government*. New York: Holt, Rinehart, Winston.

—— 1956. The United States: The Functional Approach to Party Government. In *Modern Political Parties*, ed. Sigmund Neuman. Chicago: University of Chicago Press.

—— 1960. *The Semisovereign People*. New York: Holt, Rinehart, Winston.

—— 1975. *The Semisovereign People*. New York: Harcourt Brace Jovanovich.

SCHELLING, THOMAS C. 1971. Dynamic Models of Segregation. *Journal of Mathematical Sociology*, 1: 143–86.

SCHICKLER, ERIC. 2000. Institutional Change in the House of Representatives, 1867–1998: A Test of Partisan and Ideological Balance Models. *American Political Science Review*, 94/2: 269–88.

—— 2001. *Disjointed Pluralism*. Princeton: Princeton University Press.

—— and PEARSON, KATHRYN. 2008. Agenda Control, Majority Party Power, and the House Committee on Rules, 1937–1952. Revised version of a paper presented at the 2006 Annual Meeting of the Midwest Political Science Association, Chicago.

—— and RICH, ANDREW. 1997. Controlling the Floor: Parties as Procedural Coalitions in the House. *American Journal of Political Science*, 41 (Oct.), 1340–75.

SCHIER, STEVEN E. 2009. *Panorama of a Presidency: How George W. Bush Acquired and Spent his Political Capital*. Armonk, NY: M. E. Sharpe.

SCHLESINGER, ARTHUR M., JR. 1949. *The Vital Center: The Politics of Freedom*. New York: Houghton Mifflin.

—— 1960. *The Politics of Upheaval*. Boston: Houghton Mifflin.

—— 1973. *History of US Political Parties*. 4 vols. New York: Chelsea House.

SCHLESINGER, JOSEPH A. 1966. *Ambition and Politics: Political Careers in the United States*. Chicago: Rand McNally.

—— 1985. The New American Political Party. *American Political Science Review*, 79: 1151–69.

—— 1991. *Political Parties and the Winning of Office*. Ann Arbor: University of Michigan Press.

—— 1994. *Political Parties and the Winning of Office*. Ann Arbor: University of Michigan Press.

SCHLOZMAN, KAY LEHMAN. 1984. What Accent the Heavenly Chorus? Political Equality and the American Pressure System. *Journal of Politics*, 46: 1006–32.

—— and BURCH, TRACI. 2009. Political Voice in an Age of Inequality. In *America at Risk: The Great Dangers*, ed. Robert F. Faulkner and Susan Shell. Ann Arbor: University of Michigan Press.

—— and TIERNEY, JOHN T. 1986. *Organized Interests and American Democracy*. New York: Harper & Row.

—— VERBA, SIDNEY, BRADY, HENRY E., JONES, PHILIP EDWARD, and BURCH, TRACI. 2008. Who Sings in the Heavenly Chorus? The Shape of the Organized Interest System. Paper prepared for presentation at the Annual Meeting of the American Political Science Association, Boston, Aug. 28–31.

SCHMITTER, PHILIPPE. 1974. Still the Century of Corporatism? *Review of Politics*, 36: 85–131.

SCHNEIDER, ANNE LARASON and INGRAM, HELEN. 1993. Social Construction of Target Populations: Implications for Politics and Policy. *American Political Science Review*, 87/2: 334–47.

—— —— 1997. *Policy Design for Democracy*. Lawrence: University Press of Kansas.

SCHOFIELD, NORMAN. 1978. Instability of Simple Dynamic Games. *Review of Economic Studies*, 45/3: 575–94.

—— and SENED, ITAI. 2006. *Multiparty Democracy: Elections and Legislative Politics*. New York: Cambridge University Press.

SCHULER, DOUGLAS. 1996. Corporate Political Strategy and Foreign Competition: The Case of the Steel Industry. *Academy of Management Journal*, 39: 720–37.

—— 1999. Corporate Political Action: Rethinking the Economic and Organizational Influences. *Business and Politics*, 1/1: 83–97.

—— REHBEIN, KATHLEEN, and CRAMER, ROXY. 2002. Pursuing Strategic Advantage through Political Means: A Multivariate Approach. *Academy of Management Journal*, 45: 659–72.

SCHWARTZ, MILDRED A. 1990. *The Party Network: The Robust Organization of Illinois Republicans*. Madison: University of Wisconsin Press.

SCHWARTZ, THOMAS. 1977. Collective Choice, Separation of Issues, and Vote Trading. *American Political Science Review*, 71: 999–1010.

—— 1989. Why Parties? MS, University of California, Los Angeles.

SCULLY, ROGER and PATTERSON, SAMUEL C. 2001. Ideology, Partisanship and Decision-Making in a Contemporary American Legislature. *Party Politics*, 7: 131–55.

SEGURA, GARY M. and NICHOLSON, STEPHEN P. 1995. Sequential Choices and Partisan Transitions in U.S. Senate Delegations: 1972–1988. *Journal of Politics*, 57/1: 86.

SELTZER, RICHARD, NEWMAN, JODY, and LEIGHTON, MELISSA VOORHEES. 1997. *Sex as a Political Variable: Women as Candidates and Voters in U.S. Elections*. Boulder, Colo.: Lynne Rienner.

SELZNICK, PHILIP. 1953. *TVA and the Grass Roots*. Berkeley: University of California Press.

SHADE, WILLIAM. 1981. Political Pluralism and Party Development: The Creation of a Modern Party System, 1815–1852. In *The Evolution of American Electoral Systems*, ed. Paul Kleppner et al. Westport, Conn.: Greenwood Press.

SHAFER, BYRON E. 1983. *Quiet Revolution: The Struggle for the Democratic Party and the Shaping of Post-Reform Politics*. New York: Russell Sage.

—— 1988. *Bifurcated Politics: Evolution and Reform in the National Party Convention*. Cambridge, Mass.: Harvard University Press.

—— (ed.) 1991. *The End of Realignment: Interpreting American Electoral Eras*. Madison: University of Wisconsin Press.

—— and JOHNSTON, RICHARD. 2006. *The End of Southern Exceptionalism: Class, Race, and Partisan Change in the Postwar South*. Cambridge, Mass.: Harvard University Press.

SHAIKO, RONALD G. 1999. *Voices and Echoes for the Environment: Public Interest Representation in the 1990s and Beyond*. New York: Columbia University Press.

—— 2005. Making the Connection: Organized Interests, Political Representation, and the Changing Rules of the Game in Washington Politics. In *The Interest Group Connection: Electioneering, Lobbying, and Policymaking in Washington*, ed. Paul S. Herrnson, Ronald G. Shaiko, and Clyde Wilcox. Washington, DC: CQ Press.

SHAPIRO, DAVID B. 2004. A Network Analysis of the Consortium for Citizens Disabilities (CCD) and a Theory of Policy Networks. Ph.D. dissertation, University of Illinois at Chicago. Sent on request: Shapiro.David7@gmail.com.

SHARP, JAMES ROGER. 1993. *American Politics in the Early Republic: A New Nation in Crisis*. New Haven: Yale University Press.

SHEA, DANIEL M. 1995. *Transforming Democracy: Legislative Campaign Committees and Political Parties*. Albany: State University of New York Press in cooperation with the Center for Party Development, Washington, DC.

—— 1996. *Campaign Craft: The Strategies, Tactics and Art of Political Campaign Management*. Westport, Conn.: Praeger.

SHEA, DANIEL M. 1999. The Passing of Realignment and the Advent of the "Base-Less" Party System. *American Politics Quarterly*, 27: 33–57.

—— 2003. Schattschneider's Dismay: Strong Parties and Alienated Voters. In *The State of the Parties: The Changing Role of Contemporary American Parties*, ed. John C. Green and Rick Farmer. 4th edn. Lanham, Md.: Rowman & Littlefield.

—— and GREEN, JOHN C. 2007. Throwing a Better Party: Local Parties and the Youth Vote. In *Fountain of Youth: Strategies and Tactics for Mobilizing America's Young Voters*, ed. Daniel M. Shea and John C. Green. Lanham, Md.: Rowman & Littlefield.

SHEFTER, MARTIN. 2002. War, Trade, and U.S. Party Politics. In *Shaped by War and Trade*, ed. Ira Katznelson and Martin Shefer. Princeton: Princeton University Press.

SHELLEY, MACK. 1983. *The Permanent Majority: The Conservative Coalition in the United States Congress*. Birmingham: University of Alabama Press.

SHEPSLE, KENNETH A. 1972. The Strategy of Ambiguity: Uncertainty and Electoral Competition. *American Political Science Review*, 66: 555–68.

—— 1974. On the Size of Winning Coalitions. *American Political Science Review*, 68/2 (June), 505–18.

—— 1979. Institutional Arrangements and Equilibrium in Multidimensional Voting Models. *American Journal of Political Science*, 23: 27–59.

—— 1989. The Changing Textbook Congress. In *Can the Government Govern?* ed. John Chubb and Paul Peterson. Washington, DC: Brookings Institution.

—— 1991. *Models of Multiparty Electoral Competition*. Fundamentals of Pure and Applied Economics, ed. Jacques Lesourne and Hugo Sonnenschein. London: Harwood Press.

—— and WEINGAST, BARRY R. 1987. The Institutional Foundations of Committee Power. *American Political Science Review*, 81: 85–104.

SHERIDAN, VALERIE S. (ed.) 2006. *Washington Representatives 2006*. Washington, DC: Columbia Books.

SHIELDS, TODD G., GOIDEL, ROBERT K., and TADLOCK, BARRY. 1995. The Net Impact of Media Exposure on Individual Voting Decisions in U.S. Senate and House Elections. *Legislative Studies Quarterly*, 20: 415–30.

SHIPAN, CHARLES R. 1997. *Designing Judicial Review: Interest Groups, Congress, and Communications Policy*. Ann Arbor: University of Michigan Press.

SHOR, BORIS. 2009. All Together Now: Putting Congress, State Legislatures, and Individuals in a Common Ideological Space. Paper presented at the Ninth Annual Conference on State Politics and Policy, Chapel Hill, NC.

—— BERRY, CHRISTOPHER, and McCARTY, NOLAN. 2007. A Bridge to Somewhere: Mapping State and Congressional Ideology on a Cross-Institutional Common Space. Paper presented at the Seventh Annual Conference on State Politics and Policy, Austin, Tex.

SHRIBMAN, DAVID. 1982. "Sincerely Yours": Your Congressman's Computer. *New York Times*, Aug. 17.

SIAROFF, A. 1999. Corporatism in 24 Industrial Democracies: Meaning and Measurement. *European Journal of Political Research*, 36/2: 175–205.

SIGELMAN, LEE. 2006. The American Political Science Review Citation Classics. *American Political Science Review*, 100/4: 667–9.

SIGNORINO, CURTIS S. 2002. Strategy and Selection in International Relations. *International Interactions*, 28: 93–115.

—— 2003. Structure and Uncertainty in Discrete Choice Models. *Political Analysis*, 11: 316–44.

SILBEY, JOEL H. 1967. *The Shrine of Party: Congressional Voting Behavior, 1841–1952*. Pittsburgh: University of Pittsburgh Press.

—— 1977. *A Respectable Minority: The Democratic Party in the Civil War Era, 1860–1868*. New York: W. W. Norton.

—— 1985. *The Partisan Imperative: The Dynamics of American Politics before the Civil War*. New York: Oxford University Press.

—— 1991. *The American Political Nation, 1838–1893*. Stanford, Calif.: Stanford University Press.

—— 2001. "To One or Another of These Parties Every Man Belongs": The American Political Experience from Andres Jackson to the Civil War. In *Contesting Democracy: Substance and Structure in American Political History, 1775–2000*, ed. Byron E. Shafer and Anthony J. Badger. Lawrence: University Press of Kansas.

SIMMEL, GEORG. 1955. *Conflict and the Web of Group Affiliations* (1922). Trans. Kurt H. Wolff and Reinhold Bendix. New York: Free Press.

SINCLAIR, BARBARA. 1983. *Majority Leadership in the U.S. House*. Baltimore: Johns Hopkins University Press.

—— 1989. *The Transformation of the U.S. Senate*. Baltimore: Johns Hopkins University Press.

—— 1995. *Legislators, Leaders, and Lawmaking*. Baltimore: Johns Hopkins University Press.

—— 1997. *Unorthodox Lawmaking: New Legislative Processes in the U.S. Congress*. Washington, DC: CQ Press.

—— 2000. *Unorthodox Lawmaking: New Legislative Processes in the U.S. Congress*. 2nd edn. Washington, DC: CQ Press.

—— 2002a. Do Parties Matter? In *Party, Process, and Political Change in Congress*, ed. David Brady and Matthew McCubbins. Stanford, Calif.: Stanford University Press.

—— 2002b. The "60-Vote Senate": Strategies, Process and Outcomes. In *U.S. Senate Exceptionalism*, ed. Bruce I. Oppenheimer. Columbus: Ohio State University Press.

—— 2005. The New World of U.S. Senators. In *Congress Reconsidered*, ed. Lawrence C. Dodd and Bruce I. Oppenheimer. 8th edn. Washington, DC: CQ Press.

—— 2006. *Party Wars: Polarization and the Politics of the Policy Process*. Julian Rothbaum Lecture Series. University of Oklahoma Press.

—— 2007. *Unorthodox Lawmaking: New Legislative Processes in the U.S. Congress*. 3rd edn. Washington, DC: CQ Press.

—— 2008. Leading the New Majorities. *PS: Political Science and Politics*, 41 (Jan.), 89–93.

SINDLER, ALAN P. 1966. *Political Parties in the United States*. New York: St Martin's Press.

SKINNER, RICHARD. 2005. Do 527's Add Up to a Party? Thinking about the "Shadows" of Politics. *The Forum*, 3/3, art. 5.

SKOCPOL, THEDA. 1992. *Protecting Soldiers and Mothers*. Cambridge, Mass.: Belknap Press.

—— 1999. Advocates without Members. In *Civic Engagement in American Democracy*, ed. Morris P. Fiorina and Theda Skocpol. Washington, DC: Brookings Institution.

—— 2003. *Diminished Democracy*. Norman: University of Oklahoma Press.

—— 2004. Voice and Inequality: The Transformation of American Civic Democracy. *Perspectives on Politics*, 2: 3–20.

SKOWRONEK, STEPHEN. 1982. *Building a New American State: The Expansion of National Administrative Capacities, 1877–1920*. Cambridge: Cambridge University Press.

—— 1997. *The Politics Presidents Make: Leadership from John Adams to Bill Clinton*. Cambridge, Mass.: Harvard University Press.

SKOWRONEK, STEPHEN. 2005. Leadership by Definition: First Term Reflections on George W. Bush's Political Stance. *Perspectives on Politics*, 3/4: 817–31.

SLAPIN, JONATHAN B. and PROKSCH, SVEN-OLIVER. 2008. A Scaling Model for Estimating Time-Series Party Positions from Texts. *American Journal of Political Science*, 52/3: 705–22.

SLONIM, SHLOMO. 1986. The Electoral College at Philadelphia: The Evolution of an Ad Hoc Congress for the Selection of a President. *Journal of American History*, 73: 35–58.

SMALLWOOD, FRANK. 1983. *The Other Candidates: Third Parties in American Elections.* Hanover, NH: University Press of New England.

SMITH, ADAM I. P. 2006. *No Party Now: Politics in the Civil War North.* New York: Oxford University Press.

SMITH, DANIEL. 2006. Initiatives and Referendums: The Effects of Direct Democracy on Candidate Elections. In *The Electoral Challenge: Theory Meets Practice*, ed. Steven Craig. Washington, DC: CQ Press.

SMITH, MARK A. 1999. Public Opinion, Elections, and Representation within a Market Economy: Does the Structural Power of Business Undermine Popular Sovereignty? *American Journal of Political Science*, 43: 842–63.

—— 2000. *American Business and Political Power: Public Opinion, Elections, and Democracy.* Chicago: University of Chicago Press.

SMITH, RICHARD A. 1995. Interest Group Influence in the U.S. Congress. *Legislative Studies Quarterly*, 20: 89–139.

SMITH, RICHARD NORTON. 1982. *Thomas E. Dewey and his Times.* New York: Simon & Schuster.

SMITH, STEVEN RATHGEB. 2002. Social Services. In *The State of Nonprofit America*, ed. Lester Salamon. Washington, DC: Brookings Institution.

—— and LIPSKY, MICHAEL. 1993. *Nonprofits for Hire.* Cambridge, Mass.: Harvard University Press.

SMITH, STEVEN S. 2007. *Party Influence in Congress.* New York: Cambridge University Press.

SNOW, DAVID A., ROCHFORD, E. BURKE, JR., WORDON, STEVEN K., and BENFORD, ROBERT D. 1986. Frame Alignment and Mobilization. *American Sociological Review*, 51 (Aug.), 464–81.

SNYDER, JAMES M., JR. 1992. Long-Term Investing in Politicians; or, Give Early, Give Often. *Journal of Law and Economics*, 35/1: 15–43.

—— and GROSECLOSE, TIM. 2000. Estimating Party Influence on Congressional Roll-Call Voting. *American Journal of Political Science*, 44: 193–211.

—— —— 2001. Estimating Party Influence on Roll-Call Voting: Regression Coefficients versus Classification Scores. *American Political Science Review*, 95/3: 689–98.

—— and TING, MICHAEL. 2002. An Informational Rationale for Political Parties. *American Journal of Political Science*, 46: 90–110.

SOBEL, JOEL. 2002. Can We Trust Social Capital? *Journal of Economic Literature*, 40: 139–54.

SONGER, DONALD R. and SHEEHAN, REGINALD S. 1993. Interest Group Success in the Courts: Amicus Participation in the Supreme Court. *Political Research Quarterly*, 46/2: 339–54.

SORAUF, FRANK J. 1963. *Party and Representation: Legislative Politics in Pennsylvania.* New York: Atherton Press.

—— 1967. Political Parties and Political Analysis. In *The American Party Systems: Stages of Political Development*, ed. William N. Chambers and Walter Dean Burnham. New York: Oxford University Press.

—— 1992. *Inside Campaign Finance: Myths and Realities.* New Haven: Yale University Press.

—— 1994. *Inside Campaign Finance: Myths and Realities.* New Haven: Yale University Press.

SOSS, JOE and SCHRAM, SANFORD F. 2007. A Public Transformed? *American Political Science Review*, 101/1: 111–27.

SOULE, JOHN W. and CLARKE, JAMES W. 1970. Amateurs and Professionals: A Study of Delegates to the 1968 Democratic National Convention. *American Political Science Review*, 64/3: 888–98.

SOUTHWELL, PRISCILLA L. 1986. The Politics of Disgruntlement: Nonvoting and Defection among Supporters of Nomination Losers, 1968–1984. *Political Behavior*, 8 (Mar.), 81–95.

SPALTER-ROTH, ROBERTA and SCHREIBER, RONNEE. 1995. Outside Issues and Insider Tactics. In *Feminist Organizations*, ed. Myra Marx Ferree and Patricia Yancey Martin. Philadelphia: Temple University Press.

SPEEL, ROBERT W. 1998. *Changing Patterns of Voting in the Northern United States: Electoral Realignment, 1952–1996.* University Park: Pennsylvania State University Press.

SPILLER, PABLO T. and GELY, RAFAEL. 1992. Congressional Control or Judicial Independence: The Determinants of U.S. Supreme Court Labor-Relations Decisions, 1949–1988. *RAND Journal of Economics*, 23: 463–92.

SPRIGGS, JAMES F., II and WAHLBECK, PAUL J. 1997. Amicus Curiae and the Role of Information at the Supreme Court. *Political Research Quarterly*, 50/2: 365–86.

SPROAT, JOHN G. 1968. *The Best Men: Liberal Reformers in the Gilded Age.* New York: Oxford University Press.

SQUIRE, PEVERILL. 1993. Divided Government and Public Opinion in the States. *State and Local Government Review*, 25: 150–4.

—— 2000. Uncontested Seats in State Legislative Elections. *Legislative Studies Quarterly*, 25/1: 131–46.

—— and SMITH, ERIC R. A. N. 1988. The Effect of Partisan Information on Voters in Nonpartisan Elections. *Journal of Politics*, 50: 169–79.

STAGGENBORG, SUZANNE. 1986. Coalition Work in the Pro-Choice Movement: Organizational and Environmental Opportunities and Obstacles. *Social Problems*, 3: 374–90.

STAMPP, KENNETH M. 1980. The Concept of a Perpetual Union. In Kenneth M. Stampp, *The Imperiled Union: Essays on the Background of the Civil War.* New York: Oxford University Press.

STANLEY, HAROLD W., BIANCO, WILLIAM T., and NIEMI, RICHARD G. 1986. Partisanship and Group Support Over Time: A Multivariate Analysis. *American Political Science Review*, 80 (Sept.), 969–76.

—— and NIEMI, RICHARD G. 1991. Partisanship and Group Support, 1952–1988. *American Politics Quarterly*, 19 (Apr.), 189–210.

—— —— 2001. Party Coalitions in Transition: Partisanship and Group Support, 1952–1996. In *Controversies in Voting Behavior*, ed. Richard G. Niemi and Herbert F. Weisberg. 4th edn. Washington, DC: CQ Press.

STARR, PAUL. 1982. *The Social Transformation of American Medicine.* New York: Basic Books.

STEADMAN, M. S., JR. and SONTHOFF, HERBERT. 1951. Party Responsibility: A Critical Inquiry. *Western Political Quarterly*, 4: 454–68.

STEENSLAND, BRIAN, PARK, JERRY Z., REGNERUS, MARK D., ROBINSON, LYNN D., WILCOX, W. BRADFORD, and WOODBERRY, ROBERT D. 2000. The Measure of American Religion: Toward Improving the State of the Art. *Social Forces*, 79: 291–324.

STEHR, STEPHEN. 1997. Top Bureaucrats and the Distribution of Influence in Reagan's Executive Branch. *Public Administration Review*, 57/1: 75–82.

STEIN, ROBERT M. 1990. Economic Voting for Governor and U.S. Senator: The Electoral Consequences of Federalism. *Journal of Politics*, 52: 29–53.

STEINMO, SVEN. 1993. *Taxation and Democracy: Swedish, British, and American Approaches to Financing the Modern State*. New Haven: Yale University Press.

STEVENS, ARTHUR, MILLER, ARTHUR, and MANN, THOMAS. 1974. Mobilization of Liberal Strength in the House: The Democratic Study Group. *American Political Science Review*, 68: 667–81.

STEWART, CHARLES. 1991. The Politics of Tax Reform in the 1980s. In *Politics and Economics in the Eighties*, ed. Alberto Alesina and Geoffrey Carliner. Chicago: University of Chicago Press.

STIGLER, GEORGE J. 1975. *The Citizen and the State: Essays on Regulation*. Chicago: University of Chicago Press.

STOKES, THOMAS. 1940. *Chip Off My Shoulder*. Princeton: Princeton University Press.

STONE, CLARENCE N. 1989. *Regime Politics*. Lawrence: University Press of Kansas.

—— 1993. Urban Regimes and the Capacity to Govern. *Journal of Urban Affairs*, 15/1: 1–28.

STONE, DEBORAH A. 1988. *Policy Paradox and Political Reason*. Glenview, Ill.: Scott, Foresman.

—— 1989. Causal Stories and the Formation of Policy Agendas. *Political Science Quarterly*, 104/2: 281–300.

—— 2002. *Policy Paradox*. New York: W. W. Norton.

STONE, WALTER J. 1984. Prenomination Candidate Choice and General Election Behavior: Iowa Presidential Activists in 1980. *American Journal of Political Science*, 28: 372–89.

—— and ABRAMOWITZ, ALAN I. 1983. Winning May Not Be Everything, but it's More than We Thought: Presidential Party Activists in 1980. *American Political Science Review*, 77: 945–56.

—— ATKESON, LONNA RAE, and RAPOPORT, RONALD B. 1992. Turning On or Turning Off? Mobilization and Demobilization Effects of Participation in Presidential Nominating Campaigns. *American Journal of Political Science*, 36/3: 665.

—— and MAISEL, L. SANDY. 2003. The Not-So-Simple Calculus of Winning: Potential U.S. House Candidates' Nomination and General Election Prospects. *Journal of Politics*, 65: 951–77.

—— and RAPOPORT, RONALD B. 1994. Candidate Perception among Nomination Activists: A New Look at the Moderation Hypothesis. *Journal of Politics*, 56 (Nov.), 1034–52.

—— —— 2001. It's Perot Stupid! The Legacy of the 1992 Perot Movement in the Major-Party System, 1992–2000. *PS: Political Science and Politics*, 34: 49–58.

—— —— and ABRAMOWITZ, ALAN I. 1992. Candidate Support in Presidential Nomination Campaigns: The Case of Iowa in 1984. *Journal of Politics*, 54 (Nov.), 1074–97.

—— —— and ATKESON, LONNA RAE. 1995. A Simulation Model of Presidential Nomination Choice. *American Journal of Political Science*, 39 (Feb.), 135–61.

—— —— —— 1997. A Candidate-Centered Perspective on Party Responsiveness: Nomination Activists and the Process of Party Change. In *The Parties Respond*, ed. L. Sandy Maisel. Boulder, Colo.: Westview Press.

STONECASH, JEFFREY M. 1996. The State Politics Literature: Moving beyond Covariation Studies and Pursuing Politics. *Polity*, 28: 559–79.

—— 2000. *Class and Party in American Politics*. Boulder, Colo.: Westview Press.

—— 2006. *Political Parties Matter: Realignment and the Return of Partisan Voting*. Boulder, Colo.: Lynne Rienner.

—— BREWER, MARK D., and MARIANI, MACK D. 2003. *Diverging Parties: Social Change, Realignment, and Party Polarization*. Boulder, Colo.: Westview Press.

STORING, HERBERT. 1981. *What the Anti-Federalists Were For: The Political Thought of the Opponents of the Constitution.* Chicago: University of Chicago Press.

STOUTLAND, SARA E. 1999. Community Development Corporations: Mission, Strategy, and Accomplishments. In *Urban Problems and Community Development*, ed. Ronald F. Ferguson and William T. Dickens. Washington, DC: Brookings Institution.

STRAHAN, RANDALL. 2007. *Leading Representatives.* Baltimore: Johns Hopkins University Press.

STRATMANN, THOMAS. 1992. Are Contributors Rational? Untangling Strategies of Political Action Committees. *Journal of Political Economy*, 100/3: 647–64.

—— 2005. Some Talk: Money in Politics. A (Partial) Review of the Literature. *Public Choice*, 124/1–2: 135–56.

STROLOVITCH, DARA Z. 2006. Do Interest Groups Represent the Disadvantaged? *Journal of Politics*, 68: 893–908.

—— 2007. *Affirmative Advocacy: Race, Class, and Gender in Interest Group Politics.* Chicago: University of Chicago Press.

SUÁREZ SANDRA L. 2000. *Does Business Learn? Tax Breaks, Uncertainty, and Political Strategies.* Ann Arbor: University of Michigan Press.

SUMMERS, MARK W. 1988. *The Plundering Generation: Corruption and the Crisis of the Union, 1849–1861.* Oxford: Oxford University Press.

—— 1993. *The Era of Good Stealings.* New York: Oxford University Press.

—— 1997. *The Gilded Age, or, The Hazard of New Functions.* Upper Saddle River, NJ: Prentice Hall.

—— 2000. *Rum, Romanism and Rebellion: The Making of a President, 1884.* Chapel Hill: University of North Carolina Press.

SUNDQUIST, JAMES. 1968. *Dynamics of the Party System: Alignment and Realignment of Political Parties in the United States.* Washington, DC: Brookings Institution.

—— 1983. *Dynamics of the Party System.* Rev. edn. Washington, DC: Brookings Institution.

—— 1988. Needed: A Political Theory for the New Era of Coalition Government in the United States. *Political Science Quarterly*, 103: 613–35.

SUSSMAN, GERALD. 2005. *Global Electioneering: Campaign Consulting, Communications, and Corporate Financing.* Lanham, Md.: Rowman & Littlefield.

SWARTS, HEIDI J. 2008. *Organizing Urban America.* Minneapolis: University of Minnesota Press.

SWIERENGA, ROBERT P. 1990. Ethnoreligious Political Behavior in the Mid-Nineteenth Century: Voting, Values, Cultures. In *Religion and American Politics*, ed. Mark A. Noll. New York: Oxford University Press.

TAMAS, BERNARD and HINDMAN, MATTHEW. 2007. Do State Election Laws Really Hurt Third-Parties? Ballot Access, Fusion, and Elections to the US House of Representatives. Paper presented at the Annual Meeting of the Midwest Political Science Association, Palmer House Hotel, Chicago, Apr 12.

TARROW, SIDNEY G. 1994. *Power in Movement: Social Movements, Collective Action, and Mass Politics in the Modern State.* Cambridge: Cambridge University Press.

—— 2005. *The New Transnational Activism.* New York: Cambridge University Press.

TAYLOR, VERTA. 1989. Social Movement Continuity. *American Sociological Review*, 54: 761–75.

TENPAS, KATHRYN DUNN. 1997. *Presidents as Candidates: Inside the White House for the Presidential Campaign.* New York: Garland.

TERKEL, AMANDA. 2008. Joint Chiefs Chairman Mullen: Military Ready to Accept Repeal of Don't Ask Don't Tell. *Think Progress*, May 7.

THOMAS, CLIVE S. and HREBENAR, RONALD J. 1991. The Nationalization of Interest Groups and Lobbying in the States. In *Interest Groups Politics*, ed. Allan J. Cigler and Burdett A. Loomis. 3rd edn. Washington, DC: CQ Press.

———— 1999. Interest Groups in the States. In *Politics in the American States: A Comparative Analysis*, ed. Virginia Gray, Russell L. Hanson, and Herbert Jacob. 7th edn. Washington, DC: CQ Press.

———— 2003. Interest Groups in the States. In *Politics in the American States: A Comparative Analysis*, ed. Virginia Gray and Russell L. Hanson. 8th edn. Washington, DC: CQ Press.

THOMPSON, DENNIS F. 1993. Mediated Corruption: The Case of the Keating Five. *American Political Science Review*, 87/2: 369–81.

THOMPSON, JOHN N. 1994. *The Coevolutionary Process*. Chicago: University of Chicago Press.

THURBER, JAMES A. 1998. The Study of Campaign Consultants: A Subfield in Search of a Theory. *PS: Political Science and Politics*, 31/2: 145–9.

—— NELSON, CANDICE J., and DULIO, DAVID A. (eds.) 2000. *Crowded Airwaves: Campaign Advertising in Elections*. Washington, DC: Brookings Institution.

TILLY, CHARLES and TARROW, SIDNEY. 2007. *Contentious Politics*. Boulder, Colo.: Paradigm.

TOCQUEVILLE, ALEXIS DE. 1969. *Democracy in America*, ed. J. P. Mayer. Garden City, NY: Doubleday Anchor.

TREADWAY, JACK M. 1985. *Public Policymaking in the American States*. New York: Praeger.

TRIPATHI, MICKY, ANSOLABEHERE, STEPHEN, and SNYDER, JAMES M., JR. 2002. Are PAC Contributions and Lobbying Linked? New Evidence from the 1995 Lobby Disclosure Act. *Business and Politics*, 4/2: 131–55.

TROY, GIL. 1996. *See How They Ran: The Changing Role of the Presidential Candidate*. Cambridge, Mass.: Harvard University Press.

—— 2005. *Morning in America: How Ronald Reagan Invented the 1980s*. Princeton: Princeton University Press.

—— 2007. *Morning in America: How Ronald Reagan Invented the 1980s*. Princeton: Princeton University Press.

TRUMAN, DAVID B. 1951. *The Governmental Process: Political Interests and Public Opinion*. New York: Alfred A. Knopf.

—— 1971. *The Governmental Process: Political Interests and Public Opinion*. 2nd edn. New York: Alfred A. Knopf.

TSEBELIS, GEORGE. 1997. *Bicameralism*. Cambridge: Cambridge University Press.

—— 2002. *Veto Players: How Political Institutions Work*. New York: Russell Sage; Princeton: Princeton University Press.

TULIS, JEFFREY. 1987. *The Rhetorical Presidency*. Princeton: Princeton University Press.

TURNER, JULIUS. 1951. Responsible Parties: A Dissent from the Floor. *American Political Science Review*, 45: 143–52.

—— 1952. *Party and Constituency: Pressures on Congress*. Baltimore: Johns Hopkins University Press.

UPI.COM. 2008. Obama Grassroots Effort Called Biggest Yet. Oct. 12. <http://www.upi.com/Top_News/2008/10/12/Obama-grassroots-effort-called-biggest-yet/UPI-11951223813843>.

USEEM, MICHAEL. 1984. *The Inner Circle*. New York: Oxford University Press.

USLANER, ERIC M. and WEBER, RONALD E. 1979. United-States State Legislators' Opinions and Perceptions of Constituency Attitudes. *Legislative Studies Quarterly*, 4: 563–85.

VAN BUREN, MARTIN. 1827. Martin Van Buren to Thomas Ritchie. Martin Van Buren Papers (July 13). Washington, DC: Library of Congress.

—— 1867. *Inquiry into the Origin and Course of Political Parties in the United States.* New York: Hurd and Houghton.

VAN HOUWELING, ROBERT PARKS. 2007. An Evolving End Game: Partisan Collusion in Conference Committees, 1953–2003. In *Process, Party and Policy Making*, ed. David W. Brady and Mathew D. McCubbins, ii: *Further New Perspectives on the History of Congress.* Stanford, Calif.: Stanford University Press.

VAN RIPER, PAUL. 1958. *History of the United States Civil Service.* Evanston, Ill.: Row, Peterson.

VANDEN BERGH, RICHARD G. and HOLBURN, GUY L. F. 2007. Targeting Corporate Political Strategy: Theory and Evidence from the U.S. Accounting Industry. *Business and Politics*, 9/2: 1–31.

VERBA, SIDNEY and NIE, NORMAN H. 1972. *Participation in America.* New York: Harper & Row.

—— SCHLOZMAN, KAY LEHMAN, and BRADY, HENRY E. 1995. *Voice and Equality: Civic Voluntarism in American Politics.* Cambridge, Mass.: Harvard University Press.

VLAHOS, KELLEY BEAUCAR. 2005. Federal Elections Turn to Permanent Campaigning. *Fox-News.* <http://www.foxnews.com/story/0,2933,165255,00.html>. Accessed Jan. 28, 2009.

VOGEL, DAVID. 1989. *Fluctuating Fortunes: The Political Power of Business in America.* New York: Basic Books.

VOSS-HUBBARD, MARK. 2002. *Beyond Party: Cultures of Antipartisanship in Northern Politics before the Civil War.* Baltimore: Johns Hopkins University Press.

WALD, KENNETH D. and SMIDT, CORWIN E. 1993. Measurement Strategies in the Study of Religion and Politics. In *Rediscovering the Religious Factor in American Politics*, ed. David C. Leege and Lyman A. Kellstedt. Armonk, NY: M. E. Sharpe.

WALKER, JACK L., JR. 1966. A Critique of the Elitist Theory of Democracy. *American Political Science Review*, 60: 285–95.

—— 1983. The Origins and Maintenance of Interest Groups in America. *American Political Science Review*, 77: 390–406.

—— 1991. *Mobilizing Interest Groups in America: Patrons, Professions, and Social Movements.* Ann Arbor: University of Michigan Press.

WALLACE, MICHAEL. 1968. Changing Concepts of Party in the United States: New York, 1815–1828. *American Historical Review*, 74: 453–91.

WALLSTEIN, PETER and HAMBURGER, TOM. 2008. Obama's Army May Get Drafted. *Los Angeles Times*, Nov. 14.

WARE, ALAN J. 1985. *The Breakdown of Democratic Party Organization, 1940–1980.* Oxford: Oxford University Press.

—— 1996. *Political Parties and Party Systems.* Oxford: Oxford University Press.

—— 2002. *The American Direct Primary: Party Institutionalization and Transformation in the North.* New York: Cambridge University Press.

—— 2006. *The Democratic Party Heads North, 1877–1962.* New York: Cambridge University Press.

WARREN, DORIAN T. 2005. The Labor Movement's Identity Politics. PhD dissertation, Yale University.

WARREN, MARK E. 2001. *Democracy and Association*. Princeton: Princeton University Press.

WARSHAW, SHIRLEY ANNE. 2004. Mastering Presidential Government: Executive Power and the Bush Administration. In *Transformed by Crisis: The Presidency of George W. Bush and American Politics*, ed. Jon Kraus, Kevin J. McMahon, and David M. Rankin. New York: Palgrave Macmillan.

—— 2005. The Other Reagan Revolution: Managing the Departments. In *The Reagan Presidency: Assessing the Man and his Legacy*, ed. Paul Kengor and Peter Schweizer. Lanham, Md.: Rowman & Littlefield.

Washington Representatives. 1981, 1991, 2001. Washington, DC: Columbia Books.

WASSERMAN, STANLEY and FAUST, KATHERINE.1994. *Social Network Analysis: Methods and Applications*. New York: Cambridge University Press.

WATSON, HARRY. 2006. *Liberty and Power: The Politics of Jacksonian America*. New York: Hill & Wang.

WATTENBERG, MARTIN P. 1984. *The Decline of American Political Parties 1952–1980*. Cambridge, Mass.: Harvard University Press.

—— 1987. The Hollow Realignment: Partisan Change in a Candidate-Centered Era. *Public Opinion Quarterly*, 51 (Spring), 58–74.

—— 1990. *The Decline of American Political Parties, 1952–1988*. Cambridge, Mass.: Harvard University Press.

—— 1991. *The Rise of Candidate-Centered Politics: Presidential Elections of the 1980s*. Cambridge, Mass.: Harvard University Press.

—— 1994. *The Decline of American Political Parties, 1952–1992*. Cambridge, Mass.: Harvard University Press.

—— 1996. *The Decline of American Political Parties: 1952–1994*. Cambridge, Mass.: Harvard University Press.

—— 1998. *The Decline of American Political Parties: 1952–1996*. Cambridge, Mass.: Harvard University Press.

WATTS, DUNCAN J. 1999a. Networks, Dynamics, and the Small World Phenomenon. *American Journal of Sociology*, 105/2: 493–527.

—— 1999b. *Small Worlds: The Dynamics of Networks between Order and Randomness*. Princeton: Princeton University Press.

—— and STROGATZ, STEVEN H. 1998. Collective Dynamics of "Small World" Networks. *Nature*, 393: 440–2.

WAWRO, GREGORY. 2001. A Panel Probit Analysis of Campaign Contributions and Roll Call Votes. *American Journal of Political Science*, 45/3: 563–79.

—— and SCHICKLER, ERIC. 2006. *Filibuster: Obstruction and Lawmaking in the U.S. Senate*. Princeton: Princeton University Press.

—— —— 2007. Cloture Reform Reconsidered. In *Party, Process, and Political Change in Congress*, ed. David Brady and Matthew McCubbins, ii. Stanford, Calif.: Stanford University Press.

WEINGAST, BARRY R. 1979. A Rational Choice Perspective on Congressional Norms. *American Journal of Political Science*, 23/2: 245–62.

—— and MARSHALL, WILLIAM J. 1988. The Industrial Organization of Congress; or, Why Legislatures, Like Firms, Are Not Organized as Markets. *Journal of Political Economy*, 96/1: 132–63.

—— and WITTMAN, DONALD. 2006. *The Oxford Handbook of Political Economy*. New York: Oxford University Press.

WEISSMAN, STEPHEN R. and HASSAN, RUTH.2006. BCRA and 527 Groups. In *The Election after Reform: Money, Politics, and the Bipartisan Campaign Reform Act*, ed. Michael J. Malbin. Lanham, Md.: Rowman & Littlefield.

—— and RYAN, KARA D. 2006. Non-Profit Interest Groups' Election Activities and Federal Campaign Finance Policy. In *Campaign Finance Institute Report*. Washington, DC.

WEKKIN, GARY D. 1985. Political Parties and Intergovernmental Relations in 1984. *Publius*, 15: 19–37.

WELCH, RICHARD. 1988. *The Presidency of Grover Cleveland*. Lawrence: University Press of Kansas.

WELCH, SUSAN and CARLSON, ERIC H. 1973. The Impact of Party on Voting Behavior in a Nonpartisan Legislature. *American Political Science Review*, 67: 854–67.

WHITE, JOHN KENNETH and SHEA, DANIEL M. 2000. *New Party Politics: From Jefferson and Hamilton to the Information Age*. Boston: Bedford/St Martin's.

—— —— 2004. *New Party Politics: From Jeffersonian and Hamilton to the Information Age*. 2nd edn. Belmont, Calif.: Wadsworth.

WHITE, THEODORE H. 1961. *The Making of the President 1960*. New York: Atheneum.

—— 1965. *The Making of the President 1964*. New York: Atheneum.

—— 1969. *The Making of the President 1968: A Narrative History of American Politics in Action*. New York: Atheneum.

—— 1973. *The Making of the President 1972: A Narrative History of American Politics in Action*. New York: Atheneum.

—— 1982. *America in Search of Itself: The Making of the President 1956–1980*. New York: Harper & Row.

WHITTIER, NANCY. 1995. *Feminist Generations*. Philadelphia: Temple University Press.

WIEBE, ROBERT H. 1967. *The Search for Order, 1877–1920*. New York: Hill & Wang.

—— 1995. *Self Rule: A Cultural History of American Democracy*. Chicago: University of Chicago Press.

WILCOX, CLYDE. 1989a. Share the Wealth: Contributions by Congressional Incumbents to the Campaigns of Other Candidates. *American Politics Quarterly*, 17: 368–408.

—— 1989b. Organizational Variables and Contribution Behavior of Large PACs: A Longitudinal Analysis. *Political Behavior*, 11/2: 157–73.

—— 1996. *Onward Christian Soldiers? The Religious Right in American Politics*. Boulder, Colo.: Westview Press.

—— 2005. Designing Campaign Finance Disclosure in the States: Tracing the Tributaries of Campaign Finance. *Election Law Journal*, 4: 371–86.

—— 2009. Of Movements and Metaphors: The Coevolution of the Christian Right and the Republican Party. In *Evangelicals and American Democracy*, ed. Steven Brint and Jean Reith Schroedel, ii: *Religion and Politics*. New York: Russell Sage.

WILDAVSKY, AARON. 1965. The Goldwater Phenomenon: Purists, Politicians, and the Two-Party System. *Review of Politics*, 27: 386–413.

WILENTZ, SEAN. 2008. *The Age of Reagan: A History, 1974–2008*. New York: Harper.

WILLIAMS, CHRISTINE B. 1990. Women, Law and Politics: Recruitment Patterns in the Fifty States. *Women and Politics*, 10/3: 103–23.

WILLIAMS, GRANT. 2008. Tax-Exempt Organizations Registered with the IRS. *Chronicle of Philanthropy* (June 26).

WILSON, GRAHAM. 1990. Corporate Political Strategies. *British Journal of Political Science*, 20/2: 281–8.

WILSON, JAMES Q. 1960. *The Amateur Democrat*. Chicago: University of Chicago Press.

—— 1962. *The Amateur Democrat: Club Politics in Three Cities*. Chicago: University of Chicago Press.

—— 1974. *Political Organizations*. New York: Basic Books.

—— (ed.) 1980. *The Politics of Regulation*. New York: Basic Books.

—— 1995. *Political Organizations*. Princeton: Princeton University Press.

WILSON, WOODROW. 1956. *Congressional Government* (1885). New York: Meridian Books.

WINGER, RICHARD. 1988. What Are Ballots For? <http://www.ballot-access.org/winger/wabf.html>. Accessed Feb. 19, 2009.

—— 1994. The Importance of Ballot Access. <http://www.ballot-access.org/winger/iba.html>. Accessed Feb. 19, 2009.

—— 2006. Approximately 690,000 Signatures Needed for 2008 Presidential Candidate. *Ballot Access News*. <http://www.ballot-access.org/2006/11/25/approximately-690000-signatures-needed-for-2008-presidential-candidate>. Accessed Feb. 19, 2009.

WINTERS, RICHARD. 1976. Party Control and Policy Change. *American Journal of Political Science*, 20: 597–636.

WITCOVER, JULES. 1977. *Marathon: The Pursuit of the Presidency 1972–1976*. New York: Viking Penguin.

—— 2003. *Party of the People: A History of the Democrats*. New York: Random House.

WITKO, CHRISTOPHER. 2006. PACs, Issue Context, and Congressional Decisionmaking. *Political Research Quarterly*, 59/2: 283–95.

WITTMAN, DONALD A. 1983. Candidate Motivations: A Synthesis of Alternatives. *American Political Science Review*, 77: 142–57.

WOLAK, JENNIFER, LOWERY, DAVID, and GRAY, VIRGINIA. 2001. California Dreaming: Outliers, Leverage, and Influence in Comparative State Political Analysis. *State Politics and Policy Quarterly*, 1/3: 255–72.

—— NEWMARK, ADAM, MCNOLTY, TODD, LOWERY, DAVID, and GRAY, VIRGINIA. 2002. Much of Politics Is Still Local: Multi-State Lobbying in State Interest Communities, *Legislative Studies Quarterly*, 27/4: 527–56.

WOLBRECHT, CHRISTINA. 2000. *The Politics of Women's Rights: Parties, Positions, and Change*. Princeton: Princeton University Press.

WOLL, CORNELIA. 2006. Lobbying in the European Union: From Sui Generis to a Comparative Perspective. *Journal of European Public Policy*, 13/3: 456–69.

WONG, CAROLYN. 2006. *Lobbying for Inclusion*. Stanford, Calif.: Stanford University Press.

WONG, JANELLE S. 2007. Two Steps Forward. *Du Bois Review*, 4/2: 457–67.

WOODBERRY, ROBERT D. and SMITH, CHRISTIAN S. 1998. Fundamentalism et al.: Conservative Protestants in America. *Annual Review of Sociology*, 24: 250–6.

WOODWARD, BOB. 2002. *Bush at War*. New York: Simon & Schuster.

—— 2004. *Plan of Attack*. New York: Simon & Schuster.

—— 2006. *State of Denial*. New York: Simon & Schuster.

WOOLDRIDGE, J. M. 2002. *Econometric Analysis of Cross Section and Panel Data*. Cambridge, Mass.: MIT Press.

WRIGHT, GERALD C. 2009. Rules and the Ideological Character of Primary Electorates. In *Reforming the Presidential Nomination Process*, ed. Steven Smith and Melanie Springer. Washington, DC: Brookings Institution.

—— and BERKMAN, MICHAEL B. 1986. Candidates and Policy in United States Senate Elections. *American Political Science Review*, 80: 567–88.

—— and SCHAFFNER, BRIAN F. 1989. PAC Contributions, Lobbying, and Representation. *Journal of Politics*, 51/3: 713–29.

—— —— 2002. The Influence of Party: Evidence from the State Legislatures. *American Political Science Review*, 96: 367–79.

WRIGHT, JOHN R. 1985. PACs, Contributions, and Roll Calls: An Organizational Perspective. *American Political Science Review*, 79/2: 400–14.

—— 1989. PAC Contributions, Lobbying, and Representation. *Journal of Politics*, 51/3: 713–29.

—— 1990. Contributions, Lobbying, and Committee Voting in the U.S. House of Representatives. *American Political Science Review*, 84: 417–38.

—— 1996. *Interest Groups and Congress: Lobbying Contributions and Influence*. Boston: Allyn and Bacon.

—— 2004. Campaign Contributions and Congressional Voting on Tobacco Policy, 1980–2000. *Business and Politics*, 6: 1–26.

WRIGHT, STEPHEN G. and RIKER, WILLIAM H. 1989. Plurality and runoff systems and numbers of candidates. *Public Choice*, 60/2: 155–76.

WUTHNOW, ROBERT. 1988. *The Restructuring of American Religion*. Princeton: Princeton University Press.

YACKEE, JASON WEBB and YACKEE, SUSAN WEBB. 2006. A Bias Toward Business? Assessing Interest Group Influence on the U.S. Bureaucracy. *Journal of Politics*, 68/1: 128–39.

YACKEE, SUSAN WEBB. 2008. The Hidden Politics of Regulation: Interest Group Influence during Agency Rule Development. Paper presented at the Annual Meeting of the Midwest Political Science Association, Chicago.

YOHO, JAMES. 1995. Madison on the Beneficial Effects of Interest Groups. *Polity*, 27/4: 587–605.

YOUNG, GARRY and WILKINS, VICKY. 2007. Vote Switchers and Party Influence in the U.S. House. *Legislative Studies Quarterly*, 32 (Feb.), 59–77.

YOUNG, McGEE. 2008. The Political Roots of Small Business Identity. Manuscript, Syracuse University.

ZALD, MAYER and McCARTHY, JOHN D. 1987. *Social Movements in an Organizational Society*. New Brunswick, NJ: Transaction Press.

ZALLER, JOHN R. 1992. *The Nature and Origins of Mass Opinion*. Cambridge: Cambridge University Press.

—— 1998. Politicians as Prize Fighters: Electoral Selection and Incumbency Advantage. In *Politicians and Party Politics*, ed. John G. Geer. Baltimore: Johns Hopkins University Press.

ZARDKOOHI, ASGHAR. 1985. On the Political Participation of the Firm in the Electoral Process. *Southern Economic Journal*, 51/3: 804–17.

ZEIGLER, L. HARMON and BAER, MICHAEL. 1969. *Lobbying: Interaction and Influence in American State Legislatures*. Belmont, Calif.: Wadsworth.

ZEISEL, HANS. 1980. Lawmaking and Public Opinion Research: The President and Patrick Caddell. *American Bar Foundation Research Journal*, 5/1: 133–9.

ZELLER, BELLE. 1954. *American State Legislatures: Report of the Committee on American Legislatures*. New York: Thomas Y. Crowell.

NAME INDEX

Note: Includes all referenced authors.

Subject Index

Note: Law cases cited are indexed under 'legal cases'.